MODERN GERMAN SOCIOLOGY

European Perspectives:
A Series of Columbia University Press

MODERN GERMAN SOCIOLOGY

Edited with introductions
by
VOLKER MEJA
DIETER MISGELD
NICO STEHR

New York　　　COLUMBIA UNIVERSITY PRESS

Columbia University Press
New York   Oxford
Copyright © 1987 Columbia University Press
All rights reserved
Printed in the United States of America

Library of Congress Cataloging-in-Publication Data

Modern German Sociology

    Bibliography: p.
    Includes index.
    1. Sociology—Germany (West)—History. 2. Social institutions. 3. Social
structure. I. Meja, Volker. II. Misgeld, Dieter. III. Stehr, Nico.
    HM22.G2M63 1987 301′.0943 86-24519
    ISBN 0-231-05854-3
    ISBN 0-231-05855-1 (pbk.)
    c 10 9 8 7 6 5 4 3 2

CONTENTS

Preface

Most contemporary sociologists are likely to agree that their discipline has become more international since the end of World War II. Any anthology emphasizing a particular *national* tradition is therefore bound to be selective since it must to a large extent abstract from those features of the discipline which have resulted from the increase in the range and intensity of international cooperation.

Our collection is not primarily intended for the specialist in German sociology and its history, nor is it addressed to sociologists in Germany. It is rather aimed at readers of English interested in those German intellectual developments and orientations, especially in the Federal Republic, that have been widely discussed in English-speaking countries and have achieved a certain influence there. Most of our selections either belong among these developments or are critical responses to them. It is due to this particular emphasis that certain theoretical and historical discussions are predominant, and that much highly specialized, yet significant recent research has been left aside.

Certainly we recognize that in German sociology, just as elsewhere, there has been a strong tendency toward specialization. This specialization has led to a concentration of sociological inquiry and research in areas of practical importance for modern societies, such as the sociologies of education and work, of organizations, criminology, and policy research. But much of this research, as well as some theory, has been inspired by methods and conceptions of inquiry originating outside Germany, especially in the United States. It is difficult to gauge how original German contributions are in these areas. We therefore have not attempted this task, which will be addressed in international gatherings and publications that concentrate on detailed discussion of highly specialized social scientific research. We have emphasized those aspects of German sociology which indicate a continued interest in a fluid conception of the boundaries of sociology, and which avoid distinctions between sociology and social theory, social philosophy and social psychology.

Our introductory essay is designed to make a case for this approach by arguing that a very distinctive feature of German sociology in its entire history is the importance of theory as well as of the critique of contemporary society (especially of German society). Indeed, we argue that theory and critique belong together (parts 2 and 3), when regarded from this point of view. For theory and critique to become cogent, however, they must be shown to be applicable either to a society in its special organizational forms, or to social scientific discourse. We have chosen Class, Bureaucracy and the State (part 4) as a domain of substantive application, and the relationship between Identity and Social Structure (part 5) as an instance of a more method-oriented application. Part 1 discusses the history of sociology prior to 1945 as well as the classics which have played a particularly important role in German sociology, and thus allows the reader to measure the achievements of contemporary German sociology and social theory, particularly in regard to its self-reflectiveness, against its own tradition.

While jointly responsible for the book, the editors adopted the following division of labor: Volker Meja substantially revised the introductions and several of the essays in this collection before editing the entire manuscript; Dieter Misgeld provided the basic draft of the general introduction and of the introductions to parts 2, 3, and 4; Nico Stehr wrote a first draft of the introductions to parts 1 and 4 and contributed to the critical apparatus for the general introduction. Translators' and major editors' contributions to the translations are acknowledged on the first page of each article.

The suggestions of Judith Adler, Michal Y. Bodemann, David Kettler, Raymond Morrow, Gianfranco Poggi, Kurt H. Wolff, as well as those of a number of German scholars, including several contributors to our book, were often very helpful. Without Laura C. Hargrave's admirable textprocessing and typesetting skills and her competent advice in a number of editorial matters this book would have been completed much later. We gratefully acknowledge the financial support of the Social Sciences and Humanities Research Council (Canada), the Memorial University of Newfoundland, the Ontario Institute for Studies in Education, the University of Alberta, and the University of Munich.

Volker Meja	Dieter Misgeld	Nico Stehr
Memorial University of Newfoundland	Ontario Institute for Studies in Education and University of Toronto	University of Alberta

Introduction

The Social and Intellectual Organization
of German Sociology Since 1945

Continuity, the ability to establish and reproduce an identity across historical and social existence, helps individuals and societies ground their activities in a secure image of themselves. In some sense, this also applies to intellectual disciplines and to the professions. But what happens when there is a serious upheaval, a profound disruption of continuity, when it becomes highly problematic, even impossible, to take direction from the past? Certainly such a state of affairs, whether on the personal or societal level, deserves to be called a "crisis." And crises can be resolved productively or creatively, but they may also lead to disintegration.[1]

The years from 1933 to 1945 constitute such a watershed for German society and for German sociology. Following the experiences of collapse, defeat, division, and slow rebuilding, the consciousness emerged during the years immediately after the end of World War II that nothing would ever again be as it once had been.[2] Like all other academic disciplines, German sociology too had once openly articulated its commitments to national German traditions and culture. This commitment is shared by sociologists otherwise as different as Max Weber, Ernst Troeltsch, Max Scheler, Hans Freyer, and Arnold Gehlen.[3] But like other national cultures of Western Europe, Germany too had harbored intellectuals of a more cosmopolitan persuasion, especially in the social sciences, who had an uneasy relation to national traditions. Sociologists such as Karl Mannheim and Theodor Geiger, or social philosophers such as Max Horkheimer, Theodor Adorno, and Herbert Marcuse, for example, built on traditions of thought highly prominent in the sphere of influence of German language and culture. But they also expressed their opposition to traditions of German nationalism in the clearest terms and often continued to do so even after World War II. The rise of National Socialism, the policies of brutal repression and genocide connected with Nazi rule, and the total defeat of German military power combined to produce a cultural and moral crisis of such profundity that every step in the postwar reconstruction of German culture could only be uncertain. And how much deeper had this uncertainty to be in the case of an intellectual field such as sociology, which even in the 1920s had barely succeeded in establishing itself as a recognized academic discipline; which only shortly thereafter, in 1933, had in fact for the most part been dissolved; and which had to realize that many of those intellectual conceptions which had informed it in the period of its initial consolidation had now fallen into disrepute.[4] One only needs to recall that most leading representatives of the field had been forced into emigration, and that after 1945 there were overt pressures from the Western allies and their administrations to thoroughly reconstitute sociology on the basis of a ground plan quite unfamiliar to the older practitioners of the discipline.[5]

In sum, the reconstitution of German sociology during the first years after the war occurred in the face of considerable external and internal pressures.[6] One might be tempted to think that this situation would have led to a crisis of conscience and confidence, and to a fundamental change of direction in German sociology. For sociology, after all, was a field to which a number of those returned who had been forced into exile (including Helmuth Plessner, René König, Max Horkheimer, Theodor W. Adorno and, very late, Norbert Elias).[7] And sociologists who had stayed in Germany from 1933 to 1945, and who had initially either actively supported National Socialism (Arnold Gehlen), or who had remained quiescent (Hans Freyer, Helmut Schelsky), might have felt compelled to explain their involvement in or lack of active opposition to morally and intellectually deeply discrediting events. But such a crisis of conscience and the possible renewal did not take place, at least not immediately. There were no major apologies or self-reflective analyses by those who had stayed in Germany during the period of National Socialism. Instead of the crisis of disciplinary conscience there prevailed mostly silence. And precisely this silence was later to become a topic of considerable criticism, especially among new generations of sociologists.

Yet it must also be pointed out that since the mid-fifties[8] more empirical sociological studies have been produced in Germany than in its entire previous history and that sociology is now a well-established field in post-secondary institutions, and that there is a strong presence of German sociologists in international organizations.[9] In fact, West Germany is one of the very few countries in which sociology has a strong public presence, a developed profile as a discipline, and considerable influence on political discourse and decisions. Nonetheless, questions have frequently been raised not merely about the distinctive character of sociology as practiced in Germany, but also about the possibility and significance of sociology itself, including questions about the distinctive contribution of sociology in Germany and about its international merits. This situation leads us to a few preliminary observations about sociology in Germany:

1) German sociology in the postwar period has persistently monitored and evaluated its own development by reference to the development of sociology elsewhere. Instead of focusing on its own traditions, or on the general cultural traditions from which it was derived, German sociology has treated American sociology in particular (see, as an example, essay 20), and to a lesser extent other sociologies, as a vantage point from which to assess itself and its place in German society, and from which to reappraise its relation to the foundational period of the discipline (see essays 4 and 5). This self-critical reflection, however, has had the consequence that comprehensive questions about society, which sociology had once raised in the period of its formation, once again resurfaced. In this case, they were applied to sociology itself (see essays 4, 6, and 10). But this also led to a vigorous reexamination of the place of sociology in German society, which had seemed quite secure in the period of its consolidation prior to 1967. Indeed, the role of sociology in society and culture became a focus for a debate which often reached beyond the discipline.[10]

2) The distinguishing feature of contemporary sociology in Germany, then, is the intensity and persistence of its critical self-reflection and the fact that especially the most visible members of the discipline, for example Habermas and Luhmann, tend to engage in such self-reflective discourse. Self-criticalness, as we have known since Freud, can take the form of inhibiting self-doubt and scrupulousness, of an obsessive preoccupation with oneself. This also is one of the characteristics of German sociology, which seems to indicate a lack of confidence of its practitioners in their ability to advance the discipline, and to confidently face future directions. Self-criticalness has also another side: Precisely because German sociology has never taken for granted its own legitimacy, orderly progress, and social efficacy, it has found it possible (and necessary) to raise questions about its own significance as a phenomenon of intellectual and political culture, and about its own location in the societal process. Is sociology, for example, an instrument of political and administrative domination, an aspect of cultural hegemony, or can it contribute to greater societal rationality?[11] One may note, therefore, that German sociology once again raises the issue of societal rationalization and modernity, thereby returning in

one sense to its origins in the thought of Karl Marx and Max Weber (see essays 3 and 14).[12]

We therefore suggest:

3) that if there is something distinctive about contemporary German sociology, it is precisely its consciousness of societal crisis; and in this sense, contemporary German sociology has come full circle, being now once again firmly linked to the best sociology had to offer in its early period up to the Weimar Republic. One may even say that in Germany sociology is the science of crisis *par excellence*. It engages in the diagnosis of its time.[13] The crisis consciousness of German sociology is of course linked to the attempt to understand the crisis of German society in the wake of Nazism, but sociology attains insight also into a possible general crisis of "postindustrial" or "late capitalist" societies. This deeper sense of societal crisis, too, underlies the major methodological debates[14] with which much of postwar German sociology is internationally identified.

But is there a German sociology in the first place? And how can it be distinguished from "sociology in Germany"? How can it further be distinguished from philosophy, social philosophy, economic history? As is also the case with the founders of sociology in France, Italy, the United States, and elsewhere, the early German sociologists came originally from other fields, especially philosophy or economics, history or law. Moreover, even among later generations of sociologists some continued writing nonsociological works or returned to them (including Helmuth Plessner, Arnold Gehlen, Helmut Schelsky, and, of course, Max Horkheimer, Theodor Adorno, and Jürgen Habermas). They produced essays and books intended also for broader audiences — not necessarily in order to popularize sociology, but in order to address the significant issues of the day, both as sociologists and as intellectuals who believed they possessed the general intellectual capability, as well as the moral obligation, to speak to such issues. This attitude has remained unchanged from Max Weber to the conservatives Arnold Gehlen, Helmut Schelsky, and Friedrich H. Tenbruck, from the politically engaged liberal Ralf Dahrendorf to the left-wing intellectuals of the Frankfurt School. It also characterizes the philosophers of social science associated with "critical rationalism" (Hans Albert, Ernst Topitsch) who have translated "critical rationalism" into a form of "*Ideologiekritik*," for which there is no parallel among members of Karl Popper's followers in other countries. The widespread participation of sociologists in public debates and disputes, which continues to this very day, indicates not only a particular and widely shared self-conception of sociologists as sociologists but also a receptivity to and an audience for sociological ideas and sociologically informed opinion which is considerably broader than in many English-speaking countries.[15]

One must also note that sociology frequently has been taught, even in the postwar period, under the aegis of other disciplines (such as *Wirtschaftswissenschaft* or *Staatswissenschaft*), or in special educational institutes (for example, the Wirtschaftshochschule in Hamburg), or separate teaching and research institutes or faculties (which later became universities, such as the Wirtschaftshochschule in Mannheim), which were either distinct from or not fully integrated into the classical university structure as conceived initially by Wilhelm von Humboldt.[16]

Finally, German sociologists have given much attention to such questions as the professionalization of sociology, possible career paths for sociologists, and sociology's task within practical training below the level of post-secondary education.[17] However, the issue of professionalization is approached in German sociology not as a mere technical question: It is not just asked how obstacles to secure well-defined career-patterns for trained sociologists can be removed. On the contrary, professionalization itself is at issue. In particular the cult of specialization (*Spezialistentum*) is deplored as an intellectual and moral aberration from a more broadly based cultural and social awareness (e.g. essay 4) the growing intellectual division of labor is regarded as a violation of a more principled commitment to the theoretical and critical comprehension of the society as a whole, a task which cannot be accomplished by sociology alone (e.g. essay 10).

What, then, are the particular features of sociology as practiced in Germany? Much of postwar German sociology has not been essentially different in either method or theory from other sociologies. This applies, for example, in particular to a vast body of empirical research in industrial sociology and to the study of public administration, of organizations,[18] class relations and social inequality, of public opinion research, and so on. There are differences in emphasis, to be sure, distinctive modifications and critiques of research practices followed by quantitative sociologists. Yet as late as 1959 Ralf Dahrendorf could claim that "foreign sociologists do not even open the publications of German sociologists with the expectation to find something which contributes to problems which matter to them."[19]

The empirical social research carried out during the "consolidation" phase of West German sociology indeed is a kind of mainstream sociology.[20] It proved to be the basis of professional legitimation for that generation of sociologists which followed most directly the small group of German sociologists who had been crucial in reestablishing the discipline in the 1950s and 1960s. The social research during the emergence of the welfare state also is a reflection of the distinct sociopolitical climate of the time, in particular the broad *consensus* on social, political, and economic matters in the era of reconstruction and therefore not merely the outcome of an Americanization of German sociology.

However, the situation has changed substantially since the late fifties. Authors such as Adorno and Horkheimer, Dahrendorf and Habermas, but also scholars of quite different theoretical orientations, such as Thomas Luckmann, Norbert Elias, and, more recently, Niklas Luhmann, Claus Offe, and Wolfgang Schluchter, are widely read abroad. Even Arnold Gehlen, an austere figure of deeply conservative inclination, whose thought runs counter to the liberal traditions of Anglo-American and French social thought, has received attention.[21] But often these writers are not read as sociologists, certainly not as "mainstream" sociologists, with the exception of Dahrendorf and perhaps Luckmann and, increasingly, Luhmann. They are perceived as philosophers or social and political theorists,[22] and therefore as concerned with the ethical, philosophical, and methodological foundations of social science, or they are seen as philosophical anthropologists. Thus it becomes quite evident that Dahrendorf's verdict is now dated.

What to Dahrendorf, René König, and others has appeared as a form of provincialism, is not merely a consequence of the collapse and destruction of dominant German traditions prior to 1933 and of the separation of German sociology and cultural life at large from other Western societies in the Nazi period; it may also be the result of resistance to "Americanization," as Schelsky, for example, argues,[23] that is, a refusal to conform to developments not merely in sociology but in American society as a whole.

Evidently, then, Schelsky continues to speak as a member of an older generation shocked by the successive waves of modernization (interpreted as Americanization) penetrating German social life. But the more fundamental issue of the relation of German sociology to German society has not vanished. It is taken up as a sociological critique of German society, in which sociology becomes a form of cultural criticism or, less directly, a critical reflection upon the developmental and rationalization potential of advanced industrial or late capitalist societies in general.

Moreover, in the meantime it has been possible for German sociologists to develop further what they have partly assimilated from
abroad. Niklas Luhmann, perhaps the most prominent sociologist (in a
professionally restricted sense) in Germany at present, has refined Parsons' structural functionalism and social systems theory into what
Luhmann himself calls "functionalist structuralism," and has made it
a formally more consistent theory.[24] Jürgen Habermas has achieved a
unique synthesis of philosophical analysis, social theory, and
sociology by employing and reorganizing materials primarily from
English-speaking countries. And Norbert Elias, who returned to
Germany only when he was close to eighty years old, applies sociological, historical, and social psychological approaches to the theoretical
and empirical study of long-term social processes. Ralf Dahrendorf's
engaged liberalism, his commitment to sociology as "applied enlightenment," finally, suggests a greater degree of political engagement than
is characteristic of American sociology. It also arises more clearly from
a sociological theory of society than such conceptions as Karl Popper's
"open society," on which Dahrendorf to some extent relies. If there
clearly are achievements, then, which are of major international significance, it is less clear to what extent these are the result of a particular sensitivity to, or involvement with, the peculiarities of the present
German situation, although they are undoubtedly linked to intellectual concerns deeply rooted in the German tradition.

New Forms of Rationalization: The "Conservative" Tradition

The theme of rationalization, which Weber had introduced into sociology, constitutes one of the central and unique theories of contemporary German sociology. It is connected with an ongoing reflection
among sociologists of different political and philosophical orientations
on the societal consequences of technology and science as the distinguishing forces of a new social order.

But because Max Weber's theory of capitalist rationalization,
which plays such a prominent role in Jürgen Habermas' *The Theory of
Communicative Action*, had a rather indirect influence in German sociology prior to the publication of Habermas' recent work and of
Wolfgang Schluchter's influential studies of Max Weber's sociology,
upon which Habermas also relies,[25] its influence manifested itself
mainly in the context of discussions concerning the contribution of sociology to comprehensive theories of society. This is indeed the kind of
sociology foreign observers expect from German sociologists, at least

those observers who regard German culture as deeply steeped in Hegelian philosophy and historicism, and who assume that philosophies such as phenomenology, hermeneutic phenomenology (Heidegger), hermeneutics, and even critical social theory all carry forward motifs from this tradition.

The dominant figures in German social thought all show a definite awareness of these cultural and philosophical origins. And they frequently interpret the theme of "occidental" rationalism in this light. Arnold Gehlen, for example, singles out the theme of "cultural crystallization," a term by which he wants to designate "the state of affairs in a given realm of culture that occurs as soon as all the fundamental potentialities contained within it have been developed" (essay 9). As a result, changes "in the premises" and in "basic views" become increasingly unlikely. This is true, according to Gehlen, for the period which began in the late nineteenth century, after Marx and Nietzsche, with the formation of the specialized social sciences, including sociology, and of specialized technologies, with their consequent division of society into experts and laymen.

Helmut Schelsky makes a somewhat similar point: "We produce scientific civilization not merely in the form of technology [*Technik*]. We also produce it perpetually and by necessity in a much more comprehensive sense as society and as soul [*Seele*]." And, he adds, "Man as a social being and as possessor of a soul has himself become a product of technological and scientific production."[26] Technological civilization carries this process forward without regard or concern for traditional ideologies, and transforms democracy in such a way "that the old forms of dominance [*Herrschaftsformen*] are left behind like empty husks."[27] And even where possible routes of escape, resignation, and opposition to this "iron cage" are mapped out, where it is recognized that only ever renewed reflection can stimulate the necessary inquiries into the meaning of this process itself, does a spirit of *amor fati* in the tradition of Nietzsche prevail in the end, just as in the case of Weber. This may also be expressed in Arnold Gehlen's characteristic terseness, that nowadays philosophers might as well heed a piece of practical advice and become engineers.

Here one is reminded of the German conservative writer Ernst Jünger, who many decades ago wrote *Der Arbeiter*,[28] which celebrated the industrial worker as the epoch-making prototype of human adaptation to the new age of technological dominance. The worker and the modern engineer were celebrated since they lived the new ethos of technological mastery. This ethos was regarded as the one Nietzsche had praised as well as feared, but which he had anticipated as the only general cultural attitude adequate to the new conditions of civilization after the demise of Christianity and of traditional aristocratic culture.[29]

Jünger, Gehlen, and Heidegger, it should be recalled, were opinion leaders. They were also conscious of the fact that they had been deeply implicated in the brief history of National Socialism. However, they neither repented nor apologized, but instead merely admitted to an "error": German Fascism, they claimed, was after all not the final and definitive realization of the will to gain conscious control of technological rationalization. It was rather a cataclysmic and deeply destructive consequence of the inescapable process of rationalization, living out its fate in blindness, confusion, and complete moral and political anarchy.

Authors such as Gehlen, Heidegger, and Jünger (of whom only Gehlen is close to sociology, although the others influenced it) do not regard the Nazi era as a refutation of their interpretations of the fate of modernity (of Western rationalization). They rather regard it as a confirmation. In their own view, they were wrong in their initial positive response to National Socialism, not so much because they erred morally, but because in a historical field in which morality, as Nietzsche insisted, can no longer provide guidance, they had erred intellectually: They had not only failed to realize that the new technological order could establish itself without resorting to brute physical force after all, but had also failed to correctly diagnose the historical trend toward refined systems of technological domination and control which can, on the whole, do without open use of brute force.[30]

It is important to recognize that figures such as Gehlen in social theory and philosophical anthropology,[31] Heidegger in philosophy, and Jünger in literature, all belong to a generation which reached intellectual maturity in the 1920s. The case of someone like Helmut Schelsky in a more recent generation, however, is different. Although Schelsky builds on Gehlen, his work shows a more pragmatic, more political, less heroic, and more humane concern with the new forms of domination, which he himself described as "instruction, supervision, and planning" (*Belehrung, Betreuung, Beplanung*).[32] This is not to say that Schelsky is not old-fashioned enough to seek salvation in metaphysical terms: for he assigns to sociology the task of attempting an answer to the question of "how metaphysical positions are possible at all in a scientific civilization."[33] But he also recognizes that "depoliticization" and the dissolution of democracy are actual dangers and that the technical spirit of science must be transcended, not by relying on philosophy or *Weltanschauung*, but from within the sciences themselves.[34] None of this is altogether clear or immediately practicable since Schelsky's recommendations remain hesitant and haphazard.[35]

The relations between science and public opinion, the question of scientific education (*Bildung*), or the issue of the limits to the scientization of social practice have, for example, been grasped much more clearly by Jürgen Habermas in his numerous papers on these topics, as well as in his more systematic works. This applies even more to the issues of democracy (democratization) and depoliticization. Even someone like Adorno was more specific than Schelsky at times, for example when recommending ways to counteract the increase in unconscious behavior associated with the systems of technological manipulation and estrangement. This is, of course, even more characteristic of the younger sociologists and cultural critics, often influenced by Adorno and Habermas, especially insofar as they belong to the radically democratic, Marxisant left (see essays 12, 13, and 15). And it certainly holds for Ralf Dahrendorf's frequent contributions to political debate in the Federal Republic.

Niklas Luhmann also belongs to the conservative tradition although in quite a different sense.[36] And, of course, he primarily is a sociologist, not a cultural or social critic, or a philosopher or social thinker. But Luhmann is not just a sociologist either. Most of all, he is a sociological theorist, and as such also a sociologist of sociology and of social theory. A sociology of sociology is central to his sociology. All his sociological investigations are accompanied by systematic reflection on the status of the observations made, on the reasons why they can be properly called sociological. One might say that insofar as societies are systems which reduce complexity, by engaging in increasingly risk-burdened, system-differentiating actions, sociology has a central place in the societal subsystem of science. For sociology consciously represents the very process of societal self-differentiation. It is the subsystem which theoretically articulates the process in which subsystems are formed. Insofar as it can take an action-guiding role, it can contribute to the process of rationalization by making societal subsystems more conscious and more aware of alternative possibilities, for example by introducing additional specifications, system differentiations of action systems.

The conservative inheritance is brought home insofar as Luhmann (just like his predecessors Arnold Gehlen and Helmut Schelsky) views the process of technical rationalization without considering normative aspects, traditional values, or general philosophical and ideological standards. But in contrast to Gehlen and Schelsky, Luhmann no longer relies on Nietzsche. Nor is there an attempt to explore the future by calling upon a pretechnological, preindustrial past apparently richer in cultural possibilities (as Gehlen does). Luhmann is unabashedly modern and contemporary, but not without a consciousness of history. In this he is comparable to his intellectual opponent Jürgen Habermas, who is perhaps, and paradoxically, the only real *theorist* of liberal democracy Germany has known in the twentieth century. Luhmann makes no concessions to conservative doubts about the process of rationalization. He liberates the legacy of German conservatism in sociology from its conservative ideology by unreservedly accepting the rationalizing potential of technology and science, and by introducing a form of sociological consciousness to the process which he regards as adequate to it.

But Luhmann's contribution reaches beyond the mere transformation of a conservative legacy. Many of his investigations begin with the contrast between the classical traditions of European social thought reaching from Plato and Aristotle to the nineteenth century, and sociology itself as the theory of social systems. The older tradition placed concepts such as *philia* (friendship) and justice or *koinonia* (community, *Gemeinschaft*) at its centre. This tradition based its concept of society on these notions, thus giving primacy to political society. It therefore made the "political contingency of 'the good life' a primary issue," as Luhmann says, rather than the "social contingency of the world."[37] With sociology as the theory of social systems, the social contingency of the world rather than the political contingency of the ethically defined good life becomes the primary issue. Political society can no longer be the guiding system of society, nor can concrete and substantive concepts such as values, goals, needs, and interests remain at the center of social theory.

Sociology becomes radically functionalist. It inquires into the social function of any structure, thus analyzing abstract mechanisms for the generalization of values, beliefs, and attitudes, which give priority to their change. Any direct reference to human nature or any other stable normative conception is eliminated. The only criterion defining the increasing rationalization of society is that of an increasing functional differentiation of society, i.e., the generation of mechanisms "which have to be more abstract and more situationally specific at the same time."[38] Clearly, Luhmann in the end has much more in common with his teacher Parsons than with any German sociologist. It is also apparent that social evolution for Luhmann is a directional process, to choose a formulation which the later Parsons employs in making reference to Weber.

At the same time, one cannot fail to notice that societal rationalization is described by Luhmann much less in terms of an evolving "societal community" or as a "company of equals" than is true for Parsons. There is less emphasis in Luhmann on principles such as egalitarianism and rights or values, and hardly any emphasis at all on the "development of modern institutions of citizenship"[39] as a basis of social solidarity. In a sense Luhmann seems to read Gehlen's philosophical anthropology into Parsons' systems theory of modern societies. Gehlen regards philosophical anthropology, concerned as it is with the relation between institutions and instinctual makeup of human beings, as foundational for sociology. He observes: "How is it that man achieves predictable, regular conduct . . . in the face of his openness to the world [*Weltoffenheit*], his instinctual deficiency, his plasticity and instability. . .? Raising this question amounts to posing the problem of institutions." Human groups, Gehlen maintains, are kept together by "habits of thought, emotion, valuing and action, which solidify themselves in them and become automatic."[40]

Like Gehlen, Luhmann thinks in terms of such "openness to the world," and he views the relation between human groups and environments as burdened by risks and uncertainty. But he does not seek to ground these claims in anthropological assumptions. Rather, for Luhmann those social mechanisms which ensure the stability of social action are central, even if in modern societies this stability can be found only in the increasing replaceability of one structural arrangement by another. Luhmann thus exorcises Gehlen's respect for the past (with its admiration for what Gehlen views as rigid, yet admirable institutional structures of primitive societies, and its disdain for the apparently arbitrary organization of the most advanced modern societies) and subordinates it to the future-oriented emphasis on modernization which is also typical of Talcott Parsons. Yet there remain common conceptions between Gehlen and Luhmann, in particular their shared notions of values and norms, a similar indifference to declarations of principles for political democracy, a similar preference for those institutions of the modern state which require professional qualifications and dedication to organizational goals as a criterion of membership, rather than electoral success.

Further analysis of Luhmann's work cannot be provided here. But it is worth noting that the peculiarly German element in Luhmann's theory is perhaps the need to derive the system of society from a fundamental relationship to the world as such, and to see questions of democratic values and norms as secondary to such issues as gains in power, mastery, flexibility, and competence, which are perceived as the real evolutionary gains for modern societies.

So far we have described the conservative stream of German sociology. We have identified a concept of social theory and sociology which primarily exists in this form in Germany. But this is not to say that it is the dominant form of sociology and social theory in Germany. However, it does link contemporary German sociology to the ideological currents which precede and postdate the period of National Socialism. It represents a continuity of thought which is elsewhere difficult to find, a current of thought which once was deeply nationalistic and aristocratic, in Nietzsche's sense, even hostile, as in Gehlen's case, to pluralist democracy and to the rise of the intellectual and cultural critic as a figure of public influence. This current of thought is antagonistic as well to a concern with values or, following Nietzsche, it often prefers strength and institutional and national loyalty, in short, values of the counter-Enlightenment. It must be stated clearly, however, that with Luhmann this tradition has been transcended. Luhmann is immune to general ideological considerations, by virtue of his introducing a radicalized Parsonian framework into German sociology. Flexibility takes precedence over rigidity, and international culture and a global society take precedence over narrow conceptions of German culture and the German national state.

We have discussed the "conservative" current of German sociology in detail in order to direct attention to what can be seen as the "deep structure" of German sociology. Readers will notice, for example, that only Kurt Lenk's comprehensive paper (essay 2) addresses similar considerations. Other contemporary historians of German sociology have been much more concerned to identify the detailed complexities of the classical theorists. They can be read as partial correctives to more comprehensive perspectives, such as the one we have proposed so far.

We have already mentioned that a figure such as Ralf Dahrendorf definitely stands apart from the currents considered so far. If anything, Dahrendorf, in his commitment to a thoroughgoing liberalism of a humanist persuasion, radicalizes certain social and political commitments of distinctly British liberal traditions. This is perhaps the result of Dahrendorf's intent to remedy the suppression of Enlightenment traditions in Germany, in the hope of thus identifying the humanizing potentials of sociology as "applied enlightenment." Thus Dahrendorf is not merely an advocate of modernization in its value-free sense. In his book *Life Chances*, he uses sociology for the articulation of definite value commitments, such as the balance between the values of "equality of opportunity" and the securing of communal bonds (ligatures), thereby clarifying the notion of life-chances.[41] He expresses a certain skepticism toward unbridled modernization, which Habermas seems to share, but Luhmann would tend to dismiss.

There also is, of course, a great deal of German sociology which has nothing in common with all this, especially in the various specialized fields of sociology, such as the sociology of industrial organization, of work, of social inequality, of public administration, of leisure (*Bindestrichsoziologien*, as German sociologists call them), of which it is hard to say how they differ, if at all, from work in these fields done in other parts of the world. And there are developments such as phenomenology which, although they began in Germany, have in the recent past been more influential abroad than in postwar Germany and which have sometimes returned to Germany after they had been successful, and of course transformed, in the United States.[42]

New Forms of Rationalization: The "Critical" Tradition

Our discussion has so far been primarily organized around the conflict between counter-Enlightenment and Enlightenment traditions. We have also emphasized developments in sociology which see in it more than a specialized social science, and we have emphasized its affinity to social philosophy and political thought, thus singling out certain features of sociology in Germany which have always been regarded as its special trademark.

We therefore now turn to the Frankfurt School, or critical theory, as a development in social theory and sociology which has received more national and international attention than any other school of German sociology.[43] The members of the Frankfurt School must be regarded as opponents of the counter-Enlightenment traditions in German social thought. Without their influence neither Marx's work nor psychoanalysis would have been reintroduced as systematically and thoroughly into recent German sociology as has in fact happened from the mid-1960s onward. Several of our selections represent these trends (see the contributions by Adorno, Habermas, Offe, Eder, Negt, Dahmer, and Oevermann). The recent discussions of the development of contemporary German sociology all acknowledge the influence of the Frankfurt School. Yet critical theory is nevertheless often regarded as a mixed blessing at best. Professional sociologists committed to sociology as a social science discipline frequently regard the methodological debates provoked by critical theory as sterile or as much too philosophical. This attitude is quite compatible with König's emphasis upon sociology as "nothing but sociology," but not with the orientation of Schelsky or Gehlen, for example. Luhmann has usually ignored critical theory altogether, except, of course, for his well-known debate with Habermas, in which he appears to have participated more reluctantly than his opponent.

Others have complained vigorously about the "negative image" critical theory has conferred upon sociology as a whole. It is said, for example, that the Frankfurt School unduly politicized German social science students of the late 1960s, thus alarming the public in general and employers in particular. Its emphasis upon theory and a critical attitude as a procedure of philosophical reflection is said to have distracted from sociology proper and from its necessary cognitive and institutional development toward professionalization, and turned sociology itself into a form of cultural and social criticism. Yet the Frankfurt School has successfully affected philosophical discourse in Germany and has had considerable impact in various fields, from psychology (and psychoanalysis) to political science, literary and art criticism, media studies, etc.

This influence has occurred in two broad phases. The first phase is mostly associated with Theodor W. Adorno's enormous influence as a teacher and author, especially in the 1960s and until his death in 1969. Adorno drew the attention of intellectuals to the importance of the social sciences. His analyses ranged from those on Marx, psychoanalysis, research on industrial society, and studies of the formation of public opinion to critical examinations of the methods of empirical social science, cultural alienation and prejudice, and the effect of the Hitler period on German cultural consciousness.[44]

The second phase is largely linked to Jürgen Habermas' work, which is concerned with a reformulation of critical theory as a comprehensive theory of society. Habermas has systematically broken through a variety of barriers characteristic of conservative sociology and social thought in Germany as well as of the older tradition of the Frankfurt School. Together with Karl-Otto Apel and others he pioneered a critical reading of Peirce, Wittgenstein, and Searle, as well as of G.H. Mead and Talcott Parsons. More recently, he has brought within his compass the tradition of cognitive psychology from Piaget to Kohlberg, which led to new approaches in socialization theory (see essays 8 and 21).[45] Habermas has also contributed to a renewal of interest in interpretive orientations in sociology, of both German and non-German origin, from phenomenology and hermeneutics to ethnomethodology. In addition, there is the continuous reexamination of the classics, from Marx to Freud and Weber, from Mead and Durkheim to Parsons. Most recently, even Lukács, Horkheimer, and Adorno have been placed among those classics who still deserve to be heard, but whose limitations must also be recognized.

Several of the younger authors in our collection have worked with Habermas (Offe, Eder, Negt, Oevermann) and either been influenced by him or have been his collaborators. Habermas has also had a close working relationship with such psychoanalytic writers as Mitscherlich (essay 19), Lorenzer,[46] and Dahmer (essay 18). Our selections testify to at least one major consequence of this unique network of influence: Critical theory has become much less speculative today than it was in the generation of its founders. Both Offe and Eder, for example, treat their general theoretical frameworks as open to question, as in need of empirical, especially historical, confirmation. They have put considerable effort into the analytical clarification of theoretical concepts and have thereby moved away from Horkheimer's and Adorno's Hegelian notions of conceptual knowledge. They no longer refer, for example, to knowledge of the society in its totality, as Adorno did in his essay "Late Capitalism or Industrial Society?" (essay 10).

The same methodological and metatheoretical sophistication is also practiced by such psychoanalytically oriented authors as Alfred Lorenzer, and it is characteristic of the work of Helmut Dahmer as well. And even Alexander Mitscherlich, a generation older than Habermas, employed psychoanalysis more cautiously for purposes of social criticism than was ever true for Adorno.

Marxists, such as Alfred Schmidt[47] or Oskar Negt (essay 12), who are closer to the early Horkheimer (Schmidt) or Adorno (Negt) than to Habermas, are clearly more concerned in their analyses with historical detail and with precise periodization, for example, of German social and political history.

What is, broadly speaking, the position of the Frankfurt School on rationalization? And can its contribution to sociology and social thought be designed as a *German* contribution to sociology? One answer we can rule out in advance: that the Frankfurt School is "German" in the strict sense of committing itself to a specific national tradition. Its very intention is cosmopolitan, its style and attitude urbane, not merely reflecting German and Austrian but also French cultural sophistication (Adorno) and, at least since Habermas, it is influenced by

Anglo-American philosophy and sociology as well.

For Horkheimer, Adorno, and Habermas (not to speak of Marcuse), having been born, grown up, and worked in Germany or Austria meant little more than it meant to Karl Marx or Sigmund Freud. But what does this analogy to Marx (and Freud) suggest? German society, German cultural developments and attitudes, are a favored object of criticism from the vantage point of a critique committed to social and political emancipation. In this sense, Horkheimer, Adorno, and also Habermas are radical Enlightenment theorists for whom emancipation always also means emancipation from national and nationalistic preoccupations and prejudices, from cultural provincialism and isolation. Germany is a favored object of criticism for the members of the Frankfurt School because Germany's fate also throws light upon the possible universal fate of all societies, namely the transformation of capitalist rationalization into a universal system of reification.

The social thought of the Frankfurt School is significant for sociology in that it proposes to place the concept of a societal totality at the very center of sociological analysis. Adorno, for example, argues that empirical investigations must be linked with central theoretical questions. The system of society must be placed ahead of the procedures and facts of science, thus requiring of sociology that it form a concept of the society and of the objectivity of social processes and structure. This has implications for the method of sociology. Sociological analysis has to become "immanent" analysis. Rather than letting the subject of social analysis be governed by the requirements of sociological methods, the methods themselves must be fashioned in a way adequate to the object. This entails an examination of the development of rationalization in terms of a dialectical theory still inspired by Marx. And here tension between the productive forces and the relations of production remains the issue. But this tension no longer points to a liberating resolution, because the dominance of the exchange of equivalents as a primarily economic mechanism of societal regulation has been transformed into a more universal form of authority relations: "industrial procedures and methods reach into the spheres of material production, administration and distribution, as well as into the sphere of 'culture.' They do so with economic necessity" (essay 10).

Adorno's theory, then, is still located within a (broadly speaking) Marxist framework. However, it also lends support to those critics who find that Adorno's theory leaves unexamined the theory of surplus value, i.e., the central doctrine of "economist" Marxism and that it therefore constitutes a kind of hidden orthodoxy. This remains true, even though Horkheimer's and Adorno's *Dialectic of Enlightenment*[48] had already generalized Marx's conception of the reification of social relations (of commodity fetishism) into a critique of a presumably universal and inescapable process of the reification of cultural consciousness, reaching from Homeric Greece to the twentieth century. Following Horkheimer, cultural studies based on this conception have been called "critiques of instrumental reason."

Habermas, in his discussion of the dialectic of rationalization[49] characterizes these views as a construction and a retreat from a more broadly based and less speculative program of interdisciplinary research (essay 8). It is a retreat to the philosophy of history and thus from sociology. He himself, in virtually all his publications since 1973, has attempted to reconstitute critical theory independently from "an objective teleology of history."[50] For him social theory becomes a vehicle for the formulation of far-reaching empirical hypotheses and of nontrivial — i.e., heuristically powerful — conjectures about the potential for continued rationalization in contemporary societies and of possible crises brought about in this process which must be creatively resolved. Habermas only employs philosophy *in conjunction with* sociological theory: The rationality of social action and of societal rationalization processes are to be analyzed in their full range. In his view, the reduction of communicative rationality to instrumental or purposive rationality (*Zweckrationalität*) must be avoided. It comes as no surprise, therefore, that Habermas has placed the tradition of critical theory squarely within the context of the classical dispute on the relation between Marx and Weber (see essay 3), who are clearly the two leading figures of a specifically German tradition in sociology.[51] Nowhere else has the history of sociology been so closely linked to the confrontation of and the possible convergence between these two classical theorists.

Democracy and the History of Rationalization

Habermas' interpretations of Weber and Marx, which are based on his communication theory of society, represent just one instance of the renewed interest in Weber and other classics of German sociology, most notably among them Georg Simmel. Other studies as well indicate an interest either in Weber's theory of politics[52] or in Weber's studies of the history of Western rationalization,[53] which cannot be separated, in contemporary West Germany, from either a confrontation with Marx's influence or from reflection on democratic political processes. It is again Habermas who initially formulated this constellation of questions. In *Strukturwandel der Öffentlichkeit*, Habermas began a review of the political tradition of Enlightenment social thought, which included Hegel and Marx, and he thus placed Marx squarely into the context of the development of liberal-democratic thought.[54] We find a similar concern for the fate of liberal democracy in Oskar Negt's "The Poverty of Bourgeois Democracy in Germany" (essay 12). While Habermas' historical studies are carried out primarily in order to gain insight into the conditions for the possibility of an increasing discursive (communicative) rationalization of social practice (which practically speaking, amounts to its democratization), Negt's essay is meant to remind a German public of a history in which liberal-democratic traditions were never fully realized. It is no coincidence that Negt has also contributed to studies of the public sphere, in his case with a strong emphasis on the possibility of a "proletarian" public.[55]

In both cases, however, sociology is integrated into a theory of politics and of publicly consequential communication. Many other sociologists, most prominently Luhmann, treat democracy as just one topic among others for sociology. Thus, there is an interest both in normative questions of democratic theory, to which sociological questions are subordinated, and in the organizational structures of democracies in general or those of the institutions of the Federal Republic in particular.

We have also encountered Dahrendorf's intermediate position, which suggests the unique socially emancipatory function of sociology for democratic societies. Overall it can hardly be denied that German sociology has come a long way since 1945. Older positions, conservative or otherwise, committed to national cultural traditions or not, were based on a global theory of history and insisted that they themselves were exempt from capitalist rationalization.[56] If one interprets either Gehlen's and Schelsky's, or Horkheimer's and Adorno's (as well as Marcuse's) theories as responses to Weber, they appear to be "progressive" transformations. For Weber's legacy was ambiguous: Capitalist rationalization was seen as simultaneously unavoidable and destructive. Many authors who have attempted to somehow resolve this ambivalent diagnosis were driven in the end to share Weber's attitude of stoic resignation or of impotent protest. In the meantime, a considerable body of sociology has developed in Germany in the "specialized sociologies," unencumbered by most of these problems, but influencing the generation of theorists which includes Dahrendorf, Habermas, and Luhmann. The younger German sociologists have also provided perceptive interpretations of the problems significant to the older generation, often by crossing barriers insurmountable for the latter. They no longer share the earlier pessimism, even if critical questions are asked about contemporary capitalism and state socialism, peace and war, science and society, the environment and industrial society, and about the future of democratic societies. The younger generation can discuss Marx and the history of Marxism, as well as the history of non-Marxist sociology and social theory, without being trapped by many of the past hostilities.

We may therefore conclude that Enlightenment traditions of social thought have finally been accepted in Germany more thoroughly than ever before. They have become part of a reflection on the possibilities of further societal rationalization and of a searching reflection on the very meaning of this process.

The crisis of the postwar period has led to a highly developed form of social and political self-reflection, and to a refinement in sociology of both foundational theory and questions of method. The resulting quest for a role of sociology (and of the social sciences in general) in the achievement of a rational society may constitute the most distinctive contribution of German sociology to the discipline at large. In this sense we may regard it as just as German as the works of Marx and Weber — and also as just as international.

NOTES

1. It is important to point out that this volume deals for the most part only with West German sociology. The quite different social, political, and economic developments in the German Democratic Republic are not examined in regard to their impact on sociological activities and thought. Our restriction is self-exemplifying. The attention paid in West Germany to the development of sociology in the GDR is quite limited. By contrast, the critical and distancing reception in the GDR of the intellectual developments typical of West German sociology has been persistent and surprisingly lively. See, e.g., Kurt Braunreuther and Helmut Steiner, "Zur Situation der bürgerlichen Soziologie in Westdeutschland," in Kurt Braunreuther, ed., *Zur Kritik der bürgerlichen Soziologie in Westdeutschland* (Berlin: Verlag der Wissenschaften, 1962), pp. 9-85; Kurt Braunreuther, *Ökonomie und Gesellschaft in der deutschen bürgerlichen Soziologie* (Berlin: Verlag der Wissenschaften, 1964); Michael Thomas, "Konservative Soziologie — konservative Soziologiegeschichte," *Deutsche Zeitschrift für Philosophie* (1984) 32:587-592.

2. One of the enduring themes of controversy in postwar German sociology is the question to what extent there *is* a continuity between pre- and postwar German society. How profound a transformation has there in fact been, and in which institutions and cultural formations has it been most evident, especially in West Germany? Such issues have been taken up, at first somewhat hesitantly but later more deliberately. See Ralf Dahrendorf, *Bildung ist Bürgerrecht* (Hamburg: Nannen, 1965). See also Wolfgang Zapf, *Beiträge zur Analyse der deutschen Oberschicht* (Munich: Piper, 1964) and his *Wandlungen der deutschen Elite* (Munich: Piper, 1965).

3. One of the strongest indictments of these intellectual and political commitments may be found in Georg Lukács' *Die Zerstörung der Vernunft* [1954], 2d ed. (Neuwied: Luchterhand, 1962) [*The Destruction of Reason*, P. Palmer, tr. (Atlantic Highlands, N.J.: Humanities Press, 1981)]. Lukács sees many sociologists wittingly or unwittingly supporting the destruction of reason through fascism. An enduring theme of postwar debates among sociologists in West Germany has been the question of the collaboration of sociologists who remained and were trained in Germany during the Nazi regime. Among the major opponents in this debate are René König and Helmut Schelsky. See Helmut Schelsky, *Ortbestimmung der deutschen Soziologie* (Düsseldorf: Diederichs, 1959); "Zur Entstehungsgeschichte der bundesdeutschen Soziologie. Ein Brief an Rainer Lepsius," *Kölner Zeitschrift für Soziologie und Sozialpsychologie* (1980) 32:417-456, and René König, "Über das vermeintliche Ende des deutschen Soziologie vor der Machtergreifung des Nationalsozialismus," *Kölner Zeitschrift für Soziologie und Sozialpsychologie* (1984) 36:1-42; "Die alten Geister kehren wieder...Helmuth Plessner zum 90. Geburtstag," *Kölner Zeitschrift für Soziologie und Sozialpsychologie* (1982) 34:538-548. The controversy between Schelsky and König extends also to the intellectual status of sociology in the last years of the Weimar Republic and the renewal of sociology after the war in West Germany. See also Dirk Käsler, *Die frühe deutsche Soziologie in ihren Entstehungs-Milieus* (Opladen: Westdeutscher Verlag, 1984); Carsten Klingemann, "Soziologie im NS-Staat," *Soziale Welt* (1985) 36(3):366-387; and Helmut Berking, *Masse und Macht. Studien zur Soziologie in der Weimarer Republik* (Berlin: Wissenschaftlicher Autorenverlag, 1984).

4. The great majority of sociologists of the Weimar era emigrated (see René König, "Die Situation der emigrierten deutsche Soziologen in Europa," *Kölner Zeitschrift für Soziologie und Sozialpsychologie* (1959) 11:113-131; Svend Riemer, "Die Emigration deq deutschen Soziologen nach den vereinigten Staaten," *Kölner Zeitschrift für Soziologie und Sozialpsychologie* (1959) 11:100-112; M. Rainer Lepsius, "Die Entwicklung der Soziologie nach dem Zweiten Weltkrieg 1945 bis 1967," in Günther Lüschen, ed., *Deutsche Soziologie seit 1945*. Special issue 21 of the *Kölner Zeitschrift für Soziologie und Sozialpsychologie* (Opladen: Westdeutscher Verlag, 1979), pp. 26 ff. ["The Development of Sociology in Germany after World War II (1945-1968)," *International Journal of Sociology* (1983) 13(3):3-87]. Some who remained in Nazi Germany ceased to work as sociologists and a smaller group became advocates and practitioners of a new "German" sociology, e.g., Hans Freyer, Karl Valentin Müller, Karl Heinz Pfeffer, Max Rumpf, Andreas Walther; see Heinz Maus, "Bericht über die deutsche Soziologie 1933-1945," *Kölner Zeitschrift für Soziologie und Sozialpsychologie* (1959) 11:72-99; Urs Jäggi et al., *Geist und Katastrophe. Studien zur Soziologie im Nationalsozialismus* (Berlin: Wissenschaftlicher Autorenverlag, 1983); and especially Otthein Rammstedt, *Deutsche Soziologie 1933-1945. Die Normalität einer Anpassung* (Frankfurt: Suhrkamp, 1986).

5. Our emphasis will be on what may be called the "mature" phase of postwar sociology in Germany which, in our view, include its more recent intellectual accomplishments. All these matters have been discussed in Helmut Schelsky, *Ortsbestimmung der deutschen Soziologie*, as well as in "Zur Entstehungsgeschichte der bundesdeutschen Soziologie. Ein Brief an Rainer Lepsius"; see also Günther Lüschen, ed., *Deutsche Soziologie seit 1945*, and in that volume especially Lepsius' "Die Entwicklung der Soziologie nach dem zweiten Weltkrieg 1945 bis 1967." See also H. Braun, "Die gesellschaftliche Ausgangslage der Bundesrepublik als Gegenstand der zeitgenössischen soziologischen Forschung," *Kölner Zeitschrift für Soziologie und Sozialpsychologie* (1979) 31(4):766-795; Heinz Sahner, *Theorie und Forschung. Zur paradigmatischen Struktur der westdeutschen Soziologie und zu*

ihrem Einfluss auf die Forschung (Opladen: Westdeutscher Verlag, 1982); Johannes Weyer, *Westdeutsche Soziologie 1945-1960. Deutsche Kontinuitäten und Nordamerikanischer Einfluss* (Berlin: Duncker & Humblot, 1984); and Sven Papcke, ed., *Ordnung und Theorie. Beiträge zur Geschichte der Soziologie in Deutschland* (Darmstadt: Wissenschaftliche Buchgesellschaft, 1986).

The development of postwar sociology in the Federal Republic may be divided into three phases: (1) the reconstitution of sociology in the immediate aftermath of the war in the years 1945-1949, (2) the consolidation of the discipline between 1950 and 1966 which led to the establishment of four major centers (Berlin, Frankfurt, Cologne, and Münster) of sociology teaching and research (see Lepsius, "Die Entwicklung der Soziologie nach dem zweiten Weltkrieg 1945 bis 1967" ["The Development of Sociology in Germany after World War II (1945-1968)"]), and (3) the contemporary period which commences with the student rebellion but also includes, of course, the unprecedented growth of sociology in higher education up to the present with its stagnation of employment opportunities for sociologists both in universities and elsewhere. The contemporary period of sociology in Germany sees a new generation of sociologists educated in the postwar era take the place of those who had determined the character of sociology during the 1950s and part of the 1960s, and the emergence of a broad diversity of perspectives instead of the dominance of a few centers during the previous phase. Among these perspectives (which cannot be considered here in detail) are also those which arise from new social movements, such as the West German women's movement, the environmental and the peace movements (see Beck, essay 16; and Habermas, essay 8). They encompass a variety of historical, empirical, and critical sociological studies. These three distinct phases in the institutional development and character of sociology also correspond to dominant intellectual themes and preoccupations of German sociology.

6. The revival of sociology immediately after the war was in large measure the work of an older generation of scholars born between 1865 and 1885 (Alfred Weber, Leopold von Wiese, Alfred von Martin, Alexander Rüstow), who had their intellectual roots in the liberal traditions of the 1920s and who had remained in Germany. However, their influence was essentially limited to initiatives leading to the *institutional* reestablishment of sociology Their impact on the *intellectual* development of postwar sociology was comparatively insignificant. (see Lepsius, "Die Entwicklung der Soziologie nach dem zweiten Weltkrieg 1945 bis 1967" ["The Development of Sociology in Germany after World War II (1945-1968)"].

7. Equally significant, of course, is the large number of sociologists who, for different reasons, did not return to Germany or Austria to take up posts in universities. Among this group are Karl Mannheim (who, however, died in 1947), Norbert Elias (who did not return until the 1970s), Alfred Schutz, Leo Löwenthal, Herbert Marcuse, Karl August Wittfogel, Hans Speier, Theodor Geiger, and Paul Lazarsfeld.

8. The research centers which were responsible for these studies in the 1950s were frequently founded outside the universities, e.g., the Sozialforschungsstelle in Dortmund created with the financial support of the Rockefeller Foundation. Some of the empirical social research carried out here can be counted among the classics of postwar German sociology. (See Heinrich Popitz, Hans P. Bahrdt, Ernst A. Jüres, and Hanno Kesting, *Das Gesellschaftsbild des Arbeiters* (Tübingen: J.C.B. Mohr, 1957); Heinrich Popitz, Hans P. Bahrdt, Ernst A. Jüres, and Hanno Kesting, *Technik und Industriearbeit* (Tübingen: J.C.B. Mohr, 1957).

9. See Lepsius, "Anmerkungen zur Entwicklung und zum Praxisbezug der deutschen Soziologie," in Günther Lüschen, ed., *Deutsche Soziologie seit 1945*, pp. 4-9.

10. This debate was initially provoked by the Frankfurt School and especially by Adorno (essay 10). Most influential has been the collection by Theodor W. Adorno et al., *Der Positivismusstreit in der deutschen Soziologie* (Neuwied: Luchterhand, 1969) [*The Positivist Dispute in German Sociology* (London: Heinemann, 1976)]. But his *Soziologische Schriften I and II* (Frankfurt: Suhrkamp, 1972) are also significant. See also the collection of the Frankfurt Institute of Social Research, *Aspects of Sociology* (Boston: Beacon Press, 1972). Adorno's insistence that the theory of society (in a comprehensive sense) must have primacy over sociology as a specialized discipline, has been indirectly rejected by Schelsky (essay 4) and directly criticized by König (essay 5). König argues that the "theory of society" is no substitute for "sociological theory." See also René König, essay 4, and his "Einleitung," in René König, ed., *Handbuch der empirischen Sozialforschung* (Stuttgart: Enke, 1962), 1:11-12. The consolidation phase of German sociology was characterized by efforts to construct *sociological* theories while *theories of society* have become a preoccupation of sociologists in Germany since the mid-sixties. Theories of society, according to König, are closer to ideological conceptions with global intentions, a specific political agenda, and rarely subject to empirical analysis; while sociological theories aspire to be "nothing but sociology." See René König, *Soziologie* (Frankfurt: Fischer, 1958), p. 7; *Soziologie Heute* (Zürich: Regio, 1949); *Soziologische Orientierungen* (Cologne and Berlin: Kiepenheuer & Witsch, 1965); see also Emile Durkheim, *The Rules of Sociological Method* (Chicago: University of Chicago Press, 1938), p. 141. For Adorno, of course, limiting sociology to empirical and positive methods of research and to the corresponding form of theory-construction has as a consequence that it remains uncritical of ideologies.

11. The different functions of sociology as an "oppositional" or "stabilizing" discipline echo, of course, Horkheimer's distinction between traditional and critical theory, see Max Horkheimer, "Traditionelle und kritische Theorie," *Zeitschrift für Sozialforschung* (1937) 6(2):245-294 ["Traditional and Critical Theory," *Critical Theory: Selected Essays*, Matthew J. O'Connell et al., tr. (New York: Herder & Herder, 1972)]; are raised again by Jürgen Habermas in the early 1960s, see Jürgen Habermas, "Von den kritischen und konservativen Aufgaben der Soziologie," in Freie Universität Berlin, *Universitätstage 1962* (Berlin: de Gruyter, 1962); and become one of the central issues in the positivist dispute, see Theodor W. Adorno et al., *The Positivist Dispute in German Sociology*.

12. See Wolfgang Mommsen, *Max Weber und die deutsche Politik (1890-1920)* (Tübingen: J.C.B. Mohr, 1974) as well as the first published volume of the Max Weber *Gesamtausgabe*, *Zur Politik im Weltkrieg*. Schriften und Reden 1914-1918, vol. 15, Wolfgang J. Mommsen, ed. (Tübingen: J.C.B. Mohr, 1984).

13. See, for example, Jürgen Habermas, *Theorie des kommunikativen Handelns*, vols. 1 and 2 (Frankfurt: Suhrkamp, 1981) [*The Theory of Communicative Action*, vol. 1, Thomas McCarthy, tr. (Boston: Beacon Press, 1984)]. In vol. 1 Habermas refers to sociology in its classical phase as a science of the crisis of modern societies (p. 4). Arnold Gehlen's work (see essay 9) consists to a considerable extent of a diagnosis of the times. See his *Die Seele im technischen Zeitalter* (Reinbeck bei Hamburg: Rowohlt, 1957) [*Man in the Age of Technology*, P. Lipscomb, tr. (New York: Columbia University Press, 1980)]. Thus we are arguing that one can identify patterns of thematic continuity in German sociology, which reach from Marx, Weber, and Simmel to Gehlen, Schelsky, and the Frankfurt School. Here one may note that conservatives such as Gehlen have *also* expressed this respect for Marx (and Simmel), and critical theorists have learned from Weber, but also from Schelsky and

Gehlen (this is most clearly documented in Habermas' writings). And independent figures standing for underdeveloped liberal traditions in Germany such as Helmuth Plessner or Ralf Dahrendorf also address "crisis" themes, even if they may concentrate on German society.

Our argument suggests that the question of a crisis of "modernity" has also been the topic of philosophical analysis and reflection for quite some time. For example, it is manifestly present in Heidegger's and Jaspers' writings. The diagnosis of the times motivated by a consciousness of crisis may take a highly speculative form, as in Arnold Gehlen's and Theodor W. Adorno's work. Or the effort may be made to open it to scientific treatment. In this second instance it may come close to an analysis of social policy. See the introduction to Claus Offe and Wolf-Dietrich Narr, *Wohlfahrtsstaat und Massenloyalität* (Königstein: Anton Hain/Meisenheim Verlag, 1973), and Offe, "Die Sozialwissenschaften zwischen Auftragsforschung und sozialer Bewegung," in Ulrich Beck, ed., *Soziologie und Praxis. Erfahrungen, Konflikte, Perspektiven* (Göttingen: Otto Schwarz, 1982).

On the methodological principles at issue see Jürgen Habermas, *Legitimation Crisis* (Boston: Beacon Press, 1975). Undeniably, the theme of a "crisis of modernity" is not only addressed in Germany. One merely needs to consider the influence of French post-structuralism, and especially of Michel Foucault's work, in order to see this. For convergences between recent German and recent French sociological thought, see Axel Honneth, *Kritik der Macht. Reflexionsstufen einer kritischen Gesellschaftstheorie* (Frankfurt: Suhrkamp, 1985).

We are arguing here that this has been a theme which has been constitutive of the development of German sociology, in some major respects, at least since Max Weber's (and possibly Georg Simmel's) time. This had been openly acknowledged in the 1920s, for example by Karl Mannheim, who has also pointed to its origins in the German Hegelian and historicist-culturalist traditions.

14. These are, first (and most prominently), "The Positivist Dispute" (*Positivismusstreit*) with Adorno and Popper, Albert and Habermas as the major proponents, and Ralf Dahrendorf as commentator. The conference which was the occasion of this dispute took place in 1961; see Theodor W. Adorno et al., *The Positivist Dispute in German Sociology*. Second, the debate on the occasion of the 16th Congress of the German Sociologists on "Late Capitalism or Industrial Society", also the title of Theodor W. Adorno's introductory lecture (see essay 10), in 1968; see Theodor W. Adorno, et al., *Spätkapitalismus oder Industriegesellschaft?* (Stuttgart: Enke, 1969). Third, the debate between Habermas and Luhmann (see J. Habermas and N. Luhmann, *Theorie der Gesellschaft oder Sozialtechnologie — was leistet die Systemforschung?* [Frankfurt: Suhrkamp, 1971]), which was followed by several publications on the debate and its implications. Since then Luhmann's systems-theory has gained considerable currency among many theorists, including Habermas, Offe, and Eder.

There is also the collection by Karl-Otto Apel et al., *Hermeneutik und Ideologiekritik*, (Frankfurt: Suhrkamp, 1971) reflecting a debate initiated by Habermas in his *Zur Logik der Sozialwissenschaften* [1967] (Frankfurt: Suhrkamp, 1973). It primarily addresses foundational problems of social theory and social science, especially the status of psychoanalysis as a critical/emancipatory, as well as explanatory or "objective" hermeneutic employed in social understanding (see Oevermann, essay 21). Major participants were Karl-Otto Apel, Hans-Georg Gadamer, and Jürgen Habermas. However, a hermeneutical approach in the social sciences has so far not gained wide acceptance among German sociologists. There appears to be greater interest in hermeneutics in Anglo-American countries than in Germany, quite similar to the greater Anglo-American interest in phenomenology. However, some of Thomas Luckmann's German students have developed his interest in Alfred Schutz's social phenomenology, and have linked it, as is almost always the case in North America and Britain, to ethnomethodology and symbolic interactionism.

15. The commercial success of many works addressing sociological questions, such as the writings by the Frankfurt School theorists, and the extent to which sociologists, for example Ralf Dahrendorf and Helmut Schelsky, have written sociologically informed books of general appeal, is another indication of the success of sociologists in either setting the agenda for major public debates or in intervening in an influential manner in public discussion. As the political mood of these disputes changes, different groups of sociologists tend to take the offensive or defensive in these public debates. See Dahrendorf, *Gesellschaft und Demokratie in Deutschland* (Munich: Piper, 1965) [*Society and Democracy in Germany* [1969] (New York: Norton, 1979)] and Helmut Schelsky, *Die Arbeit tun die anderen. Klassenkampf und Priesterherrschaft der Intellektuellen* (Opladen: Westdeutscher Verlag, 1975).

16. This particular issue and educational issues in general have been a topic of considerable attention and interest among sociologists. *Bildungsforschung* is a well developed field in German sociology. It differs considerably from the sociology of education as practiced in North America, however. On the whole, it is more interdisciplinary in its organization and it has also influenced major debates about the nature and purpose of university education as well as primary and secondary schooling, in which several of the authors in our selection in one way or another participated (Schelsky, Dahrendorf, Gehlen, König, Adorno, Habermas, Oevermann). See Ralf Dahrendorf, *Arbeiterkinder an deutschen Universitäten* (Tübingen: J.C.B. Mohr, 1965) and his *Bildung ist Bürgerrecht* (Hamburg: Nannen, 1965). Also Helmut Schelsky, *Abschied von der Hochschulpolitik oder die Universität im Fadenkreuz des Versagens* (Bielefeld: Bertelsmann, 1969) and Ulrich Oevermann, *Sprache und soziale Herkunft* (Frankfurt: Suhrkamp, 1972). On the classical German university see Schelsky, *Einsamkeit und Freiheit* (Hamburg: Rowohlt, 1963).

17. During the consolidation phase this was a matter of concern in particular to René König, one of the founders of postwar German sociology and the intellectual initiator of the considerable emphasis on empirical research now evident in German sociology. Today, under very different circumstances — in particular stagnant university budgets, a highly skewed age distribution of sociologists teaching at German universities and rather poor employment opportunities for younger sociologists — this issue is of more general concern.

18. Renate Mayntz has been an important pioneer of the sociology of organizations during the second phase of German sociology after the second world war. See R. Mayntz, *Soziologie der Organisation* (Reinbek bei Hamburg: Rowohlt, 1963) and *Soziologie der öffentlichen Verwaltung* (Heidelberg: C.F. Müller, 1978). Niklas Luhmann and Wolfgang Schluchter are among those who have contributed to this field during the more recent phase. See Wolfgang Schluchter, *Aspekte bürokratischer Herrschaft* [1972], 2d ed. (Frankfurt: Suhrkamp, 1985), from which essay 14 has been taken. For information about Luhmann's numerous publications in this area, see Niklas Luhmann, *The Differentiation of Society* (New York: Columbia University Press, 1982), bibliography.

19. Ralf Dahrendorf, "Betrachtungen zu einigen Aspekten der gegenwärtigen deutschen Soziologie," *Kölner Zeitschrift für Soziologie und Sozialpsychologie* (1959) 11:139.

20. Mainstream social research continues to be carried out in West Germany and is for

the most part unaffected by the major theoretical and methodological debates and perspectives in contemporary German sociology.

21. See Gehlen, *Die Seele im technischen Zeitalter* [*Man in the Age of Technology*].

22. This holds in particular with respect to the Frankfurt School theorists. This evaluation may change, however, because of the response of sociologists in North America and Britain to Habermas' recent work, especially *The Theory of Communicative Action*. On Habermas' earlier work see Anthony Giddens, "Habermas' Social and Political Theory" and "Labour and Interaction," in *Profiles and Critiques in Social Theory* (Berkeley/Los Angeles: University of California Press, 1982), as well as other writings. An interesting example of a recent evaluation is Jeffrey C. Alexander's interpretation of Habermas' *The Theory of Communicative Action*. In "The Parsons Revival in German Sociology," in Randall Collins, ed., *Sociological Theory 1984* (San Francisco, Washington: Jossey-Bass, 1984), he refers to Habermas as a "critical Parsonian." See also his review essay on "Habermas' New Critical Theory: Its Promise and Problems," *American Journal of Sociology* (1985) 91(2):400-423. An important German collection on Habermas' book, which also contains a response of Habermas, is Axel Honneth and Hans Joas, eds., *Kommunikatives Handeln* (Frankfurt: Suhrkamp, 1986).

Claus Offe is increasingly recognized as a political sociologist and political scientist. Although originally linked with critical theory, he now stands for a new orientation emphasizing the contradictions of the welfare state and an analysis of systems problems for the reproduction of late capitalist societies. Here he is clearly influenced by Luhmann. See essay 15, taken from his *Strukturprobleme des kapitalistischen Staates* (Frankfurt: Suhrkamp, 1972), and *Leistungsprinzip und Industrielle Arbeit* (Frankfurt: Europäische Verlagsanstalt, 1970) [*Industry and Inequality* (New York: St. Martin's, 1977)], and especially his collection of essays entitled *Contradictions of the Welfare State*, J. Keane, ed. and tr. (Cambridge, Mass.: MIT Press, 1984) and *Disorganised Capitalism* (Oxford: Polity Press, 1985).

23. Schelsky, *Ortsbestimmung der deutschen Soziologie*, p. 27.

24. Niklas Luhmann, *Soziale Systeme. Grundriss einer allgemeinen Theorie* (Frankfurt: Suhrkamp, 1984). The apparent revival of Parsonian functionalism in the United States (see Jeffrey C. Alexander, "The Parsons Revival in German Sociology," in Randall Collins, ed., *Sociological Theory 1984*) has found considerable intellectual support in Germany, as is especially evident in the work of Richard Münch, whose stature as a social theorist is growing. See, for example, Richard Münch, *Theorie des Handelns. Zur Rekonstruktion der Beiträge von Talcott Parsons, Emile Durkheim, und Max Weber* (Frankfurt: Suhrkamp, 1982) and his *Die Struktur der Moderne. Grundmuster und differentielle Gestaltung des institutionellen Aufbaus moderner Gesellschaften* (Frankfurt: Suhrkamp, 1984).

25. See *Die Entwicklung des okzidentalen Rationalismus* (Tübingen: Mohr, 1979) [*The Rise of Western Rationalism: Max Weber's Developmental History* (Berkeley: University of California Press, 1981)]; and Wolfgang Schluchter, *Rationalismus der Weltbeherrschung* (Frankfurt: Suhrkamp, 1980).

26. Helmut Schelsky, *Der Mensch in der wissenschaftlichen Zivilisation* (Cologne-Opladen: Westdeutscher Verlag, 1961), p. 449.

27. *Ibid.*, p. 460. In the early 1960s, Schelsky's thesis of the increasing dominance of technological rationality in modern society and the question of the extent to which political decisions are now constrained if not actually determined by the logic of technology prompted the "technocracy" debate among German social scientists (see Helmut Schelsky,

ibid.; Arnold Gehlen, *Die Seele im technischen Zeitalter* [*Man in the Age of Technology*]; Jürgen Habermas, *Technik und Wissenschaft als Ideologie* (Frankfurt: Suhrkamp, 1968); Dieter Senghaas, "Sachzwang und Herrschaft," *Atomzeitalter* (1966) 3:366-370; Hans Lenk, *Philosophie im technischen Zeitalter* (Stuttgart: Kohlhammer, 1971). Without question these issues will be taken up again under various foci as is already evident (e.g., Walter Bühl, *Die Angst des Menschen vor der Technik* (Düsseldorf: Econ, 1983); Leo Kofler, *Beherrscht uns die Technik? Technologische Rationalität im Spätkapitalismus* (Hamburg: VSA-Verlag, 1983).

28. Ernst Jünger, *Der Arbeiter* (Hamburg: Hanseatische Verlagsanstalt, 1932).

29. This is reminiscent of Heidegger's sensitivity to these conceptions, of the "heroic nihilism" of *Being and Time* (1927), of the praise of the working collective and the power of industrial labor in his controversial address in support of Hitler delivered as rector of the Universität Freiburg in 1933, and above all of his careful and penetrating reinterpretation of Nietzsche's notion of the will to power as the "will to will" in his Nietzsche lectures in the 1940s. One should not be surprised by the affinity of this thinking to currents of thought present among radically conservative, yet also anti-bourgeois and anti-Marxist groups of intellectuals in the 1920s. Some of these currents provided a fertile ground for National Socialism among some educated groups in German society.

30. This analysis suggests a certain affinity between conservative social thought in Germany and the position taken by at least one major representative of critical social theory, Theodor W. Adorno. For a detailed comparison of Adorno with Heidegger, see Hermann Mörchen, *Macht und Herrschaft im Denken von Heidegger und Adorno* (Stuttgart: Kohlhammer, 1980). See also J. Habermas, *Theorie des kommunikativen Handelns*, 2:385. Our selection (essay 8) from this work indicates that Habermas has dissociated himself from this earlier phase in the history of critical social theory, which is dominated by Horkheimer's and Adorno's *Dialektik der Aufklärung* (Amsterdam: Querido, 1947) [*Dialectic of Enlightenment* (New York: Herder and Herder, 1960)]. For differences between the two positions, see the dispute between Adorno and Gehlen included in Friedemann Genz, *Adornos Philosophie in Grundbegriffen* (Frankfurt: Suhrkamp, 1974). The debate is entitled "Ist die Soziologie eine Wissenschaft vom Menschen? Ein Streitgespräch," pp. 223-311. The convergences as well as the differences between Gehlen's and Adorno's positions are quite clearly revealed in this debate.

31. Even if our discussion has placed much emphasis on Arnold Gehlen's approach to philosophical anthropology as a foundation for his sociology, it should be pointed out that Gehlen is neither the only nor even the first representative of this orientation in German sociology. Helmuth Plessner and Max Scheler published the first important works in philosophical anthropology in 1928. See Plessner, *Die Stufen der Organischen und der Mensch* [1928], 2d ed. (Berlin: de Gruyter, 1965) and Scheler, *Die Stellung des Menschen im Kosmos* (Darmstadt: Otto Reichl, 1928).

Plessner developed a theory of the preconditions of human life by beginning with the relation of humans to the natural world. One of his basic terms is the notion of the "human position of eccentricity," i.e., the idea that human beings are distinguished by their unique capacity for distancing themselves from objectifying the world and from themselves. This basic feature of the "human condition" can explain the social and historical variability of human attitudes and dispositions. Subjectivity (the capacity for self-reflection) and sociality are seen as complementary dimensions of human life. It is with reference to these polarities that Plessner addresses the concept of social role as well as sociological questions in general. His method requires an integration of philosophy with the empirical sciences.

Plessner's famous analysis of the failure of bourgeois liberal culture in Germany, provoked by the National Socialists' rise to power and published as *Die verspätete Nation. Über
die politische Verführbarkeit bürgerlichen Geistes* (Zurich: Max Niehans, 1935), revealed his concern with the question of the survival of Western civilization. This question, Plessner
argued, could be adequately addressed only by the new discipline of philosophical anthropology, which is to document the possibility of human freedom. Plessner's work has
been published as *Gesammelte Schriften*, 10 vols., G. Dux, O. Marquard, E. Ströker, eds.
(Frankfurt: Suhrkamp, 1980-1985).

Plessner's work has been continued by the contemporary sociologist Günter Dux, who
is also co-editor of Plessner's collected works and who attempts to connect the natural history of the human species with its cultural history. See Dux, *Die Logik der Weltbilder* (Frankfurt: Suhrkamp, 1982), and "Toward a Sociology of Cognition," in N. Stehr and V. Meja,
eds., *Society and Knowledge: Contemporary Perspectives on the Sociology of Knowledge* (New
Brunswick, N.J. and London: Transaction Books, 1984).

Another younger sociologist close to the position of philosophical anthropology is
Wolf Lepenies who, however, refers to his own position as "sociological anthropology,"
thus moving close to the French and Anglo-American traditions of social anthropology.
See W. Lepenies, *Soziologische Anthropologie* (Munich: Hanser, 1971) and W. Lepenies and H.
Nolte, *Kritik der Anthropologie* (Munich: Hanser, 1971). See also W. Lepenies, *Die drei
Kulturen. Soziologie zwischen Literatur und Wissenschaft* (Munich: Hanser, 1985).

32. Schelsky, *Die Arbeit tun die anderen.*

33. Schelsky, *Der Mensch in der wissenschaftlichen Zivilisation*, p. 46.

34. *Ibid.*, p. 459

35. Schelsky's sociology, even according to his own conception, ultimately evolves
into an *anti-sociology*, which represents a sociologically informed warning against a certain
kind of sociology, in particular against the cultural and political conceptions associated
with critical theory. Such a warning against sociology as a social and cultural force is generally shared by neoconservative sociologies. See Helmut Schelsky, *Die Arbeit tun die
anderen*; Schelsky, *Rückblicke eines 'Anti-Soziologen'* (Opladen: Westdeutscher Verlag, 1981);
Friedrich H. Tenbruck, *Die unbewältigten Sozialwissenschaften oder die Abschaffung des Menschen*
(Graz: Styria, 1984).

36. See Alexander, "The Parsons Revival in German Sociology." Alexander refers to a
"strain of *Realpolitik*" in Luhmann and to his relative conservatism (p. 403).

37. See Luhmann, essay 7.

38. Luhmann, *The Differentiation of Society*, pp. 248, 250, 251.

39. See Talcott Parsons, *The System of Modern Societies* (Englewood Cliffs, N.J.:
Prentice-Hall, 1971), pp. 139, 94, 22.

40. Arnold Gehlen, *Studien zur Anthropologie und Soziologie* (Neuwied: Luchterhand,
1963), p. 79.

41. Ralf Dahrendorf, *Life Chances* (Chicago: University of Chicago Press, 1979). See essay
11. The prevailing perception and the reputation of Dahrendorf's theoretical stance, based
on his publication in the late 1950s, in particular *Soziale Klassen und Klassenkonflikte*
(Stuttgart: Enke, 1957) [*Class and Class Conflict in Industrial Society* (Stanford: Stanford University Press, 1959)] and his critique of structural-functionalism, e.g., Dahrendorf, *Die
angewandte Aufklärung. Gesellschaft und Soziologie in Amerika* (Munich: Piper, 1963), is of

course that of a conflict theorist. On the other hand, Marxists, especially orthodox Marxists, see him as a representative of a more status quo oriented sociology (e.g. Braunreuther and Steiner, "Zur Situation des bürgerlichen Soziologie in Westdeutschland," pp. 41-47).

42. See Richard Grathoff, "Der Ansatz einer Theorie sozialen Handelns bei Alfred Schütz," *Neue Hefte für Philosophie* (1976) 9:115-113; Richard Grathoff and Bernhard Weidenfels, eds., *Sozialität und Intersubjektivität* (Munich: Fink, 1983); Fritz Sack et al., eds., *Ethnomethodologie. Beiträge zu einer Soziologie des Alltagshandelns* (Frankfurt: Suhrkamp, 1976); Ansgar Weymann, ed., *Kommunikative Sozialforschung* (Munich: Fink, 1976); Alfred Schütz and Thomas Luckmann, *Strukturen der Lebenswelt*, I and II (Frankfurt: Suhrkamp, 1979-1984); Manfred Anwärter, Edith Kirsch, Manfred Schröter, eds., *Kommunikation, Interaktion, Identität* (Frankfurt: Suhrkamp, 1976).

43. Our use of the term "school" does not imply that the members of the Frankfurt School represent a tight knit intellectual network. On the contrary, both in the past and at present, the Frankfurt School lacks many of the social and intellectual traits associated with a more restrictive meaning of the term "school." For further details see Martin Jay, *The Dialectical Imagination: A History of the Frankfurt School and the Institute of Social Research 1923-1950* (Boston: Little, Brown & Co., 1973) and Jay, *Marxism and Totality* (Berkeley and Los Angeles: University of California Press, 1984). See also Helmut Dubiel, *Wissenschaftsorganisation und Erfahrung. Studien zur frühen kritischen Theorie* (Frankfurt: Suhrkamp, 1978) [*Politics and Science* (Cambridge, Mass.: MIT Press, 1985)].

44. The edition of Adorno's collected works by Suhrkamp in 23 volumes (1982 to the present) testifies to the enormous range of his production. Here we can neither mention nor discuss the wide range of his studies in philosophy, literature and music (including the sociology of music).

45. See also R. Döbert, G. Nunner-Winkler, J. Habermas, *Entwicklung des Ich* (Cologne: Kiepenheuer & Witsch, 1977).

46. E.g., Alfred Lorenzer, *Sprachzerstörung und Rekonstruktion* (Frankfurt: Suhrkamp, 1970) and *Zur Begründung einer materialistischen Sozialisationstheorie* (Frankfurt: Suhrkamp, 1972).

47. See Alfred Schmidt, *Zur Idee der kritischen Theorie Elemente der Philosophie Max Horkheimers* (Munich: Hanser, 1974); *Die kritische Theorie als Geschichtsphilosophie* (Munich: Hanser, 1976); *History and Structure: An Essay on Hegelian-Marxist and Structuralist Theories of History* (Cambridge, Mass.: MIT Press, 1981).

48. Max Horkheimer and Theodor W. Adorno, *Dialectic of Enlightenment*.

49. Jürgen Habermas, *The Theory of Communicative Action*, especially vol. 1, ch. 2 ("Max Weber's Theory of Rationalization"), ch. 4 ("From Lukács to Adorno: Rationalization as Reification"), and vol. 2, ch. 8 ("Concluding Reflections: From Parsons to Weber to Marx").

50. *Ibid.*, vol. 2, pp. 555, 561.

51. Even prior to the appearance of *The Theory of Communicative Action*, Wolfgang Schluchter observed that Habermas stands for an integration of Marx with Weber (which may have the consequence that critical theory's links to Marx become even more tenuous). See W. Schluchter, *Aspekte bürokratischer Herrschaft*, p. 299.

52. Wolfgang Mommsen, *Max Weber und die deutsche Politik (1890-1920)*.

53. Wolfgang Schluchter, *The Rise of Western Rationalism: Max Weber's Developmental History*.

54. Jürgen Habermas, *Strukturwandel der Öffentlichkeit* (Neuwied: Luchterhand, 1962).

55. See Oskar Negt and A. Kluge, *Öffentlichkeit und Erfahrung. Zur Organisationsanalyse von bürgerlicher und proletarischer Öffentlichkeit* (Frankfurt: Suhrkamp, 1973).

56. Recent developments suggest also that the search for and the legacy of a German sociology which sees itself in conscious opposition to English, French, or American intellectual traditions is far from dead. Parts of the neoconservative movement in philosophy and social science find the uniqueness of German sociology precisely in those of its attributes which are connected with counter-Enlightenment tendencies, thereby continuing a tradition that was well analyzed by Karl Mannheim in 1925 in a manuscript only recently published in full. See Karl Mannheim, *Konservatismus*, David Kettler, Volker Meja, and Nico Stehr, eds. (Frankfurt: Suhrkamp, 1984) [*Conservatism*, David Kettler and Volker Meja, trs. (London and New York: Routledge & Kegan Paul, 1986)].

I

German Sociology: A Retrospective

Every social science discipline turns to its past for guidance, in particular at times of internal crisis and major social transformation. The history of sociology, which everywhere involves more than a widely acclaimed body of intellectual accomplishments and institutional successes, is consequently of special significance for the practice and the teaching of contemporary sociology. This is especially true in Germany, with its influential sociological tradition but also with its recent dark past in which many of these achievements were deliberately eradicated.

The development of sociology in postwar West Germany reflects to a considerable extent the broader social trends of German society, which may be roughly divided into several periods: the immediate postwar period with its special problems, the period of reconstruction during which sociology was reestablished as an academic discipline, and, starting in the late 1960s, the period of the breakdown of social consensus. At present, West German sociology, by and large reflecting the contemporary sociopolitical and economic situation, is attempting to come to terms with a sense of resignation and self-doubt, of having failed to live up to the enormous promise which infused sociology in the late 1960s and early 1970s. This perception of partial failure is also linked to its stagnating institutional basis in the German academic system.

It is precisely in such times of crisis that sociology tends to turn inward in order to find within its own traditions a new measure of hope, and a different orientation. The renewed interest in its own history represents an effort to gain a new sense of itself as a discipline and to prepare the ground for new intellectual departures.

The first selection in this part of the book deals with the complicated history of post-World War I sociology. M. Rainer Lepsius (essay 1) provides a most informative review of German sociology in which he examines its social, political, institutional, and intellectual context by focusing upon the interwar period. Lepsius pays special attention to the interdependence of intellectual developments in social science, cultural history, and sociopolitical events. But he wants to do more than merely write an intellectual and institutional history of sociology. His analysis is also prescriptive, that is, he attempts to strengthen a particular perspective in contemporary German sociology.

According to Lepsius, the interwar period is marked by the first successful establishment of a democratic political regime in Germany, the Weimar Republic, and its collapse, only fourteen years later, as a result of the National Socialist seizure of power in 1933. This period spanning some forty years witnessed World War I and its aftermath, the October Revolution, the economic depression in the 1920s, World War II, the Holocaust, the overthrow of National Socialism, the redrawing of European boundaries and the global redistribution of power. It is a period of fateful and rapid social change testifying to the best as well as to the worst possibilities of human action and imagination. But it is also an era which presents unusual difficulties for analysis, and not only because it tends even now to evoke strong emotional reactions.

For a short time after the end of World War I sociology flourished in Germany. However, the National Socialist seizure of power led to the forced emigration of many of its most prominent representatives. Those who remained behind, if they did not go into what some of them later liked to call "internal emigration," often busied themselves with dubious efforts to produce a sociological perspective in conformity with the regime's ideology. Thus, the truly productive phase of German sociology was limited to a brief creative period during the Weimar Republic, a political system ravaged by conflict and torn by crisis after crisis. But sociology, as has often been observed, may well be borne out of and respond to social conflict and crisis. Periods of crisis, at any rate, tend to heighten sociological self-reflection and self-criticism. As individual and public troubles explode in all seriousness and as political solutions are required ever more urgently, sociology seems to take up the challenge and attempt to provide a diagnosis.

Yet the sociology of the Weimar Republic, observes Lepsius, did not achieve a shared diagnosis, a consensus on the causes of the social crisis. Such sociologists and sociologically oriented scholars and intellectuals as, for example, Karl Mannheim, Max Horkheimer, Ferdinand Tönnies, Leopold von Wiese, Emil Lederer, Alfred Weber, Werner Sombart, Karl Korsch, Rosa Luxemburg, Max Scheler, and Helmuth Plessner never agreed on a uniform method of analysis of the sociological causes of the crisis or on how the severe social, political, and economic problems of the period might be tackled. Not surprisingly, the

Weimar Republic produced a highly differentiated but also fragmented sociological community still uncertain about itself and linked in many ways to the more established academic disciplines such as jurisprudence, history, philosophy, and economics. Sociology was often seen, both by many of its practitioners and by outsiders sympathetic to the sociological approach, as an integrative science which might be able to synthesize otherwise diverse approaches and even entire disciplines. It was also seen as a perspective with a certain moral and political claim, in addition to its scientific status. All of this gave sociology a highly ambivalent image. These features of German sociology during the Weimar Republic, furthermore, indicate that Max Weber's sociological program, including his methodological individualism and his call for a social science abstaining from value judgments, had not yet gained a significant following at this point.

Lepsius points out that important challenges and impulses for the development of sociology in the Weimar Republic often came from external sources and contexts, for example, from political events, from innovations in education outside the university system, or from the labor unions. This meant also that many sociologists were quite prepared and even desired to work in positions outside academia.

After the National Socialist seizure of power in 1933, nearly two-thirds of all sociology teachers lost their positions. Sociology as it had flourished in the Weimar Republic came to an abrupt halt. Certain traditions such as historicism, holism, idealism, and Social Darwinism continued to be accepted under the new regime but were quickly developed into what Lepsius calls a "partisan sociology." In general, however, National Socialism favored distinctly nonsociological conceptions of human existence, especially those which stressed inherited factors as determinants of the development of human societies. Only the exiled sociologists continued to work within those sociological traditions which, along with them, had been exiled as well. These traditions, in turn, gave rise to some of the most lucid and profound analyses of the emergence and the nature of German Fascism.

Kurt Lenk (essay 2) attempts to show that sociology in the Weimar Republic, in spite of the great fragmentation of sociological approaches, may well have had a relatively similar understanding of history. Lenk identifies the shared sociocultural context and the milieus which he sees as constitutive for the approaches of sociological scholars as different as Georg Simmel, Ernst Troeltsch, Max Weber, Max Scheler, and Karl Mannheim, whose analyses and vision of society converge, beginning with the decline of the German Empire, toward a tragic consciousness and a shared conviction of the "tragedy of culture."

In the case of Georg Simmel, it is the "philosophy of life" (*Lebensphilosophie*) which points to the increasing separation in modern society of human creations from human needs. Max Weber similarly points to the inescapable inversion of means and ends, which he regards as a permanent and tragic attribute of modern life. According to Weber, sociology cannot, in the end, even hope any longer to grasp the full complexity of social life in its thoroughgoing irrationality. The duality of reason and reality characteristic of modern society inevitably leads to a growing gap between theory and social practice, which can no longer be bridged. Lenk views Max Scheler's sociology and philosophical anthropology in similar terms. Scheler's conception is tragic as well since Scheler sees history as a cruel process which constantly destroys human values or neglects to respond to them in any way, and which is increasingly governed by "real" rather than "ideal" factors, as a result of which convictions, values questions, and ethical conceptions are lost from sight. Finally, Lenk analyzes Karl Mannheim's sociological program and concludes that Mannheim is engaged in a continual intellectual struggle to overcome the tragic implications of the crisis afflicting society, with its deep divisions of beliefs and social status and power position. However, Lenk considers the solutions to the crisis offered by Mannheim as ultimately doomed to fail, thereby further exemplifying the profundity of the tragic consciousness which few German sociologists of the time could escape and all had to respond to in some way or another.

The tragic consciousness described by Lenk was not shared by all sociologists, of course. Those, for example, who found their moral, political, and even scientific inspiration in Marxist thinking were little affected by it. This too helps to provide a sense of the factionalized character of the German sociological "community." The history of German sociology has in any case always been also a history of major controversies. Disputes about the nature of history, society, and the individual and on the possible impact of the social sciences are quite regular features in German social science. But some of the most vigorous and influential controversies were carried out among factions of the sociological community in the form of seminal *disputes*. Each generation of scholars appears to have had its own dispute, as it were. There is the dispute on methods (*Methodenstreit*) toward the end of the past century, the dispute on value-neutrality (*Werturteilsstreit*) at the beginning of this century, involving Max Weber and Werner Sombart, the brief sociology of knowledge dispute (*Streit um die Wissensoziologie*) in the late 1920s stimulated especially by Karl Mannheim's version of the sociology of knowledge, and there is, most recently, the positivist dispute (*Positivismusstreit*) between such critical rationalists as Karl Popper and such critical theorists as Theodor W. Adorno.

In addition to the particular social and intellectual events which may have set off each of these often polemical disputes among German sociologists, the philosophical and methodological claims of Karl Marx and Max Weber are invariably either directly or indirectly implicated in the debates. Each dispute has extended our knowledge about the particular methodological pitfalls and shortcomings of the philosophy of science conceptions of the various sociological traditions. Yet these debates have not been able to resolve the cognitive conflict once and for all. Close attention must be paid even now to the various alternative philosophical positions in social science.

Jürgen Kocka, in his thorough discussion (essay 3) of the different philosophies of social science associated with the works of Karl Marx and Max Weber, has assimilated the results of the various disputes and aims at a new philosophy of social science beyond mere dogmatism and mere decisionism.

Kocka argues that Max Weber's methodological position revolves around two dualities, not present in the work of Marx, which cannot be overcome — namely the dualities of reality and cognition and of reason and decision. Marx's historical materialism remains for Weber only one among many possible theoretical perspectives. Final judgment among competing views, based for example on their object adequacy, is rendered impossible, according to Weber, by the unbridgeable gap between the standpoint of the investigator and the object to be investigated. For Marx, by contrast, reality is neither invariably estranged from human understanding nor does human consciousness always approach reality with categories alien to its subject matter. In contrast to Weber, Marx's philosophy of science postulates that the right action can be, at least in the final analysis, deduced from an adequate analysis of historical reality. The presupposition for such discourse is the Hegelian conviction not shared by Weber that there is an initial identity of the object of inquiry and the knowing subject.

The accentuated confrontation of the two positions leads Kocka to an attempt at mediation since he considers either conception unsatisfactory for a workable philosophy of the social sciences. However, even such mediation has its limits. But Kocka is nevertheless convinced that the mutual reading and critique of Marx through Weber

and of Weber through Marx can provide the foundation of a new applied philosophy of science.

Kocka's essay clearly demonstrates that the history of sociology
generally remains a fertile source for intellectual stimulation and inspiration, and that the history of German sociology offers a particularly rich resource. Sociology as it was practiced in the Weimar
Republic, for example, not only gave rise to Karl Mannheim's
comprehensive and ambitious sociology of knowledge program, but
also to the critical theory of Max Horkheimer, Theodor W. Adorno,
and their associates, to the exemplatory empirical social research of
Theodor Geiger and Paul Lazarsfeld, to the development of philosophical anthropology by Helmuth Plessner and Arnold Gehlen, and to the
phenomenological sociology of Alfred Schutz.

1

Sociology in the Interwar Period: Trends in Development and Criteria for Evaluation

M. RAINER LEPSIUS

Interest in the history of the social sciences in Germany and Austria has grown in recent years, and this is especially so for the history of sociology between the end of World War I and the new beginning after 1945.[1] This period, fruitful in its results and multifaceted when examined in terms of the history of science, for long met with only slight attention, and even today comprehensive, systematic presentations remain an exception.[2] The sharp political ruptures, the complexity of the cultural atmosphere of the times, and the multitude of scientific approaches, as well as the close interpenetration of scientific developments, cultural and ideological history, and political events which are so characteristic for this period, makes its comprehensive and systematic analysis especially difficult.

The history of sociology in the German-speaking Central Europe in the period between 1918 and 1945 is demarcated by several epoch-making political events: World War I and the Russian Revolution on the one side, World War II and the overthrow of National Socialism on the other. These events define a unique period of enormous political and cultural importance. Its significance is quite out of proportion to its short duration. In these thirty years or so, German-speaking Central Europe, as it had evolved prior to World War I, in the first instance had its sphere of influence restricted by the dissolution of the old Hapsburg Empire, was then slowly ravaged by authoritarian regimes, had its cultural integrity weakened by National Socialism, and was

Translation, revised and updated for this volume by the author, of "Die Soziologie der Zwischenkriegszeit: Entwicklungstendenzen und Beurteilungskriterien," in M. Rainer Lepsius, ed., *Soziologie in Deutschland und Österreich 1918-1945*, Special issue 23 of the *Kölner Zeitschrift für Soziologie und Sozialpsychologie* (Opladen: Westdeutscher Verlag, 1981), pp. 7-23. Translated by Volker Meja on the basis of a previous translation by Iain Fraser published as *European University Institute Working Paper 104* (Badia Fiesolana: European University Institute, 1984), pp. 1-35.

finally broken up by the political division of Europe after World War
II. The destruction of Central Europe as a multifaceted cultural region
mediated through the German language is bound up with the annihilation of Central European Jewry, to which the social sciences in particular had been greatly intellectually indebted.[3]

The close interpenetration of intellectual currents in the social
sciences in Germany and Austria can be gleaned from the great controversies before the First World War — the *Methodenstreit* (dispute on
method) between Gustav Schmoller and Carl Menger and the debates
between Max Weber and Rudolf Goldscheid within the Deutsche
Gesellschaft für Soziologie (German Sociological Society) — as well as
from the mutual exchange of scholars. For the interwar period we
shall mention only Joseph Schumpeter, Emil Lederer, and Carl
Grünberg, all Austrians who taught at German universities and who
were very influential there, but especially Karl Mannheim who, like
Georg Lukács and Arnold Hauser, thought of himself as Hungarian
but published in German, taught in Heidelberg and Frankfurt, and
was to become one of the greatest figures in German sociology. All this
makes clear that the history of "German" sociology cannot be confined
to the boundaries of a nation-state.[4]

The sociology of the interwar period can be divided into three very
different political and cultural constellations, each of them of only
short duration: first, sociology in the period between 1918 (the end of
the war) and the National Socialist seizure of power in Germany in
1933 and the suppression, in 1934, of socialism in Austria, a period of
some fifteen years; second, sociology under National Socialism, a
period covering some ten years and characterized by increasing restrictions on scientific work in the war years; third, sociology in exile,
which existed as an independent variant since 1933 and continued
into the 1950s. The development of German sociology is therefore
highly fragmented. There was never a "zero hour"; and there are also
continuities between these periods, though sociology's "organizational
form as science" [*Wissenschaftsgestalt*] — to use an expression by Karl
Mannheim — was in each case different. Even within these three periods, moreover, sociology lacked a uniform character. Neither the sociology of the Weimar Republic nor that in exile or that of National
Socialism shared the same epistemological foundation, a similar understanding of the scientific nature of sociology, or similar lines of inquiry or "paradigms." The sociology of this period is consequently
distinguished by a considerable complexity of its manifestations. In
such a complex situation, trends of development and criteria for eval-

uation are difficult to determine. They can be sketched out only provisionally and summarily, a task which will be attempted below.

Sociology in the Weimar Republic begins with the death of Max Weber in 1920. Just shortly before his death, Weber had taken up a chair again in Munich, and it is probable that he would have had considerable influence there. His death meant a definite weakening of his sociological research program [*Erkenntnisprogramm*]. Marianne Weber, to be sure, managed within the span of only a few years, to publish (by 1924) almost all of Weber's work, posthumously or in new editions, as well as to help preserve her husband's legacy with her own impressive biography on him published in 1926; but there was no circle of disciples that could have rapidly taken up and further developed Weber's work. In contrast to Emile Durkheim, Weber had no "school"; his scholarly acceptance was therefore both slow in coming and erratic. The program pursued by Weber of a sociology founded upon methodological individualism and the comparative analysis of social structures and cultural systems did not significantly influence developments in the 1920s.[5] His death meant a decisive weakening of the opposition to holism and historicism at precisely a time when materialist, Social-Darwinist and idealist philosophies of history were being activated in an attempt to explain the culturally devastating experience of the lost war.

Georg Simmel, who died shortly before the war ended in 1918, similarly met with practically no response in the 1920s. Along with Weber, he was among those who wanted to build sociology upon a theory of action and do away with the notion of essences derived from philosophy of history. Simmel, like Weber, found an audience only after World War II.

Of the founders of sociology prior to World War I, only Ferdinand Tönnies, Werner Sombart, and Alfred Weber remained influential in the Weimar period. None of them, however, came up with a systematic research program for sociology that might have been able to become a dominant influence. While Tönnies was the recognized Nestor of German sociology in the 1920s and the president of the German Sociological Society, the considerable personal esteem in which he was held must not be confused with his actual influence.

After the war, Marxism finally gained admission to the universities, as is indicated by Carl Grünberg's and Karl Korsch's appointments to university chairs. Many social scientists were inclined toward socialism and support of the Social Democrats, in sharp contrast to the conservative majority of German university teachers who opposed the democratic Republic. But it was only toward the end of the Weimar Republic that the confrontation with Marxism became significant in social science. Instrumental in this development were the publication of Marx's early writings in 1932, by J.P. Mayer and S. Landshut, as well as the work of Karl Korsch and Max Adler, as well as the early writings of Max Horkheimer, Herbert Marcuse, and other members of the Frankfurt Institut für Sozialforschung, but most especially Karl Mannheim's transformation, after 1928, of the Marxian critique of ideology into the sociology of knowledge.

In the 1920s there was no dominant figure in sociology, which evolved in a number of milieus with little common direction. Even within its local centers in the Weimar Republic there was practically no paradigmatic unity. This was the case in Berlin just as much as in Vienna.[6] But even the more visible centers such as Heidelberg, Frankfurt, Cologne, and Leipzig were not scientifically homogeneous. In Frankfurt, sociology was represented until 1930 by Franz Oppenheimer and by Carl Grünberg's Institut für Sozialforschung, but in terms of its own history, sociology became significant only once Karl Mannheim and Max Horkheimer were appointed to chairs in Frankfurt. Both had their own groups of disciples, between whom there was little overlap. In Cologne there developed, alongside Leopold von Wiese's analysis of interpersonal relations [Beziehungslehre], quite different orientations, such as those represented by Max Scheler, Helmuth Plessner, and Paul Honigsheim. Not even in Leipzig, where Hans Freyer had great personal influence, can one speak of a school in the strict sense.[7] Heidelberg was just as diversified. In addition to Alfred Weber, Emil Lederer worked there, both at a distance from the legacy of Max Weber. Such younger scholars as Edgar Salin, Arnold Bergstraesser and Karl Mannheim had little in common. Outside these local centers a few sociologists worked in small circles, such as Ferdinand Tönnies in Kiel.

In the early years of the Weimar Republic, sociology possessed no articulated self-image, and only a very few saw it as an empirical specialized science. The vague idea of a "sociological perspective" predominated, which was to permeate and complement the traditional sciences. Academic sociologists, in terms of their training and careers, were embedded within the established disciplines, in particular philosophy and political economy.

In connection with the postwar debate on German university reform, the by and large uncertain self-image of sociology played a significant role. C.H. Becker, the orientalist and later a Minister of

Education and Cultural Affairs in Prussia, began the debate in 1919 when he called for synthesizing branches of study in the universities to overcome the specialization of research and teaching in the traditional disciplines. He thought that sociology would be particularly suited for this task, "since it consists solely of synthesis. And this makes sociology all the more important for us as a means of education. Chairs of sociology are an urgent necessity for all universities. By that is meant sociology in the broadest sense of the word, including political science and contemporary history. It is only by way of the sociological approach that a mental habit is created in the intellectual sphere which then becomes political conviction, when transferred to the moral sphere."[8] This passage already contains all the elements of the then prevailing view of sociology: its interdisciplinary, synthetic character, its role in moral and political education, its significant role in establishing and disseminating a new political culture.

Against Becker's call for the establishment of professorships of sociology as a way of achieving university reform, there came an immediate objection by the historian Georg von Below, who described a synthesizing "universal science" as mere dilettantism. The thoroughly justified sociological lines of inquiry, he argued, could best be pursued within the traditional specialized sciences, particularly since "every sociologist must always belong to one of the traditional disciplines, if he is not to lose firm ground from under his feet."[9] Von Below's position also expresses the contemporary understanding of sociology quite well; a "general sociology" — this is the implication of his argument — possesses no specific object of knowledge and therefore cannot be pursued scientifically outside the traditional disciplines; if it nevertheless attempts precisely this, sociology turns, in Alfred Dove's famous phrase, into a *Wortmaskenverleihinstitut*, a mere "rental agency for verbal masks," or into political education.

Ferdinand Tönnies, then the President of the German Sociological Society, reacted to these ideas with ambivalence. On the one hand he agreed with Becker's proposal to establish professorships in sociology, "because the academic philosophers as a rule are aloof from sociology and fail to understand it"; on the other hand he saw sociology, within which he also counted political science, as a part of philosophy and therefore refused to distinguish between sociology in a broad or narrow sense: "thinking and working, imaginative thinking and methodical work — that is precisely what sociology like any other field needs, whether it is understood broadly or narrowly."[10]

The situation of sociology in the early 1920s may be portrayed as a "cycle of misunderstandings" with momentous consequences. Tne uncertain self-image of sociologists contributed to a lack of clarity in the view of outsiders regarding the status of sociology as a science. Sociology was perceived as focused on pedagogical, political, and moral tasks that were rejected by the traditional sciences. Anxious for recognition and institutionalization, sociology did not oppose these expectations from outside, thereby reinforcing the uncertainty of its self-image. This "cycle of misunderstandings" is perhaps typical for the institutionalization of every new science, since funding is decided by political bodies not guided by a scientific interest in advancing knowledge, but rather by particular ideas about the desirable educational and vocational functions of universities. The discrepancy between self-image and perception by others is consequently significant for institutionalization processes in general. In the case of sociology, which neither had a uniform self-image nor was adequately institutionalized, this gap could not be bridged in the interwar period.[11]

Sociology as a form of political education, which C.H. Becker had still seen in the early Weimar period as a means of reinforcing democratic political culture, was claimed by Hans Freyer toward the end of the Weimar Republic for a very different political culture.[12] For both Becker and Freyer, sociology was a way of achieving a cognitive synthesis by way of which a (politically differently conceived) image of the present could be communicated, and thereby also commitment and experience. The "battle for sociology" (C.H. Becker) waged in public was in fact a struggle about the imposition of different "political cultures" by way of a politicized and pedagogically instrumentalized university. This battle had as such little to do with sociology, which was focused upon only because it was readily available and not already staked out by a clear self-image of its practitioners. This indicates clearly enough that Max Weber's attempt to establish sociology as an empirical and value-free science built upon methodological individualism[13] failed to gain a significant footing in the self-image of sociologists during the Weimar period. Holistic, historicist, idealist, and voluntarist ideas contributed to sociology's self-image as well as to its perception by others much more strongly than did Weber's program.[14] Becker's assertion that "the battle for sociology is at bottom a battle about a new concept of science,"[15] while entirely correct, must nevertheless not be understood as referring to a problem specific to sociology alone. What we are dealing with here is a general controversy on the function of the sciences in a period of heterogeneous political ideas and values. This controversy affected sociology just as much as the other sciences, but it was more explicitly argued out in it than in these other sciences.

The first chairs for sociology were established in the newly founded universities after the war: in Frankfurt by special endowments, in Cologne by municipal initiative. The third new university, Hamburg, also received a chair for sociology, as did Leipzig and the Institutes of Technology (*Technische Hochschulen*) at Dresden and Braunschweig. The German Sociological Society made considerable efforts to introduce a major in sociology for its students, and also recommended sociology (especially to Institutes of Technology and Institutes for Trade and Commerce) as a supplementary subject in General Studies. This coexistence of sociology in the "narrow" and in the "broad" sense left room for virtually every sociological orientation. Ferdinand Tönnies argued that only the future development of sociology could justify its present institutionalization: Throw it in at the deep end and it would learn to swim.[16]

This general discussion was pursued in 1932 with greater clarity. Karl Mannheim's speech at the Congress of German University Teachers of Sociology [*Tagung reichsdeutscher Hochschuldozenten der Soziologie*] on February 28, 1932, decisively influenced that body. He there defines sociology in the "narrower sense" as a "specialized science" which studies the "conditions and forms of sociation" [*Vergesellschaftung*] in an "unhistorical, axiomatic," "comparative and typifying" and "historically individualizing" way. He adds the warning: "In Germany we must today primarily oppose the exaggerations of the historicists, who still under the influence of the traditions of the romantic and the historical school, make the conception of the essential uniqueness of the historical into a myth, thereby closing themselves off from all those fruitful insights that comparison and generalization would be capable of bringing out." He distances himself from all philosophers of history, and also from that brand of cultural sociology which is a "theory of the general interconnectedness of happenings in the social and cultural domains."

The connections between different areas of culture do not arise "because they are parts of some unattached spirit floating about somewhere, but because they are an expression of the life and fate of quite definite human groups." For Mannheim, sociology also includes empirical social research:

A structural view contains the inherent risk that one accustoms oneself to considering facts observed in compact interconnections as if they were precise data or else combining purely hypothetical constructs with one another. This finally leads to one hypothesis confirming another and to building card houses that do not correspond to any reality. As a counterweight to the runaway growth of purely constructive thinking, adopting the method of precise description and the application of quantitative data are very desirable counters to these defects of speculative thinking.

Finally, he lists "contemporary analysis," as a "structural sociology" of the present, among sociology's areas of study, as a way to the "sociological orientation" of a democratic society, to prevent the transformation of a "democracy based upon reason" into a "democracy based upon emotional appeal" which can serve as the legitimation for dictatorship.

From this comprehensive program Mannheim develops three different curricula for the teaching of sociology: political and legal; economic and social scientific; and a philosophical orientation with an emphasis upon intellectual history. He does this cautiously, aware that "the constellation at the origin of a science shapes its subsequent character, and its pedagogical form generally works back upon its scientific form." Once codified, the "conceptual structure of a science will long determine what empirical matters can make their way into the sciences and what is bound to be obscured by these very conceptualizations."[17]

Karl Mannheim's views have been set out at such length here because they typify the self-conception of sociology at the end of the Weimar Republic. Mannheim, who had gained a considerable reputation with his book *Ideologie und Utopie* (1929), is a typical representative of the younger generation of sociologists of the Weimar period, who saw in sociology a specific discipline and not just a mere perspective. Had this development, for which he was the leading spokesman, not been broken off in 1933, his views would almost certainly in the 1930s have had a decisive effect, and not only on the institutionalization process of German sociology.

Among the sociologists of influence in the Weimar period who had not already emerged as significant figures prior to World War I, the most important are Leopold von Wiese, Hans Freyer, and Karl Mannheim. Von Wiese, though a tireless organizer, lacked intellectual fascination; Freyer was a brilliant intellectual, but took no part in the institutional development of the discipline; Mannheim combined analytic precision with a sense of responsibility for the scientific development and political and educational function of sociology in a liberal and democratic society. He could have brought to fruition Max Weber's legacy of a comparative, antihistoricist and anti-idealist sociology.

But all attempts to institutionalize sociology came to nought. Even though the Prussian parliament decided in 1929 to set up chairs for sociology at all universities, the economic crisis and subsequently National Socialism put an end to such endeavors.

The decisive impulses for the development of sociology in the Weimar Republic came, not from the universities and from academic sociology, but from quite other contexts and practical orientations. Of particular importance was the popular education movement that took root after the war, especially the Deutsche Hochschule für Politik in Berlin, founded in 1920, which became a center for political sociology and political science.[18] Equally innovative and influential was the Schule der Arbeit in Frankfurt,[19] which was co-founded by Hugo Sinzheimer. The Volkshochschule movement met with great interest among younger sociologists and offered to many their first professional platform. Paul Honigsheim, for example, was director of the Volkshochschule in Cologne from 1919 to 1933, and Theodor Geiger worked as an administrator of the Volkshochschule in Berlin until he was appointed in 1928 by the Technical University of Braunschweig.

The expansion of vocational institutes provided the younger sociologists with new fields of activity, as did the schools for social work and welfare. This entire branch of nonuniversity education has yet to be investigated in its importance for the development of sociology in the 1920s; this is also the case for the adult education activity of the parties, the trade unions, and the various branches of the youth movement.[20]

Also important was the development of labor law and labor courts. Labor law opened a whole new field of sociological investigations. Hugo Sinzheimer is an influential example of this development. Trade unions and employer associations brought lawyers such as Ernst Fraenkel and Franz Neumann into the social sciences.

When the universities became increasingly traditionalist and when antidemocratic ideas began to predominate among the professioriate, younger social scientists turned toward fields of activity outside the universities.[21] "Thus what we call social and political science was largely carried on outside the universities," wrote Franz Neumann in retrospect.[22] In this connection one should also mention the journals Die Gesellschaft, and Die Arbeit (the latter a publication of the socialist clerical workers' association), which provided a forum for the pedagogical and political interests of the younger generation of social scientists.

The period after 1928 saw an extraordinary invigoration of sociology, in both its academic and nonuniversity manifestations. This development has yet to be clearly brought out in any history of the sociology of the Weimar Republic. Important books were published, such as *Ideologie und Utopie* by Karl Mannheim (Bonn: Cohen, 1929), *Soziologie als Wirklichkeitswissenschaft* by Hans Freyer (Leipzig and Berlin: Teubner, 1930), as well as the *Handwörterbuch der Soziologie*, edited by Alfred Vierkandt (Stuttgart: Enke, 1931), the first systematic survey of sociology, which contains as its theoretical centerpiece Theodor Geiger's "Soziologie: Aufgaben, Methoden, Richtungen," an article on the tasks, methods, and approaches of sociology. In Frankfurt the leading positions in sociology were in 1930 inherited by Mannheim (from Oppenheimer) and by Horkheimer (from Grünberg). Theodor Geiger had already been called to Braunschweig in 1928. The generation in their mid-thirties began to occupy chairs, redefining sociology and also turning to empirical and practice-oriented work on problems of contemporary social structure. Among this generation are: Theodor Geiger (born 1891), Albert Salomon (1891), Gottfried Salomon (1892), Karl Mannheim (1893), Max Horkheimer (1895). They faced a much older generation of notables in the field: Ferdinand Tönnies (1855), Werner Sombart (1863), Franz Oppenheimer (1864), Alfred Vierkandt (1867), Alfred Weber (1868), Richard Thurnwald (1869). There was a generation gap between them of almost thirty years; a generation molded by Bismarck's empire was replaced by one marked by World War I and by the postwar period. Leopold von Wiese (1876) was closer to the older generation; Hans Freyer (1887) to the younger. The new upsurge in sociology after 1928 was borne by the younger generation, and it was precisely they who after the National Socialist seizure of power in 1933 were by and large forced, at the age of about forty, to give up their academic work in Germany and go into exile.

One manifestation of this new orientation, which had moved away from the old philosophical and methodological positions of "metasociological" reflection and which understood sociology as a science of the present, are a great outpouring of sociological works, only some of which were still published in Germany prior to 1934. Among these writings are: Theodor Geiger's *Die soziale Schichtung des deutschen Volkes* (Stuttgart: Enke, 1932), Rudolf Heberle's *Landbevölkerung und Nationalsozialismus* (Stuttgart: Deutsche Verlagsanstalt, 1963), previously published in an abbreviated English version under the title *From Democracy to Nazism* (New York: Grosset & Dunlap, 1945), Max Horkheimer et al.'s *Studien über Autorität und Familie* (Paris: F. Alcan, 1936), Hans Speier's *Die Angestellten vor dem Nationalsozialismus* (Göttingen: Vandenhoeck & Ruprecht, 1977). Also emphasized in this context must be the revival of empirical research, especially the activities of the group of researchers under Paul F. Lazarsfeld in Vienna, whose *Die Arbeitslosen von Marienthal* (Leipzig: Hirzel, 1933)[23] represents a milestone of empirical research which remains renowned even today. Finally it must be remembered that the foundations of the sociologies of Alfred Schutz and Norbert Elias, which did not gain general recognition until long after World War II, were already laid before 1933.

There is no indication that the development of sociology would have ceased at the end of the Weimar Republic. On the contrary, it is precisely during the Republic's last years that sociology demonstrates, in its empirical research output and its institutionalization, a vigorous, wide-ranging development.[24] The National Socialist seizure of power is the cause for the rupture of this development. Only one distinct philosophical and sociological line of development did continue across the gap: philosophical anthropology. It was begun in the early 1920s by Max Scheler and Helmuth Plessner and pursued into the 1940s by Arnold Gehlen.[25]

There has recently been a debate on the significance of the National Socialist seizure of power for the development of sociology in Germany and on the nature of sociology under National Socialism. This debate is characterized by a profound uncertainty in its criteria of evaluation.[26]

It must above all be pointed out that some two-thirds of all full-time and part-time teachers of sociology had been expelled from the universities by 1938 in consequence of the seizure of power. Furthermore, most of the new generation of younger sociologists also left the country.[27] The ensuing considerable weakening of the manpower potential of sociology must be directly attributed to the National Socialist seizure of power. National Socialism did not especially seek out sociologists for persecution as a group, since it rather concentrated on racially and politically discriminated groups. This policy, however, hit the social sciences particularly hard, and not coincidentally, since the social sciences pursued research programs that attracted intellectuals from particular sociocultural groups. If the emigration of social scientists is viewed not in terms of the loss in manpower potential but rather in terms of its consequences for the scientific nature of the sociology that remained in Germany, we can observe a systematic result: the exclusion of particular scientific traditions from sociology. Political intervention produced a selection of academic orientations in favor of historicism, holism, idealism, voluntarism, and Social Darwinism, and to the detriment of methodological individualism, historical materialism, structuralism, and analyses of social change as well as socialization theory. The former orientations have had a long tradition in the German humanities, which were molded by romanticism and idealism; Social Darwinism joined in later. National Socialism did not create these orientations but made possible their prevalence against those forces that had opposed these traditions since the end of the nineteenth century. The latter were also represented in sociology, if the thinkers favored after 1933 are to be reckoned as belonging in the history of German sociology: Herder, Hegel, Möser, Fichte, Riehl, Dilthey, Spann. If, by way of these traditions, the attempt is made to demonstrate the continuity of sociology in the period beyond 1933, it must at the same time also be shown that other traditions show no such continuity. If this is not done, the selection of traditions already determines the result of the investigation, viz., the assertion that sociology did survive after 1933.

In every reflection on the spiritual roots of National Socialism the question always arises which elements from a complex intellectual history are to be selected and brought into a causal relationship to National Socialism, and how those elements that show no affinity to it are to be treated. In principle it may be assumed that ideas and thinkers can be located for every conceivable political regime in a long, complex intellectual history and that these can, after the fact, be brought into a plausible affinity with the legitimation claims of the political regime. But this remains trivial as long as the criteria for selection and imputation have not been defined.

The same holds true for inquiries into the continuity of sociology beyond 1933 and for discussions on the characteristics of sociology under National Socialism. That there was sociology both before and after 1933 is a trivial observation, as long as the criteria have not been justified on the basis of which only those elements to which continuity is ascribed and which characterize sociology under National Socialism are selected from the complex history of sociology. Such purely nominalist argumentation cannot do justice to the facts and merely adds to confusion since it is quite obvious that the history of sociology includes diverse research programs and different methodological approaches. These differences must be taken into account together with the different conceptions of science that result. The question whether National Socialism spelled the end of sociology in Germany is therefore at the same time a question about what sociology in fact is, or, more precisely, how many sociologies we want to distinguish, and which among them were done away with by National Socialism and which not. It is precisely the scientific heterogeneity of the sociology prior to 1933 that requires such distinctions.

If the history of sociology is seen as an attempt to achieve a systematic analysis of the determinants of human existence that are rooted in the fact that man is a social animal, then the history of sociology involves the cognitive differentiation of man's perception of the world and of human existence. This program aims at a gradual differentiation of social factors, structures, and processes from biological factors on the one hand and from cultural conceptions of order [*Ordnungsideen*] on the other. Individual action, as affected by social factors, emerges as the starting point for analysis. Right from the beginning, there is considerable resistance to this cognitive differentiation in terms of intellectual history. The relativization of traditional perceptions and interpretations of human existence which accompanies the sociological outlook causes uncertainties. As a result, there are efforts to preserve traditional notions of order of a transcendental kind and to reconstruct these as philosophies of history that promise a satisfactory degree of reduction in complexity and which keep constant the perception and the meaningful interpretation of the conditions and the purpose of history. This reaction in intellectual history toward the sociological research program takes shape especially in historicism, holism, idealism, materialism, and Social Darwinism. Although employing different strategies, all these attempts share an interest in preventing the sociological perspective from differentiating itself, or at the very least to ward off those of its consequences which they see as threatening. Totalities grounded in essences [*wesenhafte Ganzheiten*] developing in accordance with the laws of a philosophy of history (i.e. in accordance with a cultural projection of and interpretation of human existence) keep reflection about the social determinants of human existence at a level of abstraction not susceptible to empirical testing. The social variables, variously entangled in hypothetical orders of diverse construction, are thereby rendered incapable of being differentiated and isolated. This gives rise to sociologies and "anti-sociologies."

Sociology under National Socialism is consequently distinguished by the fact that "anti-sociological" research programs gain prominence. In racial theory, the nature and nurture debate gives way to arguments in favor of inheritance; social factors determining human behavior, which can be demonstrated by scientific analysis, are simply excluded. In the theory of the people's [*Volk*] historical subjectivity, what is elevated into the subject matter of social reflection is a mythical "totality"

which escapes sociological analysis. Through the idea that reality is
constituted by the deed, the role of social determinants in the organization of society is replaced by a voluntaristic idealism. A desire to ward
off modernization is revealed in the emphasis upon integration, synthesis, and "community." Faced with the manifestations of this modernization — capitalism, industrial society, urbanization and the
dissolution of structurally homogeneous communities, pluralist interest formation and the institutionalization of conflict, differentiation of
guiding social and moral ideas and new forms of solidarity — sociology under National Socialism shows preference for depreciating or for
simply ignoring industrial society ("anticapitalism"), for straightforwardly celebrating socioculturally homogeneous patterns of settlement
such as the village and rural areas ("anti-mass society"), for the devalu-
ation of conflict institutionalization ("antidemocratism"), for retaining
shared values ("anti-intellectualism"), for a reduction of expressions of
solidarity ("antisociety"). Insofar as a very one-sided selection from
among the social factors of human existence goes along with these
moral and political attitudes, sociology under National Socialism is indeed a partisan sociology. But before such an assessment can be made,
it must first be demonstrated that sociological research was carried out
in the first place, at least in a narrow sense. The mere fact that work
was done on particular social problems and areas of social concern (for
instance, town and country planning, work productivity and personnel management, folklore, population trends, etc.) is in itself not sufficient to demonstrate this. Sociology is distinguished not by a unique
experiential subject matter but rather by its distinctive cognitive subject
matter. Insofar as this latter could not be derived from racial theory, it
was taken over from idealist and historicist social philosophy. It is for
this reason that Arnold Gehlen's sociologically rather imprecise
Institutionalism is the only doctrine which has been able to survive
into the present. Sociology under National Socialism no longer encompasses the whole range of scientific approaches characteristic of
German-language sociology in the 1920s; it is a partisan sociology.
Even a number of those sociologists, furthermore, who did remain in
Germany, either voluntarily ceased publishing sociological works or
were forced to do so. They thereby effectively lost their influence
under National Socialism. Alfred Weber and Alfred von Martin are
examples.

The German sociology in exile must not be forgotten when
discussing the history of German sociology during this period. Considered from the standpoint of the history of science that would not be

justifiable for several reasons. First, the sociology in exile continued fundamental intellectual traditions which under the rule of National Socialism in Germany (and also in Austria, following the imposition of the corporate state there) were politically persecuted or at least suppressed. The macrosociological structural analysis of industrial society, with its roots in Marxism, was perhaps the most prominent victim. Second, the majority of the representatives of the newer approaches which made their appearance after World War I, including Freudian social science, phenomenological sociology, the sociology of knowledge, and modern political sociology, were among the emigrés. For the emigration of social scientists meant not merely their by and large involuntary exile, but also the banishment of particular traditions, approaches, and topics of research.

Only in exile did the scientific promise of the German-language sociology of the interwar period become evident, and only there did it emerge as a significant force in international sociology. The writings of Max Weber and Georg Simmel were largely taken up and developed further by emigrés who introduced these authors to international sociology (Hans Gerth, Reinhard Bendix, Lewis Coser, Kurt H. Wolff). It was not until long after the war that a systematic engagement with both Weber and Simmel could be witnessed in Germany. The modern theory of science, which had its beginnings in Vienna and Berlin, also made itself felt in German social science only after the war, by way of the emigré writings, especially those of Karl Popper. This is also the case for social psychology, and here especially for the work of Kurt Lewin. The significance of Paul Lazarsfeld for the development of empirical social research has already been pointed out. Finally, there is the further development of the sociology of knowledge, of the critique of ideology, and of the sociology of law in the work of Theodor Geiger, as well as the growing interest during the past two decades in the work of Alfred Schutz and of Norbert Elias, whose influence was delayed by their emigration. These few examples must suffice to indicate the promise of German sociology, which was already evident and on the verge of coming to fruition in the early 1930s, but which was ruptured by National Socialism. It was, finally, again emigrés who in their ambitious diagnoses of the "German catastrophe" reflected upon the intellectual, political, and moral collapse of Germany under National Socialism. Among these diagnoses are: Ernst Fraenkel, *The Dual State* (London: Oxford University Press, 1941), Erich Fromm, *Escape from Freedom* (New York: Farrar & Rinehart, 1941), Max Horkheimer and Theodor W. Adorno, *Dialektik der Aufklärung* (Amsterdam: Querido,

1944),[28] Karl Mannheim, *Mensch und Gesellschaft im Zeitalter des Umbaus* (Leiden: A.W. Sitzhoff, 1935),[29] Franz Neumann, *Behemoth* (London: V. Gollancz, 1942), Sigmund Neumann, *Permanent Revolution* (New York and London: Harper, 1942), Helmuth Plessner, *Das Schicksal des deutschen Geistes im Ausgang seiner bürgerlichen Epoche* (Zurich and Leipzig: M. Niehaus, 1935), and Joseph Schumpeter, *Capitalism, Socialism and Democracy* (New York and London: Harper, 1942). It is in the works of the emigrés that the intellectual potential of German sociology — viz., to come to terms with the actual political reality — was in fact realized. Those sociologists who remained in Germany, by contrast, were unable, even after the war, to draw any sociological conclusions and achieve theoretical insights from their personal experience with National Socialism.

NOTES

1. Apart from Raymond Aron's book *La sociologie allemande contemporaine* (Paris: F. Alcan, 1935 [*German Sociology* (New York: The Free Press, 1964)], published in German in 1953, and the two articles by Karl Mannheim, "German Sociology (1918-1933)" in *Politica* (February 1934) 1:12-33, and Albert Salomon, "German Sociology," in Georges Gurvitch and Wilbert E. Moore, eds., *Twentieth Century Sociology* (New York: The Philosophical Library, 1945), the examination of sociology in the interwar period begins with the following four articles published in the *Kölner Zeitschrift für Soziologie und Sozialpsychologie* (1959) (11)1: Gottfried Eisermann, "Die deutsche Soziologie im Zeitraum von 1918 bis 1933," pp. 54-71; Heinz Maus, "Bericht über die Soziologie in Deutschland 1933 bis 1945," pp. 72-79; Svend Riemer, "Die Emigration der deutschen Soziologen nach den vereinigten Staaten," pp. 100-112; René König, "Die Situation der emigrierten deutschen Soziologen in Europa," pp. 113-131.

This period also saw the publication of review articles by W.E. Mühlmann, "Sociology in Germany: Shift in Alignment," in H. Becker and A. Boskoff, eds., *Modern Sociological Theory* (New York: Dryden Press, 1957), and by René König, "Germany," in J.S. Roucek, ed., *Contemporary Sociology* (New York: The Philosophical Library, 1958), as well as Helmut Schelsky's *Ortsbestimmung der deutschen Soziologie* (Düsseldorf-Cologne: Diederichs, 1959). [See essay 5.]

In the 1960s the following publications appeared: Kurt Lenk, "Das tragische Bewusstsein in der deutschen Soziologie der zwanziger Jahre," *Frankfurter Hefte* (May 1963) 18(5):313-320 [a later version of Lenk's article is contained in essay 2]; Helmut Klages, "Zum Standort der deutschen Soziologie im ersten Jahrhundertdrittel," *Jahrbuch für Sozialwissenschaft* (1964) 15:256-280; K. Braunreuther, *Ökonomie und Gesellschaft in der deutschen bürgerlichen Soziologie* (Berlin: Deutscher Verlag der Wissenschaften, 1964); Ralf Dahrendorf, "Soziologie und Nationalsozialismus," in Andreas Flitner, ed., *Deutsches Geistesleben und Nationalsozialismus* (Tübingen: Wunderlich, 1965); Bernhard Schäfers, ed., *Soziologie und Sozialismus: Organisation und Propaganda. Abhandlungen zum Lebenswerk von Johann Plenge* (Stuttgart: Enke, 1967).

A new interest in detailed studies began in the late 1960s with a number of American publications on the significance of the social science emigration: Laura Fermi, *Illustrious*

Immigrants (Chicago: University of Chicago Press, 1968); Donald Fleming and Bernard Bailyn, eds., *The Intellectual Migration* (Cambridge, Mass.: Harvard University Press, 1969), with contributions by Paul F. Lazarsfeld, Theodor W. Adorno, Marie Jahoda, H. Stuart Hughes and Herbert Feigl on the social sciences; H. Stuart Hughes, *The Sea Change* (New York: Harper & Row, 1975). In this connection, Franz L. Neumann, "The Social Sciences," in *The Cultural Migration* (Philadelphia: University of Pennsylvania Press, 1953) and Robert Boyers, ed., *The Legacy of the German Refugee Intellectuals* (New York: Schocken Books, 1969), with contributions on Hannah Arendt, Theodor W. Adorno, Herbert Marcuse, Karl Mannheim and Otto Kirchheimer, also deserve mention. Martin Jay's *The Dialectical Imagination: A History of the Frankfurt School and the Institute of Social Research 1923-1950* (Boston: Little, Brown & Co., 1973) stands at the beginning of an extensive literature on the Institut für Sozialforschung and its leading figures. Other publications include Helmut Dubiel, *Wissenschaftsorganisation und politische Erfahrung* (Frankfurt: Suhrkamp, 1978); Ulrike Migdal, *Die Frühgeschichte des Frankfurter Instituts für Sozialforschung* (Frankfurt: Campus, 1981); and Michael Wilson, *Das Institut für Sozialforschung und seine Faschismusanalysen* (Frankfurt: Campus, 1982). See also Paul Kluke, *Die Stiftungsuniversität Frankfurt am Main* (Frankfurt: Kramer, 1971), which discusses the social sciences at the University of Frankfurt and the Institut für Sozialforschung. Also worthy of mention is Susanne Pettra Schad, *Empirical Social Research in Weimar Germany* (Paris-Den Haag: Mouton, 1972).

More recently, a number of studies, including Ph.D. theses and *Habilitationen*, have been published, among them Heine von Alemann, "Leopold von Wiese und das Forschungsinstitut für Sozialwissenschaft in Köln 1919-1934," *Kölner Zeitschrift für Soziologie und Sozialpsychologie* (1976) 28:649-673; Ursula Karger, "Deutsche Soziologentage in Perspektive," *Sociologia Internationalis* (1976) 14(1-2):7-21; Alfons Söllner, *Geschichte und Herrschaft: Studien zur materialistischen Sozialwissenschaft 1929-1942* (Frankfurt: Suhrkamp, 1979); Bärbel Meurer, "Vom bildungsbürgerlichen Zeitvertreib zur Fachwissenschaft. Die deutsche Soziologie im Spiegel ihrer Soziologentage," in B. Heidtmann and R. Katzenstein, eds., *Soziologie und Praxis* (Cologne: Pahl-Rugenstein, 1979); Sven Papcke, "Die deutsche Soziologie zwischen Totalitarismus und Demokratie," *Aus Politik und Zeitgeschichte* (May 17, 1980) B20:3-19; Waltraut Bergmann et al., *Soziologie im Faschismus 1933-1945* (Cologne: Pahl-Rugenstein, 1981); see also the contributions in the anthology *Soziologie in Deutschland und Österreich 1918-1945* (Opladen: Westdeutscher Verlag, 1981), which is Special issue 23 of the *Kölner Zeitschrift für Soziologie und Sozialpsychologie*, M. Rainer Lepsius, ed.; Helmut Schelsky, *Rückblick eines 'Anti-Soziologen'* (Opladen: Westdeutscher Verlag, 1981); René König, "Über das vermeintliche Ende der deutschen Soziologie vor der Machtergreifung des Nationalsozialismus," *Kölner Zeitschrift für Soziologie und Sozialpsychologie* (1984) 36:1-42; the contributions by Dirk Käsler, Erhard Stölting, Thomas Hahn, Margrit Schuster, Helmuth Schuster, and Johannes Weyer on the role of sociology under National Socialism, in *Soziale Welt* (1984) 35:5-145; Dirk Käsler, *Die frühe deutsche Soziologie 1909-1934 und ihre Entstehungsmilieus* (Opladen: Westdeutscher Verlag, 1984).

For Austria, see Leopold Rosenmayr, "Vorgeschichte und Entwicklung der Soziologie in Österreich bis 1933," *Zeitschrift für Nationalökonomie* (1966) 26(1-3):268-282, and John Torrance, "The Emergence of Sociology in Austria 1885-1935," *Archives européennes de Sociologie* (1976) 17:185-219.

2. Writings which consider the development of sociology in these decades in a broader cultural context include: René König, "Zur Soziologie der zwanziger Jahre," in Leonhard Reinisch, ed., *Die Zeit ohne Eigenschaften. Eine Bilanz der zwanziger Jahre* (Stuttgart: Kohlhammer, 1961); König, *Studien zur Soziologie* (Frankfurt and Hamburg: Fischer, 1971); Georg Lukács, "Die deutsche Soziologie der imperialistischen Periode," in *Die Zerstörung der*

Vernunft (Neuwied: Luchterhand, 1962) ["German Sociology of the Imperialist Period," in *The Destruction of Reason*, Peter Palmer, tr. (London: The Merlin Press, 1980)]; Edward Shils, "Tradition, Ecology and Institution in the History of Sociology," *Daedalus* (Fall 1976) 99(4):760-825. Wolf Lepenies, ed., *Geschichte der Soziologie*, 4 vols. (Frankfurt: Suhrkamp, 1981) contains a number of contributions that are informative for this period.

3. See René König, "Die Juden und die Soziologie," in his *Studien zur Soziologie* (Frankfurt and Hamburg: Fischer, 1971) and, more generally, Herbert A. Strauss, "Jewish Emigration from Germany. Nazi Policies and Jewish Responses (1)," *Leo Baeck Institute Year Book XXV* (London: Secker & Warburg, 1980), pp. 313-361; "Jewish Emigration from Germany. Nazi Policies and Jewish Responses (2)," *Leo Baeck Institute Year Book XXVI* (London: Secker & Warburg, 1981), pp. 343-409.

4. See Reinhold Knoll et al., "Der österreichische Beitrag zur Soziologie von der Jahrhundertwende bis 1938," in M. Rainer Lepsius, ed., *Soziologie in Deutschland und Österreich*, pp. 59-101. Also William M. Johnston, *The Austrian Mind: An Intellectual and Social History* (Berkeley: University of California Press, 1972), as well as the impressive account of the unique Vienna intellectual environment around and after the turn of the century by Carl E. Schorske, *Fin-de-siècle Vienna: Politics and Culture* (New York: Knopf, 1980); Allan Janik and Stephen Toulmin, *Wittgenstein's Vienna* (New York: Simon and Schuster, 1973); William J. McGrath, *Dionysian Art and Populist Politics in Austria* (New Haven: Yale University Press, 1974). After the turn of the century, Budapest had an intellectual milieu of considerable interest to the history of sociology. A "Social Scientific Society" had been founded there in 1900, and stimulated much sociological interest. See Zoltán Horváth, *Die Jahrhundertwende in Ungarn. Geschichte der zweiten Reformgeneration 1896-1914* (Neuwied: Luchterhand, 1966); David Kettler, *Marxismus und Kultur. Mannheim und Lukács in den ungarischen Revolutionen 1918/1919* (Neuwied and Berlin: Luchterhand, 1967) ["Culture and Revolution: Lukács in the Hungarian Revolution of 1918," *Telos* (Winter 1971) 10]; Arnold Hauser, *Im Gespräch mit Georg Lukács* (Munich: C.H. Beck, 1978).

5. See Helmut Fogt, "Max Weber und die deutsche Soziologie der Weimarer Republik: Aussenseiter oder Gründervater?" in M. Rainer Lepsius, ed., *Soziologie in Deutschland und Österreich*, pp. 245-272, and Gerd Schroeter, "Max Weber as Outsider: His Nominal Influence on German Sociology in the Twenties," *Journal of the History of the Behavioural Sciences* (1980) 16:317-332. The apparently contradictory evaluation of Weber's influence in these two articles results from different criteria of evaluation. On the whole it is probably correct to state that it is unlikely that Weber could have gained wider acceptance prior to the 1930s, since his collected works were available only after 1925 and are at any rate not easy to understand, leaving aside the writings already widely discussed before the war, in particular the value freedom postulate, the Protestant Ethic thesis, and the methodological essays. Not before 1937 did the first comprehensive analysis of Max Weber's sociology appear, Talcott Parsons' *The Structure of Social Action* (New York and London: McGraw-Hill, 1937). What is remarkable is not so much this rather late date, but the fact that the first systematic treatment of Max Weber's sociology should have come from an American. This is quite typical for the history of Weber's influence in the interwar period.

6. See René König, "Soziologie in Berlin um 1930," pp. 24-58, and Reinhold Knoll et al., "Der österreichische Beitrag zur Soziologie von der Jahrhundertwende bis 1938," on sociology in Vienna, in Lepsius, ed., *Soziologie in Deutschland und Österreich 1918-1945*, pp. 59-101.

7. See Hans Linde, "Soziologie in Leipzig 1925-1945," in Lepsius, *ibid.*, pp. 102-130.

8. C.H. Becker, *Gedanken zur Hochschulreform* (Leipzig: Quelle & Meyer, 1919).

9. Georg von Below, "Soziologie als Lehrfach" in *Schmollers Jahrbuch für Gesetzgebung, Verwaltung und Volkswirtschaft* (1919) 43(4):59-110. Also published as a book (Munich and Leipzig: Duncker & Humblot, 1920).

10. Ferdinand Tönnies, *Hochschulreform und Soziologie* (Jena: S. Fischer, 1920), p. 33.

11. See M. Rainer Lepsius, "Gesellschaftsanalyse und Sinngebungszwang," in Günter Albrecht et al., eds., *Soziologie. René König zum 65. Geburtstag* (Opladen: Westdeutscher Verlag, 1973).

12. See Hans Freyer, *Das politische Semester. Ein Vorschlag zur Universitätsreform* (Jena: E. Diederichs, 1933); also his *Herrschaft und Planung. Zwei Grundbegriffe der politischen Ethik* (Hamburg: Hanseatische Verlagsanstalt, 1933).

13. See Wolfgang Schluchter, "Wertfreiheit und Verantwortungsethik," in his *Rationalismus der Weltbeherrschung* (Frankfurt: Suhrkamp, 1980) ["Value Neutrality and the Ethic of Responsibility," in Guenther Roth and Wolfgang Schluchter, *Max Weber's Vision of History: Ethics and Methods* (Berkeley, Los Angeles, London: University of California Press, 1979)].

14. See Dirk Käsler, "Der Streit um die Bestimmung der Soziologie auf den deutschen Soziologentagen 1910-1930," in Lepsius, *Soziologie in Deutschland und Österreich*, pp. 199-244 ["In Search of Respectability: The Controversy Over the Destination of Sociology during the Conventions of the German Sociological Society, 1910-1930," *Knowledge and Society: Studies in the Sociology of Culture, Past and Present*, vol. 4, R.A. Jones and H. Kuklick, eds. (Greenwich: Jai Press, 1982)].

15. C.H. Becker, *Vom Wesen der deutschen Universität* (Leipzig: Quelle & Meyer, 1925), p. 41.

16. Stoltenberg, *Soziologie als Lehrfach an deutschen Hochschulen* (Karlsruhe: G. Braun, 1926), p. 19.

17. Karl Mannheim, *Die Gegenwartsaufgaben der Soziologie* (Tübingen: J.C.B. Mohr, 1932). The quotes come from the following pages: 7, 8, 9, 11, 22, 24, 28, 31, 37, 33.

18. See Ernst Jäckh, ed., *Politik als Wissenschaft. Zehn Jahre Deutsche Hochschule für Politik* (Berlin: H. Reckendorf, 1931); Ernst Jäckh and Otto Suhr, *Geschichte der Deutschen Hochschule für Politik* (Berlin: Gebr. Weiss, 1952).

19. See Otto Antrick, *Die Akademie der Arbeit in der Universität Frankfurt a.M.* (Darmstadt: E. Roether, 1966).

20. Leopold von Wiese had edited a volume entitled *Soziologie des Volksbildungswesens* (Munich: Duncker & Humblot) as early as 1921. Among the professors at teacher-training institutes were: Albert Salomon in Cologne, Frieda Wunderlich in Berlin, Ernst Kantorowicz and Käthe Mengelberg in Frankfurt. Otto Kirchheimer and many others worked in trade-union and political adult education.

21. See Herbert Döring, *Der Weimarer Kreis. Studien zum politischen Bewusstsein verfassungstreuer Hochschullehrer in der Weimarer Republik* (Meisenheim: Hain, 1975), Fritz K. Ringer, *The Decline of the German Mandarins* (Cambridge, Mass.: Harvard University Press, 1969).

22. Franz L. Neumann, "The Social Sciences," in Neumann et al., *The Cultural Migration: The European Scholar in America* (Philadelphia: The University of Pennsylvania Press, 1953), pp. 21-22.

23. Marie Jahoda, Paul F. Lazarsfeld, and Hans Zeisel, *Die Arbeitslosen von Marienthal* [1933], 2d ed. (Allenbach and Bonn: Verlag für Demoskopie, 1960) [*Marienthal: The Sociography of an Unemployed Community*, tr. by the authors with John Reginall and Thomas Elsaesser (Chicago: Aldine, 1971)].

24. On sociological research done in Germany prior to the National Socialist seizure of power, the results of which were for the most part published only in exile, see M. Rainer Lepsius, "Die sozialwissenschaftliche Emigration und ihre Folgen," in Lepsius, ed., *Soziologie in Deutschland und Österreich*, pp. 461-500, and René König, "Über das vermeintliche Ende der deutschen Soziologie vor der Machtergreifung des Nationalsozialismus." The thesis that sociology was finished even before the National Socialist seizure of power is maintained by Helmut Schelsky in *Ortsbestimmung der deutschen Soziologie*, pp. 36 ff.

25. See Karl-Siegbert Rehberg, "Philosophische Anthropologie und die 'Soziologisierung' des Wissens vom Menschen," in Lepsius, ed., *Soziologie im Deutschland und Österreich*, pp. 160-198.

26. See Carsten Klingemann, "Heimatsoziologie oder Ordnungsinstrument? Fachgeschichtliche Aspekte der Soziologie in Deutschland zwischen 1933 and 1945," in Lepsius, *ibid.*, pp. 273-307, and also the biographical references there.

27. See M. Rainer Lepsius, "The Development of Sociology in Germany after World War II (1945-1968)," *International Journal of Sociology* (1983) 13(3):3-87. On the loss of an entire new academic generation, see also the surveys appended to the article by M. Rainer Lepsius, "Die sozialwissenschaftliche Emigration und ihre Folgen," pp. 487-500.

28. English: *Dialectic of Enlightenment*, John Cumming, tr. (New York: Seabury, 1972).

29. See also the revised and considerably enlarged English translation by Edward Shils, *Man and Society in an Age of Reconstruction* (London: K. Paul, Trench, Trubner & Co., 1940).

2

The Tragic Consciousness of German Sociology

KURT LENK

> I fear that we will protrude
> into an alien future like the
> remnant of an aristocratic culture.
> — Ernst Troeltsch

The German sociology of knowledge of the 1920s, as Gottfried Eisermann has aptly observed, unlike any other branch of sociological investigation, is both "in its origins," and "in its entire approach, an essentially German product of mind."[1] It can therefore hardly be regarded as a mere sociological speciality. To be sure, certain constituent elements can in fact be identified as belonging to such a more narrowly conceived sociology of knowledge, in contrast to its overall thrust as a general "philosóphy of knowledge."[2] However, such a sociology of knowledge fails to grasp the basic impulses and intentions of both Max Scheler's and Karl Mannheim's more comprehensive orientations. If we want to spell out the significance of the sociology of knowledge in terms of cultural history by focusing on a number of its key concepts, it is first of all necessary to specify the sociocultural context and the particular milieu in which the sociology of knowledge approach initially arose. The general mood which permeates especially the writing of Georg Simmel, Ernst Troeltsch, Max Weber, Max Scheler, and Karl Mannheim finds its point of convergence in a tragic consciousness. Not unlike a concave mirror, this phenomenon gives focus to the leading themes of the social consciousness shared by a segment of the German intelligentsia from the beginning of World War I

Translation by Volker Meja and Gerd Schroeter of "Das tragische Bewusstsein in der deutschen Soziologie," in Kurt Lenk, *Marx in der Wissenssoziologie* (Neuwied: Luchterhand, 1972), pp. 9-41. Text abridged and notes revised for this book by the author. Earlier versions were published under the title "Das tragische Bewusstsein in der deutschen Soziologie der zwanziger Jahre" in *Frankfurter Hefte* (May 1963) 18(5):313-320, and in the *Kölner Zeitschrift für Soziologie und Sozialpsychologie* (1964) 16:257-287.

to the end of the Weimar Republic. Although the outlook and the values which underlie this tragic consciousness can be encountered already in Hegel, Schelling, Schopenhauer, and Nietzsche,[3] it is only after the demise of the German Empire that the crises associated with historicism in its phase of decline began to dominate the field of vision. Shortly after his emigration to England, Mannheim himself characterized this phase, in which the sociology of knowledge too has its roots, in the following manner: "If I were asked to summarise in one sentence the significance of German sociology since 1918 I should say: *German sociology is the product of one of the greatest social dissolutions and reorganisations, accompanied by the highest form of self-consciousness and self-criticism.*"[4]

Historicism as Destiny

In the exceedingly complex history of historicism, two fundamental but interdependent positions should be distinguished. The first, which we find, for example, in Friedrich Meinecke,[5] is based on an aesthetically oriented general attitude toward life which, despite the constant flux of every social order and of all values, retains its confidence in the meaningfulness of historical growth. Amidst the great diversity of social and spiritual phenomena, this variant of historicism adheres to the belief in a slowly emerging meaningful historical whole. The enormous range of human opportunities is interpreted not so much as a challenge to the truth claims of religious systems, ethical norms, and philosophical knowledge, but rather as a meaningfully differentiated unity of cultural styles. This historical tradition is in its basic outlines derived from the Hegelian theory of the spirit of the people [*Volksgeist*], but it is qualified under the influence of the philosophy of life.

The theoretical conclusions which the second variant of historicism draws from the simultaneous as well as sequential occurrence of heterogeneous intellectual positions are, by contrast, less optimistic. While the first variant points to the multifaceted abundance and diversity of the objectivations of life, this same state of affairs appears to the second variant as an anarchy of systems and world views, which is likely to lead to a general skepticism. A naive confidence in human creativity gives way to a universal distrust of the power of the spirit.[6] The sense of crisis which stems from the experience of the futility of all reason leads in the direction of relativism. As a result, knowledge is now understood as concealing rather than as illuminating the actually existing objective configurations. Every opinion is declared to be merely provisional. Behind this epistemologically pessimistic variant of historicism, we can detect a magnified concept of truth, according to which only that which is "eternal" and "unchanging" may be regarded as "true." The historical relativity of every concept, which constitutes the core problem of historicism and of the German sociology of knowledge, therefore leads to doubts about the very possibility that knowledge will ever be able to fully apprehend its object.

Significant elements from both variants of historicism entered the different designs of a sociology of knowledge during the 1920s. Mannheim's way of reasoning and his goal of a new synthesis, for example, may to a large extent be interpreted in terms of his refusal to accept the necessity of making a choice between the two variants of historicism. But even Mannheim was unable to overcome an ambivalent attitude toward the problem of relativism, as is clear in a question he asks and which he sees as resulting from an "elemental perplexity of our time": "How is it possible for man to continue to think and to live, in a time when the problems of ideology and utopia are being radically raised and thought through in all their implications?"[7] Stimulated by a pronounced sense of crisis, in the light of which the contemporary situation is experienced as little more than a period of transition, the sociology of knowledge inclines (in the tradition of Troeltsch) toward a "cultural synthesis," to be borne by a specially chosen intellectual stratum or elite.

The Tragedy of Culture

The idea of the "tragic nature of history," which is derived from the theory of alienation as interpreted by the philosophy of life [Lebensphilosophie], is clearly exemplified by Simmel's cultural sociology. In it, social processes and causal interconnections are transposed into a cosmic sphere, where they appear to be a self-propelled movement of "life." Simmel views Marx's theory of the forces of production as little more than a straightforward embodiment of the Hegelian spirit.[8] He consequently regards the estrangement of the producers from their products, as it exists in capitalist society based upon commodities and exchange, as merely one particular expression of a more general "tragic fate," which determines every kind of cultural manifestation in a similar manner. He therefore believes that the fetish-character of commodities (Marx) is "only a specific case of the general fate of the contents of our culture." As social institutions grow increasingly more independent of human needs, a universal law of life emerges which inevitably determines all human action. Every attempt to escape this destiny is thus mere delusion.[9]

The processes of reification, which Marx depicts as concrete economic ones, become generalized under the influence of *Lebensphilosophie* and neoromanticism; as a result, Simmel's sociology falls under the spell of Nietzsche's *amor fati*. Simmel's conception of destiny submerges the obvious facts at the surface of social events into the obscurity of an "empirical pantheism" by claiming that it is not economic relations but more deeply submerged currents of a psychic and metaphysical sort which are the motivating factors underlying the social process.

As "tragic" Simmel regards: (a) the conflict resulting from the *principium individuationis* between the human impulse for personal integration and the growing pressure in modern industrial society toward an ever greater specialization based on the division of labor; (b) that all historically grown forms of life are necessarily imperfect in the face of the unending flow of life; (c) the tendency, which manifests itself in modern culture, that "the perfection of persons lags behind that of things"; and finally, (d) that as a result of the steadily advancing intellectualization and differentiation of societal existence, there arises a universal mediation of every originally "organic" relationship by abstract, reified media, such as law, money, parliament, and bureaucracy. The tragedy of culture, as the embodiment of these phenomena, points to the increasing separation of human creations from the immediate needs of concrete individuals.[10]

At a purely formal level, Simmel's cultural criticism thereby takes up Marx's critique of commodity fetishism, but it reinterprets the latter's socioeconomic meaning as a metaphysical one. While Marx describes the inversion of the relationship between living and dead labor in economic categories, which always also imply social relations, Simmel's primary commitment remains his idea that the manifestations of alienation themselves determine the law of world history.

Simmel belongs to those sociologists of religion who emphasize the illusory element in both the acts and the contents of faith, yet do not therefore come to the conclusion that religious appearances must be dissolved by intellectual means. Quite to the contrary, because of its integrative social consequences, religion ought to be promoted. Were it to disappear, "one of the strongest bonds by which society is held together" would be lost. Like Hobbes and Spinoza, Simmel regards the religious needs of human beings as cementing the social order. As a result, he emphasizes the usefulness and appropriateness of the tendency of those with a pious disposition to elevate "the religious elements residing in the empirical sphere"[11] into quasi-objective structures, in order thereby to secure norms that appear as firm and binding for everyday social behavior. The production of fictions which are believed to be true is seen as a specifically human metaphysical achievement which proves itself especially in situations of crisis.[12]

Simmel's social and political ideas must be discussed in connection with his philosophy of religion. The conclusion reached by Marx in his theory of revolution, that surmounting "feelings of unfreedom" under capitalism requires the abolition of the real economic antagonism between the owners of the means of production and the proletarians, is not compelling for Simmel because he considers it possible "to preserve superordination and subordination . . . , while at the same time eliminating those psychological consequences which make such relationships abhorrent."[13] Simmel's suggestion for sociopolitical reform thus amounts to the recommendation to influence the sense of living [Lebensgefühl] of individuals in such a way that they become capable of looking objectively at the conditions of their own existence. The "sociological forms of individual existence . . . need only be accompanied by and blended with the religious mood in order to produce the essential aspect of religion."[14]

While the traditional critique of ideology tends to view the irrationality that is reproduced in humans as an indicator of actually existing societal antagonisms, the opposite is the case for Simmel: "the life of the soul" is an irreducible quality, is absolute immediacy. As in the later writings of Scheler and Mannheim on the sociology of knowledge, the conceptual tools of Marx's theory are removed from their close association with the critique of ideology and incorporated into a design along the lines of the human sciences and the philosophy of life, carried along by "the warm stream of life, which flows into the schemata of concepts of things."[15] Ontology takes the place of conceptual analysis. In it, "man" is represented as a creature who is unchangeable in his innermost being. Measured against the spiritual world within, history and society are secondary phenomena, and social relationships become designated as external "superstructure," as mere "exterior of life." Simmel wants to portray the basic irreducibility of that ultimate psychic or perhaps metaphysical structure, to which all surface phenomena must be related. The constantly changing variety of cultural forms springs from the soul. Precisely because the individual no longer needs to be a real person while performing his social functions in a society based on exchange, he is said to be more fully himself. Freedom thus becomes identical with the feeling that one is free.

Romantic "anticapitalism" sees in democracy and liberal ideals, as well as in the institutions that correspond to them, only temporary symptoms of transition between an old and a new Medieval Age. Social wellbeing, order based on status, faith and contentment, stability and discipline, are all brought into play as weapons against enlightenment, reason, critique, and personal freedom, as already in Comte's vision of the "positive age." Comte, of course, still saw as guarantor of social order precisely those natural sciences which sociologists of the community as well as the "conservative revolution" see as responsible for the dissolution of every "organically grown" formation.

The cultural pessimism which has shaped a part of German sociology at least since World War I clearly predates Spengler's Cassandra calls. The cultural values of most of the leading representatives of this orientation toward life originate in an authoritarian monarchy. During the years of the Weimar Republic many were able to free themselves rationally from these values, but few managed to do it emotionally. The *Spektator-Briefe* by Troeltsch as well as Meinecke's wartime and postwar publications are witnesses.[16] Already during the war, when the monarchy collapsed and the value-premises once thought to be absolute began to dissolve, these authors perceived this development as a serious danger to social and cultural life. The experience of individual impotence in the face of a merciless bureaucratic and technical machine leads to the growing realization that all human volition and all human abilities are uncertain. The bourgeois ideals of the eighteenth and nineteenth centuries, the liberal anticipations of technical and cultural progress, begin to lose their persuasive power and turn into mere illusions.

Max Weber's Methodological Individualism

While the development of the tragic consciousness of German sociology, insofar as it derives from the philosophy of life, may be understood as a consequence of the latter's approaches to social existence, it is considerably more difficult to explain the same phenomenon in the work of Max Weber, who, even in his methodological assumptions, is far removed from the intuitionism of the philosophy of life.

Weber's sociology begins consistently with the social, i.e., understandable, actions of individuals. The context of action established by the individual and the resulting social interrelationships provide the basic reference point for the object. All comprehensive social categories have their anchorage here. The starting point for sociology can be neither social regularities nor supra-individual formations and collectivities, but must rather be the atomized parts of society, i.e., individuals involved in means-ends relationships. Since only they, and not classes or parties, can be "agents of meaningful behavior,"[17] they also represent the irreducible elements of the sociological concept of reality.

On the basis of this axiom, it is possible to understand both Weber's critique of historical materialism as well as his call for value-free sociological inquiry. Every form of developmental thinking, along with the resulting teleological interpretation of history, is, according to this rigorous definition, pure metaphysics. The so-called historical trends proclaimed by socialism are the result of illegitimate universalizations of certain value judgments and their transformation into quasi-scientific assertions.[18]

According to Weber, the history of socialism reflects the fate to which all movements borne by ethical values are subject in modern times: means become ends and finally turn into ends in themselves. While for early Protestantism, still nourished by faith, the acquisition of worldly goods was merely a means which remained subordinate to the real purpose of carrying out God's will, this relationship became reversed in the course of historical development and as soon as the religious content had evaporated, the striving for gain and material possessions "achieved an increasing and finally inexorable power over the lives of people."[19] Weber describes the realization of socialism in a similar manner:

An inanimate machine is mind objectified. Only this provides it with the power to force men into its service and to dominate their everyday working life as completely as is actually the case in the factory. Objectified intelligence is also that animated machine, the bureaucratic organization, with its specialization of trained skills, its division of jurisdiction, its rules and hierarchical relations of authority. Together with the inanimate machine it is busy fabricating the shell of bondage which men will perhaps be forced to inhabit some day, as powerless as the fellahs of ancient Egypt.[20]

Weber believes that within the machinery of socialist state capitalism the original ethical core of socialism will be forced to yield to bureaucracy, in the same way that the spirit of capitalism gave way to the fully developed capitalist system.

Simmel's theory of "the tragedy of culture" is thereby given concrete form by Weber. While Simmel interprets the alienation of life as a universal law, Weber conceives of the soullessness and the rationalization of social life as a permanent attribute of modern history.

Weber's basic skepticism toward accepting objectively existing social regularities corresponds to the nominalism of his approach. Since
he rejects any teleological interpretation of history out of hand, he
looks upon general laws as mere abstractions which "lead us away
from the richness of reality." They have a limited function solely for
the preliminary effort of generating hypotheses for specialized empirical research, namely, as a guide for constructing ideal types and norms
of social action; however, these will never represent anything more
than probabilities.[21] In this regard, too, Weber is a nominalist. The formation of concepts in the social sciences remains dependent upon classification and definition, while every claim that scientific constructs
can impart knowledge about the structure of the sociological object itself is rejected as delusive. As a result, theory and abstraction remain
external to the real processes in social life.

It must not be overlooked that in a historical period in which
many assertions in the social sciences were burdened with traditional
value judgments, the call for value freedom doubtlessly contained progressive elements. Weber's fierce battle both against the transfiguration
of the life-world by intuitionism and against "essences" leads to the
conclusion that scientific inquiry at least must remain free of senti-
ments. The scientist must analyze the presuppositions and the values
underlying his own thinking, and detach these as far as possible from
empirically verifiable statements of fact. For this reason, according to
Weber, sociological research can only help to select among different
options, but is unable to provide the motive for individual action.[22]

Yet, the irrationality of social and political life, which Weber
wants to expel from scientific work, reappears metaphorically in his
own thinking as inexplicable "fate" or as an "iron cage," which sur-
rounds people in the late stage of bourgeois society. Scheler refers in
this connection quite properly to Weber's "exaggerated love of gloom,
of the tragic and insoluble tensions of life, his infatuation with the irrational as such."[23] Weber's demonology seems to be a metaphor for the
recognition of the relative feebleness of theoretical endeavors compared to the blind force of historical processes. He sees the ghosts of the
past arise from their graves, and stage once again their eternal struggle
about value positions that are in the final analysis irreconcilable. The
meaningful world of subjective purposefully rational action, which
sociology seeks to understand, represents merely a limited segment of
an infinite reality, which in any case can be suspended by the blind
fatefulness of societal processes. On this point, Weber concurs with a
number of skeptical sociologists, for example, Emile Durkheim and

Vilfredo Pareto. When Weber points out, for example, that an interpretation of the social actions of individuals in terms of meaning does not also need to be causally valid, since "'conscious' motives may well, even to the actor himself, conceal the various 'motives' and 'repressions' which constitute the real driving force of his action," it is evident that these views are closely related both to Pareto's theory of derivations and to Freud's concept of rationalization.[24] In each case the dominant idea is that the connection between motive, action-sequence, and self-understanding of the social behavior of individuals, as a rule, possesses an illogical structure. The rationality of individual consciousness is not in itself a constitutive element of the human psyche, but rather the result of an adaptation to predominant societal forces. Thus, Weber's individual who is acting purposefully-rationally is determined just as much by the "rationality" of the society based on exchange and commodities as is Schopenhauer's and Pareto's *Homo mendax*.

Weber stresses repeatedly that the methodological starting point of the model of purposeful rationality in understanding individual behavior should not be equated with the actual prevalence of rationality in the subject. It rather results from Weber's call for an empirical basis of theory formation in the social sciences. What may be described as "social action" can be adequately determined only in relation to the phenomenal sequence of individual ways of behaving. The appeal to subjectively understandable interconnections is the counterpart to the renunciation of constructions along the lines of philosophy of history. The light of reason and the demand for the meaningfulness of the social process as a whole are now removed from the objective sphere and returned to the sphere of a subjective, purposeful rationality of the social actions of individuals. Since their actions are objectively always a result of social processes, it is to a certain extent possible, according to Weber's method of interpretive understanding, to make social dynamics accessible in indirect ways.

Far removed from all substantive and realistic conceptual interpretations of sociological categories, Weber wants to analyze the functional interrelations of active individuals. According to his methodology, all social events may be traced back to the subjective behavior of the individuals partaking in them. That this reduction in the end fails is the inevitable result of a procedure which has as its axiom the conviction that the historical flow of life is essentially unknowable. As in Simmel, the profusion and the chaos of reality is countered by a categorically structuring, subjective reason, which is capable of grasping only certain aspects, depending on the respective cultural significance of a social phenomenon. The subjective cognitive interests of the scholar thus guide the value relevance, according to which the given social base is constructed.[25] According to Weber, the only possible kind of empirical sociological knowledge is to study the contextures of meaning of the actions of single individuals, to investigate what was intended in the sequence of actions, and to isolate the relation of means and ends from the complex flow of events and shift it into the light of interpretive understanding. "Why" individuals act the way they do and the motives underlying their actions consequently are already located at the margins of sociological research, since questions that must be asked here inevitably fail to be answered. It was Weber's conviction that sociology as a science must never seek to reflect social life as it really is, since this is forestalled from the very beginning by the "absolute irrationality of every concrete manifold."[26]

Social reality, outside the domain of subjective intentions, appears in Weber's methodology primarily as the object of imputation. The epistemological idealism of neo-Kantian persuasion, to which Weber remains committed, tolerates the genuinely social dimension only as a border area at the edge of an intrasubjective sequence of states of consciousness; the latter alone is scientifically relevant, since only it is amenable to analysis. This procedure at the same time renders social existence irrational, as a consequence of the premise of methodological individualism, which also puts its stamp on the German sociology of knowledge. To the extent that the realm of values, in which the acting individuals participate, is moved to an extra-social sphere (which has no evident connection with social realities), the possibility of a critical analysis of social conditions disappears in favor of an immanent-theoretical epistemology.

Weber's methodological individualism consequently does not leave the research object unaffected: What was initially designed as a purely methodological confinement to the sphere of observable, factual, purposefully rational contextures is turned into a priority of consciousness over objective factors of social life. The reduction of collective social entities to purposefully rational networks and causalities of individual action, which is called for by the method of interpretive understanding, in the end reveals itself as a transposition of social reality into the world of pure spirit. Weber's approach to macrosociological formations may be compared with Hans Kelsen's confinement of the concept of the state to an ideal legal sphere of the normative type. Macrosociological formations, Weber argues, are products of the mind:

hypostatizations of purely abstract ideal types into fictitious "things" that are judged real by an uncritical and prescientific consciousness. Such conceptual frameworks should be systematically banished from thinking and seen as what they really are, namely, "the resultants and modes of organization of the particular acts of individual persons, since these alone can be treated as agents in the course of subjectively understandable action."[27]

The reduction of these anthropomorphic formations, which appear to lead a life of their own, however, only occurs in the mind of the idealist scholar for whom single individuals represent the ultimate reality and who, as a result, must exclude from consideration — on logical as well as "ontological" grounds, i.e., in the sense of "scientifically relevant" or "irrelevant" — all those phenomena which cannot be subjected to the method of interpretive understanding. Theory and practice are thereby radically divorced. If the dissolution of objectified conceptual formations amounts to the central claim of Weber's sociological methodology and constitutes his critique of ideology, then the question must be answered negatively, whether such an analysis of anthropomorphic, reified conceptualizations may also take the determinant objective social factors (which are responsible for their genesis) as the subject of its critique. This analysis is especially powerful when social reality is viewed from the start as an "irrational stream of life."

A reform of the conceptual tools of social science based on the principle of value freedom constitutes the methodological core of Weber's sociology. The application of this principle in his investigations of social and economic history demonstrates, however, that his call for the confinement of the subject-matter of sociology to subjective, purposefully rational actions — which is, after all, the methodological presupposition of the principle of value freedom — cannot be consistently adhered to at decisive junctures. The elements which determine those contextures of the action of single individuals which are accessible to interpretive understanding and which are initially conjured away in the methodological premise, reappear, if only implicitly, as superior irrational "powers" which can be banished only by metaphorical means.[28] A demonology deriving from the spirit of Protestantism takes the place of a critical analysis of such notions as "destiny," "fate," and "iron cage," which even in Weber's own view are completely devoid of content. While also stressing the tragic nature of historical and social processes, Weber attempts to preserve at least the autonomy of the realm of values and its immunity from the vicissitudes of life by relocating positive value judgments into the conscience of individual actors. Since these values are simply introduced as givens, they in no way correspond to social reality. The neo-Kantian dualism between reality and the sphere of values, with its implicit separation of genesis and validity, clearly reveals the remoteness of social science theory from practice which is so characteristic of German sociology as well. In neo-Kantianism (to which Weber remained committed all his life), just as in Husserl's and Scheler's phenomenology, spirit and life are brought into an unbridgeable opposition. The attempt to counter the relativistic consequences of psychologism and historicism makes dualistic positions unavoidable. It is on such bases that the fundamental problem of the mediation between hitherto more or less unconnected principles — e.g., life and culture, drives and spirit, real factors and ideal factors — could become a central topic of the sociology of knowledge which emerged in the decade after Weber's death, in the 1920s.[29]

The Powerlessness of the Spirit

The interest in philosophical anthropology that has been so characteristic of the human sciences also provides the central problematic for the sociologies of culture and knowledge during the first third of this century. In both cases, "human existence" is defined in terms of the ongoing process of the self-interpretation of life. The concrete historical forms in which this takes place may provide occasions and starting points, but they are not themselves the real goal of inquiry. Rather, they merely represent the means through which the self-orientation of "man" can proceed in history and society. For this reason, referring the objectifications of life back to the fundamental conditions and structures of the soul constitutes the regularly recurring theoretical theme of "positive historicism."[30] "Referring back" [*Rückbeziehung*] stands in polemical opposition to mere "reduction," a methodological procedure which is criticized and rejected as the basic defect of positivism, of naturalistic theories, and especially of historical materialism. As a result of this dependence on a polemically distorted image of "negative historicism," the genetic analysis of psychic and social contextures is replaced by a call for an intuitive sympathetic understanding of the diverse manifestations of life, in order thereby to interpretively understand those psychic processes that have led to the formation of the individual cultural creations. As Simmel had already done earlier, the sociologies of culture and knowledge in the subsequent period look upon the creative element of the human spirit and its ultimately unfathomable spontaneity as the absolute sphere itself. Confronted by this absolute, every attempt at mere analytical concept formation must fail. The historical process no longer appears to be, as in Hegel's philosophy of history, the march of universal reason but rather a plurality of formations and expressions of equal importance, which succeed one another during the various self-contained epochs of civilization. Scheler stresses — and this distinguishes him from Mannheim — the alogical and naturalistic instinctual determinism of history, which in his theory he confronts with a relatively independent spiritual realm.[31] Although the nature of the ideas and values found in the spiritual sphere cannot be explained by the respective pre-given constellation of material factors, their realization remains nevertheless reserved for precisely those factors which are said to proceed blindly along their destined path, oblivious to "meaning." Thereby, however, the spiritual sphere itself becomes an "unreal" factor, compared to the force of the overpowering institutionalized drives: "The course of real history is totally *indifferent* to the logical requirements of spiritual creation."[32]

The tragic consciousness of Scheler's sociology of knowledge thus follows from its theoretical starting point, according to which history is a place of value destruction. The duality between "ideal" and "real" factors, which is at first diagnosed only for the late stages of human civilization, eventually is proclaimed for the entire course of history. In the writings of Scheler, history appears to be in a state of permanent decline. According to him, the most important values gradually disappear in favor of the growing influence of inferior ones. On the basis of this metaphysical hypothesis, which displays the characteristic features of an axiomatic assertion about the connections between drives and spirit, Scheler concludes that, during the late periods of human history, a "tragedy" which inheres in the human condition itself casts a shadow on human existence. The assertion of an irreversible disintegration of historical and social reality manifests itself in Scheler's theory especially in his claim that "spirit" and "power" — as well as "ideal" and "real" factors, as their correlates in the sociology of knowledge — face each other across an unbridgeable chasm. A mediation between them can only be the result of rare "chance." While Scheler had initially, during the war, seen this duality primarily as a specific expression of political conditions in Germany, he expanded this proposition in the 1920s into the idea of a universally valid fundamental anthropological and metaphysical condition. In a manner similar to Simmel, for whom the alienation of the producers from their products within the capitalist economic system is merely a particular expression of a universal alienation, the later Scheler detects in this concrete state of societal affairs a typical expression of the tragic nature of all of reality: "It is a characteristic trait of our world . . . , that the causal sequence of events pays no heed to the values which appear in it, that the claims which the values themselves may make, are largely insignificant for the causal development."[33] According to this conception, to be sure, the ideal factors (ideas, ideals, utopias, values) assume the function of "directing and guiding,"[34] but, according to Scheler, the possibility that the ideal factors can influence the real factors gradually diminishes in the later stages of civilization, and this inevitably leads to an "enmassment of life."[35]

For Mannheim, the societal crisis of his age is the result of an increasing awareness of the fateful particularity of all spiritual attitudes; this crisis is also "the crisis of a whole world which has reached a certain stage in its intellectual development." Yet the "inner perplexity,"[36] which results from the extension of the problem of ideology to the noological level, also throws into relief the meaning of the entire historical process, that is, the gradual "humanization" of man. This simultaneity of a consciousness of crisis and of the hope that the meaning of history can be revealed by "thinking through" the implications of relativism and of ideology makes Mannheim's design of a sociology of knowledge a typical product of the spirit of the age. Since, however, the emerging totality of meaning, in which all intellectual points of view are to take part, can be introduced only as a fictitious and utopian proposition, Mannheim is unable to overcome historicism, as he had hoped, by way of the total and general concept of ideology as a value-neutral tool of his sociology of knowledge inquiry. The sublimation of historicism in a new "relationism" remains a mere postulate, whose realization was problematic from the very start. The program of Mannheim's sociology of knowledge — a "cultural synthesis" which incorporates and thereby mediates all spiritual opposites — which in its basic outline was already formulated by Ernst Troeltsch, finally leads in Mannheim's late writings to the design of a pragmatic sociology intended to serve as a point of departure for planning and the creation of social order.[37]

In summary, we are able to identify in the theoretical thinking about society three central themes which characterize the tragic consciousness of the German sociologies of culture and knowledge: (1) The sociology dominant during the first third of this century reflects the process of an increasing detachment of the conditions and institutions created by human beings from human needs. Public institutions and bureaucratic organizations as well as political institutions are increasingly propelled by a dynamic of their own, which finds itself in sharp conflict with the original goals associated with the creation of these social formations (theory of alienation). (2) In these sociological designs, the sphere of economic, political, and social power ("real factors," interests, "social existence") is contrasted to a relatively independent sphere of values, e.g. the "ideal factors" (doctrine of duality). (3) The sphere of the spirit and of ideas, when compared to the overwhelming power of the social base, reveals itself as largely irrelevant and powerless (theory of the powerlessness of the spirit).

The phenomenon of a tragic consciousness, which has been discussed here by reference to German sociology, characterizes the general situation of the cultural and human sciences, marked as they were by numerous symptoms of crises, in the Germany of the interwar period.[38] Yet, this consciousness cannot be understood as a phenomenon which is typical of merely one particular generation, and which can be grasped by way of social psychology. The tragic, dualistic interpretation of history and society owes much to the social and economic conditions of German imperialism during the period of its collapse. As a result of the absence of political unity and the division into numerous small and minuscule states, the Enlightenment ideas which flowed into Germany from England and France were condemned to remain politically powerless for more than a century. All attempts at a thorough reform of social and political conditions were thus often frustrated precisely because of this lack of German national unity. When at least the external preconditions for a far-reaching reform of state and society had finally been created after the end of the First World War, the ideas and ideals of bourgeois liberalism, which also decisively shaped the parliamentary system with its idea of representing the popular will, had already lost much of their earlier appeal. The cultural expression of this situation was the hypostatization of "culture" as a higher realm, above and beyond everyday life, thereby depriving the originally critical elements of thought of their effectiveness in society. The function of this "culture," now relatively isolated from the realities of life, often consisted in providing consolation and substitute gratifications by way of compensating for those needs which could not be satisfied in the real world. Enlightenment thought, with its tendency to call for the transformation of social conditions, to the extent that it had been taken up at all, became correspondingly disarmed and neutralized. Its place was occupied by an ahistorical and depoliticized realm of inner values, from which it was difficult to acquire an adequate understanding of social contextures. This encouraged the restoration of conservative political tendencies (during the Bismarck years guided by ideas of national power), which, toward the end of the Weimar Republic, joined forces with radical middle class ideologies in their fight against the "system."

The developments outlined above also explain why German cultural life has long been described by neutral observers as extraordinarily differentiated, while the German political reality, when compared with the Western democracies, may be regarded as backward. The great systems of German idealist philosophy, especially those of Kant and Hegel, represented intellectual revolutions, yet German social conditions remained virtually untouched by them. Kant's distinction between the private and the public use of reason, as well as his distinction between "culture" and mere "civilization," which derives from Rousseau, can be seen as symptomatic in this context. Rather than reflecting upon the historical causes of these dualities, the sociology of knowledge, which stands in the tradition of the human sciences and the philosophy of life, has tended to accept them as vitally necessary. This tendency finds its theoretical expression (not only in the writings of Scheler and the authors whom he influenced) in the assertion of an independent sphere of the spirit and of an autonomous universe of ideas.

NOTES

1. Gottfried Eisermann, "Einführung," in Werner Stark, ed., *Die Wissenssoziologie* (Stuttgart: Enke, 1960).

2. See Jacques Maquet, *The Sociology of Knowledge* (Boston: Beacon, 1951); Bernhard Glaeser, *Kritik der Erkenntnissoziologie* (Frankfurt: Klostermann, 1972); Manfred Bracht, *Voraussetzungen einer Soziologie des Wissens* (Tübingen: Elly Huth, 1974); Peter Hamilton, *Knowledge and Social Structure: An Introduction to the Classical Arguments in the Sociology of Knowledge* (London/Boston: Routledge & Kegan Paul, 1974); Gunter W. Remmling, ed., *Towards the Sociology of Knowledge* (London: Routledge & Kegan Paul, 1973); Hans-Joachim Lieber, ed., *Ideologienlehre und Wissenssoziologie* (Darmstadt: Wissenschaftliche Buchgesellschaft, 1974).

3. See Peter Szondi, *Versuch über das Tragische* (Frankfurt: Insel, 1961), p. 7.

4. Karl Mannheim, "German Sociology (1918-1933)," *Politica* (February 1934) 1:13 [emphasis in original].

5. See Friedrich Meinecke, "Ernst Troeltsch und das Problem des Historismus," in Meinecke, *Staat und Persönlichkeit* (Berlin: Mittler & Sohn, 1933); *Vom geschichtlichen Sinn und vom Sinn der Geschichte* [1939], 3d ed., rev. and enl. (Leipzig: Köhler & Amelang, 1941); *Aphorismen und Skizzen zur Geschichte* (Leipzig: Köhler & Amelang, 1942); *Schaffender Spiegel* (Stuttgart: K.F. Koehler, 1948).

6. See Georges Gurvitch and Raymond Aron, "Grundsätzliches zur Soziologie des Wissens," *Der Volkswirt* (1930), vol. 29; Gunter W. Remmling, *Road to Suspicion* (New York: Appleton-Century-Crofts, 1967).

7. Karl Mannheim, *Ideologie und Utopie* [1929], 3d ed. (Frankfurt: Schulte-Bulmke, 1952), p. 38 [*Ideology and Utopia*, Louis Wirth and Edward Shils, trs. (New York: Harcourt, Brace and World, 1936), p. 42].

8. Georg Simmel, *Die Probleme der Geschichtsphilosophie* [1892], 3d ed., rev. (Leipzig: Duncker & Humblot, 1907), p. 168 [*The Problems of the Philosophy of History*, Guy Oakes, tr. (New York: Free Press, 1977), p. 191]; *Philosophie des Geldes* (Leipzig: Duncker & Humblot, 1900), pp. x-xi [*The Philosophy of Money*, Tom Bottomore and David Frisby, trs. (Boston: Routledge & Kegan Paul, 1978), p. 56]; *Philosophische Kultur. Gesammelte Essays* (Leipzig: Kröner, 1911), pp. 245 ff. [see Georg Simmel, *The Conflict in Modern Culture and Other Essays*, K. Peter Etzkorn, tr. (New York: Teachers College Press, 1968), pp. 27 ff.); *Fragmente und Aufsätze aus dem Nachlass und Veröffentlichungen der letzten Jahre* (Munich: Drei Masken Verlag, 1923), pp. 263 ff. See also the new volume of Simmel selections, *Schriften zur Soziologie*, H.-J. Dahme and O. Rammstedt, eds. (Frankfurt: Suhrkamp, 1983).

9. Simmel, *Philosophische Kultur*, pp. 272, 270 [*Conflict in Modern Culture*, pp. 43-44, 42]. See also Georg Simmel, *Brücke und Tor. Essais des Philosophen zur Geschichte, Religion, Kunst und Gesellschaft*, Michael Landmann and Margarete Sussman, eds. (Stuttgart: K.F. Koehler, 1957), p. 98.

10. Georg Simmel, (a) *Soziologie* (Leipzig: Duncker & Humblot, 1908), pp. 196 ff., 709 ff. [see *The Sociology of Georg Simmel*, Kurt H. Wolff, ed. (New York: Free Press, 1950), p. 249]; (b) *Philosophie des Geldes*, p. 479 [*Philosophy of Money*, p. 450]; (c) *Der Krieg und die geistigen Entscheidungen. Reden und Aufsätze* (Munich/Leipzig: Duncker & Humblot, 1917), p. 48; see p. 62; (d) *Philosophie des Geldes*, pp. 113, 144 [*Philosophy of Money*, pp. 151, 174-175]; *ibid.*, p. 477 [*ibid.*, p. 448].

11. Georg Simmel, *Die Religion* [1906], 2d ed., rev. and enl. (Frankfurt: Rütten & Loening, 1912), pp. 48, 17 [*Sociology of Religion*, Curt Rosenthal, tr. (New York: Philosophical Library, 1959), pp. 34, 11].

12. See Max Adler, *Georg Simmels Bedeutung für die Geistesgeschichte* (Vienna/Leipzig: Anzengruber-Verlag, 1919).

13. Simmel, *Philosophie des Geldes*, pp. 342-343 [*Philosophy of Money*, p. 336].

14. Simmel, *Die Religion*, p. 32 [*Sociology of Religion*, p. 18].

15. Simmel, *Philosophie des Geldes*, p. 538 [*Philosophy of Money*, p. 498].

16. See Ernst Troeltsch, *Spektator-Briefe* (Tübingen: Mohr, 1924); Friedrich Meinecke, *Die Idee der Staatsräson in der neueren Geschichte* [1924], 2d ed. (Munich: Oldenbourg, 1925) [*Machiavellism: The Doctrine of raison d'état and its Place in Modern History*, Douglas Scott, tr. (London: Routledge & Kegan Paul, 1957)].

17. Max Weber, *Gesammelte Aufsätze zur Wissenschaftslehre* [1922], 2d ed., rev. and enl. (Tübingen: Mohr, 1951), p. 439 [Max Weber, "Some Categories of Interpretive Sociology," Edith E. Graber, tr., *Sociological Quarterly* (1981) 22:158].

18. E.g., *Wissenschaftslehre*, pp. 204 ff. [Max Weber, *Methodology of the Social Sciences*, Edward A. Shils and Henry A. Finch, trs. (Glencoe: Free Press, 1949), pp. 102 ff.].

19. Max Weber, *Soziologie — Weltgeschichtliche Analysen — Politik* (Stuttgart: Kröner,

1956), p. 397 [*The Protestant Ethic and the Spirit of Capitalism*, Talcott Parsons, tr. (New York: Scribner's, 1958), p. 181; "Socialism," in J.E.T. Eldridge, ed., *Max Weber: The Interpretation of Social Reality* (London: Michael Joseph, 1971), pp. 191-219].

20. Max Weber, "Parliament und Regierung im neugeordneten Deutschland," [1917] appendix 2 in *Wirtschaft und Gesellschaft*, J. Winkelmann, ed., 4th ed. (Cologne-Berlin: Kiepenheuer & Witsch, 1964) 2:1080 ["Parliament and Government in Germany," appendix 2 to *Economy and Society*, Guenther Roth and Claus Wittich, trs. (Berkeley, Los Angeles, London: University of California Press, 1978), p. 1402].

21. Weber, *Wissenschaftslehre*, p. 180 [*Methodology of the Social Sciences*, p. 80]. See also pp. 166, 169, and p. 92 n. 1 [pp. 68, 70; Max Weber, *Roscher and Knies*, Guy Oakes, tr. (New York: Free Press, 1975), p. 251, n. 47].

22. On Weber's concept of value judgments see Dirk Käsler, "Max Weber," in Käsler, ed., *Klassiker des soziologischen Denkens* (Munich: Beck, 1978) 2:40 ff., or Käsler, *Einführung in das Studium Max Webers* (Munich: Beck, 1979); Wolfgang Schluchter, "Wertfreiheit und Verantwortungsethik," in Schluchter, *Rationalismus und Weltbeherrschung* (Frankfurt: Suhrkamp, 1980), ["Value-Neutrality and the Ethic of Responsibility," in Guenther Roth and Wolfgang Schluchter, *Max Weber's Vision of History: Ethics and Methods* (Berkeley, Los Angeles, London: University of California Press, 1979), pp. 65-116].

23. Max Scheler, *Die Wissensformen und die Gesellschaft* [1926], 2d ed. (Berne-Munich: Francke, 1960), p. 432.

24. Weber, *Wissenschaftslehre*, p. 548 [*Economy and Society*, 1:9]; Weber, *Gesammelte Aufsätze zur Religionssoziologie* (Tübingen: Mohr, 1920) 1:255, [*From Max Weber: Essays in Sociology*, H.H. Gerth and C. Wright Mills, eds. (New York: Oxford University Press, 1946), p. 283]. On Freud's concept of rationalization, see Gerhard Maetze, "Der Ideologiebegriff in seiner Bedeutung für die Neurosentheorie," *Jahrbuch der Psychoanalyse* (1960-62) nos. 1 & 2.

25. "Such a 'value relevance' — interpreted correctly — does not imply the value-contingent 'formation' of the object of cognition out of a chaotic and amorphous 'substance,' but . . . a questioning of experience, which does not, however, impose a specific answer." Ernst Troeltsch, *Sozialphilosophie zwischen Ideologie und Wissenschaft* (Neuwied: Luchterhand, 1961), p. 122.

26. Weber, *Wissenschaftslehre*, p. 92, n. 1 [*Roscher and Knies*, p. 251, n. 47].

27. *Ibid.*, p. 553 [*Economy and Society*, vol. 1, p. 13].

28. See the relevant comments by Julius Schaaf, *Grundprinzipien der Wissenssoziologie* (Hamburg: Meiner, 1956), pp. 137 ff.

29. While Max Weber is associated here with the tragic consciousness characteristic of this period, it should also be emphasized that there are vast differences between his theory and the sociology of knowledge program of "cultural synthesis." As a nominalist, Weber confines himself to a diagnosis of the antagonisms in the world views of his day as set patterns, since he remains primarily interested in their sociopolitical consequences. On the other hand, cultural sociology and sociology of knowledge (in the tradition of Ernst Troeltsch) go beyond this restraint, imposed by the principle of value freedom, insofar as they also see it as one of their tasks to integrate the opposing positions into a new synthesis. In Mannheim's work, for example, the particular outlooks are no longer interpreted as mutually exclusive final value positions, but rather as covertly coordinated polar aspects of a comprehensive historical meaningful whole [*Sinntotalität*]. In this way, the

German sociology of knowledge returns to the philosophy of history assumptions of Hegelian metaphysics, even though its practitioners officially attempt to distance themselves from it.

30. On this label see Erich Rothacker, "Das historische Bewusstsein," *Zeitschrift für Deutschkunde* (1931) 45:473.

31. See Kurt Lenk, *Von der Ohnmacht des Geistes. Kritische Darstellung der Spätphilosophie Max Schelers* (Tübingen: Hopfer, 1959); John Raphael Staude, *Max Scheler 1874-1928: An Intellectual Portrait* (New York: Free Press, 1967); Arnold Gehlen, "Rückblick auf die Anthropologie Max Schelers," in Paul Good, ed., *Max Scheler im Gegenwartsgeschehen der Philosophie* (Berne-Munich: Francke, 1975), pp. 179 ff.

32. Scheler, *Wissensformen*, p. 40 (emphasis in original). [*Problems of a Sociology of Knowledge*, Manfred S. Frings, tr. (London-Boston: Routledge & Kegan Paul, 1980), p. 54].

33. Max Scheler, *Vom Umsturz der Werte* [1915], 4th ed. (Bern: Francke, 1955), p. 159.

34. See Scheler's definition of "directing and guiding" in *Wissensformen*, p. 40 [*Problems*, p. 54]. See also *Wissensformen*, pp. 21 ff. and 50 ff. [*Problems*, pp. 37 ff. and 62 ff.].

35. *Ibid.*, pp. 41, 156 ff. [*Ibid.*, pp. 55, 156 ff.].

36. Mannheim, *Ideologie und Utopie*, pp. 92, 38 [*Ideology and Utopia*, pp. 105, 42].

37. On this point compare the incisive analysis by Dieter Boris, *Krise und Planung. Die politische Soziologie in Spätwerk Karl Mannheims* (Stuttgart: Metzler, 1971).

38. See Hermann Lübbe, "Die philosophischen Ideen von 1914," in Lübbe, ed., *Politische Philosophie in Deutschland* (Basel-Stuttgart: Benno Schwabe, 1963), pp. 173 ff.

3

The Social Sciences Between Dogmatism and Decisionism: A Comparison of Karl Marx and Max Weber

JÜRGEN KOCKA

Weber has been called the "bourgeois Marx,"[1] but this controversial comparison refers to much more than can be treated here.[2] Marx and Weber "give a critical analysis of contemporary man within bourgeois society in the context of the bourgeois-capitalist economy."[3] What Weber described as the autonomous and, ultimately, the irrational character of the rationality of modern society, Marx had a half century earlier analyzed as alienation. While Weber accepted this inversion of the means-ends relationship as an inescapable "cage," and simultaneously as the locus for the possibility of individual freedom, Marx sought to encourage transformation by demonstrating the possibilities of societal change. For Marx, rational consciousness mediated through interests leads necessarily to praxis; for Weber some forms of adequate understanding tend to impede action, though Weber also demanded that action occur with an awareness of its conditions and possible effects.

The present essay investigates systematically the relationship of Marx to Weber with reference to one of the fundamental problems in the philosophy of the social sciences: namely, the relationship between the object of inquiry and the process of acquiring knowledge of that

Translation by Charles Lawrence of "Geschichtswissenschaft zwischen Dogmatismus und Dezision: Bausteine zu einer zukünftigen Historik," in Jürgen Kocka, *Sozialgeschichte: Begriff — Entwicklung — Probleme* (Göttingen: Vandenhoeck & Ruprecht, 1977), pp. 9-40. Earlier versions were published under the title "Karl Marx und Max Weber. Ein methodologischer Vergleich," *Zeitschrift für die gesamte Staatswissenschaft* (1966) 122:328-357, and in H.U. Wehler, ed., *Geschichte und Ökonomie* (Cologne: Kiepenheuer & Witsch, 1973), pp. 54-84. Reprinted, with some minor translation modifications, from Robert J. Antonio and Ronald M. Glassman, eds., *A Weber-Marx Dialogue* (Lawrence, Kansas: University of Kansas Press, 1985), pp. 134-166. Information about translations into English has been appended to the note section.

object.[4] It has been addressed in two extremely different ways: in Marx's theory, which is oriented toward Hegel, and in Weber's philosophy of science [*Wissenschaftslehre*]. Both approaches are equally important, and they represent two contrary, but fundamental, positions in the philosophy of science. Marxists frequently accuse "bourgeois" scientists of irrational decisionism, arbitrariness, vagueness, and agnosticism in the determination of the relationship between concepts and reality and often mention Max Weber as the witness for the prosecution.[5] Conversely, many Marxists claim to be the only ones who have adequately formulated the problem, concepts, and theories whose identity with the structures of reality to be analyzed is assured in principle and which alone make scientific knowledge of societal regularities possible; to those who are not strong adherents of Hegelian-Marxian epistemology, these claims appear as not only unjustified and uncritical but also as antipluralist and dogmatic.[6] The purpose of the following comparison is to create a frame of reference for understanding some of the conditions, implications, and perspectives which will lead to a resolution of this theoretical and practical argument.

The confrontation of Marx's and Weber's philosophies of science and methodological conceptions will reveal their respective limitations and biases. Sharpened awareness of their deficiencies can lead to advances which encourage and support partial mediation of the positions and which decrease their respective one-sidedness. An attempt should be made to elaborate aspects of the interpretations of Marx and Weber which have been neglected. We should try to identify those elements in both frameworks which are indispensable for any new philosophy of science, which can be defended against the charges of both authoritarian dogmatism and noncommittal decisionism, and which has either abandoned truth claims for its results or can only claim them methodologically. In addition, it will be shown that a continuing problem in the philosophy of social science (i.e., the relationship of the object of inquiry to knowledge of that object) is most closely connected with a separate issue in the philosophy of history concerning the relation of historical reality to the norms of political action (i.e., the relationship of science to politics). This undertaking confronts certain difficulties:

1. Weber rarely dealt with Marx explicitly. Whenever he focused on Marxism, he criticized a particular elaboration of Marx's theory but essentially missed Marx's own position, from which the contemporary historical materialists had regressed.

2. Marx scarcely explained his methodology, just as those who base their approach on him have hardly produced more than a few sketches toward a methodology. An explanation for this failure must be found. In order to ascertain Marx's methodological position, it will be necessary to draw on his philosophical and economic works and to develop his position from his concept of history.

3. Consequently, the logic of comparison requires an investigation of Weber's concept of history, underlying his theory of science.[7] A perspective has to be developed to make the difference between Marx and Weber clear; such a perspective would have become manifest if Weber had interpreted Marx more adequately.

Weber's Critique of Marx

Weber cannot be understood merely on the basis of his opposition to Marx.[8] Frequently, and especially in his major work, *Economy and Society*, Weber followed a method similar to Marx's approach: that is, relating forms of social organization and consciousness to economic processes. For example, Weber deduced the formation of communities and development of a value-related societal structure from the primacy of economic competition,[9] and in his sociology of religion he established the significance of the premise of a God for a particular economic development.[10] Even Weber's critique of historical materialism is indebted to the method of Marx: "Under the impression of the profound cultural significance of *modern* economic transformations and especially of the far-reaching ramification of the 'labor question,'" historical materialism gained its monistic character (*WL*, 167/69).[11] By relating Marxist monocausality to its socioeconomic basis, Weber placed it under suspicion as being an ideology.

On the other hand, in the *The Protestant Ethic and the Spirit of Capitalism*, Weber consciously rejected Marx;[12] his method reversed Marx's approach by setting forth the spiritual-religious origins of capitalist relations of production.[13] In order to explain Weber's ambivalent attitude toward Marx, Weber's statements regarding Marxism must first be considered.

"The so-called 'materialist conception of history' with the crude elements of genius of the early form which appeared, for instance, in the *Communist Manifesto* still prevails only in the minds of laymen and dilettantes" (*WL*, 167/68). Weber rejected this as a *Weltanschauung*. He argued that this concept of history implies the naive belief "that all cultural phenomena can be *deduced* as a product or function of the constellation of 'material' interests" (*WL*, 166/68). Weber defined "materialistic" as "the unequivocal dependence of 'historical' processes on the respective type of acquisition and utilization of material, that is economic commodities, and especially the unequivocal determination of 'historical' acts of men by 'material,' that is economic interests" (*WL*, 314). Objections to this type of historical materialism can be found throughout Weber's work.[14]

Nevertheless, Weber believed "*that the analysis of social phenomena and cultural processes* with special reference to their *economic* conditioning and ramifications was a scientific principle of creative fruitfulness and, with careful application and freedom from dogmatic restriction, will remain such for a very long time to come" (*WL*, 166/68). Weber even considered the danger that the Marxist method might be undervalued in the contemporary era. "The eminent, indeed unique, heuristic significance of these ideal types [i.e., Marxist categories] when they are used for making a comparison between them and reality is known to everyone who has ever employed Marxist concepts. Similarly, their perniciousness as soon as they are thought of as empirically valid or real (i.e., truly metaphysical), 'effective forces,' 'tendencies,' etc., is likewise known to those who have used them" (*WL*, 205/103).

Weber attempted to preserve the Marxist interpretation of history, as he understood it, for his own definition of science. He accepted historical materialism as a heuristic principle and freed it from its claims to absolute truth and therewith from its revolutionary potential. He viewed it as one of many methods of scientifically interpreting reality — insofar as this is possible at all. Thus, Weber could benefit from Marx's models without allowing them to diminish the eclectic character of his own methodology. This point necessitates consideration of Weber's critique of Marx's interpretation of history. Two aspects must be distinguished. First, Weber took historical materialism to task for mistaking the tendencies, forces, and regularities, which it ascertained for reality, rather than characterizing them as ideal types, which are distanced from reality. According to him, historical materialism naively identifies empirical scientific knowledge with objective reality.[15] Secondly, Weber believed that causal explanations of a historical materialist type deduce individual historical phenomena from a "law" which is, in the final analysis, ahistorical; this law of causal dependence of societal consciousness and action on economic relations is held to be the unique cause of all development. This second reproach does not do justice to Marx's understanding of a "law."

Concerning the relationship between the writing of history and the philosophy of history, Marx stated:

With the description of reality, independent philosophy loses its medium of existence. At best, a summary of the most general results, abstractions derived from observation of the historical development of men, can take its place. Apart from actual history, these abstractions have in themselves no value whatsoever. They can only serve to facilitate the arrangement of historical material and to indicate the sequence of its particular strata. By no means do they give us a recipe or schema, as philosophy does, for trimming the epochs of history.

The premises guiding the arrangement and description of material are found only through "the study of the real life-process and activity of the individuals of any given epoch."[16]

Marx rejected expressly philosophical laws beyond the writing of practical history; he had three major reasons. First, for Marx, history, which is a "process between man and nature"[17] mediated through labor, is not an automatic, fully determined product of the "material base." To be sure, some of Marx's formulations make such an interpretation possible, but these are contradicted by the dominant thrust of his approach, which is thoroughly historical. Though this is not as strongly emphasized in his major economic work as in his early writings, the historical dimension can still be detected in his later works as well.[18] For Marx, history cannot develop without consciousness which has become practical. Consciousness is not to be understood as an effect of "material existence," where human action is nothing more than an unequivocal, deterministic effect of laws dictated by "the base." "The [undialectical] materialistic doctrine[19] concerning the change of circumstances and education forgets that circumstances are changed by men and that the educator himself must be educated. Hence this doctrine must divide society into two parts."[20] This is just what Marx did not want. On the contrary, Marx contends that societal being and consciousness are reciprocally changing elements of an intertwined relationship. At every historical stage there is an ensemble of established social relations which "on the one hand is modified by the new generation but on the other hand also prescribes its conditions of life, giving it a definite development and a special character. It shows, therefore, that circumstances make men just as much as men make circumstances."[21] After insight into his dialectical mediation of being and consciousness — of conditions of existence and human beings — it is obvious that Marx was not speaking of ahistorical, deterministic natural laws.

Second, if Marx had formulated laws of history, he would have committed the same errors of which he accused Feuerbach. According to Marx, Feuerbach was wrong when he spoke of "man" rather than referring to "actual historical individuals" in all their variability.[22] Marx would have had to abstract from history, state a natural law, and thereby depart from his own approach, which argues that the nature of man is his history and that this could not be grasped in the form of laws.[23] The objective possibilities for man in society are limited only by his previous history and by inherent natural laws insofar as nature is not fully absorbed by the mode of its historical appropriation.[24] These inherent laws of nature, which are not wholly at man's disposal, can only be described in the context of a particular historical situation in which men struggle with them. Therefore they do not provide the basis for the formulation of an essence of man, even one negatively defined.[25]

Finally, in 1870 Marx engaged in sharp polemics against the attempt "to subsume" the whole of history "under a single natural law," the principle of survival of the fittest.[26] He frequently used the concept *natural law* to characterize the developmental tendencies of society. He spoke of the natural laws of capitalist production, which "act with firm necessity and have the tendency to prevail."[27] Natural law is to be understood in a double sense.

Marx used the term critically to explain the self-reproduction of the capitalist system: "because the cohesion of the aggregate production imposes itself as a blind law upon the agents of production, and not as a law which, being understood and hence controlled by their common mind, brings the production process under their joint control."[28] Societal or economic processes proceed according to natural laws in this sense as long as men have not yet become subjects who can determine their own conditions of existence.[29] By referring the natural laws to a particular historical situation from which they originated and within which they operate, Marx tried to show that the notion of natural laws was itself historically relative and changeable. At the same time, he criticized their rigid, repressive, naturalistic character, with the intention of overcoming it.[30]

Marx also believed that all historical stages of production have *certain* common characteristics. "Insofar as the labor process is only a simple process between man and nature, then its simple elements remain common to all forms of societal development."[31] Such constants, within Marx's conceptualization, are not astonishing when one reflects on the relationship of man and nature in Marx. While the young Marx characterized the goal of historical development in utopian fashion as "the complete unity of man with nature,"[32] he observed later that nature is not fully absorbed in the historical manner of its practical appropriation. Even in socialist society man will still have to struggle with nature to satisfy his needs, because, even then, it will not be fully stripped of its capacity for resistance.[33] In 1868, he wrote: "Natural laws cannot be suspended. What can be changed is only the *form* in which the laws prevail in historically different circumstances."[34] It is evident that, here, natural law means the ever present conditions of existence and eternal necessity of nature, independent of all societal forms.[35] Nevertheless, it is not these formal and abstract natural laws which, in the opinion of Marx, are the objects of inquiry of historians and political economists; they study only the forms wherein these laws prevail.[36]

Such ambivalent formulations may suggest contradictions in Marx's analysis. But they should not obscure the fact that, for Marx, natural laws are not ahistorical, transcendental laws abstracted from historical, concrete, individual cases or rules to interpret historical phenomena; instead, Marx's natural laws are universals found only in the particular.[37]

It is true, for Marx, that history did not have an unlimited plasticity. However, the "eternal laws" which Weber ascribed to him are not in Marx's thought. When Weber accused the historical materialists of having an ahistorical and monocausal notion of law, he was not criticizing Marx, but rather those who interpreted him rigidly and nondialectically. Of course, Marx didn't always follow his own historical-dialectical approach, and above all Marx's concept of the relation of the universal and particular in history can be understood only on the basis of its origins in Hegelian logic. By the turn of the century, and especially in the decades following, such concepts were interpreted by a public which no longer shared the assumptions and insights of Hegelian logic; even Weber may have succumbed to this type of misunderstanding.

Nevertheless, understanding the one-sidedness of Weber's views does not remove the differences between Weber's and Marx's methodological positions. Marx did not formulate ahistorical laws of historical process but nevertheless maintained the claim of analyzing scientifically the "core structure" of capitalist society (i.e., to reach a true understanding of the substance of reality) which Weber considered to be impossible and which he rejected as "metaphysics." Even if Weber had interpreted Marx more adequately, Marx's premise would still have been unacceptable to him.

Reality and Method: Weber

Weber believed in a strict separation between the scientist and the reality under investigation. Certainly it is incorrect to maintain that Weber held that this reality is unstructured before it is observed scientifically. "The *choice* of the object of investigation and how far this investigation extends into the infinite causal web" is determined by the evaluative values [*Wertideen*] of the researcher (*WL*, 184/84). This formulation implies that causal connections into which the investigation can extend do exist. In other words, the investigation *follows* preexisting structures of reality; it does not create them from thin air.[38] Furthermore, this reality, which is pregiven in the *Geisteswissenschaften*, is social-historical reality. For Weber, the objects of social scientific inquiry have already come into being on an "ontic"[39] dimension through value-related action and to this extent are related to, and also structured through, meaning. This special character of the object makes, according to Weber, historical "understanding" possible, which likewise can only proceed through reference to values (*WL*, 180 ff./80 ff.).

On the other hand, Weber made some statements suggesting that reality is chaotic. "The light which emanates from those highest evaluative ideas always falls on an ever-changing finite segment of the vast chaotic stream of events, which flows away through time."[40] From these quotations, many interpreters have concluded that Weber meant reality had absolutely no objective structure.[41]

This contradiction between conceptions of reality as structured and as chaotic can be resolved. Even though the reality of the "heterogeneous continuum"[42] is structured through and determined by causal relations and value relations, this does not mean that the scientist discerns this reality *in these relations*. In fact, the pregiven structures of the "continuum" could be irrelevant to those structures sought and in part constituted by scientific inquiry. This would be the case if the pregiven causal relations are infinite in number while simultaneously each element stands in an ambiguous relationship to the others. One can speak of a chaos of causal relationships and of a mass of individual value-related elements,[43] of "an amorphous detritus" even though the elements are individually structured. Culture is merely a slice of reality, arranged and constituted according to the analyst's specific values and standpoints. Though it is certainly structured, reality nevertheless appears chaotic to the observer.[44]

If reality is presented as infinitely complex and diverse, then empirical scientific knowledge can only be partial knowledge. "All the analysis of infinite reality which the finite human mind can conduct rests on the tacit assumption that only a finite *part* of this reality constitutes the object of scientific investigation [*Erfassung*] and that only it is 'important' in the sense of 'being worthy of being known'" (*WL*, 171/72). The choice of what is "important" proceeds from value ideas and viewpoints derived from the interests of the researcher. These interests cannot be taken "from the material itself" (*WL*, 181/82). Again and again Weber denied the possibility of deriving the standpoint which makes scientific inquiry possible from the object itself.[45] The criterion for judging the correctness of a research perspective or the possibility of choosing among several standpoints cannot be derived sufficiently from the object to be investigated.[46] Although the reality in the "heterogeneous continuum" is structured, Weber had to stress the independence of the standpoint of the inquiry and construction of categories from the object of investigation because the "ontic" structures in the "heterogeneous continuum" are largely indifferent to the causal connections and interdependent structures which the scholar tries to establish. To be sure, the "ontic" structure of reality is *not completely* indifferent to the formulation of a scientific framework (the formulation of concepts, models, and explanations). The scientist cannot approach every object with each interest and each concept and cannot contrive randomly "a historical individual."[47] At the very least, the richness of empirical data which allows for many, though not all, interpretations provides discretionary limits.[48] But, as long as scientific concept formation does not contradict this elementary fact (and for Weber the degree of latitude appears to be quite large), reality remains indifferent to the construction of categories.

Weber's effort to demarcate clearly the world of objects as a value-free facticity from the sphere of values and the standpoints dependent on them is understandable on the basis of his notion of reality, and it is a constitutive and indispensable dimension of his philosophy of science [*Wissenschaftslehre*] and ethics. However, this separation drew accusations of decisionism. In fact, it does appear as if the choice of research perspectives [*Erkenntnisgesichtspunkte*] is a decision which cannot be rationally grounded or criticized, if the matter to be investigated, i.e., historical reality, is eliminated as a criterion for this choice.[49] Weber stated that the choice of standpoint is not arbitrary as long as it is successful (*WL*, 170/71), but this success is judged according to the same standpoints for which it in turn is supposed to be the criterion.

On the basis of Weber's methodological essays summarized thus far, there remains a deep gulf between reality and understanding. Objectivity can be achieved only methodologically, not on the basis of content. This disavowal justifies Weber's further claim that the value-relevant standpoint be exempted from rational discussion. Reason and decision seem to go their separate ways. From this viewpoint, Weber's ambivalent attitude toward Marx is easier to understand. Weber could accept Marx's perspectives and categories as one set of possibilities among many, and he gave Marx neither preference nor derision relative to others. Thus, he criticized both historical materialism and racial theories, placing them formally on the same level, deserving of equal consideration (*WL*, 167/68 ff.). For Weber, there could be no knowledge of the substance of reality in itself [*Substanzeinsicht*], and he therefore had to contest the claim that Marx's theory was more than a rational ordering of an ultimately chaotic reality.

Reality and Method: Marx

Marx rejected the comprehension of reality solely as "a form of the object" and instead conceived it as "sensuous human activity," as praxis.[50] Thus, historical reality is a process in which human labor and human consciousness are objectified continuously and to an ever-increasing extent. In turn, historical reality acts as a limiting condition on the thinking and acting subject. Marx would have rejected the Weberian demand for a clear demarcation between the knowing subject and object of inquiry as too abstract. He could have argued that on the one hand we can always find a significant degree of human consciousness in the limiting conditions on every level of historical process; on the other, in any situation human consciousness can be described as historical in form and content, that is, determined by the historical process. (As Marx wrote: "Der Mensch, das ist die Welt des Menschen.")[51]

Two points follow logically. First, reality is not in principle estranged from rational human understanding insofar as it is mediated increasingly through labor and constituted through consciousness transformed into praxis. Marx adhered to this position contra Feuerbach even for the objects of natural sciences; "even this 'pure' natural science receives its aim, like its material, only through commerce and industry, through the sensuous activity of men."[52] This applies all the more to the social sciences. Second, human consciousness does not approach reality with categories alien to the subject matter. "The essence of man is no abstraction inhering in each single individual. In

its actuality it is the ensemble of social relations."[53] Therefore, in form
and content human consciousness is "a historical existence in its conceptual form, an area of experience and range of ideas determined by
society."[54] This implies that values and points of view must be incorporated as features of the total social and historical process and not, as
in Weber, remain unrelated to the object of investigation.

Within Marx's approach it does not follow, however, that human
consciousness is always adequate to its objects. According to Marx,
conceptual elements, which enter into reality, can and must appear inverted in the consciousness of the carriers and agents of alienated economic relations.[55] When private producers in capitalist exchange
combine their social labor in an abstract way, "they are not aware of it,
but they do it."[56] Marx was convinced that the task of science is to clear
up this necessarily false consciousness. However, he thought that this
can be mediated only through proletarian class interests and, likewise,
can be successful only if connected with actual changes in social conditions.

What are the methodological consequences of this implied insepa-
rability of consciousness and world? It definitely does not entail the
dissolution of the object in the knowing subject. The "concrete subject
[i.e., the object of inquiry] remains outside the intellect and independent of it — that is so long as the intellect adopts a purely speculative,
purely theoretical attitude. The subject, society, must always be envis-
aged therefore as the pre-condition of comprehension even when the
theoretical method is employed."[57] Thus, inquiry can hardly be described as an agreement of the intellect with external objects, in the
sense of a mimetic theory of knowledge. This theory would presuppose the duality of subject and object which Marx attempted to
overcome.[58]

Nor can inquiry be described outside the practical relations of man
and reality. On the one hand, Marx's reflection on objects of the external world began with the significance of those objects for satisfying
human needs;[59] on the other, labor itself is objectified in the historical
reality under study through the progressive practical appropriation of
these objects. Accordingly, human praxis enters into the definition of
this reality which it has in part constituted, and in this way praxis becomes a criterion for truth. "The question whether human thinking
can reach objective truth is not a question of theory but a *practical* question."[60] Without entering further into the problems encompassed by
this statement,[61] it is clear that, in Marx's view, even scientific thought
is already preformed by a practical relation between work and man.

Scientific thinking focuses on a world which is incomplete in the sense that it needs further evolution through praxis, insofar as it always already contains objectified human praxis. Historical reality is structured: scientists can determine structures through the praxis operant in that context. Weber's distinction between "objective" and "historical" (e.g., constituted through the application of scientific concepts) realities is irrelevant to this mode of thought. Marx stated: "The dispute about the actuality or nonactuality of thinking — thinking isolated from practice — is a purely *scholastic* question."[62]

This way of referring to praxis as ever present and also continually changing excludes two inferences. First, such an approach does not permit formulation of a general *system* of economics or sociology. Such a system would be detached from its historical context and rendered abstractly independent. Thus, it is once again clear that the general law of history criticized by Weber found little room in Marx's thinking. But there is a limited agreement between Marx and Weber, since Weber argued that, on the basis of the constantly changing research interests [*Erkenntnisinteressen*], a definitive system in the cultural sciences was impossible (*WL*, 184/84). Second, within such an approach, a methodology in Weber's sense is impossible to perfect. Every methodology must complete the break, which Marx rejected, between the knowing subject and the object of analysis. Moreover, it can be argued that a methodology is always required to abstract from concrete historical cases; in other words, it must provide a schema, under which it subsumes all processes of inquiry.[63] From Marx's perspective, therefore, a critique of Weber's methodological position proceeds in the following manner.[64] Social reproduction has attained such independence that the human world confronts humanity as something completely alien. The historical process cannot be fathomed by the isolated individual for reasons specified by Marx; this is reflected in Weber's characterization of reality as an incomprehensible chaos. One can no longer think in terms of progress. Rationality shrinks to efficient means-ends relations, so that goal-setting no longer needs to be related to reason. Marxist critique of Weberian methodology strives to interpret the latter's ahistorical formulations of cognitive processes of the empirical sciences by reflecting on their social-historical presuppositions; and in this way the critique relativizes them historically and socially, thereby negating them as a general methodology. One step of this critique involves clarifying Weber's notion of reality, a presupposition on which he never reflected. Such a critique locates Weber in his social and historical context. Thus, the critique of abstract categories proceeds to the critique of abstract relations, the former being a pseudo-approximation of the latter. Ahistorical categories, separated from their objects, are shown to be indicative of alienated thought, and thereby relative.

Historical Totality vs. "Heterogeneous Continuum"

It follows from the above that Marx, in contrast to Weber, had a notion of total history [*Gesamtgeschichte*] and thought of society as a specific and specifiable totality. The whole determines its individual, interrelated elements, just as it is determined by them. Marx applied the method which he briefly delineated in the introduction to the *Critique of Political Economy*.[65] He proceeded from the "actual and the concrete, the real preconditions," thus, in the study of political economy, from the people. This "true and concrete" proves to be an empty abstraction if its structure of classes and their basic elements — capital, wage labor, and so forth — are not penetrated. The conception of the whole remains chaotic and completely unspecified as long as one does not proceed analytically from what is believed to be concrete to always thinner abstractions and simpler definitions. "From there the journey should be made once again in the opposite direction, until one arrived once more at the concept of the populace, which this time is not a vague notion of a whole, but a rich totality comprising numerous definitions and interrelationships." Therefore, what is concrete for Marx is not immediate perception but "the concrete concept is concrete, because it is a synthesis of many definitions, thus representing a unity of diverse elements."[66] This concrete totality encompasses the entire social relations of a historical period.

The whole can only be found in its parts. "The presupposition for the existence of the whole lies in the nature of its parts, and so it is only through the study of these parts that the whole is constituted. But even this is not enough for it must be shown how the parts interrelate with one another and mutually determine one another in order to appear as a whole."[67] Conversely, because of their interconnections, each part can be grasped only if, at the same time, the whole is investigated. Marx condemned indirectly any approach that viewed the object of inquiry as one example, which in turn is subsumed under a context of meaning [*Sinnzusammenhang*].

The implicit basis for this methodology is a conception of reality that requires appearance to be distinguished from essence and surface from core. "The final pattern of economic relations as seen on the surface, in their real existence and consequently in the conceptions by which the bearers and agents of these relations seek to understand them, is very different from, and indeed quite the reverse of, their inner but concealed essential pattern and the conception corresponding to it."[68] Although in an alienated society the existing form of social relations more often disguises than reveals its true character, social scientists must nevertheless begin with one of the surface manifestations, for they can locate the core structure only in its concrete historical manifestation. The task of science is to define the concept of this "core structure,"[69] that is, "to reveal the economic laws of motion of modern society."[70] However, this does not imply a general law in the sense of a universal formula. Rather, it is a matter of formulating a concept which cannot be severed from its forms of existence. Therefore, Marx demanded simultaneously "the beginning of the journey in the opposite direction"; that is, the uncovering of the relations between the core structure and surface phenomena. Only then can the core structure be adequately grasped (i.e., concretely).[71] At the same time, "the conceptions by which the bearers and agents of these relations seek to understand them" are questioned.[72] Thereby, the possibility arises of altering these ideas. This possibility is not limited to the theory but must proceed toward practical changes of those relations that shaped false consciousness.

According to Marx, and in contrast to Weber, understanding of the substance of reality is in principle possible for science on the basis of the aforementioned dialectical relation between consciousness and reality. However, this can be reached only by consciousness which is no longer constrained by class relations or warped by the pressures of alienated economic conditions. The possibility of such knowledge cannot be reflected on abstractly, since the content and form of knowing consciousness are determined by the outcomes and moments of particular historical situations.

Marx's demand that science provide insight into the essence of historical relations, which means a grasp of the totality, is made possible by a materialist reformulation of Hegel's notion of reality.[73] This notion encompasses a structural unity in all its diversity as well as a core structure in all its appearances. In contrast, Weber's neo-Kantian position conceives of reality as a "heterogeneous continuum" and must be satisfied with partial knowledge. Weber condemned every distinction between essence and appearance as bad metaphysics and every intention of conceptualizing the whole as a presumptuous self-deception. Conversely, the persuasive power and consistency of Marx's propositions are extraordinarily dependent on their Hegelian premises.

Weber's method proceeds from a conception of historical reality as a "heterogeneous continuum." Above all, it is distinguished from Marx's emphasis on the whole by the isolation of *one* "causal chain" from the richness of reality according to *one* heuristic standpoint. Weber did not think of reality as a structured totality. In addition, even though he could pursue supplementary "causal chains" in further investigations, it is very difficult, using Weber's method, to reflect continually on the relation and significance of one moment of reality in relation to others.

This abstraction, required by Weber's methodology, results in difficulties, as in *The Protestant Ethic and the Spirit of Capitalism*. For example, within his limited approach, Weber was unable to explain adequately the phenomenon of Pietism. Pietism, though resting on the same religious foundation as Puritanism, hardly led to the same sober asceticism and work ethic. To explain this difference, Weber would have had to portray the other conditions that led to the transformation of Calvinistic religiosity into secular efficiency. These conditions are probably of a social, economic, geographic, or other character and have the effect that similar religious contents led in one case to an active worldliness and in another case to an inner piety.[74] Weber would have had to reflect on the interwoven character and reciprocal influence on different conditioning elements and weigh their significance relative to one another.[75]

Weber had similar difficulties by limiting, to *one* causal chain, his explanation of how early capitalist manufacturing grew out of traditional cottage industries in the eighteenth century.[76] He presented the new Calvinist spirit as the motivating force that effected an intensification of controls over work, planning, the search for customers, and so on, and also destroyed the prevailing forms of industry. However, it is questionable whether the impetus and effects of this new spirit can explain adequately why manufacturing required a central workplace separate from one's living quarters. It is at least conceivable that the planning, canvassing for customers, and increased rationality of labor could also have been guaranteed in a decentralized form of operation. The explanation of the origin of the centralized enterprise requires reference: to the development of the means of production, the tools and early machines, whose purchase and use demanded centralization; to the work process whose future technical development clearly demanded a centralized administration; and to the connection of these elements with the new capitalist spirit. Weber's approach does not spur investigation of these questions and connections.

Marx, in contrast, attempted to grasp reality with all its diverse, reciprocally conditioning elements, including scientific research itself. As seen in his elaboration of "labor," even the most abstract categories are historical. It could be thought of only as "labor in general" in a "well developed totality of actual types of labor, where none dominates the others." This presupposes a societal form "in which individuals easily pass from one type of labor to another and are indifferent to the particular kind of labor which befalls them." That was less the case at the time of the physiocrats than in modern bourgeois society. Through this example Marx demonstrated convincingly "how even the most abstract categories, despite their validity for all epochs, precisely because they are abstractions, are equally a product of historical conditions even in the specific form of abstractions and they retain their full validity only for and within the framework of these conditions."[77] In this way, the above-mentioned thesis — the inquiring subject does not approach an object with alien categories — takes on concrete form. However, subjects must continually reflect on their position within the totality of the historical process and on the origins of their categories within this process.[78] Categories and perspectives can be criticized only insofar as they are placed within the context of conditions under which they originated and are applied.

Marx justified the dominant position of the categories of work, production, and exchange on the basis of their great importance in capitalist society. For Marx, categories were also categories of being [*Seinskategorien*]. To use Weber's language, for Marx, scientific standpoints were likewise dominant elements of the reality to be investigated.

Here, a question should be addressed to Marx the historian: can categories, which are purportedly applicable to contemporary society, also be applied to the past? For example, can class and class struggle, categories which according to Marx are historically relative, be equally well applied in investigations of the Middle Ages? Marx was sufficiently historical and aware of the heterogeneity of historical particularities so as not to contend naively that contemporary concepts are automatically applicable to previous historical periods. "Thus, although it is true that the categories of bourgeois economy are valid for all other social formations, this has to be taken *cum grano salis*."[79] Nevertheless, he believed that insight into the structure and relations of past societies is possible only on the basis of the present form of social organization, since this has attained the highest level of development. The earlier forms are looked upon by the latest "as stages in the development of itself." "In this way the bourgeois economy provides the key to antiquity etc.,"[80] although the historical differences must not be overlooked. Marx's position indirectly implies that only in the present do individual elements come to light as what they were, in disguised form, in the past. The present is the developed form of the past, and contemporary categories, which are related to past forms, can grasp the essence of those forms better than categories which were known and used during the period under investigation.

In other words, Marx conceded that historical observation always occurs from the specific horizon of the observer. However, for Marx, the present conditions, which constitute that horizon, are the more developed and more adequate form of the conditions under study. Here, there is a certain justification for Weber's criticism that the "laws" of historical materialism are a universal historical method in which the relations of production have an almost metaphysical preponderance. There are, indeed, some elements within Marx's thought which make it easy to mistake his portrayal of the anatomy of bourgeois society for a maxim of the philosophy of history or a "materialist conception of history."

The above peculiarity of Marx's method follows necessarily from his modified appropriation of Hegel's concept of development. With this goes the presupposition that is fundamental to Marx — namely, that history can be grasped as a rational process, at least in principle, and to which man belongs unconditionally as an active mediating agent. For Hegel, true history is the way to self-liberation of the spirit, which moves to manifest the reality of its essence though initially existing only in itself. The materialist Marx no longer held this position. Nevertheless, he conceived every historical epoch as a structured totality, whose contradictions already contain within themselves the demand and promise of their dissolution. Accordingly, the present is "restricted future."[81] The future is only the realization of developmental tendencies which are already established and fixed in the present.

In the final analysis the above presupposition explains the antagonism of Marx's thought to Weber's position. Weber's rejection of any concept of development [Entwicklung] follows necessarily from an understanding of reality as a "heterogeneous continuum."[82] This difference is highlighted clearly through a comparison of what Marx and Weber understood as critique. Weber stated: "The fate of a cultural epoch which has eaten from the tree of knowledge is that it must know that we cannot learn the *meaning* of the world from the results of its analysis, be it ever so perfect; it must rather be in a position to create meaning itself. It must be recognized that general views of life and universe can never be products of increasing empirical knowledge, and that the highest ideals, which move us most forcefully, are always formed only in the struggle with other ideals which are just as sacred to others as ours are to us" (*WL*, 154/57). "Every meaningful value-judgment about someone else's *aspirations* must be a criticism from the standpoint of one's own *Weltanschauung*; it must be a struggle against *another's* ideals from the standpoint of one's *own*" (*WL*, 157/60). In contrast, Marx asserted: "Reason has always existed, but not always in reasonable form. The critic therefore can start with any form of theoretical and practical consciousness and develop the true reality in its 'ought' and in its final goal out of its *own* forms of reality."[83] While for Weber an individual acting autonomously creates meaning in a world which is ultimately meaningless, Marx believed that the meaning of new social relations could be found through a critique of past relations, which already embody them implicitly.

Critique and Attempts at Mediation

In Marx's theory the reality to be investigated is a criterion for the suitability of the categories of investigation. Since the issue is knowledge of essential structures, of "laws" of a particular reality and not partial knowledge, the categories of investigation cannot be derived arbitrarily. Instead, the object of inquiry compels researchers, who immerse themselves in the object, to accept standpoints and categories adequate to the investigation. This also applies to the relation of values (norms and criteria of action) to reality. Pushed to its limits, the position is that norms of action are deducible from the correct analysis of historical reality.[84] In contrast to Weber's value freedom, decisions are clearly open to examination and are thereby simultaneously eliminated. In a "'scientific civilization' where politicians would no longer be 'decision makers' or 'rulers,' but rather analyzers" politics would consist of drawing consequences from the constraints of the social mechanisms that determined societal development.[85] Similarly, in a world that rendered an analysis of itself and its "objective potentialities" possible, to the extent that understanding of what was "socially desirable" could be derived from them,[86] value decisions would be replaced by deductions from an analysis of reality. In both instances, from the consequent elimination of decisions, there emerge the dangers of illiberalism, authoritarian antipluralism, and dogmatism. In science, this is manifested as intolerance toward other propositions. From the confines of this approach, such propositions appear only as errors or ideological deviations from true reality. Sociopolitically, this approach provides an ideological justification of its own goals as general and absolute because they are based on supposedly scientific insights (though, in fact, its goals are thoroughly one-sided).

Weber's philosophy of science postulates a contrary position, holding fast to the impossibility of deriving prescriptive knowledge from the object of inquiry. For Weber, knowledge is always fragmentary: its direction is determined by the initial choice of one standpoint from several alternatives. Weber hardly mentioned the interdependence of this choice with one's knowledge of reality, even though he claimed that the origin of the inquiry and the manner and aim of its proceedings is determined by these standpoints.

Above all, this radical separation is applicable to the relationship between historical reality and values, between empirical science and life decisions. Knowledge of values and goals of action do not follow from empirical scientific analysis. According to Weber, science can contribute something to the formulation of goals of action,[87] but it cannot justify the preference of one value over its opposite (*WL*, 149 ff./52 ff.). Even if science were able to establish a developmental tendency in history, this still would not provide actors with clues as to whether they should support or oppose its realization (*WL*, 474 ff.). Since a variety of possible actions derived from contrasting values are left open, the origin and choice of values appear closed to rational discussion (*WL*, 469 ff.). In the arena of action (the process of inquiry), goals and norms (cognitive standpoints and goals respectively) are constituted ultimately by a choice on whose essential rationality it is impossible to comment.[88]

Up to this point, Marx and Weber represent alternative and radically opposed ways of thinking. This confrontation points to shortcomings and pitfalls of their paradigms and provides a basis for alternating critique and attempts at mediation. This gives rise to the question whether there are perhaps certain elements within both Marx's and Weber's approaches, elements which require going beyond the pattern reconstructed so far in this article. I have tried to show that an approach where the cognitive standpoint can be derived clearly from the reality under investigation necessarily presupposes a concept of history which, though modified in the direction of praxis, depends heavily on Hegel. Norms of action can be oriented toward the objective possibilities of a specific reality only if that reality in its historical form is such that it can be mediated through correct practical consciousness toward the realization of that which existed heretofore only as potentiality (i.e., a type of reality which, for becoming itself, needs human praxis and, hence, practical knowledge). This reality is neither external nor alien to understanding, but rather, as Hegel stated, "it is the nature of the content and that alone which lives and stirs in philosophic [*wissenschaftlichen*] cognition, while it is this very reflection of the content which itself originates and determines the nature of philosophy."[89] The presupposition is certainly of the initial identity of the object of inquiry and the knowing subject, which is anchored in Hegel's philosophy. If history is an act "by which the absolute final aim of the world is realized in it and the merely implicit mind achieves consciousness and self-consciousness,"[90] then — and only then — can critique consist of the confrontation of a particular reality with its potentiality or its "claims," thereby ensuring historical progress. This concept of history guarantees, in principle, the unproblematical adequacy of contemporary categories in historical investigations, for these categories arise from a present which is the true and developed form of the past. For Hegel, the identity of subjective and objective spirit, of human consciousness and historical actuality, which becomes manifest in morality [*Sittlichkeit*], is marked out and present (if only implicitly) from the beginning.

But the question must be posed whether Marx, in his historical materialist rejection of Hegel's premise of a universal, historically unfolding reason,[91] did not also deny the foundation for conceiving the relationship between humanity and history in an Hegelian manner, as an identity that is already existent and merely needs to be realized. Certainly from Marx's position it can be argued that, since historical reality is always formed and mediated by human reason, it needs neither to be alien to human understanding nor "a vast chaotic flow" in Weber's sense. But it is less clear from Marx's premises why the particular level of metabolic process between man and nature[92] should always carry implicitly within itself its own future design or its own critique in the sense of an Hegelian objective possibility, which enables one to state without question — "What is valuable for society is always what has become possible historically."[93] For in Marx's view the material of the historical process is not identical with a notion of nature, which could be described as idea in its otherness[94] and whose implicit truth would be embodied in history from its beginning. Just as nature, for Marx, does not unfold fully in history, neither does it *demand* its meaningful cultivation through historical labor; at best it *permits* it and leaves open alternatives (e.g., destructive utilization). However much of each historical situation is mediated through concepts, it does not fully and unambiguously contain the goal of its future. The goal of humanity is the concept of its previous development only if this concept as self-actualizing reason already precedes its own development. However, Marx rejected this premise.[95] Thereby, the deducibility of goals of political action from an appropriate analysis of previous history becomes objectively highly questionable within any Marxian approach (although Marx did not see this).

The same objection applies to the deducibility of cognitive standpoints and conceptual categories from the object of inquiry. As shown above, Marx's social and historical analysis proceeds from a specific historically determined and practical horizon. Since, on the basis of his methodological remarks, Marx claimed to proceed from "the actual and concrete elements of real preconditions" and took "the people" as the point of departure for his research in order to arrive at their organization (classes) and the fundamental elements of the latter,[96] then at this point, he already had an implicit preunderstanding [Vorverständnis]. For example, he did not start with one nation-state as opposed to other nation-states. And his theory enabled him to arrive at economically defined classes as organizational elements but not, for example, religious or ethnic groups. This theoretical preunderstanding is neither self-evident, nor is it the only one possible. But Marx wrote as if this preunderstanding, these categories and theoretical statements, would be imposed on the researcher by the object of inquiry, as if they would emerge naturally from immersion in the object. But, in fact, this belief does not follow from his own premises.[97]

In the preceding paragraphs, I tried to show that within Marx's approach, but in some contrast to what Marx actually wrote: (1) the object of inquiry is itself not a wholly sufficient criterion, not a fully sufficient "empirical referent" for a definitive determination of appropriate concepts and cognitive approaches; and (2) the problem of the fit of concept and object (which Weber stated clearly but solved in too decisionistic a fashion) cannot be passed over simply by referring to Marx. The same objection applies to praxis as a second possible mode of control over the formulation of scientific concepts, categories, and theories. Certainly, as shown above, Marx's theory convincingly shows that scientific research always stands in a multireferential practical context, and hence, can and must find criteria for its procedures. However, even if research must always be oriented to praxis, it is impossible for this praxis to provide a fixed objective measure, either for evaluation of norms or for the choice of cognitive approach. Man is always a constitutive element in the midst of this praxis, just as cognition is a dimension of the very process that it desires to understand. Cognition is unable to objectify praxis as a comprehensible totality. Therefore, the problem of the "hermeneutic circle," of which Marx was unaware, has to be addressed.[98] This is especially pertinent for a mode of thought that considers itself as part of the totality to be known. In addition, praxis is continually changing, among other ways through the progress of research, and the guidelines for which it is supposed to provide. And historically, praxis never attains a definitive form; it can always be interpreted differently.

If correctly interpreted, in Marx's thought there persists the unresolved problem of how values and cognitive approaches and categories can be controlled. Neither the historical reality to be investigated nor the specific historical praxis of the investigator provides a sufficiently clear criterion for such choice. However, this does not require a return to the decisionistic alternative discussed above.

The following points must be retained: (1) the cognitive standpoint is reflective of the object of inquiry and the specific form of societal praxis, although it is not unequivocally deducible from them; and (2) individual historical phenomena, per Marx's claim, are not grasped outside of a notion of totality, even though totality cannot be fully or directly conceptualized. How do these points relate to Max Weber's philosophy of science?

To be more compatible with these two elements of Marx's theory, an interpretation of Weber's philosophy of science must (1) maintain Weber's primacy of the cognitive standpoint in empirical research, while holding to the impossibility of simply deriving it from criteria based on the subject matter or the existing culture, and (2) find, within Weber's theory, possibilities for control of the choice of standpoint so as to free it from the charge of decisionism.

Weber has been criticized for presenting science with an object that does not exist in historical reality. Because of the absence of structure in the "heterogeneous continuum," knowledge can — according to this criticism — be validated only methodologically and not through a confrontation with reality. Culture is merely a "subjective concept" and history only "our composition." Weber's reality, "an amorphous detritus of appearances," supplies no criterion for choice, evaluation, and control of those perspectives which make knowledge possible.[99]

This criticism, supported by Weber's statements, remains valid even if, as shown above, the "heterogeneous continuum" is not wholly without structure, for these "ontic" structures cannot prevent reality from appearing first and foremost as a "chaotic stream." Nevertheless, such a radical critique, according to which Weber's methodological position must appear paradoxical,[100] cannot explain sufficiently numerous other elements and passages within his philosophy of science. Weber indicated, at least implicitly, that although cognitive standpoints are deducible from the object of inquiry, they can be questioned and controlled. Thus, he hoped to determine, with more research, "the *extent* of the cultural significance of ascetic Protestantism" for modern capitalism.[101] This would mean that, at a later point, a rational decision can be reached concerning the importance of one perspective and causal chain (e.g., the socioeconomic) relative to others.

Weber considered the scientist's principle value premises [*Wertideen*] to be the criterion for the choice of cognitive standpoint (*WL*, 259 ff.). He believed that a "scientific genius" would gear his inquiry to values that determine "the 'conception' of a whole epoch" (*WL*, 182). Weber also implied that the researchers' cognitive interests and standpoints are mediated by the practical needs of their time (*WL*, 148, 158, 165). Certainly, Weber's intertwining of the standpoints with social conditions is not a sufficient basis for control of a standpoint. For if practical, cultural problems are introduced as a criterion of appropriate correspondence for the formulation of the standpoint and concepts, there arises the question as to how it is possible to achieve an unequivocal understanding of those very problems. The same difficulty reappears because, according to Weber's position, the practical, cultural concerns vary according to the interests, values, and standpoints of the individual, whereas these standpoints are supposed to be measured against the problems.

Nevertheless, Weber's awareness of the close relation between standpoints and social conditions can justify, within his own theoretical framework, the demand that the formulation of scientific standpoints and theories be reflected on from the perspective of the societal context, one element of which is the research itself.[102] Weber does not expressly make this demand, but it has a place within his philosophy of science. Moreover, Weber's repeated demand for clarity and intellectual integrity can, within the confines of his position, justify sufficiently the demand that scientists reflect on the intertwining of their cognitive standpoints with their social situations; this Weber acknowledged (*WL*, 259 ff.). If this is a correct interpretation of Weber's philosophy of science, it is somewhat protected against the charge of irrational decisionism.

In Weber's theory both the social reality of the investigator and the object of inquiry offer possibilities of limiting subjective arbitrariness. "If, however, I wish to grasp the concept of 'sect' genetically, e.g., with reference to certain important effects [Kulturbedeutungen], which the 'sectarian spirit' has had for modern culture, certain characteristics of both [church and sect] become *essential*, because they stand in adequate causal relation to those effects" (WL, 194/93-94). For Weber, the concept of cultural meaning [Kulturbedeutung] usually indicated the basis for the interest with which the researcher turns to a particular historical object, a methodical procedure, according to which "a segment of the meaningless infinity of world events" is bestowed with "meaning" and thus becomes "culture."[103] In the above quoted case (WL, 194/93-94), however, Kulturbedeutung denoted the connection through which a cultural phenomenon of the past has influenced modern culture. Thus, though Kulturbedeutung usually belongs to those concepts which bind scientific knowledge to the researcher's value decisions, here the term denotes an objective structure.[104] In Weber's view, culture not only represented a slice of chaos ordered by a methodical relationship with the scientist's values and viewpoints, but he also recognized something similar to a "material concept of culture," culture on the "ontic" level, whose structure and meaning, at least initially, are not constituted by the researcher's standpoint.[105]

This is evidence for something like an "ontic" turn in Weber's work; this can help to defend against the charge of decisionism. But how does it fit into the framework of his theory? How can freedom of choice of the research perspective, which Weber insisted on so frequently, be reconciled with the assumption of a "material" culture? If such a "material" culture exists, scientific investigations cannot confront it as a subordinate, amorphous stuff; rather, it demands that researchers adequately reconstruct the object (the "ontic" structure) of their investigations. At any rate, "material culture" is, within Weber's approach, part of a reality of which only partial knowledge is possible, and it cannot be thought of such that cognitive standpoints are *unequivocally* deducible from it. Nevertheless, it represents a *real* context which controls retroactively whether the perspectives from which the research proceeds are appropriate to the structures for which they have been constituted. Though the subject matter does *not impose* standpoints on the researcher, it *nevertheless influences* their choice and application. Moreover, it requires continuous reflection on the relationship between standpoint and object. In this way the subject matter limits arbitrariness of the choice of standpoint.

Weber never made this premise of his arguments explicit and thus did not justify it in the context of his other concepts. Discourse in the philosophy of science, at that time, occasioned Weber to stress the nondeducibility of evaluative standpoints against the attacks of the nomothetical and historical schools.[106] Putting this aside, an explication of such a premise would have had to include a theory of material culture, which Weber was not prepared to undertake. The goal of such a theory would have been to reconcile the tension between it and reality viewed as a "heterogeneous continuum." Possibly this would have led to irreconcilible contradictions and the need to examine a notion which Weber supported exclusively through appeals to empirical evidence.

For Weber, as well as Marx, subject matter exercised a control function over the application of the previously constituted standpoint, a process whose explication might not be possible without modification of Weber's whole theory. The question arises: through which mechanism does the research object influence and direct the choice of cognitive standpoint? Attention is drawn to the prescientific preunderstanding of the object [*Vorverständnis*], which steers the formulation of categories.

"All historical 'valuation' includes, so to speak, a 'contemplative' element, it contains not only and not primarily the immediate value judgement of the assessing person, but rather its essential content is . . . a 'knowledge' of the object's 'relations to value.' It therefore presupposes the capacity for a change in the attitude toward the object, at least theoretically" (*WL*, 260/158). Even if historical research, namely the search for historical causes, is preceded and constituted by the choice of certain values, this constitutive act always presupposes some "knowledge" of the various possibilities through which the object can be related to values: "the 'objectification' and analysis of concrete reality is thereby taken for granted" (*WL*, 86). Here, Weber emphasized that another form of knowledge of reality must have preceded the constitution of scientific standpoints and concepts. He designated this prescientific preunderstanding as "objectification" and "analysis":[107] it makes possible the formulation of scientific concepts and limits their arbitrariness.

It appears that Weber knew of a — to him, self-evident — regulator of the choice of perspectives and concept-formation which inhered in the subject matter; however, its explication would have entangled his theory in contradictions. The notion of "heterogeneous continuum" forced Weber to describe the cognitive process as one of abstracting and isolating factors. In contrast, a preunderstanding, which informs the analyst of the different possible value relations, must include a notion of the whole. For only on this basis can a preunderstanding exclude the fortuitousness of the choice of standpoints and provide, though not in wholly adequate fashion, a presupposition for the critical examination of the "essential" in the sense of "worthy of being known." Weber was aware of this when he acknowledged a *functional* analysis of the relation between the 'parts' and the 'whole'" as a requisite "preliminary orientation to problems" (*WL*, 515, 518; *Economy and Society*, 15, 17). Weber noted: "[I]n certain circumstances, this is the only available way of determining just what processes of social action it is important to understand in order to explain a given phenomenon" (*WL*, 515; *Economy and Society*, 15) and to enable us to carry out the task of interpretive [*verstehende*] sociology. A question arises as to whether a concept of the whole is meaningful and practicable within a reality conceived of as a "heterogeneous continuum." Once again, Weber would have run into difficulties in further explication of his theory, as this would have called into question the "heterogeneous continuum."

Confronting Marx's thought with Weber's theory revealed tensions, dogmatic tendencies, and deficiencies within the former, but also showed that Weber's approach in no way resolved the problem of Marx's thinking. The confrontation of Weber's philosophy of science with Marx's position likewise entailed critique and offered simultaneously the opportunity to free Weber's theory from some of its decisionistic consequences, i.e., interpreting it so that it is less closed to some of the indispensable elements of Marx's teachings. This attempted mediation found its clearest limits in the two authors' notions of reality, namely in the residue of Hegelian historical speculation in Marx and in the concept of a "heterogeneous continuum" in Weber. It has been argued that the revisions of these notions, though leading to new problems and tensions, would eliminate certain extreme and unacceptable aspects of both Marx's and Weber's philosophies of science, specifically the danger of dogmatism in the former's epistemology and the danger of decisionism in the latter's methodology.

The outlines of a practical position in the philosophy of science are indicated clearly. Naturally, its elaboration could rest on numerous contributions which can neither be considered nor further investigated here.[108] The outlines are as follows: on the one hand, neither the structures of the object of inquiry nor the practical mediatory context within which the investigators find themselves are able to prescribe unequivocally the researchers' cognitive standpoint, statement of the problem, categories, explanatory models, and theories; on the other hand, they are not indifferent to these matters. Therefore, researchers must justify continually, by way of argumentation and as part of the research procedure, their decisions concerning theories, concepts, and procedures in categories appropriate to the subject matter and congruent with societal rationality (which, to be sure, is open within limits to different interpretations). This position would *establish* a context for discussion, be open to a plurality of research perspectives, and yet simultaneously *circumscribe* this context by indicating points of control: the object itself, the relation to practice, and the rational, critical, open, and to the greatest extent possible, autonomous communication among the investigators. Only in this way can a position in the philosophy of science escape both the charge of authoritarian dogmatism and the verdict of decisionistic arbitrariness.

NOTES

1. See E. Topitsch, "Max Weber Geschichtsauffassung," *Wissenschaft und Weltbild* (1950) 3: 262.

2. Throughout the essay, "*Wissenschaft*" has been translated as "science" and "*Wissenschaftler*" as "scientist." However, "*Wissenschaft*" is a broader concept including disciplines that, in the Anglo-American tradition, are usually considered to be part of the "humanities" rather than the "sciences."

3. K. Löwith, "M. Weber und K. Marx," in K. Löwith, *Gesammelte Abhandlungen*, (Stuttgart: Kohlhammer, 1960), pp. 1-67 [*Max Weber and Karl Marx* (London: Allen & Unwin, 1982), p. 25].

4. However, the historical aspect of the relationship of Marx and Weber is not treated here. See G. Roth, "Das historische Verhältnis der Weberschen Soziologie zum Marxismus," *Kölner Zeitschrift für Soziologie* (1968) 20:429-477.

5. See W. Lefévre, *Zum historischen Charakter und zur historischen Methode bürgerlicher Soziologie. Untersuchung am Werk M. Webers* (Frankfurt: Suhrkamp, 1971), pp. 6-23 ff.

6. For examples of such Marxist argumentation see F. Tomberg, "Was heisst bürgerliche Wissenschaft?", *Das Argument* (1971) 66: 470-475; W. Eckermann and H. Mohr, eds., *Einführung in das Studium der Geschichte*, 2d ed. (Berlin: Deutscher Verlag der Wissenschaften, 1969), pp. 33, 40 ff., 47 ff., 69 ff.; E. Hahn, *Soziale Wirklichkeit und soziologische Erkenntnis. Philosophisch-methodologische Aspekte der soziologischen Theorie* (Berlin: Dietz, 1965). For criticisms see H. Albert, *Traktat über kritische Vernunft* (Tübingen: J.C.B. Mohr, 1968), pp. 7, 47-54; H. Seiffert, *Marxismus und bürgerliche Wissenschaft* (Munich: C.H. Beck, 1971), especially pp. 85-104.

7. On Weber's philosophy of science, see A. v. Schelting, *Max Webers Wissenschaftslehre* (Tübingen: J.C.B. Mohr, 1934); J.J. Schaaf, *Geschichte und Begriff. Eine kritische Studie zur Geschichtsmethodologie von Ernst Troeltsch und Max Weber* (Tübingen: J.C.B. Mohr, 1946); D. Henrich, *Die Einheit der Wissenschaftslehre Max Webers* (Tübingen: J.C.B. Mohr, 1952); F.H.

Tenbruck, "Die Genesis der Methodologie Max Webers," *Kölner Zeitschrift für Soziologie* (1959) 11:473-630; J. Janoska-Bendl, *Methodologische Aspekte des Idealtypus: Max Weber und die Soziologie der Geschichte* (Berlin: Duncker & Humblot, 1965); and most recently, G. Hufnagel, *Kritik als Beruf. Der kritische Gehalt im Werk Max Webers* (Frankfurt: Propyläen, 1971), including a detailed bibliography.

8. For example, K. Braunreuther writes that "Max Weber's true vocation was to be an anti-Marxist." In "Bemerkungen über Max Weber und die bürgerliche Soziologie," *Wissenschaftliche Zeitschrift der Humboldt-Universität, Gesellschafts- und Sprachwissenschaftliche Reihe* (1958/59):115-123, esp. p. 116.

9. Max Weber, *Wirtschaft und Gesellschaft* [1922], 4th ed. (Tübingen: J.C.B. Mohr, 1956), pp. 199-207 [*Economy and Society* [1968], Guenther Roth and Claus Wittich, trs. (Berkeley, Los Angeles, London: University of California Press, 1978), pp. 339-348.].

10. *Ibid.*, p. 262 [p. 429], for example, the connection between Chthonian deities and agriculture. See also p. 352 [p. 582].

11. Max Weber, *Gesammelte Aufsätze zur Wissenschaftslehre* [1922], 3d ed. (Tübingen: J.C.B. Mohr, 1968) [Partial translation in *The Methodology of the Social Sciences*, Edward A. Shils and Henry A. Finch, eds. and trs. (New York: The Free Press, 1949)]. This is referred to in the text as (*WL*...). However, the pagination is from the first edition (1922), since the second and third editions list the page numbers from the first edition in brackets on their inside margins (insofar as these differ from the third edition). This makes possible the use of all three editions. The second page number refers to the English translation, if available, even where it has been modified: e.g., [*WL*, 167/69].

12. See Max Weber, "Die protestantische Ethik und der Geist der Kapitalismus," *Gesammelte Aufsätze zur Religionssoziologie* (Tübingen: J.C.B. Mohr, 1920), 1:38 [*The Protestant Ethic and the Spirit of Capitalism*, T. Parsons, tr. (New York: Scribner's, 1958), p. 56]. The realization that in the United States the spirit of capitalism existed prior to capitalist economic development was used by Weber in his polemic against "naive" historical materialists: "In this case the causal relationship is certainly the reverse of that suggested by the materialistic standpoint. But the origin and history of such ideas is much more complex than the theorists of the superstructure suppose and their development never comes to fruition like that of a flower." Also *ibid.*, p. 60 [p. 75].

13. However, Weber himself acknowledged that this approach is not sufficient to explain *mature* capitalism: "The [victorious capitalism] forces the individual, insofar as he is involved in the system of market relationships, to conform to capitalist rules of action." *Ibid.*, p. 37 [p. 54]. Therefore, in *mature* capitalism, which Marx investigated in *Das Kapital*, the *spirit of capitalism* must, to a significant extent, be conceived as a function of conditions which, according to Weber, it had initially helped to bring about. These conditions have since developed into a self-reproducing system (cage). But this insight was not part of Max Weber's methodological reflections. See also *ibid.*, pp. 203 ff. [pp. 181 ff.].

14. See, for example, *ibid.*, pp. 37 f., 60, 83, 205 f. [pp. 55 f., 75, 91, 182 f.].

15. In this connection, Janoska-Bendl, *Methodologische Aspekte des Idealtypus*, pp. 89-114.

16. Karl Marx and Friedrich Engels, "Die deutsche Ideologie," *Werke* (Berlin: Dietz, 1961 ff.), 3:27. Hereafter abbreviated as *MEW* ["The German Ideology," Loyd D. Easton and Kurt H. Guddat, eds., *Writings of the Young Marx on Philosophy and Society* (New York: Doubleday, 1967), pp. 415-416. Henceforth: Easton and Guddat, *Writings of the Young Marx*].

17. Marx, "Das Kapital," vol. 1, *MEW*, 23:57.

18. In the foreword to "An Introduction to a Critique of Political Economy" (1859), Marx gives a schematic compilation of his previous studies. In this summary, he seemed to argue in favor of a thoroughgoing separation between social being and consciousness; this has led to an undialectical interpretation of his own work. K. Marx, "Zur Kritik der politischen Ökonomie," *MEW*, 13:18 ff. Such mechanistic statements in Marx's writings were adopted and emphasized by later theoreticians, such as Karl Kautsky and Max Adler, in part already by Friedrich Engels, and in still another way by the Stalinists. A. Wellmer has demonstrated this in *Kritische Gesellschaftstheorie und Positivismus* [1969], 3d ed. (Frankfurt: Suhrkamp, 1971), pp. 69-127 [*Critical Theory of Society*, John Cumming, tr. (New York: Herder & Herder, 1971), pp. 67-119].

19. This refers to the doctrine of materialism current in Marx's time, and which he criticized (Feuerbach's views, among others).

20. Marx, "Dritte These über Feuerbach," *MEW*, 3:5 ff. [Easton and Guddat, *Writings of the Young Marx*, p. 401].

21. Marx, "Die deutsche Ideologie," *MEW*, 3:38 [Easton and Guddat, *Writings of the Young Marx*, p. 432].

22. *Ibid.*, p. 42 [p. 432].

23. See Marx, "Ökonomisch-philosophische Manuskripte aus dem Jahre 1844," *MEW*, Supplementary vol., part 1, p. 579: "Neither nature objectively nor nature subjectively is directly given in a form adequate to the *human* being. And as everything natural has to *come into being, man* too has his act of origin — *history*. . . . History is the true natural history of man." ["Economic and Philosophical Manuscripts of 1844," Marx and Engels, *Collected Works*, (Moscow: Progress Publishers; London: Lawrence & Wishart, 1975), 3:337].

24. See A. Schmidt, *Der Begriff der Natur in der Lehre von Marx* (Frankfurt: Europäische Verlagsanstalt, 1962), pp. 51 ff. [*The Concept of Nature in Marx*, B. Fowkes, tr. (London: New Left Books, 1971), pp. 63 ff.].

25. On the historical character of Marx's general approach, see A. Schmidt, "Über Geschichte und Geschichtsschreibung in der materialistischen Dialektik," in *Folgen einer Theorie, Essays über 'Das Kapital'* (Frankfurt: Suhrkamp, 1967), pp. 103-109; and H. Fleischer, *Marxismus und Geschichte* (Frankfurt: Suhrkamp, 1969) [*Marxism and History*, Eric Mosbacher, tr. (New York: Harper & Row, 1973)].

26. Marx's letter to L. Kugelmann, June 27, 1870, *MEW*, 32:685. [*The Letters of Karl Marx*, Saul K. Padover, ed. and tr. (Englewood Cliffs, N.J.: Prentice-Hall, 1979), p. 273].

27. Marx, "Das Kapital," vol. 1, *MEW*, 23:12.

28. *Ibid.*, vol. 3, *MEW*, 25:267 [*Capital* (Moscow: Foreign Language Publishing House, 1959; London: Lawrence and Wishart Ltd., 1960), 3:251-252].

29. See *ibid.*, vol. 1, *MEW*, 23: 89, 511: ". . . with blind destructive effect of a natural law . . . ," ". . . as for example the law of gravity, when a house collapses on your head." See also R. Rosdolsky, "Ein neomarxistisches Lehrbuch der politischen Ökonomie," *Kyklos* (1963) 16:631 ff.

30. See also A. Schmidt, "Über Geschichte," pp. 128 ff.

31. Marx, "Das Kapital," vol. 3, *MEW*, 25:890 f.

32. Marx, "Ökonomisch-philosophische Manuskripte," *MEW*, Supplementary vol., part 1, p. 538 ["Economic and Philosophical Manuscripts of 1844," *Collected Works*, 3:298].

33. See Marx, "Das Kapital," vol. 3, *MEW*, 25:829, and Schmidt, *Begriff*, pp. 57, 109, 115 ff. [pp. 69 f., 128, 134 ff.].

34. Marx's letter to L. Kugelmann, July 11, 1868, *MEW*, 32:553.

35. Marx, "Das Kapital," vol. 1, *MEW*, 23:57.

36. As an example, Marx points to the necessity of the social division of labor as a prevailing natural law which assumes the form of exchange value in capitalist society. "The task of science is to explain *how* the law of exchange prevails" (letter to Kugelmann, July 11, 1868.) See R. Rosdolsky, "Der Gebrauchswert bei Karl Marx," *Kyklos* (1959) 12:31 ff.

37. See also Marx's letter to Engels, Dec. 9, 1861, *MEW*, 30:207: "Hegel had never subsumed a mass of 'cases' under a general principle called Dialectic." [*The Letters of Karl Marx*, p. 155].

38. See Henrich, *Die Einheit der Wissenschaftslehre*, p. 14.

39. The adjective *ontic* refers to reality as it is pregiven to scientific analysis, a reality which has not yet been constituted through the scientific-methodological reference to values and standpoints. (In contrast, Weber used the term *historical individual* to refer to a unity of elements of reality, which are tied to one another partly through an act of the investigator, an act which is related to the investigator's values and interests.) Just as Weber avoided epistemological reflections concerning the appearance of reality to the scientist, so the term *ontic* is used here in an epistemologically unproblematical fashion. See Henrich, *Die Einheit der Wissenschaftslehre*, pp. 17 ff.

40. *WL*, pp. 213/111, 180/181: "'Culture' is a finite segment of the meaningless infinity of the world process, a segment on which *human beings* confer meaning and significance,"; *WL*, p. 77/78: "The number and type of causes which have influenced any given event are always *infinite* and there is nothing in the things themselves to set them apart as alone meriting attention. A chaos of external judgements. . . ."; *WL*, p. 84/84: "The stream of immeasurable events flows unendingly toward eternity." There are numerous other passages in the same vein.

41. Tenbruck, "Die Genesis der Methodologie Max Webers," p. 601, and also S. Landshut, "Kritik der Soziologie" in Landshut, *Kritik der Soziologie und andere Schriften zur Politik* (Neuwied: Luchterhand, 1967), pp. 37 ff; Hufnagel, *Kritik als Beruf*, pp. 139, 211.

42. This is Rickert's term, not Weber's. It signifies an incalculable, manifold, and differentiated reality which is characterized by an immense number of features in its space-time determinations as well as in its quantitative aspects. Every concrete object stands in a total context, its determining elements are just as complex and in principle as inexhaustible as its own characteristics.

43. Such a value referent constitutes a common structure for all acting individuals. However, this remains purely formal since nothing binding or anything in the way of regularities can be stated concerning the content of the values which function as points of reference. Though this reference to values, which is conceived as a specifically human "rationality," constitutes a structure at the level of the individual (the "personality"), it is not suitable for the establishment of a supraindividual structure in the sense of material culture. This is because the content of its rationality can consist of an incalculable number of different combinations. Thus it is clear that the objects of an interpretive sociology

[*verstehende Soziologie*] are "solely the resultants and modes of organization of the particular acts of *individual* persons, since these alone can be treated as agents in a course of subjectively understandable action," See *WL*, p. 514 [*Economy and Society*, p. 13]. Therefore, within a sociology of understanding it is hardly possible to have a concept (either dialectical or functional) of the social whole.

44. See Tenbruck, "Die Genesis der Methodologie Max Webers," p. 600. On the question of Weber's view of the structure of reality, see the modification of this interpretation below.

45. Standpoints are tied to "evaluative ideas . . . [whose] . . . validity can *not* be deduced from empirical data as such" (*WL*, p. 213/111). "We cannot discover, however, what is meaningful to us by means of a 'presuppositionless' investigation of empirical data. Rather perception of its meaningfulness to us is the presupposition of its becoming an *object* of investigation," *WL*, pp. 175 f./76. See also note 40.

46. Similarly, Weber had to deny the deducibility of norms of action from the knowledge of the context in which the action is to take place. See *WL*, pp. 154 and 475.

47. See Henrich, *Die Einheit der Wissenschaftslehre*, p. 19.

48. For further criteria which from Weber's theoretical perspective can serve to limit the arbitrariness of the choice of concepts and categories, see below.

49. See also *WL*, pp. 151 ff. and 469 ff.

50. Marx, "Erste These über Feuerbach," *MEW*, 3:5 [Easton and Guddat, *Writings of the Young Marx*, p. 400].

51. Marx, "Zur Kritik der Hegelschen Rechtsphilosophie, Einleitung," *MEW*, 21:378. Tom Bottomore translates this as "Man is *the human world*, the state, society," in Karl Marx, *Early Writings* (London: Watts, 1963), p. 43.

52. Marx, "Die deutsche Ideologie," *MEW*, 3:44 [Easton and Guddat, *Writings of the Young Marx*, p. 418].

53. Marx, "Sechste These über Feuerbach," *MEW*, 3:6 [Easton and Guddat, *Writings of the Young Marx*, p. 402].

54. O. Morf, *Geschichte und Dialektik in der politischen Ökonomie. Zum Verhältnis von Wirtschaftstheorie und Wirtschaftsgeschichte bei K. Marx*, 2d ed. (Frankfurt: Europäische Verlagsanstalt, 1970), p. 114.

55. Marx, "Das Kapital," vol. 3, *MEW*, 25:219 [*Capital*, 3:205].

56. Marx, Das Kapital, vol. 1, *MEW*, 23:88.

57. Marx, "Einleitung zur Kritik der politischen Ökonomie," *MEW*, 13:633 [*A Contribution to the Critique of Political Economy* (New York: International Publishers, 1970), p. 207].

58. Lenin's mimetic theory was criticized in this respect by Marxists. See K. Korsch, *Marxismus und Philosophie* [1923] (Leipzig: Hirschfeld, 1930), pp. 25 ff. [*Marxism and Philosophy*, Fred Halliday, tr. (London: New Left Books, 1970), pp. 60 ff.].

59. See Marx, "Randglossen zu Adolph Wagners Lehrbuch der politischen Ökonomie," quoted in Schmidt, *Begriff*, p. 93 [*The Concept of Nature in Marx*, p. 110].

60. Marx, "Zweite These über Feuerbach," *MEW*, 3:5 [Easton and Guddat, *Writings of the Young Marx*, p. 401]. See also Schmidt, *Begriff*, p. 101 [*The Concept of Nature in Marx*, pp. 119 f.].

61. See E. Bloch, *Das Prinzip Hoffnung* (Berlin: Aufbau Verlag, 1954), 1:214 ff.

62. Marx, "Zweite These über Feuerbach," *MEW*, 3:5 [Easton and Guddat, *Writings of the Young Marx*, p. 401].

63. See Schmidt, *Begriff*, p. 94 [*The Concept of Nature in Marx*, p. 111]; *MEW*, 3:5 [Easton and Guddat, *Writings of the Young Marx*, p. 401].

64. See G. Lukács, *Die Zerstörung der Vernunft* (Neuwied: Luchterhand, 1961), pp. 521-537 [*The Destruction of Reason*, P. Palmer, tr. (London: Merlin, 1980), pp. 601-619]; for a more differentiated and relatively positive view, see the Marxist analysis of I.S. Kon, *Die Geschichtsphilosophie des 20. Jahrhunderts* (Berlin: Academie-Verlag, 1964), 1:136-157.

65. Marx, "Einleitung zur Kritik der politischen Ökonomie," *MEW*, 13:631 ff. [*A Contribution to the Critique of Political Economy*, pp. 206 ff.].

66. *Ibid.* See also O. Morf, *Geschichte und Dialektik*, pp. 36 ff.; and A. Schmidt, *Geschichte und Struktur. Fragen einer marxistischen Historik* (Munich: Hanser, 1971), pp. 41 ff. [*History and Structure: An Essay on Hegelian-Marxist and Structuralist Theories of History* (Cambridge, Mass.: MIT Press, 1981), pp. 28 ff.].

67. O. Morf, *Geschichte und Dialektik*, p. 128.

68. Marx, "Das Kapital," vol. 3, *MEW*, 25:219 [*Capital*, 3:205].

69. *Ibid.*, p. 825 [p. 817]: "all science would be superfluous if the outward appearance and the essence of things directly coincided."

70. This is Marx's own formulation of his "goal." See "Das Kapital," vol. 1, *MEW*, 23:15 ff.

71. See Rosdolsky, *Lehrbuch*, pp. 645 ff.

72. See note 68 above.

73. One must agree with G. Lukács, *Geschichte und Klassenbewusstsein. Studien über marxistische Dialektik* [1923] (Neuwied: Luchterhand, 1970), pp. 229-260 [*History and Class Consciousness: Studies in Marxist Dialectics*, Rodney Livingstone, tr. (Cambridge, Mass.: MIT Press, 1971), pp. 223-255]; H. Marcuse, *Reason and Revolution* [1941], 2d ed. (Boston: Beacon Press, 1952), pp. 273 ff.; K. Bekker, *Marx' philosophische Entwicklung. Sein Verhältnis zu Hegel* (Zurich and New York: Oprecht, 1940); S. Avineri, *The Social and Political Thought of Karl Marx* (Cambridge: Cambridge University Press, 1968), pp. 3 ff.; Schmidt, *Geschichte und Struktur*, pp. 47-51 [*History and Structure*, pp. 33-38]; and many others who argue for the immense and continuous influence of Hegel's philosophy on Marx, a philosophy which Marx himself had radically transformed. For an unconvincing contrary position, see L. Althusser, *Für Marx* (Frankfurt: Suhrkamp, 1968), pp. 130-135, 142-145 [*Pour Marx* (Paris: Maspero, 1966), pp. 108-116; *For Marx*, Ben Brewster, tr. (New York: Pantheon, 1979), pp. 107-116].

74. Weber, "Die protestantische Ethik," pp. 134 ff., 192 [*The Protestant Ethic*, pp. 131 ff., 172].

75. Weber probably saw this himself. He characterized this work as preliminary and expected supplementation to come from future research carried out from other perspectives (*ibid.*, pp. 205 ff. [pp. 182 ff.]).

76. *Ibid.*, pp. 52 ff. [pp. 67 ff.].

77. Marx, "Einleitung zur Kritik der politischen Ökonomie," *MEW*, 13:634 [*A Contribution to the Critique*, p. 210].

78. These demands are only implied by Marx (*ibid.*, pp. 617 ff. [pp. 192 ff.]); they can be inferred from the context. Weber does not make these demands because he completely separates the researcher's standpoints from the object of inquiry. See below.

79. Marx, "Einleitung zur Kritik der politischen Ökonomie," *MEW*, 13:636 [*A Contribution to the Critique*, p. 211].

80. *Ibid.*

81. E. Bloch, *Subjekt-Objekt, Erläuterungen zu Hegel* [1949] (Berlin: Aufbau-Verlag, 1951), pp. 221 ff.

82. E. Troeltsch, *Der Historismus und seine Probleme* [1922] (Aalen: Scientia Verlag, 1961), 1:367.

83. Marx's letter to A. Ruge, Sept. 1843, in *Die Frühschriften*, S. Landshut, ed. (Stuttgart: Kröner, 1953), p. 169 [*The Letters of Karl Marx*, p. 31]. See Wellmer, *Kritische Gesellschaftstheorie*, pp. 59-61, 78-92 [*Critical Theory of Society*, pp. 57-59, 76-89], as to the possibility of reconstructing this immanent critique in Marx's work in connection with the transition from Hegel to Marx (a theme which I have not extensively treated).

84. As a modern representative of this position, see M. Horkheimer, "Zum Begriff der Vernunft," in Adorno and Horkheimer, *Sociologica* II (Frankfurt: Europäische Verlagsanstalt, 1962), esp. p. 204, and W. Hofmann, *Gesellschaftslehre als Ordnungsmacht. Die Werturteilsfrage heute* (Berlin: Duncker & Humblot, 1961), p. 29.

85. This "technocratic" perspective, from a non-Marxist perspective, is formulated in H. Schelsky, *Der Mensch in der wissenschaftlichen Zivilisation* (Cologne: Westdeutscher Verlag, 1961), pp. 25 ff.

86. In the context of Marxist thought see W. Hofmann: "The idea that social facts can be judged according to their value gains a general validity when those social facts objectively correspond to the level of the potentials of a given historical formation. That which is socially valuable is always that which has become historically possible." *Gesellschaftslehre als Ordnungsmacht*, p. 32.

87. These functions of science are listed briefly, but succinctly, in *WL*, pp. 427 ff.

88. As a decisionist, in this sense, Weber is categorized with some modifications and often contradictory evaluations by Tenbruck, "Die Genesis der Methodologie Max Webers," pp. 600 ff.; Lukács, *Die Zerstörung der Vernunft*, pp. 532 ff. [*Destruction of Reason*, pp. 609 ff.]; L. Strauss, *Naturrecht und Geschichte*, H. Boog, tr. (Stuttgart: Koehler, 1956), pp. 107 ff. [Original publ.: *Right and History* (Chicago: University of Chicago Press, 1953)]; J. Habermas, *Technik und Wissenschaft als Ideologie* (Frankfurt: Suhrkamp, 1968), pp. 121 ff. ["Technology and Science as Ideology," *Toward a Rational Society*, J.J. Shapiro, tr. (Boston: Beacon Press, 1970)]; H. Marcuse, *Kultur und Gesellschaft* (Frankfurt: Suhrkamp, 1965), 2:107 ff. See also the overview in G. Roth, "Political Critiques of Max Weber: Some Implications for Political Sociology," *American Sociological Review* (1965) 30:213-223.

89. G.W.F. Hegel, *Wissenschaft der Logik* (Leipzig: F. Meiner, 1923), part 1, p. 6 [*Hegel's Science of Logic* (London: George Allen & Unwin Ltd., 1929), p. 36]. O. Morf, *Geschichte und Dialektik*, p. 77, claims this statement for the Marxist method. As to the close relationship between Marx's method and Hegel's logic, see Schmidt, *History and Structure*.

90. G.W.F. Hegel, *Enzyklopädie der philosophischen Wissenschaften im Grundrisse*, 6th ed. (Hamburg: F. Meiner, 1959), p. 426, section 549 [*Hegel's Philosophy of Mind* (London: Oxford University Press, 1971), p. 277].

91. See Marx and Engels, "Die deutsche Ideologie," *MEW*, 3:13 ff. [Easton and Guddat, *Writings of the Young Marx*, p. 404].

92. See Marx, "Das Kapital," vol. 1, *MEW* 23:57.

93. See above, note 86.

94. This is Hegel's notion: Hegel, *Enzyklopädie*, p. 197, section 244.

95. Recently Wellmer elaborated on the remnants of this Hegelian, speculative logic of history in Marx's thought, even though it no longer has a proper place or justification for being there. Wellmer sees in these remnants the basis for Marx's tendency to assume that social-historical contradictions would be overcome, almost out of necessity, in a progressive revolutionary manner. See *Kritische Gesellschaftstheorie und Positivismus*, pp. 56 ff., 64 ff., 77, 93 ff., 126 f. [*Critical Theory of Society*, pp. 54 ff., 64 ff., 74, 89 ff., 118 f.]. This assumption "proved false, and in a fatal sense," *ibid.*, p. 128 [p. 121]. See also M. Theunissen, *Gesellschaft und Geschichte. Zur Kritik der kritischen Theorie* (Berlin: de Gruyter, 1969), pp. 30, 33-38. He shows that, even though "critical theory" explicitly rejects Hegelian premises (the presupposition of an absolute, though historically developed, objectivity), "critical theorists," e.g., Habermas, in the final analysis act as if they could still proceed on the basis of the presupposition of a philosophy of identity. It is at this juncture that Theunissen locates in "critical theory" certain tendencies toward an intolerant dogmatism and absolute claim of an epistemological-political character.

96. Marx, "Einleitung zur Kritik der politischen Ökonomie," *MEW*, 13:631 ff. [*A Contribution to the Critique of Political Economy*, p. 206].

97. Habermas demonstrates convincingly the tremendous significance of such a preunderstanding for scientific inquiry, a prescientific understanding which is historically changeable and heterogeneous even within the same society and epoch. Habermas turns this insight against certain representatives of neopositivism who fail to take it sufficiently into account. See "Analytische Wissenschaftstheorie und Dialektik. Ein Nachtrag zur Kontroverse zwischen Popper und Adorno," in *Zeugnisse. Th. W. Adorno zum 60. Geburtstag*, M. Horkheimer, ed. (Frankfurt: Europäische Verlagsanstalt, 1963), pp. 473-501, esp. p. 476. Reprinted in Th. W. Adorno, ed., *Der Positivismusstreit in der deutschen Soziologie* [1969] (Neuwied: Luchterhand, 1972), pp. 151-191 [Th. Adorno et al., *The Positivist Dispute in German Sociology* (London: Heinemann, 1976), pp. 131-162], and in J. Habermas, *Zur Logik der Sozialwissenschaften* [1967], 2d ed. (Frankfurt: Suhrkamp, 1970), pp. 9-38. These critical reflections must also be addressed to Marxist approaches insofar as they suppress their own historicity and skip over hermeneutical issues in epistemology.

98. Theunissen, *Gesellschaft und Geschichte*, p. 34 shows that even "critical theory," which relies on Marx, cannot solve this problem and that the possibility of critical theory's dogmatism, in relation to other theories, results from its claim to knowledge of the totality, a claim which neglects the problematic of the hermeneutic circle, but does not solve it.

99. See, e.g., Tenbruck, "Die Genesis der Methodologie Max Webers," pp. 600, 602; and similarly Landshut, "Kritik der Soziologie," note 41; Lefévre, *Zum historischen Charakter und zur historischen Methode der bürgerlichen Soziologie*, pp. 16 ff.

100. Finally, on the basis of such an interpretation of Weber's methodology, no suffi-

cient reason can be found for *not* interpreting the origin of British capitalism from the high incidence of fog in England. In contrast to this interpretation, it must be remembered that Weber produced not only a philosophy of science, but also practical research projects, whose results can hardly be understood against the background of such a paradoxical methodology.

101. Weber, "Die protestantische Ethik," pp. 205 ff. [*The Protestant Ethic*, pp. 182 ff.].

102. This interrelatedness between science and society is analyzed in Habermas, "Analytische Wissenschaftstheorie," pp. 473 ff.

103. *WL*, p. 180. Also D. Henrich, *Die Einheit der Wissenschaftslehre*, pp. 74 ff., and D. Henrich, "Diskussionsbeitrag" in *Max Weber und die Soziologie heute. Verhandlungen des 15. deutschen Soziologentages*, O. Stammer, ed. (Tübingen: J.C.B. Mohr, 1965), pp. 81-87 [*Max Weber and Sociology Today*, O. Stammer, ed. (Oxford: Basil Blackwell, 1971), pp. 66-71)]. This argumentation will neither be accepted nor disapproved by those making, in my opinion unsuccessful, attempts to categorize Weber as an epistemological decisionist. See, above all, Lefévre, *Zum historischen Charakter*, pp. 16-29, and especially pp. 20 ff. and 115 ff. Lefévre refers, as have many before him, to the problems and limits of Weber's approach. What is striking is the high degree of uncritical self-confidence with which he suggests that Weber's difficulties can in principle be overcome along with bourgeois society, without demonstrating how this could be accomplished, either on the level of the philosophy of science or in scientific practice. A few allusions to the solvability of the problem through participation in the anticapitalist "struggle of the laboring masses for the control over the objectivities produced by them" remain mere affirmations. Hufnagel, *Kritik als Beruf*, pp. 139, note 2; 211; 213 ff., also attempts to retain a decisionistic interpretation of Weber's approach. Much more convincing is W. Schluchter, *Wertfreiheit und Verantwortungsethik. Zum Verhältnis von Wissenschaft und Politik bei Max Weber* (Tübingen: J.C.B. Mohr, 1971), who places Weber in the context of Habermas' pragmatic model.

104. "The *Kulturbedeutung* of unfree labor was finally reinforced significantly through the inclusion of large inland areas." Max Weber, "Die sozialen Gründe des Untergangs der antiken Kultur," in Max Weber, *Soziologie — Weltgeschichte Analysen — Politik*, J. Winkelmann, ed., 2d ed. (Stuttgart: Kröner, 1956), p. 8 ["The Social Causes of the Decay of Ancient Civilization, I," *The Journal of General Education* (1950) 5:79].) Here "*Kulturbedeutung*" denotes the decisive force that radiates from a specific cultural content to the culture as a whole, thus an objective reality.

105. Janoska-Bendl, in *Methodologische Aspekte des Idealtypus*, pp. 33 ff., speaks of a "minimum of philosophy of history" in Weber, and certainly the character of Weber's ideal types is "conceptual," i.e., they are neither representations of reality nor fully autonomous thought constructs. The attempt to identify "the fundamentals of a philosophy of history" in Weber implies the assumption that Weber presupposed implicitly something like structures of sociohistorical reality, which are pregiven to scientific inquiry. See, above all, W.J. Mommsen, "Universalgeschichtliches und politisches Denken bei Max Weber," *Historische Zeitschrift* (1965) 201:557-612. However, Mommsen overlooks this consequence and sketches the relationship of reality and scientific knowledge (pp. 569 ff.) in a way that can be logically maintained only by those who simultaneously deny all elements of a theory of material culture in Weber. Mommsen lacks any insight into the connection between "the fundamentals of a philosophy of history," which he treats extensively, and the question of the relation between sociohistorical reality and scientific knowledge in Weber's works. Similarly flawed is his critique in *Historische Zeitschrift* (1970) 211:623 ff.

106. See Tenbruck, "Die Genesis der Methodologie Max Webers," pp. 590 ff. The relationship of Weber's methodological position to his critique of the Wilhelmine bureaucracy cannot be discussed, though it is possible to find historical causes for the pointed statements in his philosophy of science. Important references are to be found in Gustav Schmidt, *Deutscher Historismus und der Übergang zur parlamentarischen Demokratie. Untersuchungen zu den politischen Gedanken von Meinecke, Troeltsch, Max Weber* (Lübeck: Matthiesen, 1964), pp. 226-305.

107. Other passages demonstrate that Weber generally used the term "analysis" to characterize a nonempirical scientific approach to an object. See, for example, *WL*, pp. 262 ff.

108. Of special importance are certain statements by Habermas, for example his "Einleitung" to *Theorie und Praxis* [1963], 2d ed., (Frankfurt: Suhrkamp, 1971), pp. 9-47 [*Theory and Practice*, John Viertel, tr. (Boston: Beacon Press, 1974), pp. 1-40]. See also the work of H. Albert, whose "critical rationalism," based on Karl Popper, doubtless escapes a significant portion of the intense critique of positivism launched by Adorno, Habermas, etc. In this debate, the gap between "critical theory" and "critical rationalism" has been made to appear greater than it actually is. Albert stresses the differences between his own position and positivism (which has been criticized strongly by the Frankfurt School). See Albert, *Traktat über kritische Vernunft*, pp. 6 ff., 54, 59 ff., 61 ff., 75 ff. The possible mediation of his argument, which navigates between dogmatism and decisionism, with certain positions found in "critical theory" would have to be addressed separately.

II

Approaches to Theory

In German sociology, debates about theory have always been about more than the place of theoretical assumptions and programs in sociology or the relevance of sociological theory for empirical research. They have also addressed the relationship of sociology to comprehensive "theories of society."

The predominant approaches to theory in postwar Germany have continued to reflect this basic tendency of German sociology. But debates about theory by and large now take place in the face of an increasing acceptance of empirical sociological research and of sociology as an empirical discipline. A single-minded and exclusive focus on empirical research is, however, generally regarded as a mixed blessing at best, since such an orientation may add to our knowledge of society while simultaneously diminishing it. This view presupposes that sociological research must not relinquish its connection to theory. All authors represented in this part of the book share this position, even if their assessment of the epistemological status and cognitive significance of theoretical propositions regarding empirical research, normative theory, and broad philosophical views of society are often very different.

However, the strongest disagreements concern the problem of the nature of sociology as a whole and its relation to social theory as an undertaking reaching beyond the specialized discipline of sociology. It is precisely in this domain that the debates about theory in German sociology reveal their distinctive characteristics. They have one question as their central focus: whether sociology is indeed primarily a theoretical discipline. As such a theoretical discipline, sociology would be the major constituent component of a theory of society, which has the emergence of modern society as its theme. Understood as a primarily empirical discipline, however, sociology would have to forgo addressing such wide-ranging questions, and instead confine itself to a more modest scope of by and large strictly empirical investigations.

Those orientations which regard sociology as the central constituent component of a theory of society attempt to incorporate empirical research into a comprehensive theory, which in turn serves as an interpretive framework for empirical findings. While the positions represented in this part of the book differ with respect to the legitimacy, significance, and nature of such comprehensive theories, they all recognize the conjectural status of wide-ranging theoretical claims. And they also accept the irreversibility of the social processes that have led to the institutionalization of social research. They all recognize, furthermore, the modernization processes in highly "developed" societies as the stage on which sociology as a specialized discipline first arose. Sociological theory and the raising of theoretical questions about society remain important because the past and future development of society cannot be addressed without them.

René König (essay 5) and Norbert Elias (essay 6) express the strongest reservations among the authors in this part of the book about the significance and self-sufficiency of social theory, while Niklas Luhmann (essay 7) and Jürgen Habermas (essay 8) tend toward the opposite view: they not only defend the autonomy of sociological theory but also advocate a more wide-ranging social theory (or a theory of society) as an undertaking that is beyond the grasp of sociology as a narrowly specialized discipline. Helmut Schelsky (essay 4), on the other hand, articulates a third view: while sociology has become a specialized science, it must by necessity continue to approach social and cultural phenomena by way of a philosophically informed framework of interpretation.

König strongly emphasizes the importance of distinguishing between a "theory of society" and "sociological theory." He rejects as false the all too common view that German sociology is too theoretical and flatly states that it lacks the kind of theorizing which is necessary for its development as a specialized science.

Here he implicitly endorses the views otherwise frequently expressed by those West German philosophers of social science who have adopted Karl Popper's "Logic of Scientific Discovery" as a canon for research in all empirical disciplines. As König puts it: there is "too little understanding of the specific functions of theory in the research process." This leads him to endorse Robert K. Merton's "theories of the middle range" as perhaps more fruitful than other theories for empirical research.

König rejects a "theory of society," in this instance represented by Theodor W. Adorno's critique of empirical sociology, which entails as its central category that of society as a "totality." Such views only document, according to König, that "historicist" thought still predominates in German social theory. König does not altogether deny the usefulness of a theory of society and he even finds himself in agreement with the practical aims of Adorno's critical social theory and its general goal of furthering social and philosophical "enlightenment." But for König even a theory of society committed to philosophical enlightenment cannot replace what one might call, with Niklas Luhmann, "sociological enlightenment." Sociological enlightenment requires the self-limitation of theory to the development of sociological research.

For Norbert Elias contemporary sociology is too preoccupied with theory construction. The primary weakness of theories that are formulated at a high level of abstraction is that they fail to reflect upon their initial partisan commitments and their dependence on a relatively narrow contemporary point of departure. Theory as such is an insufficient remedy against the sociologist's "involvement in the short-lived struggles of the moment." It needs to be integrated with comparative historical research into a frame of reference without ideological encrustations. However, comparative historical research alone cannot provide the explanations sought by the sociologist, who aims at explanations of the "long-term development of human societies." The high-level syntheses pursued by sociologists require the employment of theoretical models, not merely for the sake of empirical testability, but in order to safeguard the very object of sociological inquiry, which is to make the human past intelligible and to raise questions about the future of present-day societies.

Helmut Schelsky is also concerned with history, but more narrowly with the history of German sociology since its emancipation as a discipline from political economy and philosophy. He focuses especially upon those constellations of discourse and traditions of inquiry that have been influential in Germany since the emergence of German idealism.

But he also systematically addresses questions of importance to sociology. While rejecting the view that sociology can be reintegrated with economics and philosophy into an all-inclusive theory of society, he argues as well against an instrumentalist conception of sociology. Sociology's task is the "diagnostic inquiry into the facts of society." But this does not make it a simple "positive" science. Its task, rather, is to strengthen society's consciousness of reality. During the classical phase of its foundation sociology had played a prominent role in the formation of the social and cultural consciousness of modernity. In Schelsky's view, sociology ought to remain committed to this task. To do so it must address and evaluate common misconceptions and illusions, including the naive confidence in the usefulness and appropriateness of sociological research for purposes of social planning.

Sociology is a specialized discipline as well as a form of theoretical reflection. It needs to acknowledge its limits by recognizing that it depends on a division of labor between the sciences which is the very basis of their cooperation. But it also brings this general state of affairs to consciousness by reflecting on the developmental history of the sciences and of society, and by establishing connections between both. Thus sociology is inevitably also a "theory of society," albeit with severely restricted claims to validity. In this (and only in this) respect Schelsky's position is indebted to the tradition of Hegelian social thought.

Niklas Luhmann, who acquired his *Habilitation* with Schelsky, takes an even stronger position with respect to the tradition of classical European social philosophy than his former teacher. If it is Schelsky's concern to extricate sociology from global views of society (as they were formulated in the nineteenth century), without turning it into a mere "positive" science, Luhmann is determined to preserve a level of abstract generality and an autonomy of theory which would make sociological theory indistinguishable from a comprehensive theory of society in the classical sense, were it not for his resolute effort to recast all classical doctrines and classifications (such as *Gemeinschaft/Gesellschaft*) in terms of the methods and concepts of systems theory.

Luhmann's theory is now gaining wide international recognition. It anticipated and helped initiate the revival of functionalism in sociological theory, in Germany and elsewhere. The essay published here highlights a number of concepts central to Luhmann's enormous and still growing oeuvre. It also shows very clearly how a general theory of society in Luhmann's sense differs from other traditional or contemporary theories which still operate with substantive conceptions of society, polity, or community.

When Luhmann speaks of society as a "system" and argues for a retention of a comprehensive theory of society (without, of course, endorsing the conceptual means of classical theories of this type), he declares his preference for a form of sociology which, as in Schelsky, is both actively implicated in the continued growth of modern societies (e.g. toward a global polity) while simultaneously analyzing this process. The formation of sociology as a specialized discipline is part of an ongoing process of modernization, which no longer has a final and substantive goal.

The systems theory of society only recognizes "an increase in social complexity, i.e. in the number and kinds of possible experiences and action" as a criterion relevant to the analysis of the evolution of social systems. The latter are meaning-constituting systems. How complexity is grasped and "reduced" in a variety of social processes and subsystems is open to theoretically guided empirical or historical investigation, perhaps by the more specialized "sociologies" (of politics, knowledge, religion, education, law, etc.). But they will never make theory superfluous. Theory has to be established at a level of generality sufficient for the analysis of society as that social system which institutionalizes the "ultimate, most basic mechanisms of complexity reduction." Accordingly, Luhmann has revised structural functionalism to meet the logical requirements of a consistent systems-theoretical approach.

In Jürgen Habermas' *The Theory of Communicative Action* (Boston: Beacon Press, 1984-87), from which essay 8 has been taken, sociological systems theory (especially Parsons' media theory) receives much attention. Luhmann's rigorous and elegant reformulation of this tradition of theory in sociology clearly has left its imprint on Habermas' thought. In many respects the enormously rich and complex argument contained in *The Theory of Communicative Action* can be seen as an effort to limit and correct the claims of sociological theory with respect to its grasp of the dynamics of modernization processes in capitalist societies. Sociological theory, especially in its systems-analytic form, Habermas argues, is too closely linked with the one-sided development of capitalist rationalization processes, and with the development of the economy and the state bureaucracy as subsystems of purposive rational action in Weber's sense, for it to be aware of the logic peculiar to communication processes taking place in the "life-world" of social action. A critical theory of society is therefore needed in order to give voice to the claims to reason and rationality contained in communicatively organized practices of daily life in the developed societies.

A critical theory addressing such tasks recommends itself as a framework within which interdisciplinary research on the selective pattern of capitalist modernization can be taken up once again. A critical theory of this nature will no longer rely on the assumptions of the Marxist philosophy of history, as Habermas states clearly. And it no longer depends on the critique of ideologies for its conception of the normative standards of critique. It endeavors to identify the latter by a twofold process of theoretical analysis: (a) a theory of rationality grounded in a theory of communication in language, and (b) a theory of modernity and of the rationalization processes constitutive of modern society.

Habermas' provocative arguments prepare the ground for a balanced appraisal of the relation between sociological research, sociological theory, a comprehensive theory of society, and the philosophical arguments required for their integration. His review of the "classical" tradition of critical social theory (in particular, Horkheimer, Marcuse, Adorno) clearly demonstrates that in its more recent past (from the 1940s to the late 1960s) critical social theory had systematically underestimated the significance of both empirical social research and of sociological theory. Habermas' move away from the Hegelian philosophy of history toward a philosophy of language must be counted as a self-correction of critical social theory. For Habermas, a comprehensive theory in the sense intended by critical theorists (and frequently objected to by sociologists such as König, Schelsky, and even Elias and Luhmann) can only show its productiveness in detailed and diverse forms of social scientific and philosophical investigation.

Forms of social integration, socialization, and ego development in postliberal societies, as well as the mass media, mass culture, oppositional movements, and their protest potential can thus become research topics for critical social theory, to which it applies its own theoretical views like a focusing lens. It is only in this manner that critical theory can in fact be critical of social reality and draw attention to the "pathologies" of modernity and the conflicts endemic to it, which other forms of social theory frequently tend to ignore. Such claims are, of course, far removed from the much greater hopes for comprehensiveness still nourished by the primarily philosophically oriented critical theorists of the older generation.

Recent German sociology and social theory, then, have a much more tentative relation to theoretical claims than is often assumed. This may, indeed, be one further step in the transformation of German sociology into the kind prevalent in Anglo-American countries in particular. But the rigorous pursuit of theoretical questions remains nevertheless a distinctive feature of the West German sociological landscape. Theory still is regarded as an appropriate means for articulating the relation of inquiry in the social sciences to the realities of society. It continues to be a preoccupation as well as a strength of German sociology and its theoretical traditions to raise questions about the nature of this relation.

4

Sociology as a Science of Social Reality

HELMUT SCHELSKY

Sociology as a Specialized Science

It has often been said that sociology in its modern form arose in connection with the historical emergence of modern industrial society. It came into existence when members of the capitalist bourgeoisie began to take an interest in education in the arts and sciences. In this respect, *German* sociology must be understood as a fusion of the theory and the problems of liberal capitalist society with German idealist philosophy. The two main roots of German sociology are the theory of civil society and Hegel. Other influences received from earlier social-scientific endeavors in political science [*Staatswissenschaften*], in the science of finance [*Kameralistik*], or in the theory of natural law had to pass through these two filters. German sociology first emerged as an amalgamation of *philosophy with political economy*. Their union became decisive for the development of sociology in Germany throughout the nineteenth century and during the first third of the twentieth century. From Hegel's *Philosophy of Right*, through Marx, Lorenz von Stein, and up to the historical school of political economy one can encounter, even if with changing emphases, an amalgamation of these two basic elements. Moreover, the same amalgamation reappears in the works of Max and Alfred Weber, Tönnies and Sombart, Simmel and von Wiese, Freyer and Spann, Mannheim, Scheler, and Schumpeter. Sociology was then not yet an independent discipline. Rather, it lived in close communication and personal union with at least one of the two "sister disciplines" mentioned. In Germany, with only a few exceptions, the association of ethnology and sociology remained, suprisingly enough, as insignificant as that with history, which influenced sociology only later, by way of economics.

Reprinted from *Ortsbestimmung der deutschen Soziologie* (Düsseldorf-Cologne: Diederichs, 1959), pp. 12-19, 118-131. Translated by José Casanova and Dieter Misgeld.

This peculiar connection between economics and philosophy, from which German sociology arose and which was the source of its vitality until recently, is now coming apart. While there are some scholars even now whose work still represents the old connection (Brinkmann, Mackenroth, Rüstow, Salin, and Weippert represent the union with economics; Plessner, Adorno, Horkheimer, and Gehlen the union with philosophy), it is nevertheless evident that, within the general development of the sciences, sociology is becoming an increasingly autonomous discipline in Germany. To be sure, there are still scholars who cross the boundaries between the disciplines. And this is to be welcomed. But this kind of scholar will no longer be the typical and representative bearer of our discipline. For reasons intrinsic as well as extrinsic to the development of the sciences, the sociological specialist who is nothing but a sociologist is now inevitable. The organization of research and of science policy combine with the immanent logic of the thematic and methodological developments within sociological research to push sociology in the direction of autonomy.

One should immediately add, however, that German sociology is not taking this path willingly, at least not with great enthusiasm or even as a result of the conscious planning of its main representatives. Rather than having chosen this development on its own, sociology is being forced into it; and the younger generation of sociologists is of course more readily willing to accept this development than the older one. There can in fact no longer be a unified science reaching from economics to philosophy and with sociology as a universal rather than as an autonomous specialized science at its center. Such a unified science is no longer compatible with the development of economics and philosophy as the two original disciplinary sources of sociology. Here I am not referring to the well-known argument that each particular field of inquiry has become so extensive and specialized that no individual scholar can any longer hope to master it in its entirety. This is actually an unconvincing argument which takes for granted that research is now pursued as a mere routine, as a form of mere busyness. Even today it is still possible to achieve productive syntheses. Now as before this achievement depends on a scholar's intellectual level and on his capacity for work. The reasons for the changes run deeper and have to do with developments within disciplines.

Contemporary German philosophy and economics have taken a direction in their development which increasingly militates against sociological thinking. In this sense, the growing *autonomy of sociology* as only one among many scientific disciplines can be understood as a *fis-*

sure or separation, caused by the disciplinary specialization of philosophy on the one hand and of economics on the other. In formulating the goals and in developing independent approaches, these two sciences have driven a wedge between themselves and sociology, thus forcing sociology to establish itself as a self-contained body of knowledge and thought. This process is in fact more characteristic of contemporary German sociology than of sociology in other countries. In the United States, for example, sociology has been well established as an independent discipline for a long time, but the development toward greater autonomy there has quite different causes. Only Soviet social science continues to adhere dogmatically to the idea of the unification of philosophical, economic, and sociological thought (a conception which has been our legacy as well).

The notion that sociology is a "young science" is today gaining a more precise meaning. For the most part, after all, it has not been entirely unjustified to conclude that this cliché has merely given a new name to a familiar thing, mistaking for all of sociology what is merely the newest phase in its development. Frequently even the establishment of university chairs in sociology was seen as an affirmation of the existence of the field (this also shows, of course, that people have not learned from Plato and Aristotle about such matters). But as an *independent discipline* sociology is indeed a "young science." It has acquired its autonomy only very recently, at least in comparison with the ancient and continuously cultivated symbiotic relation between sociology and its two sister disciplines.

How did this separation of sociology from economics and philosophy come about? This question can be answered by investigating the "sociological" components of classical economics and philosophy, that is, by examining how these disciplines then assimilated and even required sociological thinking. The answer can be briefly sketched in the following manner: In classical German political economy, it was sociology which gave this field its theoretical underpinnings; and for nineteenth- and early twentieth-century philosophy, it was sociology which served as an essential source of experience. Economics has now turned to other foundations of its theory, however, and philosophy has turned to other forms of experience. Thus, while sociology has been freed from performing these tasks for economics and philosophy, it must now treat tasks as its own which were previously carried out in these disciplines. In what follows I would like to elaborate this thesis in greater detail.

Classical German political economy (i.e., the historical school as well as those concerned with social policy and conceptions of the political order) had based its theories upon analyses and conceptions addressing society as a whole. Economics was understood as only one part of a comprehensive and unified social science. If one considers the subjects which well into the 1920s were taught in German universities under the heading of "economic theory," one realizes that economic theory was largely what today would be called "sociology." That has changed radically in the meantime. The changes can be summed up as follows: Political economy has become mere economics; the analysis of the flow of goods and money has been restricted to purely economic data, and the data are elaborated into models. The models themselves, in turn, are valid only for the domain of economic activity. They do not apply to social conduct in a wider sense. As a result, economics has achieved a considerable degree of rationality which permits the development of complex mathematical theories. This kind of theory no longer needs to be rooted in social history, social policy studies, or conceptions of the social and political order of society. Economics has thereby become a highly differentiated and precise applied science, that is, a *functional science* which fulfills its continuously expanding tasks only by restricting itself to the purely technical aspects of its expertise.

As a functional science of planning and management (and precisely because of its extraordinary effectiveness and its practical and social significance) economics is forced to exclude from its domain all claims to universal knowledge and to knowledge of society as a whole, for such claims may have a destabilizing effect. The fields of industrial management and business administration had always succumbed to the pressure to become applied and quantifying sciences. But today, political economy, in its approaches and tasks, is also steered by the sheer weight of its functional or planning knowledge [*Herrschafts-wissen*] in the direction of the purely "economic" domain. It is true that at times the ensemble of social relations still appears as the background of all social and therefore also of economic action. But present-day political economy no longer feels compelled to take its place within the context of the theory and analysis of the society as a whole, and to develop a theory of the economy which is also a theory of society. And even where complementation of economic theories by a historically informed sociological theory is still regarded as desirable, sociology is already seen as an independent discipline with which one can at best cooperate.[1] Indeed, there are still numerous areas where the research interests of economics and sociology do overlap and where therefore both disciplines are compelled to cooperate. However, there no longer is any need for a common theoretical foundation. All the attempts, therefore, to preserve sociology as an integral part of political economy are, in my view, efforts to swim against the current.[2] Political economy has excluded the analysis and the politics of purely economic action (and of its institutions) from the domain of sociology but has ceded to sociology the sociohistorical, sociostructural, and socio-political analysis of society. Whether it likes it or not, sociology has to take up this task as an independent discipline.

Philosophy, sociology's other main origin, has undergone a similar development, though in a different direction from sociology. In different epochs of the history of ideas, philosophy has found nurture in various extra-philosophical sources of experience. For medieval philosophy, religious experience served almost exclusively (or at least predominantly) as such a source; for early modern philosophy from Descartes to Leibniz and even to Kant, it was the experience of the new natural science (developing from the sixteenth to the eighteenth centuries) that was crucial; classical German philosophy from Herder and Hamann to Schelling and Schleiermacher, found in the experience of art, particularly in that of poetry, one of its more productive sources. In this sense, one could argue that, starting with Fichte and Hegel and right into the 1920s to such thinkers as Scheler and Spengler, and perhaps even to Jaspers' existentialism, social and political experience has been one of the crucial sources of German philosophy.

Any examination of contemporary West German philosophy shows that this too is no longer the case. At least in the universities, philosophical thinking is by and large no longer grounded in such experience. Only in exceptional cases is the philosophical mastery of concrete social and political reality still viewed as one of philosophy's concerns and tasks. Insofar as it contributes to something more than the mere transmission and animation of its own traditions and problems, philosophy today is primarily committed either to formal and symbolic logic or, as ontology and existential philosophy, offers metaphysical interpretations of internal experience[3] while largely rejecting any connection with the empirical sciences (of external life), in the belief that it can do without them. In any case, the demand to ground philosophical thinking in an experience of social life interpreted by science is hardly present any more in German philosophy. Thus, yet another intellectual task, which once served as a basis for the close association of philosophy and sociology, has been removed from this interdisciplinary frame: the *philosophical interpretation of the scientific an-*

alysis of social and political life as it is actually experienced. Even this task of a general philosophical interpretation of social reality is today more and more the domain of sociology as an autonomous discipline.

The autonomy of sociology is built, therefore, upon the tasks which it once fulfilled by representing the interests of theory in economics and those of experience in philosophy. In achieving its independence by way of separation, sociology assumes certain legacies from both sides, which must be borne fully in mind if one wants both to ascertain correctly the independent course taken by the discipline and to understand the diversity of its contemporary aims and its difficulties in defining itself and its place among the other sciences. As an autonomous discipline, sociology has incorporated the goals and knowledge claims of the two disciplines in which it originated. On the one hand, the connection with economics lasted long enough for sociology to irrevocably inherit the form of knowledge typical of social scientific empiricism. For sociology this entails the requirement that knowledge must find practical application; it must provide functionally useful knowledge. And one may note that this preference for empirical research and functionally useful knowledge entirely predominates both in contemporary North American sociology and that of many European countries. Even within German sociology, many of its practitioners and supporters now maintain that this is the only useful and promising direction for sociology.

On the other hand, German sociology, because of its philosophical legacy, still regards the "philosophical" interpretation of society, culture, and history as one of its tasks — albeit by relying on scientific means. But such expectations nevertheless reach sociology primarily from without, either from neighboring disciplines, from an educated public, or from other interested parties. They are entertained much less by sociologists themselves. I believe, however, that sociology cannot shun this claim without simply abandoning altogether a legitimate need for a certain type of knowledge which it helped to generate in the first place. In any case, sociology cannot simply reject such expectations as unscientific. Rather, it must find a way to respond to them by responsible scientific means and to fulfill them legitimately. Both in its theory and practice, contemporary German sociology is stuck with the dilemma of having to be an empirical and functionally useful discipline on the one hand, and a social philosophy and interpretation of culture on the other. It is from within this dilemma that sociology has to determine its way and its tasks.

Since the organization of a science normally lags behind its actual development, there emerge right away new difficulties of an organizational and political nature from sociology's changing role among the sciences. They can be located quite precisely in the dilemma of sociology as standing between economics and philosophy. In German universities, sociology belongs to different faculties (either to the faculty of law and politics, or to the faculty of economics and social science, or to the faculty of philosophy), which already indicates sociology's ambiguous nature. In the postwar period, the prevailing tendency has been to attach sociology primarily to the faculty where the economic sciences too have found their home. However, any one-sided incorporation of sociology into only one of the faculties in German universities will lead to sociology's partial loss of its distinctive nature and tasks.

Sociologists will encounter serious restrictions of their freedom of learning, teaching, and research, as soon as sociological teaching and research are regulated by only one faculty. They will no longer be able to do justice to a variety of curriculum policies and to professional and academic examinations. Most students include sociology in their course of studies only as a minor. Thus one also needs to consider where the field is to have its long-term practical and social effects: is it to exclusively influence future economic and administrative elites, or also teachers and journalists of various kinds? We may note that the conflict between different knowledge goals (which is built into the discipline) has consequences with respect to the assessment of its possible social effects. Contemporary German sociology displays considerable interest in the questions concerned with the direction and organization of science as well as with the appropriate location of the discipline in German universities. Sociologists themselves, for reasons which we have tried to explain, are nearly as unable to achieve consensus on these questions as are the representatives of other disciplines or of the relevant academic committees and organizations. Thus it must remain an open question whether sociology will simply succumb to the often rigid and narrowly circumscribed division of faculties that exists in the German university system or whether it will be given a chance to play a mediating role between two or even three faculties. . . .

Sociology as a Science of Social Planning

The development of sociology in Germany has largely taken place along ideological lines of a certain kind, i.e. by elaborating universal systems of explanation and of historical change. This still is the image of sociology even today in the disciplines close to it and also in the sphere of social practice. As in the past, there still is, for example, a tendency even today not to distinguish between sociology and socialism.*

But the development of German sociology in the nineteenth and twentieth centuries can by no means be accounted for exclusively by reference to such a scheme of universal systems. The historical sociologies of Wilhelm Roscher and Max Weber, for example, do not fit such a scheme; neither do Simmel's and von Wiese's formal sociology nor the numerous examples of empirical sociographic research, let alone Scheler's and Mannheim's sociology of knowledge, for whom sociological thinking is a thinking uncompromisingly opposed to ideology.

New orientations to research and to the interpretation of knowledge became operative here in sociology, which must be understood not so much in terms of the legacy of a universal philosophy as in relation to the development of the other specialized sciences. Among these orientations are the focus upon historical knowledge, in particular upon historical relativism as its consequence, the need for systematization and classification, the demands for quantification and even mathematization of social-scientific findings, etc. In Germany, empirical sociology in its initial phase as a specialized science clearly developed alongside the hitherto predominant sociology, the sociology of society as a whole. As already indicated, it first made its appearance in close connection with political economy. As a result of subjecting — with the highest empirical exactitude possible — particular domains of social life to an analysis of the regularities operative in them, "sociology" emerged as a comprehensive and ramified science. By acquiring an empirical and rational foundation, it became the equal of the other empirical human sciences, modeling itself especially after economics and psychology.

Gradually this development also generated a different attitude of sociology toward social practice. Sociology now begins to regard itself as one scientific instrument among others, in the service of planned social action. As a consequence, universal sociologies are more and more scouted and rejected as ideological formations, while (progressive as well as conservative) revolutionary conceptions of an integrated social order are unmasked as prescientific or as utopias. There is a straight line leading from Weber's opposition to value judgments in

---

* Editors' note: The first paragraph of this section is an abridgment of the final two paragraphs of the deleted section preceding our selection.

sociology to the contempt shown by contemporary empirical sociologists for the faintest semblance of a social "interpretation of meaning" and especially for ideology.

This kind of sociology views the systematic application of the empirical knowledge of social functions as its appropriate relationship to social practice. In the place of an ideological program for the transformation of the world as a whole and for the construction of total orders, there emerges an empirical functional science of planned individual social action, of the gradual reconstruction of segments of social life. The sense of mission in sociology and the consciousness of its own power is replaced by a *scientific self-conception of an instrumental kind*. Aware of its own indispensability and usefulness, sociology willingly joins the ranks of the other, equally respectable, empirical sciences and cooperates with them.

In the theoretical field, however, the new orientation of sociology frequently gives rise to calls for a synthesis of the human sciences. These calls reflect the expectation that painstaking accumulation of empirical knowledge together with scientific management will permit the regulation and safeguarding of all areas of social life. An ever increasing knowledge of the way society actually works will make it feasible, according to this view, to influence social and private life in all spheres of action, and to achieve the harmonious functioning of social subsystems (the economy, population and reproduction processes, education, marriage and family life, political organization, the adaptation of individuals to their environment, etc.).

This way of thinking also gives rise to blueprints for the reconstruction of entire societies. Karl Mannheim's notion of "planning for freedom" (developed in his later years under the influence of British Labour Party thinking) or Talcott Parsons' often quoted essay, "The Problem of Controlled Institutional Change" (which was clearly influenced by New Deal thinking on social planning) may serve as examples.[4] But such "plans" are radically different from the constructions of a universal order in sociological systems insofar as they primarily develop *social techniques* based on an empirical and functionalist analysis of society. They no longer offer prescriptive visions of the social order and of its aims.

Contemporary sociology predominantly interprets its own relation to social practice in terms of such a combination of empirical analyses with the technical organization of social action. It aims at the planned scientific control of society as a whole (or of its functional subsystems). American sociology, as the model for contemporary sociology in all

Western countries, already embodies to a large extent such a conception of knowledge and of action. It primarily is applied empirical research. And German social science to some extent also shares this position, at least insofar as it has empirical and functionalist analyses of society as its focus.

One of the first consequences of such an instrumentalist self-conception is that sociology, in response to the great variety of societal subsystems and their functional requirements, can more easily and in good conscience choose to embrace specialization and even find itself confirmed in this choice by the everyday practical demands for specialized sociologies. The desire to become an applied and effective science is translated into the most diverse techniques, from legal and administrative measures to education and instruction (as forms of popular enlightenment) in schools, universities, vocational training centers, at conferences, and in the mass media. When sociology was still committed to ideological conceptions of a universal order, it aimed above all at a radical transformation of social conditions and institutions. Direct political intervention was an almost inevitable consequence. The new sociology is probably once again more inclined to begin with the human beings themselves, even if now as an object of social techniques and in order to direct and manipulate them by scientific means. Whether this is "education"⁵ or "adaptation" (in the sense of making people "adjust") is now little more than a matter of competition between different social technologies.

It is highly significant, in my view, that the functionalist interpretation of sociology (but also of the social sciences in general) entails a new conception of social practice. Sociology has contributed greatly to the formation of this new conception, which by now is frequently seen as self-evident. Very briefly, it entails the following: scientifically based "social planning"; the "gentle" regulation and manipulation of people in all spheres of social action, with the good conscience, moreover, typical of the applied sciences; excessive emphasis upon "organization," whether of leisure, of marriage and family life, or of "human relations," etc. It would be misleading, of course, to attribute the expansion of these practices exclusively to sociology and the other functional sciences. Today, social practice itself displays an equally strong inclination to demand instrumental formulas, analyses, and procedures from the social sciences. Practical experts already commonly see sociology as an instrument of social planning.

It cannot be denied that sociology can indeed provide useful services capable of practical application. But the application of sociology to politics and other forms of practice does at the same time not at all mean that sociology should see itself even in its most fundamental striving for knowledge merely as a functional science that delivers social techniques of planning. Sociological knowledge and research have their own intellectual justification independently of their possible application. Practical social action and the applied sciences are in turn also justified in themselves and no reference to sociological analyses and their possible application in the sphere of practice can change that. In order to bring this out more clearly than is usually the case today, I propose to separate sociology from social practice by developing a new conception of sociology and of its relationship to practice.

Sociology as Reality Testing

The critical self-appraisal of sociology in its relationship to social practice is difficult to formulate since there are no models. I think, however, that precisely this conception is gaining ground in German sociology. Sociologists as different as Arnold Gehlen and René König may be said to represent such a position. I myself have maintained in several publications that it is today a necessary and the most appropriate attitude of sociology toward practical questions. But this view has not been accepted yet in the sphere of social practice. On the contrary, it is one of the main causes for the uneasiness and irritation which sociology provokes among the applied sciences, among practical experts seeking its advice, and at times even within its own ranks.

Before describing this "third" position concerning the relationship of sociology and social practice further, it is important to stress that we are here only dealing with a particular attitude toward practical social issues. Sociology's previous achievements and scientific results (as we have described them) continue to influence its internal development and to constitute the essential contents of our discipline. This is equally true, for example, with respect to the theoretical statement of the problem espoused by sociological systems, irrespective of whether their notions of social order are conservative or revolutionary, as it is of the wide-ranging empirical analyses produced by a sociology which understands itself as a science of social planning. What is changing, it seems to me, is merely the relationship to social practice. The new position can best be characterized with the formula "sociology as reality testing" [*Wirklichkeitskontrolle*]. The notion of "testing" [*Kontrolle*] is here something very different from "planning" and also from the English "control" which, at least in American sociology, has in any case already to some extent taken on the meaning of "planning."

It is not only holistic ideologies (whether revolutionary or conservative) that have become suspect in contemporary sociology, but also the direct translation of sociological knowledge into practical blueprints and social techniques. These doubts are present irrespective of whether sociology merely wants to be generally useful by contributing to the administration of people or whether it responds to predetermined and recommended goals, thereby becoming a science which provides contracted-for services. In contrast to this emphasis on practical commitments, it is necessary to point to sociology's task as a *pure science of reality*, that is, as a diagnostic inquiry into the facts of society. As such it has to remain free from practical demands and from drawing practical conclusions. This task of "pure analysis" can be understood and is justifiable only from the perspective of a new conception of social action. Social action can no longer be conceptualized in relation to anthropological and intellectual structures which presuppose the self-contained unity of the person. Neither the scientist nor the practical expert, as individuals, can still feel entitled to adopt the stance of being the generalized subject of social action, as it were. Rather, social action has to be understood basically as a system of specialization and cooperation in which not only its material domain but also its forms of action and thought have been separated from one another. They remain linked only through the system of the division of labor.

Such a system of social action can no longer be gathered together in one individual's mind, nor can diagnostic and programmatic modes of analysis or normative and factual perspectives be joined by individual efforts. Whenever this is nevertheless attempted, one risks an unjustifiable deterioration of the intellectual range of the relevant sociological positions. Nowadays all responsible individual action and thought occurs within a system of cooperation, in which the individual must recognize and affirm his own partial function inside a larger whole. This structure of social action has long been reflected in a series of irrefutable facts. Direct personal experience no longer can be the basis for the essential forms of social practice (economics, politics, etc.); they all require the support of independent scientific investigation.[6] The time when the whole range of what had to be known and done could be united in the pseudo-solutions of a "world view" or a "total philosophical perspective" (an "ideology") is gone forever. Ideologies today are in principle no more right concerning social reality than is common sense.

This emphasis upon the purely analytical function of sociology, that is, upon its task to show reality as it really is, presupposes that sociology abandons its claim that it possesses an all-inclusive conception of social action. Precisely by restricting itself to the analysis of social actuality — including normative actuality — and by enthusiastically accepting *this* as its task, sociology frees normative and practical inquiry to take responsibility for itself. As long as the normative and practical sciences do not attempt to take over the tasks that properly belong to sociology, it will not attempt to impose its own premises upon practice. And even if these sciences regard themselves, as they in fact do, as superior to the sciences which confine themselves to diagnosis and analysis, I see no need to object. It is, however, obvious that such claims to superiority are illusory under the prevailing conditions of an unavoidable cooperation between the sciences. In a system characterized by the existence of indispensable functions, no function can be superior to any other, even if one may come closer to the desired goal than another.

As soon as the system of social action is based on cooperation and on the division of labor, one and the same group cannot at the same time be responsible for decisions and plans concerning the change of social reality and for the empirical investigation of the sphere of action in question. It is precisely for this reason that in such a system planning and decision making positions can provide real freedom of choice and permit more effective planning, as long as in their investigation of facts they abstain from making specific proposals on issues of planning.

This does not mean that empirical sociological research needs to be remote from the practical sphere. Even in its purely analytic work, but also in its choice of subject matter, sociology is unavoidably determined by practical situations and needs. And sometimes sociological research will even involve contract work. Sociological research can also be oriented toward possible forms of social action. Yet sociologists must refrain from tying their research too closely to the sphere of practical politics. They must not count the day-to-day problems of social planning and the social use of their own findings among their scientific tasks. Sociology's task must rather be the "disinterested" analysis of social reality as it actually is coming to be, and thereby thoroughly illuminate what is feasible and what indeed is not. When the practical sciences, from physics to theology, claim that contemporary social reality can be given shape and be remade, they often exaggerate. The critical analysis and diagnosis of realities as they in fact are has emerged as an especially timely task for sociology in confronting such claims. It must not be distracted from this task by prior commitments.

In other words: The most important contribution of sociological analysis to social action is perhaps no longer that it point the way to what is to be done and that it help to shape decisions. Its task is rather to reveal that which is happening and which cannot be changed anyhow. At the present time, a scientific understanding of social reality might have a most significant influence by taking a critical view of universally accepted modern beliefs, especially insofar as they seem to entail unlimited confidence in planning and in the possible remaking of people and things. Not the ends, but the limits of social action are, therefore, the legitimate subject matter of contemporary sociology. Moreover, it is precisely this which will lead to the freedom and the effectiveness of social action.

Social action cannot be derived directly from sociological analysis. And because society no longer surrenders the relevant factors of social life to the immediacy of personal experience, social action directly grounded in normative commitments is now obsolete. No social action can be justified today merely by reference to decisions about norms and plans. The purely scientific and "disinterested" analysis of social action, in all its ramifications, is what today constitutes responsible scientific behavior. Isolated individuals cannot meet responsibilities requiring institutional cooperation. Accordingly, institutions are not just syntheses of purpose but also of thought, which must bring together the specialized sciences, with their merely partial grasp of the truth, in order to thereby make possible a system of social action.

In this process sociology inherits the task of exploring *the preconditions* of action and of the actor, rather than the task of fathoming their goals. Sociology can, for example, demonstrate that people acting in various social domains often do not know the real facts and also have illusory ideas about themselves. Thus they may maintain (as the basis for their action) now obsolete beliefs about facts and interpretations of social reality. These beliefs and interpretations are normative, but they may not accurately reflect reality. The misrepresentation of reality from the perspective of the "ought," that is, from the point of view of the goals and norms of social action, constitutes one of the great dangers in a world which in its complexity can no longer be adequately grasped from the position of immediate experience. It is a world already thoroughly penetrated by the imperatives of planning and organization. The moral imperative, the normatively justified will — that "omnipresence of the ethical" (Gehlen) — has become "home" for the individual in contemporary society, and nothing could be further from the truth than to characterize the present as an "immoral age."

The weakness of such a position, however, lies in the absence of univocal, clear alternatives of action, in the ambivalence of the interventions which it permits. For isolated individuals lack a fully developed consciousness of reality. They can no longer master it (in a compensatory manner) as if it was subject to their concepts of moral obligation alone. Undeniably, of course, social action still aims at making reality and norms coincide. This is a task which it may never relinquish, even if, as today, this calls for cooperation between the sciences. An illusory pursuit of ideals is as dangerous for social action as confidence in facts alone. Two fundamental orientations of our times are equally mistaken: the idealist's excessive preoccupation with intervention and remaking things and the empiricist's fatalistic acceptance of the facts. These two attitudes reinforce each other.

We are caught in a dilemma: The increasing pressure for social intervention and task-oriented research is accompanied by an ever more fragile sense of reality. The certainties once characteristic of the applied sciences, but also of politics, economics, medicine, education, pastoral care, and even of technology itself, seem to be crumbling. Practical experts can today only feel unperturbed and secure by clinging to the rules and routines that belong to their domain of activity. But it is precisely these rules and techniques that fail to provide a profound understanding of an individual's social actions. In fact, they increasingly indicate a loss of human freedom. The practical expert of today will have to turn to scientific inquiry if he wants to understand the meaning of his actions, and not just in order to learn to cope with the complex techniques which he himself employs. He has to consult those sciences whose very subject matter is the conflict between norms and reality, a conflict which we have already described as a task of cooperation between the sciences. This cooperation must be able to come to terms with the innermost contradiction of our time, and cannot be approached with the trivial expectation of a preexistent or self-evidently possible harmony between the sciences. It must be understood as a conflict between different truths.

Different conceptions of truth and of scientific inquiry compete with one another in order to assert their relative intellectual autonomy. Undoubtedly an aggressive know-it-all attitude will be just as unpleasantly evident in the course of the controversy as the plaintive protest of those who feel themselves challenged. The proposed cooperation among the sciences ought to be viewed as a goal, indeed as a rarely attained and only imperfectly attainable condition. It can become a moral and intellectual obligation for a scientific discipline only as long as the discipline remains responsible to itself. And disciplines can meet their responsibilities only by remaining partial to their own subject matter with good conscience.

In this context, the task devolves upon sociology of strengthening society's consciousness of reality. It has to gain a hearing for the facts of our life. Thereby, however, sociology exposes itself to the charge that it more or less openly demands the acceptance of whatever reality happens to exist; that it ignores the normative requirements of human freedom; that it leads to quietism or to the conservative politics of restoration. Such criticisms clearly still assume that sociology is responsible for social action in its entirety. In its past, sociology did indeed make such claims, but we can no longer share such a perspective. Actually, it is precisely criticisms of this sort which seem incapable of accepting the more limited role of sociology in a system of scientific cooperation and instead claim for it the entire field of social action. Representatives of the applied sciences who do not find their normative professional or practical ethos validated by sociology's actual propositions — or the practical experts whose need for easy recipes and instructions remain unfulfilled by sociology — continue even now to see sociology as the universal science of social action. They do not know or they fail to recognize that sociology's function in the system of social action basically *rests on the freedom of not having to act.* Freedom from the compulsion to act is an old and legitimate foundation of inquiry. Contemporary sociology also depends on it, especially when it is analytical or diagnostic. It depends on it precisely for the sake of its own freedom and truth, and also for the sake of the practical value of its propositions.

The cooperatively organized discovery and analysis of social facts is a task of sociology with which scientists or practical experts need to come to terms, even if they do their work in the face of practical constraints and guided by normative requirements. For they are after all always free to either accept or reject sociological findings on normative grounds. They can think and plan on this basis. And more than this: scientific cooperation will actually require the exercise of this freedom as their essential contribution. Nonetheless, applied scientists and practical experts must not fall prey to the view that "what ought not to be, cannot be." Normatively grounded demands for action cannot be allowed to distort the facts. The inclination to impose normative commitments upon the diagnosis of society and its actual state is of course the sublime danger affecting the scientization of all social practice in the present period. As a consequence, factual knowledge is eviscerated and the sting may be taken out of undeniable realities, especially when normative commitments are expressed in a strongly emotional manner and with a claim to moral superiority. Freed from the constraints of reality, an illusory consciousness emanating from the field of scientifically managed practice forces its way back into scientific knowledge itself. It threatens the analytic sciences in their very core. It is necessary to resist this temptation to daydream, which is so characteristic of scientific humanists, even if the analytic scientist [Analytiker] will be seen as the real troublemaker in a world of good will. Practical experts demanding the freedom to act will have to fight for it in the actualities of social life, but not by struggling against sociology. Sociology has to remain relentless in its efforts to provide information about social reality.

The basic issue in the cooperation between normative and analytic inquiries in the social sciences is the identification of the place of sociology in the changed self-conception of modern man, a transformation in which sociology had played a decisive role.

The great analysts of the extra-conscious forces underlying human conduct (such as Nietzsche, Freud, and Pareto) have made amply clear that a thinking in which fully critical analysis — i.e., an analysis free from particular motivations — has become the essence of self-consciousness is no longer capable of unambiguously prescribing compelling orientations of action. On the contrary, it weakens and dissolves the remnants of traditional action orientations by changing the needs and motives which belong to it. This process of the critical transformation of self-consciousness encroaches upon conceptions of goals and aims in all social institutions. Contemporary humanity's attitude toward itself is fundamentally different from that of 150 years ago. "Eccentricity," as Plessner has termed this fundamental human condition, has grown and been transformed from being a need for the conscious shaping of motives into a need by self-consciousness for critical insight and factual knowledge. Humanity wants to attain a more objective relation to itself. In the face of this change, the stability of social institutions can be secured only if they include among their goals, their ideologies, and their programs a greater satisfaction of those needs relating to consciousness, such as the needs for critical insight. At the same time the modes of institutional organization that bind and give rise to motives must not lose their function. Contemporary social institutions require self-criticism and analysis as a means of reality testing and for the sake of their own stability. Criticism and analysis are equally as important as strongly motivated compliance with the law or a programmatic consciousness.[7]

Here lies the true reason for the fact that today all forms of social practice insist on sociological analysis: Industrial enterprises and their occupations reach for industrial and organizational sociology; there are sociologies of education, of health, etc.; everywhere the churches pursue a sociology of ecclesiastic communities, of the ministry, etc. Here one finds the hitherto unexamined roots for a new relationship of social practice to sociology.

But the conflict between self-control by means of analysis and criticism and the need for strengthening and adjusting motivational consciousness can no longer be resolved by the individual. The locus of social action can only be institutions and a system of institutional action, a system in which, depending on the function, there have to be both acting and nonacting individuals. Once *reality testing* has become the central sociological value, sociology must emphasize, *as its* function in the system of social action, critical opposition to action programs. But it may not once again usurp the place of the demiurgical social theorist who reveals every action as socially determined and thereby invalidates it. By conceiving the sociological interpretation action in this way, one gives up two views concerning sociology's relation to social action, views which have in any case become intellectually indefensible in modern society. They are, on the one hand, the perpetual articulation of new social and ethical policies calling for action, and, on the other, the purely functional unmasking of the hidden determinations of social action. In the first view, sociology understood itself as an omnipotent actor. In the second, it dismissed action as an illusion. The third position appears to be possible only if sociology, with all its knowledge, learns to understand itself as only one part in the system of social action.

NOTES

1. See Andreas Predöhl and his analysis of political economy in *Jahrbuch für Sozialwissenschaft* (1959) 4-10(1):2. See also G. Schmölders' version of an "economically oriented behavioral research" in which cooperation between sociology and economics is seen as merely one instance of the cooperation required between all of the otherwise autonomous human sciences. See Günter Schmölders, "Ökonomische Verhaltensforschung." *Ordo. Jahrbuch für die Ordnung von Wirtschaft und Gesellschaft* (1953):203-244.

2. See especially Gerhard Mackenroth, "Ökonomie und Soziologie. Zur Wissenschaftspolitik in den Sozialwissenschaften," in Karl Muhs, ed., *Festgabe für Georg Jahn* (Berlin: Duncker & Humblot, 1955), p. 351; also his student Erik Boettcher, "Das Bemühen Mackenroths um die Einheit der Sozialwissenschaften," *Kölner Zeitschrift für Soziologie und Sozialpsychologie* (1957) 9(1):88.

3. See Helmuth Plessner's assessment in "Zum Situationsverständnis gegenwärtiger Philosophie," introduction to the "Fischer-Lexikon" volume *Philosophie* (Frankfurt: S. Fischer, 1958).

4. See Karl Mannheim, "Planning for Freedom," *Man and Society in an Age of Reconstruction* (London: Routledge & Kegan Paul, 1940), and Talcott Parsons, "The Problem of Controlled Institutional Change," [1945] *Essays in Sociological Theory Pure and Applied* (Glencoe, Ill.: The Free Press, 1949), p. 310, note 37.

5. In their ideas on planning, Mannheim and Parsons assign a decisive role to "education" in the reconstruction (or remaking) of society. Many other different scientific conceptions of "political education" belong here as well.

6. For the situation in economics see Karl Schiller, "Der Ökonom und die Gesellschaft," *Hamburger Jahrbuch für Wirtschafts- und Gesellschaftspolitik* (1956) 1:9-21. See, e.g., p. 13: "All this leads to a single conclusion: corporate management, coordinated economic strategies, and public economic policy are all bound to become more scientific and to heighten our public awareness. People who even today still speak of a deep chasm separating theory from practice, are only repeating an obsolete cliché from the past. They are very much like those early economists of whom it was said that they were like parrots, on every occasion rattling off the words 'supply' and 'demand'."

7. Helmut Schelsky, "Über die Stabilität der Institutionen, besonders Verfassungen," *Jahrbuch für Sozialwissenschaft* (1952) 44:14 ff.

5

Recent Developments in the Relation Between Theory and Research

RENÉ KÖNIG

I would like to communicate some of the feelings of uneasiness I have had during the past few years when looking at certain developments in postwar sociology, both in Germany and in France. Traces of these developments may also be found in the United States. My feelings of uneasiness are mainly concerned with the relation between sociological theory and research. Although considerable advances have been made in postwar German sociology, and although numerous important research projects have been concluded successfully, it cannot be claimed that the condition of either research and theory or of their mutual relation is very satisfactory. Rather than focusing upon the respective importance of sociological *theory* and *research* in the complex history of German sociology, I will discuss the recent development of a distinction between *sociological theory* and what I propose to call a *theory of society*.[1]

The General State of Sociological Theory and Research

In this section, I will briefly outline the constellation out of which this new development arose. I hope to make clear that while there are

An unedited version of this speech, delivered at the fourth World Congress of Sociology (Milan and Stresa, September 8-15, 1959), was published as "On Some Recent Developments in the Relation between Theory and Research," in *Transactions of the Fourth World Congress of Sociology* (London: International Sociological Association, 1959), 2:275-289. The published text has been completely rewritten by Volker Meja in consultation with the author.

Author's Note: The reader should keep the publication date of this essay in mind and see it as the historical starting point for the discussions in the 1960s. The events during this period have thoroughly proven the legitimacy of the criticisms advanced in this short text. Many of the shortcomings in the 1960s might have been avoided if the warnings implicit in this paper had been taken seriously. It would be important to find out if German sociology continues to suffer from the fact that the methodological discussions of the late 1950s have never been brought to a satisfactory conclusion. *René König*.

undoubtedly good reasons for criticizing the present state of sociological theory, it is not necessary to conclude that the only way out of these difficulties is the way proposed, for example, by Georges Gurvitch in France or by Theodor W. Adorno in Germany. Even though Gurvitch and Adorno are certainly justified in expressing their dissatisfaction with the present relation between theory and research, it is an entirely different matter to proceed from this sort of criticism to a radical rejection of research designs distinguished by a sound integration of sociological theory and research and to replace these, for instance, with a "hyperempiricism"[2] seeking to understand reality in terms of an all-embracing totality of life.

A few rather puzzling examples may help to clarify my point. In the short preface to their sociological textbook, *Soziologie*, Arnold Gehlen and Helmut Schelsky wonder how to deal with sociological theory. It may sound extraordinary, but the editors explicitly state that they decided "to do without premature systematization and without what might be called theory." They state that they insisted that all contributions to their volume

tackle larger theoretical perspectives or models only where permitted by the evidence. A comprehensive theory is not in the offing for the time being. Such an attempt, if it is to be taken seriously, would have to point again and again to its own shortcomings, to the enormous gaps in our anthropological understanding and to the very obvious lack of first-hand data. It would also have to point to the extreme one-sidedness, until now, of most attempted systematizations which have tended to universalize merely partial and often partisan perspectives, as well as to doubts about the applicability to contemporary conditions of many of Max Weber's conceptions, even if Weber's work is until this day the most comprehensive and realistic design of a theory of social systems.[3]

It is easy to agree with the wise skepticism of these remarks. But I doubt that a general agreement can be reached with regard to the actual meaning of "theory," as it is employed there. On the one hand Gehlen and Schelsky say that "larger theoretical perspectives or models" should be tackled only if "permitted by the evidence." This seems to point in the direction of what Robert K. Merton has called a "middle range theory." On the other hand, they seem to have something different in mind when they raise general anthropological questions. This latter point becomes partially clear if we consider that in Germany "anthropology" means "philosophical anthropology." Finally, they have yet something else in mind when they complain about the lack of first-hand surveys, which, evidently, is what they mean by research.

Another useful example is provided by Erich Reigrotzki in his book on social problems in West Germany. He there hopes to provide relevant information on particular social problems without reference to any sort of theoretical conception. He believes that factual information can be obtained first and that the theoretical evaluation of the data can be done *post factum*.[4] This argument is reminiscent of the position, quite common among the representatives of the early historical school of economics, that much empirical data must be compiled before a coherent theory can be developed. In fact, a theory can never be developed along such lines; on the contrary, such a procedure might lead to serious errors, as has been so justly stressed by Merton. Since in most cases no consistent body of theoretical propositions is available, the *post factum* hypotheses are little more than *ad hoc* hypotheses, with "but a slight degree of prior confirmation."

It seems that there is both an open and an implicit agreement that such sociological specialities as, for instance, the sociology of the family, urban sociology, industrial sociology, etc., can be based on nothing but the pure facts, and can do without a theoretical framework. Here we have to confront the extraordinary fact that German sociology, far from suffering from an overemphasis on theory, actually *lacks* theory. There is also too little understanding of the specific functions of theory in the research process. As a matter of fact, when looking at postwar research efforts, we often meet with the implicit or even the explicit proposition that a research design does not necessarily depend upon theoretical hypotheses.

Another observation should perhaps be added. A similar view is often advocated by the opponents of empirical sociological research, for example in their criticism of American sociology. The general view appears to be that American sociology lives in a theoretical void and attempts to develop its concepts by an endless accumulation of empirical data. Even if, in some isolated cases, this may indeed have been so in the past, surely it no longer applies to contemporary American sociology, which has increasingly become aware of the far-reaching theoretical implications of research. We are dealing with a similar misunderstanding when we read that the "zero hypothesis" in research is nothing but a "tabula rasa," and that the observer should be completely unprejudiced and free from any kind of theoretical preconceptions when doing field work. Many representatives of the so-called "sociographic" approach come very close to this sort of attitude. The main danger here is what might be called an unconscious normative impact of factual data upon our judgment. This is a naive realism whose results can be easily predicted. The research worker falls victim to grave errors resulting from the biased character of his findings.

It is quite obvious that the rather primitive character of such an approach could not fail to provoke protests from the more theoretically minded sociologists. This is precisely the point where, in my view, two different meanings of "theory" are often confused — meanings which should be carefully kept apart. On the one hand, it seems obvious that no research is possible without "models," theoretical frameworks or hypotheses adapted to the situation or to the facts under scrutiny. For example, we need a general model of family structure if we want to analyze particular aspects of contemporary family life. Yet, it is by no means sufficient to develop a general theory of the family. We also need a more or less articulated, systematized and interconnected set of propositions concerning many distinct individual aspects of family life. We may call this a body of interconnected theories from which new hypotheses can be developed.

When we look at these propositions closely it can be easily shown that they represent two different types of logical structure. On the one hand we find statements such as the following: the probability of divorce decreases to some extent with an increase in the number of children because a larger family permits greater group cohesion, provided that the development of stable family relations is not prevented by such external causes as a poor economic situation, disease, unemployment, etc. On the other hand, we find propositions of a different type, such as: strong paternal authority is a prerequisite for family stability, but there are indications of a steady decline in paternal authority leading to general decay of family life and a rapid increase in the divorce rate. This confusion between two kinds of propositions is avoided by Merton, who distinguishes between "theories of the middle range" and "all-embracing and grandiose" logically interconnected conceptions. The second example given above clearly belongs to the latter kind of theory, whereas the first is of a more limited character and more modest in scope.

Even though it is argued that both approaches are different, they nevertheless remain connected in some way since the assumption is made that the second alternative is little more than a generalization of the first. In fact, when Merton focuses attention on "theories intermediate to the minor working hypotheses evolved in abundance during the day-by-day routines of research, and the all-inclusive speculations comprising a master conceptual scheme from which it is hoped to derive a very large number of empirically observed uniformities of social behavior,"[5] I am rather inclined to assume that the word "intermediate" is carefully chosen, i.e., that it has more than a purely incidental meaning and points to the general assumption that we are dealing merely with steps on a continuum, though at different levels of abstraction. This leads me to the central point of my argument.

Even though in the past I held this view myself, I have now thoroughly revised it, especially under the theoretical impact of the work of Georges Gurvitch. We are indeed rather mistaken when approaching this problem as if only the levels of abstraction were different. Both conceptions, it seems, belong to entirely different dimensions of thought and are derived from different categorical systems. On the one hand we have "sociological theory," in the sense defined by Merton. This theory has grown out of shrewd hypotheses and past research, and is continually being checked against new facts and new circumstances, in an attempt to either corroborate the original hypothesis, modify it in the direction of greater precision and greater generalization, or develop a new set of hypotheses. On the other hand, there is Gurvitch's "dialectical hyperempiricism," which wants to facilitate and to promote the birth of new philosophical doctrines and is concerned with the depth as well as the entire range and wealth of social life.[6]

While the propositions of a sociological theory are hypothetical and limited in range, and this applies to integrated theoretical systems as well, the propositions of dialectical hyperempiricism, in regard to their logical structure, are universal and apodictic. However, dialectical hyperempiricism is dissimilar to speculative dogmatism of the traditional kind insofar as the latter's theoretical model was monistic or even monolithic. On the other hand, Gurvitch's position in its own way is quite receptive to speculation. Marcel Mauss' pluralism was still utterly unspeculative, just a way of acknowledging that social life penetrates through every layer of existence and therefore requires a multidimensional approach. For Gurvitch and others, however, pluralism grows out of a metaphysical logic, out of what, ever since Hegel, has been called "dialectic." I will return to this point in a moment.

Sociological Theory or Theory of Society?

It is useful to distinguish "sociological theory" from a general "theory of society." A recent publication by Theodor W. Adorno et al.[7] will help define the issues as well as permit us to unmask, as it were, the logical structure behind Adorno's "theory of society," and point to some of its implications. This way of proceeding may help to bring out the basic differences between such a theory of society and a sociological theory in Merton's sense.

In Adorno et al.'s chapter with the promising title "Sociology and Empirical Social Research" we can read:

The gap between the theory of society and empirical social research by no means has as its cause the relative youth of the latter. And this gap can hardly be filled by the further accumulation of findings, which can already be hardly surveyed, nor developed in such a manner that in time theory will be completely realized by these findings and thus be rendered superfluous. Compared to the central problems of social structure, on which the life of man depends, empirical research encompasses only a narrow sector. The limitation to selected, sharply isolated subject matter — thus precisely that approximation of empirical social research to the natural sciences, which, in accord with the requirement for exactitude, seeks to create conditions similar to those in the laboratory — prevents the treatment of the totality not only temporarily but in principle. It also entails that the assertions of empirical social research frequently have an inconclusive or peripheral character, or merely represent information for administrative purposes; and because of this, from the very outset they are not suitable for incorporation in relevantly posed theoretical problems.[8]

This passage raises many questions, and I will try to deal at least with the following:

1. The picture given here of sociological research is very different from its actuality. While I am quite prepared to concede that there indeed is such a thing as administrative and purely pragmatic research without theoretical import, it is also the case that much of sociological research distances itself quite consciously from this sort of naive empiricism.

2. The terms "theory of society" and "sociological theory" are used interchangeably here. This creates the impression that both refer to the same thing. The passage quoted above may therefore be interpreted as emphasizing merely so-called "relevant theoretical questions" in research.

3. I am quite unable to agree with the claim that the accumulation of research findings has been immense. On the contrary, one of the most serious weaknesses of our science is its lack, not abundance, of reliable and useful findings.

4. Finally, I would like to draw attention to a rather curious and illuminating coincidence between the theoretical question of social structure and the metaphysical question of the basis of human life. There can be no doubt that the social sciences would not even exist if people had not been concerned with the condition and the future of humanity. However, I nevertheless feel that this issue must be carefully separated from the question of sociological theory formation.

In this connection a brief comment on the ambition of wanting to grasp "society in its totality" may be in order. Adorno et al. provide much evidence that a theory of society that has overcome the antinomy between theory and action is essentially centered around the category of totality. This is a development which I have already discussed in regard to the case of Gurvitch. In both instances, these notions are indebted to the early writings of Marx, as in the case of another Marxist philosopher, Georg Lukács, who first formulated these ideas in the early 1920s. In his *History and Class Consciousness* Lukács explicitly states — and he believes that this is the original meaning of Marx's philosophy — that only "in this context which sees the isolated facts of social life as aspects of the historical process and integrates them in a *totality*, can knowledge of the facts hope to become knowledge of *reality*." Elsewhere in Lukács' book we can read that the whole system of Marxism "stands and falls with the principle that revolution is the product of a point of view in which the category of totality is dominant."[9] Incidentally, the totality aspect of this new type of science is here too connected with the dialectic.

In their chapter on "The Concept of Sociology," Adorno et al. claim that a sociology stubbornly committed to "positive" research is in danger of losing all "critical consciousness." The advocates of research, it is claimed, suspect "anything that diverges from the positive, that urges upon sociology questioning the legitimation of the social instead of merely ascertaining and classifying it."[10] Critical consciousness is asked to call into question the legitimacy of social life as such. To speculate about the legitimacy of social life is, no doubt, a fascinating sociological question, but it is unlikely that as a result we will come up with detailed and specific knowledge about any society. That human beings are living in social agglomerations, as important as this may be, must be clearly distinguished from the problem of the variety of social life as it actually is and as it finds expression in time and space.

The same chapter also contains a more illuminating argument: "But only a critical spirit can make science more than a mere duplication of reality by means of thought, and to explain reality means, at all times, to break the spell of this duplication. Such a critique, however, does not imply subjectivism, but rather the confrontation of the object with its own concept."[11] Let us leave the last part of the argument aside for now and turn toward the "spell of duplication." This term, too, has been borrowed from Marx, where it first appears in the fourth of the "Theses on Feuerbach" as the "duplication of the world" by religion, which Marx sees as a forerunner of philosophy in the unfolding of human thought. In criticizing this "duplication," Marx makes a decisive statement, which was to become fundamental for his philosophy: "The philosophers have only interpreted the world in different ways; the point is to change it" (Eleventh Thesis on Feuerbach).[12]

Adorno et al. see every scientific conceptualization as a mere "duplication." Action, by contrast, reaches into the dimension of the unforeseen and the unpredictable, as soon as it goes beyond perfunctory routine and subordinates itself to the category of totality. Such action is "revolutionary action." Here again, we encounter the same constellation: theory of society, society as a totality, and, as a new element, revolutionary action.

Finally, there is the rather puzzling statement that "critique" implies the confrontation of the object with its own concept, and there is the astonishing conclusion: "Whoever does not measure human things by what they themselves want to signify will not merely see superficially but falsely."[13] Perhaps it would be unfair to place too much emphasis on this concluding statement, which smacks intensely of conceptual realism. But since the other arguments are in any case much more important and more significant, I will consider some of their implications.

"Totality" in German Social and Philosophical Thought

In this section I will try to show that only by considering these implications can we hope to grasp the fundamental meaning of the statements by Adorno et al. and understand in what sense their view is distinguished from sociological theory proper. That the category of totality entirely dominates this essentially "holistic" argument, to use Karl Popper's terminology, is due to the influence of Marx. Popper himself is mainly concerned with the historical variant of holism which he calls "historicism."[14] But there are also nonhistorical varieties of holistic thought in the social sciences, among them, as one of the most extreme cases, Othmar Spann's "organistic universalism." And finally there is the dynamic type of holism, as represented by the dialectical approach. Even though these different approaches vary greatly in their background as well as in their political outlook, they are nevertheless offspring of a pattern of thought we have already encountered in both Gurvitch's hyperempiricism and Adorno's Hegelian-Marxian philosophy.

There can be little doubt that speculation, too, is rooted in theory and in research. But it draws its far reaching conclusions from limited experiences which are gathered in a more or less haphazard way. In contrast to sociological theory, speculation uses empirical data in an uncritical and uncontrolled manner and tends to rush to its conclusions overly hastily. Frequently only evidence corroborating the basic theses of the philosopher is taken up, while counter-evidence is pushed aside. On the other hand, the philosophical orientation of social thought which I have called a "theory of society" is not only concerned with universal propositions — whose most important function is preparing for action, mainly revolutionary action — but also with empirical research, which is employed for the same purpose. However, for the theory of society, in contrast to sociological theory, research does not aim at corroborating or rejecting hypotheses but, in its function of "unmasking" ideologies, is a tool of revolutionary action. Adorno has stressed this on several occasions.[15]

Adorno himself, of course, can hardly be described as a social thinker with a definite political orientation. He is a deeply philosophical spirit, and his general theory of society calls for a fundamental social transformation without at the same time calling for political revolution. Adorno by and large confines himself to "enlightenment," in the German sense of *Aufklärung,* and to a general cultural criticism which cannot easily be translated either into a reform program or a set of theoretical propositions. Adorno has done extremely important empirical research on the social roots of prejudice and on the authoritarian personality as a major cause of anti-Semitism. The main purpose of *The Authoritarian Personality* was to unmask the real causes of prejudice. The major difference between a "sociological theory" and a "theory of society" can be further clarified by way of this particular example.

The proponents of a theory of society may be quite satisfied that the evidence of their research work — that the causes of anti-Semitism and of prejudice are frequently found in an authoritarian personality — propels people to immediate educational or political action against authoritarianism of any kind. Sociological theory, by contrast, cannot rest satisfied with such a result, however desirable it may inherently be. It must address additional questions. Is the authoritarian personality, for example, inherently predisposed toward anti-Semitism or prejudice? If it is indeed the case that anti-Semitism is frequently caused by authoritarian traits in a particular person, then the obverse must surely hold true as well. We do not need to go further: it is quite clear that sufficient evidence for this claim has not been given. It could be that the authoritarian personality only becomes anti-Semitic once it has linked its fate with particular social classes and their vested interests. But Adorno is less interested in providing a sociological theory of anti-Semitism than in bringing about action — i.e., a cultural criticism struggling against anti-Semitism by way of enlightenment and by unmasking its real causes.

This sort of cultural criticism rests upon the category of "totality." We must keep in mind, however, that there are two kinds of thinking in totalities in social thought, a right-wing and a left-wing version. The intellectual level of the latter is generally much higher than that of the former. There is a difficulty which in our case complicates the assessment, and that is the fact that philosophical thinking in totalities, although it could easily do without research altogether, still makes use of research findings when these prove helpful in battling or unmasking prejudices or ideologies. In this sense a theory of society can be quite similar to sociological theory. We nevertheless, for good reasons, must keep both approaches clearly distinct. Whereas sociological theory is prepared to use research findings even against itself, the philosophical thinking in totalities of the theory of society precludes this. As soon as research findings threaten the assumptions of the theory, the findings are rejected as of a merely "administrative" nature, as "isolated," or even as "meaningless." It can easily be shown that the entire argument is circular, as Hegel already observed in his introduction to the *Phenomenology of the Spirit*.

This circularity is in fact inherent in dialectical thinking. As a purely philosophical approach it can be very illuminating, both ethically and theoretically. I myself, I should add, am in full agreement with every one of Adorno's goals. A theory of society undoubtedly has an important function in social thought. It serves enlightenment, unmasks deeply held prejudices and ideologies, and brings pure speculation down to earth. Yet it cannot replace sociological theory. The first step of a critical consciousness must indeed be to free itself from what Bacon called the *idola fori*; the next step, however, must be to arrive at scientific evidence by the usual means of checking theoretical hypotheses against empirical data.

In concluding I would like to return to my starting point and to my feelings of uneasiness about the contemporary situation of sociological research in Germany and, to a lesser extent, in France. Research there is sometimes linked to sociological theory, in the sense defined earlier, to an appropriate body of theoretical propositions. But quite frequently research is also "dialectically" linked to a general theory of society. What is of great importance is that, rather than accepting or rejecting one of these two approaches, they be separated very carefully, both intellectually and in research. As separate entities, sociological theory and the theory of society can both perform useful functions in the difficult process of the ongoing self-clarification of social thought. But dangers arise as soon as both are confused. These dangers are considerably more serious than the dangers arising from confusing sociological theory and mere speculation, since speculation uses research unsystematically and often extremely haphazardly, while a theory of society, as it has demonstrated all too well, is very capable of empirical research, although with the limitation mentioned above. It is precisely its research ability that might create the impression that sociological theory and the theory of society represent similar approaches. Yet, as we have seen, a theory of society is, under certain conditions, quite inclined to reject theory and research alike by contending that truth cannot be discovered by isolated investigations that do not possess a concept of social totality. In comparison, sociological theory will always appear inherently futile, since it is inevitably confined to a relatively narrow range of conceptualizations rooted in reality.

NOTES

1. See also René König, "German Sociology," in Joseph S. Roucek, ed., *Contemporary Sociology* (New York: Philosophical Library, 1958), pp. 779-806.

2. A term by Georges Gurvitch who, under the influence of Marx's early writings, has turned away from his own sociological pluralism and empiricism [Georges Gurvitch, *Essais de sociologie* (Paris: Librairie du Recueil Sirey, 1938), p. 18] and now vigorously attacks empiricism [Georges Gurvitch, *La vocation actuelle de la sociologie* (Paris: Presses Universitaires de France, 1950), p. 105; *Sociologie différentielle* (Paris: Presses Universitaires de France, 1957), p. 124].

3. Arnold Gehlen and Helmut Schelsky, eds., *Soziologie. Lehr- und Handbuch zur modernen Gesellschaftskunde* [1955], 3d ed. (Düsseldorf: Diederichs, 1957), pp. 9-10.

4. Erich Reigrotzki, *Soziale Verflechtungen in der Bundesrepublik* (Tübingen: J.C.B. Mohr, 1956), pp. v-vi, 237 ff.

5. Robert K. Merton, *Social Theory and Social Structure* [1949], 3d ed. (Glencoe, Ill.: The Free Press, 1957), pp. 5-6.

6. See Gurvitch, "L'hyper-empirisme dialectique, ses application en sociologie," *Cahiers Internationaux de Sociologie* (1953), vol. 15.

7. Institut für Sozialforschung, *Soziologische Exkurse* (Frankfurt: Europäische Verlagsanstalt, 1956). [Frankfurt Institute for Social Research, *Aspects of Sociology*, John Viertel, tr. (Boston: Beacon Press, 1972), pp. 117-128].

8. *Ibid.*, p. 109 [pp. 120-121]. While this essay, like the book of which it is a part, was published under the collective authorship of the Frankfurt Institute for Social Research, Adorno's imprint is clearly evident in this essay.

9. Georg Lukács, *Geschichte und Klassenbewusstsein* (Berlin: Malik, 1923), pp. 21-22, 39 [*History and Class Consciousness*, Rodney Livingstone, tr. (London: Merlin Press, 1968), pp. 8, 29].

10. See "Begriff der Soziologie," *Soziologische Exkurse*, p. 17 [see "The Concept of Sociology," *Aspects of Sociology*, p. 11].

11. *Ibid.*, p. 18 [p. 11].

12. In T.B. Bottomore and Maximilien Rubel, eds., *Karl Marx, Selected Writings in Sociology and Social Philosophy*, [1956], Tom Bottomore, tr. (London: McGraw-Hill, 1964), p. 69.

13. *Soziologische Exkurse*, p. 18 [see *Aspects of Sociology*, p. 11].

14. Karl R. Popper, *The Open Society and its Enemies*, [1945], 2d ed., rev. (London: Routledge & Kegan Paul, 1952); *The Poverty of Historicism* (London: Routledge & Kegan Paul, 1957).

15. See Theodor W. Adorno, "Soziologie und empirische Forschung," in Klaus Ziegler, ed., *Wesen und Wirklichkeit des Menschen* (Göttingen: Vandenhoeck & Ruprecht, 1957), pp. 245-260. See also a collective article of Adorno's Research Institute in Frankfurt; "Empirische Sozialforschung," in *Handwörterbuch der Sozialwissenschaften* (Göttingen: Vandenhoeck & Ruprecht, 1954); Max Horkheimer and Theodor W. Adorno, *Dialektik der Aufklärung* (Amsterdam: Querido, 1947) [*Dialectic of Enlightenment*, John Cumming, tr. (New York: Seabury, 1972)].

6

The Retreat of Sociologists into the Present

Norbert Elias

1. Not much attention has been paid to the retreat of sociologists into the present. This retreat, their flight from the past, became the dominant trend in the development of sociology after the Second World War and, like this development itself, was essentially unplanned.

That it was a retreat can become clearly visible if one considers that many of the earlier sociologists sought to illuminate problems of human societies, including those of their own time, with the help of a wide knowledge of their own societies' past and of earlier phases of other societies. The approach of Marx and Weber to sociological problems can serve as example. Marx tried to throw into better relief what he regarded as the most urgent problem of his time by presenting his own time as a stage between the past and possible futures. Weber again and again tried to clarify general sociological problems by means of evidence from past ages and from societies at an earlier stage of development.

2. The narrowing of the sociologists' focus of attention and interest to the immediate present, in some respects, undoubtedly represents progress in the development of the discipline. Sociologists are now much better able than before to study and in some cases solve short-term problems of their own society in a reasonably reliable manner. Concentration on present issues has found a striking expression in an almost explosive profusion of empirical sociological investigations, partly but by no means only of the statistical variety.[1]

3. The immediate present into which sociologists are retreating,

Translation by Stephen Kalberg and Volker Meja of a considerably revised and enlarged version of "Über den Rückzug der Soziologen auf die Gegenwart," *Kölner Zeitschrift für Soziologie und Sozialpsychologie* (1983) 35(1):29-40. The second half of this paper was newly written in English by the author.

Acknowledgement: I want to express my gratitude to Volker Meja for his great help in revising the original text for publication in this volume. I am also very grateful to my assistants Rudolf Knijff and Maarten van Bottenburg for helping me with the second part of this paper.

however, constitutes just one small momentary phase within the vast stream of humanity's development, which, coming from the past, debouches into the present and thrusts ahead toward possible futures. It is not surprising, therefore, that the recent abundance of empirical sociological inquiries went hand in hand with an impoverishment in other respects. One of its symptoms was the pronounced cleavage between the great majority of these empirical inquiries and the inquiries now presented as sociological theory. This cleavage is already foreshadowed in the work of Max Weber, whose action theory, which is set out in the early parts of *Economy and Society*, is often hardly noticeable in his empirical work. For a time the theoretical work of Talcott Parsons on the one hand and of neo-Marxist sociologists on the other hand held the center of the theory stage. But the theoretical eminence of these two schools of thought has not been matched by a rich harvest of empirical work inspired by these two types of theories and at the same time capable of testing their cognitive value. The real significance of the split into two camps, Parsonians and neo-Marxists, which with some transitions and fusions has determined much of the teaching of sociological theories in the universities of this world for quite a while, is political rather than scientific. The two types of theories represent a projection into the social sciences of the political division in society at large between conservatives and liberals on the one hand and socialists and communists on the other. No wonder that in sociology much empirical work is done without reference to theory and that many theoretical discussions proceed without any reference to empirical work. It is as if scientific researchers in the field of physics were divided into followers of a conservative or liberal and a socialist or communist theory of physics. There is obviously something very wrong with a scientific discipline if its leading representatives allow political sentiment to dominate their scientific work. In sociology one can observe again and again that what seems at first to be a serious scientific and learned discussion conducted on a very high level of abstraction reveals itself on closer inspection as a complex superstructure erected in order to attack or give support to specific positions on the contemporary spectrum of social ideals and beliefs. Scientific detachment in such cases can hardly disguise the partisanship underneath; nor can the facade of a scientific theory conceal the underlying extra-scientific commitment, although the latter can often only be recognized if one is able to penetrate the blur of an idiosyncratic terminology.

Thus Parsonianism and neo-Marxism, as the two most prominent schools of theoretical thought in sociology, fought out an attenuated version of the class struggle within the setting of an academic discipline. The intellectual edifice of these two schools of thought did not really represent scientific theories in the sense in which this word is used in the older sciences. Though it may now be forgotten, physics and biology too had to fight a long battle of emancipation from extra-scientific beliefs. Galileo is still remembered as an exponent of the struggle of physics for autonomy from powerful extra-scientific ideals, in that case particularly of the religious type. As far as can be seen, representatives of sociological theories, and indeed of theories in the human sciences generally, are as yet hardly aware that an analogous struggle for autonomy still lies ahead of them. But in their case the principal fight for emancipation has the character of a struggle for autonomy from the political and social ideals of the day.

4. The human population has undergone an unplanned process of growth, in more than purely numerical terms and in spite of all fluctuations. Throughout history, it has been divided into different groups, into survival units of one kind or another. These survival units have also grown in size. From small bands of twenty-five to fifty members, perhaps living in caves, humans coalesced into tribes of several hundred or several thousand members, and nowadays more and more into states of millions of people. Their changing size has changed the structure of these social units. The means of control — of external control as well as of self-control — required for the survival and integrity of a social unit of thirty people are different from the means of control required for the survival and integrity of a social unit formed by millions of people. The whole way of life of humans has changed in the course of this process. One can see here in a nutshell, as it were, why a theory of society prompted by different political ideals of twentieth-century industrial societies and presented as a universal theory of human societies can have only very limited cognitive value. Transitions from smaller to larger units of integration occur today under our very eyes. I do not think that sociological theories without a developmental framework can be of much help in elucidating the sociological problems presented by such changes, either on the theoretical or the empirical level. As long as theories prevail that abstract from the diachronic as well as from the dynamic character of societies, it will not be possible to close the great gap that exists today between this kind of theoretical design and empirical sociological research.

The understanding of human societies requires, it seems to me, testable theoretical models which can help to determine and to explain the structure and direction of long-term social processes — i.e., in the last resort, the development of humanity. I do not think, moreover, that theories of this type can be of use only in the field of sociology. A unifying developmental frame of reference without ideological encrustations, without, for instance, any built-in postulate of a necessarily better future, could also be of use in the other human sciences. The range of explanations is unduly narrowed if inquiries are focused on contemporary problems. One cannot ignore the fact that every present society has grown out of earlier societies and points beyond itself to a diversity of possible futures. If we immure sociological problems in static typologies and static concepts of structure and function, we neglect the intrinsic dynamics of human societies.

5. A number of universal concepts that indicate the properties common to all societies are also required for the construction of process models, that is, models of the development of humanity. Where the investigation of processes as such constitutes the focus of the research task, however, the universals acquire a different cognitive status and value than is the case where timeless law-like regularities stand in the center. In the latter case, the discovery of universals is the highest research aim, while in the case of process models it constitutes only an auxiliary tool for the construction of process models. Moreover, in the case of process universals, the researchers must be certain that they are genuine universals, that they refer to the least differentiated as well as to the most differentiated societies. General law-like regularities or typologies abstracted from the researcher's observations of his own society and presented as universals are in that case not of much use.

6. It might be useful to discuss an example of the type of universals that play a central role in the construction of process models. In all possible societies, people who belong to a group with regard to which they say "we" have to fulfill a specific set of elementary functions for each other and for the group as a whole if they are to survive as a group. I need not consider here all these elementary functions but shall give a few examples. Usually interwoven and certainly interdependent, they are often conceptualized as strands or spheres of social development. In many cases, one of them is presented as the sole motive force of social development. Ideas as driving force, class struggle as driving force are obvious examples. Multifunctional and, in that sense, nonreductive process models are still to come. I cannot and need not in this context give a fuller account of the variegated patterns of their interrelationship. Nor do I need to argue here with the assumption that this interrelationship, throughout this development, is always the same. What I shall do is give a short diagnostic summary of

some of the elementary functions and then some examples which, I hope, will bring them to life.

It was Karl Marx who identified the first of these elementary functions which members of a group have to perform satisfactorily if they are to survive as a group. Traditionally it was called the "economic" function. And it is perhaps not necessary to break with this tradition, but there can be no doubt that the term "economic" is imprecise. If a long-term development is the frame of reference, one has to distinguish very clearly between a stage of development in which economic functions are performed by groups of economic specialists and a stage of lesser differentiation where everyone must fulfill economic functions in a nonspecialized way. To put it at its simplest, one can say that one of the elementary universals of human groups is the provision of food and other basic wherewithals of life.

The second of these survival functions is that of control of violence or, in a somewhat wider sense, the function of conflict management in its two aspects: control of violence within a group and control of violence in the relationship between different survival groups. Both in the case of economic functions and in that of violence control functions one has to distinguish between stages of social development where the same persons who perform economic functions also perform violence control functions — where, in other words, these functions are not yet performed by specialists — and stages of development where economic functions on the one hand and conflict management functions on the other are performed by different persons, i.e., by specialists. There are, of course, many transitional stages. By and large, however, one can say that the condition in which specialists are entirely set free from the performance of other vital functions, among them that of food production, and where their central social function is confined to that of violence control and conflict management within and between groups, is identical with the social formation we call a "state." Perhaps it needs to be added that I am not concerned with the question whether it is good or bad that such a specialization emerged. I am simply concerned with the clarification of a demonstrable fact. The emergence of social specialists for violence control is a good example of the interwovenness of the changing patterns of the way in which these vital functions are performed in human societies.

Specialists for violence control can emerge in a society only if its members produce more food than is needed for the survival of the food producers and their families. However, in the long run, the regular production of surplus food requires a comparatively high level of physical security for the producers of food. It requires the effective protection of whatever it is — livestock, fertile acres, rich fishing grounds — against marauders. In their development, advances toward specialization of economic and of violence control functions are reciprocal.[2]

The excavations of Sumerian towns offer a number of clues to the stages that led to the development of permanent monopolies of violence. Presumably, this occurred in conjunction with the parallel development, quite indispensable in that case, of a monopoly of taxes. Excavations indicate, for example, that, from a certain period on, Sumerian settlements were surrounded by solid and undoubtedly also very expensive walls.[3] Viewed together with other evidence, this fact indicates that here — and possibly for the first time — human societies attained the organizational stage of city-states. They produced enough food not only to support those building and guarding the walls, but also to feed the priests in their temples, the monopolistic specialists controlling the basic fund of knowledge of a group, especially knowledge of the ways of the spirit world,[4] as well as the monopolistic controllers of violence, the princes in their palaces and the warriors, the controlled specialists in the use of violence. Among other tasks, the latter guarded and coordinated the laborers in the fields, the building and maintenance of the vulnerable irrigation canals and of the city walls, the palaces, and the temples. From smaller settlements, perhaps with the character of village-states centered on a temple, the settlements we now know as Sumerian grew into the first type of large-scale organization, with a greater differentiation of specialized functions. They grew into walled city-states, each with a large temple and a palace organization. These Sumerian city-states, like the Greek city-states of a later age, fought with each other for centuries an indecisive struggle for hegemony until they all were conquered by, and to some extent subjected to the rule of, a stronger state from outside.

In the more advanced societies of our own age, groups of economic specialists are among the most powerful groups and, in some cases, the most powerful groups of all. The prevalence of specialized economic activities in many contemporary societies has given rise to a sociological theory according to which the specialized economic sphere is at all times the only basic sphere of society. All other aspects of society, it seems, can be explained in terms of their economic development. Conflicts between groups of economic specialists, according to this theory, are to be considered as the universal driving force of the development of humanity, and monopolization of economic functions, of the means of production, can be regarded universally as the main source of social power.

This would suggest that throughout the development of humanity, as in more recent times, economic specialists monopolizing the means of production constitute the most powerful, the actual ruling groups of society. However, whether or not that is a correct diagnosis of the distribution of power chances in contemporary industrial societies, it most certainly is not a correct diagnosis of the distribution of power in earlier state-societies. There, with very few exceptions, the principal ruling groups were warriors and priests. In one guise or another these groups of specialists, as allies or as rivals, formed the ruling groups of state-societies for the greater part of their development. Economic specialists, such as merchants, usually ranked lower than nobles and priests and could until very recently rarely match the power and wealth of their leading groups such as kings or popes (in countries such as Russia, Germany, and Austria, not until 1914). One cannot help asking which structural characteristics of human societies are responsible for the long-lasting dominance in most state-societies of these two groups of specialists, of warriors and priests. It certainly suggests that the attempt at presenting a universal theory of society, if one's vision is foreshortened by preoccupation with short-term, present-day causes, increases the risk of failure. The discovery of the economic conditions of social change was a great advance, the reduction of all social changes to economic conditions a great impediment to further advance. With regard to the distribution of power in a society one can say that monopolization of the means of violence or of the means of orientation, that is of knowledge and particularly of magic-mythical knowledge, plays no less a part as a source of power than the monopolization of the means of production. Neither the social function of violence management and control nor that of knowledge transmission and acquisition can be simply reduced to, and explained in terms of, the economic functions of a society. All three and a number of others which need not be considered here are equally basic and irreducible.

A word about knowledge may be of some use here. Knowledge in particular has never quite recovered from the curse put on it by Marx, who attributed to it the ontological status of a mere superstructure. To perceive its basic role in human societies one need only think of a "knowledgeless" group — that is, a group to which no knowledge has been transmitted from previous generations — in order to recognize the basic social function of knowledge. The idea of such a group evidently is an unrealizable thought experiment, but it demonstrates quite clearly that human groups, which certainly cannot survive without food or protection from physical violence, also cannot survive without knowledge. Nonhuman organisms, to a greater or lesser extent, are capable of finding their food "instinctively," that is, with the assistance of innate steering mechanisms, and perhaps in conjunction with a comparatively small degree of learned knowledge. Human beings, on the other hand, are entirely incapable of orienting themselves without learned knowledge: except at the infant stage, they cannot find the right food or even any food at all without transmitted knowledge. The human need for knowledge, in other words, is as elementary as the need for food. Like the means of satisfying other elementary needs, those of satisfying other people's requirements of knowledge can be monopolized. In the form of a monopoly, the means of orientation, the appropriation of the means of satisfying the human requirement for knowledge can serve as a basis for power inequalities.

One further elementary function should be mentioned. Other social organisms occasionally possess innate self-controls that make it possible for them to live together in groups without destroying themselves or each other. Human beings, however, have no such inborn restraints. They must acquire the patterns of self-restraint indispensable for social life through learning while living with others. Accordingly, individual learning of a social pattern of self-restraint or a civilizing process of sorts is also one of the universal elementary survival functions which one encounters in every human group. One of the social institutions that performs this function can be found in the initiation rites of less complex human groups. They represent an early form of civilizing individual group members. Group pressure toward the exercise of self-constraint, like all the other elementary functions I have mentioned, can also be monopolized and utilized as a source of power and status differentials, and thus as a means of domination and exploitation. Initiation rites, for example, are not only a means of producing a specific pattern of self-constraint, but also important episodes in the concealed or overt power struggle between the generations. This elementary function too is irreducible. The learning of self-constraint is certainly not possible without simultaneous fulfillment of the other functions mentioned before, including the control of violence. However, they in turn require individual patterns of self-control.

These four elementary functions do not constitute the entire range of possible functions. There are others. Those I have mentioned provide, nonetheless, examples of universals of social development that can be empirically tested and, if necessary, corrected.

7. I would like to illustrate by means of an example the cognitive value of the concept of basic social functions. Marx attempted to understand the whole dynamic of social development theoretically by reference to a single common denominator. He considered the monopolization of the means of production — for instance, the means of satisfying hunger — as the source of social inequalities and as the root of all other inequalities. He regarded the conflicts arising from this monopolization of chances to satisfy "economic" needs as the primary and perhaps even as the exclusive driving force of social development.

As a result, he perceived a ruling class of feudal warriors as a stratum more or less of the same type as a ruling class of commercial or industrial entrepreneurs. He did not attach great relevance to the difference between those who owed their "economic" power to their class and those who owed it to their capital. Yet, the French slogan *nul terre sans seigneur* was really a class slogan. It meant that no one who did not belong to the warrior nobility, and thus was skilled in the use of physical violence in order to enforce obedience, had the right to own land. In a number of cases, custom reinforced by class solidarity denied peasants and other nonprivileged groups the possession and use of the weapons of the upper classes.

The recognition of the role of structural conflicts as a motor of change was a gain for the diagnostic capacity of social scientists, the restriction to intrastate conflicts of an economic nature an impediment.

Marx saw more clearly what feudal and entrepreneurial groups had in common than he saw the structural differences. He noted that, since both could monopolize the economic means of production, both acquired power chances that allowed them to exploit other groups. Yet he failed to ask, and therefore found no reason to explain, why those in possession of power monopolies consisted of a nobility of warriors in the one case and relatively pacified merchants in the other.

Sociologists defeat their own ends if they neglect such differences, if they omit, for instance, to ask why classes of economic specialists did not always play the same central part in the power structure of their society that they play today. It is easy to see that the social characteristics of those groups which formed the most highly placed establishment in a state-society and which therefore presumably possessed the greatest power resources has changed in a highly specific manner since the days when, probably in ancient Sumer, societies with the distinguishing characteristics of a state first emerged from pre-state socie-ties. Since that time, between five and six thousand years ago until fairly recent times, two groups of social functionaries, with relatively few exceptions, held the position as the highest ranking, most power-ful, and often as the richest groups in the status hierarchy of state-societies. These two main establishments were, broadly speaking, groups of priests and groups of warriors; those who ruled the temple and those who ruled the palace (the princes, kings, and emperors at the head of their courts in conjunction with, and sometimes deposed by, oligarchic groups of warrior nobles).

There were exceptions. One of them was the city-states. The Phoe-nician, Greek, and, later, the Italian and Dutch city-states are ex-amples. Sea-states, that is, states whose principal military establish-ment was based on ships, generally had ruling groups with different social characteristics from those of the ruling groups of land-states, that is, states whose principal military forces were land armies. England since the time of Henry VIII as well as the Netherlands are ob-vious examples. The development in China also followed a different course. The officials of the civil administration at the imperial court, and throughout the country, a class of land owners with administra-tive functions, succeeded relatively early in wresting power from the warriors. Sometimes called "gentry," sometimes "mandarins," they formed throughout the vast country a fairly closely knit hierarchical network with a unified cultural tradition and a strong sense of their own superiority in relation to all other groups. Thus, in China a non-military social formation, which required for the maintenance of its high power ratio and its high status from its members a fairly high level of self-control, replaced for hundreds of years the warriors who, wherever they formed the ruling establishment, ruled more directly and also were ruled more directly by means of pressures from without. Moreover, during the period roughly corresponding to the middle ages of the West, the ruling officials of China developed what was probably the most advanced state organization of the time, which then slowly rigidified and declined.

In the majority of states, however, the greatest power and status chances, in some cases well into the twentieth century, were in the hands of either warriors or priests, or of both as allies *and* rivals. The relationship between these two establishments, throughout the long years of their supremacy, was basically ambivalent and varied a great deal. At times they competed for power, as in ancient Egypt and in the medieval West, where the struggle between emperor and pope offers a telling example. More recently, the conflict between the Shah and the mullahs in Iran offers another. In other cases they became allied in their endeavor to ensure law and order through the obedience of other groups. Compared with the status of princes, nobles, and high priests, the status of merchants in the past rarely surpassed the second or third rank. This fact in itself can serve as a fairly reliable indication that their power chances too were generally smaller than those of warriors and priests.

In the course of the nineteenth and twentieth centuries, two groups of economic specialists, first the middle class entrepreneurs and managers and later, to a lesser extent, representatives of the organized working classes, in a growing number of state-societies, gained ascendancy over the two traditional ruling establishments. Before that time one or another of the latter (or both) had usually held a dominant position in the estate assemblies wherever they existed. Now representatives of the groups of economic specialists, organized in the form of mass parties, gained the ascendancy in the state assemblies, which changed their character: estate assemblies gave way to parliaments. One should perhaps not close too soon the question of which structural changes are reflected in this development from state-societies — where for a long time warriors or priests (or both) contributed the most powerful and the highest ranking establishments — to more recent state-societies — where nobles and priests lost their privileged status and two antagonistic, yet interdependent economic classes gained the ascendancy.

Moreover, a new development has occurred in very recent times. Yet another social formation with different social characteristics now frequently exceeds in power and status the establishments of the two groups of economic specialists, while often remaining in a latent condition of competition with them. I am referring to men and women who are professional politicians and members of a party establishment. Both in one-party and in multiparty states, career politicians, (i.e., political specialists) possess at the present time in many state-societies a better chance of gaining access to the state's central monopolies and to the concomitant power chances than do military, priestly or economic specialists. The latter groups, wherever they are organized and powerful enough, are competing for power chances with party politicians.*

8. One may well ask why social establishments with different so-

* Editors' Note: The text that follows has been newly written in English by the author.

cial functions and therefore with different social characteristics took their place at the head of the status and power hierarchies of state-societies at different times. The earlier references to the basic survival functions of human societies can be of help here. Hegel and Marx, the historical idealist and the historical materialist, both assumed as a matter of course that one single and always the same set of functions, in one case the intellectual, in the other the economic sphere, played the dominant part as a driving force throughout the development of humanity. In actual fact one can observe in state-societies from the earliest days until our own time several basic functions whose representatives by virtue of their specialism play or share a dominant part in the power and status hierarchy and thus in the power struggles of their age. But the resources and thus the ratio of power chances available to these different groups of functionaries and particularly their chances of access to the central monopolies of a state can vary considerably under different social conditions. So does, therefore, their position in the status hierarchy of societies.

Emancipation from monistic models, their replacement by pluralistic models of social development (which includes present times no less than the past) thus becomes a matter of some strength and intensity. In a provisional way one can perhaps say that the power ratio of a group of social functionaries varies in accordance with the changing strength and intensity of the social requirements which that group is able to satisfy by virtue of its specialism. A group's capacity to provide, perhaps to ration or to withdraw and, generally, to control the means of fulfilling social requirements of a survival unit (and thus of other groups) is the mainstay of that group's power ratio.

However, the dependence for its survival of a differentiated survival unit in the form of a state-society on a group or groups of specialized functionaries (such as priests or warriors) is never entirely one-sided. To some extent these groups in turn depend on other groups for the fulfillment of social requirements. What one can usually observe in surveying state-societies is a reciprocal attunement of needs and satisfactions, a balance of give-and-take, however uneven, between different groups of specialists, including those endowed with the task of taking decisions for a state-society as such. As a rule, therefore, one encounters in such a society an overt or latent tug-of-war between specialized groups, including the governing groups, with the aim of moving the balance of give-and-take in a direction more favorable toward one's own group. With few exceptions, however, state-societies throughout the ages, even if they were explicitly planned to promote complete equality, were cast again and again in a mold of great inequality. The balance of give-and-take of different groups of specialists remained stubbornly uneven, though it has become somewhat less uneven than it used to be in some of the multiparty states. In spite of this spurt of functional democratization, state-societies generally still represent a highly uneven reciprocity of control between governing groups and groups being governed.

Present conditions may be seen more clearly by comparison with conditions in the past. If the contemporary reading of the earliest state-societies which have come to light so far is indeed correct, if the earliest state-like organization in ancient Sumer (the first large-scale organization known to us) was in fact centered on a temple and headed by priests, it is perhaps not unduly daring to conclude that the social requirements of the state population which priests could satisfy were at this stage much more pressing and imperative. Also a higher level of self-restraint may have helped priests to have the edge on the population they ruled. The relatively high degree of secularization, the very extensive fund of testable reality-congruent knowledge of a later age, and a conscience formation which in adults has become less dependent on external restraint, real or imagined, may make it difficult to understand that at a stage of development where the fund of reality-congruent knowledge was considerably smaller, the social need for the magic-mythical knowledge of the ways of the spirit world (which formed the core of a priest's calling) was very much stronger, and that the power of priests was correspondingly greater.

In prescientific state-societies, priests were usually the principal specialists for the preservation, development, and transmission of a society's basic means of orientation, of its fund of knowledge. Moreover, magic-mythical knowledge could be more easily monopolized than scientific knowledge. Hence it is not surprising that in the ancient Sumerian city-states priests formed the most powerful or, after warriors had gained the ascendancy over them, the second most powerful establishment. The fact that priests also helped to strengthen and to reproduce the social requirements of people which formed the basis of their high power-ratio need not divert attention from the genuineness of these requirements at that stage in the development of humanity. Projection of a contemporary requirement- and restraint-structure into that of earlier ages blocks the understanding of the latter. State-societies of our own time are highly dependent upon a scientific production of knowledge. Their members can rely on an extensive body of reality-congruent means of orientation. Knowledge which children learn with great ease at a later stage was in many cases non-existent at an earlier stage of development and might have been completely incomprehensible to its human representatives if it had been presented to them. In the same way, people who already know may find incomprehensible the condition of knowledge of those who did not know. They may find it extremely difficult to put themselves in the position of those who did (or do) not yet know, and social scientists have by and large failed to make it easier for them to understand that condition. They have failed to act as interpreters for human beings whose fund of reality-congruent knowledge, though perhaps much more detailed, was much more limited than their own. Today people hardly experience the horror of not-knowing, the encounter with events for which they have no name. Human beings cannot survive if they cannot place events by giving them a name, by fitting them into their fund of communal symbols. Thus in the long ages during which their fund of reality-congruent knowledge remained comparatively small, people filled its gaps with communally standardized fantasy knowledge. Moreover, members of contemporary societies which we call advanced often feel that the level of insecurity and of dangers to which they are exposed is far too high, at least in terms of their own wishes and needs. As a result, they often fail to recognize that the danger level of contemporary industrial societies is very much lower than that of medieval societies, or, for that matter, of the Mesopotamian states of antiquity. In that respect, too, the imagination of members of the wealthier industrial nation-states often fails. With few exceptions they enjoy, in health and ill-health, well-off or poor, a comparatively high level of security which they hardly seem to notice. They find it difficult to understand that in the earlier state-societies the capacity for controlling the manifold dangers which threatened people was much lower. Words fail them when they try to show that the restraint-pattern of people of earlier societies — including its conscience formation — was different from their own. In order to control themselves they had to rely to a greater extent on the fear of external agencies, including fear of the gods.

The process which transformed tribal villages into city-states was one of the great breakthrough processes in the development of human societies. It was an ascent to a new level of differentiation and integration. Advances in Mesopotamian archeology have greatly increased our understanding of that process. The development in the course of which a new type of organization emerged, the novel figuration of a state with properties of its own not found at the pre-state levels, may have taken quite a long time, certainly a few centuries and perhaps more than a thousand years. A continuous process comprising many intermediary stages linked the village stage to that of the city-state.

One of the obvious characteristics of the latter was the greater quantity of people bonded together within the survival unit with the structural characteristics of a state. However, living together in larger numbers was made possible for people, and imposed on them, by a new figuration they formed with each other, including a new way of life. It required a different pattern of control both by others and by oneself. Governing, centrally coordinating, directing and controlling all other activities, maintaining peace within the state, and defending its citizens against attacks from outside now became a permanent specialism. People who performed these social functions were set free from most other social tasks, above all from that of growing their own food, and set apart from all other groups by power and status differences and thus by a social distance of a magnitude unknown at the village level. In the same way those who produced food or manufactured goods now also became permanent specialists in a sense which had not existed before centralized functions of governing assumed the characteristics of a specialism permanently monopolized by certain groups, persons, or families. At the tribal stage, at the village level, stratification in terms of sex- and age-groups was normal. Priests and smiths were among the few occupational specialists. At the state level occupational stratification permeated the whole fabric of society. The fact that food growing became now a permanent and exclusive specialism, no doubt played a significant part in the increase of the agricultural produce, but it also meant the exclusion of food growers from any share in the ruling, coordinating, and controlling functions of a state-society.

The way toward understanding this process of change from a pre-state to a state level of organization (and of much else besides) is at present to some extent blocked by a type of conceptualization which divides societies rather vaguely into four or five static spheres. They are represented by terms such as "political," "economic," "cultural," or "religious," and are generally treated as universals which can be discovered in all societies regardless of their stage of development. However, they are rarely linked with precision to specialized functions performed by groups of people in their society according to its stage of integration and differentiation. As a result, such terms as "social differentiation" and "division of functions" (the latter above all in its better known form as "division of labor"), are often confined to what is considered as the economic sphere of society. It may seem like stretching a point to apply terms like "social differentiation" and above all "division of labor" to the political sphere, for example. The emergence of a central government as a permanently differentiated set of functions is therefore often not clearly seen as a process of advancing differentiation of societies.

Earlier writers, first of all Gordon Childe,[5] discovered the fact, now widely accepted, that the emergence of the Sumerian city-states, with their considerable number of specialized groups which did not grow their own food, was made possible by a development of agriculture to a level where those who worked on the land produced an agricultural surplus, i.e., more food than they needed for their own survival and that of their families. The production of a food surplus was widely seen as a condition of the emergence of human settlements with the characteristics of a city, which contained many human groups who did not grow their own food. What was perhaps less clearly seen was the significance of the fact that the cities also had the social characteristics of a state. It may be unpleasant to realize, but one cannot entirely bypass the fact that at this stage the production and distribution of a food surplus and, more generally, the production of a social capital depended to a large extent on forms of external constraints. These constraints were in the first instance imposed upon people by fear of goddesses and gods and of the magical powers of priestesses and priests, or by warlords and their followers whose might also seemed to have come from the gods. In these early stages, indeed for a long time to come, these ruling groups used their power to restrain and to exploit others with little self-restraint, confining many of those who labored on the land or on the irrigation works to a subsistence level. Priests in all probability first developed the art of writing as a means of controlling the large quantities of food and manufactured goods which were owed to the gods, were stored in the temple buildings, and apportioned from there again to the various sections of the state population. Such a huge organization could no longer be managed and controlled by means of the unaided memory of the gods' servants. Written accounts greatly facilitated the handling and the control of a temple household's income and expenditure. The extraction of a large surplus from food growers and craftsmen by the temple and palace organizations was in all probability one of the conditions of the rich flowering of the Sumerian culture. But the fact that the constraints of a centralized state organization were initially at the root both of the production and the distribution of a surplus is often not clearly seen, probably because this is too distasteful to us. The urban revolution, as it was called, thus seemed to be fully explainable in economic terms. Much attention was given to the great fertility of the soil in the delta-valley of the great rivers and the added agricultural yield that was due to an ingenious network of irrigation devices. The discovery of the part played by an agricultural surplus in the development of Sumerian cities was a genuine scientific advance. But it was made under the aegis of a monocausal theory which represented factors that could be classified as economic, as the spring and fountainhead of all other developments.

What happened in Sumer, as I have mentioned, was a development of villages not only into cities, but also into city-states with a higher level of specialization (particularly of governmental functions) than had anywhere been attained by humans before. The fertility of the soil and the production of a food surplus undoubtedly played a part in that development, but cannot fully explain it. Free peasants hardly ever take the trouble to produce a food surplus year after year without strong rewards or strong compulsion. It is hardly conceivable that the villagers of ancient Sumer formed an exception, that they began to produce a regular food surplus which then brought into being a surplus population of nonagrarian urban groups. A monistic cause-and-effect explanation is out of place here. A different picture emerges, however, if one tries to fit the fragments of evidence together not in a causal form, but in the form of a process. The question then arises, which social functionaries commanded sufficient power resources in order to compel food growers to do the hard work that was required for the production of a food surplus even under the most favorable natural conditions. Which group (or groups) had the power to develop and to control the building and maintenance of irrigation works? Who had the authority to coordinate the labor forces on which the regular production, the transport and distribution of a food surplus depended? The answer is provided by the existing evidence. The nucleus around which the Sumerian city-state developed was in the first place the temple, seat of a god and stronghold of priests, and in the second place the palace, seat of a warlord or king, and stronghold of his warriors and administrators.

It has sometimes been argued that the appropriation of the economic surplus was the main source of power of the two ruling groups in these early states. However, the surplus was not simply there. It grew together, and itself formed part of the human organization which in time assumed the characteristics initially of a temple centered, then of a temple-palace centered city-state. A causal explanation confuses the issue. In such cases a process-type explanation is more approriate. The late stage of the process, which alone is visible to us, shows clearly enough not only that the food surplus produced under pressure by people working on the land was the condition of the existence of a nonagrarian city population, but a state organization capable of coordinating the work on the land as well as the maintenance of the irrigation works and their defense was also a condition of the steady production of a surplus. Perhaps it was first a settlement centered on an old and venerated Sumerian sanctuary, that of Eridu, which developed in that direction, initially protected against always imminent foreign attacks by the delta's marshland or by river arms, and perhaps by the awe the powerful deity of a great sanctuary could inspire even in foreign groups. Over time more and more city-states competed with each other for hegemony and groups specialized as warriors gained ascendancy over the priests. The latter's natural and magical features were supplemented or replaced by human-made features, particularly by city walls. Once it is recognized that the development of a city-state with its creation of a food surplus was a lengthy process, it becomes easier to see that it was not primarily the appropriation of economic resources which constituted the power basis of priests and warriors, but rather the intrinsic characteristics of their specialism as social functionaries. The power of priests was derived in the first place from their special relationship with the gods, from their exclusive possession of means of orientation of the magic-mythical type. In fact, the elevated position of priests in the power and status hierarchy of societies until (and indeed far beyond) the emergence of secularized knowledge can serve as a sensitive yardstick for the strength and intensity of the need for such knowledge in society at large. In the same way warlords or kings and their followers were able to maintain and to control the organization which ensured the regular production of a food surplus, in the first instance because from a certain stage on the danger to which human groups settled in cities were exposed from other groups — such as the daily danger of attack by marauders or of war by human enemies — was so great that the dependence of people within a society for their physical security (and indeed for their survival) on specialists for the use of violence or warfare — in other words on military men — was considerable. Almost everywhere military men assumed the characteristics of a caste set apart from other groups by birth as members of the highest ranking group. As in the case of the priests, here too the high status of a group of specialists can be seen as a measure of the strength and intensity of the social requirements which they could satisfy by virtue of their specialism. That a form of hereditary nobility came with great regularity to be attached to military men was indicative of the high priority which for thousands of years defense or attack in warfare had among the requirements of human societies. Kings and nobles no doubt long retained their supremacy even after specific changes in the structure of human societies had diminished the strength and urgency of the social requirements which they fulfilled. One may be inclined to think that the question of the defunctionalization of kings and of the descendants of the traditional warrior classes generally deserves closer attention. Yet in this case the fact that these groups of social specialists in many societies held for a long time the highest position in the power and status hierarchy, usually one much superior to that of merchants and other groups of economic specialists, can serve as a yardstick of the strength and urgency of the demand for the services which they were able to monopolize.

A fully developed pluralistic model of the development of human societies would have to include, in addition to the economic functions, a number of other functions, particularly if the groups concerned were able to give their specialism the form of a hereditary monopoly. Churches often claimed a hereditary right to legitimize priests, nobles in many cases successfully claimed for their members the exclusive access to the commanding positions of the armed forces. More generally one can say that monopolization of the means of orientation and of the means of violence (and the power struggles connected with them) must be placed side by side with the monopolization of the means of production and the conflicts resulting from it as irreducible factors of the development of societies. A further group, which I can mention only in passing, is that of high state officials, a group whose relatively high power chances are based on a monopolistic control of the access to the higher state offices. Finally, in our own time, party politicians, as I have already mentioned, have joined the ranks of ruling establishments. In the course of a process of functional democratization mass parties in both one- and multiparty states were able to monopolize access to the governmental offices of a state and thus to the state's central monopolies.

Increasing internal pacification and its concomitants, greater physical and legal security, have helped to increase the power potential of the two groups of economic specialists, the controllers of capital and the controllers of labor. A prolonged tug-of-war between these two interdependent groups has held the center of the social stage in most countries undergoing industrialization for the greater part of the nineteenth and twentieth centuries. It was a transient episode of great consequence. Until much of the labor and some of the service work of humans became mechanized, neither of the two warring groups could gain the upper hand. The balance of power between them was tilted in favor of the controllers of the means of investment, and thus of employment chances, but their power surplus was not great enough for the undisputed dominance to which they sometimes aspired. Nor was the corresponding aim ever within reach of the leaders of labor organizations. Although occupational organizations of workers greatly increased their power potential, the intrinsic power resources of the industrial working classes as a group of social functionaries fulfilling basic requirements of their society was never great enough for the attainment of a lasting superiority over other groups, including the controllers of capital. This ideal of some of their spokesmen was as unattainable by violent as by nonviolent means. Revolution in the name of industrial workers increased the power resources of party establishments at the expense of all other groups, including the industrial workers themselves. It gave the party establishment not only the control of the means of violence and taxation, but also the control of capital and thus of occupational opportunities. In addition, the party establishment also gained a monopolistic control of organization and knowledge.

The four types of basic social requirements and of specialisms capable of fulfilling them that have been mentioned above do not exhaust the list. Human groups specialized for the means of violence, orientation, capital accumulation and investment, and organizing other groups of people, were able, at one time or another, to establish themselves as controllers of the central monopolies of a state and thus, alone or in partnership, to perform ruling functions in their society. Recurrent power conflicts within or between states, whether between competing establishments or between established and outsiders — in other words, hegemonial[6] and survival struggles of various kinds — formed one of the strongest, perhaps *the* strongest, driving force in the development of societies. As such they were blind; they involved people again and again with unintended results. In some cases these had the character of a dominant ascent, perhaps of a spurt toward a higher level of integration and differentiation, in others that of a descent to a lower level, of decline or disintegration.

There is much detailed work to be done on the changes in the struc-

ture of humanity which find expression in the changes of establishments briefly surveyed here in the form of a testable model. At present,
"structure of humanity" may still sound unfamiliar. It becomes an indispensable concept, however, if one considers that structural changes
of relationships within and between societies are functionally interdependent. Humanity is simply another word for the totality of human
societies, for the ongoing process of the figuration which all the various survival units form with each other, whether they have the character of kinship groups, tribes, or states. In former days the term
humanity often served as symbol of a far-fetched ideal beyond the
reach of social science inquiries. It is far-fetched no longer. Nor is it an
ideal. At a time when all the different tribes, all states of the world, are
drawn together more closely, humanity increasingly represents a
purely factual frame of reference of sociological inquiries into past no
less than present phases of social development. As a symbol at a high
level of synthesis, representing the long-term continuity of the development of human societies, the concept becomes a gateway to discovery indispensable for the understanding of past and present times.

9. Among the many questions left open here for the time being is
why a different relationship between priests and warriors appears to
have developed relatively early in different branches of Indo-Aryan
peoples. In the state formation process of the Aryan-speaking groups
invading India, priests came out at the top of the status and power
hierarchy. They formed the highest caste, warriors the second highest.
Among Celtic or Gaelic peoples too priests called Druids may have had
some ruling functions and a very high position in the status and
power hierarchy. In the state formation processes of Hellenic, Italic,
Germanic, and Slavic peoples, on the other hand, warriors gained the
ascendancy over priests. Among Greeks in particular, priests and
priestesses, although they played a dominant part in some sanctuaries
such as that of Delphi, apparently lost the competitive struggle for supremacy and particularly for the ruling positions in society to the warrior nobles. Already in Homer one can observe the supremacy of the
warriors. There, gods often associate with warrior nobles or direct their
fate without priestly intermediaries and sometimes as if they themselves were simply a more powerful breed of nobles. It is difficult to
imagine that a great spurt of secularization could have taken place
among the ancient Greeks and continued for a time among the
Romans had the old contest there between warriors and priests taken
the same turn as in India, had there too priests gained ascendancy over
warriors. The same can be said of the great contest for supremacy be-

tween pope and emperor in the Middle Ages. Once again, if priests, organized in churches, had gained supremacy over kings and nobles (the functional descendants of the old warrior classes), the second great secularization spurt represented above all by the rise of the natural sciences could hardly have occurred.

Time has tempered the rivalry between these two groups of specialists. Priestly and military establishments still rank high in the power and status hierarchy in most contemporary state-societies. But by comparison with past ages the social need for their services has lessened. In many cases economic and party establishments have moved ahead of them to the top of the power and status hierarchy. Scientific establishments as specialists for the production and transmission of basic knowledge, as the main providers of new means of orientation in their societies, have taken over functions formerly performed by priests. Their members by virtue of their specialism respond to social requirements of a high order. It illuminates the structure of power balances that nonetheless the power resources of scientific establishments are relatively limited, much more so than those of economic or of party establishments. Individually some scientist may command high respect. But as a group contemporary scientists hardly form a focus of power in the same sense as the establishments I have named before. The reason is not without interest. Scientists are engaged in an activity which fosters and demands a high level of individualization. They are as a rule less closely and also less militantly organized than these other establishments. Though by no means unaware of common professional interests, their distribution in different universities and a variety of other institutions, as much as the individualizing character of their teaching and research work, usually lessens the interest in their representation as a corporate body. Moreover, it is very difficult and in the long run next to impossible to monopolize the results of scientific work. Magic-mythical knowledge can often be successfully treated as a mystery and thus as the exclusive preserve of a particular human group. Reality-congruent knowledge, once discovered, may be kept secret for a time, but it can always be discovered by others and, in practice, can be rarely kept secret for any length of time. It is a good example of the role played in the distribution of power resources by the inability to monopolize satisfactions required by others. Priests and scribes of ancient Sumer and Egypt were for a long time successfully able to reserve for themselves a large body of knowledge and, as part of it, the art of reading and writing. The monopolization of this knowledge gave strong support to their privileged position. By contrast, even the most sophisticated scientific knowledge of our time is published and made accessible to a wider public by way of libraries. Scientific establishments compete with each other and try to reserve places and grants for their own flock. In some cases they immure themselves in an ivory tower of otherwise incomprehensible symbols trying to gain kudos and authority from their obscurity. However, they can rarely for long make a mystery of genuine scientific, that is, reality-congruent knowledge.

NOTES

1. Since, viewed from the perspective of sociology, "qualitative" is not the proper conceptual opposite of "quantitative," one must search for a more appropriate term. Nonquantitative, or not exclusively quantitative, empirical sociological research is usually concerned with certain static and dynamic features of human groups. As an alternative to "qualitative" I suggest "figurational."

2. The emphasis upon the reciprocity of economic and violence control functions (and of other vital functions as well) can perhaps appear as a purely theoretical advance in knowledge. In actual fact, it has far-reaching practical implications. To name only one of them, in the Soviet Union a monopolistic organization of violence control — and of knowledge control as well — has developed willy nilly in association with, one might even say in spite of, an officially sanctioned belief system which represents the development of the "economic sphere" as the principal and often even as the sole driving force of social development. It represents the state organization merely as a superstructure in relation to the economic basis. In this case, the representation of the economic sphere as the basis of social development, and thus also of the social distribution of power, obviously conflicts with the observable course of events. It helps conceal the fact that control of the monopoly of physical violence can be as powerful a driving force of social development as the monopolistic control of the economy or, for that matter, of knowledge.

3. See Paul Garrelli, *Le Proche-Orient Asiatique* (Paris: Presses Universitaires de France, 1969), p. 66. Perhaps we should also remember the walls around medieval castles and towns in order to better understand the degree of pacification of these societies.

4. It is not unlikely that priests, in the early stages of the growth of the temple organization, combined with their priestly functions those of controllers of violence, of military protectors of the fields and the incipient irrigation systems. When in the course of time the balance of power between priestly and secular rulers shifted in favor of the latter, they — the leaders of troops, the military rulers — on their part often defunctionalized some of their priests and assumed priestly functions themselves.

5. Gordon Childe, *What Happened in History* (Harmondsworth: Penguin, 1942).

6. See Norbert Elias, *Humana conditio. Beobachtungen zur Entwicklung der Menschheit* (Frankfurt: Suhrkamp, 1985).

7

Modern Systems Theory
and the Theory of Society

NIKLAS LUHMANN

My topic here is "modern systems theory and the theory of society." Behind this, of course, lies the very basic question of whether society can indeed be adequately understood when conceived of as a system. The question arises — if not as a problem, then at least as a premise — at the very beginning of European social philosophy, and it will perhaps be of some interest here to see how it was answered at that time.

I

In the tradition of the schoolmen who followed Aristotle, society was defined as *koinonia politike* or *societas civilis*. If we bear in mind the different degree of abstraction involved, we can translate *koinonia* as *social system*. Society, then, was viewed as a social system, as one system among others, namely the political system. At the same time, however, it was regarded as the all-encompassing social system — one among others and at the same time the whole! The conflicting claims of systems theory and the theory of society are already evident. The conflict was clearly decided in favor of the theory of society. Aristotle did not take the path that would actually have been more natural in the Greek tradition — to maintain the generic concept of *koinonia* as indicating the true locus of society's being; instead, a single example of this genus, the *koinonia politike*, was awarded ontological and ethical primacy. Social science came into being not as the theory of social systems but as that of civil society.

That the problems inherent in this position were not more acutely felt and critically analyzed was the result of the relatively concrete

A lecture given at the 16th Congress of German Sociologists, Frankfurt, 1968. Translation by Gordon Turpin of "Moderne Systemtheorien als Form gesamtgesellschaftlicher Analyse," in Jürgen Habermas and Niklas Luhmann, *Theorie der Gesellschaft oder Sozialtechnologie — Was leistet die Systemforschung?* (Frankfurt: Suhrkamp, 1971), pp. 7-24.

level of concept formation prevailing at that time. The meaning of *koinonia* was not unfolded in the direction of such concepts as function, structure and process, meaning and action, information and complexity, but in that of friendship and law. *Koinonia* was seen as a whole consisting of parts, with the parts subordinate to the whole; it is the end and they are the means. This configuration was then applied to political, or civil, society as the true *koinonia*, and the concept pairs whole/part, above/below, end/means were projected onto one another and explicated with reference to one another. Judged by modern standards, each pair of concepts remains unclear. How they are able to support one another is also unclear. In this way the lack of clarity itself becomes unclear, and classical European social philosophy can achieve its at first so fascinating plausibility.

Although we can, of course, no longer accept or build on this solution, the problem has been passed on to us. In the concept of society (if we neglect the partial concepts of the nineteenth century as passing phenomena) there remains preserved a claim of all-inclusiveness, a claim staunchly defended today by Adorno, for example, but one that still appears to conflict with the universality claims of the theory of social systems — for the theory of social systems still admits only one possibility: to regard society as one social system among others. But how, then, are we to explain the special status of society among these social systems?

It cannot be claimed that this problem has been adequately worked out, let alone resolved, in contemporary theoretical discussions. Certain paths of approach can be discerned, however, and these converge if they are interpreted radically enough. The theory of society is moving, although for the most part outside sociology, toward a radical understanding of the social dimension as a necessary dimension of meaningful experience; systems theory (also primarily outside sociology), in the direction of a radical functionalism. In the end these two features can be combined.

II

Let me briefly sketch the development of these two movements. Classical European social philosophy took as its starting point certain assumptions about the nature of man and divided the social conditions of human existence into two groups: the favorable and the unfavorable. Presupposed hereby was also a given structure of needs and goals. Accordingly, the problems that had to be resolved were dependence on and interference by others, *indigentia et metus*, and the corresponding goals to be attained had to be formulated as peace and justice, *pax et justitia*. These, however, were problems that could be, and had to be, resolved through political domination.

Although modern notions of natural law (e.g., Grotius or Pufendorf) had already begun to undermine this formulation of the problem, it was only in the wake of a modern metaphysics, reoriented toward the subjectivity of self-consciousness, that a radical problematization of the social dimension began. In reflection on the subjective conditions of meaningful experience, one always finds the Other already presupposed as alter ego, as co-constituting subject. The constitution of meaning and of the world — this is the end result of Husserl's struggle with the problem — must be recognized as an intersubjective achievement. Intersubjective constitution, however, means nothing other than the social contingency of the world — i.e., regarding the given from the point of view of other possibilities.

The focal problem of society can no longer be that of the *political contingency* of "the good life," of goal attainment and need fulfillment, but only that of the *social contingency* of the world. A theory of social systems must be adequate to this problem, or it will be able to use the word *social* only in an arbitrarily restricted sense and certainly only in bad conscience.

Systems theory has gone through its own changes independently of these developments in the theory of society, proceeding from an ontological systems concept toward a functional, environment-oriented systems concept. In a rough sketch, we can distinguish four stages in this development:

(1) the old concept of system, still surviving in some definitions, which attempted to define system with the help of the categories *whole* and *part* — i.e., as a purely internal arrangement of the relations of the parts to each other and to the whole, without any reference whatever to an environment;

(2) *equilibrium theories*, which also regarded systems as existing in and of themselves, but at least considered the environment as a source of disturbances that can or cannot be compensated for within the system;

(3) the theory of *open systems*, which assumed that a system could maintain itself only by maintaining and selectively regulating exchange processes with its environment — the interdependence of system and environment is already seen here as something normal and not a deficiency;

(4) *cybernetic systems theories,* which comprehend the relationship between system and environment in terms of a difference in complexity. The environment is regarded here as being overly complex. A system, if it is to survive, must bring its own complexity into an appropriate relationship to that of the environment — Ashby's "requisite variety" — and, as well, compensate for its lower complexity with an increase in selectivity.

Since these developments in systems theory have taken place, with some overlapping, in the order mentioned, they can be interpreted as a trend and extrapolated. This leads to the more general proposition that systems serve the reduction of complexity, namely by stabilizing internal/external differences. Although I cannot show this in detail here, everything that is said about systems — differentiation into parts, hierarchy formation, boundary maintenance, differentiation of structure and process, selective projections or models of the environment, and so on — can be analyzed functionally as reduction of complexity. In this form, systems theory — and this is the idea that I want to put forward for discussion — can approach that transcendental problem of the social contingency of the world; and that means: become the starting point for a theory of society. It remains only to redefine contingency in terms of complexity. The social contingency of meaningful experience is simply one aspect of that immeasurable world complexity that must be reduced through system formation.

III

A theoretically fruitful combination of social theory with systems theory will not be possible if we restrict our concept of system to one based on organisms or information-processing machines. Without doubt, both of these are systems that reduce complexity, so the general concept fits here and does make a comparison possible. It is not my intention to call into question the comparability of social systems with organisms or machines, for only such a comparison will reveal the important difference. Social systems are identified on the basis of *meaning.* Their boundaries are not physical in nature (although, of course, physical boundaries, for example, those of territory, may symbolize meaning boundaries) but are, instead, the boundaries of what may become relevant within given contexts of meaning. Having said this, we must now attempt to show a little more clearly just what it implies.

The concept of meaning is usually explained with some reference to the subjectivity of the act of meaning or intending something —

and thus already in danger of being disqualified as unscientific. It is, however, generally easier to clarify the concept of meaning than that of subject, and we should, therefore, formulate our definition the other way around, defining not meaning through subject but subject through meaning — viz., as a meaning-using system.

Meaning is a special strategy of selective behavior in the face of high complexity. Meaningful identification makes it possible to grasp simultaneously, and deal with as a cohesive unit diverse indications of other possible experiences far too numerous to be attended to individually, to bring unity to the vast profusion of possibility and, while holding on to this larger referential structure, to orient oneself around some particular individual aspect. It is important to note here that although the selection of one particular use or aspect of meaning does neutralize or even negate other possibilities for the moment, it does not simply eliminate them as such, as possibilities. The world is not reduced to only what is actually being attended to each time a selection is made; it still remains as the horizon of references, as the horizon of further possibilities, and thus as the domain from which followup selections or further choices are made. This makes it possible to refer acts of selection to one another, to coordinate them, and thus to increase selectivity, even though the actually given potential for attention remains unchangingly small.

It is important to understand both the power of selectivity based in meaning and the problems surrounding it, among other reasons because it lends a special note to the question of system boundaries. The problem of identifying the boundaries of the system of society — be they territorial, of personal membership, of the integrating culture, or whatever has been offered as a criterion — has still not been adequately solved. Therefore, we must come to realize that what we are dealing with here can only be boundaries of meaning and not, as in the case of things or organisms, physical boundaries. And meaning boundaries are nothing other than aids to selection.

IV

At this point I would like to insert a few remarks on Talcott Parsons' systems theory and the concept of society to be found there. If we compare Parsons' work with the developments in systems theory and the theory of society already mentioned, it will be seen that he takes a halfway position in both areas, a position that always remains precarious and, in my opinion, offers no satisfactory possibility of combining the theory of society with systems theory. His position may be characterized in a few "yes - but" statements:

(1) *It is true* that Parsons manages to overcome the purely behaviorist standpoint and follow Weber in defining action through intended meaning. *But* the concept of meaning itself is not analyzed further. Meaning is treated as a property of human action and not as selection out of a universe of other possibilities.

(2) *It is true* that Parsons no longer presents the problem of order in the way Hobbes did — i.e., with reference to the question of political means — and, instead, refers to the contingency of intended meaning. Order is not equated with political domination but defined as a normative structure that overcomes this contingency and makes possible the complementarity of expectations. *However*, because the concept of meaning is not functionalized we end up with only such statements as: if order is to exist at all, there must be structures, norms, commonly accepted values, institutions, etc. These statements remain empty and the accompanying analytical-classifactory scheme serves merely to further decompose and elaborate them, not, however, to give them substance.

(3) *It is true* that Parsons can use this approach to apply the techniques of functional analysis *within* pregiven system structures. *But* he cannot deal with the broader and more fundamental question of the function of systems themselves or of structure as such. He is quite aware of the limitations inherent in such a structural-functional analysis, but the attempts to overcome them are restricted to the creation of a gigantic and incredibly complex model of interdependent variables instead of involving a radical reformulation of the entire problem of functionalism.

Taken together, all of this prevents Parsons from looking for the function of society itself, from distinguishing society from other social systems by pointing to its specific function. In his search for a *differentia specifica* he turns instead to the old criterion of self-sufficiency, or autarchy. His concept of system, however, presumes that the system is dependent on its environment, and this autarchy criterion has to be relaxed to the point of unrecognizability, to the point where it means no more than independence in the function of normative control of action, a function he feels must be fulfilled at the level of the social system (and not such other action systems as culture, personality, and organism). It simply does not exclude dependence on these other action systems or on the physical-natural environment of action. Parsons cannot, and does not, deny the interdependence between society and its subsystems. We are then left with only the thesis of independence from other societies and their subsystems at the level of normative control of action. Such independence from other systems of the same type is simply one general feature of segmentary differentiation: it also holds true for the relationship among families, churches, hospitals, or political parties. We might, therefore, offer a reformulation: society is the largest given social system with internal functional differentiation alongside which there exist only social systems of the same type; or: society is that level of system formation beneath which functional differentiation exists; or still more pointedly: society is that social system which institutionalizes the ultimately attainable form of functional differentiation.

This reformulation will allow us to accommodate Parsons' concept of society to a conception that is still more general.

The key to combining systems theory and the theory of society lies in a *similar radicalization* of both concepts. The Aristotelian notion of autarchy cannot be combined with the modern theory of open systems, and the questions raised by a transcendental theory of society cannot be answered with a systems concept oriented to organisms or organizations. A combination on an equal level could be achieved, however, if we were to undertake a thoroughgoing functionalization of all concepts used and to ultimately refer them back to the problem of the extreme complexity of the world. Action systems can then be given a functional definition as relationships of meaning among acts which reduce complexity by stabilizing an internal/external difference. And society can then be treated as a special system, as a special case of such complexity reduction — if we can point out just where its specific achievement in reducing complexity lies.

V

In our search for those reductions of complexity that are characteristics of society, we run up against the old idea that there must be something like an ultimate basis for order in human social life — some final source or foundation of meaning, once thought to reside in the cosmic order or, for example, construed as a "social contract." Put into the language of functional systems theory, what we would be looking for here would be the ultimate, most basic mechanisms of complexity reduction. And ultimate and basic would be equivalent to: anchored in the unspecifiable and presuppositionless.

Society — or so we could reformulate the old expectation — *is that social system that institutionalizes the ultimate and most basic reductions.* Society thus supplies the presuppositions upon which all other social systems can build; it supplies the foundation for all structures of the social dimension. Society is that social system whose structures determine just how much complexity a person is able to deal with — i.e., is able to translate into meaningful experience and action.

If we start with this still purely formal statement and try to fill it with meaning, we come to an at first glance disappointing conclusion: those meaning-bestowing processes that were once associated with ultimate models or explanations of the world are no longer institutionalized at the societal level. They have been delegated to relatively well-defined subsystems and functionally specified in the interests of greater performance.

Truth, for example, is no longer an unproblematic everyday affair for the whole society but a matter for science to deal with. Final decisions on truth are left to science, and society must live with the risks involved in having to accept results as true simply because their intersubjective transferability can be asserted. A comparison with older social orders will very soon show just how unlikely, how laden with preconditions and risks, such a differentiation of a distinct mechanism for determining truth actually is.

Law is another example. Our law has become *positive*; i.e., we now make even its validity dependent on decisions taken within the political system. And this means that one subsystem of society determines, in relatively autonomous processes, what law is to be, and its decisions are factually regarded as legitimate and binding. That this really works is, to a sociologist, almost a miracle. The legal profession itself can hardly believe it.

Love can be taken as a third example. Within the classical European tradition *philia* was usually translated as *friendship* and regarded as an essential characteristic of all social systems, especially political, or civil, society. However, we have now come to regard love as individual passion and the family as its proper sphere. The term *passion* already indicates that society has relinquished social control. Love can no longer be accepted as the social basis for a uniform interpretation of the world, but at best as the basis for individually experienced concrete personal spheres.

These few examples should suffice to indicate the problem: the most important, the classical feats of complexity reduction that give structure to behavior within society, are no longer institutionalized as the very nature of society — and thus as an ethical imperative — but, instead, as the achievement of various subsystems. The meaning boundaries controlling such reductions can no longer be brought into agreement: truth, law, love — all have different themes and different boundaries of obligation. This might lead us to conclude that all integration by way of common external boundaries of society has simply disappeared. If this were true, society would no longer be a system. It would no longer have those features which unify all other systems, no longer be an encompassing system excluding others, but at most a nonexclusive structure that made communication possible and interpreted the world — i.e., language. Society as language — this is the end result of such an interpretation — would replace society as a system.

Our topic here, society, would then be very simply removed from sociology into the theory of language, perhaps hermeneutics — but certainly somewhat too simply. Two problems in particular could not be properly dealt with in this manner: the problem of secure boundaries for increasingly differentiated and complex subsystems, which are institutionalized as being almost unrestricted or arbitrary, and the problem of evolution.

Let me finish here by commenting briefly on these two very closely related topics.

VI

If we look at the history of meaning-constituting systems, we notice that increased functional differentiation within systems has always resulted from the system being increasingly differentiated from its environment. Or put somewhat differently: internal differentiation of a system depends on well-established external boundaries and then serves, as functional differentiation, to stabilize the external boundaries. Societies, for example, that were institutionalized on the basis of kinship ties often had difficulties defining their outer boundaries and, just for this reason, difficulty in making the transition from segmentary to functional differentiation. This rule also holds true for societal subsystems: functional differentiation of a political system along the lines of party politics, bureaucratic administration, and the public, can be institutionalized only if role separation and the existence of special political programs make the political system as such distinguishable from the rest of society. These observations lead us to the hypothesis that society (and especially today, where it has attained a hitherto unknown degree of functional differentiation) is also dependent on stable external boundaries. The question is: where do these boundaries lie?

To answer this question, it will be necessary to introduce a second hypothesis: the more complex a system is to become, the more abstractly defined its boundaries must be. As differentiation increases, i.e., as society becomes more complex, we can expect more abstract system boundaries. This would appear to be the reason why society today cannot be adequately defined as an association of individuals, or on the basis of a particular territory or a common culture. All of these relatively concrete boundaries are cut across by unregulated interdependencies. The boundaries of society can no longer be symbolized so concretely. They function as much more abstract selection aids, apportioning to experience and action within society that amount of complexity which can be meaningfully reduced there.

What we are looking at here is primarily a matter of the exclusion of indeterminate and indeterminable (and thus nonmanipulable) complexity. The references to other possibilities implicit in all meaning are cut off where they would jeopardize society's institutionalized selection strategies. Basically unrecognizable possibilities are not admitted. Talking of the "mysteries of God" appearing in nature is no longer accepted — as it was in the middle ages — as an explanation of a given phenomenon. We have no miracles, no luck (in the sense of *kairos* or *fortuna*), no sacred places, and so on. All this has been described, but not explained, as the secularization or demystification of the world. It does, however, serve very well to characterize the essential nature of what we are trying to describe here, namely the exclusion of indeterminate complexity.

The indeterminate complexity that constituted the horizon of experience for older societies has been replaced by models or explanations of the world that present it in terms of reducible complexity. To this belongs the recognition of *all* human beings as subjects whose experience constitutes meaning. There is no fundamental exclusion of the relevance of opinions on grounds of status or group membership. That points to consensus as one form of reduction. In addition, in a material sense, reality is schematized in terms of causality, as an endless context of possible arrangements of causes and effects. Here too, specific forms of reduction are implied, in this case in the binary structure of the scheme where physical regularities or laws, on the one hand, and values, on the other, serve as selection aids. And finally, time is taken as principally open and directed toward the future (i.e., not as circular or recursive). Its forms of reduction are planning and the acceptance of history to bind the future. In each of these cases, the world is modeled in a way that implies extreme complexity, but at the same time schematized in a form that selective strategies can reduce. All-too-drastic, short-circuited forms of reduction (e.g., magic) are excluded, at least as officially institutionalized forms of behavior within society.

These examples bring us to another topic: society's exclusion of the indeterminable changes the way fear is dealt with and with this the moral quality of the society. It changes in particular the style in which institutions and freedom are ethically related to one another. Where very great, almost unrestricted complexity of the world and of society have been institutionalized, the moral certainty of right action no longer suffices as a means of dealing with fear. Security then becomes a problem and a theme — security in the sense of protection from the socially sanctioned actions of others.

I will have to limit myself here to these few remarks. They were intended to show that a theory of the system boundaries of society, even when conceived at a very high level of abstraction, can lead to concrete results. There now remains one last problem — the problem of evolution.

VII

In sociology it has often been claimed that we could well dispense with both the concept and the theory of society. If this were done, however, we would be relinquishing the only level on which the problem of evolution can be adequately discussed. The various special theories of evolution dealing with such specific products of evolution as writing or democracy, or with the development of specific subsystems, such as the modern family, are not adequate to the task we have in mind: they cannot, within their limited scope, grasp the conditions of the possibility of evolution.

This is another reason (and in my opinion a decisive one) for retaining the idea of society as a system. What else could be the object of such development? Even at this point in our argument we will be confronted with the very widespread notion that systems theory is not able to deal with the problem of social change. This notion, however, is quite incorrect and merely diverts our attention away from the real problems of systems theory. There are abundant systems-theoretical analyses of structural change (and almost no causal ones!). The real crux of systems theory is not the problem of social change or the problem of social conflict, but that of society. If systems theory could supply the basis or foundation for a theory of society, it would also be in a position to understand the evolutionary processes that impinge upon and influence the structural formation of societal subsystems.

The theories of evolution of the nineteenth century are hardly adequate to this task. The frame of reference offered by their basic categories still comprises the old dichotomies of species and individual, whole and part, cause and effect. And their style of argument still consists of piling these dichotomies one on top of the other: the survival of the species, or whole, is the result of processes in the parts, or individuals. These ideas and this way of thinking still belong to the classical European intellectual tradition, even where a more modern concept of causality has colored them differently. The new evolutionism in America has not been able to replace this theory. It did introduce numerous modifications and so eroded the old contours that certain weaknesses could be corrected, but this process has left the concept and the theory of evolution so inconsistent and lacking unity that some reflection on the basis of this entire undertaking is now called for.

If we consider the development of systems theory outlined under the headings of functionalism, environmental reference, and meaning and complexity reduction, several starting points for such a reappraisal will emerge.

First of all, we must make a very careful conceptual distinction between the problem of survival or system maintenance and a criterion for progress. Increased longevity, durability, survival are by no means reliable indicators of progress — neither for organisms nor for meaning-constituting systems. In the process of evolution, a system's prospects for survival may increase or decrease, and we should not regard progress as a kind of immanent *telos* of the system.

We will have to try to specify some criterion for progress which, while still systems-theoretical in nature, is independent of the concept of system maintenance or survival. I believe that for sociology this criterion is the complexity of society. In the course of human development, we find an increase in social complexity, i.e., in the number and kinds of possible experience and action. This increase in complexity is not to be found in every single subsystem, but certainly in society as a whole, and this results in pressure on the subsystems to adapt to the new situation — for they must live in a society with increased complexity and, thus, in a more complex world. Not every structure necessarily changes, but the selectivity of all meaning is automatically altered: every given meaning now entails a selection from among more alternative possibilities; every Yes implies more No's — and this changes the stability conditions for all systems. Stability must now be achieved at a higher level of complexity.

What this precisely means and where it will lead us cannot be worked out in detail here. We can only offer a few examples of the direction such analyses might take.

More complex societies must, to a great extent, replace concrete premises for the processing of experience with more abstract ones — i.e., with meaning structures that do not work in such a direct fashion but do have a greater potential for alternatives. Concrete information processing still remains possible but takes on a specific form and specific function that can justify such drastic selectivity, as in the case of love, for example, or art.

Complex societies have to distinguish more sharply between persons and roles and to guarantee their structure and the reliability of behavioral expectations more through roles than through persons. Persons can then be institutionalized as individuals. This does not exclude, but rather makes possible, using them in certain contexts — e.g., in the family or in positions of political leadership — as guarantors of a particular set of expectations, but only within certain limited functional contexts where this is found to be necessary.

More complex societies must institutionalize a high degree of arbitrariness in their subsystems. We can recall here the examples that have already been mentioned: the passionizing of love, the positivization of law, the definition of truth through the mere intersubjective transmissibility of meaning. All this implies release from the control of the overall society and, thus, the acceptance of greater structural risks by the society itself and by its subsystems, which become unpredictable for one another.

More complex societies are dependent on functional differentiation. Because of this they must provide both for more dependence and for more independence among their subsystems. This is possible in principle because of increased complexity — i.e., because of an increase in the ways in which subsystems may be dependent on, or independent of, one another — but in concrete cases it places high demands on behavior, for example, with regard to the precision with which system boundaries and social processes have to be perceived.

These few examples are intended to show that the concept of society involves a level of problem formulation that cannot be relinquished. If the theory of social systems is to be recognized throughout this discipline as the theory of sociology, it will have to show just how it will deal with society as a social system. Previous attempts to deal with this problem have fallen, roughly speaking, into three groups:

(1) classical European moral philosophy (*praktische Philosophie*), which regarded one social system, say the political system, as the whole;

(2) attempts to go beyond this by using metaphorical analogies to the concept of organisms or cybernetic machines. These, however, afford no possibility of recognizing the special characteristics of meaning-constituting systems;

(3) Talcott Parsons' general theory of action systems, which encountered substantial difficulties in its attempt to define systems as boundary-maintaining while at the same time retaining the concept of society as the all-encompassing social system.

None of these solutions is fully convincing. I believe there is another way of dealing with this problem: we must be far more consistent in adopting a functionalist approach, and we must come to see and understand the ways of using meaning to grasp and reduce complexity. Society can then be regarded as that social system whose boundaries exclude indeterminate, nonmanipulable complexity and which thus prestructures the possibilities that can be taken up and realized within.

8

The Tasks of a Critical Theory of Society

Jürgen Habermas

The research program [of the early critical theory] of the 1930s stood and fell with its historical-philosophical trust in the rational potential of bourgeois culture — a potential that would be released in social movements under the pressure of the developed forces of production. Ironically, however, the critiques of ideology carried out by Horkheimer, Marcuse, and Adorno confirmed them in the belief that culture was losing its autonomy in postliberal societies and was being incorporated into the machinery of the economic-administrative system. The development of productive forces, and even critical thought itself, was moving more and more into a perspective of bleak assimilation to their opposites. In the totally administered society only instrumental reason, expanded into a totality, found embodiment; everything that existed was transformed into a real abstraction. In that case, however, what was taken hold of and deformed by these abstractions escaped the grasp of empirical inquiry.

The fragility of the historical-philosophical foundations of this attempt to develop critical theory in interdisciplinary form makes it clear why it had to fail, and why Horkheimer and Adorno scaled down this program to the speculative observations of the *Dialectic of Enlightenment*. Historical-materialist assumptions regarding the dialectical relation between productive forces and productive relations had been transformed into pseudonormative propositions concerning an objective teleology in history. This was the motor force behind the realization of a reason that has been given ambiguous expression in bourgeois ideals. Critical theory could secure its normative foundations only in a philosophy of history. But this foundation was not able to support an empirical research program.

This was also evident in the lack of a clearly demarcated object do-

Translation by Thomas McCarthy of "Aufgaben einer kritischen Gesellschaftstheorie," *Theorie des kommunikativen Handelns* (Frankfurt: Suhrkamp, 1981), 2:560-593 [*The Theory of Communicative Action*, vol. 2, Thomas McCarthy, tr. (Boston: Beacon Press, 1987)].

main like the communicative practice of the everyday life-world in which rationality structures are embodied and processes of reification can be identified. The basic concepts of critical theory placed the consciousness of individuals directly opposite societal mechanisms of integration, which were only extended inward, intrapsychically. In contrast to this, the theory of communicative action can ascertain for itself the rational content of anthropologically deep-seated structures by means of an analysis which, *to begin with*, proceeds reconstructively, that is, unhistorically. It describes structures of action and mutual understanding that are found in the intuitive knowledge of competent members of modern societies. There is no way back from them to a theory of history that does not distinguish between problems of developmental logic and developmental dynamics.

In this way I have attempted to free historical materialism from its historical-philosophical ballast.[1] To do this, one must abstract: (1) the development of cognitive structures from the historical dynamic of events, and (2) the evolution of society from the historical concretion of forms of life. Both help in getting beyond the confusion of basic categories to which the philosophy of history owes its existence.

A theory developed in this way can no longer start with concrete ideals immanent in traditional forms of life. It must orient itself to the possibility of learning processes opened up by a historically attained level of learning. It must refrain from critically evaluating and normatively ordering totalities, forms of life and cultures, life contexts, and epochs *as a whole*. And yet it can take up some of the intentions for which the interdisciplinary research program of earlier critical theory remains instructive.

Coming at the end of a complicated study of the main features of a theory of communicative action, this suggestion cannot count even as a "promissory note." It is less a promise than a conjecture. So as not to leave it entirely ungrounded, I would like in what follows to comment briefly on [several] theses [a to d]. With these illustrative remarks I also intend to emphasize the fully open character and the accessibility of an approach to social theory whose fruitfulness can be confirmed only in the ramifications of social-scientific and philosophical research. As to what social theory can accomplish in and of itself — that resembles the focusing power of a magnifying glass. Only when the social sciences no longer ignited a single thought would the time of social theory be past.

a) On the Forms of Integration in Postliberal Societies

Occidental rationalism arose within the framework of bourgeois capitalist societies. For this reason, following Marx and Weber, I have examined the initial conditions of modernization in connection with societies of this type and have traced the capitalist path of development. In postliberal societies there is a fork in this path: Modernization pushes forward in one direction through endogenously produced problems of economic accumulation, in the other through problems arising from the state's efforts at rationalization. Along the developmental path of organized capitalism a political order of social-welfare state mass democracy took shape. In some places, however, under the pressure of economic crises, the mode of production, threatened by social disintegration, could be maintained for a time only in the form of authoritarian or fascist orders. Along the developmental path of bureaucratic socialism a political order of dictatorship by state parties took shape. In recent years Stalinist domination by force has given way to more moderate, post-Stalinist regimes; the beginnings of a democratic workers' movement and of democratic decision-making processes within the Party are for the time being visible only in Poland. Both the fascist and the democratic deviations from the two dominant patterns depend rather strongly, it seems, on national peculiarities, particularly on the political culture of the countries in question. At any rate, these branchings make historical specifications necessary even at the most general level of types of societal integration and of corresponding social pathologies. If we permit ourselves to simplify in an ideal-typical manner and limit ourselves to the two dominant variants of postliberal societies, and if we start from the assumption that alienation phenomena arise as systemically induced deformations of the life-world, then we can take a few steps toward a comparative analysis of principles of societal organization, kinds of crisis tendencies, and forms of social pathology.

On our assumption, a considerably rationalized life-world is one of the initial conditions for modernization processes. It must be possible to anchor money and power in the life-world as media — that is, to institutionalize them by means of positive law. If these conditions are met, economic and administrative systems, which have a complementary relation to one another and enter into interchanges with their environments via steering media, can be differentiated out. At this level of system differentiation modern societies arose, first capitalist societies, and later — setting themselves off from those — bureaucratic socialist societies. A capitalist path of modernization opens up as soon as the economic system develops its own intrinsic dynamic of growth and, with its endogenously produced problems, takes the lead — i.e., the evolutionary primacy — for society as a whole. The path of modernization runs in another direction when, on the basis of state ownership of most of the means of production and institutionalized one-party rule, the administrative action system gains a like autonomy in relation to the economic system.

To the extent that these organizational principles are established, there arise interchange relations between the two functionally interlocked subsystems and the societal components of the life-world in which the media are anchored. The life-world, unburdened of tasks of material reproduction, can in turn become more differentiated in its symbolic structures and can set free the inner logic of development of cultural modernity. At the same time, the private and public spheres are now set off as the environments of the system. According to whether the economic system or the state apparatus attains evolutionary primacy, either private households or politically relevant memberships are the points of incidence for crises that are shifted from the subsystems to the life-world. In modernized societies disturbances in the material reproduction of the life-world take the form of stubborn systemic disequilibria; the latter either take effect directly as *crises* or they call forth *pathologies* in the life-world.

Steering crises were first studied in connection with the business cycle of market economies. In bureaucratic socialism crisis tendencies spring from self-blocking mechanisms in planning administrations, as they do on the other side from endogenous interruptions of accumulation processes. Like the paradoxes of exchange rationality, those of planning rationality can be explained by the fact that rational action orientations come into contradiction with themselves through unintended systemic effects. These crisis tendencies are worked through not only in the subsystem in which they arise, but also in the complementary action system into which they can be shifted. Just as the capitalist economy relies on organizational performances of the state, the socialist planning bureaucracy has to rely on self-steering performances of the economy. Developed capitalism swings between the contrary policies of "the market's self-healing powers" and state interventionism. The structural dilemma is even clearer on the other side, where policy oscillates hopelessly between increased central planning and decentralization, between orienting economic programs toward investment or toward consumption.

These systemic disequilibria become crises only when the perform-ances of economy and state remain manifestly below an established level of demand and harm the symbolic reproduction of the life-world by calling forth conflicts and reactions of resistance there. It is the societal components of the life-world that are directly affected by this. Before such conflicts threaten core domains of social integration, they are pushed to the periphery — before anomic conditions arise there are appearances of withdrawal of legitimation or motivation. (See figure 8.1.) But when steering crises — i.e., perceived disturbances of material reproduction — are successfully intercepted by having recourse to life-world resources, pathologies arise in the life-world. These re-sources appear in figure 8.2 below as contributions to cultural repro-duction, social integration, and socialization. For the continued existence of the economy and the state, it is the resources listed in the middle column as contributing to the maintenance of society that are relevant, for it is here, in the institutional orders of the life-world, that subsystems are anchored.

Figure 8.1. Manifestations of Crisis in Reproduction Disturbances (Pathologies).

Structural Components / Disturbances in the Domain of	Culture	Society	Person	Dimension of Evaluation
Cultural Reproductions	Loss of Meaning	Withdrawal of Legitimation	Crisis in Orientation and Education	Rationality of Knowledge
Social Integration	Unsettling of Collective Identity	Anomie	Alienation	Solidarity of Members
Socialization	Rupture of Tradition	Withdrawal of Motivation	Psycho-pathologies	Personal Responsibility

Figure 8.2. Contributions of Reproduction Processes to Maintaining the Structural Components of the Life-World.

Structural Components Reproduction Processes	Culture	Society	Personality
Cultural Reproduction	Interpretive Schemata Fit for Consensus ("Valid Knowledge")	Legitimations	Behavior Patterns Effective in Child-Rearing Educational Goals
Social Integration	Obligations	Legitimately Ordered Interpersonal Relations	Social Memberships
Socialization	Interpretive Accomplishments	Motivations for Actions that Conform to Norms	Interactive Capabilities ("Personal Identity")

We can represent the replacement of steering crises with life-world pathologies as follows: anomic conditions are avoided, and legitimations and motivations important for maintaining institutional orders are secured, at the expense of, and through the ruthless exploitation of, other resources. Culture and personality come under attack for the sake of warding off crises and stabilizing society (first and third columns vs. middle column in figure 8.2). The consequences of this substitution can be seen in figure 8.1: instead of manifestations of anomie (and instead of the withdrawal of legitimation and motivation in place of anomie), phenomena of alienation and the unsettling of collective identity emerge. I have traced such phenomena back to a colonization of the life-world and characterized them as a reification of the communicative practice of everyday life.

However, it is only in capitalist societies that deformations of the life-world take the form of a reification of communicative relations — that is, only where the private household is the point of incursion for the displacement of crises into the life-world. This is not a question of the overextension of a single medium but of the monetarization and bureaucratization of domains of action of employees and consumers, of citizens and clients of state bureaucracies. Deformations of the life-world take a different form in societies in which the points of incursion for the penetration of crises into the life-world are politically relevant memberships. Here too, in bureaucratic socialist societies, domains of action that are dependent on social integration are switched over to mechanisms of system integration. But instead of the reification of communicative relations we find the shamming of communicative relations in bureaucratically dessicated, forcibly humanized domains of pseudopolitical discourse. This pseudopoliticization is symmetrical to reifying privatization in certain respects. The life-world is not directly assimilated to the system, that is, to legally regulated, formally organized domains of action; rather, systemically self-sufficient organizations are fictively put back into a simulated horizon of the life-world. While the system is draped out as the life-world, the life-world is absorbed by the system.

b) Family Socialization and Ego Development

The diagnosis of an uncoupling of system and life-world also offers a different perspective for judging the structural transformation of family, education, and personality development. For a psychoanalysis viewed from a Marxist standpoint, the theory of the Oedipus Complex, interpreted sociologically, was pivotal for explaining how the functional imperatives of social systems could establish themselves in the superego structures of the dominant social character. Thus, for example, Löwenthal's studies of drama and fiction in the nineteenth century served to show in detail that the constraints of the economic system — concentrated in status hierarchies, occupational roles, and gender stereotypes — penetrated into the innermost aspects of life history via intrafamilial dependencies and patterns of socialization.[2] The intimacy of highly personalized relations merely concealed the blind force of economic interdependencies that had become autonomous in relation to the private sphere — a force that was experienced as "fate."

Thus the family was viewed as the agency through which systemic imperatives got involved in our instinctual vicissitudes; its communicative internal structure was not taken seriously. Because the family was always viewed only from functionalist standpoints, and was never given its own weight from structuralist points of view, the epochal changes in the bourgeois family could be misunderstood, in particular, the result of a leveling out of paternal authority could be interpreted wrongly. It seemed as if systemic imperatives now had the chance, by way of a mediatized family, to take hold directly of intrapsychic events — a process that the soft medium of mass culture could at most slow down. If, by contrast, we *also* recognize in the structural transformation of the bourgeois family the inherent rationalization of the life-world, if we see that in egalitarian relationship patterns, in individuated forms of intercourse, and in liberalized child-rearing practices some of the potential for rationality ingrained in communicative action is *also* released, then the altered conditions of socialization in the middle-class family appear in a different light.

Empirical indicators suggest the growing autonomy of a nuclear family in which socialization processes take place through the medium of largely deinstitutionalized consensual action. Communicative infrastructures are developing which have freed themselves from latent entanglements in systemic dependencies. The contrast between the *"homme"* who is educated to freedom and humanity in the intimate sphere and the *"citoyen"* who obeys functional necessities in the sphere of social labor was always an ideology. But this has taken on a different meaning. Familial life-worlds see the imperatives of the economic and administrative systems coming at them from without, instead of being mediatized by them from behind. In the families and their environments we can observe a polarization between communicatively structured and formally organized domains of action; this places socialization processes under different conditions and exposes them to a different type of danger. This view is supported by two rough sociopsychological clues: the diminishing significance of the Oedipal problematic and the growing significance of adolescent crises. For some time now psychoanalytically trained physicians have observed a symptomatic change in the typical manifestations of illness. Classical hysterias have almost died out; the number of compulsion neuroses is drastically reduced; on the other hand, narcissistic disturbances are on the increase. Christopher Lasch has taken this symptomatic change as the occasion for a diagnosis of the times that goes beyond the clinical domain.[3] It confirms the fact that the significant changes in the present do escape sociopsychological explanations that start from the Oedipal problematic, from the internalization of societal repression which is simply masked by parental authority. The better explanations start from the premise that the communication structures that have been set free in the family provide conditions for socialization that are as demanding as they are vulnerable. The potential for irritability grows, and with it the probability that instabilities in parental behavior will have a comparatively strong effect — a subtle neglect.

The other phenomenon, a sharpening of the adolescence problematic, also speaks for the significance of the uncoupling of system and life-world. Systemic imperatives do not so much insinuate themselves into the family, establish themselves in systematically distorted communication, and inconspicuously intervene in the formation of the self as openly come at the family from the outside. As a result, there is a tendency toward disparities between competences, attitudes, and motives and the functional requirements of adult roles. The problems of detaching oneself from the family and forming one's own identity have in any case turned development in youth (which is scarcely safeguarded by institutions anymore) into a critical test for the ability of the coming generation to connect up with the preceding one. When the conditions of socialization in the family are no longer functionally in tune with the organizational membership conditions that the growing child will one day have to meet, the problems that young people have to solve in their adolescence become insoluble for more and more of them. One indication of this is the social and even political significance that youth protest and withdrawal cultures have gained since the end of the 1960s.

This new problem situation cannot be handled with the old theoretical means. If we connect the epochal changes in family socialization with the rationalization of the life-world, socializing interaction becomes the point of reference for the analysis of ego development, and systematically distorted communication — the reification of interpersonal relations — the point of reference for investigating pathogenesis. The theory of communicative action provides a framework within which the structural model of ego, id, and superego can be recast.[4] Instead of a drive theory, which represents the relation of ego to inner nature in terms of a philosophy of consciousness — on the model of relations between subject and object — we have a theory of socialization, which connects Freud with Mead, gives the structures of intersubjectivity their due, and replaces hypotheses about instinctual vicissitudes with assumptions about interaction history and identity formation.[5] This approach can (1) appropriate more recent developments in psychoanalytic research, particularly the theory of object relations and ego psychology; (2) take up the theory of defense mechanisms in such a way that the interconnections between intrapsychic communication barriers and communication disturbances at the interpersonal level become comprehensible; and (3) use the assumptions about mechanisms of conscious and unconscious conflict mastery to establish a connection between orthogenesis and pathogenesis. The cognitive and sociomoral development studied in the Piagetian tradition takes place in accord with structural patterns that provide a reliable foil for intuitively recorded clinical deviations.

c) Mass Media and Mass Culture

With its distinction between system and life-world, the theory of communicative action brings out the independent logic of socializing interaction; the corresponding distinction between two contrary types of communications makes us sensitive to the ambivalent potential of mass communications. The theory makes us skeptical of the thesis that the public sphere has been liquidated in postliberal societies. According to Horkheimer and Adorno, the communication flows steered via mass media *take the place* of those communication structures that had once made possible public discussion and self-understanding by citizens and private individuals. With the shift from writing to images and sounds, the electronic media — first film and radio, later television — present themselves as an apparatus that completely permeates and dominates the language of everyday communication. On the one hand, it transforms the authentic content of modern culture into the sterilized and ideologically effective stereotypes of a mass culture that merely duplicates what exists; on the other hand, it uses up a culture cleansed of all subversive and transcending elements for an encompassing system of social controls, which is spread over individuals, in part reinforcing their weakened internal behavioral controls, in part replacing them. The mode of functioning of the culture industry is said to be a mirror image of the psychic apparatus, which, as long as the internalization of paternal authority was still functioning, had subjected instinctual nature to the control of the superego in the way that technology had subjected outer nature to its domination.

Against this theory we can raise the empirical objections that can always be brought against stylizing oversimplifications: that it proceeds ahistorically and does not take into consideration the structural change in the bourgeois public sphere; that it is not complex enough to take account of the marked national differences — from differences between private, public-legal [*öffentlich-rechtlichen*] and state-controlled organizational structures of broadcasting agencies, to differences in programming, viewing practices, political culture, and so forth. But there is an even more serious objection, an objection in principle, which can be derived from the dualism of media discussed above.[6]

I distinguished two sorts of media that can ease the burden of the

(risky and demanding) coordinating mechanism of reaching understanding: steering media, through which subsystems are differentiated
out of the life-world, and generalized forms of communication, which
do not replace reaching agreement in language but merely condense it,
and thus remain tied to life-world contexts. Steering media uncouple
the coordination of action from building consensus in language altogether and neutralize it in regard to the alternative of coming to an
agreement or failing to do so. In the other case we are dealing with a
specialization of linguistic processes of consensus formation that remain dependent on recourse to the resources of the life-world background. The mass media belong to these generalized forms of
communication. They free communication process from the provin-
ciality of spatiotemporally restricted contexts and permit public spaces
to emerge, by establishing the abstract simultaneity of a virtually present network of communication contents far removed in space and
time and by keeping messages available for manifold contexts.

These media publics hierarchize and at the same time remove restrictions on the horizon of possible communication. The one aspect
cannot be separated from the other — and therein lies their ambivalent
potential. Insofar as mass media channel communication flows in
only one direction through a centralized network — from the center to
the periphery or from above to below — they considerably strengthen
the efficacy of social controls. But tapping this authoritarian potential
is always precarious because there is a counterweight of emancipatory
potential built into communication structures themselves. Mass media
can both decontextualize and concentrate processes of reaching understanding, but it is only in the first instance that they relieve interaction
from yes/no responses to criticizable validity claims. Abstracted and
clustered though they are, these communications cannot be reliably
shielded from the possibility of opposition by responsible actors.

When communications research is not abridged in an empiricist
manner and does allow for dimensions of reification in communicative everyday practice, it confirms this ambivalence. Again and again
reception research and program analysis have provided illustrations of
the theses in culture criticism that Adorno, above all, developed with a
certain overstatement. In the meantime, the same energy has been put
into working out the contradictions resulting from the facts that:

1. The broadcasting networks are exposed to competing interests; they
are not able to smoothly integrate economic, political and ideological,
professional, and aesthetic viewpoints.

2. Normally the mass media cannot, without generating conflict, avoid the obligations that accrue to them from their journalistic mission.

3. The programs do not only — or even for the most part — reflect the standards of mass culture; and even when they take the trivial forms of popular entertainment, they may contain critical messages — "popular culture as popular revenge."[7]

4. Ideological messages miss their audience because the intended meaning is turned into its opposite under conditions of being received against a certain subcultural background.

5. The inner logic of everyday communicative practice sets up defenses against the direct manipulative intervention of the mass media.

6. The technical development of electronic media does not necessarily move in the direction of centralizing networks, even though "video pluralism" and "television democracy" are at the moment not much more than anarchist visions.[8]

d) Potentials for Protest

My thesis concerning the colonization of the life-world, for which Weber's theory of societal rationalization served as a point of departure, is based on a critique of functionalist reason, which agrees with the critique of instrumental reason only in its intention and in its ironic use of the word "reason." One major difference is that theory of communicative action conceives of the life-world as a sphere in which processes of reification do not appear as mere reflexes — as manifestations of a repressive integration emanating from an oligopolistic economy and an authoritarian state. In this respect, the earlier critical theory merely duplicated the errors of Marxist functionalism. My references to the socializing relevance of the uncoupling of system and life-world and my remarks on the ambivalent potentials of mass media and mass culture show the private and public spheres in the light of a rationalized life-world in which system imperatives *clash with* independent communication structures. The transposition of communicative action to media-steered interactions and the deformation of the structures of a damaged intersubjectivity are by no means predecided processes that might be distilled from a few global concepts. The analysis of life-world pathologies calls for an (unbiased) investigation of tendencies *and* contradictions. In welfare state democracies, class conflict has been institutionalized and thereby pacified. This does not mean, however, that the potential for protest has been laid to rest altogether. These potentials do, however, emerge along different lines of conflict — and just where we would expect them to emerge if the thesis of the colonization of the life-world were correct.

In the past decade or two conflicts have developed in advanced Western societies which deviate in various ways from the social-welfare-state pattern of institutionalized conflict over distribution. They no longer flare up in domains of material reproduction; they are no longer channeled through parties and associations; and they can no longer be allayed by compensations that conform to the system. Rather, these new conflicts arise in domains of cultural reproduction, social integration, and socialization; they are carried out in subinstitutional — or at least extraparliamentary — forms of protest; and the underlying deficits reflect a reification of communicatively structured domains of action that will not respond to the media of money and power. The issue is not primarily one of compensations that the social welfare state can provide, but of defending and restoring endangered ways of life. In short, the new conflicts are not ignited by distribution problems but by questions having to do with the grammar of forms of life.

This new type of conflict is an expression of the "silent revolution" in values and attitudes that R. Inglehart has observed in entire populations.[9] Studies by Hildebrandt and Dalton, and by Barnes and Kaase confirm the change in themes from the "old politics" (which turns on questions of economic and social security, internal and military security) to a "new politics."[10] The new problems have to do with quality of life, equal rights, individual self-realization, participation, and human rights. In terms of social statistics, the "old politics" is supported by employers, workers, and middle class tradesmen, whereas the new politics finds stronger support in the new middle class, among the younger generation, and in groups with more formal education. These phenomena tally with my thesis regarding internal colonization.

If we take the view that the growth of the economic-administrative complex sets off processes of erosion in the life-world, then we would expect old conflicts to be overlaid with new ones. A line of conflict forms between, on the one hand, a center composed of strata *directly* involved in the production process and interested in maintaining capitalist growth as the basis of the social-welfare-state compromise, and, on the other hand, a periphery composed of a variegated array of groups that are lumped together. Among the latter are those groups that are further removed from the "productivist core of performance" in late capitalist societies,[11] which have been more strongly sensitized to the self-destructive consequences of increasing complexity or have been more strongly affected by them. The bond that unites these heterogeneous groups is the critique of growth. Neither the bourgeois emancipation movements nor the struggles of the organized labor movement can serve as a model for this protest. Historical parallels are more likely to be found in the social-romantic movements of the early industrial period, which were supported by craftsmen, plebians, and workers, in the defensive movements of the populist middle class, in the attempts at escape (nourished by bourgeois critiques of civilization) undertaken by reformers, the *Wandervogel*, and the like.

The current potentials for protest are very difficult to classify because scenes, groupings, and topics change very rapidly. To the extent that organizational nuclei are formed at the level of parties or associations, members are recruited from the same diffuse reservoir. The following catchphrases serve at the moment to identify the various currents in the Federal Republic of Germany: the antinuclear and environmental movements; the peace movement (including the theme of North-South conflict); the citizens' action movement; the alternative movement (which encompasses the urban scene, with its squatters and alternative projects, as well as the rural communes); minorities (the elderly, gays, handicapped, and so forth); the psychological scene, with support groups and youth sects; religious fundamentalism; the tax-protest movement, school protest by parents' associations, resistance to "modernist" reforms; and, finally, the women's movement. Also of international significance are the autonomy movements struggling for regional, linguistic, cultural, and also religious independence.

In this spectrum I would like to differentiate the emancipatory potentials from those for resistance and withdrawal. After the U.S. Civil Rights Movement — which has since issued in the particularistic self-affirmation of black subcultures — only the feminist movement stands in the tradition of bourgeois-socialist liberation movements. The struggle against patriarchal oppression and for the redemption of a promise which has long been anchored in the acknowledged universalistic foundations of morality and law gives feminism the impetus of an offensive movement, whereas the other movements have a more defensive character. The resistance and withdrawal movements aim at stemming formally organized domains of action for the sake of communicatively structured domains, and not at conquering new territory. There is an element of particularism that connects feminism with these movements; the emancipation of women means not only establishing formal equality and eliminating male privilege, but also overturning concrete forms of life marked by male monopolies. Furthermore, the historical legacy of the sexual division of labor to which women were subjected in the bourgeois nuclear family has given them access to contrasting virtues, to a register of values complementary to those of the male world and opposed to a onesidedly rationalized everyday practice.

Within resistance movements we can distinguish further between the defense of traditional and social rank (based on property) and a defense that already operates on the basis of a rationalized life-world and tries out new ways of cooperating and living together. This criterion makes it possible to demarcate the protest of the traditional middle classes — against, for example, threats to neighborhoods by large technical projects, the protest of parents against comprehensive schools, the protest against taxes (patterned after the movement in support of Proposition 13 in California), and most of the movements for autonomy — from the core of a new conflict potential: youth and alternative movements for which a critique of growth sparked by themes of ecology and peace is the common focus. It is possible to conceive these conflicts in terms of resistance to tendencies to a colonization of the life-world, as I hope now to indicate, at least in a cursory way. The objectives, attitudes, and ways of acting prevalent in youth protest groups can be understood, to begin with, as reactions to certain problem situations that are perceived with great sensitivity.

"Green" Problems. The intervention of large-scale industry into ecological balances, the growing scarcity of nonrenewable natural resources, as well as demographic developments present industrially developed societies with major problems; but these challenges are abstract at first and call for technical and economic solutions, which must in turn be globally planned and implemented by administrative means. What sets off the protest is rather the tangible destruction of the urban environment, the despoliation of the countryside by housing developments, industrialization and pollution, the impairment of health from the ravages of civilization, pharmaceutical side effects, and the like — that is, developments that noticeably affect the organic foundations of the life-world and make us drastically aware of standards of livability, of inflexible limits to the deprivation of sensual-aesthetic background needs.

Problems of Excessive Complexity. There are certainly good reasons to fear military potentials for destruction, nuclear power plants, atomic waste, genetic engineering, the storage and central utilization of private data, and the like. These real anxieties are combined, however, with the terror of a new category of risks which are literally invisible and are comprehensible only from the perspective of the system. These risks invade the life-world and at the same time burst its dimensions. The anxieties function as catalysts for a feeling of being overwhelmed in view of the possible consequences of processes for which we are morally accountable — since we do set them in motion technically and politically — and yet for which we can no longer take moral responsibility — since their scale has put them beyond our control. Here resistance is directed against abstractions that are forced upon the life-world; they have to be dealt with in the life-world, although they go beyond the spatial, temporal, and social limits of complexity of even highly differentiated life-worlds, centered as they are around the senses.

Overburdening the Communicative Infrastructure. Something that is expressed rather blatantly in the manifestations of the psychological movement and renewed religious fundamentalism is also a motivating force behind most alternative projects and many citizens' action groups — the pain of withdrawal symptoms in a culturally impoverished and onesidedly rationalized practice of everyday life. For this reason, ascriptive characteristics like gender, age, skin color, neighborhood or locality, religious affiliation, serve to build up and separate off communities, to establish subculturally protected communication communities which accommodate the search for personal and collective identity. The revaluation of the particular, the natural, the provincial, of social spaces that are small enough to be familiar, of decentralized forms of commerce and despecialized activities, of segmented pubs, simple interactions, and dedifferentiated public spheres — all this is meant to foster the revitalization of possibilities for expression and communication that have been buried alive. Resistance to reformist interventions that turn into their opposite, because the means by which they are implemented run counter to the declared aims of social integration, also belongs in this context.

The new conflicts arise along the seams between system and life-world. Earlier I described how the interchange between the private and public spheres and the economic and administrative action system takes place via the media of money and power, and how it is institutionalized in the roles of employees, consumers, citizens, and clients of the state. It is precisely these roles that are the targets of protest. Alternative practice is directed against the profit-dependent instrumentalization of work in one's vocation, the market-dependent mobilization of labor power, against the extension of pressures of competition and performance all the way down into elementary school. It also takes aim at the monetarization of services, relationships, and time, at the consumerist redefinition of personal lifestyles. Furthermore, the relation of clients to public service agencies is to be opened up and reorganized in a participatory mode, along the lines of self-help organizations. It is above all in the domains of social policy and health policy (e.g., in connection with psychiatric care) that models of reform point in this direction. Finally, certain forms of protest negate definitions of the role of citizen, the routines for pursuing interests in a purposive-rational manner — forms ranging from the undirected explosion of disturbances by youth ("Zurich is burning!"), through calculated or surrealistic violations of rules (after the pattern of the U.S. Civil Rights Movement and student protests), to violent provocation and intimidation.

According to the programmatic conceptions of some theoreticians, the partial softening of the social roles of employees and consumers, of clients and citizens of the state, is supposed to clear the way for counterinstitutions that develop from within the life-world in order to set limits to the inner dynamics of the economic and political-administrative action systems. These institutions are supposed to divert out of the economic system a second, informal sector which is no longer oriented to profit and to oppose to the party system new forms of a "politics in the first person," a politics that is expressive and at the same time has a democratic base. Such institutions would reverse precisely those abstractions and neutralizations by which in modern eties labor and political will-formation has been tied to media-steered interaction. The capitalist enterprise and the mass party (as an "ideologically neutral organization for acquiring power") generalize their points of social entry via labor markets and manufactured public spheres; they treat their employees and voters as abstract labor power and subjects of decision; and they keep at a distance — as environments of the system — those spheres in which personal and collective identities can alone take shape. By contrast, the counterinstitutions are intended to differentiate some parts of the formally organized domains of action, remove them from the clutches of the steering media, and return these "liberated areas" to the action-coordinating mechanism of reaching understanding.

However unrealistic these ideas may be, they are important for the polemical significance of the new resistance and withdrawal movements reacting to the colonization of the life-world. This significance is obscured, both in the self-understanding of those involved and in the ideological imputations of their opponents, if the rationality of cultural modernity is rashly equated with the rationality of self-maintenance of economic and administrative action systems — that is, whenever the rationalization of the life-world is not carefully distinguished from the increasing complexity of the social system. This confusion explains the fronts — which are out of place and obscure the real political oppositions — between the antimodernism of the Young Conservatives and the neoconservative defense of postmodernity that robs a modernity at variance with itself of its rational content and its perspectives on the future.

In this work I have tried to introduce a theory of communicative action which clarifies the normative foundations of a critical theory of society. The theory of communicative action is meant to provide an alternative to the philosophy of history on which earlier critical theory still relied, but which is no longer tenable. It is intended as a framework within which interdisciplinary research on the selective pattern of capitalist modernization can be taken up once again. The illustrative observations (a) through (d) were meant to make this claim plausible.

What Marx called "real abstraction" has to do with the social-scientific tasks of a theory of modernity, not the philosophical. Social theory need no longer ascertain the normative contents of bourgeois culture, of art and of philosophical thought indirectly, by way of a critique of ideology. With the concept of a communicative reason ingrained in the use of language oriented to reaching understanding, it again expects philosophy to take on systematic tasks. The social sciences can enter into a cooperative relation with a philosophy that has taken up the task of working on a theory of rationality.

It is no different with modern culture as a whole than it was with the physics of Newton and his heirs: It is as little in need of a philosophical grounding as science. As we have seen, in the modern period culture gave rise of itself to those structures of rationality that Weber then discovered and described as value spheres. With modern science, with positive law and principled secular ethics, with autonomous art and institutionalized art criticism, three moments of reason crystallized without help from philosophy. Even without the guidance of the critiques of pure and practical reason, the sons and daughters of modernity learn how to divide up and develop further the cultural tradition under these different aspects of rationality — as questions of truth, justice, or taste. More and more the sciences drop the elements of world views and do without an interpretation of nature and history as a whole. Cognitive ethics separates off problems of the good life and concentrates on strictly deontological, universalizable aspects, so that what remains from the Good is only the Just. And an art that has become autonomous pushes toward an ever purer expression of the basic aesthetic experiences of a subjectivity that is decentered and removed from the spatiotemporal structures of everyday life. Subjectivity frees itself here from the conventions of daily perception and of purposive activity, from the imperatives of work and of what is useful.

These magnificent "onesidednesses," which are the signature of modernity, need no foundation and no justification in the sense of a transcendental grounding; but they do call for self-understanding regarding the character of this knowledge and an answer to two questions: (1) whether a reason that objectively split up into its moments can still preserve its unity, and (2) how expert cultures can be mediated with everyday practice. The reflection offered in chapters 1 and 3 [of volume 1 of *The Theory of Communicative Action*] are intended as a provisional account of how formal pragmatics can deal with these questions. With that as a basis, the theory of science, the theory of law and morality, and aesthetics, in cooperation with the corresponding historical disciplines, can then reconstruct both the emergence and the internal history of those modern complexes of knowledge which have been differentiated out, each under a different single aspect of validity — truth, normative rightness, or authenticity.

The mediation of the moments of reason is no less a problem than the separation of the aspects of rationality under which questions of truth, justice, and taste were differentiated from one another. The only protection against an empiricist abridgement of the rationality problematic is a steadfast pursuit of the tortuous routes along which science, morality, and art communicate with one another. In each of these spheres differentiation processes are accompanied by countermovements which, under the primacy of one dominant aspect of validity, reintroduce the two aspects at first excluded. Thus nonobjectivistic approaches to research within the human sciences bring viewpoints of moral and aesthetic critique to bear — without threatening the primacy of questions of truth; only in this way is critical social theory made possible. Within universalistic ethics the discussion of ethics of responsibility and ethics of conviction and the stronger consideration given to hedonistic motives bring the calculation of consequences and the interpretation of needs into play — and they lie in the domains of the cognitive and the expressive; in this way materialist ideas can come in without threatening the autonomy of the moral.[12] Finally, post-avant-garde art is characterized by the coexistence of tendencies toward realism and engagement with authentic continuations of the classical modern art that distilled out the independent logic of the aesthetic; in realistic and *engagé* art, moments of the cognitive and of the moral-practical come into play again in art itself, and at the level of the wealth of forms that the avant-garde set free. It seems as if the radically differentiated moments of reason wanted in such countermovements to point toward a unity — not a unity that could be had at the level of world views, but one that might be established *this side* of expert cultures, in a nonreified communicative everyday practice.

How does this sort of affirmative role for philosophy square with the reserve that critical theory always maintained in regard to both the established scientific enterprise and the systematic pretensions of philosophy? Isn't such a theory of rationality open to the same objections that pragmatism and hermeneutics have brought against every kind of foundationalism? Don't investigations that employ the concept of communicative reason without blushing bespeak universalistic justificatory claims that will have to fall to those — only too well grounded — metaphilosophical doubts about theories of absolute origins and ultimate grounds? Haven't the historical enlightenment and materialism forced philosophy into a self-modesty for which the tasks of a theory of rationality must already appear extravagant? The theory of communicative action does aim at that moment of unconditionality which, with criticizable validity claims, is built into the conditions of processes of consensus formation. *As claims* they transcend all limitations of space and time, all the provincial limitations of the given context. Rather than answer these questions here with arguments already set out in the introductory chapter [to volume 1], I would like to close by adding two methodological arguments which speak against the suspicion that the theory of communicative action is guilty of foundationalist claims.

First we must see how philosophy changes its role when it enters into cooperation with the sciences. As the "feeder" [*Zubringer*] for a theory of rationality, it finds itself in a division of labor with reconstructive sciences; these sciences take up the pretheoretical knowledge of competently judging, acting, and speaking subjects, as well as collective knowledge systems that have been handed down, in order to get at the foundations of the rationality of experience and judgment, action and mutual understanding in language. In this context, reconstructions undertaken with philosophical means also have a hypothetical character; precisely because of their strong universalistic claims, they are open to further, indirect testing. This can take place in such a way that the reconstructions of universal and necessary presuppositions of action oriented to reaching understanding of argumentative speech, experience and objectivating thought, moral judgments, and aesthetic critique, enter into empirical theories that are supposed to explain *other* phenomena — for example, the ontogenesis of language and communicative abilities, moral judgment and social competence, or the structural transformation of religious-metaphysical world views, or the development of legal systems, or forms of social integration generally.

From the perspective of the history of theory, I have taken up the work of Mead, Weber, and Durkheim and tried to show how in this type of theory, which is simultaneously empirical and reconstructive in approach, the operations of empirical science and those of philosophical conceptual analysis intermesh. The best example of this cooperative division of labor is Piaget's genetic theory of knowledge.[13]

A philosophy that opens its results to indirect testing in this way is guided by the fallibilistic consciousness that the theory of validity which it wanted to develop on its own can now be sought only in the felicitous coherence of different theoretical fragments. Coherence is the sole criterion of judgment at the level on which theories stand to one another in relations of supplementing and mutually presupposing; for it is only the individual sentences derivable from theories that are true or false. Once we have dropped foundationalist claims, we can no longer expect a hierarchy of sciences; theories — whether social-scientific or philosophical in origin — have to fit with one another. Otherwise one puts the other in a problematic light and we have to see whether it suffices to revise the one or the other.

The test case for a theory of rationality with which the modern understanding of the world is to ascertain its own universality would certainly include throwing light on the opaque figures of mythical thought, clarifying the bizarre expressions of alien cultures, and indeed in such a way that we not only comprehend the learning processes that separate "us" from "them," but also become aware of what we have *unlearned* in the course of this learning. A theory of society that does not close itself off *a priori* to this possibility of unlearning has to be critical also in relation to the preunderstanding that accrues to it from its own social setting — that is, it has to be open to self-criticism. Processes of unlearning can be gotten at only through a critique of deformations that are rooted in the selective exploitation of a potential for rationality and mutual understanding which was once available but is now concealed.

There is also another reason why the theory of society based on the theory of communicative action cannot stray into foundationalist byways. Insofar as it refers to structures of the life-world, it has to explicate a background knowledge over which no one can dispose at will. The life-world is at first "given" to the theoretician (as it is to the lay person) as his or her own, and in a paradoxical manner. The mode of preunderstanding or of intuitive knowledge of the life-world from within which we live together, act, and speak with one another, stands in peculiar contrast, as we have seen, to the explicit knowledge of something. The horizonal knowledge that communicative everyday practice *tacitly* carries with it is paradigmatic for the *certainty* with which the life-world background is present; and yet it does not satisfy the criterion of knowledge that stands in internal relation to validity claims and can therefore be criticized. That which stands beyond all doubt seems as if it could never become problematic; as what is simply unproblematic, a life-world can at most fall apart. It is only under the pressure of approaching problems that relevant components of such background knowledge are torn out of their unquestioned familiarity and brought to consciousness as something in need of being ascertained. It takes an earthquake to make us aware that we had regarded the ground on which we stand every day as unshakable. Even in situations of this sort only a small segment of our background knowledge becomes uncertain, is set loose after having been enclosed in complex traditions, in solidaric relations, in competences. If the objective occasion arises for us to arrive at some understanding about a situation that has become problematic, background knowledge is transformed into explicit knowledge in only a piecemeal manner.

This has an important methodological implication for sciences that have to do with cultural tradition, social integration, and the socialization of individuals — an implication that became clear to pragmatism and to hermeneutic philosophy, each in its own way, as they came to doubt the possibility of Cartesian doubt. Alfred Schutz, who so convincingly depicted the life-world's mode of unquestioned familiarity, nevertheless missed precisely this problem: whether a life-world, in its opaque taken-for-grantedness, eludes the phenomenologist's inquiring gaze or is opened up to it does not depend on choosing to adopt a theoretical attitude. The totality of the background knowledge constitutive for the construction of the life-world is no more at his disposition than at that of any social scientist — unless an objective challenge arises, in the face of which the life-world as a whole becomes problematic. Thus a theory that wants to ascertain the general structures of the life-world cannot adopt a transcendental approach; it can only hope to be equal to the *ratio essendi* of its object when there are grounds for assuming that the objective context of life in which the theoretician finds himself is opening up to him its *ratio cognoscendi*.

This implication accords with the point behind Horkheimer's critique of science in his programmatic essay on "Traditional and Critical Theory":

The traditional idea of theory is abstracted from scientific activity as it is carried on within the division of labor at a particular stage in the latter's development. It corresponds to the activity of the scholar which takes place alongside all the other activities of a society, but in no immediately clear connection with them. In this view of theory, therefore, the real social function of science is not made manifest; it conveys not what theory means in human life, but only what it means in the isolated sphere in which for historical reasons it comes into existence.[14]

As opposed to this, critical social theory is to become conscious of the self-referentiality of its calling; it knows that in and through the very act of knowing it belongs to the objective context of life which it strives to grasp. The context of its emergence does not remain external to the theory; rather, the theory takes this reflectively up into itself: "In this intellectual activity the needs and goals, the experiences and skills, the customs and tendencies of the contemporary form of human existence have all played their part."[15] The same holds true for the context of application: "As the influence of the subject matter on the theory, so also the application of the theory to the subject matter is not only an intrascientific process but a social one as well."[16]

In his famous methodological introduction to his critique of political economy of 1857, Marx applied the type of reflection called for by Horkheimer to one of his central concepts. He explained there why the basic assumptions of political economy rest on a seemingly simple abstraction, which is in fact quite difficult as regards the logic of research and does in fact break new ground as regards theoretical strategy:

It was an immense step forward for Adam Smith to throw out every limiting specification of wealth-creating activity — not only manufacturing, or commercial, or agricultural labor, but one as well as the others, labor in general. With the abstract universality of wealth-creating activity we now have the universality of the object defined as wealth, the product as such or again labor as such, but labor as past objectified labor. How difficult and great was this transition may be seen from how Adam Smith himself from time to time still falls back into the Physiocratic system. Now it might seem that all that had been achieved thereby was to discover the abstract expression for the simplest and most ancient relation in which human beings — in whatever form of society — play the role of producers. This is correct in one respect. Not in another. . . . Indifference toward specific labors corresponds to a form of society in which individuals can with ease transfer from one labor to another, and where the specific kind is a matter of chance for them, hence of indifference. Not only the category "labor," but labor in reality has here become the means of creating wealth in general, and has ceased to be organically linked with particular individuals in any specific form. Such a state of affairs is at its most developed in the modern form of existence of bourgeois society — in the United States. Here, then, for the first time, the point of departure of modern economics, namely the abstraction of the category "labor," "labor as such," labor pure and simple, becomes true in practice.[17]

Smith was able to lay the foundations of modern economics only after a mode of production arose which, like the capitalist mode with its differentiation of an economic system steered via exchange value, forced a transformation of concrete activities into abstract performances, intruded into the world of work with this real abstraction and thereby created a problem for the workers themselves: "Thus the simplest abstraction which modern economics places at the head of its discussions and which expresses an immeasurably ancient relation valid in all forms of society, nevertheless achieves practical truth as an abstraction only as a category of the most modern society."[18]

A theory of society that claims universality for its basic concepts, without being able simply to bring them to bear upon their object in a conventional manner, remains caught up in the self-referentiality that Marx demonstrated in connection with the concept of abstract labor. As I have argued above, when labor is rendered abstract and indifferent, we have a special case of the transference of communicatively structured domains of action over to media-steered interaction. This interpretation decodes the deformations of the life-world with the help of another category, namely "action oriented to reaching understanding." What Marx showed to be the case in regard to the category of labor holds true for this as well: "how even the most abstract categories, despite their validity — precisely because of their abstractness — for all epochs, are nevertheless, in the specific character of this abstraction, themselves likewise a product of historic relations, and possess their full validity only for and within these relations."[19] The theory of communicative action can explain why this is so: the development of society must itself give rise to the problem situations which objectively afford contemporaries a privileged access to the general structures of the life-world.

The theory of modernity that I have here sketched in broad strokes still permits us to recognize the following: In modern societies there is such an expansion of the scope of contingency for interaction loosed from normative contexts that the inner logic of communicative action "becomes practically true" in the deinstitutionalized forms of intercourse of the familial private sphere as well as in a public sphere stamped by the mass media. At the same time, the imperatives of autonomous subsystems penetrate into the life-world and, through monetarization and bureaucratization, force an assimilation of communicative action to formally organized domains of action — even in areas where the action-coordinating mechanism of reaching understanding is functionally necessary. It may be that this provocative threat, this challenge that places the symbolic structures of the life-world as a whole in question, can account for why they have become accessible to us.

NOTES

1. Jürgen Habermas, *Zur Rekonstruktion des historischen Materialismus* (Frankfurt: Suhrkamp, 1976) ["Toward a Reconstruction of Historical Materialism," *Communication and the Evolution of Society* (Boston: Beacon Press, 1979), pp. 130-177].

2. Leo Löwenthal, *Gesammelte Schriften*, vol. 2 (Frankfurt: Suhrkamp, 1981).

3. See Christopher Lasch, *The Culture of Narcissism* (New York: Norton, 1979).

4. See Jürgen Habermas, *Erkenntnis und Interesse* (Frankfurt: Suhrkamp, 1968) [*Knowledge and Human Interests* (Boston: Beacon Press, 1971)]; Alfred Lorenzer, *Sprachzerstörung und Rekonstruktion* (Frankfurt: Suhrkamp, 1970); K. Menne, M. Looser, K. Osterland, E. Moersch, *Sprache, Handlung und Unbewusstes* (Frankfurt: Athenäum, 1976).

5. Jürgen Habermas, "Moralentwicklung und Ich-Identität," in *Zur Rekonstruktion des historischen Materialismus* ["Moral Development and Ego Identity," in *Communication and the Evolution of Society*].

6. See *Theorie des kommunikativen Handelns* (Frankfurt: Suhrkamp, 1981), 2:413ff.

7. D. Kellner, "TV, Ideology and Emancipatory Popular Culture," *Socialist Review* (1979) 45:13ff.

8. From Lazarsfeld's early radio studies on the dual character of communication flows and the role of opinion leaders, the independent weight of everyday communication in relation to mass communication has been confirmed again and again: "In the last analysis it is people talking with people more than people listening to, or reading, or looking at the mass media that really causes opinions to change." C.W. Mills, *Power, Politics and People* (New York: Oxford University Press, 1963), p. 590. See P. Lazarsfeld, B. Berelson, H. Gaudet, *The People's Choice* (New York: Columbia University Press, 1948); E. Katz, P. Lazarsfeld, *Personal Influence* (Glencoe, Ill.: Free Press, 1955). Compare O. Negt, A. Kluge, *Öffentlichkeit und Erfahrung* (Frankfurt: Suhrkamp, 1970), and, by the same authors, *Geschichte und Eigensinn* (Frankfurt: Zweitausendeins, 1981).

9. R. Inglehart, "Wertwandel und politisches Verhalten," in J. Matthes, ed., *Sozialer Wandel in Westeuropa* (Frankfurt: Campus, 1979).

10. See Kai Hildebrandt, Russel J. Dalton, "Die neue Politik," *Politische Vierteljahrsschrift* (1977) 18:230 ff.; S.H. Barnes, M. Kaase et al., *Political Action: Mass Participation in Five Western Democracies* (Beverly Hills and London: Sage, 1979).

11. Joachim Hirsch, "Alternativbewegung — eine politische Alternative," in Roland Roth, ed., *Parliamentarisches Ritual und politische Alternativen* (Frankfurt: Campus, 1980).

12. On this point, Max Horkheimer's essay, "Materialismus und Moral," *Zeitschrift für Sozialforschung* (1933) 2:162 ff., is still worth reading.

13. R.F. Kitchener, "Genetic Epistemology, Normative Epistemology, and Psychologism," *Synthese* (1980) 45:257 ff.; T. Kesselring, *Entwicklung und Widerspruch: Ein Vergleich zwischen Piagets genetischer Erkenntnistheorie und Hegels Dialektik* (Frankfurt: Suhrkamp, 1981). I have examined the methodological peculiarities of reconstructive sciences in connection with the division of labor between philosophy and psychology in Kohlberg's theory of the development of moral consciousness, in "Interpretive Sociale Wetenschap versus Radicale Hermeneutiek," *Kennis Methode* (1981) 5:4 ff.

14. In M. Horkheimer, "Traditionelle und kritische Theorie," *Zeitschrift für Sozialforschung* (1937) 6(2):245 ff., here p. 253 [*Critical Theory* (New York: Herder and Herder, 1972), pp. 188-243, here p. 197].

15. *Ibid.*, p. 260 [p. 205].

16. *Ibid.*, p. 252 [p. 196]. I once characterized the relation between social theory and social practice in the same way: "Historical materialism aims at achieving an explanation of social evolution which is so comprehensive that it encompasses the theory's own contexts of origin and application. The theory specifies the conditions under which a self-reflection of the history of the species has become objectively possible. At the same time it names those to whom the theory is addressed, who can with its help gain enlightenment about themselves and their emancipatory role in the process of history. With this reflection on the context of its origin and this anticipation of the context of its application, the theory understands itself as a necessary catalytic moment in the very complex of social life that it analyzes; and it analyzes this complex as an integral network of coercion, from the viewpoint of its possible transformation." *Theory and Practice* (Boston: Beacon Press, 1973), pp. 2-3.

17. Karl Marx, *Grundrisse der Kritik der politischen Ökonomie* (Berlin: Dietz, 1953), pp. 24 f. [*Grundrisse*, Martin Nicolaus, tr. (New York: Vintage, 1973), pp. 104 f.].

18. *Ibid.*, p. 25 [p. 105].

19. *Ibid.*

III

Diagnoses of Contemporary Society

In his analysis of the emergence of sociology as a specialized discipline, Helmut Schelsky (essay 4) identifies two conflicting sets of expectations as constitutive of the history of German sociology both before and after World War II. On the one hand, sociology is seen as an "empirically and functionally useful discipline," on the other hand as "social philosophy and an interpretation of culture."

Insofar as sociology is attempting to meet the second set of expectations, it needs to address a broader public, including academically trained civil servants, teachers, and administrators, as well as members of the intelligentsia engaged in the formation of public opinion. This audience expects sociology to contribute to a diagnosis of the times and of the fate and future of industrial society and its institutions. Addressing questions of this kind became particularly important during the period of postwar reconstruction in the Federal Republic of Germany. In the German Democratic Republic, by contrast, they received hardly any attention, for there the path of development and reconstruction was clearly determined by the principles of Marxist-Leninism imposed upon East German society by the Soviet Union.

Questions about the future of industrial society and modern culture are consistently at the center of the thought of both Arnold Gehlen (essay 9) and Theodor W. Adorno (essay 10). The Weimar experience as well as that of National Socialism had been formative for them, although in fundamentally different ways. Gehlen supported National Socialism during the 1930s, while Adorno was its determined opponent as well as a refugee from Nazi terror. Wolfgang Schluchter describes Gehlen as a "neo-Saint-Simonian," and his philosophy as one of resigned adaptation to modern technology and to scientific civilization in an age of post-Enlightenment. There is no room in this conception for innovative social intervention and transformative politics. Independent critical intellectuals are therefore criticized by Gehlen for what he sees as their empty and narcissistic subjectivism. Gehlen admires the *esprit de corps* and loyalty to an office or to a calling which one can still find in the military, in the civil service, and among the technical intelligentsia. (See Wolfgang Schluchter, "Von der Regierung über Personen für Verwaltung über Personen. Die technologische Gesellschaft," *Aspekte bürokratischer Herrschaft* [Munich: List Verlag, 1972], pp. 177-236; 2d ed. [Frankfurt: Suhrkamp, 1985].) Adorno's view is antithetical to Gehlen's and, indeed, a defense of critical and self-reflective thought. While critical of Enlightenment rationality in many respects, he is also its prominent defender. Gehlen, on the other hand, diagnoses our time as one of post-Enlightenment. Writers such as Ralf Dahrendorf (essay 11) and Oskar Negt (essay 12) acknowledge a certain continuity of problems and issues inherited from the cataclysmic history of modern Germany. But once again, their responses to them are strikingly different, both from those of each other, as well as from the positions of Adorno and Gehlen, who represent the preceding generation.

While sociology as a specialized science is, for Adorno and Gehlen, little more than just one of various avenues in the exploration of the historical transformations constitutive of modern society, Dahrendorf regards sociology as distinctly helpful for a comprehensive understanding of liberal political culture. Sociological thinking stands for the awareness of the social dimensions of political liberty. And Negt, who as a Marxist is not primarily committed to sociology, places much emphasis upon cultural and political history in order to come to terms with specific features of German history and with the weaknesses of German political culture.

Cultural pessimism (*Kulturpessimismus*) is not as marked a trait in these two younger authors as in the positions articulated by Gehlen and Adorno. But Adorno and Gehlen have something else in common: their examination of modern society in terms of a broad historical perspective, requiring wide-ranging comparisons. Otherwise they differ, of course, greatly in their views of modern society, liberal democracy, and contemporary culture. Dahrendorf and Negt, on the other hand, are closer to the actualities of present-day society; either by employing a pragmatic approach, as in Dahrendorf's reflections on the future of "open" societies, or critically, as in Negt's radical rejection of the restorative features of West German democracy.

Adorno's essay, first delivered as the opening lecture of the 1968 Congress of German Sociologists, polemically introduces the distinction between "late capitalism" and "industrial society" as a central theme for sociology. While granting that in many respects the analysis of the realities of modern capitalism are now beyond the conceptual means of classical Marxism (especially of Marx's own theory), there are no compelling reasons for Adorno to abandon the framework of

Marxian analysis altogether. To the contrary, Adorno argues that the general validity of Marxian theory is becoming ever more evident. While certain Marxian doctrines, such as the "laws" of surplus value and capital accumulation, or the "law" of the general collapse of the capitalist system may be obsolete, state interventionist capitalism may have indeed achieved class compromise, the pacification of class conflict on the basis of welfare-state policies. At the same time, however, the integration of the human population and the human personality into the capitalist system has become nearly total. Consciousness has been domesticated and the capacity of subject populations to resist the manipulation and redirection of their cultural and political possibilities has been weakened and possibly even obliterated. Thus, the Enlightenment's vision of history, which was fully articulated only with the emergence of bourgeois society and the formation of an emancipated "collective societal subject," has begun to disappear from view. What now prevails is the universal "fetishization" of social relations, and freedom as a universal condition is beginning to vanish as a possible human goal.

To Gehlen, such reflections appear arbitrary and reveal the inability of "socially unattached" intellectuals to recognize the realities, thereby accepting the reality of historical constraints. In his appraisal, modern societies represent a new stage in the emergence of human historical cultures, one which is beyond the grasp of a theory such as the Marxian attempt to combine an all-encompassing theory of society with a political action program. Gehlen uses the term "cultural crystallization" (borrowed from Pareto) in order to identify the situation of modernity as one of *"post-histoire."* This situation arises when all the possibilities inherent in a cultural domain have been developed in their basic elements, "so that changes in the premises and fundamental ideas become increasingly unlikely." Modernity no longer possesses the cultural capacity to produce new global ideologies or world views. "The history of ideas is finished," Gehlen says. For Adorno this represents a particularly cynical view of modern history and of modern societies, one that denies the very possibility of articulating the experiences of estranged identity and of social and cultural dislocation so characteristic of the life-experience of people in modern societies (a factor to which Dahrendorf and Negt are clearly responsive, and to which Dahrendorf's concept of "life chances" is meant to be a response).

Gehlen, to be sure, alludes to democratic pluralism and to a global ethics of responsibility derived from Nietzsche (*Ferneethik*). But this allusion by and large does not affect the overall thrust of Gehlen's analysis and his own version of the "end of ideology" thesis. For they do not modify its central feature: that, whether we like it or not, the fundamental institutional and cultural constraints of modern organized society must be accepted if anarchy and an increasing anomie are to be avoided. For Adorno this undoubtedly represents a failure of theoretical nerve and moral will, and a way of avoiding the decisive task of intellectuals, which is to apply judgments about the truth and the falsity of particular conditions to contemporary society. Moral judgments and a comprehensive theory of society are inseparable, Adorno believes, and human needs, for better or worse, express "the condition of society as a whole . . . . A judgment about true or false needs would have to take the structure of society as a whole into account, together with all of its mediations." It is not surprising that Adorno takes sociology to task for its lack of success in coming up with a concept of society in its totality. The abstract logical and classificatory thinking of sociology, as Adorno describes it, fails to do justice to what is specifically "social" about society, its structure. Its adequate grasp requires dialectical thinking. Adorno consequently objects to the tendency in empirical research to separate the knowledge of social facts from an intellectual and moral comprehension of society as a whole. It is due to this "failure of nerve," as it were, that the unavoidable diagnosis of the times is so infrequently taken up in sociology and that the category of "late capitalism" begins to sound absurd and removed from the realities of modern institutions.

Gehlen's lecture is addressed to a quite different audience than Adorno's. He is not really interested in encouraging the discipline of sociology to become self-reflective and to adopt a critical stance toward the centers of power in modern society. Rather, Gehlen asks for a sober acknowledgement of the facts of modern culture by those actively participating in the organization of public and corporate power. Modern social institutions must be appraised with a similar realism and policy alternatives must be designed on this background. There clearly are echoes here of the Prussian-Hegelian faith in the state, in the legitimacy and strength of public authority. If there is something like passion in Gehlen, it is the passion of Nietzsche's *amor fati*, the recognition and acceptance of one's own fate. Gehlen also has an enormous respect for technology and industry as collective achievements of modern society.

Adorno's and Gehlen's diagnoses of contemporary conditions are very different from the effort by Dahrendorf to establish and to reform a liberal political culture in the West German Federal Republic since 1945. Dahrendorf's sociological writings, including his *Life Chances*, should be seen as a contribution to the self-clarification of political liberalism and of its program of social reform. A sociological diagnosis of the times is important for Dahrendorf, because "the social scientist must do more than merely pursue social science. Concern with the theory of social processes is barren if it is based on no more than a detached theoretical interest." It is from this vantage point that Dahrendorf develops the critique of Marx contained in our selection.

Marx, Dahrendorf argues, "could never rid himself of the Hegelian sickness of having to try to make sense of the process of history by assuming unsatisfactory beginnings and a totally satisfactory end." His view represents a genuine sociological perspective on history, which is quite different from the one shared, at least in its premises, by Adorno and even by Gehlen, even if the latter might have preferred to reverse the relation of beginning and end, given his admiration for the "heroic cultures" of the distant past. Negt's account of the failure of the liberal tradition in German history is inspired by the anticipation of socialism as the fulfillment of democracy. He takes a more activist view of the future than Adorno, with whom he shares the belief in the continued relevance of Marx. Negt's vigorous critique of the "antiradical" legislation of the 1970s, introduced in the wake of the student protests and of the antiauthoritarian movement of the late 1960s as well as the subsequent, but not necessarily connected, terrorist incidents of the 1970s is inspired by his belief that a liberal political culture has always tended to give way in German history to authoritarian governments responding to and encouraging a mindless fear of socialism and especially of communism. Like the other selections in this part of the book, Negt's essay documents the concern in German sociology and social thought with the appropriate organization of society as a central issue of the diagnosis of contemporary society.

9

The Crystallization of Cultural Forms

Arnold Gehlen

In the course of not much more than a hundred years, Americans and Europeans constructed an unprecedented reality: they brought together achievements in technology and industry and created a new world that has become the basis for their continued existence; they established themselves in a new environment, beyond comparison both in its powerfulness and in its artificiality. The physical and intellectual persuasiveness of modern culture has proven irresistible. One nation and continent after another has cast off its oldest traditions and abandoned its fundamental and organically grown assumptions in order to gain entry into this new world. This enormous process, which, as Max Weber predicted as early as 1908, will transform the external and internal face of humanity to the point of unrecognizability, has been accompanied by catastrophes of equal magnitude. The first four-year war based on technology was also responsible for humanity's first common experience — an experience which spanned the entire globe.

In Germany, the often painful process of industrialization, which lasted for generations, was observed right from the start with the bright and alert consciousness of one of the most intellectually active nations on this earth. Historical self-reflection immediately recognized the epochal nature of the process. We invented new machines and a new morality, we simultaneously suffered and benefited from them, we observed them and noted their consequences. To get a sense of the fantastic range of the consequences of this process, it is perhaps sufficient to realize that approximately a hundred years ago, in 1867, Otto invented the internal combustion engine and Marx published *Das Kapital*. Moreover, in the same year, Bismarck introduced universal suffrage in the North German Parliament. Events were thus simulta-

Lecture delivered in Bremen (February 24, 1961). Translation by Clare A. McMillan of "Über kulturelle Kristallisation," *Studien zur Anthropologie und Soziologie* (Neuwied und Berlin: Luchterhand, 1963), pp. 3-17. Also in vol. 6 of the Arnold Gehlen *Gesamtausgabe* (Frankfurt: Vittorio Klostermann, 1983).

neously transformed into science, sparking quick and powerful formulations of programs and political movements.

The construction of this new milieu in which we live was carried out against bitter opposition from every sector — political, economic, intellectual, and artistic. What we call "cultural critique" represents only one, entirely justified, aspect of these disputes. It is an effort to express by way of rational argument the discontent, helplessness, and suffering of those who, for whatever reason, remain unconvinced. This sort of passionate critical engagement is present in the works of all the important writers and philosophers of this period: we can find it, for example, in Scheler, Musil, Benn, and Thomas Mann. Among the extraordinary chaos of voices which reflected upon and interpreted both the past century and the present one, one often despairs of ever finding any orientation. Even Benn was swayed by the vision of total, nihilistic chaos. I believe, nonetheless, that certain stabilizing influences can now be observed, which permit a description of this situation. Perhaps it will then no longer seem so unpredictable and without direction. There are traces of what I call "crystallization." In attempting such a description, however, one must above all take note of what has disappeared: for example, that blindness toward the fundamental laws of technology and industry which runs through Nietzsche's entire work. I can still clearly remember my indignation as a student upon reading a remark by Spengler to the effect that he hoped his writings would contribute to converting philosophy students into technicians. Such advice seems entirely reasonable to me today.

In the past century and even in our own, many attempts were made to bring order into this confused chaos of ideas and topics from all ages and regions of the world by organizing them from the point of view of a specific science, which then naturally took on an air of supercompetence. Such attempts have entirely ceased. In these earlier days one did not yet doubt the capacity of the sciences to shape popular beliefs. Such attempts therefore took on a missionary zeal and aspired to a new intellectual organization of society. Nietzsche hoped to achieve this by way of philosophy. His scheme extended from biology and physics to the history of culture and religion. As he touched with extraordinary skill on the events relevant to the times, he used them to fuel his passionate pursuit of an anti-Christian ethic. Nietzsche constitutes a clear example of what I would describe as the irreproducible past. He wants to derive clear-cut prescriptions for action from a comprehensive interpretation of the world. I call such an attitude the "great key-attitude" [*grosse Schlüsselattitüde*]. It first emerged with Christianity, and, as has often been noted, the more recent comprehensive systems are little more than secularized Christian attempts to combine an interpretation of the world with universally valid directions for action.

During the past two thousand years, this form of behavior has become so ingrained that it is now entirely secularized. Attempts have repeatedly been made to generalize the explanatory bases and the ways of viewing reality of the individual specialized sciences and to derive ethical conclusions from them. Darwin in this way developed his zoology into an evolutionary history of the human race. His fundamental concepts of the struggle for survival and of the survival of the fittest, by which he explained the changes undergone by a species, were also understood as a biological and ethical justification of British competitive capitalism. The effect of these ideas was extraordinary. They caused economically successful Europeans to imagine themselves at the center of life. The industrial age was justified in terms of inherent laws of existence.

Systems of this nature constitute world views, i.e., comprehensive interpretations of life drawn from philosophy or from the sciences, which provide the basis for ethical prescriptions. These world views, which have almost always been atheistic, are substitute religions. Freud's psychoanalysis should also be viewed from this perspective. Although it refrained from making assertions about the external world, it nevertheless assumed the correctness of natural science and its mechanistic explanations. In its fundamental idea and aim, Freud's extraordinary and original psychology integrated the entire history of human culture and of ethics, including the arts, and it also supported its claims by way of specific analyses. In regard to ethics, the liberation of human beings from guilt feelings and from the notion of God still showed something of the old vigor of the Enlightenment. But Freud's later all-pervasive pessimism in regard to the human possibilities for happiness indicates a fundamental resignation. Socialist ideas are not entirely absent in Freud either, and he thus is close to that most influential of all systems, the Marxian, which brought together a well-thought-out philosophy of history and economic theory, on the one hand, and clear guidelines for action, in the sense of the class struggle, on the other. Marx achieved all this the more effectively as he not only addressed the educated classes but also by attempting to organize the disadvantaged and by promoting solidarity among them, was concerned with the fate of collectivities.

These are only a few examples of world views with both theoretical and practical intent. When such a world view is translated into a fundamental disposition, into an inner need of the human being, I call it a "great key-attitude." Until well into the twentieth century, there were hardly any philosophers who did not want to become effective in this sense. One might even say that the great prestige enjoyed by science, both in the past century and in the present one, was accorded to it from within. For science was ultimately expected to shed light on such important questions as "What can we know?" and "What should we do?" The answer to the third of the Kantian questions, "What may we hope for?", had for all practical purposes already been given, if one believed, as this bourgeois era in fact did, in inner-worldly progress.

It is of enormous importance for the understanding of our own time and of ourselves to realize that this sort of intellectual attitude is now obsolete. Such an attitude cannot reemerge once again. Earlier on, however, the internal dynamics of science pressed precisely toward this end. The "great key-attitude" is still alive among many people as a sort of empty model, but this model is now without a worldly content and without clear ethical prescriptions. Marxism survived as a theory because it was institutionalized by a world power for which it serves as a political doctrine. Ideas can in any case generally survive only if they are embodied in institutions. The other great systems of that time, including Nietzsche's philosophy, are now little more than important chapters in literary history, or the substance of their world view has evaporated and they have, like psychoanalysis, become highly specialized and professionalized.

Let us consider the different phenomena which become understandable once we adopt this viewpoint. The first phenomenon upon which I shall touch briefly concerns the consolidation of religion — an event that appeared utterly improbable one hundred years ago, and that is by no means limited to Christianity alone. Since, with the exception of Marxism, atheistic substitute systems have disappeared, religion remains at least *in foro interno* the undisputed moral authority. However, religion has completely renounced any judgment on the technological and industrial transformation of the external world and instead concentrates on the human element. It has been integrated into society.

I would now like to explain why systematic world views can no longer emerge. There are both practical and theoretical reasons for this. It soon became evident that the realization of ideas (that is, the adjustment of reality in the direction of the purity of the idea) inevitably leads to bloodshed. Reality is not compatible with the ideal, which consequently takes revenge upon it. Thus Mommsen spoke of the executioner's axe that is always dangling unconsciously behind the conscious idea. After two world wars, which were fought at enormous sacrifice under the banner of ideas, the only ideas and world views that now seem to have a future are those that have already become a functional part of the established social order and of the operating rules of large industrial societies. They have emerged as the true constituents of industrial societies and, as a reality which was paid for dearly, are now beyond discussion. This is how things are in the Western and Eastern halves of the globe. It is hard to imagine that any system of ideas with world-shaping claims similar to the Marxist system a hundred years ago or to Nietzsche's system eighty years ago could even gain a hearing today. This is beyond the possibilities of our epoch. But this also explains the present state of philosophy.

We can hardly overestimate the significance of the end of a philosophy involving the key-attitude. It was philosophy which gave rise to the explosions that reverberated from Voltaire right into the twentieth century and also left its impact on the more gradual yet irreversible changes of the human spirit. Furthermore, a substitute religion arising from an excessively specialized science, such as Darwinism or biologism, is also no longer a real possibility, quite apart from the fact that biologism was in Germany compromised on the political level. The present state of the sciences no longer permits the extension of scientific findings into an ethical system or a world view. Earlier, such attempts were linked to a still relatively primitive developmental stage of the sciences, at which the interconnectedness between phenomena was still overestimated.

The theme of specialization must be addressed here. Every serious science has now become split into so many different specialized branches that it would firmly resist all claims to its own supreme competence, for it would then have no voice left at all. Today there are fully developed technical languages in chemistry and physiology, as well as in psychology, etc., all of them concerned with a clearly defined subject matter confined to a specific area. Each of these technical languages (among which are also the languages of law and medicine) demands consent; in other words, anyone wishing to do research in these fields cannot but accept that the concepts employed in them capture the respective subject matter quite precisely. What is lacking, however, is a general language demanding consent that cuts across or is set above these particular disciplines. A language that encompasses at least several of these specialized fields does not exist. This is to say that one can at best speak only in a dilettante fashion about the cosmos of the sciences.

The division between expert and layman has now become final. The concepts and approaches to problems employed in every special branch of science, with its present degree of specialization, have become so difficult to grasp and so abstract that they are completely incomprehensible to all but those who have long years of specialized study behind them. Even a well-educated person interested in a particular subject area outside the realm of his own work can only gratify his interest in a simplified fashion that may already be obsolete. Consequently, the attempts to popularize difficult theories have come to a halt. In the 1920s, many works appeared which sought to translate Einstein's theories into educated lay language. No one attempts such things today because in many areas, including sociology, as a consequence of the ongoing trend toward specialization, communication even among colleagues has become more difficult and even a secure overview within any one field has become problematic. Consequently, outside of one's own immediate area of expertise, one simply assigns competence, information, and responsibility to others. In other words, power of judgment is delegated to others.

The sciences therefore are in a situation that is prevalent throughout modern society, above all, in the economy, in government, and in politics. Everywhere the informed are separated from the uninformed, the experts from the laymen, the professionals from the dilettantes; and most importantly, this state of affairs has been established everywhere without friction, has become accepted. Curious phenomena may arise when fields in which until recently the competence of everyone was acknowledged suddenly become inaccessible as a result of the introduction of experts. This is the situation in the arts, where there is now an art for artists, reserved for a highly aware group of connoisseurs — an art that lay people find difficult to understand. It is hardly possible any more to imagine a form of folk literature or folk art that would not immediately appear antiquated and trite. In the 1920s, things had not progressed to quite this extent: Barlach's art, for instance, was popular but at the same time expressed the mood of the times. This also belongs to the past.

Given these circumstances, it is clear that global views of the world can no longer be formulated within the sciences, just as fundamental reforms can no longer be instituted somewhere within the total system of social practice. Fundamental reforms in government or education are similarly impossible. Given the abundance of data available in those areas, such reforms would have to be thought out at such a high level of abstraction and with such a lack of transparency that only dilettantes could continue to imagine that their views could remain relevant.

I would like to dwell a little longer on the state of the sciences and describe their institutional stabilization. It is well known that the natural sciences are pursued not only in universities but also, involving a far greater investment of personnel and capital, in the large industrial plants and in state-owned laboratories, where, for example, nuclear research is concentrated. The institutional framework of the medical sciences is readily apparent in clinics, which function at the same time as research centers. Above all, it is evident in the organization of the health insurance system, a giant body devoted to the calculation, processing, and payment of health insurance claims — a body that services 75 percent of the total population in Germany. We tend to view jurisprudence and the law in turn as presenting a grand rational system of concepts and norms that one can organize neatly in law books; indeed, this is how it is taught. To see how this system really works, however, one must look at the numerous agencies through which lawyers day by day translate the law into actions — not only in the courts and lawyers' offices, but also in the parliaments and their legal committees, in such supranational organizations as the Organization for European Economic Cooperation (OEEC) with its machinery for reaching agreements, in the legal departments of industrial corporations, in the countless government offices (which must all behave in a legally correct manner since every government act can be challenged in the courts), in city halls, in the headquarters of trade unions, etc.

I stated earlier that a coherent view of the world can no longer be gained by way of the sciences, but to attempt such a thing outside of the sciences would be even more absurd. We are now beginning to realize that this failure need not seem so disquieting, because all the sciences are in fact interconnected, perhaps not in the scientists' heads — no synthesis can be achieved there — but in the reality of society as a whole. They all function as part of the enormous superstructure of industrial society. The interconnections thus exist in social practice, where they are as all-pervasive as the air we breathe. There are chemicals today in every loaf of bread and the results of chemistry circulate in our bloodstream, every building testifies to statical calculations, every change of residence involves the techniques of mechanical engineering, and every administrative action, jurisprudence. And when, as a sociologist, I make a statement or express an "opinion," it occurs to me on occasion that these have already been classified in statistical surveys.

This is true of all the applied sciences — they all function as part of the superstructure of society as a whole. For this reason, they are all caught up in full and unbroken development, they are compelled to progress as they develop, and they are protected from stagnation and Confucianism precisely because they are so tightly interwoven with practical reality. The sole exceptions are philosophy and the studies of classical antiquity. They are no longer self-evidently valid and now find themselves in a crisis of self-justification. What I have described to you is a *"culture encadrée"* — the culture of sciences built into a supermachine, which operates with the strength of 50 million people. There is no self-doubt there; step-by-step continued development, and hence progress, is taken for granted. However, at no place within this entire system, which is becoming increasingly saturated with confidence in its scientific organization, does one encounter that great intellectual hope of new vistas opening before us, the expectation of new spaces to explore — a hope often exaggerated and disappointed, but nonetheless encouraging and vitalizing, like the expectations contained in the ideological aspirations of the past century. One can say today that this youthful energy survived the First World War but not the Second.

To complete our picture, we should now consider the two halves of the globe, East and West, each with powerful centers of concentration of this industrial, technological, scientific culture. A political ideology has been incorporated into each of these systems; each is infused to its last fibers by such an ideology, which penetrates to the innermost part of human existence and perpetuates itself in the external features of everyday life. The democratic idea is the older and more flexible of the two. It is compatible with many different forms of government; it is cosmopolitan and surprisingly tolerant toward the Left; it consists more of an attitude and set of morals than of doctrine and dogma. The Marxist idea, on the other hand, is scientific, bureaucratic, erudite, and doctrinaire; it picks out its own opponents and demands definite engagement; it aspires to be universal and makes materialist statements about the objective world. In their understanding of human beings, these two ideologies are fundamentally opposed; their ideas of what is best for people are incompatible. They are two ethical universes which permeate these giant systems just like the sciences mentioned earlier.

Whoever is in agreement with the analysis I have presented thus far, will already have in hand the evidence for what I term "cultural crystallization." This expression may be open to misinterpretation because it calls to mind something inorganic. It originated with the Italian sociologist Vilfredo Pareto, although to him it meant something quite different. I find it a helpful term and propose to use it in characterizing the state of affairs in a given realm of culture that occurs as soon as all the fundamental potentialities contained within it have been developed and counterpossibilities and antitheses have been discovered and either absorbed or eliminated, so that henceforth changes in the premises and the basic views become increasingly unlikely. The crystallized system may still have the semblance of considerable fluidity and activity, and, as observed earlier, in numerous individual areas progress is indeed still made. New developments, surprises, and genuine creativity are all still possible, but only within the area already staked out and only on the basis of the already given fundamental premises, which are no longer called into question.

Many people see the general situation in which we live as somehow restorative. This, I believe, is wrong. Any such idea is derived from an earlier period in world history and not from an analysis of what actually exists now. I would like to suggest that we discard such concepts and adopt instead the term "crystallization," which does not rule out but rather contains progress in specific areas in the specialized sciences. Once one accepts this view, it will become clear that crystallization even exists in such an extraordinarily turbulent and colorful realm as that of modern painting. The last great events in this field took place around 1910. At that time, artists turned away from the external world and began to explore the subjective sphere, to sound out the subject in painting. This did not generate an infinite number of basic possibilities, but rather a limited number — three, four, five, not more. These in turn were developed in rapid succession. They were not subsequently abandoned and no new ones were found; instead, they formed the basis for what was to come, namely the unfolding and the playing out of what had become visible, the developing of what was now possible. They are still of importance to us, but we forget that these great revolutions occurred a long time ago. It is extremely unlikely that further fundamental changes will take place, and for this reason the notion of an "avant-garde" is actually comical — it is quite out-of-date. The movement is not a forward progression, but rather a process of enrichment and consolidation in place. Anyone who speaks of the avant-garde today is referring only to freedom of movement as a program, but this has long been conceded. The situation described here exists, from a cultural perspective, everywhere in the same form. I have suggested the term crystallization to describe it, and I would like to point out that the variety, abundance, and flexibility of the accompanying phenomena conceal the rigidity of the fundamental decisions. One must consider both aspects together.

If we now return to my earlier topic of the two great halves of the globe, each with its fundamental ideology, then it may come as less of a surprise when I say that we can no longer expect anything from the history of ideas. Humanity needs to establish itself within the now existing radius of the great guiding ideas, along with the range of variations that accompanies them. The meaning of civilization is fixed for us in its basic possibilities. This holds just as surely as humanity's general understanding of religion still remains entirely dependent upon the great doctrines of salvation, even if these were conclusively articulated long before our time. I would only add to this the reasonable assumption that the so-called "developing countries" will not produce a positive third ideology. For global ideologies of this nature — including those whose historical time has passed (such as fascism) and those initial impulses that were never developed (such as Rousseau's and Nietzsche's redemptive theories) — are without exception of European origin. None have originated outside of this region of the world. I will therefore take the risk of predicting that the history of ideas is finished, and that we have arrived at the state of post-history. Gottfried Benn's advice to the individual, "Reckon your resources" ["Rechne mit deinen Beständen"], is now more appropriately directed at humanity as a whole. Consequently, in this epoch in which we have gained an overview of our planet both on a visual level and in terms of our knowledge about it, and in which no significant event will pass unnoticed, the world has also lost all elements of surprise. As in the realm of religion, here, too, the alternatives are known and are in every case final.

I have argued that we now face the finality of the existing ideological systems, which are split between the two political halves of the globe where they are part of the status quo and have materialized into institutions. As I said earlier, it is completely unlikely that a new ideology will arise. As I have also shown, it cannot originate from the sciences either, for these have become extremely specialized, highly diversified, and developed. Only during their much more primitive stages could one have believed that mechanics, biology, or psychology could satisfy our need for an all-encompassing overview. It is not possible to obtain a bird's-eye view of the system of all sciences, a unified view of the whole, for the fundamental reason that we can only create

islands of coherence, while the sciences are otherwise generally isolated from each other with their own complex technical languages. I
have said elsewhere that the different chapters of what we can know
no longer fit into a single volume. Astronomers have the impression
that the universe is flying apart in all directions. The situation is much
the same regarding the state of our knowledge about earthly reality.

There is no vantage point in consciousness from which one can
survey everything — in other words, there is no philosophy in the old
sense. Progress, however, is still possible wherever the successful integration of technology and industry in a highly developed society needs
science in order to function, or where research can readily find a practical application. Consider for example the different branches of chemistry, medicine, statistics, and jurisprudence. Sociology is also fortunate
to have a practical branch — the not very well-loved survey research
— which allows it to achieve a considerable degree of effectiveness.
The degree to which our society is being saturated with every kind of
technical discipline and technical knowledge is thus increasing inexorably. A level of general scientific knowledge appropriate to the developmental state of society has become necessary simply to keep it
functioning, and this level is on the rise. Even in the middle ranks of
government or industrial management, an astonishing degree of
abstract knowledge is required of the individual worker. It would be
absurd to ask for the meaning of all this: we live in a highly dynamic
society which is pluralistic in its very presuppositions. It no longer establishes definite boundaries for experience, thus confronting people
with an open world.

Bearing all this in mind, the era of the great ideological formations
which began in 1789 now appears over and done with indeed; it has
clearly passed, and all that remains is what has already been successfully institutionalized. The different systems of revolutionary ideas
put forth from 1789 on appealed to the individual. They imputed the
ability to take direct action to individuals and enlisted their (physical)
cooperation in creating a dream world. This was of course in keeping
with the more primitive grasp at that time of the problems of society.
Ardent disciples, fanatics, members of the avant-garde, were all
needed for the great struggle, for overturning the social order by means
of small arms. Today, however, as Riesman has very correctly observed
in *The Lonely Crowd*, it has become impossible to devise a program that
could decisively change the relations between economic and political
life. Such a program could find no seam to penetrate in the powerful,
smoothly running machine which even preplans responses to its own

malfunctioning. Thus, the ideologies which have survived to this day face no new rivals; they indicate definitive possibilities just as the major religions do, whose consolidation is one of the great unexpected events, a hundred years after they were seriously threatened by the onslaught of natural science images of the world.

Religion has apparently now passed through the danger zones it encountered in the West during the age of Enlightenment, and in Asia during the onslaught of white civilization, which has now been repulsed. In the areas of ideology and religion, one must now reckon with the finality of the positions that have been formulated today. Consequently, the intellectual energy of people is manifested in the further development of details in the great scientifically organized superstructure. And the arts and the humanities can continue to skirt with an attractive air of irresponsibility a core of serious problems — problems such as those arising simply from everyone's elementary will to live. On an earth that has shrunk in practical and information-related terms, the will to live present in everyone has become an urgent problem and the most pressing political issue.

If what I have said here appears even in some measure correct and realistic, then the next step will be to see how two major endeavors (which at this time are ready for the planning and gradual implementation stage) fit into the whole. In Germany today, there are two urgent political issues: aid to developing nations; and the reorganization of post-secondary education. The latter problem has arisen as a result of the great numbers of students — possibly as many as a quarter million per year — now applying to institutions of higher learning. The question arises whether the existing institutions and facilities, and also the internal organization of the disciplines, can accommodate such an onslaught. Behind this question, however, lie even more serious problems. The sharp increase in the number of students in Germany represents only one aspect of a world-wide process. In America, in Russia, and Japan, in India — everywhere the same thing is occurring. The professions [Intelligenzberufe] are proving to be overwhelmingly attractive to an ever-growing number of people. Upward social mobility and effectiveness appear to be linked here. It is impossible to assess the powerful lure of life in the public eye, which those pursuing professional careers expect to enter. In fact, failure to participate in it is increasingly perceived as an existential loss. As yet no one can say how these groups will come to terms in the long run with their own growing numbers and with their diminished opportunities for exercising their formative powers (which is in fact precisely what I have discussed until now) as well as with their generally disappointing lack of success in life. But far more urgent priorities still lie ahead. Closely related to these tendencies is a matter of imperative importance: no matter what may happen, the quality of intellectual endeavor that for many decades has been channeled into the industrial, technical, scientific system must be upheld. We must examine objectively the very important question of whether Germany, in the past always one of the centers of scientific effort, can continue to maintain its position. As yet we do not know how to formulate this vital problem precisely. However, there do appear to be in our young people certain elements of complacency, indifference, and distraction which are cause for concern. One could imagine that the two aspects I have just mentioned — the importance of maintaining the level of scientific endeavor and the difficulties arising from the influx of people — might be dealt with by incorporating strict demands and rewards into a much more rigorous process of selection. However, the existing university structure does not provide the means for implementing this sort of selection process.

The other pressing political issue we face is that of aid to developing countries. The popularity of this undertaking (according to survey results) has to do with the belief that it represents a new opportunity to get ahead in the race between East and West. This might be true, and I sense in the way in which we view this issue a bit of that old ideological fervor with which, from the Reformation to Marxism, we Germans have supplied the world again and again. But behind all this lie even greater challenges which are much more difficult to meet. To begin with, the variety of unfamiliar situations to be responded to in each case is indescribable. We do not even have the correct approach, let alone the proper tools, for making the inquiries that would be necessary in order to know in which areas we actually wish to operate. Instead quite naive conceptions prevail which certainly would not suggest themselves as readily to the former colonial powers.

In the most important cases, the primary task is to have production match the enormous growth in population. But because this entire effort is also subject to pressures of time, it is likely that an increasing number of experts will have to establish themselves on location and remain there for quite a while. This, however, is not welcomed by the populations involved. Their hearts and minds are not yet prepared for this. And there is finally the most challenging question: with what guiding principles would we in fact want to equip those individuals based either at home or on foreign locations who are supposed to assume the concrete responsibilities? The colonialist confidence in the white man as the unquestioned model and standard is now gone. A specifically Christian ethic would also probably find no response, no reciprocation, because the partners, who in many countries are tied to their own traditions, will often no longer want to have anything to do with it. And the universal humanitarian sentiment is not developed enough to offer guidelines for conduct in specific cases.

The appropriate ethical approach to these entirely new and world-wide problems has not been formulated yet. But these problems will remain with us for decades. Perhaps a sort of "ethics at a distance" [*Ferneethik*] is emerging here, a feeling of responsibility for and readiness to act on behalf of abstract partners. In the desire to erect a defense against misery, one can sense hate of extreme forms of degradation, of apathy and of the brutality of suffering which is no longer to be tolerated. I believe this is the result of the atrocities of both world wars, which should indeed be viewed as a single process spanning thirty years, and we must assume that this process will never really become the past, will never really be outlived or put behind us. It has instead become permanently branded into human consciousness, since it was in this inferno raging out of control that humanity encountered itself. I also believe that this experience is now being translated into ethics, into specific motives for action. There is a passion directed against humiliating conditions of life and a commitment to action that is not tied to partisan convictions. The commitment is directly experienced and felt. It wants to express itself in effective action and in palpable results. Perhaps heralded herein is a new morality of sober practicality. One should indeed hope so, because in the long run it is intolerable that actions always lag far behind the all too easily conceived ideologies. It burdens our conscience and damages our self-respect when we cannot meet the demands of such an ethic. Within fully developed, abstract civilization far removed from nature, and in the midst of its statistics, networks of information, computers, and automation, there suddenly appear the stark biological realities of overpopulation, of a longer life span, of contraception, and of world hunger. This overwhelming challenge might convince us that it is now time to attack the blatant reality of shocking misery in the world — this indeed would constitute progress.

10

Late Capitalism or Industrial Society?

THEODOR W. ADORNO

Those unfamiliar with the current state of debate in the social sciences could be excused for thinking that the issue [discussed in this essay] is little more than a terminological controversy. But there is more at stake here than whether the contemporary stage of the world should be called "Late Capitalism" or "Industrial Society." [It is important] to clarify whether the capitalist system, in whatever guise, still predominates, or whether industrialization has not made the concept of "capitalism" itself obsolete, together with the distinction between capitalist and noncapitalist states and perhaps even the critique of capitalism itself; whether, in other words, Marx has become obsolete — currently a widely held view among sociologists. According to this thesis, the world has become so thoroughly dominated by unanticipated technological developments that the notion of social relations — the transformation of living labor into commodities and, hence, the opposition between classes, on the basis of which capitalism was originally defined — has, by comparison, lost much of its relevance, if it has not become illusory altogether. A case in point would be the undeniable convergences between the technologically most advanced countries, the United States and the Soviet Union. Class differences, defined in terms of living standards and class consciousness, are much less in evidence than they were during the decades following the industrial revolution — especially in the leading Western countries. Such predictions of class theory as those which foresaw general immiseration and societal collapse have not been fulfilled unequivocally enough to confirm the validity of the original theory. To speak of relative immiseration has something comical about it. Even if the law

Opening address to the 16th Congress of German Sociologists (Frankfurt, 1968). Translation by Fred van Gelder of "Spätkapitalismus oder Industriegesellschaft?" In Theodor W. Adorno, *Gesammelte Schriften* 8 (Frankfurt: Suhrkamp, 1972), pp. 354-370. Adorno's opening paragraph and a few references in the text to the 16th Congress of German Sociologists have been deleted. All footnotes are translator's notes.

of the falling rate of profit — not unproblematic even in Marx's work — had proven to be correct, one would still have to concede that the capitalist system has been resilient enough to postpone the anticipated collapse indefinitely. In the first instance this is due to an immense increase in technological development which has enabled the production of a plethora of consumer goods from which all members of the highly industrialized nations have benefited. In the face of these technological developments, the social relations of production have turned out to be less rigid than Marx had expected.

The criteria by which class differences are judged — which empirical research euphemistically terms social stratification, stratification by income distribution, standard of living and education — are generalizations based upon findings about individual respondents. In this sense they are subjective. The original concept of "class" was intended to be objective, not meant to be linked to indices gleaned directly from the lives of the subjects themselves, however much even these indices may in fact express objective social laws. Fundamental to Marx's theory is the relative position of the entrepreneur and the worker in the process of production — in the final analysis, control of the means of production. The currently dominant sociological trends eschew this tenet as dogmatic. The dispute is a theoretical one and cannot be resolved by empirical research alone. For no matter how much important knowledge such research may contribute, according to critical theory it nevertheless tends to obscure the objective structures in question. Not even the opponents of dialectical thinking want to defer indefinitely discussion of a theory that expresses the real interests of sociology. The controversy is in effect about *interpretation* — unless precisely the need for interpretation is banished as unscientific.

A dialectical theory of society seeks out the structural laws underlying the empirical world, which manifest themselves in these empirical facts and are in turn modified by them. By "structural laws" it means historical trends which are derived, by and large cogently, from the constituents of the total system of society. Marxian prototypes for these were the law of surplus value [*Wertgesetz*], the law of accumulation, and the law of collapse [*Zusammenbruchsgesetz*]. By "structure," dialectical theory does not mean conceptual schemes under which sociological data are subsumed in as complete and unproblematic a manner as possible. The aim is not so much systematization as the total social system which precedes the procedures and results of the sciences themselves. This, however, does not mean that such a theory is exempt from factual validation. It must not become

tendentious, if it does not want to degenerate into dogmatism and repeat by intellectual means what in the Eastern block has been perpe-
trated by the powers that be in the name of dialectical materialism. It
would arrest what in fact in its own terms can only be seen as a state
of flux. The fetishization of objective laws has its counterpart in the
fetishization of facts. Dialectical thinking, acutely aware of the preponderance of these objective laws, criticizes rather than celebrates
both them and the illusion that the course of the world is already determined by what is particular and concrete. What is more likely is
that under the spell of the historical process the particular and the concrete have been prevented from realization altogether. "Pluralism" has
a false utopian ring. The word insinuates that an ideal world already
exists. Its function is to assuage. For that reason a self-critical dialectical theory must not accommodate itself comfortably to the general historical situation. On the contrary, it must break with the latter. Even
dialectical thinking, however, is not immune from a false separation
of thoughtful reflection and empirical research. Some time ago a
Russian intellectual of considerable influence explained to me that sociology in the Soviet Union is a new science. He referred of course to
the empirical kind. That sociology might have anything to do with the
theory of society, which in his country is the officially sanctioned state
religion, was an idea as foreign to him as the fact that Marx had himself done empirical research. Reified consciousness does not cease to
exist just because the concept of "reification" occupies pride of place.
The humbug with concepts like "imperialism" or "monopoly" — inno-
cent of all reflection upon the real state of affairs which these terms
denote — is just as phoney and irrational as the attitude which, in the
name of a blindly nominalistic view of the world, refuses to recognize
that such concepts as "exchange-society" express something objective,
that they point to something which is obscured by exclusively empirical data. They are an indication of something which is by no means always easily translatable into operationally defined states of affairs.
Both of these approaches are to be eschewed. In this regard "Late Capitalism or Industrial Society?" reflects from a position of autonomy the
methodological aim of self-criticism.

A straightforward answer to this question cannot be expected and
should perhaps not even be sought after. When compelled to choose
between alternative conceptions, even when these are theoretical ones,
one is already acting under duress. Such alternatives reflect coercive
situations that in an unfree society are projected onto the intellect,
which could do worse than contribute to its own emancipation by

obstinately reflecting upon the nature of this bondage. The dialectician in particular should resist any pressure to opt for either "late capitalism" or "industrial society," however unsatisfying he may find the lack of commitment inherent in this "on-the-one-hand/on-the-other-hand" approach. He most especially — Brecht's advice notwithstanding — should be on his guard against oversimplification; sheer force of mental habit is much too likely to suggest the standard answer, just as surely as his opponent will find the counter-argument with equal facility. Whoever holds to the insight of the predominance of the system and its structure over particular states of affairs will not, like his opponents, dismiss contradictions out of hand as an error of method or judgment, or seek to eliminate them through an internal reorganization of the system of scientific concepts. Instead he will trace them back to the structure of society as a whole, a structure which has been an antagonistic one ever since society has existed, and which remains so to this day. International conflicts and the permanent threat of a catastrophic war demonstrate this, most recently in the Russian invasion of Czechoslovakia. It is precisely this which is ignored by a "pigeonhole" kind of thinking which projects the formal-logical principle of noncontradiction directly onto the subject matter under consideration. The point is not to choose between the above two formulas on the basis of one's own theoretical position or personal inclination, but to realize that their relationship is itself an expression of the objective contradiction which marks the present stage of society, one which sociology should address at the theoretical level.

Certain prognoses of dialectical theory are in conflict with its other prognoses. A few have not come about at all. Some theoretical and analytical concepts have in the meantime led to antinomies which can be ignored only with difficulty. Yet other predictions, originally closely related to those which have remained unfulfilled, have been dramatically confirmed. Even those who reject the idea that theory should aim at predictions will not simply content themselves, in the light of these claims by dialectical theory, with the offhand conclusion that it is partly true and partly false. These are ambiguities requiring explanation. While proletarian class consciousness may indeed not exist in the advanced capitalist countries, this does not necessarily mean, as the commonly held view would have it, that social classes do no longer exist. Class was originally defined in terms of the means of production, not in terms of the consciousness of its members. There is no lack of plausible explanations for the absence of this class consciousness. For instance, the pauperization of the working class has not in fact become worse. Instead the working class has been increasingly integrated into middle-class society, sharing its values to an extent that could not have been foreseen during and immediately after the industrial revolution, when the marginalized industrial proletariat was first recruited from the pauperized and the rural poor. Class situation does not straightforwardly translate into class consciousness. The great majority of the population who, by virtue of this very integration, have no more control over their own fate than they did 120 years ago, lack not only a sense of class solidarity, but also full awareness that they are the objects and not the subjects of societal processes — processes which, as subjects, they nevertheless keep in motion. The development of class consciousness, according to Marx, was to herald a fundamental historical transformation, yet Marx treated it as a mere epiphenomenon. At any rate, when in those countries in which the class relationship is most obvious — North America, for instance — class consciousness has not manifested itself for a long time (if it ever existed there in the first place) and when the question of the proletariat becomes such a thoroughly vexing one, then quantity changes into quality. As a result, the suspicion of mystification cannot be easily dismissed, except perhaps by decree. The core of the problem is Marx's theory of surplus value. It was meant to provide an objective economic explanation of the existence of social classes and of the growing conflict between them. If technical progress (or rather industrialization) causes the proportion of living labor — which according to Marx's theory alone determines surplus value — to fall to some negligible figure, then this challenges the entire theory of surplus value. That there is at present no objective theory of value is not merely because only the established schools of economic theory enjoy academic respectability. It is also a reminder of how extraordinarily difficult it is to give an objective explanation of the formation of social classes without recourse to the theory of surplus value. As a noneconomist one gets the impression that even the so-called neo-Marxist theories want to plug the various gaps in their account of central problem areas by borrowing from academic "subjective" economics. There can be little doubt that it is not merely the deterioration in the capacity for conceptual thinking which is responsible for this. Perhaps today's world simply can no longer be captured by an internally consistent theory. Marx had in some respects an easier task since at the theoretical and scientific levels he was dealing with a conceptually coherent world view: that of liberalism. He needed merely to inquire whether the dynamic categories of capitalism themselves corresponded to this mental liberal model of it. By way of the determinate negation of the conceptual schema with which he was faced, he wanted to bring forth a similar, in its turn systematic, theory. Such a strategy is no longer possible today: the market economy has become so obviously defective that it would make a mockery of every such attempt. The irrationality of the current social structure resists its rational grasp at the theoretical level. The view that control of economic processes is increasingly becoming a function of political power is true in the sense that it can be deduced from the dynamics of the system as a whole, and yet at the same time it points in the direction of objective irrationality. This, and not only the sterile dogmatism of the adherents of this view, could help explain why an objective and compelling theory of society has been lacking for so long. It may be, however, that abandoning all hope for such a theory does not so much reflect a strengthening of the critical scientific spirit as it is an expression of enforced resignation. There is an atavistic trend not only in society at large but also in the quality of the thinking about it.

Then again: there are compelling facts which cannot, in their turn, be adequately interpreted *without* invoking the key concept of "capitalism." Human beings are, as much as ever, ruled and dominated by the economic process. It is, however, not just the population at large which is subjected to this domination but also those in control and their entourage. The classical Marxist theory held that the powerful would eventually become appendages of their own machinery of production. The much-discussed question of the managerial revolution, according to which power has devolved from the legal owners to the bureaucracies, seems to be of secondary importance by comparison. Now as much as ever, the societal process produces and reproduces a class structure which — even if it is not the one depicted in Zola's *Germinal* — is at the very least a structure which the antisocialist Nietzsche anticipated with the formula "no shepherd and one herd."[1] This heteronomy is the result, however, of something Nietzsche himself did not care to see: that here we confront the same old social oppression, now become anonymous. If the increasing immiseration has not come about exactly in the way Marx had predicted, it most certainly has in the no less frightening sense that intellectual unfreedom and dependence upon a social apparatus no longer controlled by its operators, have now become universal. The much-lamented immaturity of the masses reflects their inability ever to control their own lives, which they experience as blind fate, just as in mythology. Empirical investigations, for that matter, indicate that subjectively, in terms of their own conception of reality, social classes are by no means as leveled as at times has been assumed. Even theories of imperialism, now that the great powers have been forced to relinquish their colonies, are by no means outdated. The social processes to which these theories were meant to draw attention are as real as ever, namely in the conflict between the two monstrous power blocks. The ostensibly outdated doctrine of social antagonisms, with its telos of eventual disaster, is now overshadowed by the more obviously political ones. Whether and to what extent the class relationship should be reformulated to encompass the relation between the leading industrial nations and the developing nations courted by them is something which cannot be pursued here.

In terms of the conceptual framework of dialectical critical theory, I would like to suggest, as a tentative and necessarily abstract answer, that contemporary society is most certainly an "industrial society" from the point of view of the *forces* of production. Industrial production has everywhere become a model for society at large, irrespective of political systems. It is an all-encompassing totality inasmuch as industrial procedures and methods reach into the spheres of material production, administration, and distribution, as well as into the sphere of "culture." They do so with economic necessity. On the other hand, contemporary society is "capitalistic" in terms of the *relations* of production. People are still what they were according to Marx's analysis in the middle of the nineteenth century: appendages of machines. No longer merely literally, in the sense that industrial workers have to arrange their lives in accordance with the dictates of the machines they serve, but in a much wider, metaphoric sense: they are forced to obey — as role-bearers — an abstract social mechanism without demur, and that right down to their most intimate feelings. Production needs the profit motive as much as ever. Human needs have become a function of the machinery of production, rather than vice versa, to a much greater extent than could have been foreseen in Marx's day, although potentially they have been this all along. They are thoroughly manipulated. It is of course true enough that in this transformation, in being thus molded and shaped to the requirements of the social apparatus, human needs are to some degree met — needs which the social apparatus can then effectively mobilize in its own defense. But the use-value aspect of commodities has, in the interim, lost whatever immediate self-evidence it may once have possessed. It is not only that human needs are met indirectly, by way of exchange value; in some sectors of the economy these needs are in fact directly created by the profit-interests themselves, to the detriment of objective consumer needs — adequate housing, for instance, and especially the need for education and for information about general events which most directly concern the consumer. In those areas in which exchange value is not a matter of naked self-preservation, the tendency is for it to be enjoyed for its own sake. Empirical sociology deals with this phenomenon under such headings as "status-symbol" or "prestige," without really grasping its objective significance. In the highly industrialized parts of the world it has been possible — at least, Keynes notwithstanding, as long as new economic disasters do not occur — to prevent the most blatant forms of poverty, although not as effectively as the thesis of the affluent society proclaims. However, the spell which the system as a whole casts over its members has been strengthened by greater social integration. At the same time it can hardly be denied that the increased satisfaction of material needs, however distorted by the system these may be, offers a concrete example of what life without poverty or need could mean. Even in the poorest countries nobody would need to starve any longer. There are few impediments to a better understanding of what is objectively possible. An indication of this is the extraordinary fear of general political education not part of the official communication system. What Marx and Engels had criticized as utopianism — for fear that such thinking would undermine a more humane organization of society — has now become a distinct possibility. The critique of utopian thinking itself has today degenerated to a stock ideological response, while the triumphs of technological production bolster the illusion that a utopian world — which is in fact incompatible with the existing relations of production — has already been realized within contemporary society. But the new direction these contradictions have taken in international politics, as indicated by the arms race between East and West, render impossible what is in fact objectively possible.

Recognizing all this, however, requires that one resist the temptation to blame technology (more precisely, the forces of production) for everything, or to engage — as critics are frequently wont to do — in a kind of high-level theoretical Luddism. It is not so much technology itself as its interconnectedness with the social circumstances in which it is embedded that has become so fateful. One should bear in mind, for instance, that technological development has been channeled in a certain direction in deference to profit and power interests. By now there is indeed an ominous correspondence between this technological development and the need for control. It is no coincidence that it is the invention of new means of destruction which has become exemplary for a new type of technology. Its potential for uses which, by contrast, do not lend themselves to domination, centralization, and violence against nature has remained rudimentary — although in all probability it could heal much of what the current technology has damaged either literally or figuratively.

Despite all assurances to the contrary and despite its dynamic appearance and increased productivity, certain aspects of contemporary society are nevertheless static. This holds for the relations of production, for instance, which now involve not merely ownership but also administration — all the way to the role of the state as the general capitalist. Inasmuch as the relations of production are being rationalized in the technical sense and thus assimilated to the forces of production, these social relations have doubtlessly become more flexible. But this development fosters the illusion that full employment and the maintenance of the status quo represent some kind of ideal. What is lost from view is that there is in fact a universal interest in the emancipation from heteronomous forms of work. The current, extremely fluid international situation is only temporarily stable. It is a product of forces which threaten to destroy it. Within the reigning relations of production, the human race is its own reserve army, as it were, and it is victualed accordingly. Marx's faith in the historical primacy of the forces of production, which were to dissolve the relations of production, has been far too optimistic. To this extent Marx, the avowed opponent of German idealism, remained true to idealism's affirmative theory of history. Faith in the world spirit has functioned as an alibi for many a later version of that social order which, according to the eleventh Feuerbach thesis, was to be changed. The relations of production, out of sheer self-preservation and by means of patchwork and piecemeal measures, have continued to subordinate the unleashed forces of production. The preponderance of the relations of production over the forces of production, which have long since made a mockery of the former, is the symbol of the age. That the long arm of the human race reaches to distant and barren planets yet is unable to ensure eternal peace on earth, shows how absurd the situation is toward which the dialectic of social development is moving. That the actual course of historical events has so dashed the hopes of an earlier generation is to a large degree a result of the integration of what Veblen called the "underlying population." Only those who would place the abstract happiness of society as a whole higher than the happiness of individual human beings could wish this to be undone. This integration was itself a result of a development of the forces of production, although not in the sense of their primacy over the relations of production. It was a mistake to ever have thought of this mechanistically. The realization of this primacy of the forces of production would have required the spontaneous cooperation of all those with an interest in the transformation of social conditions, whose numbers by now have long exceeded — by several orders of magnitude — those of the genuine industrial proletariat. Objective interest and subjective spontaneity, however, remain poles apart; the latter has practically withered under the oppressive predominance of the status quo. Marx's formulation, according to which theory becomes a material force in the world as soon as it takes hold of the masses, has been flagrantly inverted by the actual course of historical events. If society is so organized that it automatically or deliberately blocks, by means of the culture and consciousness industry and by monopolies of public opinion, even the simplest knowledge and awareness of ominous political events or of important critical ideas and theories; if, to compound it all, the organization of society paralyzes even the very ability to imagine the world differently from the way it in fact overwhelmingly appears to its inhabitants, then this rigid and manipulated mental condition becomes every bit as much a material force — a force of repression — as its counterpart, i.e., free and independent thought, which once sought its elimination.

The term "industrial society," on the other hand, evokes, in a certain sense, a technocratic reading of Marx. It also suggests that this element in Marx is still applicable in our world — even though Marx is at the same time treated as obsolete. The term "industrial society" implies that the very nature of society can be deduced directly from the state of the forces of production — i.e., independently of the prevailing social conditions. It is really quite astonishing how seldom these conditions themselves are discussed and analyzed in contemporary sociology. What is best — not that it augurs well for the future — is lost from view, namely the totality, that which Hegel termed the all-pervasive "ether" of society. This, however, is anything but ethereal; it is the *ens realissimum*. Inasmuch as it is indeed abstract, it is an abstraction which is not to be blamed on a daydreaming and willful cast of mind, out of touch with reality, but rather on the system of commodity exchange, that objective abstraction to which society pays obeisance. Its power over human beings is more real than the power exerted by particular institutions, which in their turn are implicitly modeled on this general pattern drummed into people's heads. The helplessness which is experienced by the individual when confronted with the totality is a most palpable expression of this. But in sociology, with its bent for abstract-logical and classificatory thinking, these constitutive social relationships — these social conditions within which production takes place — are treated much more jejunely than is appropriate to this concrete totality [konkret Allgemeine]. They are trivialized to such terms as "power" or "social control." These are categories which have lost their sting, for what is specifically social about society, its structure, is thereby lost from view.

A straightforward opposition between forces of production and relations of production, however, would not be very dialectical. They are interconnected with one another in complex ways; each presupposes the other. It is this which tempts one simply to reduce everything to the forces of production, when in fact it is the relations of production which are paramount. The forces of production are, now more than ever, mediated by the relations of production — so thoroughly and completely in fact that it is perhaps for this very reason that the relations of production seem to be so ineluctably real. They have become second nature to us. It is precisely this which is responsible for the fact — in absurd contrast to what is objectively possible — that human beings are starving in many parts of the world. Even where material affluence is widespread, it seems to be afflicted by some kind of a curse, as if the inauthenticity of human needs has blighted the consumer goods themselves. It is quite definitely possible to distinguish between objectively "true" and "false" human needs, even if this must not provide anywhere in the world a pretext for the bureaucratic regimentation of life. Human needs, for better or worse, reflect the condition of society as a whole. They do not come first in this administered world, even if they may be welcome data for market research. A judgment about true or false needs would have to take the structure of society as a whole into account, together with all of its mediations. The illusory and distortive aspects of satisfaction of needs are today undoubtedly registered at the subconscious level, and this contributes to the discontent with civilization. A more immediate cause of the general unease however — even more important than the impenetrable interconnectedness of satisfaction of needs with profit and power interests — is the implacable and incessant threat to the one human need upon which all others depend: the simple interest in survival. Even the most sumptuous supply of consumer goods is something of a mockery in a world in which the bomb could fall any minute. There is however a direct connection between the international tensions, which are increasing right now to the point of threatening total war, and — taken literally — the relations of production. The threat of the one catastrophe is postponed and lessened by the other. The relations of production could hardly avoid the apocalyptic convulsions which further economic crises would bring in their wake, if an inordinate proportion of the gross national product — which would otherwise lack a market — were not being diverted for the production of means of destruction. This is also happening in the Soviet Union, despite the elimination of the market economy there. The economic reasons for this are clear: the desire for more rapid economic growth in this backward country brought about a dictatorial and austere administration. The freeing of the forces of production has resulted in new constraints by the relations of production: economic production has become an end in itself and has prevented the realization of the original goal, namely uncurtailed and genuine freedom. The bourgeois concept of socially useful labor, which is being satanically parodied in both of these political systems, was originally measured by the yardstick of the marketplace, by profit, and not ever in terms of plain usefulness for the people themselves, let alone in terms of human happiness. This domination of the relations of production over human beings requires, as much as ever, the most highly developed forces of production. While these two realities are conceptually distinct, this bedeviled situation cannot be grasped by isolating one from the other. They illuminate one another reciprocally. Overproduction — which stimulated the original expansion and in turn captured and then transformed the ostensibly subjective needs — is now spouted forth by a technical apparatus which has become so autarchic that it would become irrational (i.e., unprofitable) if it sank below a certain volume of production. Overproduction is consequently the inevitable result of the existing relations of production. The only sense in which the forces of production are *not* hampered by the relations of production is in the prospect of total annihilation. The methods of centralized control with which the masses are nevertheless kept in line, require a degree of concentration and centralization which possesses not only an economic, but also a technological aspect, for instance — as the mass media exemplify — the technical possibility of controlling and coordinating [*gleichschalten*] the beliefs and attitudes of countless people from some central location — something which requires nothing more obtrusive than the selection and presentation of news and news commentary.

The power of these unrevolutionized relations of production is greater than ever and yet, since they are objectively anachronistic, they are damaged, afflicted, and out of kilter. They no longer function automatically. State intervention in the economy is not — as the old school of liberal thinking believed — an extraneous and superfluous imposition, but is essential to the working of the system as a whole. It is the very epitome of self-defense. Nothing could illustrate the concept of dialectics more strikingly. Hegel's *Philosophy of Right* — a work in which bourgeois ideology and the dialectic of bourgeois society are inextricably linked — proceeded in an analogous fashion: it had to postulate the necessity of state intervention as a countervailing force to society's own immanent dialectic. Its absence, in Hegel's view, would cause society's disintegration. Hegel had to postulate an impartial state apparatus — itself supposedly unaffected by the balance of power in society — which intervened to reduce social conflict by means of a police force. This intervention by the state is at the same time part of society's immanent dialectic, comparable to the way in which Hegel's polar opposite, Marx, had visualized the revolution of the relations of production: on the one hand as something inherent in the historical process itself and yet, on the other, as an event which could be brought about only by an act qualitatively different from the internal dynamics of this system. It has sometimes been argued that it is precisely this state intervention in the economy and, even more so, the fact that large-scale and long-term planning have long since become a fact of life, which proves that late capitalism, having overcome the anarchy of commodity production, can no longer be termed "capitalism." But this view ignores that the social fate of the individual is no less precarious now than it was in the past. At no time has the capitalist economic model functioned in the way its liberal apologists have claimed. Already in Marx's work it was seen as an ideology and criticized accordingly. Marx demonstrated how little the self-conception of bourgeois society corresponded to the actual reality. It is not without a certain irony that it should be precisely this critical point — that even in its heyday liberalism was not really liberal — which has now been revived in the thesis that capitalism is not really capitalistic. Even this is indicative of a fundamental change. Measured by its own rationale of a free and just exchange, bourgeois society had always been irrational, unfree, and unjust. But as bourgeois society has deteriorated even further, this self-conception is itself disintegrating. This is in turn then chalked up by the spokesmen for the current situation as a plus, a situation in which integration has in fact become a cover for social disintegration. What is extraneous to the economic and social system — right through to the tendency toward overt politicization — now reveals itself as a constitutive feature of the system as a whole. State intervention in the economy confirms the survival ability of the system, but indirectly also the theory of the breakdown of capitalism; the telos of state intervention is direct political domination independent of market mechanisms. The expression "managed" society [*formierte Gesellschaft*[2]] has carelessly blurted this out. This regressive tendency within liberal capitalism has its correlative in a regression at the intellectual level — a regression to a point behind what is objectively attainable. People are losing those personality traits they no longer need and which even have become a hindrance. The very core of individuation is beginning to dissolve. In recent years, on the other hand, traces of a counter movement have also become visible, primarily among the most diverse sections of the youth, namely resistance to blind conformism, freedom to opt for rationally chosen goals, disgust with the condition of the world as the hoax and illusion it is,[3] and an awareness of the possibility of change. Only time will tell how significant a movement this is, or whether society's collective drive to self-destruct will triumph nevertheless. Subjective regression, however, favors regression of the system as a whole. Because the consciousness of the masses has become dysfunctional (to borrow a term by Merton), its regressive tendencies have begun to influence the social system as a whole. Increasingly the ability to maintain a rational and coherent ego identity, which even the concept of a functional society still implied, is lost.

It is a socially necessary illusion that the forces and the relations of production are now one, and that society can therefore be analyzed in an unproblematic and straightforward way from the point of view of the forces of production. The illusion is socially necessary because aspects of the total social process, which were originally separate and distinct, tangible human beings included, have been reduced to a kind of general common denominator. Material production, distribution, and consumption are all collectively administered. Though these are different spheres within a total social process, they are nevertheless separated by boundaries which once heeded the qualitative differences which exist between them — boundaries which are now disappearing. It is all of a piece. The totality of the mediation process — in fact that of the market — produces a second, illusory immediacy. This makes it possible to ignore the divisive and antagonistic aspects of actual experience and to repress them from consciousness. Such an attitude toward society — even if it does justice to the technological and organizational processes and to the uniformity produced by them — is nevertheless quite illusory. It fails to see that these unifying processes are by no means rational, for they remain subordinated to blind and irrational causal processes. There is no such thing as a collective societal subject. It is an illusion which could be described by saying that everything that today exists in society is so thoroughly mediated that it is precisely this moment of mediation itself which is beginning to disappear from view. An Archimedean point from which the nightmare can be defined no longer exists. The only possible approach is to seek out its internal inconsistencies. That is what Horkheimer and I had in mind decades ago when we referred to the "technological veil." The false identification of the world as it now is with its inhabitants is a result of the enormous expansion of technology. In effect this amounts to an affirmation of the relations of production, for whose beneficiaries one searches almost as much in vain these days as for the nearly invisible proletariat. The increasing autonomy of the system as a whole from those who constitute it, including those in control, has reached its limit. It has become a general fate, which now finds expression, as Freud put it, in an omnipresent free-floating anxiety; free-floating because it is no longer able to attach itself to anything that is alive, either people or classes. In the final analysis, however, it is only the relationships between human beings that lie buried beneath the relations of production which have been rendered autonomous. The omnipotent social order thereby creates its own ideology, and renders it virtually powerless. However powerful a spell it may cast, this nevertheless remains just a spell. If sociology, rather than being a willing purveyor of welcome information for agencies and interest groups, is to achieve something of that purpose for which it was originally conceived, then it must contribute, however modestly, by means which are not themselves subject to universal fetishization, toward breaking the spell.

Notes

1. Friedrich Nietzsche, *Also sprach Zarathustra* [1883-1885], *Nietzsche Werke VI, I* (Berlin: Walter de Gruyter, 1968), p. 14 [*Thus spake Zarathustra* [1896], R.J. Hollingdale, tr. (Harmondsworth, Middlesex: Penguin, 1874), "Zarathustra's Prologue."].

2. The allusion here is to a term coined by the Ludwig Erhard administration in the 1960s and to the intent of this administration to eliminate opposition to its policies. See Karl-Heinz Schwank, *Formierte Gesellschaft: Schlagwort oder drohende Gefahr?* (Berlin: Dietz, 1966).

3. "Welt als Schwindel und Vorstellung": wordplay on Arthur Schopenhauer's *Die Welt als Wille und Vorstellung* (Leipzig: Brockhaus, 1819) [*The World as Will and Idea* (London: Trübner & Co., 1883-1886)].

11

Life Chances, Class Conflict, Social Change

RALF DAHRENDORF

The subject of my earlier work on social theory remains my primary concern: how do open societies remain open, and how do others become that way? In one respect, answering this question is a minimal program of freedom. We are living in a world of uncertainty in which our answers may be, and often are, wrong; if we want to avoid the tyranny of error, we must avoid all tyranny and make sure that it remains possible to give new answers, and to give them effectively. The capacity of societies to change is a necessary — although not a sufficient — condition of liberty. There are philosophical questions arising from this theme, relating to the ethics of uncertainty in general, and the moral tenets of an experimental anthropology as it is implied by such a view. There are questions of political theory. Is what we have come to call democracy — or representative government, or the separation of powers, or the rule of law — the appropriate method for institutionalizing openness? There are practical questions in this context. What does one do to prevent German society from falling back into dangerous stagnation, as appeared to threaten it at the time of the Grand Coalition of 1966-69? How can one contribute to opening up those societies which are still existing under various tyrannies? Then there are theoretical questions in the stricter sense, questions of scientific theories. What forces determine the rate, the range, and the direction of social change? How can we explain the processes which make for change, and which are set free by open institution? In this note, as in much of my earlier work, I shall concentrate on the latter, theoretical aspect; but I want to add that while I have always respected the need to distinguish between the various dimensions of action and analysis, I have never believed in keeping them apart at all cost. The social scientist must do more than merely pursue social science.[1] Concern with the theory of social processes is barren if it is based on no more than a detached theoretical interest.

From R. Dahrendorf, *Life Chances* (Chicago: University of Chicago Press, 1979), pp. 53-62.

In this respect, I have little disagreement with the greatest theorist of social change, Karl Marx. In other respects, his brilliant fallacies are a starting line rather than a finishing post of analysis. In his theory of change, Marx superimposed two historical experiences which had little if anything to do with each other at the time, although they came to be linked in practice as well as in theory in our own century. One is the French Revolution of 1789, and more precisely the previously unheard-of fact that large numbers of people — "the crowd" — could play a major part in historical change ("whether [in the words of George Rudé] the revolutionary crowd is represented as *'la canaille'* or 'vile multitude' by Taine and Burke; as 'Victorious Anarchy' by Carlyle; or as *'le peuple'* or *'tout Paris'* by Michelet and Aulard").[2] A theory of (revolutionary) change by class conflict evoked almost necessarily the picture of more or less organized masses clashing with the forces of law and order and finally storming the Bastille. The other experience which went into Marx's theory is that of the Industrial Revolution, and more precisely of technical inventions increasing the productive potential of an economy enormously, although their adoption requires painful changes in almost all aspects of social relations. From the reception given to Stephenson's "Rocket" to the desperate rearguard action of the Luddites there are many examples of such growing pains. In a sense, the French Revolution was about citizenship, and the Industrial Revolution about prosperity, and one of the fallacies of their *ex post* combination was the belief that the two necessarily go together.

But Marx's theory is neither all fallacy nor is it above all unimpressive. Classes, according to Marx, are groups intertwined in a relation of fatal conflict by virtue of the places which their members occupy in the political economy. Inevitably, one class defends the status quo of legal norms, political power, and economic distribution, even though some of its enlightened members may desert the cause and become sociologists. Equally inevitably, the other class demands its own place in the sun, a fundamental change in social, political, and economic relations. Neither class, however, advances its case out of the blue, as it were. Rather, the analysis of class conflict is linked to that of what Marxians like to call, somewhat misleadingly, "objective" processes — that is, developments of social structure which are not as such the product of class action. Ruling classes inherit certain structures, "relations of production." It is these which they defend, a system of ownership, a method of wage payment, a type of responsibility for others, feudal bonds rather than contracts, for example. Existing struc-

tures provide the substance of their interests. This is relatively easy to
see; here as elsewhere the other aspect of the link between the two revolutions is more important. For Marx assumes that oppressed classes
do not simply act out of resentment against their oppression, for negative or protest reasons. In any case, their actions are not likely to be
effective, insofar as they are merely a reaction born out of frustration.
They act, rather, in the name of a new potential for satisfying wants
and needs, of new "forces of production." It is the steam engine which
gave the early bourgeoisie its pathos and its clout, not its resentment of
feudal privilege; and the weakness of feudal relations was not that
they were unjust, but that they prevented the establishment of an industrial mode of production which is among other things based on
contractual relations of work (or so Marx believed on the strength of
the English example).

This is an impressive approach: organized sociopolitical groups,
growing out of a wider potential of support under specified conditions, are engaged in a struggle for power as the visible exponents of
the present and the future, the former embodied in the laws and institutions of a society, and the latter represented by the potential of production and thus presumably of bringing well-being to people. There
is a sense in which this describes what happened in Russia in 1917
("electricity" was after all one of Lenin's promises), and perhaps what
has happened in many other countries since. It describes much less
well what happened in Britain, in France, or in any of the other countries which we today call developed. We cannot pursue the reasons
and implications of this consequential misunderstanding here. But I
would suggest that one reason is that Marx's approach was
terminologically, if not substantively, dated. He was so fascinated by
the new potential of industrial *production* and by the way in which it
was first repressed and then released by prevailing structures of social
relations, that he overlooked the much more general figure of development of which the Industrial Revolution is merely a special case. This
is Aristotle's dialectic of δύναμις and ἐνέργεια, of potential and actuality, of that which could be and that which is. The potential which is
suppressed by prevailing social structures may be one of production,
but it may also be one of distribution, or indeed one of organization,
for example the organization of work, leisure, education, and retire-
ment, and thus the social construction of human lives. One is in fact
concerned with the much more general phenomenon of an emerging
and maturing potential of life chances being held back — or not, as the
case may be — by a prevailing reality of social organization.

This is a relatively simple amendment of Marx's theory. It is also a consequential amendment of my own fragmentary theories as proposed in my book on *Class and Class Conflict*.[3] There, I concentrated very largely on the French Revolution part of Marx's theory — that is, on the theory of class organization and of what one might call the mechanics of class conflict. Critics have rightly complained about the curiously formalistic character of such an approach, in which the question of what class conflict is about is answered by little else than the reference to the "status quo," its defense or the attack on it. I have said of course that the substance of class interests arises from social positions and is in that sense structural, or even "objective," but the central proposition in this context sounds more like a definition than like a theoretical statement: "Our model of conflict group analysis involves the proposition that of the two aggregates of authority positions to be distinguished in every association, one — that of domination — is characterized by an interest in the maintenance of a social structure that for them conveys authority, whereas the other — that of subjection — involves an interest in changing a social condition that deprives its incumbents of authority."[4]

It is in keeping with this approach that the dimensions of conflict discussed in the theory are those of intensity and of violence, and the dimensions of change those of radicalness and rapidity. I see no reason today for denying the usefulness of such an analysis, but it is also limited, for what is left out is the most important if the most complex dimension: that of the direction of change and of the substance of conflict. One way of introducing this dimension is by borrowing Marx's (or Aristotle's) approach in the sense of linking the analysis of class to the analysis of non-class developments of social structure which have to do with potential and actuality, with what a society could offer and what it actually offers. These social offerings in turn have to be expressed in structural terms other than, or at least more general than, "production." I propose to follow this path, and I suggest that it marks one of the points at which the concept of life chances becomes crucial for the analysis of social processes.

So far as Marx is concerned, I have presented a rather truncated version of his theory of change so far. That was deliberate, for I find the remaining elements much less relevant, and much more fallacious too. However, it may be worth looking at them briefly, if only in order to define one aspect of the problems discussed time and again . . . which has not yet been mentioned here, that of progress.

There is first of all the fact that Marx, rather than explaining the direction of change, in fact makes assumptions about it. Take the concept of mode or relations of production. Marx finds it either difficult or impracticable to conceive of social structure — of relations of production — as changing in an undramatic and continuing fashion. He assumes that relations of production are in fact unchanging or virtually unchanging. At any rate this is so for the duration of a stage or epoch of history. Prevailing norms relating to property, to work and its conditions, to systems of production, distribution, and consumption, but also to the various layers of superstructure, are in a strange sense "ready," both in the sense of being fully prepared and in that of being complete, when they become valid; they come about by a kind of revolutionary big bang, and the only change of which they are capable afterwards is a radical change which makes them disappear as such, the creation of what Marx sometimes calls a new "basis," a new "stage of historical development." All change of social structures is revolutionary change.

I have discussed the shortcomings of this approach elsewhere.[5] Suffice it to say here that the stop-go image of social structure neither corresponds to observed facts nor does it lend itself to satisfactory explanations. The fact is that societies change all the time; and if we wait for revolutions as the only permissible form of change, we are likely to have to construct absurd theoretical crutches such as the numerous attempts on the part of more or less sophisticated Marxians to prove that everything, but everything that has happened since the turn of the century, the Great Depression and fascism, the Second World War and the Cold War, the energy crisis and the North-South dialogue, inflation and unemployment is but a symptom of the crisis of capitalism. So what? Without pursuing the theme any further here, I would suggest that it is much more useful to work on an assumption which modifies Newton's first law of movement and states that societies are in a state of continuing, uniform, and linear development unless certain factors intervene to decelerate or accelerate, confirm or deflect the process.

Again, the critical aspect of Marx's assumptions concerns not the relations, but the forces of production. While relations of production remain unchanged throughout an epoch, productive forces change all the time. In fact, Marx uses the term almost invariably in the context of "developments," or "stages of development" of productive forces. It is plausible to interpret his many references to this effect to mean that Marx thinks of productive forces as continuously growing throughout history; indeed history is designed to make them grow all the time. Relations of production are a response to a certain stage of development of productive forces; but these forces expand and grow. They outgrow the structure of an epoch, and as the resulting contradictions increase, the epoch begins to wilt and decay, or, less metaphorically (though Marx himself uses the organic metaphor), a revolutionary situation begins to develop. Marx is not naive enough to assume a unilinear, monorhythmic growth of forces of production; in bourgeois society, for example, the process is greatly accelerated; but he assumes throughout that the potential of societies to satisfy wants grows and grows.

This presentation of Marx's approach may be incomplete, but it is not misleading. It is true that Marx had in mind technological developments among other things, and it is generally assumed that science and technology at least have tended to grow in volume, effectiveness, and by any other index. Elsewhere, Marx plays with the word wealth, or rather, *Reichtum*, richness, in relation to forces of production. He speaks of "the degree of development of the material forces of production and thus of richness"; and most people would probably subscribe to the proposition that poverty has on the whole decreased in history (although Arnold Toynbee was not the only author to voice doubts about the effects of the Industrial Revolution in this respect).[6] In any case, Marx then refers to "the highest development of productive forces . . . and thus the richest development of individuals," and clearly does not mean that individuals are, or are going to be, very wealthy. On the contrary, this sounds more like that "universality of the individual not as a figment of imagination, but as universality of his real and ideal relations" which he regards as characteristic of a society in which "the full development of productive forces has become a condition of production." I do not think that one is misrepresenting Marx if one imputes to him the assumption that the potential of human development has grown throughout history.[7]

This assumption, however, is probably implausible. It is at the very least subject to grave doubts. What about those less optimistic minds who regard human history since the seventeenth century as a story of continuous decline? Nearer general understanding perhaps, what about the thesis that from a certain point onwards the generalization of opportunities leads to a reduction of their worth? (Are productive forces always options, or could they be ligatures as well?) In any case, what about centuries of stagnation and, worse, of regression in many measurable respects? Progress is too precarious a notion for us to assume that it is automatic, or even general in any respect; if there is such a thing as progress with respect to human life chances and the development of human nature corresponding to them, a case would have to be made rather than assumed. It appears that Marx, like all his colleagues in the new field of political economy, was somewhat overimpressed by the experience of economic expansion around him.

In the case of Marx, the readiness to be so impressed was helped by his philosophical predilections. He could never rid himself of the Hegelian sickness of having to try to make sense of the process of history by assuming unsatisfactory beginnings and a totally satisfactory end. The quotation about the "full development of productive forces" is but one of many which show that throughout Marx assumed not only progress within historical phases — at least progress of productive forces and revolutionary energies — but also a progression of such phases right up to the imminent final revolution and the perfect society which is to follow it. Karl Popper has said all there is to be said about this approach.[8] Insofar as we are concerned here with the course and the meaning of history, no attempt will be made to describe the process in its entirety, let alone to assert or project perfection. Our approach to understanding the historical process, and progress, is not Hegel's, but Kant's: "History, which is concerned with the story [of human actions], however deeply their causes may be hidden, nevertheless lets us hope: that if it regards the play of man's freedom of will *in toto*, it may discover that it follows a regular course; and that in this manner, what strikes the eye in individual subjects as confused and irregular, may nevertheless be capable of being recognized in the entire species as a steadily progressing, though slow unfolding of its original endowments."[9] I began . . . by restating my own concern with change and identifying the lacunae which I found in earlier approaches to the understanding of social processes. The most obvious gap is that in *Class and Class Conflict*, where the analysis of conflict remains highly formal and little is said about either the substance of conflict or the direction of change. The same is true for most of my other writings on the theory of conflict. By introducing the notion of life chances as the subject matter of human social development, it may be possible to go some way toward remedying this deficiency. Social conflicts are about more life chances, or about the defense of the level which they have reached, respectively, that is to say (from the point of view of those in power) about the attempt to secure the options which have turned into privileges within the framework of prevailing linkages or ligatures, and (from the point of view of those excluded from power) about the realization of new options even at the expense of familiar ligatures, or at times about the creation of a new quality of ligatures. In this way, a bridge to the understanding of progress can be built. If one succeeded in rendering the concept of life chances sufficiently operational to make statements possible about whether there are in a given society, or for a given class, more or fewer life chances, then the problem of progress could be reformulated in a way which is equally interesting in empirical and in theoretical contexts.

There is one other point which deserves mention in this connection. Life chances are opportunities for individual development provided by social structure, "molds," as we have called them. As such, they provide an important bridge between an understanding of society which emphasizes the structural quality of things social — *faits sociaux* in the strict sense of Durkheim — and a normative theory of society which emphasizes individual liberty. I do not think that I have succeeded in my *Homo Sociologicus* in providing a satisfactory solution of the problem which I have posed in that essay. The juvenile anarchism of the dream of a freedom which is essentially freedom *from* society leads to consequences and actions which solve little if anything. But a solution is necessary, at any rate if one is concerned, as I am, with the conditions of liberty *in* society. Again, I would certainly not claim that such a solution can be found in a concept. But the concept of life chances may help formulate statements which lead some way toward the better understanding of liberty in society. We have begun to try this path, and we shall continue along it.

NOTES

1. See my paper on "Sociology and the Sociologist," in *Essays in the Theory of Society* (London: Routledge & Kegan Paul, 1968).

2. G. Rudé, *The Crowd in the French Revolution* (Oxford: Clarendon Press, 1959), p. 4.

3. R. Dahrendorf, *Class and Class Conflict in Industrial Society* (Stanford: Stanford University Press, 1959).

4. *Ibid.*, p. 176.

5. *Ibid.*, ch. 4; as well as R. Dahrendorf, "Karl Marx und die Theorie des sozialen Wandels," in *Pfade aus Utopia* (Munich: Piper, 1967).

6. A. Toynbee, *Civilization on Trial* (New York: Oxford University Press, 1948).

7. All quotations in this paragraph from K. Marx, *Grundrisse der Kritik der politischen Ökonomie* (Moscow: Verlag für fremdsprachige Literatur, 1939/1941), pp. 438 ff. My translation [See *Grundrisse. Foundations of the Critique of Political Economy* (New York: Random House, 1973)].

8. Karl Popper, *The Open Society and Its Enemies* (Routledge & Sons, 1945).

9. Immanuel Kant, *Idee zu einer allgemeinen Geschichte in weltbürgerlicher Absicht* [1784],

Preface (Wiesbaden: H. Staadt, 1914) [*The Idea of a Universal History on a Cosmo-Political Plan*, T. de Quincey, tr. (Hanover, N.H.: The Sociological Press, 1927)].

12

The Poverty of Bourgeois Democracy in Germany

OSKAR NEGT

Today, after the nearly forgotten student uprisings of the 1960s — which once permeated the thought and the attitudes even of liberal circles — the West German social climate can only be understood if viewed in terms of a restoration. The publicized effects of the antiradical legislation [*Radikalenerlass*] in the civil service, political parties, churches, and unions are merely the tip of an iceberg. The great number of publicly less visible yet extremely important constitutional changes, as well as the shift away from formal legality to "reasons of state," have been at least as significant. An extreme polarization of social forces, however, makes this restoration different from the first restoration period directly after the war. To assume that the Left is weaker today than it was twenty years ago would nevertheless be entirely mistaken; it is significantly stronger.

The anti-extremist hysteria, resulting partially from the fact that some of its instigators have become the target of its consequences, clearly points to the political strategy uniting the often disparate and sometimes contradictory particular causes. As the liberal political philosopher Constantin Frantz suggested almost a century ago, the "German Question is the hardest knot to untie and the most difficult problem for European nations. Today, the German Question takes on a new significance for there has always been a tendency for revolutions to fail and restorations to succeed in Germany."[1]

Why are there so many restorations in German history? One answer, although not entirely satisfactory, is that a victorious revolution,

Abridged and modified version of "Die Misere der bürgerlichen Demokratie in Deutschland," originally published as the introduction to Oskar Negt's, *Kein Sozialismus ohne Demokratie* (Frankfurt: Suhrkamp, 1976), pp. 12-46. The original English translation by David J. Parent, "The Misery of Bourgeois Democracy in Germany," *Telos* (Winter 1977-78) 34:123-135, has been extensively revised by Volker Meja. The present version is printed here with the permission of the author.

embedded both in the popular traditions and in the national consciousness and culture, has in Germany never been concretely experienced.

La Marseillaise, that martial anthem of the French Revolution, is
still sung today by French workers and middle-class citizens alike, and
July 14 remains a French working class holiday even today. The German national anthem, on the other hand, does not express the celebra-
tion of a *collective struggle*, but rather an *individual longing* for unity and
freedom. At best, it supersedes by way of music the political restoration from which it itself originated.

The second period of restoration in the history of the Federal Republic cannot be explained by the immediate context of long-term economic crisis alone. In a country in which, for the past sixty years,
nothing has been as regular as social catastrophe, where no autonomous attempt at liberation from exploitation and oppression has ever
been successful, and where even the present parliamentary democracy
is the result of a military defeat that permitted no other alternative —
in such a country, history permeates everyday reality. That the German middle class lacks any revolutionary traditions of its own from
which it could have acquired its identity in the struggle for democratic
freedoms, in political and cultural struggle, in collective symbols and
in songs, casts some light on the current conservative trend (which is
little more than some kind of preventive counterrevolution). This
trend has political and ideological precursors reaching far back into
the German past.[2]

Significant aspects of German cultural life must be seen as part of
an overall theoretical effort to come to terms with the difficulties of
the German bourgeoisie in establishing itself as an autonomous political force. It can be shown that the contradictions which must result
from the unachieved *political* emancipation of the bourgeois class affect
even the very nature of theory formation in German literature and
philosophy.

Thus the characteristic traits of the bourgeois German intelligentsia
have been fear of revolution and a tendency toward dividing it into a
political component, equated with conspiracy, insurrection, and crime,
and an intellectual-cultural element in which historical traditions are
preserved and transmitted. The fear of revolution and the fetishization
of peace and order have a long history in Germany. It begins with
Martin Luther, is shared by Kant and Hegel, and even encompasses
Goethe, Schiller, and Kleist. Thus Luther, who had taught countless lay
preachers to read the bible in their own language and on whom the

peasants had initially set their hopes in the great peasants' revolution, gave the nobility and governmental authorities an ecclesiastic permit to exterminate the peasants when faced with the spreading conflagration.

The wretched history of German revolutions and restorations begins with the failure of the Peasants' Revolt, and Luther signals the beginning of the bourgeois intelligentsia's miserable state in Germany. This collective trauma of the great peasants' revolution may have been what led the German literary intelligentsia to take up the repressed theme of the Peasants' War and reaffirm that all violent revolts are inevitably doomed. Thus, it is not surprising that Goethe did not write a play called *Franz von Sickingen* or *Ulrich von Hutten*, whose personalities are much richer than that of *Götz von Berlichingen*, a robber masked as a revolutionary, and the subject of Goethe's play with the same name (1772). Not a single friendly word on the peasants can be found in this play.

To the often already quite established bourgeois townsmen struggling for further recognition, the people's collective initiatives seemed threatening and destructive, even though these efforts did express the interests of the bourgeois class. Schiller's "Song of the Bell," which even now provides suitable proverbs to every German household, student, and teacher, may serve as an example. Schiller contrasts the conservative revision of organic forms that can only be undertaken by the master with a "careful hand, and judgment wise" (metaphorically understood as the competent statesman who, when he considers it necessary, initiates a "revolution from above") with the naked force and ensuing disorder of popular revolt: "Freedom and equal rights they call, and peace gives way to sudden war; the street is crowded and the hall, and crime is unrestrained by law."[3]

Even Schiller as contemporary of the French Revolution finds it hard to understand that the "quiet" citizen, secure in his work and property by his rights and freedoms and no longer in fear of the arbitrary actions of the "bands of killers" of feudal and absolutistic potentates, is both the demand and the result of national self-liberation, of revolution.[4] This fetishization of peace and order is all the more striking since in *Die Räuber* (The Robbers) Schiller knew precisely who the real enemies of law and order were, as the motto "In tyrannos" clearly indicates.

Even Kant and Hegel reduced revolution to an essentially "spiritual" process. This was the case even though they were highly determined to preserve the emancipatory dimensions of the French

Revolution. To Hegel, merely external, i.e., political, work leads to terror, to the "fury of destruction": "The sole work and deed of universal freedom is therefore *death*, a death too which has no inner significance or filling, for what is negated is the empty point of the absolutely free self. It is thus the coldest and meanest of all deaths with no more significance than cutting off a head of cabbage or swallowing a mouthful of water."[5] Kant suggests that an epoch-making event like the French Revolution, even if characterized by enormous bloodshed, cannot be erased from the memory of mankind. Yet, as a "sign of history," it characteristically indicates the moral propensity of the human race for improvement — not among those who risk their necks as revolutionary activists, but exclusively among those who maintain a contemplative attitude toward the revolution, without directly committing themselves.

Norbert Elias has sought to base this precarious relation of the bourgeois intelligentsia to the people and the revolution, i.e., to anything that has to do with liberal-democratic freedoms and rights, on the uncertain middle position that it occupies between the undeveloped bourgeois class and the politically more important "court society."

Here as in many other fields, a small, powerless, middle-class intelligentsia falls heir to tasks which in France and England were undertaken largely by the court and the aristocratic upper class. It is learned, middle-class 'servers of princes' who first attempt to create, in a particular intellectual class, models of what German is, and thus to establish at least in this intellectual sphere, a German unity which does not yet seem realizable in the political sphere. The concept of *Kultur* has the same function.[6]

This is no accident. "Identity" is a central concept of German idealism, and by no means merely for intrinsically philosophical reasons.[7] Indeed, the identity problems revealed in the intelligentsia's mode of production and in their literary and philosophical works reflect the contradictory process of bourgeois class development in Germany.

Bureaucracy as a Substitute for National Identity

The "German question" is "a question of the obstacles" to liberal democracy in Germany.[8] Dahrendorf formulates this question from the standpoint of the bourgeois conception of the state and pinpoints particular obstructions which could have been removed at any point of German history. These impediments have often been described: the dominance of the Prussian military organization, the Junker class in league with heavy industry, feudal superimpositions, and the blockage of national unity. Undoubtedly, these obstacles have had a share in preventing the development of liberal democracy in Germany. But these factors alone cannot explain the permanent poverty of German democracy.

The question must consequently be posed differently. The German question is the question of general social conditions that have prevented a bourgeois revolution as well as the formation of the bourgeoisie as an autonomous, self-conscious political class. All other things, even the typically statist orientation of the German working class and its forms of economic and political organization, are secondary phenomena by comparison. Clearly, the chapter in *Capital* on "original accumulation," in which Marx studies the initial conditions of the development of a bourgeois-capitalist society, has not yet been written for German society.[9] For example, what has been the impact of large state-owned estates and of state factories for both the Prussian and the entire German development?

Compared with England and France, the German bourgeoisie failed to liberate itself from feudal coercive domination and the absolutist state through self-conscious revolutionary action and to assert itself as an autonomous *political* class. Yet, only in doing so could it have acquired the objective potential for regarding liberal freedoms as its own affair to be strongly defended. The German bourgeoisie's inability to solve the general problem of territorial unity and national identity by achieving its own economic and political class interests is one of the most crucial causes behind this inability to establish itself as a political class.

The demand for a national "unity" was first advanced "from below" in the Peasants' War and, as it turned out, its realization was a matter of the revolution's survival. The individual princes, however, stalled the peasants with empty promises until they had organized troops in neighboring lands, with whose help they ultimately defeated the peasant armies. Indeed, until the days of the Munich Soviet Republic (1919), this German particularism has had a disastrous effect on all revolutionary and radical-democratic movements.

After the great period of the Hanseatic League, the German towns were impoverished and became dependent on territorial powers; thus, bourgeois townsmen were unable to create a unified structure in accordance with popular national hopes. There were many small city-states but no metropolitan area such as London or Paris that could have become the cultural center of the country. In France and England the monarchy integrated the towns and subjected them to the developing nation-state.[10] In Germany, however, the once flourishing towns were subjected to a territorially defined state system. They lost not only their rich communications and trade relations, but also their political contacts with the outside world. This development also contributed to Germany's "missing" the first phase of colonial imperialism.

There began what for the history of Germany were the fateful centuries in which the class of the German population which in the Middle Ages had so splendidly stood the test even outside the country, the merchant upper class of the towns, was systematically weaned from political activity and thus politically ruined. Only now did the German towns become small, dominated by parish-pump interests, and with the town and within the town the townsman became small, too. . . . In place of the proud, upright bearing of a merchant class that had decided its own fate, and whose influence was widespread, there emerged the petty, spineless, submissive bearing of the subjects of later centuries. And thus was wasted one of the nation's best sources of strength — perhaps the best.[11]

The bourgeoisie, confined to a few towns in its communication because of tariff boundaries and political provincialism (marked as these were by the completely unsynchronized economic development of the various regions), soon developed and internalized a political attitude that prevented it from organizing egalitarian movements from below, such as Cromwell's "leveler army."

The inability to establish a national identity results from two further factors: The constitution of the Reich, "a monstrosity," as Pufendorf called it, caused an unstable balance, tottering between centralism and federalism, in which there were distracting "unredeemed" areas along the boundaries and which, down to the present day, have absorbed a great deal of political energy. Moreover, foreign troops have for centuries tumbled about on German soil. These factors also prevented the formation of a pacified, materially satisfied national consciousness *from below*. The thesis of the "belated nation"[12] is only partly correct. Actually, there has never been *one* German nation.

Consequently, what the bourgeoisie as a national class did not accomplish became the mission of the Prussian state, which expanded into all of Germany. Although the Grand Prince-Elector and Friedrich II had (in the words of Otto Hintze) still been "hard-line particularists," Prussia took the idea of national unity and incorporated it into an utterly particularistic state interest. As Engels observed, in the "Prussian style of capitalism" the feudal forces were not destroyed but incorporated into the government structure. Following the catastrophic defeat at Jena and Auerstedt, Prussia initiated a "revolution from above" that turned out to be a subtle brand of counterrevolution. Subsequently, under the pressure of economic necessities, the government forged a unified national state with "blood and iron." Hardenberg clearly had recognized this when he said to his king: "We must do the same thing from above, Your Majesty, as the French have done from below." This "revolution from above" bound the bourgeois intelligentsia to the state in two ways. First, through practical reforms, it took the edge off any possible bourgeois revolution. And, second, through the rising of the literary and philosophical intelligentsia into court society, which in those days was almost their entire public, a very efficient bureaucracy, operated by such important minds as Freiherr vom Stein, Hardenberg, Scharnhorst, Boyen, and Humboldt was inserted between the bourgeoisie, striving for nobility status, and the absolutist state. This bureaucracy then became the most stable substitute for identity and has survived all catastrophes.

A remark of Admiral von Hintze demonstrates the degree to which the military and administrative bureaucracy guaranteed collective continuity, identity, and stability against revolutionary initiatives. Standing in close contact with the top military leadership and in view of the Wilhelmine Reich's imminent collapse, he proposed a parliamentarization of the national government which was to be "the last revolution from above," the only means of "preventing a revolution from below."

Social Democracy and Liberalism

Even the German working class and its political organization, the Social Democratic Party, were internally stamped by this "revolution from above," which continued through the Bismarckian social legislation and can be felt even today. Since the political constitution of classes is dependent on the structure of the whole society, the constituting process of the dominating class also decisively determines that of the dominated one. The effect of the bourgeoisie's failure to free itself from the absolutist state and to grow into an autonomous political entity by way of the revolutionary power of equalization resulted in the Social Democratic Party and the unions carrying on their struggle in terms of the state — the party by employing the slogans "people's state" and "state of the future," the unions by being oriented toward the "present-day state." For both groups, a confrontation with the immediate class enemy was also always a direct confrontation with the state. Because of its power, the state necessarily appeared to be the stronger opponent, and so appeals were made to the state to provide the "vital necessities" that it had itself proclaimed as a legal right for the underprivileged.

Marx and Engels struggled in vain against this focus of German

Social Democracy upon the state, which they falsely attributed to external influences, especially Lassalleanism. Max Weber, who was extraordinarily sensitive precisely to those social tendencies that seemed to promise counterrevolutionary stability, was quite correct when he stated in a 1907 speech before the General Assembly of the *Verein für Sozialpolitik* that "in the long run, Social Democracy does not conquer the cities or the state, but it is rather the state that conquers the party. And I do not see," Weber added to reassure his audience, "why bourgeois society as such should see a danger in this."[13] And Hermann Heller, one of the most important contemporary theorists of the state, says in full agreement with the spirit of the Second International: "Socialism does not mean the abolition but rather the ennoblement of the state. The closer the worker comes to socialism, the closer he comes to the state."[14]

Where in this spectrum can we find liberalism, traditionally the fertile soil for the citizens' self-conscious critical attitudes toward the state? When in 1848 the liberal bourgeoisie tried to emancipate itself politically, the working class, as was clearly apparent in France, was already knocking at the door. As the bourgeois class gained economic strength, it lost interest in conquering political power. Two enemies, the working class as well as the absolutist or even the constitutional state, would have been too much for it. After German national liberalism and the Frankfurt Parliament had failed, the state-oriented reconciliation of the *citoyen* and the bourgeois had taken place once and for all. The result was citizens totally loyal to the state, the *Staats-Bürger*. The strong state, which promised to stabilize their uncertain self-consciousness, then, lost all its horrors for the liberals.

Counterrevolution as Retaliation for Insubordination

In political terms, lack of identity and an uncertain self-consciousness lead to a terroristic inclination to project one's own violent tendencies onto the enemy. Such projections are essentially totalitarian and by and large fail to make any distinction between revolutionaries and radical democrats. It is consequently not surprising that the German bourgeoisie's ideas of revolution, which elsewhere penetrated deeply into the working class, are associated far more with conspiracies, with individual banditry, and with mob leaders than with the objective processes of all historically known revolutions.[15] Against such objective historical forces, a well equipped police force, secret service, and repressive laws can accomplish practically nothing. In short, these forces produce a situation which Lenin defines as a general national crisis, in which the "lower strata" no longer want the old order and the "upper strata" no longer can live and rule in the old manner. Historical experience shows that nothing is more dangerous than to allow a German minister of police to define the features of either a prerevolutionary or revolutionary situation. A general strike would doubtless be counted as one of the marks of a prerevolutionary situation.[16]

In Germany it is thought that a revolution is "made." It is seen primarily as a technical process — like building a bridge, establishing a club, or organizing a counterrevolutionary putsch. But since revolutions can succeed only if the interests of popular majorities are at stake, they follow entirely different laws than those that apply in opposing or crushing a revolution.

Because of such distortions and projections, restoration has in Germany always contained an element of retaliation — literally of revenge for insubordinate behavior. There has not been a proper balance between the means applied and the real threat to class domination. This bloodline extends throughout German history, from the vengeful slaughter of the already defeated peasant armies; the persecution and the hunting down of German Jacobins who sympathized with the French Revolution; the Carlsbad Decrees which provided for press censorship and the persecution of so-called "demagogues" and which led to police terrorism against university teachers and students; to the antisocialist laws; and finally to fascism.[17] What connects all these examples is the fact that in Germany counterrevolutionary violence tends to be applied preventively, and the present phase of repression in the Federal Republic bears the unmistakable features of such counterrevolutionary prevention. The laws directed against the Left serve to forestall the socialist and communist social changes foreshadowed by Italy and France. These changes rest on the hopes that genuine majority rule could one day spread also to West Germany. Marx had precisely this ghastly quality of German restoration in mind when he observed:

Indeed, German history prides itself on a development which no other nation has previously achieved or will ever imitate in the historical firmament. We have shared in the restorations of modern nations without ever having shared in their revolutions. We have been restored, first because other nations ventured a revolution, and second because other nations endured a counterrevolution; in the first case because our leaders were afraid, and in the second case because they were not.[18]

The Thrust of German History

The Federal Republic of Germany does not understand itself just as the legal successor of the German Reich. It has also in many respects accepted the heritage of German history, although inadequately processed and frequently repressed and distorted. It is not accidental, then, that it was a Frenchman, the conservative democrat Alfred Grosser, who once again reminded a German public of certain well-known historical facts. On October 12, 1975, in the Paulskirche, in the very building where the first German parliament met, he pointed out two dangerous tendencies in the Federal Republic: the glorification of state and order, and the self-deception that fascism and the undermining of basic democratic rights were a product of extremists. "Perhaps I am too much a Frenchman or I am thinking too vividly of 1933, but it seems to me that there is in the Federal Republic too much talk of defending the liberal democratic order, and too little talk of defending the basic individual freedoms against intervention by the state."[19] Six months later Grosser sharpened his criticism by suggesting that the greatest danger to democracy comes from the very center of society, not from radical fringe groups. Unless one wants to ignore all historical experience, in the case of Germany it is indeed necessary to see state encroachment as a major threat to democracy.

It is the missing or repressed consciousness of national history that keeps many from recognizing that the dread of revolution is deeply imprinted in the self-conception of the German bourgeoisie and determines even today the behavior of the political parties and the state machinery. There is no such thing as an anthropologically grounded national character. Nevertheless, except where a country has opened new dimensions of human and social richness through social transformations, we can observe an astonishing historical constancy and even repetition.

An enlightened Frenchman or Italian must find it hard to understand that an engine driver who belongs to the German Communist Party is a threat to the government of the Federal Republic, whereas in Italy and France entire cities and regions are under the administration of Communist and Socialist parties. In Germany, comparable developments long ago conjured up the danger of a *coup d'état*.

But even in the midst of the present phase of repression, it would be a mistake to forget a period that was far more dangerous for the Left. The violence exerted after the 1956 prohibition of the Communist Party against hundreds of Communists who were jailed on charges of treasonously endangering the government was far more serious for those affected than is the current *Berufsverbot*. Juridically questionable formulations, such as "guilt by association," were used as guidelines. People were sentenced retroactively for offenses committed prior to the prohibitory legislation, and there was surveillance of "suspicious" individuals and organizations for having collaborated or even merely associated with Communists. All these things are quite comparable to the McCarthy era in the United States. Even the sections on violence in the criminal code were discussed in the hope that agitation for strikes, or even a strike itself, could be subsumed under the factual attributes of violence.[20] This was done, then as well as now, without violating the regulations of the constitution. And has it been forgotten what role protection of the constitution played in all the campaigns against remilitarization, against arming the *Bundeswehr* with atomic weapons, or against the emergency laws? Adolf Arndt, the important Social Democratic jurist pointed to these subtle methods of undermining democracy at the time of the verdict outlawing the German Communist Party: "No undermining of law is as treacherous and dangerous as that which wears the stolen mantle of law and uses legalistic means."[21]

If the history of a country has a counterrevolutionary bias, then no far-fetched occasions are necessary to set in motion the entire machinery of state and legal safeguards. Countries with strong traditions of counterrevolution have a very sensitive early-warning system.

The protest movement of students and youths who consciously went against the current of German history aimed more at protecting civil and political rights than at bringing about revolution. But in the attempt to bring the present situation more in line with the rest of German history, the remnants of the protest movement and the actions of some of its extreme groups have provided a pretext for a new counterrevolution in Germany. The latter does not always proceed spectacularly. While in the past the protectors of the constitution generally tried to prove that the actions of an accused person violated the constitution, now the person who has fallen under suspicion must himself give proof of his complete loyalty to the constitution. There exists a deep-seated universal distrust toward the entire nation's loyalty to the constitution.

With its institutions of representation and its mediation of popular sovereignty through political parties, the constitution leaves practically no room for popular plebiscites. Yet it is precisely by seeking to set this institutional rampart against fascistic-authoritarian developments that

the federal constitution finds itself continuing the Prussian authoritarian tradition of constitutional government, which was one of the
causes of fascism and which tended to restrict the democratic claims of
the "mob."

This basic distrust can be shown clearly by reference to political
strikes and to referenda. Although it is becoming more and more difficult to separate the political and the economic elements of a large strike
(every strike which releases mass activity that is not controlled at every
step by the union is regarded as a political threat to the present ruling
system), the Federal Republic holds firmly to this traditional division
of economics and politics.[22] Yet there is not a single example of a politically conceived strike that has led to the decline or to the destruction
of the democratic constitution.

This fundamental distrust is even more evident in the doubts about
the "reliability" of the people as a whole (though today the dangers are
seen as coming almost exclusively from the Left), as they are evident in
connection with the discussions on the implementation of the Hamburg law of May 9, 1958, calling for a referendum on atomic weapons.
Although it was obvious from the beginning that the referendum was
intended only to provide the Hamburg Senate with a survey of public
opinion, the federal administration obtained a temporary injunction
from the Federal Constitutional Court against the referendum. "The
Federal Constitutional Court did not — as the federal administration
originally requested — condemn as unconstitutional once and for all
every type of plebiscitory participation of the people by way of giving
opinions about basic political questions. But it prohibited the states
[Hamburg, Bremen and Hesse] from carrying out referenda on such
political questions — i.e., all really important ones — that fall under
the competency of the federal government. It also extended this prohibition to municipalities by the verdict against Hesse."[23] By fetishizing
the procedures of representative democracy, a legally unassailable
means of combating all extra-parliamentary activities of the people
has thereby been created. The realization of democratic rights is consequently seen as the exclusive domain of the government and its constitutional institutions. But with such restrictions, the *political* articulation of democratic mass needs becomes impossible in the long run.

Under such conditions, it is perhaps quite logical to reduce the concept of unconstitutional behavior to an anti-constitutional attitude,
but that was not the intention of the constitution. Recent decisions of
the Federal Constitutional Court, however, seem to indicate a new interpretation. West Germany lives on the myth of the "center," but the

real danger to democracy arises from that very "center."

The Internationalization of Internal Ostracism

The forces of the Left are not weaker today in the Federal republic than ten years ago. On the contrary, they have grown, even if they are fragmented and caught in unproductive competition with one another. In 1968, the state, in full possession of its integrating power, was still able to invite the extra-parliamentary opposition to return to the institutions. Today, however, this strategy is at an end. Once again, the state sees itself compelled to expel one by one those it had received into its institutions and official organizations, to ostracize them socially in order to be rid of the political challenge. This ostracism, practiced with some success in the administrative "treatment of enemies," apparently fascinates leading German politicians so much that they would like to export it all over Europe as a key component of a "healthy" state. Not only individuals or small groups, but entire political organizations and parties are to be banned from society as soon as they prove capable of interesting the majority in a socialist alternative to capitalism.

Portugal opened the door through which the spirit of the revolutionary Third World liberation movements penetrated to the center of Europe and expanded before our eyes as if no power could stop it. And if it should be the historical fate of Portugal to be unable to withstand the united defenders of a European order and to be steered back into those channels which for a short while will safeguard capitalism even on its territory, it should be remembered that Salazar and Franco too were both convinced that their order against socialism and communism was built to last forever.

As in 1848, a spectre is again haunting Europe: the spectre of communism and socialism. All the old European powers have formed an alliance against this spectre — the Pope, the Second International awakened from its apparent death, the Christian parties, European liberals, and the German Office for the Protection of the Constitution. And as if they felt a special competence for guiding the conservative restoration, German politicians push into the foreground in the attempt to bind together the parties of the old order. A polarization of European political forces is currently taking place, comparable to nothing since the 1920s and 1930s except the revolutionary liberation movements in the Third World.

The German Federal Republic occupies a special position in this attempt to suppress socialist alternatives to capitalism; it remains even now the most economically stable and politically quiescent country, upon which foreign reactionary forces are basing their hopes for social order. In the struggle against repression and for a socialist transformation of society, the West German Left does not stand alone, but it would nevertheless be mistaken to rely on international crises and to adopt forms of struggle and organization that have proven effective in other countries yet do not reflect the German historical experience. It is important to determine the concrete forms of struggle and organization appropriate to the specific conditions of West German society.

Notes

1. In Germany, the term "restoration" does not at all have the same negative connotation that it has in countries with revolutionary traditions. See, for example, the following definition: "Restoration is the reestablishment of a state which had been disrupted by civil wars, by enemy occupation, or by other causes." *Vollständiges politisches Taschenwörterbuch* (Leipzig, 1849).

2. [The poverty of the German bourgeois intelligentsia and its hostility to or at least aloofness from revolution begins with Martin Luther but also finds expression, for example, in Kleist's *Michael Kohlhaas*, in Goethe's *Götz von Berlichingen*, and in Schiller's "Lied von der Glocke" and his *Die Räuber*.]

3. "Das Lied von der Glocke" ["Song of the Bell," *Friedrich Schiller: An Anthology for Our Time* (New York: Frederick Ungar, 1959), p. 246.].

4. This completely counterrevolutionary poem was especially dear to Schiller's heart. He formulated the first ideas on the "Bell" before the French Revolution, but the poem was not finished until 1799. Schiller's biographer, Emil Palleske says about it: "No poetry can be compared with the Bell. Perhaps no poem has ever penetrated so deeply into our noble bourgeoisie and is so much a poetic glorification of our city life . . . the poet is therefore no longer himself, he *is* the bourgeoisie which through him sings the joy and sorrow of the working man to whom it has opened its heart. Everything that adorns this bourgeoisie, pity, discipline, industry, order, the protection of freedom, the honor of the house, is intoned more or less sonorously or softly, the coming and the passing generations, the danger of the elements, revolution; everything that falls naturally to the industrious quiet citizen's or the master's range of vision is woven into it in both simple terse modalities and exalted descriptions." Emil Palleske, *Schillers Leben und Werke* [1858-9], 13th ed. (Stuttgart: C. Krabbe, 1891), 2:278 ff. [See *Schiller's Life and Work*, Lady Wallace, tr. (London: Longman, Green, Longman and Roberts, 1860)].

5. G.W.F. Hegel, *Phänomenologie des Geistes*, Hoffmeister, ed., p. 418 [*Phenomenology of Spirit*, A.V. Miller, tr. (Oxford: Clarendon Press, 1977), p. 360].

6. Norbert Elias, *Über den Prozess der Zivilisation* [1939] (Frankfurt: Suhrkamp, 1976), 1:12 [*The Civilizing Process*, Edmund Jephcott, tr. (New York: Urizen, 1978), 1:11].

7. Ralf Dahrendorf, *Gesellschaft und Demokratie in Deutschland* (Munich: Piper, 1965), pp. 39 ff. [*Society and Democracy in Germany* (Garden City, N.Y.: Doubleday, 1967), pp. 26 ff.].

8. *Ibid.*, p. 26. This sociological interpretation does not, of course, exhaust the truth

content of the aesthetic and philosophical structure; but it cannot be separated from it either.

9. Moreover, Lenin and Mao Tse-Tung knew quite well what effects the process of "original accumulation" [*ursprüngliche Akkumulation*] had in their countries for the concrete social conditions. Both analyzed this subject. But the German Marxists clung literally to *Capital*, which however projects "original accumulation" in terms of English circumstances. Barrington Moore's *Social Origins of Dictatorship and Democracy* (Boston: Beacon Press, 1966) is one of the few leftist works which investigates the fate of bourgeois revolutions in terms of the roles played by the land-owning upper classes and the peasants.

10. Fritz Roerig, *Die europäische Stadt und die Kultur des Bürgertums im Mittelalter* (Göttingen: Vandenhoeck and Ruprecht, 1968), p. 121 [*The Medieval Town*, Don Bryant, tr. (London: Batsford, 1967), p. 182].

11. *Ibid.*, p. 124 [p. 186].

12. [This refers to Helmuth Plessner's 1935 study of German intellectual history, republished after the war under the title *Der verspätete Nation* (Stuttgart: Kohlhammer, 1959).]

13. Max Weber, "Diskussionsrede bei den Verhandlungen des Vereins für Sozialpolitik in Magdeburg über Verfassung und Verwaltungsorganisation der Städte" [1907], *Gesammelte Aufsätze zur Soziologie und Sozialpolitik* (Tübingen: J.C.B. Mohr, 1924), p. 409.

14. Hermann Heller, *Sozialismus und Nation* [1925], 2d ed. (Berlin: Rowohlt, 1931), p. 55.

15. See Karl Griewank, *Der neuzeitliche Revolutionsbegriff* [1955] (Frankfurt: Suhrkamp, 1973).

16. In *Der Spiegel* (August 2, 1976), the minister of internal affairs of Rhineland-Palatinate, Heinz Schwarz, discusses a draft for a new police law. Besides the fact that he is a strong advocate of the well-aimed fatal shot, Schwarz is certainly one of those who during violent demonstrations imagine themselves threatened by a prerevolutionary situation.

Schwarz: "I can, after all, throw the grenade far enough to one side. And the use of hand grenades and machine guns will in any case be possible only in a certain situation and only after a warning — i.e., after all nonparticipants have been able to leave. But there are cases when they should and must be used, e.g., in a prerevolutionary situation. It surely must at least be attempted to suppress a violent revolution."

Spiegel: "This does not exactly seem imminent now."

Schwarz: "There is no sense in passing laws only after a certain situation has already occurred. I personally hope that this paragraph will never have to be applied."

17. Brückner's book on the murder of the Chancellor von Kotzebue by the student Sand is one of the few works that consciously establishes the link with the present. It is also the most successful attempt to capture, through documentation and analysis, the typical everyday atmosphere associated with fears of restoration. See Peter Brückner, *...bewahre uns Gott in Deutschland vor irgendeiner Revolution!* (Berlin: Wagenbach, 1975).

The parallels with the current situation of antisedition controls and *Berufsverbote* are striking. Hegel, the "philosopher of the state," was always under surveillance. He failed to appoint his Heidelberg pupil Corové as an assistant because Corové, a member of a *Burschenschaft*, had written about the Sand affair. The police investigated and arrested him. By their constant surveillance and by preventing his university employment, they ruined Corové's career, even though Hegel considered him especially suited as an interpreter of his way of thinking. Corové ended up as a customs administrator in Cologne. The second assistant, Leopold von Henning, seemed beyond suspicion. But he too was eventually arrested under suspicion of demogogic activity. See Jacques D'Hondt, *Hegel in seiner Zeit, Berlin 1818-1831* (Berlin:Akademie Verlag, 1973), pp. 50 ff. [*Hegel en son temps, Berlin 1818-1831* (Paris: Éditions Sociale, 1968)].

18. Karl Marx, "Zur Kritik der Hegelschen Rechtsphilosophie" [1844], in Marx, *Die Frühschriften*, Siegfried Landshut, ed. (Stuttgart: Kröner, 1953), p. 209 ["A Contribution to the Critique of Hegel's 'Philosophy of Right,'" *Critique of Hegel's ' Philosophy of Right'*, Joseph O'Malley, ed. (London: Cambridge University Press, 1970), p. 132].

19. Alfred Grosser, *Ansprachen anlässlich der Verleihung des Friedenspreises* (Frankfurt: Börsenverein des deutschen Buchhandels, 1975), p. 47.

20. The most thorough analysis of these circumstances can be found in Wolfgang Abendroth, *Arbeiterklasse, Staat und Verfassung* (Frankfurt and Cologne: Europäische Verlagsanstalt, 1975).

21. Oral communication.

22. See Abendroth, "Der politische Streik," *Arbeiterklasse, Staat und Verfassung*.

23. *Ibid.*, p. 133.

IV

Class, Bureaucracy, and the State

This part is concerned with the analysis of social inequality, the function of bureaucratic organizations, and the role of the state in contemporary societies. As a domain of substantive application, the interrelationship between class, bureaucracy, and the state has been quite central in the history of German sociology. Macrosociological issues, while not initially at the center of theoretical reflection and of empirical work in postwar German sociology, moved to the top of the agenda of many West German sociologists from the mid-1960s on. The breakdown of societal consensus and the termination of the tentative agreement within and without sociology about the direction of social development permitted a serious reconsideration of macrosociological issues. This required a critical reappropriation of the writings of Karl Marx and Max Weber, who had made these problems the major focus of their work. It also meant a reconsideration and a reconstruction of the ideas of other classical theorists, in response both to contemporary social developments and to the development of novel theoretical approaches, such as systems theory and critical theory.

In his sociological analysis of the emergence of class societies, Klaus Eder (essay 13) draws on historical and anthropological research as well as on contemporary theoretical perspectives in sociology — particularly systems theory as developed by Niklas Luhmann — in order to develop a new frame of reference for inquiry into the evolutionary transformation and the change of structure of entire societies. Eder's theoretical aims are also to connect such a theory of social evolution with the postulates of historical materialism and sociological functionalism. His general theoretical aim is to explain why, in the course of social evolution, specific social structures and solutions prevailed over their functional equivalents. In comparing archaic (subsistence) societies and their domestic mode of production with societies in which the corresponding mechanisms of economic exchange have been dissolved through the emergence of property relations, thereby giving rise to a differentiation between producing and nonproducing groups in early civilizations, Eder ties the origins of class formation to a transformation in the structures of system integration. However, before class relations as such could emerge, specific transformations in the political system of society, and not only in the economic sphere, were necessary. In addition, Eder points to certain technological developments as prerequisites for class societies. In the end, these profound changes combined to dissolve not only the sociostructural principles of organizing the social action of traditional communities but also the then-prevailing interpretations attached to these forms of life.

Wolfgang Schluchter (essay 14) brings us directly to a detailed analysis of modern class societies and to one of the pervasive issues in them, namely whether social structures other than economic ones are, in the final analysis, not equally or perhaps even more decisive for the development of class societies. He discusses in particular the structure and function of bureaucratization in modern industrial society and its significance for the general social organization of conduct.

Schluchter, who is perhaps the foremost German interpreter of Weber, also reexamines Max Weber's influential sociological and political analysis of bureaucratization as an increasingly important form of domination in modern society, and he confronts Weber's analysis with contemporary social research and theorizing on large-scale social organizations. Schluchter urges sociologists to reconsider Weber's conceptual apparatus, in particular his understanding of forms of domination. But he also urges them to move away from Weber's profoundly pessimistic assessment of the wide-ranging social consequences of bureaucratization as the dominant administrative principle in every modern society.

Schluchter's proposals for a critical extension and transformation of Weber's conceptual approach to bureaucratic domination are based on what he sees as the recent emergence of a new type of authority which has profound social consequences for organizations and for the individuals within them. This new and increasingly important type of authority is "functional" authority. Weber did not adequately distinguish between "official" authority, with its reliance on authoritarian commands, legal norms, and discipline, and "functional" authority, which is linked to knowledge and technical competence as well as to the professionalization of occupations. "Functional" authority, therefore, represents a very different form of social control, one which is in the end more rational, or at least has the potential of being more rational, than official authority. In the long run, Schluchter argues, official authority may well become less significant than functional authority. If such a transformation does indeed take place within modern organizations, and if, therefore, a reduction in bureaucratic domination occurs, one would have to reexamine Weber's political assessment of the increasing bureaucratization of modern society.

It therefore is possible to ask whether increasing rationalization and bureaucratic organization, while undoubtedly requiring the growth of professionalization and of technical expertise, could not also lead to the institutionalization of democratic controls. In many instances it would after all be functional for organizations to either employ or encourage democratization processes, in order to countervail the closure of social relations that are the result of professionalization. This is how organizations can secure their own internal differentiation and assure their responsiveness to those social and cultural environments that are already informed by democratic standards. Schluchter sketches a theory of "late capitalism" which permits him to analyze possibilities for social learning and organizational development capable of striking a balance between bureaucratization, professionalization, and democratization. It is useful to include these considerations in the evolutionary perspective, already articulated by Eder, by extending it to contemporary societies. This is a step quite explicitly taken by Claus Offe.

In his "Toward a Theory of Late Capitalism" (essay 15), Offe emphasizes the continued theoretical relevance of Marx's concept of capitalism. In turning against prevailing social scientific conceptions, Offe identifies the central features of a theory of society that follows Marx. For Marx, "capitalism" refers to a model of societal development applicable to social formations (and their history) in their totality. It is for this reason that the notion of a basic contradiction of capitalist development still holds, even if the *late capitalist* societies of our time can no longer be analyzed merely with reference to the original Marxian model. For example, increasing incompatibilities between social-structural elements of late capitalist societies, manifesting themselves in social conflicts, no longer lead automatically to intensified class conflict. The "steering mechanisms" of late capitalist systems permit the scattering of oppositional tendencies to a variety of domains and groups, thus making the traditional Marxian focus upon an industrial proletariat partially obsolete.

But retaining the Marxian concept of capitalism is important for Offe, because otherwise there are no alternatives to the rather sterile and "depoliticized" concepts of "postindustrial" and "technocratic" society, which no longer address fundamental conflicts constitutive of present-day welfare state societies.

Offe refines and differentiates Marxian conceptions by way of systems theory. Thus a fundamental conflict of late-capitalist societies (resembling Marx's notion of the fundamentally contradictory character of capitalism) can be formulated: It is the conflict between the self-paralyzing features of late-capitalist societies and the attempt to gain control of emerging dysfunctionalities. Thus systems theory permits Offe to identify structural possibilities, or compensatory mechanisms in late capitalism, for controlling system-endangering developments. He also argues that these possibilities can be exhaustively determined and that the systems boundaries of late capitalism can thereby be identified. They coincide with those of the "authoritarian" welfare state and fall under the category of political and economic crisis management. The topics of crisis management and of oppositional potentials have remained at the center of Offe's subsequent writings, but they have also suggested an orientation away from the basic Marxian framework which is still defended in this essay, albeit with qualifications. Among these qualifications are a complementing of the analysis of class conflict by the examination of compensatory mechanisms or adaptive self-transformations of late capitalism, and a rejection of predictions about the inevitable collapse of capitalism as a system.

In his "Beyond Status and Class: Will There be an Individualized Class Society?" (essay 16), Ulrich Beck also analyzes the consequences of welfare state policies for the reproduction of class, class conflict, and social solidarity in late-capitalist societies. But unlike Offe, Beck is not primarily interested in identifying the limits of capitalist social reproduction and systems-endangering conflicts and crises. Beck rather examines the causes of the disappearance of class solidarity in the traditional sense. Among these are cultural and regional traditions, as well as traditional status orientations and status groups.

Beck employs the unusual phrase "individualization" in order to indicate that the cultural factors which once underwrote the class allegiances of people have dissipated under the impact of welfare state policies and labor market developments. People are left to themselves, so to speak; they are compelled to organize their lives with respect to their own individual aspirations, while simultaneously discovering the centrality of personal expectations when planning their lives. Thus Beck wonders whether Marx's and Weber's notions of social class (and stratum) have not become obsolete. He argues that direct economic criteria are becoming increasingly important for the identification of social inequalities, and that other factors are gaining in importance. They reflect a primary emphasis upon new forms of cultural and social identity, often derived from "ascriptive" characteristics, such as gender, ethnicity, or age. Social inequality may now increasingly be defined with reference to differential opportunities rooted in precisely such basic "quasi-natural" differences. When combined with a strong emphasis upon individual achievement and self-determination, new political and social alliances can emerge, which test the limits of the welfare state: They may be the harbingers either of a new politics of emancipation or of the conclusive dissolution of collective forms of social and political action. Late-capitalist societies may be faced with the prospect of self-paralysis, to speak with Offe, simply because the cultural resources for social solidarity have been used up. It therefore becomes an important question whether the kinds of democratic controls Wolfgang Schluchter recommends as an antidote to the unappealing vision of a new corporate state can be grounded in the experiences and organizing efforts addressed by Beck.

13

The Origin of Class Societies: A Systems Analysis

Klaus Eder

In the evolutionary development of societies, certain structures and processes have prevailed over their functional alternatives. If the aim is to go beyond a mere description of these developments, one needs to examine why it was precisely these particular structures and processes that were successful. This is a question that has been addressed by sociological systems theory, especially from the perspective of method.[1] A systems approach first identifies the problems relevant to a system and then specifies its possible goals (distinguishing all the while between organic and social systems). It then shows which structures and processes possess a capacity for solving problems that is greater than previously existing capacities.[2]

Until now, however, sociological systems theory has been unable to establish the points of reference required for the appropriate delimitation of the relevant classes of problems. In the analysis below this difficulty will be avoided by means of a heuristic procedure. With reference to ethnographic materials — which describe societies in their totality — we shall differentiate three clusters of problems which early societies must solve:

(1) The maintenance of social integration: This requires protection from hostile tribes as well as from deviant behavior within the tribe.

(2) The maintenance of system integration: This requires the steering and processing of increasing demographic growth and of morphological densities.

(3) The cognitive mastery of contingencies in relation to external nature (drought, hunger, disease, etc.).

Different solutions have to be found for these three clusters of problems, solutions that can be introduced only as constituents of so-

Translation by José Casanova and Dieter Misgeld of "Zur Systematisierung der Entstehungsbedingungen von Klassengesellschaften. Eine Analyse der archaischen Systemgeschichte," in Klaus Eder, ed., *Die Entstehung von Klassengesellschaften* (Frankfurt: Suhrkamp, 1973), pp. 15-31.

cial systems.[3] System integration is achieved by way of processes of exchange (in the earliest societies through the exchange of women and gifts) which establish social relationships among the members of the society.[4] Social integration is established within the framework of kinship structures, which supply the motivation for social conduct. Finally, the reduction of contingencies in relation to external nature is accomplished through the human capacity to learn, the human potential for cognition. Exchange, kinship (family), and the capacity for cognitive learning are the three elements of social systems which constitute the framework for possible solutions to problems.

Early societies were subsistence societies. Their goal of exchange was the sexual and material reproduction and the numerical increase of social units. Demography therefore was the initial stimulus of developments in early societies, where problems arose at the level of system integration.

If one classifies the different solutions to these problems according to "better" and "worse" ones, it would become apparent that early societies aimed merely for subsistence as a desirable goal. In the evolution of early societies, those developments were encouraged which helped them to attain their goal of subsistence more successfully and more predictably, especially in relation to the problems of demographic growth and the increase in ecological density.

These solutions point beyond the level of exchange to the political system. The political system solves the steering problems of early societies — such as the regulation of external and internal relations — by way of political institutions and by means of the normative force of sanctions — in short, by way of social integration. But this solution generates problems of its own, for together with the articulation of normative structures there emerges the issue of the stabilization of political institutions by way of cultural meanings. Norms must be legitimized and integrated into the prevailing collective interpretations.

Such solutions to systemic problems can also be encountered on the level of the technological system. Here the production of new technical knowledge provides solutions to steering problems, since increased production is necessary for the material satisfaction of a growing population. This type of solution presupposes cognitive learning processes, which are constitutive features of social life and regulate the potential for solutions on this level. By way of these learning processes, experience is rendered objective and the reach of cognitive contents in world views and in the interpretation of nature is expanded. The

institutionalization of new forms of production also leads to a different attitude to nature and poses the problem of a changed and meaningful balance between humans and nature.

I am claiming that early societies evolve into class societies by way
of system integration. The self-steering mechanism (primitive exchange) of early societies is capable only of solving the problems of
demographic growth and increasing morphological density by mobilizing additional steering capacities on the political level of social integration, as well as on the technological level of the development of
productive forces. These steering capacities secure the subsistence basis
of early societies. The socioeconomic system now becomes capable of
more than merely mobilizing the desire for immediate material reproduction. More intensive methods of production (that is, an economy
based on storage) for the first time make possible political planning for
the future. But the emergence of domination and the possibility of economic surplus give a new direction to the steering problem. Subsistence is no longer the central problem, and system integration is no
longer the prime mover of social development. What now propels evolution forward are the consequences of the development of new steering capacities. Domination must now be legitimized, since the
generalization of social norms based upon kinship no longer suffices
as justification for the new structures of domination. The increased appropriation of nature gives rise to new needs. With the emergence of
class societies, the goals for further systems development depend directly on the degree to which the population's needs are satisfied and
also on the legitimacy of the system of domination.

The Socioeconomic System and the Problem of System Integration

The socioeconomic state of nature, which is the point of departure
of primitive evolution, has been conceptualized in social anthropology
as the domestic mode of production.[5] This mode of production is characterized by the fact that the household both controls the means of production and enters into economic relations with other households
through marriage.

Under conditions of demographic growth and of an increasing
morphological (ecological) density, the segmentary organization of individual households merely pursuing their "petty self-interest," as well
as the low productivity of labor rooted in this organization, create
problems which can be solved only by way of a more complex politi-

cal organization and the inventions of the neolithic era. In the domestic mode of production, new steering capacities are first developed when political structures in the village become differentiated from the everyday political disputes of the village square. Only the institutionalization of the political functions for the organization of social relations permit doing away with the segmentary division of households and provide the conditions for the reconstruction of a segmentary into a functionally differentiated domestic production. Agriculture and herding make permanent settlements possible, at least during certain periods of time, and thus also the coordination of households.

Attempts to explain the evolution of the socioeconomic system of early societies begin with these "functional requisites" of political and technological steering capacities.[6] Individual households and their interests are the economic base of hunting and gathering societies. The more complex and hierarchically organized societies of the neolithic age succeeded in developing a storage economy or "pooling," thereby essentially eliminating the previous anarchy of production. Households now produced goods beyond what was required by the immediate interests of kinship and family.

The high point of this development was the formation of the so-called "asiatic mode of production." First one single clan and then a group of organized clans developed a new form of household economy. Agrarian surplus became appropriated on the basis of a system of "headmanship" or patronage. (Previously the surplus had been collected in pools.) This is how the development of palace and temple economies was financed. It also explains how it was possible to support a stratum of nonproducing warriors outside the local communities.[7]

This differentiation between producing and nonproducing groups dissolves the primitive mechanism of exchange. System integration can no longer be achieved within its framework. The private appropriation of the means of production becomes the new mechanism of system integration. Property relations now serve to divide social groups and to organize exchange relationships on a new level: as an exchange relation between those groups which own the means of production and those which produce goods.

This formation of class relations will be briefly outlined below. The new relation of exchange arises from a transformation of the structures of system integration. Polanyi[8] has distinguished between three types of structures which can produce system integration under conditions of increasing socioeconomic differentiation: exchange relations between individual households are originally generated through *reciprocal* gift relations; with more intensive production there arise the so-called redistributive structures alongside reciprocal ones, and not only horizontally: vertically organized social relations are also created. With the rise of kingdoms and early civilizations, there emerge exchange-free independent economic units (palace and temple economies). They become institutionalized on the basis of negative reciprocity and of an accumulation of surplus (of simple subsistence and luxury goods). These large household units are still motivated by the satisfaction of subsistence needs. But market structures finally develop alongside them and transform the surplus into commodities. In this way the foundations for new socioeconomic structures are created. They transform the social relations constituted through primitive exchange into social relations mediated through private property. Class relations are established and social asymmetry becomes structurally embedded.

Prior to the emergence of the early civilizations, commodities were evaluated on the basis of other commodities. But the arrangement of these standards in a hierarchical order does not yet lead to the creation of private property and the emergence of class relations. This holds even if these standards introduce a distinction between the satisfaction of simple subsistence needs in the agrarian households and the satisfaction of elaborated subsistence needs (the so-called luxury needs) in aristocratic and royal households (i.e., once these latter households have been differentiated from other households). The emergence of private property presupposes three interrelated processes. First, the consolidation of an aristocratic stratum of warriors: As payment for their loyalty the warriors obtain fiefs from the king, thus gaining private control of land. Secondly, the increasing dependency of the exercise of royal power upon complex rituals and thus upon a priestly stratum: within the framework of the temple economy priests become entitled to dispose of landed property. Finally, the development of merchant strata, which accumulate wealth first as providers of the royal and temple households and later by supplying the entire ruling strata with luxury goods (mainly handicrafts). Through money (e.g., indebtedness) they are able to acquire some of the means of production.

These developments fasten the now emerging social inequalities, which previously existed politically only in the form of patronage, directly to the level of system integration. The peasants cease to own the means of production, which are the precondition for primitive exchange and, thus, for reciprocal social relations. As soon as the peasants are separated from their means of production, i.e., from "land," subsistence no longer is the purpose of their production. They begin to produce for the owner (an aristocrat, a priest, or a merchant), and can reproduce themselves only by working for him.

Thus the market becomes the institution which transforms agrarian surplus into commodities to be exchanged for luxury goods and handicrafts. Exchange no longer generates social relations but rather becomes a mechanism for the realization of surplus, for the accumulation of wealth by the ruling, land-owning strata.

Intrafamilial and Interfamilial Social Integration: On the Evolution of Political Systems

Before socioeconomic structures can be transformed into class relations, certain conditions must be met at the level of the political system. Differentiated systems of domination must have arisen, whose power rests upon an aristocratic stratum of warriors or a functioning administrative apparatus.

The evolution of the political system toward this elaborated structure of domination is directed by initial conditions constitutive of social integration. The development of early political systems represents an extension of normative relations within the family to include normative relations between families.[9] The authority structure of the family serves as a model for the political conduct of adults in stateless societies. This model of legitimate authority guides the development of political structures up to the formation of the state and of non-kinship-based rules of interaction.

Early societies do not exist outside the sphere of politics. No social formation can reproduce itself without political structures. In a comprehensive analysis of early societies, Lapierre[10] has shown that even the simplest gathering societies at least temporarily institutionalized some kind of political power.[11] As morphological density (that is, the structural processing of the problem of demographic growth) increases, political structures are formed more frequently. The direction of this development is determined by kinship-based mechanisms of integration. In recent years, in an attempt to explain the formation of structures of domination, cultural anthropologists have arranged the different forms of archaic political integration and organization into an evolutionary scheme.[12] Fried's work is the best example. He distinguishes between egalitarian societies, societies based on "rank," strati-

fied societies and, finally, state societies.[13] Service's developmental
schema is constructed analogously. He distinguishes between "bands,"
"tribes," "chiefdoms," and "states."[14] Both evolutionary schemes offer a
relatively crude and little differentiated frame into which the known
early societies can be placed quite unproblematically.

The emergence of different political roles (family elder, chieftain,
aristocratic clan, king), which grow out of the family in its immediate
organization, manifests itself in different institutional structures. They
are to secure social integration in case of war or in the case of deviant
behavior. These role structures can be integrated into the evolutionary
schemata mentioned above as institutional structures. There has, for
example, always been the "big man" taking charge of action in times
of crisis. Increasingly, this position was defined by rules, until it was
eventually consolidated in the "office" of war chief.[15] There also developed the complementary office of the peacetime leader (chief), who
performed primarily religious functions. This office was mostly hereditary. The office of war chief, by contrast, was usually filled either by
appointment or by elections.

The sacral kingships in Polynesian, African, and Asian societies
represent the most elaborate institutionalizations of a religious office.[16]
Here sacral rule was delimited by the hierarchical organization of these
societies. The power of the sacral ruler was kept in check by a council
of elders, by his own clan, or by a stratum of prestigious clans.

The sacral form of domination may well have been the oldest type
of domination from which early civilizations were able to arise. In the
Inca as well as in the Aztec empires, war chiefs combined their position of power with the office of peacetime chief, restricting the sacral
office to religious functions. The foundation of the Sumerian empire
may well have taken a similar course.[17] Divine kingship, an institution found in all the early high civilizations, was a late form of sacral
kingship.

Evolutionary schemata become problematic as soon as the attempt
is made to assign specific principles of social organization to evolutionary stages. While Fried does not attempt to do this, Service actually
tries to describe the stage of development of the "band society" by
means of the principle of "patrilocality," that of "tribal society" by
means of the principle of "lineal descent," and that of the "chiefdoms"
by means of the genealogical principle (and by the principle of
hierarchization based on genealogical criteria). However, we cannot
accept this coordination of substantive principles with evolutionary
stages: the principles may merely describe one among several function-

ally equivalent forms of organization at each of the stages. Giving priority to these particular principles of organization cannot be justified empirically. The older evolutionary schemata were solely oriented to such selective structural elements and were discredited as a consequence. This happened, for example, with the claim that there existed early forms of matriarchy which in the course of evolution were replaced by patriarchal principles of organization. Matriarchies may be characterized according to various criteria, e.g., by the fact that after marriage the new family goes to live with the wife's family (matrilocality), or by the fact that descent is codified through the mother (matrilineal descent). Such forms of social organization lack specificity (in an evolutionary sense) and appear to have given rise to highly unstable societies, and in any case they have usually emerged only under highly specific contingent conditions.

It would seem that on the level of kinship structure no developmental schemata for political principles of organization can be construed. Only some typical structures can be empirically identified and the potential of those structures to aid social integration can be assessed.[18]

Only one general claim is possible: all forms of the institutionalization of domination remained bound to the terms of kinship relations. Even the king was "related" to all tribes due to kinship and marriage. When kinship could no longer be established genetically, its origins were projected back into the past, either by tracing origins back to the heroes and ancestors of the earliest times or by an ideological manipulation of the tradition.[19] In an analysis of marriage relations in the Old Testament, Leach, for instance, has confirmed the legitimacy of Solomon (as the most powerful king whom the tribes of Israel and Judah had in common).[20] Through brothers, half-brothers, widow's marriages, etc., Solomon was related to all the tribes of Israel, and it is this fact which served as the basis for his legitimacy. The meaningful stabilization of primitive political structures remains dependent upon kinship-based terminologies.

The elaboration and stabilization of domination was a process that established itself only very slowly in the evolution of early societies. In contrast to the particular interests, related to the household (which Sahlins refers to as the political "state of nature"), domination means the possibility of the integration of increasingly larger social units. However, as a result of this social integration of increasingly larger units, there emerge new problems for the apparatus of domination: it can reproduce and maintain itself only by subsidizing an increasingly larger group of nonproducing members of society. It therefore needs to rely upon mechanisms which replace mere *legitimacy* and its limited possibilities for tribute collection with the structural power of coercion. The king now has to rely upon a stratum of warriors and priests who receive land as payment for their services in maintaining his rule. Thus opportunities arise for a reorganization of patriarchal dependency relations between aristocratic and peasant families (between nonproducing and producing members of society) along the lines of the private disposal over land to be cultivated.

Cognitive Learning and the Control of External Nature: On the Evolution of the Technological System

The development of the forces of production during the neolithic era is a second prerequisite for the emergence of class societies. It reduces the risks arising from the natural environment. The point of departure of social evolution at the level of the technological system, i.e., the technological state of nature, can be described by the direct exploitation of natural resources in hunting, gathering, and fishing. All the members of a social group constitute its productive forces: women and children gather plants; men hunt. This elementary form of the human struggle with nature is stabilized by way of a specific interpretation of nature, i.e., by the ritual integration of human beings into nature.[21]

Technological development prior to the neolithic revolution can be understood as an attempt to solve the problems generated by demographic growth and by the predominant structure of system integration.[22] Cognitive learning processes guiding the development of new productive forces generated steering capacities which served to ensure system integration. During the mesolithic period, hunting and gathering societies progressively turned to the domestication of animals and to plant cultivation.[23] But the transition to agriculture, i.e., to a producing economy, first took place during the neolithic era. The term *Neolithic Revolution* designates the combination of herding with agriculture, and this mode of production was to become the basis of tribal societies and chiefdoms.[24]

The food-producing economy transforms part of the labor force into producers of means of production which technologically intensify the manner of agrarian production. Artisanal occupations (particularly smithery and metal work) give rise, on the level of the village community, to complex forms of division of labor. The heightened human struggle with the natural environment leads to the development of particular institutional structures which coordinate the available human labor power with existing resources and means of production.

In hunting and gathering societies the entire household takes part in production, and the family's labor power determines the extent to which the productive forces can be developed. As soon as neolithic methods of production become institutionalized, however, the activities of the labor force must be coordinated beyond the family level, especially for such specifically defined collective tasks as the construction of assembly houses and seasonal work. Outside the family, a more complex organization of labor develops, initially encompassing the village and eventually entire tribes.[25] Village units of production thus emerge as the first rudimentary forms of production on the level of society as a whole. The familial mode of production has been transcended.

An even more intensive utilization of the available labor power was achieved in early civilizations, where serfdom was institutionalized and the peasant population was compelled to provide for temple and palace economies. These new civilizations, centered in the cities, also introduced slave labor in nonproducing households, and established artisanship (and handicraft) as a productive force, i.e., as instrumental activities outside the sphere of food production. In the early civilizations these activities were to become the foundation for city life; a stratum of craftsmen established itself in the cities of the early Asian and Indo-American civilizations. They primarily produced luxury goods for the ruling groups. The breakthrough toward a city culture no longer organized primarily along aristocratic lines finally took place in Aegean civilization.

Early societies found a place for their technologies in interpretations of nature which were in accord with the prevailing mode of production. In agrarian (i.e., primarily food-producing) societies, cosmogonic world views predominated. These societies remained caught up in magical conceptions of causality, resembling a "science of the concrete" (as Lévi-Strauss says quite correctly). However, basic modes of cognition were rearranged as soon as artisan and craft-knowledge became distinguished from the peasant view of nature, which perceived the natural world as filled with acting and intervening powers. Societies became systematically reflective about their relation to nature and under specific structural conditions even about themselves.

Summary

The institutionalization of political domination and the division of labor between city and country are the two elements which characterize early civilizations. They are the final results of a process leading to increases in the (self-)steering capacities of these societies. Early civilizations thereby become capable of maintaining system integration in the face of objective problems of demographic growth and ecological adaptation.

As a consequence, the mechanism of system integration is transformed. Kingships are able to secure the personal dependency of the subjects upon the personage of the king only by concentrating warriors, priests, and merchants in the cities. These strata in turn are able (to a different degree in each particular civilization) to translate their privileged position within the system of domination into economic power. On the basis of land distribution, priests acquire the power to compel the peasants to supply their temple economies. On the basis of their ownership of slaves, warriors are set free from participation in food production and, later, by means of their investiture with feudal rights, they also acquire the capacity for directly exploiting parts of the peasant population. And, finally, with the expansion of commerce, merchants are able to accumulate wealth and to pay for land with money (e.g., by means of indebtedness and purchase). Thus the separation of town and country and the political position of the urban strata lead to the formation of class relations.

It took 2000 years before this structure became dominant in the early civilizations (approximately from 3000 B.C. to 1000 B.C.). But the new mechanism of system integration brought about the complete dissolution of the organizational forms of primitive communities. It destroyed all the traditional interpretations of nature and those religious views which had remained bound to archaic conceptions. The ruling classes were the first to free themselves from traditional legitimations of royal power. They also took the first steps toward the rationalization of the world. The systematic changes in social consciousness, which first appeared in the consciousness of the ruling classes, can undoubtedly be causally related to the history of archaic systems and of early civilizations. But they can be comprehended only as a history of consciousness within the framework of a developmental logic of the human spirit.

NOTES

1. See Niklas Luhmann, "Funktionale Methode und Systemtheorie," in Niklas Luhmann, *Soziologische Aufklärung* (Cologne-Opladen: Westdeutscher Verlag, 1971), pp. 31-53.

2. For an analysis of the theoretical problem that arises as a result, see Klaus Eder, "Komplexität, Evolution und Geschichte," in F. Maciejewski, ed., *Theorie der Gesellschaft oder Sozialtechnologie*, supplement 1 (Frankfurt: Suhrkamp, 1973), pp. 9-43.

3. See Jürgen Habermas, "Theorie der Gesellschaft oder Sozialtechnologie? Eine Auseinandersetzung mit Niklas Luhmann," in Jürgen Habermas and Niklas Luhmann, *Theorie der Gesellschaft oder Sozialtechnologie?* (Frankfurt: Suhrkamp, 1971), pp. 146 ff., 277 ff.

4. See M.D. Sahlins, "On the Sociology of Primitive Exchange," [1965] *Stone Age Economics* (Chicago: Aldine, 1972), pp. 185-275.

5. See Maurice Godelier, *Rationalité et irrationalité en économie* (Paris: F. Maspero, 1966) [*Rationality and Irrationality in Economics*, Brian Pearce, tr. (London: New Left Books, 1972)]; Marshall Sahlins, *Stone Age Economics*; Alexander Tschayanoff, "Zur Frage nichtkapitalistischer Wirtschaftssysteme," *Archiv für Sozialwissenschaft und Sozialpolitik* (1924) 51:578-613.

6. See Maurice Godelier, "La notion de mode de production asiatique," *Les temps modernes* (1965) 20:2002-2027; and Irmgard Sellnow, *Grundprinzipien der Periodisierung der Urgeschichte* (Berlin: Akademie-Verlag, 1961).

7. See Claude Meillassoux, "Y a-t-il des castes aux Indes?" *Cahiers internationaux de sociologie* (1973) 54:5-29. He shows that patronage is a rudimentary class relation dependent upon personal loyalties. Under the pressure of rival classes (clergy, merchants) it frequently is transformed into a class relation on the abstract basis of ground rents.

8. Michael Polanyi, Conrad M. Arensberg, Harry W. Pearson, eds., *Trade and Market in Early Empires* (Glencoe, Ill.: Free Press, 1957).

9. Robert LeVine, "The Role of the Family in Authority Systems: A Cross-Cultural Application of Stimulus-Generalization Theory," *Behavioral Science* (October 1960) 5:291-296.

10. Jean-William Lapierre, *Essai sur le fondement du pouvoir politique* (Gap: Éditions Ophrys, 1968); Vincent Lemieux, "L'anthropologie politique et l'étude des relations du pouvoir," *L'Homme* (1967) 7:25-49.

11. Among the few exceptions are some Eskimo tribes and the Caingang Indians. In the case of the Eskimos, the extreme ecological conditions of their environment may perhaps explain the exception. In the case of the Caingang Indians, one cannot speak of a "society," but rather of a sort of Hobbesian chaos. At the time of the investigation, this group was in a state of social anomie.

12. For a general critique see, Alan Southall, "A Critique of the Typology of States and Political Systems," in Michael Banton, ed., *Political Systems and the Distribution of Power* (London: Tavistock, 1965).

13. Morton Fried, *The Evolution of Political Society* (New York: Random House, 1967); and Lucy Mair, *Primitive Government* (London: Penguin, 1962).

14. Elman R. Service, *Primitive Social Organization* (New York: Random House, 1962). For a revision of this scheme see also, Elman R. Service, *Cultural Evolutionism* (New York: Holt, Rinehart and Winston, 1971), p. 157.

15. Horst Nachtigall, "Das sakrale Königtum bei Naturvölkern und die Entstehung früher Hochkulturen," *Zeitschrift für Ethnologie* (1958) 83:34-44.

16. See George P. Murdock, "World Ethnographic Sample," *American Anthropologist* (1957) 59:664-687; and Lapierre, *Essai sur le fondement du pouvoir politique*, pp. 231-286.

17. Robert McCormack Adams, *The Evolution of Urban Society* (Chicago: Aldine, 1966)

18. See Francis L.K. Hsu, ed., *Kinship and Culture* (Chicago: Aldine, 1971).

19. See Daryll Forde, ed., *African Worlds* (Oxford: Oxford University Press, 1970).

20. Edmund Leach, "The Legitimacy of Solomon," *Archives européennes de sociologie* (1966) 7(1):58-101.

21. Elman R. Service, *The Hunters* (Englewood Cliffs, N.J.: Prentice-Hall, 1966); Roy A. Rapaport, *Pigs for the Ancestors* (New Haven: Yale University Press, 1968).

22. See V. Gordon Childe, "Neolithic Barbarism," in Childe, *What Happened in History?* [1942], 3d ed., rev. (Baltimore: Penguin, 1984), pp. 55-63.

23. See Wilhelm G. Solheim II, "An Early Agricultural Revolution," *Scientific American* (April 1972):34-41; Gary H. Wright, "Origins of Food Production in Southwestern Asia: A Survey of Ideas," *Current Anthropology* (1971) 12:447-478.

24. Marshall D. Sahlins, *Tribesmen* (Englewood Cliffs, N.J.: Prentice-Hall, 1968).

25. Emmanuel Terray, *Le marxisme devant les sociétés primitives* (Paris: F. Maspero, 1968), pp. 116-137.

14

Modes of Authority and Democratic Control

WOLFGANG SCHLUCHTER

The Problem

The confrontation of Max Weber's theses in his sociology of organizations with the results of recent research in the sociology of organizations has made clear that bureaucratization and bureaucratic domination can be viewed, from an internal organizational perspective, as one of the possible forms and strategies for institutionalizing the values of efficiency and effectiveness. But it also demonstrates that other forms and strategies, particularly professionalization and professional authority, tend to become increasingly significant as industrial society undergoes radical changes and as more and more organizations are confronted with the need for flexible adaptation to new internal and external environments. Professional or "functional" authority [*Sachautorität*][1] seems to represent a type of domination [*Herrschaft*] which is not only contrary[2] to bureaucratic or "official" authority, but also one which changes the relationship between "rulers" and "ruled" in the direction of the replacement of domination over people by the administration of things. In these instances, domination by virtue of authoritative commands is thus to be changed into domination by virtue of rational argument. If this were actually the case, then one could find arguments in support of Saint-Simonian or Marxist expectations, on the level of organizations as well as on the level of society. One might say: increasing rationalization will not only lead to debureaucratization for structural reasons alone. It could also help to dismantle "irrational" domination and to realize democracy. We therefore need a more precise analysis of the differences between "official" and "functional" authority and we need to examine to what extent processes of debureaucratization resulting from professionalization can

Translation by José Casanova and Volker Meja of "Exkurs: Amtsautorität, Sachautorität und demokratische Kontrolle," pp. 145-176 in Wolfgang Schluchter, *Aspekte bürokratischer Herrschaft* [1972], 2d ed. (Frankfurt: Suhrkamp, 1985).

be connected with the democratization of social relations.

Modes of Institutionalized Power

The concepts of "official" and "functional" authority designate, first of all, two types of structural authority and represent, therefore, two different forms of normative and organized, i.e., institutionalized power.[3] Thus we must first define the concept of power. There are numerous definitions of power in sociology. Weber already indicated what all of them have in common despite their diversity.[4] In somewhat modifying his position, we might say: power refers to the possibility of one party to influence the conduct of another in such a way that the latter carries out the conduct willed by the former, even if it thereby acts against its own intentions or its "capacity to resist." Several conditions qualify this definition, e.g., that the command must be comprehensible and feasible. But in this context only the central aspect of power is relevant — insofar as there are superiors and inferiors, power is an asymmetrical relationship. But since those with less power usually can oppose the more powerful, power also has a reciprocal character.[5] A power relationship results from the reciprocal exchange of opportunities for the exercise of power, the "significance" of which is for the most part specific to particular situations. The nature of the means of power and their distribution among the "conflicting parties" thereby is of decisive significance for any power relationship.

Here we can add a further thought. Constellations of power frequently become less problematic by way of institutionalization. Through it, a "zone of acceptance"[6] is created within which commands are accepted without serious challenge to their authority. Such a zone is constituted in a dual process: by way of the transformation of the power to command into the "right" to give orders, and by way of the transformation of coercively enforced obedience into the duty to obey. To this duty corresponds a right to control what is required as a duty and, in certain cases, even a right to resistance. While it is true that the institutionalization of power relations does not eliminate the instruments of the exercise of power, they are now defined as specific sanctions and limited in their applicability. Thus, while the institutionalization of power relations cannot abolish the inequality inherent in such relations, it creates, nonetheless, immanent and partly "visible" constraints of legitimacy.[7] Institutionalization makes clear to the conflicting partners (but also to "third" parties), who can influence whom, in which situations, and by what "means."[8] This does not imply that influence always runs along the defined tracks. Nevertheless, institutionalization reinforces the "empirical validity" of norms, and this, in turn, has a structuring effect upon the actual process of influence.[9] A kind of generalized acceptance normally corresponds to moderation in the exercise of power. It can serve as the background to the routinization of the conduct of the "conflicting partners."[10] Thus, institutionalized power can also be understood as an objectivation of reciprocal opportunities for the exercise of power with respect to a well defined social situation. This situation usually is idealized by the logic and rhetoric of a legitimating formula.[11] Thus the actions of individuals are integrated in an exchange of recognitions.[12]

Authority by Office and Authority by Expertise

If one wanted to compare "official" and "functional" authority as two different types of institutionalized power, one could proceed from the perspective of those with less power by comparing the different forms of their "rights" to control the exercise of power. These rights can be related primarily to two different aspects of the institutionalized authority of command, that is, to the formal and to the substantive side of the "command." Depending on the type of control which predominates in each case, "official" and "functional" authority stand at opposite poles. In the control which those with less power may exercise over "official" authority, the content of the command is not primarily at issue. What is relevant is whether the person giving the command and the manner in which it is given are in accordance with fixed rules. Such criteria, by contrast, are of secondary nature in the control of "functional" authority which subordinates may exercise. What counts in this case above all is the content of the command. In order to be accepted, the command has to meet the criteria of a "competent" problem resolution. In the case of "official" authority, by contrast, the identifiable observance of certain procedures is already sufficient. Thus, "official" and "functional" authority can be differentiated according to the way in which "recognition" is generated: in the one case, by virtue of legal procedure, in the other by virtue of "knowledge" and content.[13] The concept of "zone of acceptance" can also serve to further clarify the differences. "Official" authority enjoys a relatively wide and constant zone of acceptance. Its subjective correlate is highly generalized acceptance, that is, "unmotivated compliance" with a large number of commands.[14] The exercise of "functional" authority, by contrast, requires a comparatively narrow zone of acceptance, as it is based upon the formation of convictions, built up from case to case. Insofar as "functional" authority comes to replace "official" authority, the "zone of acceptance" also becomes narrower,[15] for the "logic" of "functional" authority requires a motivated acceptance of the content of solutions to problems. This acceptance derives from substantive problem resolution.

A Critique of Weber's Concept of Bureaucratic Domination

Using this rough distinction between "official" and "functional" authority as a background, and proceeding from the perspective of internal organization, one can provide a different emphasis to the often advanced critique of Max Weber's definition of bureaucratic domination. Weber apparently failed to make a clear distinction between the two types of authority.[16] His concept of bureaucracy portrays a "Janus-faced organization."[17] It gains legitimacy simultaneously from "law" and "knowledge," from "procedures" and "contents," from discipline and competence. In Weber's view, at least from the perspective of the organizations themselves, "official" and "functional" authority complement one another with ease. This assumption is also one of the reasons for his belief in the technical superiority of bureaucratic organizations. The thesis that the hierarchy of power coincides with the hierarchy of knowledge apparently forced Weber to disregard an important organizational dilemma. As Etzioni has pointed out, this could happen only because Weber actually "thought that the higher the rank of an official the better equipped he tends to be either in terms of formal education (e.g., academic degrees) or in terms of merit and experience."[18] Actually, for Etzioni, the notion that hierarchical rank within a bureaucracy is internally linked to specialized knowledge does not entirely contradict reality. Nevertheless, the assumption that in bureaucracies, due to increasing specialization and to the related division of organizationally relevant knowledge, "the more rational rule the less rational,"[19] is increasingly becoming a fiction. It is precisely the growing pressure toward rationalization that is making a structural problem of bureaucratic organizations even more visible: the collapse of the unity of "official" and "functional" authority. Strategies for propping up the organization such as the introduction of the lineal-staff system can hardly serve to remedy the problem.[20] The imbalance between competence and authority typical of modern bureaucratic organizations, calls for a fundamental reorganization.[21] This development actually seems to demand a solution unforeseen by

Weber, namely the dismantling of bureaucratic domination. "Official" authority gives way to "functional" authority.

Yet, even if this transformation in the type of internal organizational domination were indeed "compelled" by the actual development, would it imply anything more than a superficial change in the processes of influence or a change of legitimating formulae? Would it actually mean an important step toward an "administration of things" and, therefore, toward a further realization of the ideal of democracy? Considering the most important differences between "official" and "functional" authority, this would indeed seem to be the case. For as soon as one ties the recognition of "commands" not only to formal but, more importantly, to substantive controls by those affected, then one replaces authoritative orders with rational reasoning and, thus, "submission" with participation and heteronomy with autonomy. "Functional" authority seems to minimize domination. The tendency toward the elimination of the zone of acceptance seems to be an indication. Yet, is this actually the case? What does the realization of functional authority mean from a sociological point of view?

An Attempt To Extend Weber's Typology of Domination

This question demands a more detailed analysis of the social processes that go hand in hand with the realization of functional authority. One can begin such analysis with the work of Heinz Hartmann who has undertaken a systematic study of what he calls "functional" authority, that is, authority based on technical expertise.[22] Hartmann too develops his position in confrontation with the work of Max Weber. Indeed, he too criticizes Weber for not having made sufficiently clear the unique nature of functional authority and, thus, for failing to see clearly the relation between increasing rationalization and the expansion of forms of functional authority.[23] In Hartmann's view, Weber actually did recognize, at least in part, the significance of expertise for modern societies. This recognition, however, was restricted to its "acquisitive" and technical components, leaving the legitimating components out of consideration.[24] It is Hartmann's intention to bring into the open the legitimating function of expertise and thereby the unique character of functional authority. He therefore proposes a reformulation of Weber's typology of domination.[25]

Hartmann has to postulate such a far-reaching claim because for him functional authority is diametrically opposed not only to Weber's type of legal domination, but to all Weberian types as such. According to Hartmann, functional authority can be distinguished from the three types of domination in three respects: it recognizes no absolute autonomy of the grounds for legitimacy, no form of legitimation consent based upon trust and, consequently, also no obedience independent of particular contexts.[26] Indeed, functional authority is never based on "faith" but rather on "knowledge." According to Hartmann, it is at least in tendency "ideology-free" and, thus, "value-free."[27] Hartmann therefore quite consistently describes the nature of functional authority in the following way: "It is not necessarily based on ultimate values, shuns faith as a method of obtaining proof of legitimacy, abstains from commands and discourages 'obedience' as a form of compliance."[28]

Hartmann ties this abstract argumentation to an intriguing thesis according to which functional authority is, for structural reasons, inherently unstable.[29] Apparently, this is due mainly to the following contradiction: As a "personal property,"[30] expertise is linked to the person, not to the position, while the process of recognition, being "fact"-oriented, calls for abstraction from any concrete person. However, when the emphasis is upon individual persons and no generalizations are made about them, then the way to the formation of either lasting trust in those persons or even trust in the system appears initially blocked.[31] The fact that expectations have been fulfilled in the past, or are being fulfilled in the present, here offers no guarantee for the future and therefore does not count in a relationship which is constructed in such a radically nontraditional way. The absence of trust that characterizes this relationship leaves it in an unsettled state. Indeed, in the long run functional authority means perpetual mistrust rather than influence.[32]

These remarks, however, already make clear that Hartmann's type of functional authority is more a hypothetical construct than an empirically probable case. He himself observes a number of secondary social mechanisms which soften the structural instability of this particular power relation, namely the "traditionalization" of the expert by virtue of personal reputation, the "traditionalization" of verification procedures through the ritual transformation of evidence into quasi-evidence, and the overarching of temporal intervals by presenting a person's competence through a kind of "extension" of previously presented evidence, a process which is partly identical to reputation building. These social, technical, and temporal generalizations thus create here a situation in which, even though the power relation is not based on trust, there emerges nonetheless a generalized legitimation consent grounded in trust. Hartmann acknowledges that in practice "this type of influence is more stable and the legitimating evidence less conclusive than it has been assumed in theory."[33]

Such observation leads to a further qualification. The apodictical opposition of faith and knowledge, upon which Hartmann ultimately bases not only the difference between functional authority and Weber's types of domination but also the nearly total incompatibility between that particular legitimation and the essential characteristics of Weber's types of legitimate domination, is now shown to be overdrawn, if not sterile.[34] Moreover, the same could also be said concerning the need to change the analytical framework of the sociology of domination, for functional authority, as a permanent power relation, appears to be based on faith just as Weber's faith-bound types of domination are built upon collective learning processes. In other words, in the final analysis, functional authority is also grounded in trust.[35] The difference, in comparison to Weber's types, lies primarily in the extension of the zone of acceptance, but also in the way in which collective learning is guided in recalling a particular source of legitimation or in the organization of legitimation processes.

Functional Authority or Domination by Expertise

Although a principled opposition between faith and knowledge cannot be accepted, it is not necessary to deny altogether that there are differences between the three types of domination and functional authority. However, all lasting social power relations are, to a certain extent, based upon trust. What therefore needs to be explained is why, in the case of functional authority, "knowledge" is not only the basis for legitimacy but can also serve as faith-producing mechanism. Here we can follow Hartmann, even if with some reservations. It seems that in the case of functional authority it is the "trust" institutionalized in the internal relations between "experts" that communicates to outsiders faith in the value of specialized knowledge — i.e., in expertise. This distinction between an internal and an external component of functional authority is important, for it makes clear that the principle of substantive controls is not the same in both instances. One of the characteristic features of a competent performance based on specialization is apparently the fact that in its external component the relationship can be understood as "representation of a complexity which is not explained in detail."[36] Expertise means precisely the reduction of complexity for others. As Hartmann emphasizes, expertise first acquires social relevance[37] in a society which is exposed to differentiation and then only after "the institutionalization of both a rational understanding of reality and a scientific realization of goals." It is by no means accidental that Hartmann regards the laicization of third parties as the main consequence of functional authority.[38] If one wanted to maintain otherwise, one would have to presuppose two conditions, namely, the relatively equal distribution of knowledge among all individuals and an extensive decrease in the differentiation of the system. If both conditions were met, however, expertise would no longer be necessary. Each person would be an expert without being a layman in any sense whatsoever.[39] That is the reason why the emergence of widening "communication gaps,"[40] at least in external relations, appears to be precisely one of the conditions for the expansion of functional authority. The resulting asymmetry presupposes, therefore, at least on the part of the public, a building up of faith, of a trust which rests upon "risky investments" and upon "overdrawn" information.[41]

Functional Authority and the Professions

If one combines the analysis of functional authority with the analysis of particular forms of social organization,[42] then the inclination of functional authority, once established, toward abolishing substantive controls, becomes especially evident. A look at the professions, which are a product of the process of rationalization and undoubtedly the most important social organization of functional authority in advanced industrial societies, may serve as illustration. According to the accepted definition, professions are organizations for the production of theoretical or practical expertise based on specialized knowledge and skills, which are obtained scientifically and can be learned only through a long process of training, usually regulated and licensed by the state. According to this definition, the professions themselves determine the criteria for good and bad expertise and develop the necessary control mechanisms.[43] An important role is played here by the professional code of ethics which serves to standardize not just the functional but especially the extrafunctional practices.[44] At the same time, it also serves as a legitimation instrument for the transformation of external control into self-control. Not accidentally, the code normally contains elements which represent symbolically the profession's responsibility vis-à-vis society. The precedence of service motives over profit motives, which is evident in practically all professional codes of ethics, may serve as illustration.[45] Furthermore, within their governing organizations professions often have sanctioning bodies such as professional tribunals. They are, therefore, not only autonomous, but in a certain sense autocephalous as well. Of course, there are clear limits to this development in a system in which the state tends to have a monopoly on legitimate force. Yet, even under these conditions, the freedom of movement of the fully established professions appears to be remarkably large. Moreover, even though in their internal relations the professions tend toward collegial rather than monocratic leadership; even though they promote a type of conduct which, rather than being procedural, is oriented toward service and problem resolution; and even though they promote a form of organization which "is prone to obstruct the channels of power, tends to subvert hierarchical relations, has a plain and steady structure and exists, strictly speaking, only at particular points,"[46] nevertheless, at least in their external relations, the professions are bent upon the elimination of external controls and draw their power from the successful monopolization of skills which are significant for the system as a whole. The achievement of functional authority among professional colleagues within a professional association therefore implies considerable inequality. Professions are corporatist monopolies and based upon the closure of social relations. In this respect, they clearly contradict the ideal of democratization.[47]

Aspects of the Professions

The image of the type of functional authority materialized in the professions has been overstated and demands certain corrections in at least four respects. First of all, it would be meaningful to introduce a conceptual clarification by breaking down the concept of profession into several concepts such as professional organization, professionalization, professional orientation, professionalism, and professional association.[48] In the literature the concept of profession normally covers all these meanings and this may be one of the reasons why it is difficult to get a clear grasp of the discussions on the professions. A better understanding of the problems involved could be obtained by demarcating the concepts in the following way:

a) *Professional organization* designates an organizational structure which is, for example, characterized by collegial leadership, by the preponderance of horizontal relations of communication and cooperation, by a problem-oriented division of tasks, by nonuniform functions, and by the members' considerable autonomy in carrying out their tasks. Its main structural problem results from the small degree to which relations are formalized, which can lead to an excessive politicization of all problems, to slow and imprecise decision-making, to unspecific gathering and processing of information, to fragmentation, and the like.[49] Consequently, such organizations frequently find themselves under pressure of increasing bureaucratization and are therefore constrained to incorporate elements of opposite principles of organization.[50]

b) *Professionalization* is the typical process for the formation of corporatist monopolies or the strategy through which a group of persons can gain social recognition and social protection for their special performance. This process undergoes a series of typical stages, which also serve to define the most important strategic goals, i.e., the formation of a professional association which seizes upon an already established activity and tries to expand it into a full-time occupation, normally changing the name of this activity and seeking to secure a specialized training for it, if possible in its own schools or even in universities offering a degree sanctioned by the state. In this process of carving out an activity from the existing occupational structure, there emerge two typical areas of conflict, one internal, the other external. Internally, there emerges a conflict between "oldtimers" and "newcomers." Externally, there emerges a conflict with similar occupations. Both problems are usually solved through increasing exclusion, often tied to the attempt to establish a kind of secret knowledge, and through a toughening of membership requirements, that is, through the internal and external closure of social relations. The development of a special code of professional ethics and the legal confirmation of the social monopoly constitute the final stages in the process, to be followed only by a safeguarding of the achievements.[51] Professionalization represents, therefore, a strategy of monopolizing certain competencies and performances, and in this respect it designates a political process of status building.

c) *Professional orientation* may be understood as a typical individual attitudinal syndrome which is generated by a long period of training, generally of an academic nature, that combines the transmission of both functional skills and value-orientations and brings forth relevant and organizationally independent behavioral effects. The case of the cosmopolitan described by Alvin Gouldner may serve as illustration of the content which this attitudinal syndrome assumes.[52] The cosmopolitan identifies himself to a large extent with learned specialized skills and with corresponding systems of control and rewards, and clings to the educational group as his reference group. That is why persons with a professional orientation fall into loyalty conflicts in organizations characterized by goal-setting, systems of compensation, and control mechanisms — that is to say, where the organizational structure does not correspond to this orientation. Such an orientation is especially incompatible with bureaucratic organizations, but succumbs to the adaptation pressure of the organization when it finds no institutional support within it.[53]

d) *Professionalism* is the "ideology" of a social group which either already possesses or is still trying to achieve a corporatist monopoly and which uses in particular the social service ideal in order to establish its claims.

e) *Professional associations* are societal pressure groups which represent the interests of established professions, supervise the professional ethics, educational standards, and working conditions of their members, and thus exercise status-political functions without thereby viewing themselves as trade unions.[54] When one looks at all these attributes, it becomes evident that the definition of profession covers a variety of structural complexes and problems connected with these. Furthermore, it also becomes evident that, depending on the particular definition, the relation between "functional authority" and "profession" assumes a different form.

Embedments of the Professions

This can be explained more concretely by way of the following reflections, all of which are tied to the thesis that there is a necessary correlation between the establishment of functional authority and the disintegration of external material controls. First of all, the thesis holds only for relatively simple role sets. Once the monopoly of the profession is secured, thus making "society," that is, the sponsor, as well as the members dependent upon the monopolized services, then the internal relations between professionals become indeed relationships between equals. Externally, however, a relationship between experts and laymen emerges, in which the clients as laymen have practically no possibility of substantial control. Yet it may be assumed that this situation changes decisively once the "sponsor" becomes an "employer," while the "employer" becomes also a "client," that is, once he becomes a consumer of a commissioned service.[55] One may assume that in such cases the chances for external control of the professions increase. Actually, the end result may even be outside management of the profession. But this is not the only factor which appears to foster the establishment of external dependencies. For instance, when the clientele of a profession remains undefined, this usually brings forth structural changes in the professional roles. The professional becomes a kind of entrepreneur in search of his clients. In such cases, the clients easily become customers or consumers, the professional-client relationship turns into an entrepreneur-consumer relationship, and the professional world view, its antimarket orientation notwithstanding, becomes progressively "commercialized."[56] The end result is not the laicization of third parties, but rather of the profession itself. The institutional defense mechanism breaks down and a profession becomes "deprofessionalized."[57]

This already indicates the significance of the concrete organizational embedment of professional work. Influence relations run differently depending on whether the expert manages a private practice or belongs to a professional organization, and also depending on whether the professional organization in question is autonomous, heteronomous, or perhaps a professional department within a nonprofessional organization.[58] The issue of effective control of the working conditions by the experts presents itself also differently, depending on the kind of organizational embedment of professional work, in the same way as the tendency toward laicization in external relations varies depending on the way in which those controls are regulated. The more the organizational context deviates from the professional ideal type, the greater appears to be the tendency toward the laicization of the clients by the experts and of the experts by the clients.[59] In fact, the incorporation of numerous professional roles into the process of industrial production has shifted the fronts. Suddenly, new mechanisms for the defense of the professions are necessary. This development can be systematically studied by looking at the structural changes taking place in professional associations. The traditional corporatist organs of representation are no longer sufficient to protect the experts, who now are predominantly employed in bureaucratic organizations. As Kornhauser has pointed out in the American context, the increased employment of professionals in commercial, mostly bureaucratically structured organizations, which has accompanied the growing process of rationalization, has led to a split in the general societal interests represented by professionals. Side by side with the traditional professional associations, there have emerged trade unions which are geared not so much toward the monitoring of professional ethics and educational standards as toward the supervision of the working conditions of professionals.[60] Thereby, however, a contradiction has been institutionalized precisely in the representative organs of professionals, a contradiction which pervades the professions and reflects the precarious position of the professionals themselves in an increasingly organized environment, namely, the contradiction between a corporatist and a class-related situation.

Professionalization: Old and New

This observation leads to a final critical remark. It appears that in the history of industrialization there have emerged two different yet overlapping processes of professionalization and with them also two different strategies of professionalization that have resulted in two different types of professions, for which the issue of outside controls also presents itself differently. According to Albert Mok, the first of these two processes is associated with that phase of "innerworldly orientation," in which "world mastery" was not yet based upon large-scale enterprises or upon an organized division of labor.[61] In the process of secularization, such values as justice, health, and the like, were to become the foundation for particular occupations, which typically emphasized simultaneously a demonstrative value-orientation and intellectual freedom. During the process of professionalization, there emerge organized, individual activities directed against the market principle and anchored sociostructurally in the upper strata of small towns. The dependency relationship between laymen and experts creates a knowledge-related, but also partly social, distance which largely loses its edge, however, as a result of the generalized control of the norm-oriented conduct of the experts. The established control mechanisms are actually norm controls rather than performance controls, for the latter are out of reach for the laymen and in principle "prohibited" for colleagues. Not competency, but integrity is the object of social control in which consequently the layman can also take part. Of course, the possibilities of the layman's being influential are highly restricted by the somewhat esoteric nature of the professional ethics and in the majority of cases even more so by social distance itself. The professional association remains here the most important instance of controls.[62]

By contrast, the second process of professionalization is, according to Mok, connected with a new estimation of the function of knowledge in an increasingly rationalized and organized society. Knowledge becomes evaluated primarily in accordance with the contribution it can make toward the attainment of the organization's goals. Correspondingly, there is a change of content in the object of controls, as well as in the control mechanisms and carriers. Integrity and conformity to values now give way to competence and creative, original performance, so that the professional associations largely lose their function as principal organs of control. As performance becomes increasingly visible, colleagues as well as laymen become the control carriers, and even the difference between colleagues and laymen is in a certain sense blurred.[63] In an urban, complex society the distance between experts and laymen can no longer be anchored directly in the social structure. While in the traditional professions those who were equals professionally were also to a certain extent equals socially, so that the professional boundaries usually coincided with class boundaries, the modern professions, by contrast, generate inequality among the professionals themselves by reason of differential evaluations of performance. "In this sense, the 'modern' professions are, unlike the 'traditional' ones, stratified, that is, they form a vertical system." Typical of this development is, according to Mok, the change in the career principle. For the traditional professions, mobility generally meant only a change in social location. In modern professions, by contrast, mobility often also leads to a change of role.[64]

One could surely question the uniformity of this tendency since the increase in rationalization not only gives rise to new variants of professions but the performance that goes hand in hand with increasing organization also makes individual attribution difficult and occasionally transfers the controls to secondary mechanisms of performance evaluation.[65] Nonetheless, Mok's argument remains important, for it stresses the fact that the process of rationalization is clearly tied not only to a tendency toward debureaucratization, but also to a tendency toward deprofessionalization and to the initiation of new processes which transform the old structural principles.

The basic question is whether the fundamental shift from "official" to "functional" authority, which is apparently connected with the process of rationalization, from an organizational perspective, not only means debureaucratization but also democratization, and, furthermore, whether the processes of professionalization and democratization run parallel. Among the preconditions for a more sophisticated examination of this basic question are: the analysis of the structural instability of functional authority, the interpretation of the secondary mechanisms used for its stabilization, the account of its organizational translation into professions, the interpretation of the related tendency of minimizing the possibilities for substantive controls, and the relativization of this thesis by referring both to the different structural complexes which constitute the professions and to the structural changes taking place within the professions themselves. This basic question is tantamount to asking what the actual relationship between "official" authority, "functional" authority and democratic controls in fact is in modern, large-scale organizations. Implicitly, it also raises the issue of whether there might not be built into the very process of rationalization a mechanism for the abolition of domination, at least with respect to the internal structure of organizations.

The Relationship Between Professionalization and Democratization

If one initially understands democratization in a purely formal way as a strategy for opening up social relations by appealing to such values as justice, equality, and freedom, then democratization and professionalization do go hand in hand. The realization of justice, equality, and freedom are, after all, primarily the result of an orientation toward achievement. To challenge, in the name of personal achievement a social order which in this sense ascribes status by birth undoubtedly implies a democratization of social relations and, furthermore, also documents the revolutionary nature of the achievement principle. These values, however, particularly the demand for equality, while not socially inflatable at will, are nevertheless capable of expansion. Equality, for instance, can be expanded into legal, political, and social equality, until it comes to embrace all of humankind.[66] Thus, it is susceptible to being rationalized to the point in which all acquired characteristics become irrelevant. This, however, would be incompatible with the rationalization strategy of professionalism. Ultimately, professionalism in fact means corporatist monopolization. When viewed from this perspective, it is a strategy for the closure of social relations and for the justification of inequality. That is why the increasing opposition of democratization and professionalization appears to be a trait of the process of rationalization. By appealing to the achievement value which is highly recognized in modern societies, professionalization has today turned predominantly into a counter strategy to democratization with its aim of continuously expanding equality. Whether such a strategy serves to open or close social relations will depend on the particular contexts.

Actually, the opposition between democratization and professionalization does not appear to be so great when one compares the most prominent organizational products of both processes with the products of bureaucratization. Indeed, the professional organization strives to realize in all its organizational consequences the principle of collegial leadership, rather than the monocratic principle. It consequently stresses reasoning, autonomy, and participation. In this sense, the professional organization remains closer to a democratic organization, with its tendency to bind all action to the reasonable consensus of a majority, than to a bureaucratic organization, with its tendency to stress command and vertical channels of communication as well as to curtail all action to the jurisdictional competence associated with specific positions.[67] Nevertheless, other equally clear indications point to the fact that this tendency toward debureaucratization, which appears with increasing rationalization, leads neither to the complete disappearance of all bureaucratic forms of organization nor to their replacement by professional or entirely democratic forms of organization. It leads rather to a peculiar combination of bureaucratic and professional principles of organization. Thus, even though the type of bureaucratic structure, which Max Weber thought to be "unrivaled," undergoes a transformation, its fundamental principles nevertheless maintain, at least in part, their formative structural power. Moreover, although increasing rationalization might foster the expansion of forms of functional authority, the pressure to restrain their structural instability generates apparently new forms of bureaucratization. Indeed, institutionalized functional authority finds its structural support in official authority rather than in democratic controls. It seems, therefore, that the occupational culture of the future will emerge from the combination of bureaucratic and professional elements, and not from the combination of professional and democratic ones. Following Harold Wilensky one can assume that "the occupational group of the future will combine elements of both, of the professional and of the bureaucratic model; the average professional man will combine professional and nonprofessional orientations; the typical occupational association might be neither a trade union nor a professional association."[68]

If such an assumption is correct, then the future occupational cultures and the organizational culture connected with them may well have greater affinity with a "civic culture" shaped by democratic standards than with the past ones. Nonetheless, both are by no means identical. Now as before, in order that democratic standards may become operationally effective, they have to be institutionalized internally. The notion that the tendency toward greater democratization is necessarily correlated with increasing rationalization is a myth. Professionalization is not identical with democratization, nor does the significance of certain aspects of bureaucratization diminish as a result of rationalization.

The Advantage of Bureaucratization: A Functionalist View

But why, with increasing rationalization, should a link between professional and bureaucratic organizations be more likely than that between professional and democratic organizations? According to what usually passes for a "conservative" point of view, this is connected with the relief function which bureaucratization, primarily understood as formalization, has for all complex social relations. Nonformalized relations, when they are not restricted mainly to small groups or single systems, can overburden the personality system, and thus possibly lead to forms of permanent frustration.[69] Within complex organizations, the pressure to build recognition each time, from case to case, apparently must not become too great, since this may be detrimental to the efficient performance of the particular organization. There are, furthermore, numerous indications that, in themselves, discussion-oriented systems have only a small data processing capability and a limited potential for taking values into account. Where formalization is largely absent, the learning capacity of systems is extremely low.[70] From this perspective, Wilensky's expectations concerning the nature of the occupational and organizational culture of the future are by no means surprising, since they appear to be derived from the facts. Apparently, the formalization that accompanies increasing rationalization is a typical stabilization mechanism to which even initially nonbureaucratic forms of organization tend to succumb. Only after taking the effects of formalization into account can one come to a realistic assessment of the chances for institutionally linking "organization and democracy," which are apparently increased as a result of the increase in rationalization.

At this point, in order to advance the argument further, I shall make use of a study by Niklas Luhmann on the sociology of organizations, in which he analyzes the process of formalization from a functionalist point of view.[71] Formalization is here viewed as a strategy which primarily fulfills two functions in the process of system building. It serves to regulate both the differentiation of expectations and the differentiation of systems. The development of formal expectations helps to regulate the relationship between personality system and organization, while the development of a formal structure serves to standardize the relationship among the subsystems. The significance of such formal expectations lies primarily in the fact that they serve to enhance the range of variation and the flexibility of organizational action and, thus, to increase the elasticity of the system.[72] This takes place primarily through the exact determination of the boundaries of the system. Moreover, insofar as the personality system also serves as environment of the formalized system, this boundary determination leads not only to a greater differentiation of "social" environments, but also to an uncoupling of the personality from social systems. Since in Luhmann's analysis this aspect of the process of formalization has pre-eminence over systems differentiation, it will guide us in the following discussion.

According to Luhmann, the significance of formalization as differentiation of expectations can be illustrated in the elaboration of a complex of expectations, typical of all differentiated organizations, which is dramatized and simultaneously protected by the threat of exclusion.[73] This set of expectations is incorporated into membership roles whereby at first relatively dissimilar persons can gain prestructured access to a given system. The membership role not only objectively standardizes a specific relationship between the individual and the organization and creates a subjective commitment to a specific, organizationally related presentation of the self. It also opens and regulates the access to other roles in the organization. Along with the membership role, other specialized and informal roles are created[74] which have a standardized relationship to it. Such a differentiation of expectations, resulting from and centered around the membership role, offers decisive organizational advantages, for it allows for the separation of individual motivations from systems motivations, makes possible the separation of the personal from the official sphere, and permits the organization to impose a negative orientation, which screens out everything going beyond the possibilities preselected by the organization.[75] Formalization in the sense of differentiation of expectations is, therefore, a strategy which serves both to delimit the organization as a system vis-à-vis the individuals who form it and to maintain the system's stability vis-à-vis those same individuals who constitute one of its environments. Through it there emerge additional possibilities for role separation and role continuation that were missing in the less complex system. Consequently, there are also new possibilities for social integration independently, as it were, from particular individuals.

Viewed from the individual's perspective, this differentiation of expectations and its specification in the membership role and other related roles presuppose a generalization of expectations. Such a generalization has to be threefold, namely: "Temporal — as protection against particular deviations and disappointments; material — as protection against incoherence and contradictions; and social — as protection against dissent."[76] In all three respects, the membership role is much more elaborated than other organizational roles, that is, it possesses the highest level of generalization and remains, therefore, relatively abstract. Its high degree of formalization can be seen in the scope of its counterfactual stabilization. It is, as it were, immune against the thought, feeling, and will of the particular individual. Temporally, this is expressed in the fact that usually the expectations of the membership can be changed only through formal decision procedures.[77] Materially, it is expressed in the fact that the membership establishes the organization's priorities and compels separations or combinations of roles that are oriented to organizational goals and frequently directed against the individual's "interests."[78] Socially, the formalization of the membership role has also an abstractive effect. It formulates a sometimes fictitious consensus, which finds its representation, if not in the individual's inner conviction, at least in his self-presentation within the organization.[79]

The formalization of expectations and their organization in a membership role are, therefore, primarily an attempt to free the organization from the personal motivations of its individual members, in order to enhance the structural variability of the organization.[80] According to Luhmann, a high degree of identification of individual motives and organizational goals would actually lead to immobility, insofar as each change in goals or even each new interpretation of the organizational goals would create serious motivation problems for the individual members.[81] Of course, formalization finds its limits where it threatens to isolate the individual totally from the organization. Even formal organizations have to motivate the individuals to cooperation and therefore cannot dispense altogether with some "connection" between the individual and the organization. Luhmann actually thinks that the formalization of expectations serves to solve this problem at a higher level, since the formal regulation of the conditional requirements for entering and leaving the organization creates a generalized motivation.[82] It permits both the individual and the organization to remain connected with one another, while their boundaries may vary. Formalization is, therefore, not only a strategy of differentiation but also one of reintegration. Moreover, the differentiation of individual and system and their reintegration at a more abstract level are normally accompanied by system differentiation. This differentiation also shows the dialectic of differentiation and reintegration. In the same way as the formalization directed at the individual clears away the identity of motivation and purpose, the system-oriented formalization breaks the identity of means and ends. Therewith, the boundaries between system and subsystem also become changeable with respect to one another. Subsystems can now, for instance, perform functions which "cannot be derived directly from the system's goals either as primary or as secondary means, but are rather more or less clearly in opposition to it."[83] Without this "freedom of action," subsystems would not be able to fulfill their functions. The dissolution of the identity of means and ends is the precondition for an increased capability of the system to adapt. This does not mean, of course, that the subsystems now have no "instrumental relation" to the organizational goals, as if they could just concentrate on solving their own problems, without regard to their own "regulative prominence,"[84] which they derive precisely from the organizational goals. What has been said concerning the differentiation of individual and system also applies in this context. Separation means reintegration at a generalized, more abstract level. In the same way as motive and purpose can be separated only once there is a generalized motivation, so means and ends can be separated only when a formal structure links the subsystems to systemic goal attainment. That is to say, formalization, both at the individual and at the organizational level, has the following function: to place the "parts" in such a way against one another that they can shift their boundary positions without being exposed to disintegration.

Some Objections

Undoubtedly, one could raise objections against Luhmann's assumption that the advantages of formalization reside primarily in the benefits of the membership role. First of all, the advantages derived from formalization are apparently available only to those organizations which regulate admission into and departure from it by means of "free" contract. Luhmann in fact tries to show that the freedom to join and leave the organization is a secondary characteristic.[85] The same could be said, no doubt, about the formalizability of expectations. However, when organizational membership is regulated by "compulsory contract,"[86] one can only in a limited sense talk of the relief effects of formalization in relation to both individual and organization. In such cases, the inner sense of duty, indeed even a generalized motivation like that of the membership role, will probably be missing. Consequently, however, formalization will have burdening rather than unburdening effects. Instead of generating an organizationally directed and generalized motivation, it will unleash resistance, apathy, or other forms of withdrawal of motivation. It should, therefore, be clear that formalization is not equally meaningful for all organizations. Some organizations may fare better by trying to enhance the flexibility of the organizational structure. Luhmann himself clearly recognizes this possibility. Yet, although he regards deformalization as a strategy that is functionally equivalent to formalization, he makes practically no reference to its possible advantages and disadvantages for the various systemic functions and systemic goals. Ultimately, however, his assessment of such a strategy is quite clear: At present, when compared with deformalization, formalization is clearly a superior strategy, in spite of all the problems which it may in the end pose.[87] The fundamental problem is that deformalization produces an increase in emotionalism and that, in consequence, the resultant order is dependent upon its ability to tap considerable sources of motivation and security. Deformalization would have to

rely either upon the members' inner sense of duty toward the common goals or upon intensive group solidarity. Thus, it cannot free the rational structure of action and the order of communication as completely from motivational tasks as is possible in the case of formal organizations. The result may be the appearance of new, emotionally conditioned and aggressively inclined indurations against the environment. Some of the advantages of formal organizations are thus lost, and with them also the predictability and the guarantee of success with which such a system can be organized.[88]

Bureaucratization Specified: Formalization and Segregation

All these objections notwithstanding, Luhmann's analysis is of crucial significance for the problems that concern us here. Although one does not need to remain strictly within Luhmann's theoretical frame of reference, his analysis opens up a new perspective on bureaucratization and on bureaucratic organization. Following some of his ideas, one could say that bureaucratization is a strategy which is directed primarily at two different levels and at two different dimensions of the organization. At the vertical level, it brings about a differentiation of individual and system and of system and subsystem, as well as their reintegration at a relatively generalized and abstract level. At the horizontal level, it leads to the double segregation of internal and external roles and functions, as well as to their system-oriented recombination. It is thus a strategy of boundary-setting in a fourfold direction. It releases the individual's motivation from the organizational goals, renders the individual's organizational roles immune against his other roles, and makes the subsystems autonomous while at the same time it determines their functional specificity. It is, therefore, a strategy of securing internal and external division of labor as well as goal-orientation, even if guided by the principle of hierarchical coordination.

Elective Affinities

By designating the "horizontal" and "vertical" coordinates of bureaucratization as segregation and formalization, one is better able to perceive the relationship between bureaucratization, professionalization, and democratization. There are certain elective affinities between the four strategies, which explains why the relationship between debureaucratization, professionalization, and democratization is not clear cut. Debureaucratization can in fact mean two different things: a certain degree of deformalization or of desegregation. While it is unlikely that the two aspects of bureaucratization develop independently of one another, deformalization does not necessarily lead to desegregation. Thus, although in a certain sense professionalization does imply debureaucratization, it is not identical with it. While increasing professionalization appears to foster deformalization, it is apparently not compatible with desegregation. On the contrary, professionalization is likely to enhance tendencies toward segregation, a process clearly opposed to democratization. Democratization as a strategy, on the other hand, is opposed to both aspects of bureaucratization and can be combined with professionalization only when the common primary opponent is formalization. The ambivalent relationship between professionalization and democratization can be summed up in the following way: Rationalization in the direction of equality and rationalization in the direction of efficiency are mutually exclusive from a certain point on.

This abstract discussion of the elective affinities between the four strategies also makes clear why professionalization has a greater affinity to bureaucratization than to democratization. But this hypothesis must be further differentiated. The affinity is particularly great toward one aspect of bureaucratization only — segregation. By contrast, formalization and professionalization are opposite strategies, as evidenced by the fact that the very notion of profession militates against an excessive separation of individual motivation and organizational goals. Furthermore, the hierarchic coordination which is linked to formalization is also contrary to the striving for autonomy that is characteristic of professionally oriented individuals. Collegial coordination or at least team coordination suits them better.[89] In this respect, professionalization, like democratization, is oriented toward debureaucratization. At least where it becomes socially relevant, professionalization entails an attack on the traditional form of "official" authority.

But such a discussion of elective affinities remains relatively useless as long as it makes no reference to concrete organizational situations. Strictly speaking, specific empirical cases would need to be analyzed. However, a more differentiated view can be obtained even by considering typical situations. By examining the four strategies in relation to typical organizational conflicts and functions as well as their relationships to the surrounding environment, certain observations can be made concerning the relative weight of each of these strategies and their capacity to either stabilize or change existing structures. Such an analysis would, moreover, also comply with one of the central points of Crozier's argument, that in order to avoid overdrawing the concept of strategy in the sociology of organizations, one must take into account "the bonds of organization."

Organizational Settings and Strategies

Theoretical discussions in the sociology of organizations often refer to the fact that rational organizations are confronted with typical dilemmas. These dilemmas generally result from the discrepancy between individual needs and organizational imperatives, as well as from a kind of goal-conflict between knowledge and power and between "functional" and "official" authority, indeed from the fact that expertise cannot be easily organized.[90] Organizations must therefore set priorities and decide whether to give preference to the requirements of the organization or to the needs of individuals, and whether to stress expertise at the expense of a hierarchical articulation of the channels of command. Depending on which priorities have been or will be institutionalized, each of the four strategies has a different weight and function. If, for instance, an organization wants to further the application of specialized knowledge yet also confine the individual's organizational involvement to his professional role, then professionalization and segregation will prevail, while formalization and democratization will be pushed back. These strategies can then be used to change established structures. The bureaucratization of the "old" professions and the democratization of the universities may serve as illustrations. If an organization, for instance, wants to secure from its members a strong commitment toward organizational goals without simultaneously attaching differential importance to knowledge, then democratization and perhaps also a certain degree of segregation will prevail, while professionalization and formalization will recede. Here they fulfill the function of upsetting the established "compromise." This can be observed, for instance, when a secret society is transformed into a mass party, or a community of religious brethren into a church.

These observations make clear that the primary function of an organization also determines the relative importance of each particular strategy. Applying to organizations the four functions distinguished by Talcott Parsons, one could say that they gain a different meaning in each case, depending on whether the organization's primary function is adaptation, goal-attainment, integration, or pattern maintenance and latency.[91] Economic and political agencies as well as agencies of integration and socialization are to different degrees open to formalization, segregation, professionalization, and democratization. This does not mean, however, that each of these strategies cannot also find expression in group conflicts within each of those organizational types. For instance, from a structural perspective, democratization has from the outset lesser chances in economic and socialization organizations than in political and integrative ones, because in the former it is hardly compatible with the so-called "bonds of organization." Yet it is precisely here that democratization can be used as a strategy to open up social relations, especially if the entire culture is informed by democratic standards, so that the legitimation of organizational functions requires at least lip service to such standards.[92] Moreover, this strategy will also be useful once the relations with the surrounding environment, which accompany the increase in organizational functions, no longer permit the use of segregation mechanisms such as physical separation.[93]

This leads to a third point. The particular products of an organization place this organization — on account of the legitimation problem — not only in a very specific relationship to the entire culture and its institutions of administration, but also to the consumers of its "products." Whether an organization produces goods or services, and whether its consumers are inside or outside the organization, not only influences the organizational structure itself but also determines the relative importance of each of the four strategies, particularly that of democratization.[94] For instance, when an organization produces services for consumers who are also members of the organization, then even in those cases in which professionalization or formalization are functionally required in order to meet the technical needs of the organization, the chances of using democratization as a counter strategy will nonetheless be greater than in the case of organizations producing goods for an impersonal market.[95] For one of the structural problems of such organizations is the segregation of members into two "classes." But such a segregation is made difficult by the fact that the clients are also, at the same time, members of the organization, which makes certain segregation mechanisms inapplicable. Perhaps this is the reason why, when compared with economic organizations, certain socialization agencies have a greater "propensity" for strategies of democratization. The relationship with the outside environment accompanies the fulfillment of the technical function, inhibits segregation and hence fosters democratization as a strategy for opening up social relations.

These differentiating remarks may suffice in illustrating the significance of organizational "bonds" in any organizational analysis. The concept of strategy presupposes a theory of complex organizations. Some aspects of such a theory have been outlined more or less explicitly above, particularly in the discussion of the relative importance of each of the four strategies. It still remains to be completed, however, if the goal is to provide an adequate foundation for the perspective presented here. On the basis of the preceding arguments it is clear that such a theory coincides only partially with Weber's theory. It takes into consideration, more than was possible for Weber, the evident increase in inter- and intraorganizational structural variation that accompanies the growing rationalization. At the same time, however, it qualifies the thesis that bureaucratic organizations are "unrivaled" and technically superior and it opens the way for debureaucratization with all its political consequences. Yet, although such a perspective, in its theory, emphasizes the structural change in the traditional bureaucratic principle, while politically stressing the significance of the institutionalization of counter principles and counter strategies, it does not argue that as a result of increasing rationalization bureaucratization has lost its function and is now a historically obsolete phenomenon. Rather, it focuses upon the significance of segregation and formalization in a context in which the growth of professionalization and democratization — especially the institutionalization of specialized knowledge and democratic controls — are partly a technical necessity and partly an almost inevitable political demand. It therefore furthers at the internal organizational level, theoretically as well as politically, a perspective which is similar to Weber's perspective at the societal level. It treats bureaucratization, professionalization, and democratization, together with "official" authority, "functional" authority, and democratic controls, not primarily as historical stages or as aporias, but rather as competing strategies and counter principles susceptible to institutionalization. Only the interplay of all these can create the kind of complexity now necessary for organizations as a result of advancing rationalization.

Organizational Dilemmas and Strategies

This can be made more specific by showing how the four strategies apply to the two organizational dilemmas. The organizational dilemmas signify that with increasing rationalization each organization must strike a precarious balance between the individual and the organization as well as between expertise and official authority. The more differentiated and complex organizations become, the better they are able to spread out simultaneously all four problems and thus deal with the organizational problems in such a manner that they can be "solved" only in relation to one another. Each solution, then, influences the other and none can be regarded as rational as long as it does not consider its consequences for other solutions and orients itself accordingly. It is for precisely this reason that organizations in which a single structural principle and strategy dominate remain either at a relatively undifferentiated level or are even bound to regress. When formalization is unduly increased, however, the motivational threads binding the members are in danger of coming apart. When segregation is unduly increased, fragmentation may result and meaningful coordination may come to an end. In turn, when professionalization is unduly heightened, increased inequality may lead to unbridgeable communication gaps; and when democratization is unduly heightened, fusions and the termination of a meaningful division of labor become the main danger. However, the thesis that complex organizations should spread out all four problems, while at the same time balancing the solutions against one another, must not be misunderstood as a plea for a naive equilibrium model. The weight to be given to each of the principles and strategies depends upon structural as well as situational factors. For this reason it would be mistaken to prohibit "regression," as it were, by normative means. There are situations in which an organization can achieve greater differentiation and increased adaptation and learning capacity only by way of regression. Such beneficial regressions can sometimes even be interpreted as revolutionary breakthroughs. Marx's model of council democracy, for instance, might be viewed in this way.[96]

Weber and Beyond

Looking back from such a perspective once again at Weber's prediction that the increasing rationalization will lead to ever more total bureaucratic domination, his view acquires a specific meaning even at the internal organizational level. Weber is aware of the danger that, far from enhancing their complexity, organizations might encourage the tendency toward bureaucratization and become one-dimensional structures characterized by rigidity and resistance to innovation. Therewith, however, they would become the cornerstones of a societal development oriented to stagnation and would be perfectly adapted to the formative tendencies of the new corporate state. Against this Weberian vision one could, of course, object that increasing rationalization does in no way present such a threat, at least not at the internal organizational level. For rationalization is after all at least partially tied to debureaucratization and thus serves to minimize bureaucratic domination in favor of functional authority. While such an objection would be justified, it is nevertheless subject to being challenged in turn, since — as the preceding analysis has tried to show — heightened rationalization fosters the expansion of certain forms of professionalization, and heightened professionalization goes hand in hand with the closure of social relations. A development accomplished by way of professionalization, in fact, would fit Weber's image of the modern corporate state extremely well, since the latter is based upon the fusion of the state with organizations and associations constituted on an occupational basis. Weber's diagnosis permits only one answer to the question concerning the right relationship between official authority, functional authority, and democratic controls in the face of increasing rationalization: that it is necessary to institutionalize all three, reinforced as counter principles. This would seem to be a measure well suited to enforcing and expanding the kind of complexity which alone can assure, in the face of the pressure toward increasing rationalization, a flexible internal and external adaptation to the environment. In other words: While rationalization and democratization do not simply cause each other reciprocally within the organization, and while rationalization can to some extent be advanced even without democratization, the formative tendencies built into the process of rationalization reinforce the application of democratic controls as a strategy for opening up social relations precisely because these tend to maintain and enhance organizational complexity.

NOTES

1. Translators' Note: *Sachautorität* has been translated as "functional" authority. As the author himself indicates in a note contained in his German text, the use of this concept in the literature is neither clear cut nor consistent. "Functional" authority refers indistinctly to the type of authority derived from expertise, professional competence, technical or specialized knowledge, in contrast with "official" authority (*Amtsautorität*), which is the type of authority derived from an "office" in the bureaucratic hierarchy. Perhaps in accordance with modern technocratic trends, *Sachautorität* could also be translated as "technical" authority.

2. See A. Etzioni, *Modern Organizations* (Englewood Cliffs, N.J.: Prentice-Hall, 1964), pp. 76 ff.

3. Influence, power, domination, authority and discipline are usually conceptually distinguished. I believe, however, that it is advisable to distinguish influence relations primarily in terms of their social organization and — apart from some of Weber's criteria, such as everyday/extraordinary, personal/functional — to investigate the validity claims of influence as well as legitimation processes in terms of the extent of the standardization of influence.

4. E.g., Kurt Holm, "Zum Begriff der Macht," *Kölner Zeitschrift für Soziologie und Sozialpsychologie* (1969) 21(2):269-288, especially pp. 285 ff. Also Max Weber, *Wirtschaft und Gesellschaft* [1921-22], 4th ed., Johannes Winkelmann, ed. (Tübingen: J.C.B. Mohr, 1956), pp. 28 ff. [*Economy and Society* [1968], Guenther Roth and Claus Wittich, eds. (Berkeley, Los Angeles, London: University of California Press, 1978), pp. 53 ff.].

5. See K. Holm, "Zum Begriff der Macht," pp. 269 ff.

6. See Chester I. Barnard, *The Function of the Executive* [1938] (Cambridge, Mass.: Harvard University Press, 1956), p. 167; Herbert A. Simon, *Administrative Behavior: A Study of Decision-Making Processes in Administrative Organization* (New York: The Free Press, 1945), p. 12; Helmut Ziegler, *Strukturen und Prozesse der Autorität in der Unternehmung. Ein organisationssoziologischer Beitrag zur Theorie der betrieblichen Organisation* (Stuttgart: Enke, 1970), pp. 68 ff.

7. See J. Winkelmann, *Legalität und Legitimität in Max Webers Herrschaftssoziologie* (Tübingen: J.C.B. Mohr, 1952), pp. 40 ff.

8. On the significance of "third parties" for the institutionalization of relationships see Peter Berger and Thomas Luckmann, *The Social Construction of Reality: A Treatise in the Sociology of Knowledge* (Garden City, N.Y.: Doubleday, 1966), pp. 58 ff.

9. See Max Weber, *Wirtschaft und Gesellschaft*, pp. 181 ff. [see *Economy and Society*, p. 312].

10. See Niklas Luhmann, *Legitimation durch Verfahren* (Neuwied and Berlin: Luchterhand, 1969), pp. 28 ff., who, however, has reservations about a conception which seeks refuge in "consensus by way of exchange" (p. 30).

11. See Peter Berger and Thomas Luckmann, *The Social Construction of Reality*, pp. 92 ff.

12. Such an argument permits combining Weber's distinction between "domination by virtue of a constellation of interests" and "domination by virtue of authority" (*Wirtschaft und Gesellschaft*, p. 542 [*Economy and Society*, p. 943]) with the distinction between "power" and "domination." Etzioni's classification of typical structures of influence is systematically influenced by a similar idea. See A. Etzioni, *A Comparative Analysis of Complex Organizations: On Power, Involvement, and Their Correlates* (Glencoe, Ill.: The Free Press, 1961), pp. 12 ff.

13. Such conceptual pairs make possible a distinction between the sources and the processes of legitimation, which is however meaningful only as an analytical distinction. E.g., H. Ziegler, *Strukturen und Prozesse der Autorität in der Unternehmung*, p. 20.

14. See N. Luhmann, *Legitimation durch Verfahren*, pp. 27 ff.

15. Similarly F. Landwehrmann, *Organisationsstrukturen industrieller Grossbetriebe* (Cologne- Opladen: Westdeutscher Verlag, 1965), p. 28.

16. See Talcott Parsons, "Introduction" to *Max Weber: The Theory of Social and Economic Organization*, T. Parsons, ed. (Glencoe, Ill.: The Free Press, 1947), pp. 54 ff.

17. See Alvin Gouldner, *Patterns of Industrial Bureaucracy: A Case Study of Modern Factory Administration* (New York: The Free Press, 1954), p. 22.

18. A. Etzioni, *Modern Organizations*, p. 76.

19. *Ibid.*

20. The decisive problem of this structural type seems to be that a normatively coerced linking of particular phases of the decision process with hierarchical positions leads to consequences that interfere with the adaptive capacity of the organization. See M. Irle, "Führungsverhalten in organisierten Gruppen," *Handbuch der Psychologie* vol. 9, 2d ed., rev., A.v. Mayer and B. Herwig, eds. (Göttingen: Verlag für Psychologie, 1970), pp. 527 ff.

21. See V. Thompson, *Modern Organization* (New York: Knopf, 1961), p. 6.

22. Heinz Hartmann, *Funktionale Autorität. Systematische Abhandlung zu einem soziologischen Begriff* (Stuttgart: Enke, 1964).

23. *Ibid.*, pp. 18 ff.

24. *Ibid.*, pp. 42 ff.

25. *Ibid.*, p. 8.

26. *Ibid.*, p. 53.

27. *Ibid.*, pp. 35, 71 ff.

28. *Ibid.*, p. 57.

29. *Ibid.*, p. 59.

30. *Ibid.*, pp. 6, 16.

31. On the problem of trust and the distinction between trust in persons and trust in the system, see N. Luhmann, *Vertrauen. Ein Mechanismus der Reduktion sozialer Komplexität*

(Stuttgart: Enke, 1968), pp. 10, 13, 20 [see "Trust," in *Trust and Power*, Tom Burns and Gianfranco Poggi, eds. (New York: Wiley, 1979), pp. 1-103].

32. See *ibid.*, p. 69 [p. 71]. Luhmann emphasizes that while mistrust is a functional equivalent of trust it is less suited for reducing complexity.

33. H. Hartmann, *Funktionale Autorität*, pp. 58-61. On the importance of reputation as a guiding mechanism of systems based upon expert knowledge, such as the system of science, see N. Luhmann, *Soziologische Aufklärung. Aufsätze zur Theorie sozialer Systeme* (Cologne-Opladen: Luchterhand, 1970), p. 237; Peter Weingart, "Selbststeuerung der Wissenschaft und staatliche Wissenschaftspolitik," *Kölner Zeitschrift für Soziologie und Sozialpsychologie* (1970) 22(3):567-592; and W. Schluchter, "Auf der Suche nach der verlorenen Einheit. Anmerkungen zum Strukturwandel der deutschen Universität," in Hans Albert, ed., *Sozialtheorie und soziale Praxis* (Meisenheim: Hain, 1971), pp. 255-280.

34. Hartmann, *Funktionale Autorität*, p. 53. Hartmann does not completely deny that there are elements of belief connected with the type of functional authority. *Ibid.*, pp. 58, 110.

35. See N. Luhmann, *Vertrauen*, p. 22 [*Trust and Power*, p. 24], where he emphasizes that trust can only be based upon the cognizance of the possibility of a breach of trust.

36. *Ibid.*, p. 49 [p. 52], where this is asserted for the function of functionally specific produced truth.

37. Hartmann's position, however, is not altogether clear here since he also attempts to reduce the import of expertise to timeless social situations, to extreme situations and to ideological conflicts. See *Funktionale Autorität*, pp. 31 ff.

38. *Ibid.*, pp. 19, 67.

39. It is not accidental that the abolition of division of labor and of expertise as well as the idea of a universal unfolding of human abilities belongs to the Marxist view of freedom from domination. The free person is the universal expert, as it were.

40. A term of Parsons, whose analyses of the importance of professional roles for the modern occupational structure have been foundational. See T. Parsons, "The Motivation of Economic Activities," [1940], *Essays in Sociological Theory*, rev. ed. (Glencoe, Ill.: The Free Press, 1954), pp. 50-68; "The Professions and Social Structure," [1939], *ibid.*, pp. 34-49. See also *The Social System* (Glencoe, Ill.: The Free Press, 1951), pp. 430 ff.

41. See N.. Luhmann *Vertrauen*, pp. 21, 23 [*Trust and Power*, pp. 24, 25].

42. See H. Hartmann, *Funktionale Autorität*, pp. 102 ff.

43. The professions, however, apparently had their preindustrial precursors in the associations of the artisans and in the guilds. Only a few examples from the immense body of literature shall be mentioned here: H. Vollmer and D. Mills, "Professionalization and Technological Change," in Vollmer and Mills, eds., *Professionalization* (Englewood Cliffs, N.J.: Prentice-Hall, 1966), p. 44; W. Moore, "Economic and Professional Institutions," in Neil J. Smelser, ed., *Sociology: An Introduction* (New York: Wiley, 1967), pp. 318 ff.; H. Wilensky, "The Professionalization of Everyone?" *American Journal of Sociology* (1964) 70(2):137-158; W. Kornhauser, *Scientists in Industry: Conflict and Accommodation* (Berkeley, Los Angeles: University of California Press, 1963), pp. 1, 11.

44. On this distinction, which is here employed in a metaphorical sense, see R. Dahrendorf, "Industrielle Fertigkeiten und soziale Schichtung," *Kölner Zeitschrift für*

Soziologie und Sozialpsychologie (1956) 8(4):552.

45. See especially W. Kornhauser, *Scientists in Industry: Conflict and Accommodation*, p. 1, who speaks of a sort of trusteeship for the community.

46. H. Hartmann, *Funktionale Autorität*, p. 107.

47. From a perspective internal to organizations this would explain the difference between Saint-Simonism and Marxism.

48. For a similar distinction see Howard M. Vollmer and Donald Mills, "Editors' Introduction," in *Professionalization*, pp. vii ff.

49. See Horst Bosetzky, *Grundzüge einer Soziologie der Industrieverwaltung. Möglichkeiten und Grenzen der Betrachtung des industriellen Grossbetriebes als bürokratische Organisation* (Stuttgart: Enke, 1970), pp. 187 ff. and M. Weber, *Wirtschaft und Gesellschaft*, pp. 159 ff. [*Economy and Society*, pp. 271 ff.].

50. See R. Hall, "Some Organizational Considerations in the Professional-Organizational Relationship," *Administrative Quarterly* (1967) 12:464 ff.; H. Bosetzky, "Bürokratische Organisationsformen in Behörden und Industrieverwaltungen," in Renate Mayntz, ed., *Bürokratische Organisation* (Cologne: Kiepenheuer & Witsch, 1968), pp. 179 ff.

51. See H. Wilensky, "The Professionalization of Everyone?", pp. 142 ff.; and T. Caplow, "The Sequence of Professionalization," in Howard M. Vollmer and Donald L. Mills, eds., *Professionalization*, pp. 20 ff.

52. See A. Gouldner, "Cosmopolitans and Locals: Toward an Analysis of Latent Social Roles," *Administrative Science Quarterly* (1957-58), p. 290. See also the survey of the studies on professional orientations and the conflicts of loyalty resulting from them as well as their "solution" in W. Kornhauser, *Scientists in Industry: Conflict and Accommodation*, p. 121.

53. This in any case is the drift of analysis in the famous books by Whyte and Presthues, which however do not merely focus upon the gradual leveling of the professional orientation. See W. Whyte, Jr., *The Organization Man* (New York: Simon and Schuster, 1956), pp. 225 ff., and Robert Presthues, *The Organizational Society* (New York: Knopf, 1962). Harold Wilensky's excellent *Intellectuals in Labor Unions: Organizational Pressure on Professional Roles* (Glencoe, Ill.: The Free Press, 1956), esp. pp. 104 ff., offers a different view.

54. See W. Kornhauser, *Scientists in Industry: Conflict and Accommodation*, pp. 86 ff.

55. On this distinction see W. Moore, "Economics and Professional Institutions," pp. 320 ff.

56. On professionals as entrepreneurs see H. Vollmer, "Professional Adaptation to Organizations," in Vollmer and Mills, *Professionalization*, pp. 276 ff.

57. The charge of "commercialization" and consequently of outside control of the profession appears a typical cornerstone of a strategy aimed at the autonomy claims of the professions.

58. See R. Hall, "Some Organizational Considerations in the Professional-Organizational Relationship," pp. 462 ff., as well as Etzioni, *Modern Organizations*, pp. 78 ff.

59. Even this development, however, is not quite clear cut. E.g., Everett Hughes' thesis that the individual autonomy of the professionals employed in a bureaucratic organization is sometimes much greater than that of such self-employed professionals as physi-

cians or lawyers who are under pressure to conform to the clients' individual or collective customs and opinions. Hughes, "The Professions in Society," *The Canadian Journal of Economics and Political Science* (February 1960) 26(1):54-61, esp. p. 61.

60. See W. Kornhauser, *Scientists in Industry: Conflict and Accommodation*, pp. 83 ff.

61. See Albert Mok, "Alte und neue Professionen," *Kölner Zeitschrift für Soziologie und Sozialpsychologie* (1969), p. 772.

62. My own analysis is different from Mok's. I emphasize the assymetry of control between laymen and colleagues. Mok appears to assume that they are on an equal footing. See *ibid.*, p. 772.

63. This is not Mok's thesis either. However, it conclusively follows, in my opinion, from the assumption that inequality is shifted into the profession itself, thereby making mutual control into a direct tool of status struggle here as well.

64. Mok, "Alte und neue Professionen," pp. 774, 775.

65. See Vollmer and Mills, *Professionalization*, pp. 22 ff., esp. 23, 28; R. Dahrendorf, "Industrielle Fertigkeiten und soziale Schichtung," p. 564. Claus Offe has generalized this view and by way of it has attempted to demonstrate the increasing ideological nature of the performance principle.

66. In principle, the list should begin with human equality. Social evolution, however, seems to have taken the reverse course. Only in advanced industrial society is the democratic principle of equality taken seriously and only there does it become socially effective — a development with decisive consequences for mobilization strategies. See T.H. Marshall, *Class, Citizenship, and Social Development* (Garden City, N.Y.: Doubleday, 1964), pp. 71 ff.

67. On the distinction of these three models of organization see H. Bosetzky, *Grundzüge einer Soziologie der Industrieverwaltung. Möglichkeiten und Grenzen der Betrachtung des industriellen Grossbetriebes als bürokratische Organisation*, pp. 292 ff.

68. Harold Wilensky, "The Professionalization of Everyone?", p. 157.

69. This, for example, is Niklas Luhmann's thesis, which he gives play to from different points of view in his voluminous work. See the especially clear comment in "Komplexität und Demokratie," *Politische Vierteljahresschrift* (1969), p. 319.

70. See the interesting controversy between Jürgen Habermas and Niklas Luhmann as well as Luhmann's assessment of the significance of discourse and of a discussion-based system. See Habermas and Luhmann, *Gesellschaftstheorie oder Sozialtechnologie — Was leistet die Systemforschung?* (Frankfurt: Suhrkamp, 1971), pp. 329 ff.

71. See N. Luhmann, *Funktion und Folgen formaler Organisation* (Berlin: Duncker & Humblot, 1964). I am relying here only on the first part of the book on the primary functions of formalization and leave unconsidered the part on secondary functions.

72. *Ibid.*, pp. 103, 141 ff. The emphasis here is on the flexibility of the social system, not of the personal system.

73. *Ibid.*, pp. 36, 38.

74. *Ibid.*, p. 48.

75. *Ibid.*, pp. 41 ff.

76. *Ibid.*, p. 56.

77. *Ibid.*, p. 62.

78. *Ibid.*, pp. 64 ff.

79. *Ibid.*, pp. 68 ff.

80. *Ibid.*, pp. 92 ff., 100 ff. This carefully considered formulation is opposed to Luhmann's approach insofar as for Luhmann it is actions, roles, etc., not individuals, which constitute a system.

81. *Ibid.*, pp. 101 ff.

82. *Ibid.*, pp. 89 ff.

83. *Ibid.*, p. 76.

84. *Ibid.*, p. 87.

85. *Ibid.*, p. 44.

86. See especially Talcott Parsons, *Structure and Process in Modern Societies* (Glencoe, Ill.: The Free Press, 1960), pp. 39 ff.

87. See N. Luhmann, *Funktion und Folgen formaler Organisation*, p. 152. Luhmann's entire analysis is essentially based upon the opposition of informal (*elementare*) and formal organization. Consequently he must in the last analysis interpret every tendency toward deformalization as a regression to informal social relations. On some results of formalization see *ibid.*, pp. 62, 68, 70, 104 ff.

88. *Ibid.*, pp. 151 ff.

89. See especially Rensis Likert, *The Human Organization: Its Management and Values* (New York: McGraw-Hill, 1967), pp. 160 ff.

90. See A. Etzioni, *Modern Organizations*, p. 75.

91. See T. Parsons, *Structure and Process in Modern Societies*, pp. 45 ff.

92. *Ibid.*, pp. 63 ff.

93. On the importance of this mechanism see especially E. Litwak, "Drei alternative Bürokratiemodelle," in Renate Mayntz, ed., *Bürokratische Organisation*, p. 123.

94. On these distinctions see T. Parsons, *Structure and Process in Modern Societies*, p. 24.

95. This assertion applies only to the internal distribution of these chances within the organization itself. An organization, for example, which produces commodities for a market, can no doubt be externally "democratized" by way of consumer organizations.

96. See Frieder Naschold, *Organisation und Demokratie. Untersuchung zum Demokratisierungspotential in komplexen Organisationen* (Stuttgart: Kohlhammer, 1969), pp. 26 ff.

15

Toward a Theory of Late Capitalism

CLAUS OFFE

To develop the outlines of a political sociology of "late capitalism" is a claim that itself requires justification. Established academic traditions cannot be enlisted to support the use of the concept of late capitalism to elucidate questions which official social science has in any case simply tended to ignore and treated either from the rather arbitrary reference point of comparative politics, or from within the framework of a series of particular studies of national development. The contributions of economics, sociology, and political science to the analysis of social developments are nowadays guided by a political and theoretical framework within which not even the term "capitalism" is a significant component. The distinctive power of this concept must therefore be affirmed *against* established research practice, which bypasses the level of abstraction on which the concept of capitalism is located in one of two quite different ways. On the one hand, the level of abstraction implied in this concept is unduly reduced by those studies which concentrate upon one particular nation-state and its history. On the other hand, the level of abstraction that is characteristic of the term capitalism is largely transcended in various theories of "industrial society," in which differences between socioeconomic formations and questions concerning capitalism or socialism are either wholly disregarded or dismissed as essentially irrelevant because of the alleged convergence of "industrial" social systems.

If the category "late capitalism" is adopted as a reference point for analyzing the highly industrialized social systems of the Western

This paper, translated by John Keane, was written in the winter of 1971 and has been slightly revised and shortened by the author. It has served as the introductory essay of the author's *Strukturprobleme des kapitalistischen Staates* [1972], 5th ed. (Frankfurt: Suhrkamp, 1980). While it diverges in its approach, style, conceptual framework, and some of its conclusions from most of the work the author has published since that time [see for English editions the two volumes *Contradictions of the Welfare State* (London: Hutchinson, 1984) and *Disorganized Capitalism* (Oxford: Polity Press, 1985)], it may still be of interest for its exploration of the deficiencies of capitalist rationality and the deficient modes of healing those deficiencies. *Claus Offe.*

world, three questions immediately arise. First, on what basis can these systems still be called *capitalist*? Secondly, what does *late* capitalism mean? And, thirdly, how can we justify the rejection of the alternative generalizing categories (e.g., "postindustrial society," "postmodern society," "technotronic society," "new industrial state," "modern capitalism") which appear so frequently in the Anglo-Saxon literature in particular?

The Concept of Capitalism

Just as Marx's analysis of nineteenth-century capitalism can no longer make sense of (or even theoretically classify) many phenomena that we find in late capitalist social formations, so, conversely, today's orthodox social sciences (especially political science) are incapable of posing, much less answering, Marx's ultimate question: What are the *laws of motion* of capital, and how do they shape the social structure? It would perhaps be more accurate to say that the dominant social sciences mostly ignore this question on purpose; almost without exception, the level of their analytical approach is *reduced*, precisely because one of their primary theoretical concerns is to *refute* Marx. The analysis of the logic of development of existing social formations has also fallen victim to this process of displacement of the focus of theoretical attention; concern with the *capitalist* identity of the capitalist system is jettisoned in favor of arbitrary procedures and definitions.

When we speak of capitalist social systems, we usually refer to those in which the greatest (and most important) part of the (produced) means of production are owned "privately." The private ownership of the means of production — the legal sanctioning of titles to property — is a static indicator, however. It serves only as a preliminary indicator of the consequences of this type of ownership. The essential element of capitalist structures is not the *legal* power of disposal over private property, but the concrete ways in which this power is typically exercised — i.e., the institutionalized procedures through which priorities are determined, the guiding strategic criteria and alternatives, as well as investment decisions and their outcomes. It is true that the continuous valorization of capital under capitalism (accumulation, the "socialization" of privately controlled production, the commodification of labor-power, constant technical and organizational innovation, rising capital intensity, urbanization, and so on) is a process that was at first linked historically to the legal form of private ownership of capital. But subsequently, this link between legal form and the logic of the valorization process has been weakened considerably. On the one hand, small shareholders no longer play any significant functional role for the process of capital while, on the other hand, managerial strata and even publicly owned organizations have become crucial executors of the capitalist valorization process. This blurred relationship between the legal form and social function of capital necessitates the formulation of a concept of capitalism which unambiguously highlights the dynamics of socioeconomic *processes*, and not merely the cluster of structural features they assume in historically diverse but functionally equivalent variants.

For Marx, "capitalism" is not the mere sum of elements that are encountered in a particular social system at any given time — elements such as the distribution of income, a particular technology or allocation of work tasks, or the recruitment of political elites from the ruling class. Rather, the Marxian theory supposes that the identity of capitalism derives from the fact that all capitalist societies share a unique lawfulness of development, and that the empirical-analytic prediction of its complex variants is not the intention and in principle exceeds the competence of materialist social science. Instead, this materialist theory can be completed only through concrete inquiries.

Marx's concept of capitalism is thus not a static description of a specific configuration of structural components. It is not an all-encompassing descriptive index of a given social structure, but instead characterizes the logic of a model of development of a historical and socioeconomic formation in its totality. Whether a given social structure can be considered capitalist is thus not decided by its income distribution (or any other descriptive indicator), but only by whether or not it is "programmed" by the logic of capitalist development. Marx expressed this logic of development in two general (and virtually interchangeable) formulae: the contradiction between the increasing "socialization of production" and its "private appropriation," and the contradiction between the "forces" and "relations" of production. These very general formulae may be reinterpreted as an answer to the questions: Which type of system problems are typically and objectively produced by this socioeconomic system, and which structural mechanisms enable it to process these problems? Viewed in this way, the antagonistic or contradictory character of a system derives from its self-destructive tendencies, which are produced by the gap between the institutionalized procedures for processing problems and those mechanisms that generate these same problems.

Marx analyzed this type of relationship through the *economic* institutions of capitalism, because under capitalist conditions these become, for the first time in history, the organizing center of all social relations, and thus also a key to the analysis of the social and economic laws of development. Under *capitalist* conditions, all elements of the social structure are either determined or limited by exchange relations. Capital subordinates all social realms to its own motion and, thereby, to its profit-directed self-valorization. It opens up markets and organizes them on a national and, later, an international scope. It organizes a class of "free" industrial workers ("free" in the sense that they are both separated from their means of labor and emancipated from feudal control of their labor power) and becomes the sole source of livelihood of those workers. Capital develops technology and eventually institutionalizes its permanent renovation; it also weaves national and international systems into an ever tighter network of relations of interdependence. But all this comes about not through conscious and deliberate direction, but as an "anarchic" and blindly spontaneous process, as a byproduct of a dynamic inherent in capital itself. As the empirical subjects of business transactions, "capitalists" themselves can act against this dynamic only to a limited degree.

Of course, these characteristics of the "socialization" of production — as well as of all the other elements of the social structure — do not yet render this process *contradictory*. The "socialization" of production first assumes an antagonistic form when its blind and "anarchic" consequences put into question the continued existence of both capital and the social formation it structures. From the perspective of *individual* units of capital, this process of self-destruction occurs through the unfolding of competition, which permanently threatens the existence of capital; for capital *considered as a whole*, it arises in the course of general economic crises, especially realization crises; and, finally, from the standpoint of the *social formation* of capitalism, this process of self-destruction occurs through the class struggle, whose objective preconditions, motivating force, and strategic orientations are in turn structured by the process of the valorization of capital. What is decisive for Marx's concept of capitalism, thus, is not the variations in space and time of particular capitalist systems, but the inevitability of these self-negating tendencies rooted in the process of *"private"* production. These tendencies determine whether any given capitalist system continues to develop or is transformed into a postcapitalist formation.

System, Structure, and Contradiction

The continuing importance of Marx's attempt to locate the basic contradiction of capitalist societies in the discrepancy between the unconscious, purely objective expansion of *"socialized"* relations of interdependence due to the intransigence of *privately* directed relations of production and the absence of conscious organization and planning of this blind process of socialization is evident in the recent controversy between "structuralist" and "historicist" interpretations of Marx's categories. The basic positions in this controversy will be recalled briefly here, since they bear significantly on the problem of whether systems-theoretical concepts can legitimately be integrated into the framework of Marxist political economy (and, if so, to what extent).

The structuralists maintain that the fundamental contradiction of capitalism is the result of the *unorganized facticity* of capitalist social development: "Men make their own history, but they do not make it just as they please; they do not make it under circumstances chosen by themselves, but under circumstances directly encountered, given and transmitted from the past."[1] Maurice Godelier interprets this passage as referring to an irreversible and ever-sharpening incompatibility between (socialized) forces of production and (privatized) relations of production.[2] "It is not a contradiction within a structure, but *between* two structures and, thus, not directly a contradiction between individuals or groups, but between the structure of the increasingly socialized forces of production and the structure of the relations of production, or private property in the forces of production." The problem of this contradiction and its resulting dynamic of development is therefore seen as a question of the "functional compatibility" of different structures, and not primarily as the conflict between groups, or even classes.

Once the fundamental contradiction (and the dynamic of development resulting from it) is conceived as a problem of the increasing incompatibility of structural components, any interpretation of this contradiction as a conflict of interest between wage labor and capital, as a clash between industrial workers and the ruling bodies of the capitalist valorization process, appears as careless sociologizing and historicization. Such "teleological" interpretations are based upon the action and interests of social aggregates, and they can be said to be careless or premature inasmuch as they postulate a *fixed* relation between the noncompatible structures and the social action which expresses this objective contradiction. The existence of such a one-to-one relationship between structural incompatibilities and manifest conflict between actors may be contested from two angles. On the one hand, it can be asked why a contradiction should express itself only in certain conflicts, and, on the other, how it is that only specific modes of conflicts, i.e., those between classes, should lead to the resolution of the contradiction. "The class conflicts within the relations of production can 'simmer,' but no solution necessarily follows unless the forces of production develop (without this, there can well be a cyclical repetition of social conflicts, stagnation, etc.)."[3] Conversely, while many conflicts which have arisen historically are manifestations of the basic contradiction between socialized production and private appropriation, it is nevertheless clear that they cannot be considered simply as a struggle between wage labor and capital. In other words, structural incompatibilities do not by any necessity lead to class conflict, and class conflict is by no means the only way to overcome such incompatibilities.

Once the logical and sociological levels of the concept of capitalist contradiction are conceptually kept apart, there emerges a viewpoint which offers at least three important analytical advantages. First, it becomes possible to investigate the relationship between the contradiction and overt conflict as itself a historical variable; in other words, the outbreak of particular conflicts can be related to the state of development of the basic contradiction. Second, this concept of capitalist contradiction is the only one capable of grasping the growing "functional incompatibility" between the "socialization" of the forces of production and the institutionalized "private" character of the relations of production as an *objective* process which does not necessarily correspond to certain indicators on the level of social conflict; any "historicist" position, by contrast, remains dependent upon either mere descriptions of processes of social conflict or dogmatic assumptions about their inevitable intensification. Finally, by comprehending the divergence of the two tendencies — systemic incompatibilities and social conflicts — as an objective process which conditions the development of class consciousness, this approach can also account for the objective retardation and interruption of the evolution of manifest conflict.

This retardation and interruption results from the formation of adaptive structures which partly reconcile the tension that exists between the process of "socialization" and the fixed relations of production. These "countervailing tendencies," which partially channel the contradiction through the *organizations* of capital, and above all through the *capitalist state apparatus*, necessitate a systems-theoretical investigation of the modes and of the limits of adaptability of the system considered as a whole. The failure of a system's efforts to stabilize its limits, to consolidate itself and preserve its identity, can then be interpreted as a contradiction. Godelier remarks correctly that "the concept of contradiction presented here might perhaps be of interest to cybernetics, which indeed explores the boundary conditions and regularized internal relations on the basis of which a . . . system can maintain the internal and external conditions of its functioning within certain margins of variation."[4]

It may be asked at this point why the self-negating model of capitalist development, which rests on the noncorrespondence of its component structures, should still be considered as both an inevitable ("necessary") and specific feature of the process of valorization of capital within capitalist social formations. To assume otherwise, of course, would be to adopt either a pessimistic theory of history or, inversely, a faith in the indefinite containment of contradiction within the framework of capitalist institutions. Nearly all representatives of bourgeois political philosophy and ideology can be situated at either end of this continuum: they either see *all* social formations as beset by structural contradictions, or they see "modern" capitalism as the *only* exception to this rule. The Marxian theory, in contrast, locates the source of the necessarily contradictory character of capitalism and, therewith, the crucial reference point for the explanation of capitalist development and its overcoming, in the "private appropriation" of the surplus value generated in production. From the Marxian standpoint, private production determined by the criterion of market profitability effectively nurtures various kinds of global systemic consequences which affect and immanently challenge its viability and the continuance of private accumulation itself, and about which little can be done within the framework of private accumulation.

It should be obvious, especially today, that the concept of "private" appropriation is not restricted to the sphere of property rights and private law. A motivational interpretation of the concept of private appropriation (one based, say, on the "selfishness" or "profit-seeking" of the owners of capital) would also be fundamentally misleading, as misleading as any interpretation that seeks to derive the relationship between private appropriation and the self-negating tendencies of capitalism from the unavoidable "blindness" of decision-making that is caused by the immense complexity of social events. The category "private" should be used to refer not to legal and psychological phenomena, but rather to the socioeconomic fact of some structural nonconsideration and neglect of those functions and consequences of action that are not its primary object. A "private" economic structure is one in which, for instance, use-values appear as mere appendages of exchange-values, in which social wealth is based on the creation of scarcity, and in which capital accumulation is accompanied by the periodic or permanent destruction of capital.

The institutionalized nonrelevance of concrete needs that are negatively affected by the motion of capital — in other words, the nonperception of some major social consequences of the valorization of capital — applies not only to the dimension of social groups that are primarily affected by this blind dynamic, but equally to that of historical change, from which existing arrangements are thought to be immune. Lukács dealt from a philosophical-historical standpoint with the inability of bourgeois consciousness to conceive of itself historically.[5] Marx sociologically concretized the need repressed by the logic of private accumulation through the concept of the exclusion of the proletarian class from power over the disposition of capital. The theorists of reification, alienation, and one-dimensionality have pursued Marx's theoretical goal without succeeding, however, in attaining his level of class-theoretical concreteness. Common to all types of radical criticism of capitalism is their emphasis upon the asymmetry between the unlimited *consequences* of the process of valorization of capital and the limitedness of the institutionalized *means* through which these consequences can be perceived, regulated, processed, or overcome within the framework of the existing system, whose constitutive principle, on the most abstract level, is that of disregard, exclusion, repression, and nonconsideration of exactly those consequences of its own operation which are crucial for its survival and integration. This critique of capitalism is evidently not based upon some abstract normative standard, such as distributive justice and the like. "Irrationality" and "private" are merely interchangeable terms for indicating the structurally conditioned lack of *conscious* social control over *factually* socialized and interdependent social processes. This self-destructive deficiency is constantly renewed and deepened by the dynamics of the capitalist economy.

Agency and Social Antagonisms

The above explication of the concept of capitalism as a category concerned with the logic of change and development makes it possible to answer the first of our initial questions: Is the concept of capitalism still applicable to the highly industrialized social systems of Western

Europe and North America? There can be no doubt that: (a) the dominant variable of *economic* growth, which comprises the annual aggregate accumulation of capitalist production units, both determines and restricts the ability of these systems to process their economic, social, and political problems; and that (b) the uncontrolled consequences of this process of capitalist growth — domination, oppression, alienation, scarcity, environmental disruption, none of which are necessarily manifest as *class* phenomena — constitute a "self-negating" tendency of these systems, at least in the indirect sense that they are forced constantly to adapt themselves to these consequences. This self-negating tendency is otherwise known as the "permanent crisis" of the capitalist system, while any particularly acute crisis, whether in the form of revolutionary upheaval or economic collapse, is only the more or less inevitable, more or less protracted manifestation of this same antagonism.

Just as economic collapse is only *one* instance of crisis, so all the empirical findings of research into particular capitalist societies (competition, pauperization, polarization of class conflict, business cycles, etc.) are only concrete instances or forms of appearance, inevitable under the given historical conditions, of capitalism's contradictory logic of development. In an advanced phase of capitalist development, it may be that institutionally neglected social needs (as well as their oppositional potential) are not represented in the proletariat as a whole, but instead shifted to the level of psychic repression, externalized upon groups in the Third World, or scattered among marginalized groups. Such changes in the forms of the conflictual appearance of crisis are not accidental; rather, they must be deduced in each case from the given state of development of the capitalist system of institutions and the prevailing strategies of adaptive conflict-displacement. On the one hand, we find pathologies of systemic stress which lead to an overtaxing of the system by its own problematic by-products, as well as to long-term "externalities" and "blind" or "anarchic" repercussions for the system which cannot be absorbed without a fundamental change of the capitalist core institutions. On the other hand, we find various cleavages and configurations of sociopolitical conflict, of which class conflict is only one variant. To conclude (as much of liberal social theorizing does) that the absence of (disruptive or revolutionary) class conflict indicates the absence (or successful overcoming) of endemic contradictions is to disregard the possibility that the scene of conflict can itself be displaced, manipulated, and distorted by strategies of adaptive conflict management which can well control the disruptiveness of conflict, but do by no means overcome the pathologies of the system's logic of self-steering.

Maurice Dobb correctly contrasts his own Marxian formulation of the concept of capitalism with the concepts employed in bourgeois traditions of political economy.[6] Neither the use of produced means of production, nor the dominance of individual entrepreneurs and their unlimited economic freedom of action, nor production for an anonymous market can serve as exhaustive criteria for capitalist social formations. On the other hand, little would be gained by defining capitalism by its logic of movement and development alone, *unless* the actual "bearers" or agents of social antagonism are also identified. The task of the theory of capitalism is therefore to establish the historically specific links between logical and sociological categories and, at the same time, to explain the changes of those rules according to which systemic contradictions translate into agency and conflict, and vice versa.

For the earliest phase of capitalism, this task is relatively unproblematic. Capitalism emerged as a system of law-like motion at the historical point at which certain specific social-structural realities began to develop. "Its historical condition was the concentration of ownership of the means of production in the hands of a class, itself only a minority of the whole society, and the consequent emergence of a propertyless class, whose livelihood was dependent entirely upon the sale of their labour-power."[7] In the phase of early capitalism, the developmental category of antagonism is clearly expressed in the substratum of social classes which maintain and deepen this antagonism. The logical category of contradiction and the sociological categories of proletariat and bourgeoisie coincide. Operating simultaneously at the logical and sociological levels, the concept of class indicates the antagonistic character of capitalist development *and* the empirical social groups which act out that antagonism. The concept of class thus has a double function: it formulates the systemic steering mechanism of a social order founded on the private valorization of capital *and* provides an empirical-descriptive criterion for designating the (potentially) conflicting social groups: the class of capitalists and the class of productive, wage-dependent workers.

But the correspondence between the level of systemic motion and conflictual social agency is not fixed or naturally given; the translation of the logical categories of development into sociological categories can be assumed as constant only at the cost of dogmatism. The *continuity* of a contradiction often coexists with a *change* of the sociostructural actors and conflicts which express it. Consequently, if the antagonisms implied by the "private," market-regulated metabolism between labor and capital are considered in their most general form, that is, *prior* to all sociological determinations of actual classes, all that can be said is that the antagonism exists wherever there emerges *some* kind of social conflict which calls into question the logic of private accumulation and its political and institutional preconditions. Exactly *which* social groups actually (or potentially) perform this role of expressing systemic contradictions under any given concrete conditions cannot be decided in advance merely by characterizing capitalist society as a class society. Just as the powers inherent in the logic of accumulation can be exercised in various institutional forms and by various social groups, so also the contradiction it generates in opposition to itself cannot simply be identified with "the proletariat" (in the sociological sense of productive wage-labor) for all stages of the development of capitalism.

This abstract reformulation of the concepts of "capitalism" as a blind and anarchic pattern of contradictory systemic steering and of "class" as a challenging and oppositional agency-to-be-specified is of importance for social research in that it provides a general reference point for both *historical* and *comparative* studies. Diverse phenomena and developments can thereby be interpreted as functionally equivalent solutions (or nonsolutions) of a common structural problem generated by the private valorization of capital. The hypothesis proposed here, that capitalism possesses an identical "logic of motion" beyond all differences of appearance, can also be easily tested. A political economy conforms to the dynamic pattern of "capitalism" (as we have reformulated the concept here) if it shows the interrelated characteristics of anarchy, interdependence, and self-paralyzing tendencies which undermine, as a consequence of modernization and rationalization, the viability of the very institutions ("relations of production") within which this modernization process is carried out.

Compensatory Mechanisms

When speaking of the "self-contradictoriness" or "self-negating tendencies" of a system, it is tempting to interpret these concepts — and the logic of development they specify — as elements of an anticipated state of affairs. They thereby would come close to some notion of an independent, cumulative, irreversible, and teleologically directed historical force, which pushes toward either total breakdown or the establishment of a postrevolutionary and postcapitalist society. Quite apart from its questionable strategic-political validity, this deduction of some state of affairs from a specific developmental dynamic does not follow from the conceptual and methodological point of departure adopted here. The proposal to make inherent self-contradictoriness the reference point for analyzing the capitalist system implies no speculation whatsoever about the long-term historical survival capacity of this system. This proposal aims only to establish a framework for the functional analysis of partial changes *within* the capitalist system, with the aid of which it becomes possible to describe adaptive strategies and developments that help to maintain the given system in spite of its contradictory character.

A comparative analysis of the development of capitalist systems indicates the existence of three general "cushioning mechanisms." Their successive institutionalization served to cushion, buffer, or redirect the self-paralyzing tendencies of the basic capitalist structure and, at any rate, prevented its manifest structural crisis. Each of them functions to extend the boundaries of survival of the system. Such mechanisms exist at the level of the *organization* of production units and markets; at the level of the organization and development of *science* and technology (i.e., "institutionalized" scientific and technical progress); and at the level of the scope and function of the *state*. Figure 15.1 indicates these three compensatory mechanisms; the corresponding levels of systemic problems which they solve temporarily; the mode of operation of these (short-term) "problem-solving" functions; and, finally, the corresponding social scientific or ideological paradigm which both accompanies the new compensatory mechanism and seeks to overcome the self-destructive forces of capitalism.

This schema is only suggestive of a sequence of steps within a systemic learning process. It is meant as a conceptual distinction of stages of capitalist development, and it is not designed to reveal either the full complexity of these developmental stages or the dynamic processes structuring their succession. Nevertheless, it represents an attempt to distinguish three broad categories of compensatory mechanisms and to order them sequentially (the vertical dimension of figure 15.1). It indicates how ever more extensive levels of the system (units of capital, capital as a whole, the social structure) are encompassed by these mechanisms. This *logical* sequence corresponds only very approximately to the *historical* emergence of these mechanisms, for the schema analytically traces and logically orders phenomena which are in fact related through complex processes of mutual conditioning. The institutionalization of technical progress, for instance, was not accom-

Figure 15.1.

Compensatory Mechanism	Level of Systemic Problem	Mode of Operation	Emerging "Post-Capitalist" Ideology or Social-Scientific Interpretation
Organization of the Market (Oligopoly, monopoly, cartels, multinational corporations; elimination of price competition; self-financing; managerial planning; long-term profit stabilization)	Survival capacity of *individual units of capital*	Elimination or reduction of threats to existence by competition; monopolization of retail and factor markets; (temporary) emancipation from cost-pressures and realization problems	"Managerial class" "Soulful corporation" Theories of the emergent "socially conscious enterprise" Burham, Berle/Means, Crosland
Institutionalization of technological progress (science and technology as prime productive force; institutionalized linking of R & D and production; its organized production)	Survival capacity of *capital in general*	Security for permanent profitable valorization of capital through systematic innovation; overcoming of stagnation, establishment of new investment outlets (Baran and Sweezy); continuous devaluation of the existing capital stock	Technological / Technocratic / Post-industrial / Post-modern } Society Bell, Lipset, Etzioni, Aron (Convergence Theory)
State regulation of the whole capitalist system	Survival capacity of the *general political, economic, and social order of capitalism*	Overcoming of valorization problems through state intervention; active organization of class compromises through the state apparatus	"Technocracy" (Schelsky) "Mixed economy" "Planning" "New industrial state" "Active society" "Pluralistic society" "Welfare state"

plished without certain catalyzing state functions, such as armaments spending and the development of war technology. Similarly, the national and international organization of markets depends on both the development of technology and the securing of markets and raw materials through imperialist means.

The relationship represented in this schema should therefore not be understood as anything more than a preliminary sketch. This schema nevertheless illustrates two important arguments. The *first* is that the functional quality and historical timing of these institutional innovations within capitalist development can be interpreted as attempted solutions to problems and contradictions whose manifestation and actuality are the direct consequence of the fundamental capitalist contradiction between the progressive "socialization" and interdependency, on the one hand, and the profit-oriented control of production, on the other. No other framework of interpretation than this one first introduced by Marx permits such a broad account of the phenomena of capitalist institutional change; and it seems even difficult to name other phenomena of change within capitalism to which this general and comprehensive framework of interpretation could not in principle be applied.

The *second* argument illustrated by this schema is that, once all of these three mechanisms (market organization, the institutionalization of scientific-technical progress and its direct integration into production and public policy, state regulation and sociopolitical integration organized by the state) are instituted, the available repertoire of institutional possibilities of moderating the capitalist system's manifest contradiction of displacing it or remedying it temporarily through the rationalization of political and economic organization is exhausted. This is of course not to say that the various possible combinations of these mechanisms have already been completely put in operation or have been utilized to their full extent in any of the modern capitalist societies. But it does suggest that there are no known dimensions in which new and additional mechanisms for preserving the capitalist system could be developed and applied which, at the same time, would be compatible with the principle of "private" accumulation and the "free" labor market. The only possibility that remains is either the variation and refinement of the existing trio of self-adaptive mechanisms already initiated in all advanced capitalist systems or, in case of their insufficiency, the collapse of the basic structure of capitalism, either in a historically unproductive manner, or productively, through a revolutionary transformation of the core institutions — and therefore the logic of development — of capitalism.

This state of affairs, in which the paradigm of self-adaptive mechanisms is fully established and subject only to new combinations and variations, justifies the introduction of the concept of *late* capitalism. Understood in this precise sense, the term late capitalism rejects any suggestion that the historical end of capitalism can be hastened by attaching a magic prefix to the word. Instead, it emphasizes the fact that advanced capitalist systems have wholly exhausted their available potential for compensating for the consequences of their self-paralyzing character.

This emphasis upon compensatory mechanisms and their inter-relationship should at least help to guard against naive formulations of the old question concerning the collapse of capitalism. Today, this question can no longer be answered by theories which extrapolate from the crisis-generating and self-destructive forces unleashed by capitalist social production and thereby predict the inevitable collapse and subsequent transformation of the system as a whole. This question can only be answered through an analysis of the *limits* and potential *inadequacy* of the compensatory mechanisms, whose function is either to retard these self-destructive tendencies in moments of crisis or to render them latent by displacing them elsewhere. The analysis and critique of the adaptive self-transformations of the system — which are nowadays entrusted to technocratic management and planning, social-democratic reform politics, welfare-state provisions, pluralist or corporatist mechanisms of class compromises, weapons-intensive technology, giant multinational corporations, and bureaucratized interest groups — must therefore supplement the analysis of class conflict and economic crisis. Naturally, these factors will complicate this type of class analysis. The question concerning the limits of the system was posed during earlier phases of capitalist development; today, there is the *additional* question concerning the possibilities of the system's adapting itself so as to extend its limits. Under these new conditions, a theory of crisis could not be convincing unless it theorized the limits of political and economic crisis-management; correspondingly, a convincing theory of class would need to theorize the potential conflict which *cannot* be controlled systematically by the divisive and pacifying functions of the authoritarian welfare state.

Notes

1. Karl Marx, "Der 18te Brumaire des Louis Bonaparte" [1852], in Karl Marx and Friedrich Engels, *Werke* (Berlin: Dietz, 1969), 8:115 ["The Eighteenth Brumaire of Louis Bonaparte," in Marx and Engels, *Collected Works* (New York: International Publishers, 1979), 11:103].

2. Maurice Godelier, *System, Struktur und Widerspruch im "Kapital,"* Joseph Grahl, tr. (Berlin: Merve, 1970), p. 22.

3. *Ibid.*, p. 28.

4. *Ibid.*, p. 31.

5. Georg Lukács, *Geschichte und Klassenbewusstsein* (Berlin: Malik, 1923) [*History and Class Consciousness* (London: Merlin Press, 1971)].

6. Maurice Dobb, *Studies in the Development of Capitalism* [1947] rev. ed. (New York: International Publishers, 1963).

7. *Ibid.*

16

Beyond Status and Class: Will There Be an Individualized Class Society?

Ulrich Beck

Are we witnessing today a process of historical change which releases people from industrial society and its social manifestations — class, stratum, occupation, family, marriage? Is this process similar to the process which occurred during the reformation, when people left the dominion of the church and entered secular society? Is it possible that new social forms are growing out of "traditional" ways of life, for which we still lack the concepts and which we cannot yet grasp? The frequently raised claims to self-determination and the defense of rights to participate must be considered in this context as well. Strongly held commitments with respect to them give us reason to believe that they signify new developments. This is also the case for the shifting relation between public and private life.

Therefore we need to inquire once again into the reality of classes and strata in the advanced societies. But here we immediately confront apparently contradictory facts. When examining the situation from a sociohistorical perspective, we find that the structure of social inequality in the developed countries displays an amazing stability. Research on this clearly indicates that, despite all the technological and economic transformations and in the face of the many efforts in the past two or three decades to introduce changes, the inequalities between the major social groups in our society have not changed appreciably, except for some relatively minor shifts and reallocations.[1]

This essay is based upon "Jenseits von Stand und Klasse? — Soziale Ungleichheiten, gesellschaftliche Individualisierungsprozesse und die Entstehung neuer sozialer Formationen und Identitäten," in Reinhard Kreckel, ed., *Soziale Ungleichheiten*, pp. 35-75 (Göttingen: Otto Schwartz, 1983) [Soziale Welt, Sonderband 2], as well as upon "Jenseits von Stand und Klasse: Auf dem Wege in die individualisierte Arbeitnehmergesellschaft," *Merkur* (1984) 38(5):485-497. The basic idea of this essay is further elaborated in U. Beck, *Risikogesellschaft — Auf dem Wege in eine andere Moderne* (Frankfurt: Suhrkamp, 1986). Translation by Volker Meja and Gerd Schroeter.

Nevertheless, it is during precisely this period that the topic of inequality disappeared almost completely from the agenda of daily life, of politics, and of scholarship. It may well be that in the late 1980s, under conditions of economic stagnation and consistently high or even rising unemployment, it will once again turn into a socially explosive issue. It is surprising, however, how much inequality has lost significance as an issue during the past two decades. Now and then questions may be raised about inequality in other contexts or in the form of new confrontations (e.g., in the struggle for women's rights, grassroots initiatives against nuclear power plants, intergenerational inequality, even regional and religious conflicts). But if public and political discussion is taken as an accurate indication of the actual developments, one could easily be led to the following conclusion: at the present time, in the Federal Republic, we have moved *beyond* class society. The notion of a "class society" remains useful only as an image of the past. It only stays alive because there is not yet any suitable alternative.[2]

The analysis that follows therefore aims to explain a paradoxical state of affairs. My thesis is that in the history of the Federal Republic patterns of social inequality have remained relatively stable. Yet at the same time the living conditions of the population have changed dramatically. Changes in income and education, in addition to other social changes, have contributed to this. These changes have been taken account of in a number of sociological investigations but they have never been analyzed systematically or explained as important social structural developments in their own right. I would therefore like to show that, as a result of shifts in the standard of living, subcultural class identities have dissipated, class distinctions based on "status" have lost their traditional support, and *processes for the "diversification" and "individualization" of lifestyles and ways of life* have been set in motion. As a result, the hierarchical model of social classes and strata has increasingly been subverted. It no longer corresponds to the realities.[3]

During the past three decades, nearly unnoticed by social stratification research, the *social meaning* of inequality has changed. In all wealthy Western industrialized countries, but especially in the Federal Republic of Germany, a process of "individualization" has taken place during the past two or three decades. Its unprecedented breadth and dynamism have generally not been adequately recognized. And while this process still continues, persistent inequalities have concealed it from our view. To put it more concisely, there have been specific historical developments leading to "individualization." They have disrupted the experience of historical continuity; as a consequence, people have lost their traditional support networks and have had to rely on themselves and their own individual (labor market) fate with all its attendant risks, opportunities, and contradictions.[4]

Such a process of individualization up to now was thought to have occurred primarily among the emerging bourgeoisie. But a new (and more precise) formulation of the concept of "individualization" may also make it applicable to the "free wage-laborer" of modern capitalism, as well as to processes resulting from the dynamics of the labor market in welfare-state societies and mass democracies. Upon entering the labor market, people are subjected to successive waves of "individualization." They become individualized in relation to family, neighborhood, and occupational ties. But they also lose their connections with their region and its culture and traditions. These pressures toward individualization compete with experiences of a collectively shared fate in the labor market represented by the social risks attendant upon wage labor, such as unemployment and the downgrading of qualifications. But it is only when these risks have been reduced that there occur those processes of individualization which *dissolve* the shared life-worlds and the shared cultural certainties of class and status groups. The relative prosperity of the German Federal Republic and its system of social security certainly have contributed to these developments.

Processes of individualization are very dynamic; they make it difficult to avoid ambiguities in the interpretation of social structure. Empirical stratification research or Marxist class analysis probably detects no significant changes: income inequalities, the structure of the division of labor, and the basic determinants of wage labor have, after all, remained relatively unchanged. The attachment of people to a "social class" (in Max Weber's sense) has nevertheless become weaker. It now has much less influence on their actions. They develop ways of life that tend to become individualized. For the sake of economic survival, individuals are now compelled to make themselves the center of their own life plans and conduct.[5]

Individualization must consequently be understood as a historically contradictory process of sociation [*Vergesellschaftung*]. The collective quality and the standardization of individual ways of life, however, are not immediately obvious. But as soon as the contradictory nature of individualization processes is experienced more intensively and is brought into consciousness, new sociocultural commonalities may begin to develop. Thus it may happen that, in the face of intensified social risks such as unemployment, new "class-situations" will emerge in spite of considerable inequalities in income and qualification levels. Or consciously formed expectations of personal growth and of an individualized life (in its material, spatial, temporal, and relational dimensions) will increasingly encounter social and political limits and obstacles. Thus, with increasing frequency, different social movements may experiment with sometimes quite extreme forms of social interaction or with one's own life and body, within counter- and youth subcultures. These subcultures are often united in their opposition to administrative and industrial intrusions into "private" life, against which their potentially explosive resistance is directed.

One can indeed claim that such still ongoing individualization processes have triggered a very far-reaching erosion and a redirection of social and cultural evolution. The fate and the consequences of these processes are therefore of general interest for the understanding of the actual transformations occurring in advanced modern societies. There are clear indications that they point in the direction of a fundamental change in the social significance and in the organization of such basic formations as the institution of the family (marriage, parenthood), sex roles, community, and work relations. These processes, furthermore, are of great significance for the understanding of the so-called "new social movements," as well as for political behavior in general.

The Labor Market as "Motor" of Individualization

"Individualization of social inequality" — does this not suggest that everything important is being forgotten, misunderstood, or simply dismissed, including everything we have learned about the class character of society, its nature as a system; about mass society and capital concentration; about ideological distortions and alienation; about unchanging human traits and the complexity of social and historical reality? And does not the concept of individualization also spell the premature end of sociology, leading to the tolling of its bell?

This requires more precise formulations. The existence of individualization has been empirically verified in numerous qualitative interviews and studies. They all point to one central concern: the demand for control of one's own money, time, living space, and body. In other words, people demand the right to develop their own perspective on life. They also want to act upon it. However illusory and ideological these claims may turn out to be, they are a reality which cannot be overlooked. And they arise from the actual conditions of life in the

German Federal Republic as they have developed in the past three decades.[6]

But today it is also becoming apparent that such processes of "individualization" can be quite precarious, especially where groups suddenly face or are threatened by unemployment and forced to confront radical disruptions of their lifestyle precisely because of the individualization they have experienced, and despite the protections provided by the welfare state.[7]

How can these developments be distinguished from the rise of "bourgeois individualism" in the eighteenth and nineteenth centuries? Processes of individualization among the bourgeoisie derived essentially from the ownership and accumulation of capital. The bourgeoisie developed its social and political identity in the struggle against feudal structures of domination and authority. In the Federal Republic, by contrast, individualization is a product of the labor market and manifests itself in the acquisition, proffering, and application of a variety of work skills. This thesis will be elaborated by looking at three dimensions of the labor market — education, mobility, and competition.

Education: As schooling increases in duration, traditional orientations, ways of thinking, and lifestyles are recast and displaced by universalistic forms of learning and teaching, as well as by universalistic forms of knowledge and language. Depending on its duration and contents, education makes possible at least a certain degree of self-discovery and reflection. Education, furthermore, is connected with *selection* and therefore requires the individual's expectation of upward mobility; these expectations remain effective even in cases where "upward mobility through education" is an illusion since education is little more than a protection against downward mobility (as it, to some extent, happened during the period of expansion of educational opportunities). For it is after all only possible to pass through formal education by *individually* succeeding by way of assignments, examinations, and tests. Formal education in schools and universities, in turn, provides individual credentials leading to individualized career opportunities on the labor market.

Mobility: As soon as people enter the labor market, they experience *mobility*. They are removed from traditional patterns and arrangements, and unless they are prepared to suffer economic ruin, they are forced to take charge of their own life. The labor market, by way of occupational mobility, place of residence or employment, type of employment, as well as the changes in social location it initiates, reveals itself as the driving force behind the individualization of people's lives. They become relatively independent of inherited or newly formed ties (e.g., family, neighborhood, friendship, partnership). By becoming independent from these ties, their lives take on an independent quality which, for the first time, makes possible the experience of a *personal* destiny.[8]

Competition: Competition rests upon the interchangeability of qualifications and thereby compels people to advertise the individuality and uniqueness of their work and of their own accomplishments. The growing pressure of competition leads to an *individualization among equals*, i.e., precisely in areas of interaction and conduct which are characterized by a shared background (similar education, similar experience, similar knowledge). Especially where such a shared background still exists, community is dissolved in the acid bath of competition. In this sense, competition undermines the equality of equals without, however, eliminating it. It causes the isolation of individuals *within* homogeneous social groups.

Education, mobility, and competition, however, are by no means independent of each other. They rather supplement and reinforce each other. Only in thus reinforcing each other do they cause the processes of individualization which have been initiated in the past two or three decades.[9]

Individualization and Class Formation: Marx and Weber

The thrust toward individualization in the welfare state can be understood more precisely by examining Karl Marx's and Max Weber's theories of social inequality. It is quite possible to regard Marx as one of the most resolute theorists of processes of "individualization." Marx often stressed that an unparalleled *process of emancipation* had been set in motion as a result of the development of industrial capitalism. In his view, emancipation from feudal relations was a precondition for the establishment of capitalist relations of production. But even *within* capitalism itself people are uprooted in successive waves and wrested loose from tradition, family, neighborhood, occupation, and culture.

Marx never followed up on this variant of a class society caught in the process of individualization. For him this capitalist process of isolation and "uprooting" had always been cushioned by the *collective experience of immiseration* and the resulting class struggle. Marx thought that it was precisely the process of emancipation and uprooting and the deterioration of the living conditions of workers under capitalism that led to the transformation of the working class from a "class in itself" into a "class for itself." He dismissed as irrelevant the question how individual proletarians, as participants in a market of exchange, could even form stable bonds of solidarity, given that capitalism systematically uprooted their lives. Marx always equated processes of individualization with the formation of classes. This still appears to be the basic position of many contemporary class theorists.

The thesis of the individualization of social inequality may be regarded as the exact mirror image of the Marxian position. Processes of individualization, as I have described them, can only become entrenched when material immiseration, as the condition for the formation of classes as predicted by Marx, has been overcome. Trends toward individualization are dependent upon complex structural conditions, which have until now been realized in very few countries, and even then only during the most recent phase of the development of the welfare state.

I can now refine my argument and turn to Max Weber as the other important theorist of social inequality. On the one hand, as is well known, Max Weber recognized the great range of modern ways of life much more emphatically than Marx. On the other hand, he ignored the latent tendencies toward individualization. Weber, in fact, argued that these could not succeed, but without sharing Marx's belief in class-formation resulting from immiseration. Tendencies toward individualization were blocked, according to Weber, by the *continuity and the authority of traditions and subcultures based on "status."* In industrial capitalism traditional "status-bound" attitudes, Weber argues, have been combined with expertise and market opportunities into substantively differentiated "social class positions."[10] Thus Weber's work already contained the basic arguments spelled out in detail by Marxist labor historians at the end of the 1960s.[11] For these historians the characteristic norms governing the life-worlds, value-orientations and lifestyles during the expansion of industrial capitalism are less the product of "class structure" and "class formation" (as understood by Marx) than remnants of precapitalist and preindustrial traditions. "Capitalist culture" is consequently a less autochtonous creation than is often assumed. It rather is of precapitalist origins, modernized and assimilated by a system of industrial capitalism which recasts and consumes it. Even though different trends toward "disenchantment" and the "demystification" of traditional lifestyles do gain a footing, the dynamic process of "individualization" is by Weber still understood as contained and buffered by status-based community organizations, themselves linked to social class positions maintained by the market. In the German Federal Republic most research on social inequalities still follows Max Weber in this regard.

Historical studies suggest that this indeed applies to developments until the early 1950s, but I do not believe that it still holds for postwar developments in the Federal Republic. At that point in time the unstable unity of shared life experiences mediated by the market and shaped by status, which Max Weber brought together in the concept of "social class," began to break apart. Its different elements (such as material conditions dependent upon specific market opportunities, the effectiveness of tradition and of precapitalist lifestyles, the consciousness of communal bonds and of barriers to mobility, as well as networks of contact) have slowly disintegrated. They have been changed beyond recognition by the increasing dependence on education as well as by an intensified mobility and by competition.

The traditional internal differentiations and social environments, which were still real enough for industrial workers in imperial Germany and in the Weimar Republic, have been increasingly dissolved since the 1950s. At the same time, differences within the industrial labor force and between rural and urban populations have been leveled. Everywhere educational reform is accompanied by a *dependence on education*. More and more groups get caught up in the race for educational credentials. As a result there emerge new internal differentiations. While these may still respond to traditional differences between milieus, the impact of education makes them fundamentally different from traditional ones. Here we can employ the distinction by Basil Bernstein that the new generation must move from a "restricted" to an "elaborated" code of speech. In conjunction with novel patterns of upward and downward mobility new hierarchies develop which are internal to social classes. They presuppose the expansion of the service sector and the creation of new occupations. The influx of large numbers of "guest workers" also is a condition contributing to this formation; for they occupy the lowest rung on the social scale. These new hierarchies do not readily fit into the established categories of research. Thus their significance for the population's outlook on life has not yet been noticed.

During the same period, traditional forms of settlement have frequently been replaced by new urban housing projects. These changes have also generated new forms of individualization. They affect patterns of interaction dependent upon housing and living arrangements. The modern metropolis as well as urban developments in the smaller towns replace traditional settlement patterns. People from a great variety of cultural backgrounds are mixed together and social relations in the neighborhood are much more loosely organized. Thus traditional forms of community beyond the family are beginning to disappear. This need not imply that social isolation increases or that relatively private family life prevails — although this may happen. But it does imply that already existing ("ascriptively" organized) neighborhoods are shattered, together with their limitations and their opportunities for social control. The newly formed social relationships and social networks now have to be individually chosen; they have to be established, maintained, and constantly renewed by individuals.[12] This may mean, to choose an extreme example, the absence of interaction, i.e., that social isolation and loneliness may become the major pattern of relationships. It may also mean, however, that self-selected and self-created hierarchies and forms of stratification may develop in relationships with acquaintances, neighbors, and friends. These relationships are no longer primarily dependent upon "physical" proximity. Whether they transcend the local sphere or not, they are formed on the basis of the interests, ambitions, and commitments of individuals, who regard themselves as organizers of their own circles of contacts and relationships. In consequence, new residential patterns may develop, consisting of a rediscovery of neighborhoods and of communal and cooperative living arrangements. There is room for experimenting with lifestyles and social relations.[13]

All this documents the emergence of new historical possibilities for individual self-formation and for a development of the private sphere under conditions of relative social security and of the declining authority of tradition. The complex new relationships can also manifest themselves politically, i.e., in the form of "political privatism." By this I mean: The expansion of social and legal limits imposed upon the private sphere; of unconventional and even publicly offensive forms of social experimentation which are quite consistent with new forms of personal freedom; and of challenges to conventional distinctions between acceptable and unacceptable behavior. Thus there emerge divisions between culture and counterculture, society and alternative groups. These new forms of cultural and social identity often have politically provocative effects. Their force has been regularly experienced during the past twenty years.

These and other developments permit the conclusion that the unstable association of community and market society which Max Weber had in mind when he spoke of social class has been partially transformed or even dissolved in the course of postwar developments. People at any rate no longer seem to understand or experience it. The new forms of life reveal dynamic possibilities for the reorganization of social relations, which cannot be adequately comprehended by following either Marx or Weber.

As a result, the following question becomes paramount: what actually does take place when in the course of historical development the identity of social classes rooted in the life-world melts away? When, on the one hand, the conditions and risks of wage labor become generalized and, on the other, "class" loses its subcultural basis and is no longer experienced? Is a class identity no longer shaped by status even conceivable? Can the inequalities persisting under conditions of the individualization process still be grasped by means of the concept of class or by means of even more general hierarchical models of social inequality? Perhaps all these hierarchical models categorically depend on status-dependent features of social reality — at least as long as they aim at interpretations of real situations. But are there interpretations which can replace these models? It may, of course, also be the case that processes of individualization are embedded in contradictions which in turn produce new social groupings and conflicts. How then are processes of individualization transformed into their opposites? How can new forms of social identity be discovered and new ways of life be developed? One can imagine three radical lines of development which are by no means mutually exclusive. Indeed, they may even overlap:

1. Class does not disappear just because status-based ways of life fade away. Social classes are rather emancipated from regional and particularistic restrictions and limitations as a result. A new chapter in the history of classes is beginning, but we still need to comprehend its historical dynamics. It can in any case no longer be said without further qualification that this still is a history of the formation of class solidarities.

2. In the course of the developments just described both the firm and the workplace lose their significance as a locus of conflict and identity formation. New sources for the formation of social bonds and for the development of conflicts arise. They lie in the domain of private social relations and of private ways of living and working. New social formations and identities *beyond* class society begin to emerge.

3. The end of class society is not some "big revolutionary bang." It consists of a relentlessly progressing and collectively experienced process of individualization and atomization in posttraditional societies.

Paradoxically, these are societies in which people become increasingly less self-sufficient.

Toward an Individualized Society of Employees

There are a great many multifarious attempts to develop new social formations, but however strong the convulsions triggered by them may be, they are invariably qualified by the fact that they, too, are exposed to ever new thrusts toward individualization. The motor of individualization is going at full blast, and it is not at all clear how new and lasting social arrangements, comparable in depth of penetration to social classes, can even be created. Quite to the contrary: Especially in the immediate future it is very likely that, as a way of coping with unemployment and economic crises, social and technological innovations will be set in motion which will open up new opportunities for individualization processes, in particular in regard to a greater flexibility in labor market relations and in regard to regulations governing working hours. But this also applies to the new forms of communication. These technological and social "revolutions," which either still lie ahead or are already in full swing, will unleash a profound individualization of lifestyles.

If this assessment is correct, a variant of social structure which neither Marx nor Weber foresaw will gain in importance. Class society will pale into insignificance beside an "individualized society of employees." Both the typical characteristics as well as the dangers of such a society are now becoming increasingly clear. In contrast to class society, which is defined essentially in terms of tradition and culture, a society of employees must be defined in terms of labor law and by way of sociopolitical categories. The result is a peculiar stage of transition, in which traditional and sharpening inequalities coincide with certain elements of a no longer traditional, individualized "post-class society" (which bears no resemblance to Marx's vision of a classless society). This transitional society is distinguished by a variety of typical structures and changes.

1. Processes of individualization deprive class distinctions of their social identity. Social groups lose their distinctive traits, both in terms of their self-understanding and in relation to other groups. They also lose their independent identities and the chance to become a formative political force. As a result of this development, the *idea of social mobility* (in the sense of individual movement between actual status classes), which until very late in this century constituted a social and political

theme of considerable importance for social identity formation, pales in significance.

2. Inequalities do by no means disappear. They merely become redefined in terms of an *individualization of social risks*. The result is that social problems are increasingly perceived in terms of psychological dispositions: as personal inadequacies, guilt feelings, anxieties, conflicts, and neuroses. There emerges, paradoxically enough, a *new immediacy* of individual and society, a direct relation between crisis and sickness. Social crises appear as individual crises, which are no longer (or are only very indirectly) perceived in terms of their rootedness in the social sphere. This is one of the explanations for the current "psycho-wave" [*Psychowelle*]. Individual achievement orientation similarly gains in importance. It can now be predicted that the full range of problems associated with the *achievement society* and its tendency toward (pseudo) legitimations of social inequalities will emerge in the future.

3. Here, too, in attempting to cope with social problems, people are forced into political and social alliances. These, however, need no longer follow a single pattern, such as the class model. The isolation of privatized lives, shielded against all the other privatized lives, can be shattered by social and political events and developments of the most heterogeneous kind. Accordingly, temporary coalitions between different groups and different camps are formed and dissolved, depending on the particular issue at stake and depending on the particular situation. It is possible to cheerfully embrace seemingly contradictory causes, for example, to join forces with local residents in protests against noise pollution by air traffic, to belong to the Metalworker's Union, and yet — in the face of impending economic crisis — to vote conservative. Such coalitions represent pragmatic alliances in the individual struggle for existence and occur on the various battlefields of society. A peculiar multiplication of areas of conflict can be observed. The individualized society prepares the ground for new and multifaceted conflicts, ideologies, and alliances, which go beyond the scope of all hitherto existing schematizations. These alliances are generally focused on single issues, are by no means hetereogeneous, and are oriented toward specific situations and personalities. The resulting social structure is susceptible to the latest social vogues (in issues and conflicts) which, pushed by the mass media, rule the public consciousness just as the spring, autumn, and winter fashion shows do.

4. Permanent conflicts tend to arise along the lines of "ascribed" char-

acteristics, which now as much as ever are undeniably connected with discriminations. Race, skin color, gender, ethnicity, age, homosexuality, physical disabilities — these are the major ascribed characteristics. Under the conditions of advanced individualization, such "quasi-natural" social inequalities lead to the development of quite specific organizing effects. These attempt to gain political clout by focusing upon the inescapability and permanence of such inequalities as well as upon their incompatibility with the achievement principle, their tangibility, and the fact that — as a result of their direct visibility — they make possible independent social and individual identifications. At the same time, individual fate is increasingly determined in a new way by economic trends and by historical necessity, as it were, for example by economic crisis or boom, restricted admission to universities and to the professions, the size of age cohorts, etc.

*

Will it be possible to choose as a point of departure the claims and the promises of the process of individualization now under way together with its impulse toward social emancipation, thereby in a new way — *beyond* status and class — uniting individuals and groups as self-conscious subjects of their own personal, social, and political affairs? Or will the last bastions of social and political action be swept away as a result of that very process? Would the individualized society then not fall, torn apart by conflicts and displaying symptoms of sickness, into the kind of political apathy that precludes virtually nothing, not even new and insidious forms of a modernized barbarism?

Notes

1. For more detailed and specific examples, see the following recent discussions of the social structure of the Federal Republic: Karl Martin Bolte, et al., *Soziale Umschichtung* (Opladen: Leske & Budrich, 1975), 4th ed.; Johan Handl, et al., *Klassenlagen und Sozialstruktur. Empirische Untersuchungen für die Bundesrepublik Deutschland* (Frankfurt/New York: Campus, 1977); Wolfgang Zapf, ed., *Lebensbedingungen in der Bundesrepublik* (Frankfurt/New York: Campus, 1978); M. Rainer Lepsius, "Soziale Ungleichheit und Klassenstruktur in der Bundesrepublik Deutschland," in Hans-Ulrich Wehler, ed., *Klassen in der europäischen Sozialgeschichte* (Göttingen: Vandenhoeck & Ruprecht, 1979); Bernhard Schäfers, *Sozialstruktur und Wandel der Bundesrepublik Deutschland* (Munich: Deutscher Taschenbuch Verlag, 1976); Karl Otto Hondrich, *Soziale Differenzierung* (Frankfurt/New York: Campus, 1982); and Stefan Hradil, "Entwicklungstendenzen in der Schicht- und Klassenstruktur der Bundesrepublik," in Joachim Matthes, ed., *Krise der Arbeitsgesellschaft? Verhandlungen des 21. Deutschen Soziologentages in Bamberg 1982* (Frankfurt/New York: Campus, 1983).

2. I am referring here to the peculiarities of the development of the class structure in the Federal Republic, which differs from the developments, for example, in Great Britain or France. In Britain, class membership is still very apparent in everyday life and remains the object of conscious identification. It is evident in speech (i.e., accents, expressions, vocabulary), in the sharp class divisions between residential areas ("housing classes"), in the types of education, clothing, and in everything that can be included under the concept of "lifestyle." See Gordon Smith, "Nachkriegsgesellschaft im historischen Vergleich," *Kolloquium des Instituts für Zeitgeschichte* (Munich/Vienna: Oldenbourg, 1982), and the following three essays in Wehler, ed., *Klassen in der europäischen Sozialgeschichte*: Eric J. Hobsbawm, "Soziale Ungleichheit und Klassenstruktur in England: Die Arbeiterklasse"; Sidney Pollard, "Soziale Ungleichheit und Klassenstruktur in England: Mittel- und Oberklasse"; Heinz-Gerhard Haupt, "Soziale Ungleichheit und Klassenstruktur in Frankreich seit Mitte des 19. Jahrhunderts." See also Pierre Bourdieu, *La Distinction* (Paris: Minuit, 1979) [*Distinction: A Social Critique of the Judgement of Taste*, R. Nice, tr. (Cambridge, Mass: Harvard University Press, 1984)].

3. I am speaking here of "social classes" in Max Weber's sense. See *Economy and Society*, Guenther Roth and Claus Wittich, trs. (Berkeley: University of California Press, 1978), pp. 302-307, 926-940.

4. On the individualization of social life-worlds see, for example, Peter Berger, B. Berger, H. Kellner, *The Homeless Mind: Modernization and Consciousness* (New York: Random House, 1973), pp. 63-82. The writings of Alain Touraine offer a parallel to my own position. See especially Touraine's *La prophétie anti-nucléaire* (Paris: Seuil, 1980) and his "Soziale Bewegungen: Spezialgebiet oder zentrales Problem soziologischer Analyse?", *Soziale Welt* (1983) 34:143-152.

To take a somewhat broader view, the importance especially of Emile Durkheim's *Suicide*, John Spaulding and George Simpson, trs. (Glencoe: Free Press, 1952) and of the theoretical perspective of Norbert Elias, especially in his *Über den Prozess der Zivilisation*. 2 vols. (Frankfurt: Suhrkamp, 1977) [*The Civilizing Process*, Edmund Jephcott, tr. (New York: Urizen Books, 1978, 1982)], becomes clear again.

For the current English-language discussion see, among others, Richard Sennett, *The Fall of Public Man* (New York: Knopf, 1977); Christopher Lasch, *The Culture of Narcissism* (New York: Norton, 1979); David Riesman, "Egozentrik in Amerika," *Der Monat*, 1981; Amitai Etzioni, *An Immodest Agenda: Rebuilding America Before the 21st Century* (New York: McGraw-Hill, 1982).

5. Here a development becomes visible which, as far as I can tell, has never been systematically examined: that structures of unequal distribution (of income, education, etc.) and the class-based cultural infrastructure of society begin to diverge and to develop independently of each other. This suggests that relations of inequality (in their structure and distribution) may remain unchanged, even if "class" is no longer experienced as an important feature of the life-world of a society.

6. On the implications of this development for industrial workers, see J. Mooser's "Auflösung des proletarischen Milieus," *Soziale Welt* (1983) 34(3); also H. Kern and M. Schumann, "Arbeit und Sozialcharakter: Alte und neue Konturen," in Joachim Matthes, ed., *Krise der Arbeitsgesellschaft?*. On women see Elisabeth Beck-Gernsheim, "Vom 'Dasein für andere'. Zum Anspruch auf ein Stück 'eigenes Leben': Individualisierungsprozesse im weiblichen Lebenszusammenhang," *Soziale Welt* (1983) 34(3):307-340. On youth see Werner Fuchs, "Jugendliche Statuspassage oder individualisierte Jugendkultur?" *Soziale Welt* (1983) 34(3):341-371.

7. Among the negative effects of individualization processes are the separation of the individual from traditional support networks (e.g., family, neighborhood), the loss of supplementary sources of income (e.g. part-time farming), and, along with this, the experience of an increased wage and consumption dependency in all spheres of life. To the extent that the main income security of this new condition of life, steady employment, is lost — regardless of the availability of social security — people are suddenly confronted by an abyss. We already receive rather disturbing news from the United States: more than twelve million unemployed, more than thirty million people living below the poverty line. But there are also alarming upheavals within the Federal Republic among welfare recipients and the so-called "transient population." Women may face particular threats in the future. Because of "individualization" processes they have, on the one hand, extricated themselves from the traditional network of support offered by the family, and the new divorce laws also force them to stand on their own feet economically. On the other hand, their position in the labor market is especially uncertain and the percentage of unemployed women is known to be much higher than that of men, in spite of a good deal of underreporting. See E. Beck-Gernsheim, "Vom 'Dasein für andere.'"

8. The extent to which the consequences of individualization are actually associated with geographical mobility is disputed in historical and sociological research. On the one hand, for example, the historian Stephen Thernstrom [*The Other Bostonians: Poverty and Progress in the American Metropolis, 1880-1970* (Cambridge, Mass.: Harvard University Press, 1973), p. 231] goes so far in his famous "Boston Study" as to make the restlessness and constant movement of impoverished industrial workers in the U.S. responsible for the invisibility of an American proletariat: "Some working-class migrants must have benefited from moving, . . . but there could still have been a large group of Americans who drifted helplessly from place to place for a lifetime, forming a permanent but invisible floating proletariat." On the other hand, migratory movements of different kinds are already typical of the Middle Ages, as well as for different phases of industrialization and urbanization in the nineteenth and twentieth centuries. See the contributions to Helmut Kaelble, ed., *Geschichte der sozialen Mobilität seit der industriellen Revolution*, as well as Kaelble, *Historische Mobilitätsforschung* (Darmstadt: Wissenshaftliche Buchgesellschaft, 1978) [*Historical Research on Social Mobility: Western Europe and the USA in the Nineteenth and Twentieth Centuries*, Ingrid Noakes, tr. (New York: Columbia University Press, 1981)]. The German Federal Republic, however, has not been characterized by any significant increase in geographical mobility. An excellent summary of theoretical orientations found in international mobility research is contained in John H. Goldthorpe, *Social Mobility and Class Structure in Modern Britain* (Oxford: Oxford University Press, 1980), pp. 1-37. This study points to the need for differentiating mobility according to its type and the context; it might be significant, for example, to what extent mobility processes occur within a homogeneous milieu based on status. Thus "mobile" persons may return to their place of origin or resettle in it. They may also be following a regular pattern of migration. The migratory movements of whole collectivities (compelled by starvation and political or religious expulsions) are quite a different phenomenon. They are not due to "individualization" (e.g., the "export" of guest-workers from their countries of origin to the Federal Republic). The various types of labor market mobility are completely different. They affect individuals as individuals in smaller or larger cohorts by continually uprooting them from their ways of life.

9. Other developments also play an important role here, for example, the *legalization of labor relations*. The differentiation of labor law as a special form of legislation leads to an individualization of interests which no longer depend upon highly aggregated interest

groups (e.g., organizations and parties) for their recognition. Individuals who are affected are thus able to defend their rights (which they strongly defend) directly in the courts.

10. Within the German Empire, Weber saw "social classes" in this sense comprised of "the working class as a whole"; "the petty bourgeoisie"; "the intelligentsia and specialists" (including civil servants and white collar employees); as well as "the classes privileged through property and education" (Weber, *Economy and Society*, 1:305). For the relationship between status groups and classes in Weber, see Wehler, *Klassen in der europäischen Sozialgeschichte*; Jürgen Kocka, "Stand — Klasse — Organisation. Strukturen sozialer Ungleichheit in Deutschland vom späten 18. bis zum frühen 20. Jahrhundert im Aufriss," in Wehler, *Klassen in der europäischen Sozialgeschichte*; Reinhard Kreckel, "Class, Status and Power? Begriffliche Grundlagen für eine politische Soziologie der sozialen Ungleichheit," *Kölner Zeitschrift für Soziologie und Sozialpsychologie* (1982) 34:617-648.

11. Especially on the basis of the very influential publications of E.P. Thompson, see *The Making of the English Working Class* (London: Gollancz, 1963); *Plebejische Kultur und moralische Ökonomie* (Berlin: Ullstein, 1980). For comments, see Dieter Groh, "Zur Einführung," in Thompson, *Plebejische Kultur*; also the contributions in D. Puls, ed., *Wahrnehmungsformen und Protestverhalten. Studien zur Lage der Unterschichten im 18. und 19. Jahrhundert* (Frankfurt: Suhrkamp, 1979). For further elaboration, see also Barrington Moore, *Injustice: The Social Bases of Obedience and Revolt* (Armonk, N.Y.: Sharpe, 1978); Anthony Giddens, *The Class Structure of Advanced Societies* (London: Hutchinson, 1973); Michael Mann, *Consciousness and Action Among the Western Working Class* (London: Macmillan, 1973); Duncan Gallie, "The Agrarian Roots of Working-Class Radicalism: An Assessment of the Mann-Giddens Thesis," *British Journal of Political Science* (1982) 12: 149-172; Robert M. Berdahl, et al., *Klasse und Kultur* (Frankfurt: Syndicat, 1982); and, most recently, Jürgen Kocka, *Lohnarbeit und Klassenbildung. Arbeiter und Arbeiterbewegung in Deutschland 1800-1875* (Bonn: Dietz, 1983).

12. See Josephine Klein, who quotes John Mogey's *Family and Neighbourhoods* (London: Oxford University Press, 1956): "The change is probably not one of importance in real activities . . . but the choice of words indicates a shift from passive acceptance of a neighbourhood to the selection of friends, a matter involving choice and therefore a more active behaviour, a sign of the use of social skills" (p. 274). Klein herself observes that "[i]n these ways, the move away from a close-knit community increases the number of occasions on which individual choices are called for, and may thereby set in motion a progress of individuation." See also Klein, *Samples from English Cultures* (London: Routledge & Kegan Paul, 1965), p. 271.

13. For a summary of recent international research on social networks, see Bernhard Badura, *Soziale Unterstützung und chronische Krankheit* (Frankfurt: Suhrkamp, 1981), pp. 20-38.

V

Identity and Social Structure

It is not accidental that the texts in this section are brought together under the title "Identity and Social Structure." German discussions which concern the relation between self and society are indeed best approached by way of the theme of "identity." This is not to claim that the essays assembled here deal with topics entirely different from those in North American or British sociological writings on socialization, or on the relation between individual and society. Quite the opposite is the case. There is not only considerable concern in German sociology with the themes and methods of socialization research, but we can also find extensive discussions on the concept of role there as well as detailed examinations of the relation between psychology (and especially psychoanalysis) and the theory of society. Developmental perspectives on the emergence of personal and individual identity are equally in evidence. They either refer to a sociological approach as distinctive from a biological-ethological one or they advocate the integration of a developmental perspective into socialization theory.

But the conceptual opposition between identity and social structure indicates that more is at stake than merely the most appropriate explanation for the integration of individuals into different forms of social structure. There is a further issue — whether present-day society can still provide the preconditions for the formation of personal and (some might add) "rational" identities.

Here one may wish to heed Friedrich Tenbruck's warning that there has been an inclination in Germany to drive a wedge between society and the individual and to approach society as the realm of alienated individuals. But this is not the entire story: while such a tendency indeed does exist — as Tenbruck documents it in his critical argument against Ralf Dahrendorf (essay 20) — there has also been ongoing concern with the most appropriate mediation of individual and society. The question has been raised under what conditions the identity of human subjects can best be achieved and to what extent sociology recognizes the significance of this normative claim.

While it may be true — see J. A. Clausen, ed., *Socialization and Society* (Boston: Little, Brown, 1968), p. 22 — that one of the first sources in early American sociology for the term socialization was the translation of the German *Vergesellschaftung* from an essay by Georg Simmel, *Vergesellschaftung* meant more for Simmel than the development of the social nature or of a social character in individuals — which is how early American sociologists understood him. For Simmel, it remained an accomplishment of individuals, even if they are in fact drawn into different realms of social meaning that are beyond their full grasp. The term identity, in this context, indicates an active relation to modes of social structuring.

Recent German sociology has shown much interest in the classical tradition of American sociology and its approach to self and society. Both Friedrich Tenbruck and Thomas Luckmann, two authors represented in this final section, explicitly refer to Charles Horton Cooley and W. I. Thomas. Others refer to George Herbert Mead. (See Hans Joas, *G.H. Mead: A Contemporary Re-Examination of His Thought* [Cambridge, Mass.: MIT Press, 1985], and Jürgen Habermas, *The Theory of Communicative Action*, vol. 2 [Boston: Beacon Press, 1987].)

Yet even this interest is informed by distinctive concerns. They belong to two domains of inquiry:

First, there is a rejection of the position that the "self" must be subordinated to society, that only the fully integrated individual represents the properly socialized self. Certain traits of this position are quite strongly evident in Helmut Dahmer's (essay 18) and Alexander Mitscherlich's (essay 19) contributions, which are clearly linked to the influence of Adorno (see especially his essay "Sociology and Psychology," *New Left Review* [Nov.-Dec. 1967], 46:67-80; [Jan.-Feb. 1968], 47:79-97). Even Tenbruck's critical analysis of the concept of role, written in 1961, reflects in a certain sense this first position, for it challenges the notion that individuals are properly conceived as role bearers, as conforming to institutionally organized role expectations which rely on the normative force of sanctions. All these authors recognize, of course, that personal identity is a socially constituted phenomenon, to use phenomenological language. Here Luckmann (essay 17), Tenbruck and Ulrich Oevermann (essay 21) are closer to George Herbert Mead than to Talcott Parsons. Indeed, Oevermann and his collaborators propose an empirical research program exploring the interactive generation of objective social structure. While explicitly referring to Mead's theory of significant symbols, they also regard the intentionality of actors as an important methodological concept. In the ideal case, they argue, the latent meaning of social action coincides with the meaning achieved by individual subjects. Thus the rational identity of societal subjects may result from a successful process of socialization. In Oevermann's work, too, a normative perspective is introduced which links empirical studies of socialization with a particular conception of the identity of "self" in society.

Second, the topics of identity, social structure, and socialization also receive distinctive treatment by the authors represented in this section in regard to issues of (philosophical) anthropology. Luckmann clearly addresses such questions in his essay, originally published as a contribution to the appraisal of human ethology as a newly emerging field. In assigning a central place to the concept of "personal identity," he regards personal identity as a specifically human level of behavioral integration. Sociological considerations concerning the formation of personal identity are only one type of question to be pursued in a comprehensive philosophical analysis of all dimensions of human life which draws on several disciplines. Thus Luckmann places his efforts into the context of a specifically German tradition of inquiry, that of a "philosophical anthropology," drawing upon biological, historical, cultural, and social inquiries.

Luckmann argues that in an evolutionary sense personal identity has become a historical form of life. He brings a phenomenological analysis to bear on this topic, inspired by Alfred Schutz. Like the founders of philosophical anthropology, Arnold Gehlen and Helmuth Plessner, Luckmann arrives at pessimistic conclusions about modern social structure. In his view, industrial societies cannot provide a secure basis for the development of personal identity. Friedrich Tenbruck, too, though from a different perspective, similarly argues that alienation in modern society results from a lack of identification with social roles, i.e., from inadequately differentiated and rather precarious conceptions of identity. Tenbruck's essay, furthermore, shows how reception in a different milieu can alter the original theory. It is an indictment of German sociology's failure to come to terms with the highly developed state of the theory of social roles in American sociology. Tenbruck calls upon Arnold Gehlen and, in another context, upon Georg Simmel (see his "Georg Simmel," *Kölner Zeitschrift für Soziologie und Sozialpsychologie* [1958] 10:587-614), themselves philosophers as well as sociologists, in order to assign the appropriate place to the concept of role in a theory of personality formation in culture. But in the end any such general or even formal sociological statements about the relation between society, culture, and persons must be transformed into statements about individuals. Tenbruck's critical discussion of the German reception of American role theory culminates in a conclusion anticipated in his essay on Simmel and followed up in an important essay on Max Weber ("The Problems of Thematic Unity in the Works of Max Weber," *British Journal of Sociology* [1980] 31:313-51). It also underlies his recent critique of social science (*Die unbewältigten Sozialwissenschaften oder die Abschaffung des Menschen* [Graz: Styria, 1983]). This is the question how people can understand themselves as individuals in the face of the increasing differentiation and rationalization of modern society.

It therefore is instructive to read those essays which link sociology with philosophical anthropology on the background of Kurt Lenk's paper on the "tragic consciousness" of German sociology (essay 2). For here historicism and the "philosophy of life" (*Lebensphilosophie*) are identified as the sources of a "spiritual" disquietude about modern society which is also characteristic of early German sociologists, especially Simmel, Weber, and Scheler. In some cases, as in Simmel's cultural criticism, this leads to a reinterpretation of Marx's critique of commodity fetishism, and thereby to the themes of alienation and personal identity addressed by Tenbruck and Luckmann.

But Marx's theory has a more direct impact among those who attempt to combine psychoanalysis and social theory. Helmut Dahmer (essay 18) and Alexander Mitscherlich (essay 19), the two authors in this part who represent this position, develop their arguments by way of a critical appropriation of Freud.

As a clinical psychoanalyst and director of the Sigmund-Freud Institute in Frankfurt, Alexander Mitscherlich (1908-1982) worked in the field of psychosomatic illnesses. He also emerged in the 1960s as a noted critic of contemporary culture (see *Society Without the Father: A Contribution to Social Psychology* [New York: Harcourt, Brace and World, 1969]) with close ties to the Frankfurt School of critical theory.

His paper on "The Nature of Human Aggression" documents his concern with the demands placed in modern societies upon the individual psyche. People, he argues, now find it difficult to become "autonomous" and to develop a strong sense of identity because the price for this is often considerable suffering. They find it less difficult to be the kind of "well-balanced" and "well integrated" person which modern psychology, role theory, and social psychology sometimes suggest as a model, thus reconciling themselves to a personal and public fate already anticipated in the arrangement of modern institutions. Without dramatizing the issue, Mitscherlich warns against the implications of a full enforcement of these expectations, which lie in the mobilization of a destructive (and self-destructive) potential that accumulates in the psyche of modern people. Mitscherlich bases his views especially on studies of ontogenetic development that have revealed the enormous force and the ambivalent nature of aggressive drives, or of "primary destructive tendencies," which prevail when renunciations demanded by the pressure toward social conformity exact too high a price.

Mitscherlich thus continues the tradition of Freud's skeptical theory of culture, a theme to which Adorno had already strongly responded (see essay 10 and his essay "Sociology and Psychology"). It is also addressed by writers not committed to a critical perspective, such as Gehlen, who is himself influenced by Scheler. Gehlen continued to lecture on Freud even in the mid-1930s.

Helmut Dahmer ("Psychoanalysis as Social Theory") discusses the limitations of Freudian social theory by contrasting it with the critique of political economy, class analysis, and ideologies. This presupposes that psychoanalysis can be interpreted as social theory, a task which Dahmer undertakes by initially focusing upon Freud's theory of culture. Its basic concepts Dahmer regards as historical ones. Thus the concepts which designate the ability of the acculturated human "self" to both internalize and resist the demands of culture and of socialization are best placed, according to Dahmer, between psychology and sociology.

Psychoanalysis is integrated into a dialectical theory of society, which makes the limits of therapeutic practice visible: privileged groups may benefit from therapy, but a transformation of social norms which could lead to the autonomy and emancipation of all members of society points beyond therapeutic practice. Psychoanalysis is to be supplemented by the dialectical critique of false consciousness.

Claims such as these reach beyond sociology and perhaps even beyond the domain of intellectual inquiry. Thus it may be in order to recall Tenbruck's warning (essay 20) that German sociology needs to pay more attention to the sociologies of knowledge and language, as well as to theories of social change, culture, and the generation of symbolic meanings.

Ulrich Oevermann and his collaborators ("Structures of Meaning and Objective Hermeneutics") have attempted to meet this requirement: they call the study of those latent structures of meaning that are inherent in interaction "objective hermeneutics," that is methods for the analysis of recorded (and transcribed) interaction texts. Thus objective structures of significance are to be discovered which, while constitutive of interaction and socialization, cannot be derived from the psychic reality of interaction participants or from their overtly acknowledged motives for compliance with social role expectations. The procedures of an "objective hermeneutics" are reconstructive and interpretive. Methodological instruments are conjoined — according to this conception — which have their origins in psychoanalysis, developmental psychology, phenomenology, and ethnomethodology, as well as in a theory of structuration derived from Mead.

Thus the genesis of the interpretation of social meanings in interaction is to be accounted for sociologically. This research program has considerable affinity to the position recently put forward by Jürgen Habermas. For about a decade Habermas has argued for the adoption of reconstructive methods in the study of socialization and role behavior (e.g., "What is Universal Pragmatics," and "Moral Development and Ego Identity," *Communication and the Evolution of Society* [Boston: Beacon Press, 1979], pp. 1-68; 69-104). It is clear that the sociology of language, often in conjunction with the philosophy of language (and especially the theory of speech acts) and theoretical linguistics, acquires prominence in these contexts. It becomes the foundation for a theory of culture, as in Habermas' *The Theory of Communicative Action*, and, in other respects, in Thomas Luckmann (e.g., *The Sociology of Language* [Indianapolis: Bobbs-Merrill, 1975]).

Here one also needs to consider Luhmann's analysis of "meaning" as the fundamental constituent of social experience and its systemic dimensions, society and personality (e.g., *Gesellschaftstruktur und Semantik*, 2 vols. [Frankfurt: Suhrkamp, 1981]). There can be no doubt that the traditional reliance of German sociology upon a philosophically and psychoanalytically informed anthropology or upon comprehensive theories of society has given way to more cautious empirical as well as theoretical orientations — at least in the field of socialization studies. But a concern with the generation and sedimentation of meaning in social interaction is regained as a primary focus. It can best be described as phenomenological in the broadest sense.

In this area, German sociology is responsive to developments which began in Germany in the 1920s, but had been ignored in the meantime. They have returned to the Federal Republic from the United States, where the themes of culture, language, and social change have received increasing attention during the past two decades.

17

Personal Identity as an Evolutionary and Historical Problem

THOMAS LUCKMANN

On Invasions, Rituals, and Institutions

When new intellectual ventures begin developing into academic disciplines they seem quite regularly to follow a natural inclination to colonize neighboring territories. The established occupants of those territories appear to have an equally natural conservative bent. They oppose resolutely, and sometimes — if the threat is serious — violently, the immoderate jurisdictional claims of the upstarts. The disputes are usually resolved in the end, but not before there has been much talking and shouting that decides how such claims and counterclaims are adjudicated.[1]

The expeditions into the territory of the social sciences which were inspired by many sources, from Darwin to the modern geneticists, but most particularly by Jakob von Uexküll, were continued by Konrad Lorenz and now, prominently among many others, Irenäus Eibl-Eibesfeldt. These incursions led not only to ritualized dueling among gentlemen scholars in the time of Darwin and Spencer but in recent decades also to unrestrained mortal combat between some of the more ambitious invaders and some of the most worried self-appointed defenders. Ethologists will surely be able to tell us whether biological analogies and, in this case, perhaps also homologies could help us to understand these all-too-human set-to's and to-do's. In fact, I wonder whether an instructive comparison of various traditions of the comparative method so beloved of ethology should not be arranged. What would a primatologist conversant with the procedures by which rank is established in a troop of baboons, a historian of science contemplat-

Originally published in English in M. von Cranach, K. Foppa, W. Lepenies, and D. Ploog, eds., *Human Ethology* (Cambridge: Cambridge University Press; Paris, Editions de la Maison des Sciences de l'Homme, 1979), pp. 56-74. The note section has been completed by the editors.

ing the long series of partly successful and partly disastrous importations of biological ideas and models into social science, and a sociologist of knowledge familiar with the ways by which social institutions reinforce the theoreticians' bent toward cognitive totalitarianism, make of the latest episodes of intellectual incursion? Speaking of territorial invasions, it may be salutary for those of us who assume that the topic of this volume[2] is not merely a minor but an important and particularly promising crossing of the borders, to remember not only what happened to China after the Mongols crossed the Great Wall in the Middle Ages but also what happened to the Mongols after they invaded China. Can we see the conference as a signpost pointing to the sinification of our vigorous latter day intellectual Mongols?

If that is indeed the case, I may express my hope that ever larger segments of the Mongol elite will acquaint themselves with the vast body of Chinese literature. It is in keeping with historical precedent that in the first phases of such an invasion the invaders try to seal themselves off from the decadent civilization of the local inhabitants. But in order to understand the rather quaint customs of a people of whom they so far had only superficial knowledge, a different attitude on the part of the newcomers eventually becomes necessary. Shall we say that sinification is a matter of adaptive behavior?

In trying to offer a contribution of my own to the discussion of the question how far ethological approaches can be taken in the systematic study of human affairs, I could follow one of several paths. For one, I could bypass the fascinating substantive parts of Eibl-Eibesfeldt's "Ritual and Ritualization from a Biological Perspective"[3] and directly start a debate of certain key methodological issues which he raises. These issues concern more than the problem of ritualization; they go beyond the ethological approach. But it would surely be premature to engage in abstract argument on what constitutes an *explanatory* law and what is merely a *descriptive* regularity; what level of interest can be legitimately satisfied in the systematic explanation of the complex structures of behavior that are involved in human affairs; how different levels of analysis can be reasonably connected in an encompassing yet nonreductionist theory that satisfies both practical and philosophical dimensions of our curiosity about the world; the limits of *functionalism* in general (i.e., in the context of any systems theory) and the specific problems of functionalist explanation in the study of human cultures, the proper uses of the comparative method in dealing with data on human affairs, data that have a peculiar (inter-) subjective, (linguistic-) symbolic, and (narrative-) historical dimension. I am confident that there will be time and opportunity to discuss these matters at a later date.

An obvious alternative was to take the paper by Eibl-Eibesfeldt as a whole and discuss it in detail from the point of view of a sociologist. I should like to stress that I find Eibl-Eibesfeldt's exposition of the key concepts of ethology instructive, the summary of his far-ranging empirical work on the universality of basic expressive movements and certain rituals in face-to-face interaction wholly admirable, and the programmatic statement of his views on what he calls cultural evolution and on the presumed selective pressures operating on cultural patterns sufficiently wrong-headed, to provoke me into resolute opposition. I do not believe that anyone who has dealt systematically with the complexities of social organization and cultural process in history could accept such a view of "cultural" evolution. The notions of selective pressure, reproductive success, group fitness, and the like cannot be transferred, without danger of simplification as well as confusion, from one explanatory level to another. The social sciences have been blessed by misleadingly vague biological analogies before! Incidentally, this probably explains why so many social scientists block off with prejudice any contribution to the human sciences from biology that goes beyond anatomical structure and physiological function. With Eibl-Eibesfeldt and other adherents of the position for which he stands one should very carefully debate the question to what extent explanations of structures and functions on one organizational level can be integrated into explanations of structures and functions on a higher level: higher in the sense that it evolved from the preceding level and that it still contains many of the elements of the preceding level.[4]

Nonetheless I shall not choose this second path to enter the discussion either. I do not plan to argue directly against what I think is a mistaken and unproductive view of social historical processes. I intend to approach the general question of how evolutionary explanations of human behavior can be integrated from a different direction. With Eibl-Eibesfeldt I share the modern, historically not always obvious, creed that *human* life is a matter of *life,* and I suppose that most social scientists today will agree with him that this means that it is a product of evolution. I also agree with him that ritualization (in the ethological meaning of the term) shapes and determines much of what are the "building blocks," the constituent behavioral elements of face-to-face social interaction. Although it is probably premature to worry now about exactly *how* much, the possibilities of some kind of measurement on such matters may improve in the future and the question may be *then* answerable more accurately.[5] Following Eibl-Eibesfeldt, I shall take ritualization to refer to "the process by which non-communicative behavior patterns evolve" into communicative ones. I shall assume that the expressive movements of which rituals consist are indeed "integrated in a more complex event which is structured in a rule-governed way."[6] I shall further assume that the regularities which he finds in these events are pretty much as he describes them and that for nonhuman species at least they are sufficient to account for these events.

It seems to me fairly obvious, however, that these events, being necessarily face-to-face, consist of continuous or near-continuous short-term sequences of social interaction. The ethological meaning of the term "ritual" does *not* include the full range of regularities in social interaction which the proverbial man in the street wants to understand for practical purposes, and which social anthropologists and sociologists as well as historians and other social scientists try to describe and explain systematically. Although the term overlaps to some extent the anthropological notions of ritual, it does not reach as far as the sociological concept of institution. It does not account for regularities in long-term behavioral sequences of individuals nor does it connect these to basic principles of human social organization as successfully as does the concept of institution — nor, of course, was it designed to do so. I do not wish to try my hand at an abstract comparison of the explanatory power of "ritual" and "institution," picking up here and there illustrations (from the Peloponnesian War to the rise of modern bureaucracy) favorable to the point to be made. Instead I should like to take up a problem that is on the borders of our various disciplines and that has been — with the mostly inglorious exception of psychology — neglected by all of them, despite the fact (or what I think is a fact) that it clearly demonstrates the interplay of evolutionary and historical determinants of human behavior: the problem of personal identity. It may be highly unusual to think of personal identity rather than specific traits (phenotypes) as having evolved, and it may be even more unusual for a sociologist with historical interests to speculate on evolutionary matters — but the Great Wall can be pierced in *both* directions.

On the Evolution of Personal Identity

What I have to say about personal identity rests on several connected assumptions. To the best of my knowledge these assumptions are compatible with present information on human phylogeny and ontogeny. I consider the argument to which I am led by these assumptions in agreement with whatever historical knowledge is available on the subject. Nonetheless it will be prudent to admit immediately that my argument contains speculative elements. This is due to two circumstances. Leaving aside for the moment the possibility that my knowledge of the specifics of human phylogeny and ontogeny is inadequate to support my assumptions, the argument that is derived from these assumptions is rather sweeping. It is formulated on such a high level of abstraction that several intermediate steps of conceptualization and operationalization are required before the argument's corroboration or refutation by an identifiable set of empirical data can be established definitely. It should therefore be considered, perhaps, as a paradigmatic venture rather than as a hypothesis. Furthermore, the argument is formulated with prejudice; which proposition about the nature of human beings offered by a human being is not? In my case the argument is evidently rooted in a philosophical and a social-theoretical position. These are the assumptions.

1. The species to which we belong is characterized by a somewhat unusual form of life. This form of life, i.e., the human level of behavioral integration, is most aptly described by the concept of personal identity. Personal identity refers to *central long-range control of its behavior by an individual organism*.

2. This form of life emerged in the *interaction* of several analytically distinct dimensions of the evolutionary process: of the anatomical and physiological evolution of the body; of the evolution of individual consciousness; and the evolution of social organization. In theoretical reconstructions, at least, ethologists and palaeoanthropologists should be able to account for the emergence of this level of behavioral organization by tracing its adaptive value to a species forced from foraging to cooperative and food-sharing hunting.[7] At all events, it seems highly implausible to assume that anything like human language, technology, and culture could have evolved without a roughly corresponding development of strongly individualized social relations and central control of individual behavior.

3. The high measure of individualization in social relations was only possible in a species with extraordinary intraspecific behavioral variability. Cultural "subspeciation," so important for the development of historical social structures, presupposes a high degree of individualization.[8]

4. The evolution of personal identity presupposes an especially high measure of the individual organism's detachment from the situation "here and now" of the environment as well as from the immediacy of experiences of self. In other words, it presupposes the beginnings of some sort of reflective consciousness and an initial stage of "eccentric-positionality," if I may use a term coined by Plessner to refer to what he considered the basic mode of human existence.[9] After the last decades of field investigation and experimental study of primates we must no longer cherish the (neo-Cartesian?) notion that all species, save ours, live in closed worlds. It may well be that the transition between the positionality of other species and the eccentricity of ours is less abrupt than former generations of scholars imagined. Nonetheless it seems reasonably certain that the conditions necessary for a high measure of individual detachment are not fully present — nor all available in the necessary combination — in other species, not even other primates.

5. The main conditions for such detachment are as follows:

(a) With regard to the body: the physiological evolution of the organism and especially of the brain, must enable the organism to experience the environment through a rich ("redundant") variety of senses as reasonably stable and predictable structure of objects and events.[10] Reconstructions of the phylogeny of the brain in relation to the phylogeny of the entire organism, and of the phylogeny of the species in relation to ecologically variable and climatically and otherwise changeable environments, show the emergence of increasingly more complicated synthetic performances. Multimodal informations about the environment can be grasped "holistically"; they are consistently related to temporally and spatially identifiable stimuli in the environment; eventually, they can even be labeled in some fashion and stored for centrally controlled reuse.[11] This is of course an essential condition for the emergence of face-to-face symbol systems and, eventually, notation.[12]

(b) With regard to consciousness: the results of the physiological evolution of the body which were just described can also be put in different terms. The extraordinary measure of synthetic ability (synthesizing synchronically *and* diachronically)[13] meant that the individual could experience changing environments as a structure of typical objects and qualities, as a "world"; and that he could integrate sequences of situations to a "history" of typical events. This cognitive development has obvious pragmatic functions. It is a necessary condition for the ability to *delay* responses to immediate situational stimuli and, eventually, to suppress some responses altogether for the sake of fictively anticipated and volitionally *projected* transsituational ends. The ability of the individual to locate himself in a "historical world" enables him to engage in *actions* over long and discontinuous sequences of behavior. It is surely plausible to assume that this ability must have been advantageous to individuals, groups, and the species as a whole.

(c) With regard to social organization: detachment from the immediacy of the experiences of self rests on attentiveness to others and the ability to recognize the reflection of one's own self in the behavior and actions of others. Protracted and intensive attention to the behavior of other individuals and a reasonably coherent assessment of their reactions emerged in social systems which were based on highly individualized and already somewhat "historicized" relations among the members of a group. The assumed ritual of cannibalism of Peking man and the Neanderthal burial of the dead are symptoms of "historicization."[14] There seem to be considerable differences in this respect even among primates and the importance of the degree of individualization of social relations for ranking and sexual bonding (all the way to the avoidance of incest) seem to vary significantly.[15] It is likely that cooperative hunting and food-sharing, in which *Homo* differs from other primates but shows interesting analogies to the carnivores, furthered what is already a high degree of individualization of social bonds among primates and especially among chimpanzees. But the most important factor seems to be the long dependence of the child on the mother. This process, need I add, should not be considered as a purely cognitive or pragmatic one. It has an important emotional component.[16] In any case, it is difficult to imagine that the highly individualized human recollection of the actions of others and the reciprocal long-term and transsituational imputation of responsibility for past actions should not have evolved from these or similar prehuman and protohuman circumstances.

6. The phylogenetically evolved structures of body and consciousness continue to determine basic elements of individual behavior. They also set recognizable limits to the varieties of human social organization. But personal identity is the regulatory principle for the integration of basic behavioral elements into long-term sequences of social interaction. Furthermore, the influence of many of the phylogenetically evolved structures of body and consciousness upon behavior is no longer direct but mediated by personal identity.

7. The evolution of a continuous central organization of individual be-

havior, linked to the evolution of individualized long-term structuring of social interaction, are the main sources of the "historicization" of individual consciousness and social organization. Evolution in the strict sense ceases to determine human affairs as specifically human, i.e., subjectively and collectively meaningful affairs. Social interaction, beginning with the rituals of face-to-face encounters, over the complex patterning of social relations in relatively small groups (as, for example, in archaic kinship systems), all the way to the bureaucratic political economies of modern industrial societies, are regulated by "norms" and "traditions," i.e., by *social institutions*. The individual lives in a historical world; his actions have strong transsituational and transindividual components. Human beings develop into political and (im-)moral actors.

To put it briefly: *personal identity*, itself a product of a few million to several hundred thousand years of natural history, mediates between the phylogenetic and ontogenetic determinants of human existence and those determinants which are the result of the artificial, self-made history that can be measured in tens of thousands and hundreds of years.

It is from these assumptions that I come to my argument. I shall try to show how personal identity, an evolutionary emergent, becomes a *historical* form of life. The constituent elements of personal identity, the human body, the elementary structures of consciousness, and the basic determinants of social interaction are established in the "*biogram*" of the species. The concrete development of any individual personal identity, however, depends upon a sociohistorical *a priori*. That a priori is linked to the evolutionary "biogram" of the species inasmuch as it cannot transgress the limits set by it. It cannot be derived from the biogram, however; it is only one of the many possible human historical constructions which is compatible with it.

In my attempt to show how personal identity becomes a historical form of life I shall take three steps. I shall present a basic sketch of the social ontogeny of personal identity in face-to-face interaction which systematizes models developed by Mead and Cooley.[17] Then I shall discuss the ways in which face-to-face interaction is determined by historically specific forms of social organization, a social structure; and by historically specific, symbolically transmitted systems of orientation in reality, a culture. Finally, I shall use a crude typology ("archaic" versus "modern") of sociohistorical a priori's to illustrate the variety of factors that make for historically distinct kinds of personal identity.

On the Historical Ontogeny of Personal Identity

It is an elementary fact of our life that we are born as individual organisms of a particular species. Another elementary fact of our life is that we are born into a unique historical society. For an individual organism it is as much part of its fate that it starts life as a twentieth-century Ulster man rather than a first-century Bedouin or Upper Paleolithic hunter, as is its birth as *Homo* rather than *Papio* or *Hylobates*. Twentieth-century Ulster society and first-century Bedouin tribes are objective realities for the individuals living in them. No doubt such realities have a peculiar objectivity that is not quite the same as the objectivity of a tree or a rock. It does not merely rest on perceptual constancy in the environment of an organism; it rests on an intersubjective, *communicatively* established, and socially transmitted organization of subjective experience. Such realities are peculiar for an additional reason. They confront the individual in the *actions* of other individuals. Anyone can see that things are so and not otherwise because of the past actions of forefathers, past and present actions of contemporaries, and perhaps because of the past and present actions of the gods. In other words, the peculiar nature of such realities resides in the fact they are human creations — although they are not creations *ex nihilo*. This applies as much to language and religion as to kinship, politics, and economics. The prohibition of joking with mother-in-law is as much part of such a reality as the belief that yams walk at night, the discovery of the wheel as much as the construction of the atom bomb, hydraulic despotism as much as parliamentary bureaucracy.

The human child is born with a body that is the result of phylogeny, leaving aside some prenatal accidents. It is born with a phylogenetically determined potential for the development of elementary structures of consciousness ranging from basic emotions and hemispheric specialization to a certain level of "intelligence." It is also born with a set range of social requirements and inclinations. The child's ontogeny has a natural history. But although this determines the *nature* of its life, in some respects inexorably and in others as a limit to alternative possibilities, it does not simply determine the *historical* course of its life. Nonetheless, the course of the child's life is not simply a sequence of open possibilities to choose from. There is a second, a socially superimposed level of existential determination which is a product of history and only very indirectly of evolution.

The individual organism, although by no means a *tabula rasa* in which learning processes happen to occur, is nonetheless the highly malleable material for a historically specific language, culture, and social structure. Historical socialization is superimposed upon maturation. Evidently, this does not mean that language, culture, and social structure should be considered arbitrary from a biological point of view; it *does* mean that they cannot be derived from biological processes except in the purely metaphorical sense in which "history" is an offspring of "evolution." To paraphrase Plessner: their artificiality is natural. *The human organism and human society are not simple structural or functional correlates.* They are not the two sides of one coin nor are they moments of a dialectical process. *The human organism is an evolutionary rather than a historical individual; human societies are historical collectives rather than evolutionary subspecies or varieties.* Their relation is established in a complicated process in which the individual organism acquires a historical personal identity in a social process that presupposes both phylogenetic and historical structures.

A historically specific social structure and a historically specific world view (i.e., a language and a culture viewed from "within" as formal but subject-centered systems of orientation and communication) influence the course of human life by way of institutional "norms." Individual action and orientation is geared to these "norms" as the individual comes to know them and he comes to know them in communicative and, most importantly, symbolic processes. The individual's behavior is increasingly not only governed by rules — it also follows rules, and, a circumstance that should not be overlooked, breaks rules.

The norms of a historical social structure and world view determine, to begin with, the character of the *primary social relations* into which the child is placed from its birth. They define the child's kinship position (first-born son) and its legal status (heir) and they also influence its survival chances (infanticide; modern hospitals). These norms shape the way in which the child is likely to be treated (authoritatively and affectionately, authoritatively and coldly, permissively and affectionately, etc.). They are translated into direct injunctions (don't scream, don't steal, sit straight, etc.). In sum, a historical social structure and a historical world view shape the most intricate aspects of the social relations in which the child matures. At the same time, a world of typical objects and events, and of connections between them, a world of smiles, words, and actions is being established in these relations for the child.

And this is of course not the end of it. Historical social structures and world views continue to influence individual existence by determining the character of social interactions in later life. The social division of labor and a system of stratification determine work and leisure and private and public conduct. All of these are evidently historical categories. Face-to-face encounters as, for example, religious rituals or flirting as well as indirect forms of social interaction such as the filling out of income tax declarations are determined by social structures rather than biological individuals. Social interaction is rule-governed intentional behavior geared into known and anticipated rule-governed behavior of others, but the rules are perceived and followed as social rather than individual entities.

Personal identity does not "mature" in the same sense in which a biological individual matures. It is the sedimentation of actions and impositions in a synthesizing, interpreting "memory." It does not develop from "within" as does the biological individual; it comes from "without." Historical sedimentations are not transmitted genetically but socially, symbolically.

Except for bodily functions, lusts, and pains, the individual does not experience himself directly; what he does experience directly is a structured and changing environment. Not only rocks and trees and dogs and fishes but other individuals, too, are a functionally essential part of this environment. They are experienced directly, by means of their body. The body of fellow men is experienced as the field of expression of their consciousness: their feelings, moods, intentions, and projects. Inasmuch as fellow men experience an individual as a significant part of their environment, the individual experiences directly another's experience of him. He comes to experience himself indirectly. In a matter of speaking, personal identity is a result of social *learning*. Cooley spoke of the "looking-glass effect."[18] This image aptly represents the process in which one individual is reflected in another's experience. In face-to-face encounters the *experience* (and not, to begin with, the more complex reflective consciousness) of one's self is built up in experiences of another.

Reciprocal mirroring is an elementary condition for the formation of personal identities. But reciprocal mirroring in the "here and now" of face-to-face encounter is a necessary but not a sufficient condition. A second condition is the mutual recollection of the actions of the other in past face-to-face situations and the reciprocal imposition of responsibility for past actions. The other fellow in the encounter is the same one as yesterday, and vice versa. Personal identity originates in the reciprocity of face-to-face encounters and as the individual matures from "within" it is imposed from "without" in collective memory. To put it somewhat differently, personal identity is intersubjective and has a situational biographical dimension.

It is clear without much further elaboration that personal identities are not "things" but regulatory principles of the intentional structures of subjective consciousness *and* of the intersubjective rather than instinctive organization of social interaction. Personal identities are not closed and definitive. Although informed consensus will have it that the most important elements of personal identity are established in the early phases of socialization, later social interactions, from face-to-face encounters to purely symbolic and mediated forms of "mirroring," support, reinforce, modify, or threaten personal identities or, in extreme cases, destroy them.

Let us return to the earliest forms of intersubjective "mirroring." The earliest social relations of the child rest upon an assumption of reciprocity, although that assumption is perhaps in part fictive. In a manner of speaking, this assumption imposes reciprocity on the child and, given the phylogenetic makeup of the human child, full reciprocity will *normally* develop.[19] If socialization fails to produce full reciprocity (for psychological, social-psychological and communicative, or social-structural reasons or some combination thereof) and the human being does not attain this form of life, a host of everyday difficulties, legal problems, psychiatric or religious questions, and moral dilemmas arise.

Intersubjective "mirroring" is a concept which refers to the formal properties of a process which in fact is the encounter of physically and historically concrete individuals. This is merely one way of saying that the fellow men involved in the earliest social relations of the child have formed personal identities in their own earlier and earliest social relations which again were not with mere biological organisms and mere sociological *homunculi* but with historically unique individuals. A historical world view, i.e., a particular sediment of past interpretations of reality, shaped *their* knowledge of the world and a historical social structure with specific institutions and "norms," i.e., the sediment of a *particular* enchainment of past actions, influenced their own actions. No more and no less is meant by the statement that a historical social structure and a historical world view form a sociohistorical a priori for the child which is superimposed on its biological maturation. I am aware of the fact that superimposition may be a poor term for the kind of interdependence that characterizes the biological and social-historical dimensions of *unitary* process.

The sociohistorical a priori which guides the actions of the adults vis-à-vis the child, actions which the child experiences as reflections of itself, determine the specific way in which the child learns to think of itself and to act as a person. Sociologists like to use the conceptual apparatus of role theory to analyze the details of this process, but the use of this apparatus is by no means essential. It is important to see that the basic processes of intersubjective "mirroring" are always concretely determined by a sociohistorical *a priori*. Human socialization is a historical process.

Personal Identity in Primitive and Modern Society

Let us now consider the historical social conditions for the development of varied elementary types of personal identity in primitive societies. In a second step, we shall compare these conditions to the requirements of socialization that characterize modern industrial societies and the kind of personal identities to which they lead. I shall have to neglect the ancient civilizations which, from a historical point of view, were an equally important frame of human socialization and which represented not only transitional forms between primitive and modern societies but long-lived, fully "adopted" social systems.

Primitive societies determine nearly all the individual's social actions directly by way of — and in terms of — the kinship system. Actions which have primarily economic, political, kinship, and religious functions do not form separate and distinct sets of institutions. Indeed, these different functions are merged in activities *subjectively* regarded as having unitary significance. In other words, the social structure of primitive societies is not organized into separate sectors with functionally specialized institutions. A hunt, for example, is not only a behavior complex that is relevant to the economic basis of the society, it also embodies aspects of the kinship system, and is a representation of religiously significant action as well as of the structure of authority. Furthermore, the institutional norms which determine behavior are subordinated to an extraordinary level of reality which is connected to experiences of death, seasonal and life-cycle transformations, dreams, fertility, and the like and which is represented symbolically and treated ritually.

The world view is transmitted almost exclusively through direct social interactions in which the validity and "reality" of linguistically and symbolically transmitted meanings, values, and "solutions" are concretely exemplified. These social interactions are structured by social, mostly kinship, roles. In primitive societies the nature of reality is therefore something which is *relatively* easy to grasp. Individual action in such a reality does not constitute a problem which normally demands great "originality." This of course does not mean that life is easy, behavior unproblematic, and individuals generally dull and noncreative, but it does mean that the adult who has been socialized into the reality of a primitive society is rather more than less competent to cope with all the problems which are assumed to be soluble within the framework of that society's world view. This contributes to the stability and unity of personal identity as a central regulatory principle of action and behavior as it is typically formed in primitive society.

In sum, the socialization process in primitive societies is almost always embedded in the most important of the systems underlying the social structure — kinship. Personal identity evolves almost exclusively in direct face-to-face social relationships. These relationships are familiar, stable, highly individualized, *and* they are systematically connected. The connections, i.e., the structure of kinship, make sense subjectively; they are articulated as elements of a symbolic universe. The maximum congruence of meaning in processes of intersubjective mirroring is, as it were, already provided for in the social structure itself. The individual's assumption that he lives in the "same" reality as his fellows is corroborated concretely time and again in direct social relationships from the earliest stages of socialization to adult life. This assumption is probably of decisive importance for the stability of the self.

Contrary to this, one of the most important characteristics of modern societies is the segmenting of the total structure into institutional domains which are organized to meet the main requirements of separate functions. In *primitive* society, economic, political, religious, and kinship functions are simply aspects of more or less unitary activities. In *modern* society, the economy, government, religion, and the family form patterns of activity which are institutionalized as specialized systems. These component systems of the social structure are of course not completely independent of each other, but they work essentially according to their own norms. This means that the norms of behavior inherent in one system at any one time are not directly transferable to other component systems. The structures of meaning belonging to different component systems are not related to personal identities, but to institutions. The behavioral norms belonging to different sectors are primarily determined by requirements which derive from their basic function (e.g., production, social control and authority, procreation, rearing, and socialization). The norms tend to be functionally rational, i.e., "rational" in terms of the several primary functions. In consequence, they are more or less emancipated from "religious" meanings, i.e., overarching symbolic universes that attempt to link social structure to individual existence and connect everyday life and crisis situations to an extraordinary, transcendent level of reality.

The segmentation of the social structure into specialized institutional sectors is accompanied by a far-reaching change in the relationship of the individual to institutions and to the social order as a whole. The social existence of the individual in modern society is made up in high measure of behavior in functionally specialized roles, which are not related to special institutions and are nearly completely anonymous in some measure. Highly specialized economic and political institutions, far removed from the immediate face-to-face social relationships of the majority of the population, determine the distribution of the very chances of access to social roles. By virtue of the continuous control of functionally important role-performances, they also shape the contents of large parts of everyday life.

Whereas primitive society consisted of a network of primary social relationships, classical civilizations had centralized political institutions. In spite of their symbolic incorporation into personalized dynastic, feudal, and similar forms, these institutions had a more or less strongly marked bureaucratic and anonymous character. Economic processes, too, were generally more impersonal in the civilizations of antiquity than in primitive society, although they were still rooted in the kinship order and especially in the family as a production and consumption unit. Nonetheless, social relationships in villages or clannish communities remained for the majority of the population exclusively face-to-face. They were linked to the superimposed political structure by clearly designated points of contact and then only from time to time (tax collectors, corvée labor, and the like).

In modern society, by contrast, the impersonal and predefined obligations attached to roles have priority in the business of everyday life; the actor's self plays an increasingly smaller part. As long as the specialized obligations of a role are "adequately" performed in the proper institutional context, the role-player is, so to speak, free to "choose" his personal identity. That identity must of course remain in the background of his role-performance or must even be denied completely. The course of institutionalized social interaction is "objectively" defined. This means that it is determined by its place in the "rational" organization of a social function in its relevant institutional sector.

But whether that course of social interaction makes sense to the human individual, whether it fits into the "subjective" organization of his person, becomes a structurally negligible issue. The objective meanings of action in most sectors of everyday life are important to the stability of the society, but they are no longer equally "important" to the personal identity of an individual. They lose their primary significance for his life. This is why in modern societies the determination of personal identity by social roles is turning into something of a mass subjective problem. Social roles which are necessary structural elements of all societies inevitably become anonymous in some measure. It hardly needs to be stressed that social roles are a necessary constituent of modern industrial societies. But when most social roles become highly anonymous and thereby depersonalized, the individual's personal identity is no longer clearly shaped by the social order in which he lives. Whether the nonproduction of personal identities by modern societies or the production system of industrial capitalism is responsible for a certain degree of alienation is a moot question.

In primitive society there is a socially objectivated world view which is transmitted through socialization processes common to all. In modern societies there is no *unitary* and *obligatory* form of world view as there is in preliterate small communities. To the highly developed division of labor and the specialization and bureaucratization of political and economic decision-making processes there corresponds a highly differentiated social a priori within society. Formation of personal identity takes place in a context which not only varies historically but is also socially unequal. To put it more precisely, even the opportunities for access to the no longer quite so common stock of knowledge are structurally "preconditioned." Socially differentiated "unequal" systems of how an individual orients himself in reality contain the categories by which an individual learns to see himself and others. They play an important role in the development of personal identity.

After primary socialization no version of the world view has an absolute monopoly. Although in modern society there is a multiplicity of world views, the individual is not completely "free to choose." Primary socialization already forms attitudes and inclinations which influence choices at a later stage. Furthermore, the constraints on behavior in institutionally specialized role systems are not without consequence for the consolidation of character, for the development of personal identity. And yet primary and secondary socialization in modern society are not linked together by cogent structural constraints, "preselecting" for the individual a cohesive (sub) cultural model. This means that achieving a stable personal identity becomes a subjective and indeed an essentially private enterprise. This is the sociopsychological correlate of the so-called pluralism of modern societies: no common social reality, no socially produced stable structure of personal identity!

Beginning from childhood, in all societies the self is placed in social relations in which, by virtue of intersubjective mirroring, it is beginning to form a personal identity. So far, all societies have provided their members with the means to do so. In modern industrial societies, however, the processes of intersubjective mirroring do not have uniform parameters of meaning. Modern societies typically produce a relatively high measure of "contradictory" aspects of the perception of self and environment. The most important source of potential incongruence in the formation of personal identity is the gap between primary and secondary socialization. There is something of a break between the home and the more or less anonymous and bureaucratized social structure into which the young person is pushed and pulled. In addition to this "longitudinal" gap there are typical problems of "horizontal" integration: between work and private life, between the half-real, half-fictive world of the mass media and the social reality of a neighborhood, etc. There are many ruptures or at least inconsistencies which make it difficult for the typical person to create — or recreate — a reasonably satisfactory and cohesive frame in which to place its experiences and actions. The individual cannot discover cohesiveness of meaning in his social experiences and actions as such; the meaning of these actions is *system-* rather than *person-*oriented. With all due caution one might say that the social structure of modern industrial societies does not provide — as other types of human social orders do — a firm basis for the development of personal identity as a consistent principle of the individual organization of human life.

In this respect modern society differs not only from primitive societies, but also from traditional preindustrial cultures. The world view — no longer firmly based on the social structure — now consists of a supply of items from which individuals may add on to the basic inventory that was built up in primary socialization. No particular version of the world view is strictly obligatory or inescapably predetermined by the social structure. Personal identity is not a matter of the sociohistoric a priori to quite the same extent as in other forms of society. Personal identity of course continues to emerge from social processes, but the social *production* of cohesive models of personal identity is largely abandoned by the social system. The production of personal identity thus increasingly becomes the business of the most private *petit entrepreneur*, the human individual.

As in all other forms of society, thus also in modern societies the central aspects of the world view (among them language), the most important patterns ("rituals") of behavior, the basic vocabularies of motives, and people's orientation within nature and the social world are transmitted through primary socialization. Here again the family works as a "filter" to the societal "input." Here again the basis of personal identity is laid down in the primary socialization process. But in no other type of society are so many and such important aspects of personal identity articulated and determined through social relationships developed *after* primary socialization. Nowhere else is it possible for so many of the elements of personal identity formed in primary socialization to be modified subsequently. And the connection between secondary and primary socialization was never so weak as in modern industrial societies. In no other society does orientation to social reality and social action depend so strongly on *secondary* socialization.

The acquisition of specialized knowledge occurs during secondary socialization. Specialized knowledge renders possible action in the different institutional subsystems. For most members of society who are recruited into the occupational system, only those specialized parts of expert knowledge are transmitted which are relevant to performance in their roles in sharply defined areas of institutionalized activity. Thus in modern society everyone, or nearly everyone, becomes a "specialist." Expertise is, however, definitely limited to clearly designated operations in specialized institutional sectors. In societies in which there is a relatively simple social distribution of knowledge, the bulk of the population consists of "laymen" — but these "laymen" are persons who are competent to deal with practically all the problems they meet in ordinary life. In modern society nearly everyone is an "expert," but mostly in a extraordinarily restricted, functionally specialized, and *impersonal* area of activity.

In all societies, at all times, personal identity is formed in processes of intersubjective mirroring. The basic structure of this process is surely "biological" but its specific operations are determined by the historically varied social structures. Modern industrial societies have significant effects on the formation of personal identity. The specialization of institutional systems, the weakening or severing of subjectively meaningful ties between experiences and actions which are determined by these systems, the growing anonymity of many social roles, the break between primary and secondary socialization; all these circumstances combined a rather new type of sociohistorical a priori for human organisms that happen to be born now rather than 400, 4000 or 40,000 years ago. The construction of personal identity has become entrusted in some measure to an "institution" which, by its very nature, is *not* an institution, the individual subject. This does not mean that society and personal identity in our time have made something like an evolutionary leap. But it does mean that they have changed significantly. And they have changed primarily because of a historically fateful degree of independence of specialized institutional systems from the cultural organization of personal identity in face-to-face communities. The institutional "second nature" which man made for himself in history is far removed from the structure that evolved from "nature" as a uniquely historical form of *life*.

NOTES

1. [Thomas Luckmann refers here to the "Werner-Reimers-Stiftung Conference on Human Ethology," Bad Homburg, West Germany, October 1977, at which his paper was presented in the session "Functions of Rituals" after the paper by Irenäus Eibl-Eibesfeldt on "Ritual and Ritualization from a Biological Perspective."]

2. [Reference to the proceedings of the Conference on Human Ethology which led to the publication of the book which contains his own contribution: M. von Cranach, K. Foppa, W. Lepenies, and D. Ploog, eds, *Human Ethology* (Cambridge: Cambridge University Press; Paris: Editions de la Maison des Sciences de l'Homme, 1979).]

3. *Ibid.*, pp. 3-55.

4. See Doris F. Jonas, "On an 'alternative paleobiology' and the concept of a scavenging phase," *Current Anthropology* (1976) 17(1): 144-155.

5. See Alison Jolly, *The Evolution of Primate Behavior* (New York, Toronto: Macmillan, 1972), pp. 138 ff.

6. Eibl-Eibesfeldt, "Ritual and Ritualization from a Biological Perspective," pp. 14, 10.

7. E.g., Hans Kummer, *Primate Societies: Group Techniques of Ecological Adaptation* (Chicago: Aldine, 1971); Jane B. Lancaster, "Primate Communication Systems and the Emergence of Human Language," in Phyllis C. Jay, ed., *Primates: Studies in Adaptations and Variability* (New York: Holt, Rinehart and Winston, 1968); George B. Schaller and Gordon R. Lowther, "The Relevance of Carnivore Behavior to the Study of Early Hominids," *Southwestern Journal of Anthropology* (1969) 25(4):307-341; Lionel Tiger and Robin Fox, *The Imperial Animal* (New York: Holt, Rinehart and Winston, 1971); Sherwood L. Washburn and C.S. Lancaster, "The Evolution of Hunting," in Richard B. Lee and Irven DeVore, eds, *Man the Hunter* (Chicago: Aldine, 1968).

8. See Jan Jelinek, "Neanderthal Man and Homo Sapiens in Central and Eastern Europe," *Current Anthropology* (1969) 10(5):475-503.

9. Helmuth Plessner, *Die Stufen des Organischen und der Mensch — Einleitung in die philosophische Anthropologie* (Berlin: de Gruyter, 1965).

10. See Doris F. Jonas and David A. Jonas, "More on 'Assumption and Inference on Human Origins,'" *Current Anthropology* (1974) 15(4):457-458.

11. U. Ebbecke, *Physiologie des Bewusstseins in entwicklungsgeschichtlicher Betrachtung* (Stuttgart: Georg Thieme, 1959); Earl W. Count, *Das Biogramm. Anthropologische Studien* (Frankfurt: S. Fischer, 1970); "On the Phylogenesis of Speech," *Current Anthropology* (1974) 15(1): 14-16; Harry J. Jerison, *Evolution of the Brain and Intelligence* (New York: Academic Press, 1973).

12. See Alexander Marshack, "Some Implications of the Paleolithic Symbolic Evidence for the Origin of Language," *Current Anthropology* (1976) 17(2):274-282.

13. See David Premack, *Intelligence in Ape and Man* (New York: Halsted, 1977).

14. Grahame Clark, *The Stone Age Hunters* (London: Thames and Hudson, 1967).

15. See Kummer, *Primate Societies: Group Techniques of Ecological Adaptation*; Vernon Reynolds, "Open Groups in Hominid Evolution," *Man* (1966) 1(4):442-452.

16. See Irenäus Eibl-Eibesfeldt, *Love and Hate: The Natural History of Behavior Patterns* (New York: Holt, Rinehart and Winston, 1972); David A. Hamburg, "Emotions in the Perspective of Human Evolution," in P. Knapp, ed., *Expressions of the Emotions in Man* (New York: International Universities Press, 1963).

17. George H. Mead, *Mind, Self and Society* [1934] (Chicago: University of Chicago Press, 1967); Charles H. Cooley, *Human Nature and the Social Order* [1902] (New York: Schocken, 1967).

18. Cooley, *ibid.*

19. Along with most sociologists I may have underestimated the degree of biological sociality and perceptual-cognitive achievement present in the newborn and young infant. See the following chapters in M. von Cranach et al., eds., *Human Ethology*: Hanuš Papoušek and Mechthild Papoušek, "Early Ontogeny of Human Social Interaction: Its Biological Roots and Social Dimensions," pp. 456-478; Colwyn Trevarthen, "Instincts for Human Understanding and for Cultural Cooperation: Their Development in Infancy," pp. 530-571; Judy Dunn, "Understanding Human Development: Limitations and Possibilities in an Ethological Approach," pp. 623-641; Klaus Foppa, "Language Acquisition: A Human Ethological Problem?" See also Harriet L. Rheingold, "The Social and Socializing Infant," in David A. Goslin, ed., *Handbook of Socialization Theory and Research* (New York: Rand McNally, 1969).

18

Psychoanalysis as Social Theory

Helmut Dahmer

Psychoanalysis is not commonly regarded as social theory. Psychology and sociology seem poles apart and, especially in the bourgeois era, seem to belong to quite different dimensions. In the battle between world views, the tendency is to regard human reality as constituted either by the vicissitudes of instincts or by capital accumulation and class struggle. Whatever lies between the two tends to be rejected. In what follows I will argue, first, that Freud's psychology, which is essentially a theory of individual neurotic disturbance, is at the same time a theory of society; second, that Freud, thirty years after his pathbreaking psychological discoveries, explicitly developed this latent social theory in *The Future of an Illusion* (1927); third, that Freud's therapeutic procedure shares certain characteristics with the dialectical theory of socialization, in particular the tendency toward a reappropriation of alienated human capacities.

Culture as the Matrix of Life Histories

It was the unique achievement of Freudian psychoanalysis to offer a social interpretation for those widespread somatic illnesses without organic cause, i.e., neurotic disturbances of the hysterical type, which the medicine of its time still regarded as simulated or merely imagined. Freud, however, not only showed that these illnesses were in fact "social ailments" acquired as a result of distorted socialization but that they were potentially curable by way of systematic talk therapy.[1] In a hypnotic state, patients who underwent the cathartic treatment developed by Breuer and Freud relived traumatic childhood experiences: scenes of social humiliation and hurt peculiarly intermingled with scenes of sexual provocation and seduction. The technique of "free" as-

"Psychoanalysis as Social Theory," *Telos* (Summer 1977) 32:27-41. Translation of "Psychoanalyse als Gesellschaftstheorie," *Psyche* (1975) 29(11):991-1010. Translation by David J. Parent revised by Dieter Misgeld.

sociation, also developed by Freud, aimed at the cognitive-affective reproduction, communication, and mental processing of unmastered traumatic scenes of adulthood, buried under cryptic memories, and associated with experiences of childhood and infancy. The neurotic symptom is healed by revealing its "meaning" — by way of a reconstruction of those childhood events (or sequence of events) whose conscious memory the symptom replaces and whose pleasurable or painful experience is bound up in it. Once the tic, fit, impotence, hysterical paralysis, or blindness (or their respective "causes") have been integrated into the patient's life history, and once the censored episode has been relocated within the officially approved biography, then the symptoms lose their power. The fact that the patient's ego could not cope with the episode in question is precisely what led to disturbances in his later life, compelling him to repeat the experience time and again. Certain stimuli, shutting off his rational actions of probing and examining reality, compel him to repeat stereotyped behavioral patterns in a maladjusted and disproportionately defensive way.

For ego identity to be formed, the demands of uninhibited instinctual wishes, internalized traditional norms, and situation-specific demands have to be mediated. Of course, the ego may succeed or fail in solving specific conflicts arising in different stages of life — conflicts which are embedded in a social matrix of increasing differentiation and heterogeneity. The theory of the vicissitudes of the instincts, of individual biographies and their typical crises, is the background for the psychoanalytic theory of neurosis. The psychic apparatus, among whose regulating principles are the securing of self-preservation and the quest for the good life, first matures ontogenetically before it becomes, to a certain extent, the "producer" of an individual biography. A psychology oriented toward such individual biographies always involves an understanding of the social constellations within which these take place. This is the element of truth in Freud's psychologistic claim that sociology is little more than applied psychology.

Freud was particularly interested in what kind of people our civilization creates, in the psychic residue in individual life histories. Society initially appears only as the clouded horizon of the theory of neurosis, as the culturally remodeled natural "environment" from which the psychic apparatus receives its stamp and by which it must prove itself. But even Freud's earliest psychoanalytic publications go beyond descriptions of disease syndromes, etiologies, and therapeutic procedures. They aim both at a model of the psychic apparatus whose structure and function must be deduced from the mechanisms at work in the process of symptom formation, as well as at a model of the cultural process which, as "macrocosm," is homologous with individual life as "microcosm." "Culture" is seen from the perspective of its "psychic aspect." Here one can already notice the limits as well as the critical nature of the psychoanalytic understanding of contemporary society.

As Freud's understanding of the formative history of individuals (and of the mode of functioning of their psychic "apparatus") became more differentiated, the shadow image of culture, illuminated from the perspective of its psychic aspects, also gained sharper profile. The critique of "civilized" sexual morality, the interpretation of totemism and the incest taboo and the study of group psychology formed the most important stages of the functionalist theory of social institutions sketched in the framework of the critique of religion: "The development of civilization appears to us as a peculiar process which mankind undergoes, and in which several things strike us as familiar."[2]

This process is familiar to the psychologist from the psychosexual development of individuals (their ontogeny) which recapitulates phylogeny. This cultural process is essentially one of renunciation, a process of self-abnegation, in the course of which the human race progressively works its way out of bondage to nature and distances itself from its own animality. The psychoanalytic theory of culture explicates the social preconditions of psychoanalysis as enlightenment. It reveals its objective function in the actual crisis of social evolution.

Freud's theory of culture is a critical theory of culture in the sense that, as a psychological theory, it measures cultural institutions by the suffering they inflict upon individuals. It does not, like Durkheim and his successors, by way of sociology repress the perennial conflict between human nature (libido) and the demands of socialization. It also does not by way of ideology add to the violence inflicted upon individuals or sanctify the culture that threatens them; instead it takes their side. Psychoanalytic theory seeks to understand individual unhappiness, the discontents with culture. Thus the psychologistic bias of his social theory protects Freud from idolizing contemporary civilization and permits him to clearly see through the crisis.

This bias, however, also explains the ideological limits of his theory. Like other social philosophers of the bourgeois era, Freud regards the existing society as a system of atomized individuals. The interconnections between the isolated individuals are essentially explained with reference to the inhibition of instinctual inclinations by way of the threat of force. Freud does not explain the relations between individuals in economic terms, for example by reference to the division of labor or to the distribution of the means of production. He fails to recognize that it is the economy that first makes possible the isolation of individuals and the anarchy of their production by regulating it behind their backs with an "invisible hand" (Adam Smith). The objective state of dependency of individuals in the bourgeois era, which has taken the place of the master-servant relationship, is also not explained by Freud's theory. Ignoring the historical specificity of capitalist socialization (i.e., the domination of members of the classes by the conditions of production), he substitutes libidinal dependence for the objective economic dependence of individuals. Freud does not analyze specific historical forms of dependence. He proceeds anthropologically. This gives his theory of culture its chimerical generality.

Cultural Institutions and Group Cohesion

Cultural institutions protect socialized human beings both against hostile external nature and against the asocial internal human nature at historically varying levels of domination of nature and self. Freud initially distinguishes those social institutions which regulate the relations of society to external nature (institutions for the production of goods) from those that regulate the social relations of individuals (institutions for the unequal distribution of goods). But "the two trends of civilization are not independent of each other: firstly, because the mutual relations of men are profoundly influenced by the amount of instinctual satisfaction which the existing wealth makes possible; secondly, because an individual man can himself come to function as wealth in relation to another one, insofar as the other person makes use of his capacity for work or chooses him as a sexual object; and thirdly, moreover, because every individual is virtually an enemy of civilization."[3]

External nature is not the only object of human domination. Some human beings make other human beings work for them and use them as their sexual objects. People can thus be used as goods, as means. Moreover, internal social relations are determined by the relations — themselves variable — of society to the natural environment. The more inhospitable the natural basis and the less developed the technical and organizational means to exploit it for the satisfaction of historically developing human needs, the more barbaric the internal social conditions of domination become. "Culture," the sum total of measures people have historically taken in order to come to terms with external nature as well as to repress or modify their own nature, involves a process of self-domestication. It has been imposed upon defiant majorities by privileged minorities, by proponents of asceticism such as Moses, who imposed the one, abstract God on the Jewish shepherd tribe in place of the many local gods.

For Freud, culture has its origin in "cultural ideals" and not in production techniques or tools: "Cultural ideals" consist of the recollection of epoch-making renunciations of instinctual pleasure, originally achieved by "great men" and kept alive in ritual as a socializing force in the succession of generations. The culture-bearing minorities invent new sublimations for crude instinctual desire. They are the real subjects of "culture," supported by the work of the majority and by the social surplus. Innovative renunciation is made easier for them because they are exempt from the torment of compulsory labor. Their renunciations are actually refined, prolonged satisfactions. Nonetheless, even these renunciations lead to a latent hostility to culture, which is evidenced in the barbaric acts committed by ruling classes threatened with destruction. The culture-promoting minorities enjoy a greater measure of real satisfaction and draw more intense illusory compensations from art and religion than do the masses. The minority distances itself from animality through sublimation: desire may only be satisfied in a socially useful, culturally valued form. The subjugated majority, however, is the involuntary bearer of the master culture, which it actually makes possible by its work. The masters' achievement of sublimation can only just barely be attained among them. It requires primitive reaction formations, by reversing the force of desire and turning it into its opposite. Aggressive cruelty is thus reversed into forbearance and finally even into "love" for the members of the community held together by force. Suppressed rage about the injustices suffered is unleashed only at dissidents and strangers, while pleasurable submission to rulers replaces social hatred.

If we turn to those restrictions that apply only to certain classes of society, we meet with a state of things which is flagrant and which has always been recognized. It is to be expected that these underprivileged classes will envy the favored ones their privileges and will do all they can to free themselves from their own surplus of privation. Where this is not possible, a permanent measure of discontent will persist within the culture concerned and this can lead to dangerous revolts. If however, the culture has not got beyond the point at which the satisfaction of one portion of its participants depends upon the suppression of another, and perhaps larger, portion — and this is the case in all present-day cultures — it is understandable that the suppressed people should develop an intense hostility towards culture whose existence they make possible by their work, but in whose wealth they have too small a share.[4]

The system of social institutions continues to be effective because motivations are produced in the socialization process which cause people to embrace asceticism and thereby assure the continuity of culture. Culture is appropriated by way of identification, first with the parents who, for the new generation, represent the existing "culture" (which differs according to class position and individual experience) and then with the nonfamilial bearers of culture and power. The individual libidinal aggressive drives are fused with the culture's ideals. Satisfaction of instinctual desires is channeled into socially accepted patterns which determine who or what is to be loved or hated, how and what one must do without, what must be renounced, and what sort of dreams may be legitimately pursued. Socialization establishes a moral bond between the members of society and unites the group beyond the divisive force of the actual political and economic inequalities. It also creates solidarity against heretics and barbarians, who either refuse to stay within the community or do not belong to it. Only such a morally united community of renunciation can be ruled by the sword. The unfree and unequal majority's attachment to the cultural ideals lacks plausibility. It needs constant external support by a fetishized cultural power. It requires the display of force and the glorification of ideals. Dissidents are sacrificed. Believers celebrate themselves. The pseudo-harmony of those involuntarily socialized is formally one of equality: the members of a culture are regarded as equal in relation to the cultural ideals and their representatives and also in regard to outsiders (the enemies of "the people" and of the culture). The less the existence of inequality can be denied, the more fanatical the resentment and the greater the hidden desire to rebel. A manic insistence on a merely formal equality before the altars of cultural power is the consequence, and the maintenance of such an illusion demands its victims.

Cohesion in class societies is achieved at the price of disenfranchising most of their members. Inequality cannot do without illusions, and this entanglement in illusions leads to dependence and immaturity:

The narcissistic satisfaction provided by the cultural ideal is also among the forces which are successful in combating the hostility to culture within the cultural unit. This satisfaction can be shared in not only by the favored classes, which enjoy the benefits of the culture, but also by the suppressed ones, since the right to despise the people outside it compensates them for the wrongs they suffer within their own unit. No doubt one is a wretched plebeian, harassed by debts and military service; but, to make up for it, one is a Roman citizen, one has one's share in the task of ruling other nations and dictating their laws. This identification of the suppressed classes with the class who rules and exploits them is, however, only part of a larger whole. For, on the other hand, the suppressed classes can be emotionally attached to their masters; in spite of their hostility to them they may see in them their ideals; unless such relations of a fundamentally satisfying kind subsisted, it would be impossible to understand how a number of civilizations have survived so long in spite of the justifiable hostility of large human masses.[5]

Wherever a clear recognition of individual or class interests conflicts with the preservation of the pseudo-mutuality of the greater community, the power of society internalized in individuals intervenes. The ego-ideal which they have in common and their social conscience block critical thought through the release of social anxiety. Critical thought standing in the service of the repressed instincts is disrupted. It can no longer examine reality in order to seek fulfillment.

Class societies are societies of inequality and unfreedom held together by morality and force. The illusory identification of the masses with the ruling minorities, with their "leaders," has always required renewed confirmation through wars against other involuntarily socialized collectivities and through the persecution of oppositional elements within society. The illusory, enforced equality of the masses and of the individuals of which they are composed in the face of the cultural ideal and its personification in God or the leader is, as Freud recognized, based on xenophobic eros. Heterosexual love tends to dissolve group attachment and lead to individuation; only if suppressed and restricted is it capable of supporting general social ties. The more society moves away, as a result of sexual restrictions, from its originally promiscuous state, the more it rewards goal-inhibited homosexual impulses. Homoerotic partial drives lead men and women to hate the strange and seek out the familiar, and they are even capable of unifying the dissimilar under a sort of pseudo-similarity.

In the great artificial groups, the Church and the army, there is no room for women as a sexual object. The love relation between men and women remains outside these organizations. Even where groups are formed which are composed of both men and women, the distinction between the sexes plays no part. . . . Even in a person who has in other respects become absorbed in a group, the directly sexual impulsions preserve a little of his individual activity. If they become too strong they disintegrate every group formation. The Catholic Church had the best of the motives for recommending its followers to remain unmarried and for imposing celibacy upon its priests; but falling in love has often driven even priests to leave the Church. In the same way love for women breaks through the group ties of race, of national divisions, and of the social class system, and it thus produces important effects as a factor in civilization. It seems certain that homosexual love is far more compatible with group ties, even when it takes the shape of uninhibited sexual impulsions — a remarkable fact, the explanation of which might carry us far.[6]

Culture is a cumulative process of renunciation. The tasks of social integration in every class society can be outlined as follows:

1. Society must place the great majority of its members in a position that enables them to remain fit for work and pleasure and not to collapse under the burden of the general prohibitions against murder, cannibalism, and incest. This is easier or harder to bear depending on the social position of the person in question.

2. Society must provide means of coercion by selecting groups of people whose function it is to see to it that the majority sticks to the morality of renunciation. It must also be able to strike down possible revolts, thereby setting an example.

3. Society must provide an arsenal of consolation prizes as a festive supplement to the cultural prohibitions and means of repression in order to provide illusory compensation to the great majority for their real frustrations. To give an example: The endless delays in satisfaction are supposed to come to an end in a realistically depicted hereafter. Thus the majority need not resort to private religions (neuroses, psychoses).

Possible forms of deviant social behavior for the socialized human beings are the seeking of refuge in private religion (mental illness) and criminal behavior; both solutions remain without revolutionary social consequences.

Work, domination, and the techniques of consolation constitute the cultural apparatus of pacification. Religion, as the "psychic inventory" of culture, is a major part of the latter. Art also belongs to this cultural arsenal: It reconciles human beings to renunciation and suffering by giving expression to their experiences and by promising compensation. Religion feeds on the helplessness and dependence endured by every new generation. The gods are projected into heaven as all-powerful parents larger than life, from whom the dependent masses seek solace and protection against the horrors of nature and society. As knowledge of the natural world becomes increasingly rational, religion loses its function as a comprehensive explanation of the world, while its social and moral function begins to predominate. Its role is to provide illusory compensation for avoidable social suffering.

The Cultural Crisis and Its Solution

The coordinated system of inequality, of illusory compensation, and of power is undermined by advances in the domination of nature. The privileged minorities, which bear culture more easily and have internalized its values more strongly, exemplify in every class society the historically attainable level of freedom and happiness. The majority, pressed into culture, orient themselves in accordance with the minority's cultural ideals. For a long time the identification of the exploited with their rulers in the name of common cultural ideals keeps the class conflict latent. But as social wealth increases, the discrepancies between the social classes are exacerbated. Whatever compensations, real or imagined, have been conceded to the masses, they cannot match the imposed renunciations and burdens. Aggression is released as a result. The latent contents of the ambivalent cultural tradition are mobilized and give expression to the new needs. Along with regression to the state of nature (criminality) and to madness (private religion), there arises the prospect of a change in the actual social reality, which the Freudian tradition has described as "regression in the service of the ego."[7] This is true to the extent that traditional legitimations can no longer bridge the real contradiction between misery and wealth, between political impotence and power.

In his analysis of joke-techniques, Freud himself elaborated the model of such "regression" as a return to needs repressed and prohibited by cultural progress. Regression helps overcome the misery of the actual situation. His psychoanalytic theory of "inspiration" and of its aesthetic effects clearly points toward a theory of social revolution:

The prevention of invective or of insulting rejoinders by external circumstances is such a common case that tendentious jokes are especially favored in order to make aggressiveness or criticism possible against persons in exalted positions who claim to exercise authority. The joke then represents a rebellion against that authority, a liberation from its pressure. . . . If we look back once more at the three separate groups of joke-techniques, we see that the first and third of these groups — the replacement of thing-associations by word-associations and the use of absurdity — can be brought together as re-establishing old liberties and getting rid of the burden of intellectual upbringing; they are psychical reliefs, which can in a sense be contrasted with the economizing which constitutes the technique of the second group. Relief from psychical expenditure that is already there and economizing in psychical expenditure that is only about to be called for — from these two principles all the techniques of jokes, and accordingly all pleasure from these techniques, are derived. . . . A pre-conscious thought is given over for a moment to unconscious revision and the outcome of this is at once grasped by conscious perception.[8]

The alternative possibilities of social development repressed by the dominant reality correspond to the prohibited wishes of individuals, which find their expression in heretical traditions. What cannot be given voice and unfold within the established framework becomes, in social fantasy, a "revolutionary myth," the anticipation of a better life.

In view of the great disparity between renunciation and compensation, widespread criminal action increasingly seems like an acceptable solution to the exploited majority. The risks involved are no longer frightening. The balance of renunciation and compensation has become historically untenable. It yields to a new reality principle. Thus social progress comes about in the "twilight of the gods" and by means of "liberating misdeeds."

Culture's cumulative process of renunciation has now, according to Freud, brought humanity to the threshold of a golden age. Given the increases in social wealth and the immensely intensified productivity of labor, the renunciations required of the majority can no longer be justified. Under these circumstances instinctual renunciations may have increased in force, but instrumental reason also has developed into the technical mastery of nature. It has decisively weakened religious traditions, which legitimate both culture in general and the current social inequality and domination. Freud fears that the disintegration of ancient religious legitimations and social norms might lead to a regression to the state of nature. He therefore advocates that, while there is still time, the opportunity be seized for establishing a new legitimation of the prohibitions at the basis of culture: He appeals to the rational insight of all men. A solution to the crisis of culture seems to him possible only in opposition to religion:

If the sole reason why you must not kill your neighbor is because God has forbidden it and will severely punish you for it in this or the next life — then, when you learn that there is no God and that you need not fear His punishment, you will certainly kill your neighbor without hesitation, and you can only be prevented from doing so by mundane force. Thus either these dangerous masses must be held down most severely and kept most carefully away from any chance of intellectual awakening, or else the relationship between civilization and religion must undergo a fundamental revision.[9]

The cultural process, as it reaches its end, reproduces the danger which had set it in motion. The species succumbs to the hostile natural forces within man's own inner nature. Its destructive potential has grown as a result of the increasing mastery over external nature. Intensified demands for renunciation and diminishing compensations produce a mounting aggressive potential in the individuals, which can be discharged socially either by way of progress or regress: "It goes without saying that a civilization which leaves so large a number of its participants unsatisfied and drives them into revolt neither has nor deserves the prospect of lasting existence."[10]

Freud sees the rationalization of social morality (which is anachronistically based on religion) as the alternative to a self-negating history of culture leading to a new barbarism. A collective renunciation of religious illusions can replace superstitious fear and coerced obedience with insight into social necessity. It can prevent regression into barbarity. The religious legitimation of relations internal to social groups is a form of "cultural lag," compared with the primacy of instrumental reason in the field of relations between groups. But without religious legitimation social inequality and class societies cannot be justified, at least not on rational grounds:

Since it is an awkward task to separate what God Himself has demanded from what can be traced to the authority of an all-powerful parliament or a high judiciary, it would be an undoubted advantage if we were to leave God out altogether and to honestly admit the purely human origin of all the regulations and precepts of civilization. Along with their pretended sanctity, these commandments and laws would lose their rigidity and unchangeableness as well. People could understand that they are made not so much to rule them as, on the contrary, to serve their interests; and they would adopt a more friendly attitude to them, and instead of aiming at their abolition, would aim only at their improvement. This would be an important advance along the road which leads to becoming reconciled to the burden of civilization. . . . We may foresee, but hardly regret, that such a process of remolding will not stop at renouncing the solemn transfiguration of cultural precepts, but that a general revision of them will result in many of them being done away with.[11]

The pedagogically organized collective rejection of illusions will inevitably lead to the abolition of irrationally legitimated social inequality. There will be escape from coercive socialization (mass cohesion), and consequently a reconciliation of human nature and culture. Reviving Feuerbach's critique of religion, Freud writes: "By withdrawing their expectations from the other world and concentrating all their liberated energies into their life on earth, [men] will probably succeed in achieving a state of things in which life will become tolerable for everyone and civilization no longer oppressive to anyone."[12] The level of social wealth achieved makes exploitation superfluous; domination over men can be replaced by the administration of things. A free association of individuals of equal rank no longer requires the social cement of suppressed sexuality. Human beings, once libidinously satisfied, will be able to live without religious solace, for their social reality is attractive enough to disarm the aggressive desires — which result from a dissolution of life forces under the mounting pressure of the culture of renunciation — together with the regressive death wish.

Therapy as Social Critique

Freud's "anthropology," his description of the structure and the functions of the psychic apparatus, is unmistakably historical. The "ego," the life-preserving central authority in the "apparatus of stimuli-mastery," works according to the maxims of a realistically modified pleasure principle. It calculates the balance between costs and benefits throughout life, and yet must ultimately fail. Freud's *Homo psychologicus*, like *Homo oeconomicus*, has a "mercantile soul" (Max Weber). Just as the autonomy of the bourgeois individual is rooted in authority and leads to it, so the "ego" of Freud's *Homo psychologicus* serves two masters and hides its lack of real power by pretending to be in charge of the powers which in fact push it ahead of themselves. Freud uses the term "clown" to describe someone who, when pushed over, pretends that he wanted to fall all along. Yet the clown, who even in distress maintains the illusion of being the maker of his misfortune, is the only self-reflective authority in the power play of psychic forces. Uncontrolled or deformed nature and social tradition are the poles between which it finds its scope. It can set itself off only partially from its supports. For Freud, the ego is therefore both the authority of truth (reality testing) and of falsehood (censorship).

On closer examination, some fundamental concepts of Freud's psychology turn out to be concepts whose contents cannot be grasped by way of psychology; they are located between psychology and sociology. "Ego weakness," the *sine qua non* of all neuroses, and even its opposite, "ego strength," are beyond the grasp of psychology. This was, in vain, attempted by Hermann Nunberg and Otto Fenichel, among others.[13] Their contents can only be grasped metapsychically, sociohistorically. As Hegel says: The owl of Minerva begins its flight only at dusk, when a life form has aged. Similarly, psychoanalytic theory describes psychological traits that correspond to a societal state that has been left behind by fundamental changes. In the transition of advanced capitalism to its imperialist phase, the psychological after image of bourgeois life enters cultural tradition through the mediating efforts of psychoanalysis; and now the utopian potential of this form of life is suddenly freed. On the one hand, Freud's psychological *theory* pronounces its own verdict on the bourgeois age by transmitting the utopian potential to posterity merely in the form of an internal fantasy. That is the meaning of Marcuse's designation of psychoanalysis as "obsolete."[14] The psychoanalytic theory of human nature now is in the position to help remedy the present state of social practice. On the other hand, psychoanalytic *therapy* still confines itself to putting the unhappy victims of culture on the road to the golden age, a road on which an actor unaware of himself is made conscious of his own actions and feelings and reexamines his past history.

The theories of the development of bourgeois society are theories of its unnoticed historical contingency [*Naturwüchsigkeit*]. By this I mean: A state of society which results from the lack of awareness among individual and collective actors of the real causes of their own behavior. The social world appears to them as an alien system of coercion that foils their plans. Whether or not the social world has been created by the actors or by former generations, the present historical world seems "natural" to its members. It is, however, not at all natural, for it can be changed. If social actors, as unconscious producers of their social relations, were to attain the "enormous consciousness" (Marx) of their authorship of these relations, they would be able to consciously plan their future socialization. The pseudo-natural appearance of the social world, its alienness to its members, can convey the meaning of the "antinomies of bourgeois thought."[15] The revolutionary dissolution of antinomies — such as "is" and "ought" and "ideas" and "reality" — was elaborated by the great idealist dialecticians: If philosophy "proceeds from the fact, it places itself in the world of existence and finitude, and will find it difficult to discover a road from thence to the infinite and supersensible; if it sets out from the Act, it stands precisely at the point joining the two worlds, from whence they can be surveyed with a single glance."[16]

According to Freud, human nature is inherently disharmonious. The first year of life signifies the beginning of an extended biological phase of childhood. During this phase instinctual development and body growth are insufficiently synchronized. Uninhibited and not yet specialized drives and delayed sexual maturation produce the development of a mechanism of restraint, the psychic apparatus. Cultural traditions encourage its formation. The cognitive exploration of reality requires this apparatus. The norms of action and social definitions of reality as a whole are recognized as valid and internalized in the socialization process. Whether and to what extent internalized norms will be flexibly interpreted with respect to specific situations depends, later on, on the ego's strength or weakness. Social progress, seen in terms of the individual's psychology, depends on the opportunity to redress the precarious balance between the suppression of instincts and substitute satisfactions. Social integration adds historically specific risks to the dangers which always threaten both individuals and the species as a whole. In a society not yet consciously designing its own future, it can apparently cause the formation of more or less automatic defense mechanisms. They ensnare countless individuals in forms of unfreedom and dependency (private religions) that go far beyond the historically inevitable level (moderate, but universal misery). Symptoms, as pseudo-natural evidence of unsuccessful socialization, are the ontogenetic corollaries of social institutions which have become independent of their bearers.

In the nineteenth century, the dialectical theory of history had initially retreated to a theory of nature.[17] But the dialectic of alienation and reappropriation returned in the form of a theory of psychotherapy. When confronted with hysteria and neurosis, Freud took steps toward a critical theory of practice — his physicalist research program notwithstanding. A critical theory of this kind documents the inadequate reflection in their consciousness of the actual experiences of the actors.

Psychoanalysis can be conceived as a conversation between two persons in order to permit each to cross limits encountered in their everyday understanding of one another.[18] This therapeutic relationship has a certain similarity with detective work. A detective must check a suspect's alibi and accuse the delinquent of the hidden truth, based on contradictions and clues. By relying upon the patient's statements, the psychoanalytic therapist also attempts to discover the truth about the patient's latent problems. But here the situation is more complex. The patient does not know this truth himself. Yet he is the only person who can corroborate it, by accepting it once the analyst has reconstructed it based on "evidence."

A psychic disturbance of the neurotic type, which generally involves an incapacity for work and enjoyment, is expressed in the failure of certain psychophysical functions, in fears, compulsive actions, etc. The neurotic symptoms are experienced by the patient himself as alien to him, as not really belonging to him, and by his fellow men as strange and irrational. Psychoanalytic theory is a microsocial experiment. Experiences of early childhood socialization are reenacted in this barely structured situation. Thus, puzzling modes of behavior such as fears and compulsions can be allowed to develop fully. The actual situation here becomes the stage for ego-alien reactions which disturb the patient's everyday life. The work of psychoanalytic understanding begins with these expressions of illness, which become "objective" in the therapeutic situation.

The patient's (involuntary) self-representation in the therapeutic situation is complemented by ideas and memories from his life, which he is asked to communicate uncensored. The sequence of "scenes" he presents becomes the documentation for a journey back into the patient's life history. Finally, the therapist infers the occurrence of a violent disruption of the patient's ego-system, which had been firmly established in early childhood as a mechanism of control imposed upon instinctual life. The patient's memories confirm this event as the "cause" of his current difficulties. The psychoanalytic reconstruction traces a chain of closely connected traumatic events back to disturbed family interactions. The traumatic events were so shocking to the growing child that he could no longer cope with their effects and the feelings induced by them. Knowledge of the events had to be denied ("suppressed"). The traumatic scenes themselves were forgotten in a defensive process, the ideas connected with them were reinterpreted in a private language, and the pertinent feelings were translated into anxiety. This inconclusive process of repression serves to disguise the motives which entangled the patient in the traumatic events, i.e., that element in the damaged subject which corresponded and responded to the "danger." Accordingly, psychopathologies are conditioned by a peril coming from the "outside," stemming from others; we have here a typical form of social suffering. It consists in the reactive, coercively imposed refusal by the weakened ego to consciously work through the dangerous situation. The ego, by denying the real conflict, must alienate a part of itself, i.e., the part entangled in the conflict. All subsequent reminders of the repressed conflict are therefore perceived as a danger from the outside. What was once just a threatening contributing factor now appears as the actual "cause" of the disturbance, both in the patient's experience and in the therapist's hypothetical reconstruction of the etiology of the illness.

The therapist is a specialist in the analysis of distorted self-formative processes. He has a model, distilled from case histories, of developmental phases and crises, as well as a theory of phase-specific disturbances and of their effects upon individual biographies. Beginning with his patient's current symptoms, he applies his knowledge of typical interrelations between cause and effect. By means of these "laws," he infers the unknown initial conditions of the illness from its known effects. The hidden determinants of the individual biography must then be extracted piece by piece, from memory, but in cooperation with the patient, who usually tries hard not to bring repressed contents back into consciousness, since this could lead to serious emotional disturbances.

The ego of the neurotic, as agency of cognition *and* censorship, has, in the sphere of the repressed conflict, partly lost the ability to perceive problematic situations realistically, to remember them, to repeat them

in mental and emotional experiments, and thus to prepare for solutions to conflicts which are appropriate to the neurotic's age and experience. The problematic, anxiety-provoking contents of his mental life
are withdrawn from his interior monologue and from possible communication. But such denial does not free the ego. It remains bound to
conflict situations and their affective and symbolic appurtenances as if
these were alien, external forces. Everything connected with the
prohibited contents automatically releases ego-alien reactions. It produces disturbances in psychic life. The ideas and feelings expelled from
memory have attained the quality of stimuli that compel specific reactions in a rigid and predictable pattern. In the vicinity of the trauma,
ego-controlled action mediated by symbols is replaced by short-
circuited, compulsive reactions to certain triggering factors. These compulsive reactions are completely beyond symbolic mediation.

To the therapist the connection between the suspected trauma and
the actual symptom at first appears as a connection between cause and
effect. This causal nexus cannot be understood or reexperienced by the
patient; it lies beyond the range of his (self-) comprehension. The neurotic disturbance, a somatic suffering without organic cause, at first reveals nothing about its genesis from repressed, unrecognizable
motives. It appears somatized in the form of a pseudo-organic illness
that resists therapeutic treatment with drugs or scalpel. The search for
"causal" explanations is adequate to the pseudo-natural connection between trauma and symptoms and can serve as a guideline for the therapist. But it leads to a cure only if, by means of the patient's
semi-voluntary statements, it gradually loses its abstractness and is replaced by an understanding of the concrete biographical context, however fragmentary it may initially be. The explanatory hypotheses in
question can ultimately be "verified" (i.e., recognized) only by the patient himself, i.e., by the object of investigation. If he recognizes his
own life in the therapist's hypothetical reconstructions, he can appropriate as his own the therapist's interpretations of his life. He will then
begin to understand the causes of his illness. And he will realize that
his illness was self-induced, albeit involuntarily and subconsciously.
Then and only then does a revision of the subconsciously inculcated
neurotic pattern of behavior become possible for him. Now the patient
can remember and understand the conflicts in his life. He no longer
needs to express their alienness subconsciously. He can free himself
from such infantile solutions as avoidance and denial.

Thus psychoanalytic therapy seeks, on the basis of everyday understanding, to provoke the patient into seeing himself as the involuntary

author of his incomprehensible neurotic productions. It frees him from neurotic repetition-compulsion by making him recognize his own repressed inner urges, which assert themselves even in this repressed state, and by compelling him to resume the effort of learning to cope with them. This effort had been traumatically interrupted in early childhood. The object whose behavior is being explained changes in the course of the therapy into a partner in dialogue, into a subject who *understands* his behavior. Apel quite correctly calls this sort of interpenetration of explanation and understanding a "critique of ideology."[19]

The psychoanalytic theory of socialization has much in common with a critical theory of society: It too is a critique of the apparent naturalness of socially integrative processes. It reproduces the dialectic of alienation and reappropriation in the medium of psychology. But there is an important difference between the critique of political economy (as the critique of ideology in the *strict* sense) and psychoanalysis: Psychoanalysis essentially wants the patient to become conscious of repressed key scenes in his life. He is to become capable of reexperiencing them and working through them. Repression withdrew these scenes from memory. It severed the linguistic connections between thing-memories and word-memories; it displaced interconnected meanings and concealed their relation to the common language; it also displaced the respective emotions. The prohibited contents were thus withdrawn equally from interior monologue and from communication and conversation with others. This is precisely the social function of "repression." The therapist appeals to language used in communication; the object of his critique is its distortion to a private language. The critique of ideology, however, criticizes false consciousness in its everyday manifestations, for instance in the colloquial reversal of the employee-employer relation or in the talk of "compensation" for labor performed, which makes all labor (and not only the necessary labor) appear as "paid for" and therefore conceals exploitation as a feature of social relations.

This difference between the critique of ideology in the strict sense and psychoanalysis makes it possible to determine the scope of psychoanalytic therapy: it works against the self-censorship by which the weakened individuals assure the victory of the established social forces over their own dreams of a better life. It attacks the status quo by freeing people from routinely conformist behavior, by striving to strengthen their reflective capacities, and by making them aware of alternatives to the prevalent reality principle. Recognition of reality is the initial goal of psychotherapy. This entails the patient's acceptance of language used in communication and his surrender of privatized meanings. Therapy also wants the patient to acquire the ability to distinguish between reality and illusory projections, between fact and fantasy. Once the patient has learned to distinguish between external reality and his own instinctual desires, he is able to accept the reality of his desires.

For a better grasp of reality does not merely bring about the collapse of the superego representing internalized social coercion. Social realities also appear to be less absolute. Psychoanalysis thus merges into a critique of false consciousness and of its necessity. This marks the end of the therapist's traditional task: The results of therapy are inconclusive. Changes in the relative strength of different *intrapsychic* forces await ratification by changes in the relation between *social* forces. Whether psychoanalysis will be a psychological technique providing greater psychological freedom to members of privileged groups or will work toward a fundamental change of social norms, of the accepted reality principle, the other cannot be determined in therapy but only in the arena of social struggles.

Notes

1. Sandór Ferenczi characterized neuroses in general as "social illnesses" in his "Psychoanalyse und Pädagogik" [1910], *Bausteine zur Psychoanalyse* (Bern: Huber, 1964), 3:22. He characterized repression as "a social phenomenon" in "Über den Lehrgang des Psychoanalytikers" [1928], *ibid.*, p. 426.

2. Sigmund Freud, "Die kulturelle Sexualmoral und die moderne Nervosität" [1908] *Gesammelte Werke*, Anna Freud et al., eds.(London and Frankfurt: Imago Publishing and S. Fischer, 1940-1960), 7:141-167 ["'Civilized' Sexual Morality and Modern Nervous Illness," in J. Strachey, ed., *The Complete Psychological Works of Sigmund Freud*, Standard Ed. (London: The Hogarth Press, 1953-1974), 9:177-204]; Freud, "Totem und Tabu" [1912-13], *ibid.*, vol. 9 ["Totem and Taboo," *ibid.*, 13:1-162]; Freud, "Massenpsychologie und Ich-Analyse" [1921], *ibid.*, 16:101-246 ["Group Psychology and the Analysis of the Ego," *ibid.*, 18:69-143]; Freud, "Die Zukunft einer Illusion" [1927], *ibid.*, 14:323-380 ["The Future of an Illusion," *ibid.*, 21:5-56]; "Das Unbehagen in der Kultur" [1930], *ibid.*, 14:419-506 ["Civilization and Its Discontents" *ibid.*, pp. 64-145]; "Der Mann Moses und die monotheistische Religion" [1937/39], *ibid.*, 16:101-246 ["Moses and Monotheism," *ibid.*, 23:7-137]; quote is in Freud, "Das Unbehagen in der Kultur," p. 456 ["Civilization and Its Discontents," p. 96].

3. Freud, "Die Zukunft einer Illusion," pp. 326 ff. ["The Future of an Illusion," p. 6].

4. *Ibid.*, p. 333 [p. 12].

5. *Ibid.*, pp. 334 ff. [p. 13].

6. Freud, "Massenpsychologie und Ich-Analyse," *Gesammelte Werke*, 16:101-246 ["Group Psychology and the Analysis of the Ego" [1920], *The Complete Psychological Works of Sigmund Freud*, 18:141].

PSYCHOANALYSIS AS SOCIAL THEORY

7. See Ernst Kris, *Psychoanalytic Explorations in Art* (New York: International Universities Press, 1952).

8. Sigmund Freud, "Der Witz und seine Beziehung zum Unbewusstsein," *Gesammelte Werke*, vol. 6 ["Jokes and their Relation to the Unconscious," [1905], *The Complete Psychological Works of Sigmund Freud*, 8:104-105, 127, 166].

9. Freud, "Die Zukunft einer Illusion," p. 363 ["The Future of an Illusion," p. 39].

10. *Ibid.*, p. 333 [p. 12].

11. *Ibid.*, pp. 364 ff., 368 [pp. 41, 44].

12. *Ibid.*, pp. 373 ff. [p. 50.]

13. Hermann Nunberg, "Ichstärke und Ichschwäche," *Internationale Zeitschrift für Psychoanalyse und Imago* (1939) 24:49-61; Otto Fenichel, "Ego Strength and Ego Weakness" [1938], *The Collected Papers of Otto Fenichel*, 2d series (New York: Norton, 1954), pp. 70-80.

14. See Herbert Marcuse, "Das Veralten der Psychoanalyse," in *Kultur und Gesellschaft* (Frankfurt: Suhrkamp, 1965), 2:85-106 ["The Obsolescence of the Freudian Concept of Man," in *Five Lectures* (Boston: Beacon Press, 1970), pp. 44-61].

15. Georg Lukács, "Die Verdinglichung und das Bewusstsein des Proletariats," *Geschichte und Klassenbewusstsein* (Berlin: Malik Verlag, 1923), pp. 94-228 [*History and Class Consciousness* (London: Merlin Press, 1968), pp. 82-222].

16. Johann Gottlieb Fichte, "Zweite Einleitung in die Wissenschaftslehre" [1797], in *Ausgewählte Werke in sechs Bänden*, F. Medicus, ed. (Darmstadt: Wissenschaftliche Buchgesellschaft, 1962), 3:52 ["Second Introduction to the Science of Knowledge," *The Science of Knowledge*, (New York: Meredith Corporation, 1970), p. 42].

17. See Odo Marquard, "Über einige Beziehungen zwischen Ästhetik und Therapeutik in der Philosophie des neunzehnten Jahrhunderts" [1963], *Schwierigkeiten mit der Geschichtsphilosophie* (Frankfurt: Suhrkamp, 1973), pp. 85-106.

18. See Siegfried Bernfeld, "The Facts of Observation in Psychoanalysis," *The Journal of Psychology* (1941) 12:289-301.

19. K.O. Apel, "Szientistik, Hermeneutik, Ideologiekritik. Entwurf einer Wissenschaftslehre in erkenntnisanthropologischer Sicht," *Transformation der Philosophie*, (Frankfurt: 1973), 2:96-127 [*Towards a Transformation of Philosophy*, G. Adey and D. Frisby, trs. (London: Routledge & Kegan Paul, 1980), pp. 46-76].

19

The Nature of Human Aggression

ALEXANDER MITSCHERLICH

The psychoanalytic theory of instincts has been a dualistic theory from its very beginnings. Its reformulation in Freud's late work not only retains this dualism but also asserts more definitely than before that the opposition is "not between ego instincts and sexual instincts but between life instincts and death instincts."[1]

Anna Freud later outlined the fundamental points of the theory of instincts in her "Notes on Aggression": Aggression cannot easily be distinguished from pregenital sexuality since in the early stages of individual development the two basic instincts which are assumed to exist are still very close and functionally interrelated.[2] It has been repeatedly shown that in the first years of life aggression serves to satisfy the earliest libidinal impulses. It remains uncontrolled and impulsive as long as the ego's boundaries have not been clearly established, and as long as the child has not consciously identified with those significant others closest to him (hence, as long as there is no genuine experience of a "Thou"). Because of the child's incomplete coordination of his activities, his expression of aggression remains incompetent. The first major expression of aggression takes place in the anal-sadistic phase, but as the child's potential for aggression increases, reality imposes restrictions. The significant others regard the child's aggressiveness as "evil," as the term *"anal-sadistic"* indicates, since it suggests insensitivity to the pain of others, to their values, etc. But the perception of the adults also affects the child's own experience: The more the child responds to their criticisms, and the less tolerant they are toward the child, the more the child is intimidated. The playful openness toward the environment and its active exploration are increasingly inhibited. The Oedipus conflict is the first significant *conscious* conflict with aggression (that is, one that is accessible to reflection). In it, the wish for

Translation by Dieter Misgeld and Steven Roesch of "Zur Wesenbestimmung der Aggression," pp. 221-230 of Alexander Mitscherlich, *Gesammelte Schriften* 5 (Frankfurt: Suhrkamp, 1983). Originally published as "Aggression und Anpassung," in *Psyche* (1956) 10:180-187.

the parents' death is experienced with guilt. Aggression has a definite direction here and even as fantasy it leads to guilt feelings.

Up to this developmental stage, aggression (whether unintended or purposive) is always experienced as hostile. But we need to distinguish more carefully between aggression and *activity*, and in particular between destructive intervention (as aggression in the strict sense) and *action*. Activity is clearly instinctual: the organism provides the requisite tools which permit expression and release for the diffuse inclination toward constant activity.

There is no need to introduce new basic concepts. But if we want to regard instinctual *activity* as aggression, it is helpful to emphasize the wider meaning of this concept. In the field of the other basic drive, sexuality, we clearly distinguish between pregenital and genital sexuality. In a similar manner, incompetent and competent aggressiveness can be contrasted. The latter would refer to activity that is adequate to a goal or situation. Regressive acts, which are possible in the sphere of aggression just as much as in that of sexuality, would then signify retreats to earlier, undifferentiated forms of action unsuited to present goals and situations but which once offered satisfactory release.

After Freud had conceived of the death instinct, he had even less reason than before to relinquish the notion of aggression, since aggression now signified all innate destructive tendencies. How the life instincts attain their goal remains unclear, however, if one does not want to ascribe to them all the instinctual energy used in constructive, goal-directed action. But such a sharp separation of the concepts is not necessary for our model of instinctual dynamics and perhaps goes beyond what this model can in fact achieve. For in everyday life we cannot observe either sexuality or aggression in their pure state. "The two fundamental instincts combine forces with each other or act against each other, and through these combinations produce the phenomena of life." In any case, it is apparently the case that "without this admixture of aggression, the sexual impulses remain unable to reach any of their aims."[3]

A detailed analysis of aggression by way of phenomenology and instinctual dynamics is an endeavor quite different from asking which combinations of instincts or forms of mutual support must occur before the more differentiated instinctual drives can take the place of the less differentiated ones. If aggression is a necessary part of libidinal impulses aiming at instinctual release, then the libidinal character of cathexis must (as Freud has stressed) mitigate the aggressive impulses. Only a twofold understanding of the instinctual object, as both aggressively active and libidinally motivated (in the sense of a sexual or sub-limated attention to the object), provides that optimal tension appropriate to reality and to the experiences of the "other" which can lead to a release satisfactory to both the ego and the id.

The same holds true for restraints upon aggression. The intolerable suppression of an individual's early, undirected, and yet unskilled ex-pressions of activity do not leave his libidinal development unaffected. Reality is after all tested and its laws are experienced by means of activity. Lack of experience of reality as tested by such activity leads to a fixation of libidinal development in its primitive early stages — and the fate of libidinal impulses is equally dark. It is significant that an exaggerated dependency (as well as the ambivalence which comes along with it) can, for example, be caused by interference with the child's motor activities. It is also the case, furthermore, that a phobic avoidance of danger or the imposition of a rigid discipline which hin-ders a child's spontaneous motor development may in fact be merely a pathological cover for libidinal affection toward the child.

The assumption of primary destructive tendencies seems quite justified if we look beyond the fortunes of an individual's childhood (in which his behavioral patterns are formed) and toward the general movement of history. Here, in the sphere of the "eternal return of the same," libidinal efforts are thwarted by aggressive tendencies, and col-lective outbursts of such destructive instinctual tendencies overwhelm all opposing desires and cathexes. The question arises whether this oc-casional predominance of purely destructive impulses is the result of an incomplete control over human instincts, since human instincts can never be completely standardized. The incessant transformation of man's environment requires the destruction of past achievements in order to make room for the new. In any case, the controversy that has existed among psychoanalysts ever since Freud conceived of the death instinct cannot be settled pragmatically — for example, by careful ob-servation of the first sign of instinctual impulses. Not even psychoa-nalysis provides the key to the definitive understanding of humanity. Even what cannot be assimilated to our respective anthropological designs survives nevertheless as an empirical fact.

Yet these remain open questions. What is certain is that a flexible response to the child and empathy with his needs (especially in the earliest period of life) will encourage competent activity. This activity is directed toward more subtle instinctual objects and will prevail over destructive aggressiveness charged with affect. Whether aggressiveness is always rooted in the death instinct is a question that can probably never be resolved. But it seems beyond doubt that the death instinct, when entwined with libidinal cathexes, can be placed into the service of Eros. The supra-individual task of culture lies precisely in developing "practices for mastering life" ["*Daseinspraktiken*" — H. Thomae] which strengthen this amalgamation of instincts. This means, first of all, that to a certain extent destructiveness must be tolerated without fear. Second, that the inevitability of causing frustration to a child must not unconsciously lead to the expression of independent aggressive and destructive tendencies. Frustrations are a necessary element of successful adaptation to reality. But they should be rationally justified; demands for their acceptance should not be emotionally charged. For psychoanalysis the great diversity of dynamic instinctual processes represents learned behavior. Thus the two modes of behavior mentioned reveal the fundamental weaknesses of the social formation of behavior in general. We are far from having achieved a level of ego strength or of consciousness which would make us relatively free of anxiety and permit us to control our destructive instinctual impulses. Socially necessary adaptation consequently means that we need to adapt to "mature" forms of life. But the entire process of adaptation cuts two ways, at least as long as adaptation means little more than to acquire mechanisms of defense against instinctual impulses, which are thereby divorced from the ego and from conscious experience, as well as to suppress anxiety in a similar manner. The alternative would be to develop ways of coming to terms with anxiety by way of an unambiguous understanding of reality. The result is an only partially successful socialization, in which unsocialized residue, rather than persisting in a natural state, as "pure id," is filled with energized contents which have been deformed by repression and obstruct communication of the id with the ego.

A decisive adaptation limit is reached when the primary core of instinctual satisfaction becomes threatened. A lasting adaptation to the social code which enables the individual to resist frustrations as well as temptations can succeed only if the satisfaction of the basic instinctual drives remains culturally accepted. To dismiss every sexual and natural expression as worthless, hostile to values, and "vile" — such an exaggerated prescription of sublimation and neutralization of instinctual energy (as, for example, in Calvinism and Puritanism) has, of course, led to the emergence of collective neuroses destructive of life that are, furthermore, characterized by a veritable double standard. But it has also resulted in uncontrolled aggressiveness without genuine libidinal bonds. This development has undoubtedly stimulated the dynamics of technical progress, but also a senseless pursuit of unfettered claims to ownership as well as cruel indifference in relations with weaker, "underdeveloped" partners. Intolerable frustrations and intimidations (which can be easily documented) have strongly encouraged aggression and the channeling of the innate tendency toward destruction against, for example, the earth, buffaloes, colonized peoples, or in the direction of child rearing. The great achievement of civilization — the incredible variety of cultural forms — has, as a result of aggression, been experienced in a cold, gloomy, and highly manic way.

Another condition must be mentioned: *isolation*. Here the transformation of inhibited activity into aggression becomes especially clear. As an example of such "an accumulation of aggressive responses," Konrad Lorenz[4] cites the isolation of small groups from "conspecific surroundings on which the dammed-up drives can be abreacted." An example of this would be the crews of small ships on which "polar malady" erupts. In such situations "minor irritations can eventually have a ridiculously angering effect." There follows a "massive threshhold-lowering of the behaviour patterns of angry outbreaks." The obstruction of instinctual energy is accompanied by an increased capacity to master impulses, but apparently only until a turning point is reached; then the obstruction recedes in a jerky pattern. Viewed psychodynamically, this is a process of regression. In the frustration phase, the needs for activity are burdened with ever stronger affects. The more the primary pressure of the drive builds against the barriers blocking its release, the less reality oriented is its actual release, that is, it becomes less capable of sublimation or neutralization. The usual tolerance threshold is reduced, and a storm of primitive affects overpowers the control of the ego. When members of an animal species are removed from their usual surroundings, the isolation likewise releases absurdly destructive tendencies. Konrad Lorenz has shown this with reference to the behavior of a pair of cichlids which were held in isolation. "Following the absence of threatening conspecifics to chase away from the family," the male will finally attack his mate and kill her. "This response pattern is particularly typical of *Geophagus*, and one can prevent this by placing a mirror in the aquarium for the male to abreact his aggression."[5]

The foremost task of the contemporary analysis of culture is to identify the level of frustration which is acceptable in human societies. Severe renunciations do not inevitably lead to the release of aggression or to such detrimental psychic consequences as apathy, resignation, depression, and ultimately psychosis. But it can hardly be any longer denied that explosions of antisocial behavior and periods of psychic impoverishment as well as of emotional indifference result from the particular organization of society at least as much as from a genetically predetermined readiness to react. And as a consequence of psychoanalytic discoveries, attention regarding these matters has shifted ever further toward the first formative experiences of childhood and their consequences. Enormous changes in the entire social environment have greatly altered the situation into which a child is born and in which he spends his first years. Birth in a hospital; the mother without the support of kinship relations; restrictions of the toddler's sphere of action; less stimulation as a result of the diminishing opportunity for observing work outside the home as well as for observing animals and plants; premature relocations; the extensive absence of the father, and increasingly also of the mother; the organization of play areas with mechanically moving (or "performing") mass-produced objects — all this implies a thoroughgoing transformation of the child's world of experience which we must also consider when speaking of frustration.[6]

It may turn out that the affective stimulation which in the initial period of life is now provided ever more exclusively by the mother, the libidinal attention she is asked to provide, and the way she must set rules amount to a burden which goes beyond the abilities of the average person. Perhaps the entire range of stimuli which, proceeding from the environment, arouses and progressively socializes the instincts has been focused too exclusively on a satisfying relationship between mother and child — and perhaps nothing can compensate for a deficiency in this area and make this frustration more tolerable. Behavior that is ruled more by frustrations than by conscious direction — "frustration behavior," as Norman Maier calls it — produces with increasing frequency clear signs of the "Kaspar Hauser" condition. Here a primary narcissism that lacks adequate environmental stimulation combines with a secondary narcissism that is imposed by means of inadequate stimulation and excessive intimidation. Affective sluggishness, learning blocks, inconsiderateness, and a reluctance to endure even small delays in instinctual gratification produce an inflexible behavior devoid of any goals. Such a person only pursues unsublimated and immediately attainable instinctual gratifications. This particular condition, of course, has been described often enough; its existence and increasing frequency have not been disputed. A change of the underlying conditions is urgently called for. As Konrad Lorenz writes: "The only means of eliminating a functional disruption of a system lies in causal analysis of the system and the disturbance."[7]

Here the limits of psychological help become evident. Many factors contributing to the formation of trauma have their roots in the "circumstances" created by society. Psychological analysis can only contribute to an expansion of consciousness that then may lead to an understanding of the precariousness of social reality and of the unreasonable and often intolerable nature of its demands. It may also reveal the vicious cycle of stimulus and response, of renunciations and their removal, and the psychological reactions which result. The apotheosis of the "well-balanced person" no longer displaying any signs of suffering — this *well-adjusted member of society* is an ideological fantasy which serves the objective function of concealment.[8] A closer look shows that this peaceful prototype, who has reconciled himself to society, is an attractive image for both the "free world" and for the world enslaved by dictatorships. Whether a society's dominant values are maintained with tolerance or intolerance is in a certain sense mere superstructure. In both cases there prevails a suspicious need for order. This need appears to indicate little more than a defensive denial of reality. The psychic economy of an actively craved conformity in the one case, and a terroristically enforced conformity in the other, may thus upon closer inspection both amount to a mandate for repression, by either inhibiting aggression or by relaxing libidinal constraints. The mobilization and specialization which accompany industrialization are complemented, as it were, by a standardization of psychic attitudes: the individual person, in order to be useful as consumer and as worker, is not to be subjected to excessive frustration. He is encouraged to enjoy a primitive sort of self-gratification, to resist impulses toward self-destruction, and to disengage himself libidinally from the world to such an extent that he can be manipulated and "readied" for use.

Adorno says of this sort of "well-balanced person" that he "would be confusing his psychic state . . . with objective reality" and, further: "[h]is integration would be a false reconciliation with an unreconciled world, and would presumably amount in the last analysis to an 'identification with the aggressor.'"[9] Adorno's sociological perspective confirms what we have tried to describe psychologically as a defect which arises as a result of overtaxing the individual's capacity to withstand frustration and conformity.

Psychoanalysis, we should remember, is forbidden in all dictatorships; the reason for this is no doubt its characteristic claim that the individual must be liberated *both* from the constraints within his own nature as well as from the latent ideological structure of society. A person of sufficient ego strength can thus resist becoming a "well-balanced person." He instead experiences in himself what is unhealthy beyond himself, in society. As the pressures toward conformity and toward denying these aspects of reality grow ever more powerful, an individual's road to recovery is increasingly marked by unavoidable suffering. And this fact alone is enough to unite all "conservative" forces against psychoanalysis and its therapeutic aims.

NOTES

1. Sigmund Freud, "Jenseits des Lustprinzips?" *Gesammelte Werke* (London: Imago Publishing, 1940), 13:57. [Sigmund Freud, "Beyond the Pleasure Principle," J. Strachey, tr. (New York: Bantam Books, 1959), p. 93].

2. Anna Freud, "Notes on Aggression," *Bulletin of the Menninger Clinic* (1949) 13:143-151 [*The Writings of Anna Freud*, vol. 4, 1948/49 (New York: International Universities Press, 1968)].

3. *Ibid.* [p. 67].

4. Konrad Lorenz, "Ganzheit und Teil in der tierischen und menschlichen Gemeinschaft," *Studium Generale* (1950) 3(9):481 ["Part and Parcel in Animal and Human Societies," *Studies in Animal and Human Behaviour* (London: Methuen, 1971), 2:163].

5. *Ibid.*

6. Alexander Mitscherlich, "Der unsichtbare Vater," *Kölner Zeitschrift für Soziologie und Sozialpsychologie* (1955) 7:188.

7. Konrad Lorenz, "Ganzheit und Teil in der tierischen und menschlichen Gemeinschaft," p. 504 ["Part and Parcel in Animal and Human Societies," p. 195].

8. Theodor W. Adorno, "Zum Verhältnis von Soziologie und Psychologie," in Theodor W. Adorno and Walter Dirks, eds., *Sociologica* (Frankfurt: Europäische Verlagsanstalt, 1955), p. 29 ["Sociology and Psychology II," *New Left Review* (January-February 1968) 47:83].

9. *Ibid.*

20

On the German Reception of Role Theory

FRIEDRICH H. TENBRUCK

By the late 1950s, the basic concepts of structural functionalism — position, role, expectation, and sanction — had deeply influenced German sociology. Even though the actual utilization of these concepts is still limited, they are no longer lacking in recognition. This is due partly to the good reputation enjoyed by American social science and partly to the impressive completeness of its terminology (which is not, upon closer inspection, so complete after all).

It is a common observation that theories undergo change in the process of their reception. As Gordon Allport has shown, all psychological theories imported from Germany acquired a dynamic aspect in the United States. Such a thoroughgoing alteration cannot be generally assumed, however, in the case of the German reception of role theory. Nonetheless, the definition and utilization of its concepts in German sociology occasionally presents certain dangers. Most importantly, these dangers, which do not exist in American sociology in the same way, tend to distort social reality.

Among these dangers I do not count here the superficial application of concepts which we occasionally find in borderline areas of sociological inquiry. The distortion of concepts by vested interests must be regarded as unavoidable. At the most basic level, it should be said that the concepts of role theory, when used merely as labels, do not constitute sociological understanding. At best, they point us in the direction of the distinctly sociological level of analysis. Astronomers, if they are to tell us anything at all, must go beyond the mere information that planets move in regular orbits to either the calculation of these orbits or the general explanation of specific mechanisms by an analysis of mass, movement, and attraction. In just this way, sociological understanding can only begin when, by way of the concepts mentioned above, specific roles become transparent or when society can be

Translation by Stephen Kalberg and Claudia Wies-Kalberg of "Zur deutschen Rezeption der Rollentheorie," *Kölner Zeitschrift für Soziologie und Sozialpsychologie* (1961) 13:1-40. Shortened for this book by the author.

understood as an ensemble of roles.

The latter task requires a systematic approach and necessitates the consideration of additional and more complex issues, such as a typology of social groups, socialization, social differentiation and stratification, and the distinction between structure and culture on the one hand and values, norms, and institutions on the other. The actual usage of these terms, it should be emphasized, is not decisive here. Social reality can be described in a variety of ways, and sociological understanding existed long before "position," "role," "expectation," and "sanction" were commonly used. Nonetheless, the advantage of this vocabulary lies not only in its terminological consistency. It also keeps us aware of every society's basic reality and thereby provides us with a means of inquiry that alleviates the necessity to seek an explanatory framework for every new case. Yet precisely because these concepts are invested with a general sociological mode of understanding, a more thorough comprehension of these terms must not be absent.

The Misunderstanding

It appears that the interpretation of these basic concepts itself occasionally gives rise to a tendency for misunderstanding. They at times convey the impression that society consists of monads. Harmony between these monads is achieved through external role requirements, over which, nonetheless, the self-contained monads reign. Either singly or collectively, these monads break out of their isolation only in order to avenge a wrong or to applaud an achievement. In this way, each role is understood by the individual as isolated and discrete rather than as embedded within active and interdependent relationships that, through the sheer immediacy of social action, prove their viability and renew themselves. By selecting as a starting point the individual situated in an abstract matrix and oriented toward his role rather than the relationship between role incumbents oriented *toward each other*, individual and role gradually and imperceptibly grow apart in role theory until they stand in antagonistic opposition. Just this conceptualization of social role as extraneous and external to the individual seems to constitute the central feature in this tendency toward systematic misunderstanding. Precisely such a misunderstanding is characteristic of Ralf Dahrendorf's *Homo Sociologicus*.[1] Since it is developed in this book into a programmatic statement with ramifications for sociological theory in general, I shall focus upon it in the discussion that follows.

For Dahrendorf, the sociological understanding of human beings runs into a pernicious conflict with human freedom. This is a theme that will be taken up later. It is first necessary, however, to consider how Dahrendorf views the sociological understanding of man. As is well known, for him this understanding is encapsulated in the gloomy idea of the alienation of man from himself. With the exception of a few less pessimistic passages, this notion runs as a pivotal line of orientation throughout his entire book. The general impression is unambiguous: fundamentally alien to individuals, social roles are cast upon them from the outside. Action in reference to roles implies a conformist surrender of the individual to the group and expresses the demands and expectations of others. Indeed, Dahrendorf *can* mean nothing more if he wants his reader to consider his real problem — the conflict between freedom and *Homo sociologicus* — seriously.

Consistent with this focus, sanctions (especially negative sanctions) attain central importance in Dahrendorf's analysis. Although he considers in passing other mechanisms of social control, none influences his argument significantly. The general line of orientation is once again unambiguous: roles are performed because sanctions stand behind the expectations of others. The coercive character of the role corresponds with its tendency to alienate. In combination, they constitute the externality of the role and lead to the paradox of *Homo sociologicus*. On the other hand, socialization does not introduce a new understanding of role-oriented action. It ultimately means only "depersonalization, the yielding up of man's absolute individuality and liberty to the constraint and generality of social roles."[2]

Undoubtedly, role theory has acquired here a tone that it never possessed in American sociology. Nowhere in American sociology — and some may consider the distinctly American optimism implied here to be naive — do we find any suspicion that the understanding of individual action as role-oriented involves a conflict with individual freedom. What has happened here? Can we settle the matter by arguing that, in the course of its reception, role theory altered its form? Apparently this is indeed so. Yet we would still like to know exactly how and at what point this change took place. Why does Dahrendorf, even though there is not the slightest precedence for doing this in the American discussion of role theory, suddenly focus his attention upon "alienation," "the deprivation of society," and "depersonalization?" Exactly where and why is role theory altered? And, once this change and the reasons for it have been understood, what remains of the paradox of the *Homo sociologicus*?

Structure and Culture

Dahrendorf's modification of role theory consists in his treatment of roles as depending upon expectations and concomitant sanctions. This will be discussed later in detail. Before doing so, a very general comparison of Dahrendorf's approach to American role theory is in order.

Immediately apparent is his elevation of negative sanctions to a position of priority, even though much of American sociology does not subscribe to this concept. As Arnold Rose writes: "Rewards are much more frequent and effective in creating conformity than most of us are aware. . . . Punishments are more obvious, but it is likely that rewards are more numerous, more pervasive, and in the long run more effective."[3] Moreover, in bestowing eminent importance to legal institutions, Dahrendorf stands in diametrical opposition to American thinking. As A.W. Green writes in this respect: "American sociologists have tended to argue that since compliance is largely secured by means of a threat to withdraw approval — within the family, work group, and informal association — then law, which threatens physical coercion, plays a secondary role in social control."[4] In general, the degree to which sanctions, and especially negative sanctions, are a significant aspect of roles remains an altogether unresolved issue. The view that negative sanctions contribute to the satisfactory performance of roles is by and large accepted without further ado.

Nonetheless, it must be admitted that there are statements in the American literature that come close to Dahrendorf's interpretation and occasionally are even in complete agreement with him. Yet such statements must not be taken out of context. American sociology's view of society can hardly be reduced to a few definitions and scattered statements. Despite its remarkable theoretical development, this view of society is also quite clearly rooted in an approach to the subject marked by breadth and depth, by the flexible and creative use of concepts, by a sympathetic understanding of social realities, as well as by a widespread and variegated use of illustrative materials and of different perspectives.

Perhaps all these features can best be demonstrated by recalling that American sociology approaches social phenomena not only by way of the analysis of social structures, but also by way of *culture* and frequently also by way of the *individual*. This, at any rate, is the understanding of society presented in sociological textbooks, where structure and culture are indeed often so intertwined that not even an analytic separation is attempted (as in the term "sociocultural"). Culture is not simply eliminated even where such a conceptual separation does take place. Talcott Parsons, who more than perhaps anyone else has advocated a structural view of society, writes: "The cultural and social components *must* be mutually integrated, because each presents indispensable functional prerequisites of the other."[5] He does in no way believe that culture can be reduced to structure.

In sum, the breadth and depth of American sociology, which originated primarily in its close historical and organizational association with cultural anthropology,[6] guarantees first that the structural conceptualization of society is understood as an abstraction from the reality of society, of which culture is a part, and second that the notion of culture simultaneously enters structural functional theory.

The latter point is evidenced in the customary emphasis upon norms and values in the secondary literature on the concept of role.[7] Although roles are often linked to the expectations of others, this does not mean that roles must be perceived as external and alien. "Expectation" does not carry the narrow connotation of an unreasonable demand, but delineates instead a range of action that reaches from demands to unconscious desires and mere hints to action guided by consensus and sentiment. Not individual but complementary roles constitute the subject of investigation. As a result of this breadth and depth of the American approach, which interweaves the levels of culture, structure, and individual action in reference to roles, various participating elements are always involved. These cannot, however, be weighed out proportionately. In this manner, American sociology has developed an awareness that roles and role behavior can mean very different things, as well as an appreciation of the fact that the proportionate significance of internal and external controls, positive and negative sanctions, and laws and customs can scarcely be determined in a general way. Above all, this broad approach guards against any utilization of the basic concepts of role theory to reconstruct social reality in such a manner that sanctions would of necessity take over the role of the motor of social action.

In light of all these considerations, it should be clear that an adequate reception in Germany of American sociology, and especially of role theory, need not focus primarily upon its sophisticated theoretical constructions as such. Rather, the major problems, content, and framework of these theories become comprehensible to the German audience only if it is familiar with the full breadth of general sociological knowledge in the United States. Those who neglect this point run the

risk of confusing high-level abstractions — all of which involve preliminary formulations, incomplete theories, and necessarily one-sided
statements — with comprehensiveness. Furthermore, concepts intended to analyze certain aspects of society are confused with content,
and largely definitional procedures with the methods of sociology.
Every good and comprehensive textbook can serve as an introduction
to American sociology. Only familiarity with several such textbooks,
when supplemented by pathbreaking studies in sociology and cultural
anthropology, can assist Germans to understand recent American theoretical developments and prepare them to undertake a program of
informed criticism. Without such preparation, any confrontation with
theoretical advances in American sociology will necessarily lead to a
dangerous narrowing of its theoretical power and even to sterility.

The major reason for Dahrendorf's misunderstanding of role theory, it seems to me, can be found in precisely such considerations.
Where the structural organization of society is separated — and not
just pragmatically and for certain analytical purposes, but in reality —
from widely accepted ideas, values, and techniques ("culture"), and
where, therefore, social structure is seen as independent and
self-contained, the process of socialization degenerates into a mere
learning of role *skills*. Roles themselves are concomitantly weakened
and perceived by individuals as mere *claims* placed upon them by society. Within this configuration, sanctions indeed become the center of
society. Whenever the concepts of role theory alone are required to
fully explain social reality, they reveal their own narrowness and rigidity. The conclusion that the individual is alienated from society
seems to be the result of precisely such narrowness and one-sidedness.

Role and Sanction

Let us now turn to our major theme. We can best begin by noting
the point of departure for all theoretical analyses of structure:
wherever society exists, social roles are linked to social positions. Here
we are dealing with facts, and thus Dahrendorf is mistaken when he
writes: "Although *Homo sociologicus* was until recently a mere postulate,
an idea whose usefulness many suspected but no one had conclusively
demonstrated, there would seem to be a chance today of testing the
postulate by applying it to empirical problems."[8] However, to the extent that one correctly understands action bound to roles as implying
simply a uniformity of behavior patterns by incumbents of the same
position, it becomes obvious that this action can be directly observed

and requires no confirmation through research studies. S.F. Nadel, a pillar of British social anthropology whom Dahrendorf fittingly cites as an authority, comes to the same conclusion:

It should be stated, first of all, that the role concept is not an invention of anthropologists or sociologists but is employed by the very people they study. No society exists which does not in this sense classify its population into fathers, priests, servants, doctors, rich men, wise men, great men, and so forth, that is in accordance with the jobs, offices or functions which individuals assume and the entitlements or responsibilities which fall to them. . . . What anthropologists and sociologists have done over and above recognizing the existence of this categorization has been to turn it into a special analytic tool.[9]

We turn now to a further structural fact. Expectations concerning the action of others exist in every society. In the absence of personal knowledge, we can, within certain limits, count upon the behavior of others simply as a result of knowledge of their social position. Again, this is an observable fact and not a hypothesis. It is also certain that these expectations cannot persist if action is not bound to roles. It follows that role and expectation are complementary. The main point here, however, is not to argue that such expectations directed toward others can become the cause of action; rather, the expectation implies above all only that actions of others can be relied upon. The eventual conjoining of sanctions with these expectations means only that action conforming to a role will be met with differentiated reinforcement and that action deviating from a role will confront various punishments.

It should be noted now that the concepts just discussed, including the complementarity of roles and expectations, do not by any means — and this simple fact seems to be forgotten time and again — constitute a sociological theory. This remains the case even though they solve, in a preliminary fashion, the conundrum of how individual actions lead to social order: they call attention to preexisting role obligations and thereby to the calculability of role incumbents' actions. They leave completely open, however, the issue of how such action in reference to roles originates, the significance of expectations and sanctions, and the question of how the dynamic of social action arises.

In view of these observations, it must be concluded that the concepts of role theory do not constitute a sociological theory; rather, out of the infinite diversity of occurrences and happenings, they delineate the immediate subject matter of sociology. By sensitizing us to the order and unity of this realm, they provide the science of society with its distinct level of analysis. Nonetheless, it need not be denied that other comprehensive orders capable of providing the subject matter for sociology could be also articulated. Although the legitimacy of different approaches and procedures must be acknowledged, it seems — and here I agree with Dahrendorf — that the rudimentary concepts of a theory of social structure constitute a natural point of departure for sociology: they alone comprehensively and realistically distinguish sociology's primary object of attention while also penetrating into all of the more complex social relationships. A specifically sociological *theory*, however, will evolve from these concepts only when explanations can be provided for the origins of action in reference to roles, when a means is discovered to assess the degree to which expectations and sanctions become significant for action, and when explanations can be offered for the ways in which role and expectation are formed and changed.

This indispensable elaboration upon the structural concepts — an elaboration that should not be *a priori* constricted in a narrow sense to the realm of structure — runs a certain risk, as Arnold Rose has noted: "In any discussion of culture, especially of the non-material culture with which the sociologist is mainly concerned, or of sanctions supporting culture, an impression is almost unavoidably but incorrectly given of a tremendous social pressure and individual conformity. That is true of no culture."[10] In this passage, Rose summarizes the experience of all who have read an introductory textbook in sociology based upon a theory of social structure. Unexpectedly, and with a certain necessity, the reader acquires a mistaken impression. That impression arises as a result of the fact that expectations exist and are directed to role incumbents in a variety of ways, that roles locate their origin in the expectations of others, and that these expectations impinge upon role incumbents, remaining external and alien to them. Observation of the fact that deviance is punished by sanctions becomes transformed into the belief that individuals perform their roles because they are threatened by negative sanctions or enticed by positive ones. In the process, the point of departure is, without explicit additional consideration, tacitly displaced to the level of individual motivation, and the objective correspondance of role and expectation is reduced to a clearly psychological causal relationship in which roles as the expectations of others are reified and expectations degenerate to the level of demands.

Through this spurious procedure, concepts originally intended only to define more clearly the area of investigation for sociology become transformed into explanatory concepts. Individual and society confront each other "unavoidably but incorrectly," the role becomes dictated by the group, and the sanction becomes the motive of the role incumbent. For whatever reasons, Dahrendorf's interpretation rests on this misunderstanding. Never justified, it is simply ordained that role and socialization imply alienation as well as depersonalization and that sanctions are the motor of society. It is simply assumed that individuals conceptualized by sociology are puppets. These puppets are then depicted through the creation of a new concept: *Homo sociologicus*.

Internal and External Controls

But why does this use of concepts involve a misunderstanding? The facts called attention to here do not exclude this interpretation; indeed, at first glance it seems quite plausible. It possesses, like all theories located on the pleasure-pain spectrum, a peculiar appeal. It appears that a simple and unified principle has succeeded in explaining the existence of social order. Our desire for cognitive clarity is satisfied long before the need arises for a more detailed understanding of a particular behavior or of particular expectations. Not surprisingly, a clear and familiar behavior model is utilized: the child who renounces an action in order to fulfill parental expectations and retain parental love as well as other advantages, the employee who acts according to the instructions of his supervisor in order to avoid the threatening consequences that would otherwise arise, and the resident of the small town who considers churchgoing as a means to ensure his good social standing are all examples for a behavior model familiar to us all from our own experience — one we frequently employ in order to explain the behavior of others. Sociology will not be able to relinquish it, if only because an abundance of such behavior exists. Indeed, to see the true center and behavioral model of society in this analysis seems quite logical since all breaches of social expectation are in fact punished.

This last point contributes decisively to the "unavoidable but incorrect" impression that society as such is a coercive institution [*Zwangsanstalt*]. It is certain, however, that punishment for role deviance does not logically lead to the conclusion that fulfillment of the role is caused by the threat of sanctions. Yet, from a sociological perspective, the question remains what meaning should be attached to this universality of negative sanctions if roles (or, at any rate, some roles or parts of roles) frequently are fulfilled when such sanctions are lacking.

An extremely fictitious situation comes to mind: the case in which the performance of all roles is based solely upon internal controls.

Even in this case a universal mode of punishment would be necessary simply because the inner controls, which consist not only of moral principles and values but also habit (the obviously right, the proven, and the useful), can, as a result of the interconnected character of action, only remain lasting and effective if they are universally valid. Deviance involves a weakening of the general effectiveness of inner controls that is in principle unbounded. Therefore, sanctions against deviants would be necessary even if the predisposition to deviate was originally only very limited. It is here, and not in the motivation of persons performing roles, that we must primarily look for the function of sanctions. Thus, logically, the universality of sanctions compel us to reject the assumption that lies at the very base of Dahrendorf's approach to social action.

If this position is accepted, it follows that social roles present an array of options for their incumbents. In other words, it is assumed that, wherever sanctions provide the final explanation for action oriented to a role, the role is given to an incumbent in competition with other potential behavior and action. In essence, role incumbents appear as individuals who select between alternatives. In this sense, a number of roles are always available to be chosen, even though, in light of the consequences, decisions take place in accord with the expected role. Such decisions, then, involve renunciations of alternative behavior. Yet, if this indirect specification of action at a certain psychological level constitutes our single means to understand action, an anthropological reduction of enormous proportion is introduced into the sociological approach. The diverse possibilities for action, all of which are known to us from personal experience as well as from the concepts of cultural anthropology and sociology, are here reduced to a single possibility: rational choice. Even though this action can assume different degrees of consciousness, society becomes a compulsory institution in which persons select available roles as a result of more or less explicit considerations and choices are made with the awareness that failure to do so would result in various forms of sanctions.

It is worthwhile to examine this narrowing of possible action-orientations somewhat more closely. It should be first noted that social roles, wherever this narrowing occurs, must be equated with external actions, if only because these alone can be coerced. Yet the role of father, for example, obviously involves not only external actions; indeed, these are, at least in modern Western society, the most variable aspects of this role. In addition, an entire complex of emotions, commitments, and identifications belong to this role. Since not capable of being coerced, these components must be spontaneous. Indeed, without them external actions remain either largely meaningless or do not even take place at all. It is also noteworthy that these noncoercive components of a role by no means remain a matter of personal discretion. They are fully expected, and just these expectations are crucial for the role. As William Goode observes: "Precisely because the appropriate emotional response in the role is the day-to-day working origin of our appropriate role performance — that is because people 'feel' the appropriate emotions, they do the appropriate things — role failure in this dimension arouses more disapproval than does mere failure in role activity."[11] Indeed, almost all roles demand some kind of identification with the role based in feelings, anticipations, and aspirations that succeed in spontaneously asserting themselves in typical situations and, in the process, make possible action oriented to roles.

Even though this identification and involvement might be less conspicuous in the case of more strongly institutionalized roles and particularly unfocused in the majority of cases in highly organized societies (about which more later), they remain central components in almost all roles. Even the behavior of the banker, the policeman, and the president of a club is not the result of their knowledge of required role skills and the concomitant sanctions; rather, in each of these examples, a certain identification is required. Where this is lacking, and where roles in fact revert simply to external claims, their quick extinction can be predicted.

All these considerations lead us to the conclusion that social roles in principle go beyond the modes of action that can be called forth by sanctions. In light of this conclusion, we can also unequivocally state that the role character of action can be reconciled with the individual spontaneity of action; indeed, it even assumes it. The individual acts within situations in which sanctions — depending upon the role — acquire a (more or less) weighty and (more or less) direct significance, yet the situation itself is not created above all and solely through expectations and sanctions. It is not by accident that Dahrendorf's interpretation of social roles omits mention of their common point of reference in "typical situations." This phrase, customary in American sociology, is employed to remind the reader that role incumbents do not simply act according to expectations and sanctions directed toward them, but in the context of a situation.

It is similar with expectations. The role incumbent is not circumscribed by a comprehensive catalogue of role obligations. Rather, expectations are formed for every case in typical situations: in precisely those situations that usually create for role carriers the presuppositions for their identification with the role, or at least with parts or aspects of the role. Moreover, the character of the expectations is misperceived if they are considered as demands primarily addressed to the person. We are dealing first of all with expectations about the behavior of others, and this means that a certain behavior is counted upon as self-evident. Only the disruption of this normal situation leads to a conscious reflection upon expectations and their orientation as demands upon others. This is the case when the role is not sharply "defined" or of generally questionable validity, or when the role incumbent in a specific case causes (or has caused) a disruption of "expectations." Equating expectations and demands reduces social action to those roles (or parts of roles) that are, in one way or another, contestable.

Finally, it should be also noted here that many expectations cannot attain the degree of consciousness assumed in respect to demands. This is the case for expectations that can be fulfilled in such an obvious and general manner that no friction or reflection occurs. More important are those cases in which expectations lack sufficient specificity. This takes place wherever roles change and newly formed expectations have not yet acquired a distinct form. In other ways as well a certain behavior can belong to a role and remain incapable of being expressed in the form of a demand. This can be explained by the fact that expectations relate not only to external actions, but also to the attitudes behind these actions. Certain expectations regarding appearance, clothes, language, gestures, and other external modes of behavior are part of the role of the youthful lover. These external aspects are *also* evaluated as symbols for general and more deeply rooted attitudes that are expected. Yet *these* expectations, because of their generality, cannot be expressed, even though they clearly exist and are effective. For this reason, they cannot become demands. This problem of the "formulation" (and not only verbal formulation) and communicability of expectations exists for many roles and even parts of roles. Indeed, an essential aspect of the pragmatic side of sociological work consists in making such roles or parts of roles objectively known.

These remarks, which are neither exhaustive nor systematic, have aimed to outline the *type* of understanding assumed by the concept of social role. Role and expectation must be conceptualized much more broadly than does Dahrendorf, and the interwovenness of role, expectation, sanction, and action oriented to roles is much more complex than can be captured in the theoretical constructs he offers. *Homo sociologicus* subjects the facts of society to a deceptively clear mechanical analysis.

Dahrendorf's Definition of Role

We now turn to Dahrendorf's attempt, in the middle section of his book, to bring out the concept of role more clearly. He discusses two definitions which, in his opinion, are irreconcilable. One addresses the actual behavior of incumbents of positions, the other discusses the expectations directed toward these incumbents. This problem exists for Dahrendorf partly because he falls victim to terminological confusion.

It is well-known that American sociology distinguishes between role and role playing. The role of the Chancellor of the Federal Republic is characterized by explicit and implicit rights and duties, and remains independent of the occupant's personality. This distinction leaves open the possibility for every Chancellor to fulfill his roles in specific ways as well as, perhaps, to change them. Confusion arises because we encounter within American sociology a minority terminology that uses the word "role" for the same phenomenon that the majority designate as "role play." This is obviously the case with Kingsley Davis, whom Dahrendorf quotes and whose definition of role he considers definitive. If we ignore Davis' definition, it becomes quickly clear that the remaining commonly employed definitions are quite similar.

But what, after all, does "definition" mean in this context? Let us leave aside that, in my opinion, at best a conceptual exposition is possible, and that a definition might conceptualize the various interpretations of the role concept at most at the conclusion of a comprehensive presentation. Instead, I will simply ask whether Dahrendorf intends to provide us with a nominal or a real definition. Let us assume that he is concerned with a nominal definition: a conceptual specification that permits a distinction between a particular object and other objects in such a manner that it will be recognized again in reality. Such a definition allows a delineation of the specific components of concrete roles. Nonetheless, it can be easily demonstrated that Dahrendorf, if he is indeed operating with reference to such assumptions, is needlessly upset with the presumed irreconcilibility of the definitions which he encounters. This is the case if only because *both* situations can be chosen as the point of departure for a nominal definition of social role. (It need not concern us here that neither situation is sufficient for the formulation of an adequate definition.)

Sociology must obviously begin with the assumption that expectations and behavior are normally congruent. Thus, in principle, the components of a role can be deduced both from the behavior of individuals as incumbents of the same position as well as from the expectations directed toward the incumbents of this position. Within the context of an exposition of the concept of role, the complex case in which expectations and behavior are incongruent can be discussed only after a consideration of social change, the exactness of the definition of social roles (which is dependent upon a society's structure and culture), and other related issues. Moreover, this situation of incongruence concerns less the issue of the social role than certain of its modulated and special forms. Because there exists in this situation a partial or total anomie in relation to roles, it is *not* possible here to decide *in principle* whether the behavior or the expectations can be considered the valid criterion for the role.

Let us reevaluate at this point Dahrendorf's plea to attach roles to expectations and not to behavior for the case when a "real" definition is desired (i.e., a definition that indicates in what form a role becomes real for the role incumbent). I have already attempted to demonstrate in various ways that the role does not — and cannot — become real primarily or only through the expectations of the group. Rather, for this to occur various expectations, emotions, dispositions, agreements, orientations, values, etc. must be presupposed. I want to take up the issue — totally neglected by Dahrendorf — of an explanation for ordered expectations. The positive explanation is, of course, simple enough: expectations exist wherever roles exist. The expectations of A that define, according to Dahrendorf, the role of B are themselves just an aspect of the role (or one of the roles) of A, and this situation is not fundamentally changed if the model involves more than two role incumbents. It is clear, however, that a real definition which reduces the role of B to the expectations of A is circuitous, if only because A's expectations are an aspect of his or her role and these are determined by the expectations of B.

Most definitions of the role concept in sociology nevertheless begin in this manner. In spite of the diversity of definitions, it is commonly understood that roles refer to a specific interdependent relationship and are complementary. This implies, first, that substantive components must complement each other, for otherwise action, since devoid of a foundation, clutches at straws; second, that expectations must be complementary (and this includes rather than excludes the commonality of basic orientations); third, that expectations and actions are respectively complementary; and finally, that a reciprocity of role incumbents exists and each is considered to be oriented toward the other. Thus, sociology assumes that the expectations of A, as a component of the situation, contribute substantively to the formation of B's role. These same expectations, however, as a component of A's own role, are dependent upon the expectations and the role of B.

Dahrendorf's definition, whenever we ask for the foundation for expectations, also leads just to this state of affairs. That which for sociology exists as a specific form of roles — and for this reason can constitute the point of departure for the delineation of concepts — becomes, however, given the context of Dahrendorf's posing of questions, a definitional vicious circle. How does this occur? Dahrendorf seeks a point of reference that can anchor the role outside of the individual in such a manner that persons become role incumbents. He then asks which external forces coerce incumbents into their role. The answer is given by his reference to expectations, which reveal themselves as constant and regular, though nonetheless only as aspects of roles. We should be able, according to Dahrendorf, to define these roles through expectations and thus through the role of the original role incumbent. The vicious circle is obvious. As soon as one looks closely, it becomes clear that the definition already presupposes precisely what, in its actual reality, is to be established by the definition.

Let us illustrate this by way of the example of the role of the married woman or, more specifically, of the part of this role that is oriented toward the husband. According to Dahrendorf, this role is constituted by the expectations of the husband. These expectations do not derive from the man's general sense of self, but from his awareness of himself as a husband. They are an aspect of this role. But the role of the husband is constituted — again according to Dahrendorf's analysis — by the expectations of the wife, thus leading to the conclusion that the expectations, originally constitutive of her role, in fact depend upon her already possessing this role. Nothing is changed if we substitute other examples, such as the manner in which the role of the married woman is determined by the expectations of other married women and the role of the married man is determined by the expectations of other married men. It is in principle possible for a wife to expect a certain behavior from every married woman toward her husband only if wives in general consider this behavior also obligatory for themselves in their relationships to married men. Thus, in a different way, we have discovered here as well that expectations cannot inherently constitute the role.

Dahrendorf's definition thus collapses, revealing the impossibility of finding a fulcrum outside the individual on the basis of which roles as external entities can be firmly anchored. Thereby, the inadmissability of an approach is demonstrated that understands roles, without looking at them more closely, as such external entities. Yet this is precisely Dahrendorf's position.

Levels of Conceptualization

Thus far, in subjecting Dahrendorf's book to close scrutiny in a polemical way, we have been repeatedly led back to his conceptualization of roles as external and alien to the individual. Unless we move beyond polemics to understanding, however, such a critique will not do justice to Dahrendorf's concern and his effort. How is one to explain the fundamental error that permeates the entire book in an obvious manner and can be seen even in the author's oblique and unproven basic assumptions?

Dahrendorf is certainly not a novice as a sociological thinker. His questions and answers do not derive from the shocks that follow the first confrontation with sociological concepts. On the contrary, they have crystallized out of an intensive preoccupation with advanced approaches to theory. Since I do not want to assume that Dahrendorf flagrantly misunderstands explicit theoretical tenets, I am led to surmise that these tenets themselves — or at least some of them — even though they do not contain the same misunderstanding, nonetheless lead, in a surreptitious manner, to misunderstandings. Indeed, this seems to be the case. What I have tried to expose in Dahrendorf's book as a deep seated and comprehensive modification of the meaning of sociological concepts (which is apparent also in other German interpretations of role theory, though in a form less daring and systematic in intention than Dahrendorf's) can be traced back as a potential danger to the writings of the theoretical avant-garde in sociology. Stated differently: a permanent preoccupation with the advanced theoretical perspectives of sociology carries with it the danger of professional distortion. Dahrendorf, it seems to me, has fallen victim to this danger.

This assertion should be, in a preliminary manner, elaborated upon in general terms along the lines of analogy. Certain theoretical approaches are concerned with a sharper conceptualization of individual aspects of society. The type of work involved here — which is indispensable — is necessarily characterized by a considerable isolation of the aspects under scrutiny and thus by a high level of abstraction. Abstraction, of course, implies abstraction from *social* reality and not the trivial notion that here, as is the case with *all* concepts, parts of reality will be left unconsidered. In the process of dealing with such concepts, these abstractions unjustly acquire the appearance of reality and, in a manner scarcely detectable to the researcher, are viewed as elements of reality itself. The resulting misunderstanding, which I will now examine, is of this nature.

Although not all sociological thinking must necessarily select it as a point of departure or definition of the problem, direct observation has led to a consensus on one matter: certain "positions" exist to which certain "roles" belong, and this fact must be always taken into account by sociologists. Thus far, these two concepts possess no technical meaning. Rather, they simply summarize the situation in reference to which the two notions define themselves: the incumbents of positions act in accord with this consensus and corresponding expectations exist which span the spectrum from a strict counting upon the presence of a certain behavior to a desire about what ought to be done. As S.F. Nadel has noted, the achievement of role theory consists in understanding this fact through a conceptual development.

Greater definitional precision has been hindered by certain fundamental difficulties that have received little or no attention in sociological theory and practice. This circumstance need not be evaluated negatively, if only because the concepts need not be formulated more precisely than is required by the problems at hand. Nonetheless, we should be aware of these difficulties.

Given the context of our questions, we are interested in the difficulty attached to the possibility of adequately understanding the general circumstance from which role theory departs if two distinct conceptualizations of the role concept are utilized. On the one hand, this term can refer to the essentially direct and evident "duties" of a role incumbent. As shown previously, these can be observed just as well in expectations as in patterned behavior. This conceptualization, in the most narrowly defined case, will refer only to external actions. According to experience, a tendency exists when roles are conceptualized in this manner to deemphasize role qualities and to hold to the real or expected role performance. On the other hand, the role concept can be defined more broadly. By doing so, the specific conditions that, as presuppositions or causes, belong to the performance of "duties" are brought into and are included in the role. In the first instance we direct our attention to the final result; in the second this result appears in the context of its concrete conditions.

These two conceptualizations — and they, of course, indicate only the extremes within which an array of further conceptualizations is possible — are utilized side-by-side in the sociological literature.

Indeed, depending upon the context, they are even commonly employed by the same sociologist in juxtaposition, a mode of procedure that makes good sense in certain circumstances. To Dahrendorf, these two conceptualizations constitute the "social psychological" and "objectivized" definitions of role, a distinction that is by no means, as he believes, congruent with that between the behavioral and expectational definitions. Dahrendorf errs also when he considers these two conceptualizations irreconcilable. Apparently one can decide which usage to employ only pragmatically, so that the choice will not in any way influence reality. Whoever prefers to understand roles merely as "duties" in the more narrow sense is free to do so. Nothing is thereby said about how the performance of these "duties" is possible. Those who utilize the role concept in the broader sense must naturally deal with the possibility that the "condition" of the role incumbent as role incumbent can itself prove to be a decisive component of the role. However, it must also be acknowledged that this may not be the case and that the role is given strictly externally. Such questions cannot be satisfactorily dealt with by a decision on which definition to employ. It can be answered only empirically.

Deciding between the two interpretations of the role concept is a purely conceptual and thus pragmatic matter. In dealing with many sociological problems, especially those relating to the analysis of modern societies as well as certain theoretical questions, it has proven advantageous to employ the more narrowly defined role concept. This definition allows for a rapid and even highly comprehensive orientation. Moreover, a consideration of further aspects of the role is very often, from a practical point of view, unnecessary. It can simply be assumed that these components exist, that they are produced regularly from society, and that they create the final product implied by roles in the more narrow sense as a catalogue of duties. In this manner, this notion of role frequently emancipates itself from unnecessary encumbrances. Unquestionably, it is important for sociology to know how far it can develop if tied to a theory essentially based upon these aspects, especially since it is obvious that such a theory may prove to be particularly suitable for the analysis of social conditions in highly organized groups and societies.

Nonetheless, it must be clear right from the start that this abstraction from social reality, because it has neglected certain aspects of this reality, should not attempt to deal with and cannot solve certain problems. Although some cases are self-evident, these problems cannot be generally known in detail. It is not possible, for example, by way of these concepts and this theory, to conceptualize social change to the extent to which it is rooted in cultural rather than structural causal factors. Furthermore, social change based in behavioral changes cannot be analyzed because behavior in this case is understood *nominally* as a product of expectations; that is, it cannot be explained if changes in expectations are lacking. And as far as social change follows from changing expectations, it is not possible to explain these expectations without further additions to the theoretical level. But these and other restrictions do not in any way call into question the legitimacy of this type of theory construction.

Yet one mode of procedure is no longer acceptable: it can no longer be asked how the individual relates to a *particular* role. *This* concept of role is a pragmatic-definitional determination that is not only an abstraction from essential aspects of social reality, but also one that is carried out in principle without consideration of real conditions. Indeed, if reality is the yardstick, certain aspects are chosen arbitrarily. For this reason, this role concept must forgo the claim of being able to conceptualize an essential part of reality. It is a construction that, within the constraints noted, can be used to assess the behavior of persons as social beings, but it cannot claim to grasp this behavior in its reality. It is permissible only to view the role as a defined product of a catalogue of expectations.[12] This is a nominal definition that relocates the role nominally in the social environment and separates it from the individual. It cannot be simply assumed that this role exists *in reality*, that individuals relate to it as an external entity, and that, in sum, this conceptualization mirrors the real situation. Whoever does so endows the role with a reality that, according to the logic of its mode of conceptualization, it cannot possess. If one wants to know in what way a role must be understood *in reality*, then the broader definition must be chosen as the point of departure. Moreover, empirical data must be brought to bear if we are to indicate which of the aspects that in fact exist in reality produce — and in what combination — action that is oriented to roles.

In sum, Dahrendorf's analysis blatantly reifies the nominal concept of role, yet the conviction that his definition is a real definition permeates his entire book. And this is just its overriding problem. He is driven by the question how the individual relates to these roles, namely, to the accumulated demands of others who, from the outset, remain external to the incumbent. Dahrendorf creates unnecessary problems for himself because of his confusion of the levels of the concepts and his understanding of a pragmatic-definitional determination as social reality.

Role is not the only concept utilized by Dahrendorf that is based upon a misunderstanding. His conceptualization of the individual, which permeates the book as an equally central focus, is also sociologically misleading. He speaks of the "absolute individuality and liberty of the single individual,"[13] which is counteracted by socialization processes and even eliminated, as if this process were a real one and as if liberty and individuality existed prior to and independent of socialization and society. He overlooks the fact that liberty and individuality presuppose a developed personality structure that is itself a product of socialization. In this same way he also speaks, if not without a certain discomfort, of "pure man" and of the "*social tabula rasa* of man devoid of roles"! He seriously considers it a *speculative* question "whether anyone would be capable of shaping his entire behavior on his own, without the assistance of society"! He emphasizes that the person devoid of roles "is a non-entity for society and sociology."[14] At this point, as a consequence of his narrowly conceived role concept, he underestimates the radical nature of sociological insights. He overlooks that both sociology and social psychology have demonstrated — and fully independently — that persons devoid of roles do not and cannot exist. He ignores as well the older and related insights from historicism, cultural anthropology, and the writings of Arnold Gehlen, all of which have called attention to how profoundly human beings are shaped by culture.

I will resist here the temptation to show that Dahrendorf basically misunderstands elementary sociological concepts and theories. It is not only that individual concepts and facts have been twisted and misperceived; they have been transposed, in their entirety, to a wrong level and placed within a wrong frame of reference.

Homunculus Sociologicus

I have sketched above a few of the central tenets of sociology's image of man. This should have been enough to reveal the illusory character of Dahrendorf's *Homo sociologicus*. Nonetheless, I would like to treat briefly those summary statements which encapsulate for Dahrendorf the results of his analysis.

We can read: "The sociologist describes man as an aggregate of roles, and unthinkingly goes on to claim that he has discovered the nature of man."[15] This is not the case. To begin with, the sociologist does not understand the roles of a person as an aggregate of unrelated actions. Important axioms and even entire theories and sociological specialties are founded upon this fact. Functionalism, the concept of culture, the approach to the study of social change, the notion of a "strain toward consistency," the concept of adaptation, and the various theories of equilibrium immediately come to mind. They all categorically presuppose that individuals take over roles not simply in an aggregate fashion. Obligations and relationships exist between roles, and these surely cannot become central if roles are perceived just nominally as catalogues of duties. Such roles do not constitute human nature, not even the nature of the role incumbent. The concept of role needs to extend its boundaries to the point where, on the one hand, it merges with the notion of structure and, on the other hand, with the concept of culture. If this is done, the full reality and possibility of roles, and thus the essence of the role incumbent, comes into view. Roles do not only have objective consequences. Basically, the incumbent of a role understands goals and meanings through which roles become intertwined in conditional contexts. The very existence of the concepts and theories mentioned above rest upon this premise. And to the extent to which this is so, the sociologist does not claim that he can ascertain the nature of the role incumbent by cataloguing role duties.

The sociologist is also not of the opinion that *Homo sociologicus* can "neither love nor hate, laugh or cry."[16] On the contrary, even the very description of roles presupposes knowledge about how people laugh and cry, hate and love. The sociologist must also not misunderstand such behavior as merely signifying external occurrences. Rather, he learns to understand it as necessary and spontaneous with reference to the real conditions specific to it. Nor can he afford to fall prey to a common and routine error: the observation that groups, within limits, display uniform behavior patterns leads some to conclude that actions cannot be produced individually.[17] Feelings are so intimately tied to roles that they form the very basis of role behavior, as William Goode (who certainly holds an extreme position among theorists of social structure), assured us above. Of course, for certain limited tasks, the sociologist can omit consideration of this and other aspects of roles and attend solely to the nominal concept that simply catalogues duties and rights. Good reasons even exist for the sociologist to shy away from analyzing the web of presuppositions that are the *real* basis of the external phenomena of action oriented to roles. As far and as long as possible, he can retain a focus upon visible actions and a nominal role concept.

But such a procedure not only runs up against its own limits; its very possibility is based upon presuppositions that have always been conceded as valid in principle. There may not be a single proposition of sociology, or, more specifically, of the theory of social structure, that can be understood without these presuppositions, all of which usually are taken for granted. Even where conclusions are arrived at from the purely formal — and in the extreme case possibly numerical — conditions of a structural system, they are obviously based upon the human beings who live and act in this system and are influenced by and respond to its conditions. Whatever the subject of sociological statements may be (group or institution, structure or role), all can — and must — be capable of being transformed into statements about individuals.[18] Human beings formed by their cultures and living under the conditions of its structure can become role incumbents only because they understand actions according to their meaning and context and because of the cultural formation of their emotional, affective, volitional, and intellectual habit. All these factors, in addition to their concomitant psychological mechanisms, create, under certain structural conditions, at the very least a spectrum for action within which roles are fulfilled and may even themselves suggest distinct action. The whole individual is unquestionably and fundamentally a participant in this process, and we can discuss roles in a meaningful sense only in relation to him. With respect to this point, the historian, insofar as he talks about *the* serfs, *the* feudal lords, *the* peasants, or even *the* Renaissance man, cannot be distinguished from the sociologist.

It would be an error, indeed one that would repeat Dahrendorf's misconceptions, if this basic insight is obscured as a result of the fact that sociology for quite some time now has paid little attention to these presuppositions of the nominal role concept and instead has concerned itself predominantly if not exclusively with very specific abstractions and problems. Whoever confuses such one-sided abstractions, however legitimate and extremely necessary they may be, with an inquiry into human nature, misrepresents both sociology and humanity.

The Malaise of Sociology

The uneasiness that permeates Dahrendorf's text is quite common in German sociology. The opinion is widespread that sociology either constructs or reveals a second and frightening form of reality which must be given boundaries.[19] To be sure, only Dahrendorf considers this task as hopeless and therefore pushes it aside. For him, hope lies in intellectual freedom rather than in sociology or science generally.

I have tried to make plausible that this malaise originates in a reification of role theory's concepts. This attempt has unveiled the scientific locus of the misunderstanding, yet there are other reasons for it as well.

A certain one-sidedness with regard to theme and method, which were determined and justified through certain advances in sociology, should be mentioned again. But if we had in West Germany a sociology of language and a sociology of knowledge that would explore not only the dependence of these phenomena upon social conditions but also their constituent significance for society; if culture, social change, and the realm of symbolic meanings and processes would receive as much attention in this country as, for example, industrial sociology; if an active interchange with cultural anthropology or history existed to warn constantly of the misunderstanding that occurs when the peculiarities of modern society are viewed as characteristics of society in general; then a broad foundation would exist in the Federal Republic — one that, within American sociology, underpins all discussions on role theory — that would confront the temptation to confuse the echo of one's own voice resounding from the forest as the voice of the forest itself.

There is yet another difference between German and Anglo-Saxon sociology. The latter remains largely within the methodological boundaries delineated by logical positivism:[20] scientific concepts are considered pragmatic determinations that, while accounting for parts of a reality, do not claim to capture it in its entirety. Operational utility is all that is demanded. When Anglo-Saxon sociology entered Germany, these central tenets arrived as well. Dahrendorf insists emphatically that scientific and especially sociological concepts involve cognitive constructions and that science formulates a second reality. He then carries out exactly what, under these presuppositions, is no longer possible: he asks how these concepts relate to the whole human being and how this human being in turn relates to these concepts. A similar problem is at times evident in Helmut Schelsky's works. In sum, a profound insecurity regarding the levels of conceptualization and thus the validity of concepts has become almost an inherent aspect of the German reception of role theory. It is all the more important to clarify these matters because of the disastrous history of this insecurity in the German sociological tradition.[21]

Another range of issues should be noted also. As a result of its complex structure and its high degree of organization, modern society creates the problem of alienation. Indeed, it is so common that popular literature lives off it and "angry young men" whistle it from the rooftops. As a result, a number of roles, considered in isolation, come close to Dahrendorf's description. Sociology has here an important task to undertake. How did this separation between persons and roles come about? Of what does it exactly consist? How has it developed historically? We cannot find answers to these questions by regarding alienation as a constituent part of role in general and then blame society and sociology for this situation. We are clearly dealing here with phenomena that occur only in a certain type of society.[22] How little relationship there is between alienation and role sanctions is already demonstrated by the extraordinarily large realm of individual freedom in modern society. Paradoxically, the feeling of alienation stems from an astonishing *lack of identification* rather than from excessive social pressures.

And this brings us to the specifically German situation. A tradition exists in Germany that separates the society from the individual and sees in society a realm of alienation. One glance at German literature and philosophy, not to mention its political history, bears eloquent testimony to this statement. Social traditions as well as intellectual approaches regarding social issues lead to precisely that misunderstanding as a result of which sociological concepts are inverted in their meaning. Helmuth Plessner[23] has recently once again called attention to this as well as to the disquieting public consequences of this tradition. It is plainly evident that in the present situation, which is characterized by a loss of sense of history and orientation, feelings of alienation are further encouraged. For this reason alone an investigation of this phenomenon is all the more urgent. But to consider this actual feeling as the basis for sociological concepts turns the entire situation upside down. This cuts off discussion of the phenomenon even before it has a chance to begin.

And what can be said in conclusion? Because he has addressed questions that are not often analyzed, Dahrendorf deserves our gratitude. I am in agreement with his conviction that the sociologists must not circumvent the moral problems of their science. But it seems to me that the misunderstanding exemplified by his book is actually grist for the mill of those who more or less naively utilize sociological statements for the purpose of conjuring up a distorted picture of social reality that corresponds to the modern feeling of alienation. But it is also true that a certain one-sidedness of the sociological analysis and an inclination toward reification, together with the general discontent felt by individuals in modern society, have led to a situation in which the relationship of sociological knowledge for the understanding of the human being has become obscured. Because it objectifies roles and thereby obstructs a direct identification by the role incumbent with a role, sociology itself promotes the feeling of alienation. This has been so ever since sociology, as a fashionable subject of general discourse, became a factor in the designs of bureaucratic planners. These facts may be viewed as indicative of the immorality of sociology. Yet this situation is in no way alleviated if sociologists are expected to cultivate a sense of tragic guilt. It should rather be the task of sociologists to make plain that this is a blatant misunderstanding.

NOTES

1. Ralf Dahrendorf, *Homo Sociologicus* (Cologne: Westdeutscher Verlag, 1959) [*Homo Sociologicus* (London: Routledge & Kegan Paul, 1973)].

2. *Ibid.*, p. 38 [p. 39].

3. Arnold M. Rose, *Sociology* (New York: Knopf, 1956), p. 71.

4. A.W. Green, *Sociology* [1956], 2d ed. (New York: McGraw Hill, 1960), p. 514.

5. Alfred L. Kroeber and Talcott Parsons, "The Concepts of Culture and of Social System," *American Sociological Review* (October 1958) 23(5):582-83. Note also Parsons' response to a critique of his work, "A Rejoinder to Ogles and Levy," *American Sociological Review* (April 1959) 24(2):248-250.

6. Reference to Lewis Henry Morgan should suffice for the historical connection. The organizational association is obvious in the fact that usually a department of anthropology and sociology unites scholars of both disciplines.

7. It should be remembered that for Parsons all role norms are not only attached to more general values, but also conceptualized as specifying them.

8. Dahrendorf, *Homo Sociologicus*, p. 46 [p. 49].

9. Siegfried F. Nadel, *Foundations of Social Anthropology* (Glencoe, Ill.: The Free Press, 1953), p. 71.

10. Rose, *Sociology*, pp. 84-85.

11. William J. Goode, "Norm Commitment and Conformity to Role-Status Obligations," *American Journal of Sociology* (November 1960) 66(3):257.

12. The scientific nominalism of Anglo Saxon sociology is significant in this respect. See below.

13. Dahrendorf, *Homo Sociologicus*, p. 38 [p. 39]. [Dahrendorf himself, in the English edition of his book, renders "die absolute Individualität und Freiheit des Einzelnen" as "man's absolute individuality and liberty." *Eds.*]

14. *Ibid.*, pp. 37 ff., 24, 39 [pp. 38 ff., 25, 38]. [Dahrendorf renders "der 'reine' Mensch" simply as "man," and "soziale *tabula rasa* des rollenlosen Menschen" simply as "social *tabula rasa* (of man)." *Eds.*]

15. *Ibid.*, p. 56 [p. 61].

16. *Ibid.*, p. 54 [p. 58].

17. That fathers, within certain structural limits, exhibit identical behavior means neither that they do not love or hate, nor that these emotions are not spontaneous and genuine.

18. Only in this sense does the observation have meaning — a routine observation ever since Simmel and one that appears again with Dahrendorf — that society consists basically only of individuals. It should also be noted that all statements on *Homo oeconomicus*, of course, can be deduced from statements on understandable human action. The original fear that laws would coerce individuals has been proven to be unfounded.

19. See Helmut Schelsky, *Ortsbestimmung der deutschen Soziologie* (Düsseldorf-Cologne: Diederichs, 1959), p. 107. Although Schelsky avoids Dahrendorf's mistake, he occasionally also comes close to mixing up his conceptual levels. This is particularly clear where he assigns to his transcendental sociology the task of ascertaining "that which in individuals makes them adhere to [!] their social roles." Thus, through a process of sociological objectification, the role here has become, unintentionally, an object to which the person should repeatedly adhere. In this way, despite the gulf that in the end separates them, both books on the one hand emphasize the "constructed" character of the sociological understanding of role theory and, on the other, unintentionally run the risk of seriously considering this understanding as a component of reality. Just such unexpected commonalities indicate to us the need for a methodological clarification.

20. The methodological self-understanding is by no means congruent with actual sociological research. The latter is distinguished by a much stronger sense of reality. Furthermore, it seems that a transformation in the self-image of the theory of science is in the offing. See Robert Bierstedt, "Nominal and Real Definitions in Sociological Theory," in Llewellyn Gross, ed., *Symposium in Sociological Theory* (Evanston, Ill.: Row, Peterson, 1959), pp. 121-144; and A. Edel, "The Concept of Levels in Social Theory," in *ibid.*, pp. 167-195.

21. See Friedrich H. Tenbruck, "Die Genesis der Methodologie Max Webers," *Kölner Zeitschrift für Soziologie und Sozialpsychologie* (1959) 11(4):573-630. In this essay on Max Weber's methodology, I have attempted to indicate the historical place where the problem of the reality and validity of social science knowledge appears to have disappeared from view. The uncertainty that has come from early treatments of how our concepts relate to reality has been only intensified by the adoption of certain positions of the nominalistic Anglo-Saxon philosophy of science.

22. See Melvin Seeman, "On the Meaning of Alienation," *American Sociological Review* (December 1959) 24(6):783-791.

23. Helmuth Plessner, *Das Problem der Öffentlichkeit und die Idee der Entfremdung* (Göttingen: Vandenhoeck & Ruprecht, 1960).

21

Structures of Meaning and Objective Hermeneutics

ULRICH OEVERMANN, WITH TILMAN ALLERT, ELISABETH KONAU, AND JÜRGEN KRAMBECK

We shall attempt below to sketch a hermeneutic perspective on socialization theory,[1] which we regard as significant for sociology in general. Our approach has grown out of the empirical study of family interactions as well as reflection upon the procedures of interpretation employed in our research. For the time being we shall refer to it as *objective hermeneutics* in order to distinguish it clearly from traditional hermeneutic techniques and orientations. The general significance for sociological analysis of objective hermeneutics issues from the fact that, in the social sciences, interpretive methods constitute the fundamental procedures of measurement and of the generation of research data relevant to theory. From our perspective, the standard, nonhermeneutic methods of quantitative social research can only be justified because they permit a shortcut in generating data (and research "economy" comes about under specific conditions). Whereas the conventional methodological attitude in the social sciences justifies qualitative approaches as exploratory or preparatory activities, to be succeeded by standardized approaches and techniques as the actual scientific procedures (assuring precision, validity, and objectivity), we regard hermeneutic procedures as the basic method for gaining precise and valid knowledge in the social sciences. However, we do not simply reject alternative approaches dogmatically. They are in fact useful wherever the loss in precision and objectivity necessitated by the requirement of research economy can be condoned and tolerated in the light of prior hermeneutically elucidated research experiences.

Excerpted from "Die Methodologie einer 'objektiven Hermeneutik' und ihre allgemeine forschungslogische Bedeutung in den Sozialwissenschaften," in Hans-Georg Soeffner, ed., *Interpretative Verfahren in den Sozial- und Textwissenschaften*, pp. 352-432 (Stuttgart: J.B. Metzlersche Verlagsbuchhandlung, 1979). The selection, translated by Dieter Misgeld and Gerd Schroeter, consists of pp. 352-354 and pp. 378-387 of the German original.

Despite the general applicability we claim for it, the explication of objective hermeneutics which follows builds upon the research context from which it arose.[2] We do not believe that it is merely coincidental that our approach originates in the analysis of interaction and socialization. The methodology of objective hermeneutics has a special affinity with the sociological theory of socialization. Reconstructive explanations of the structural characteristics of interaction should make up the core of a theory of socialization, especially if they involve general claims about the social constitution of ontogenesis.[3] Ontogenetic theories of the development of actors possess explanatory power only if the formation of structures by subjects is attributed neither to the direct causal effect of the external environment nor simply to the monological unfolding of innate capacities. Instead, structures must be seen as resulting from reconstructions which the actors themselves undertake by way of schemata of practical action, which they possess independently of their innate capacities.[4] This general starting point corresponds to the empirical finding (based on the analysis of records of interaction) that children taking part in interactions display considerable capacities for the internal differentiation of objective structures of meaning. It is quite obvious (and also unproblematic for developmental psychologists) that these differentiations are not anticipated or intentionally produced by the child and that they cannot be completely decoded or deciphered subsequently. For the structures of meaning in question far exceed the interpretive capacities of the growing child at his particular stage of development. This is precisely where the usefulness of the study of interaction (and of socialization) lies.

When systematically pursuing a sociological theory of socialization in the sense discussed, it will become obvious that its assumptions ought to be taken into consideration in every analysis of the social constitution of subjects and of their interactive competence. These assumptions are not valid for theories of socialization alone but possess general validity for the analysis of the actions of adult subjects. Where this is not the case, such analyses fall prey to psychological reductionism from the start. From this perspective, the theory of socialization is not simply a social psychological or a developmental psychological appendix to general sociology, as is the case, almost without exception, with socialization theories in sociological theory. It is rather a fundamental and independent component of a general structural sociological theory, in the sense that it is impossible to carry out a consistent structural analysis in sociology without considering this component. Our hermeneutic methodology is essential for a sociological theory of socialization. It is, furthermore, a research orientation applicable to sociology as a whole.

The tangible objects of the procedure of objective hermeneutics are records of real symbolic social actions or interactions, either written, oral, visual, or involving a combination of different media. The actual form of the records is merely a technical matter for the interpretive procedures of objective hermeneutics. For their interpretability is principally dependent upon the fact that they can be understood as a language or that the interactively generated meaning recorded can be paraphrased by way of language.

Under this condition, all recorded interactions, in whatever medium and in whatever technical format, may be regarded as valid interaction texts, as long as they represent the essential object of interpretation.

The reconstructive interpretation of interaction texts permits the discovery of rules which constitute interaction texts as *objective structures of significance* [*Bedeutungsstrukturen*], which reflect the *latent structures of meaning* [*Sinnstrukturen*] of interaction itself. The objective structures of significance of interaction texts (which are prototypes of objective social structures in general) are real and have some permanence. Analytically (though not empirically) they are independent of any specific and conscious representation of the meaning of interaction on the side of the participating subjects. We might also say that a text, once produced, comprises a social reality of its own that must be reconstructed with procedures adequate to it. It can be traced back neither to the disposition for action and the psychic conditions of the speaker nor to the psychic reality of the recipients. For this reason, it would be a basic mistake to try and infer the meaning of a text by deductions about the intentions of its producer or by way of an understanding of specific recipients. We also reject the common social science practice of making assertions about the psychic reality of actors, their motives, expectations, and value orientations, without a thorough and well-defined hermeneutic reconstruction of the objective structures of significance of their interaction texts.

To avoid misunderstanding, we must stress that the category of interaction as used here differs in two respects from the way in which it is commonly employed. On the one hand, we are starting from the premise that interaction is the most elementary unit of human action and also the smallest analytical unit of the theory of action. In this sense, individual action already represents an abstraction. Without being able to substantiate this more fully now, we refer to the fact that the difference between behavior and action can be maintained conceptually only by adopting such an assumption. For that reason, the concept of interaction is in a certain sense in fact untenable and misleading because it presupposes the primacy of single, isolated actions, from which interaction is supposed to be built up as the smallest possible unit.

On the other hand, we are not using the concept of interaction substantively in order to designate circumscribed changes and processes in the sense of concrete actions. We employ the concept more generally in order to identify meanings shared by actors within specific segments of time. From this general perspective, the category of interaction refers to a steady, uninterrupted temporal stream of events in a system of relationships, independently of whether in concrete terms these events signify constancy or change, rest or movement; we do not make the social scientific relevance of these events dependent upon the meanings intended by participants. Thus we proceed in terms of a less restrictive framework by emphasizing the objective importance of events.

The latent structure of meaning of a single interaction or utterance (as the structure of situationally and contextually possible relations of significance) permits, as a rule, different "ways of reading." Participants in the original situation of action produce only *segments* of these readings intentionally. The distinction between latent objective structures of meaning and their intentional representation is decisive for objective hermeneutics. A perfect overlap between intentional representation and latent structure of meaning is possible in principle. But it represents an especially ideal case of fully self-reflective communication: having reconstructed their own interaction texts, the acting subjects grasp the full meaning of their actions. However, in the sociological analysis of interaction, latent structures of meaning have to be differentiated from their subjective and intentional representation and from the overall psychic reality of the participating subjects. Latent structures of meaning also have to be reconstructed before other operations of data analysis are brought into play. Only in a very ideal case can we achieve what are commonly considered to be unproblematic implications of procedures of interviewing and observation: i.e., to infer the actors' dispositions for action on the basis of their own statements, and to derive from them the structure of their action. However, even in this ideal case, we cannot make do methodologically without a concept of the latent structure of meaning: for without the prior reconstruction of latent structures we are unable to determine whether we are confronted with an ideal case.

The constructions of objective hermeneutics imply a concept of significance, which, although sharply distinguished from the behaviorist notion of external criteria of conduct, cannot be reduced to a concept of subjective intentionality. By adopting a specific interpretation of Mead's theory of significance, we begin with a concept of significance and of objective social structure as emerging from interaction. Social structure in turn is to be treated as a prerequisite for the constitution of intentionality. Obviously, objective significance points to intentions and, just as obviously, it is impossible to think of the real emergence of significance from interaction without referring to the intentionality of actors. In the tradition of Mead we might even say: intentions are logically equivalent to or synonymous with the rule-dependent objective significance of an interaction text. They are instances of intentions ascribable to an idealized, transcendentally constructed, generalized subject of the "universe of discourse." Here we have in mind Mead's notion of the absolute other, the "generalized other" in the system of rules constituting significance. Therefore, in following Mead, we are merely paraphrasing the concept of objective significance. The intentionality of a specific individual subject must be categorially distinguished from it.

In order to achieve a theoretically meaningful idea of the constitution of actors, it is necessary to assume — with Mead — that the constitution of objective patterns of significance has already been achieved in interaction. The concept of the objective significance of interaction must also be incorporated into an evolutionary theory in Mead's sense — a theory of the emergence of species as well as specific structures of interaction.

The concept of the latent structure of meaning lays claims to a level of reality of its own, which must be sharply distinguished from the reality of observable conduct relevant for the theory of behavior, as well as from the reality of subjective projections of action possibilities, of definitions, and of constructions significant for action theory and symbolic interactionism. But our theory of the reality of objective structures also analytically transcends the concept of social reality found in Marx; in fact, it provides the foundation for Marx's concept. With the concept of the latent structure of meaning, real and objective possibilities of significance are introduced, whether the actors taking part in the interaction are aware of them or not.

Objective hermeneutics is a method of interpretation which can decode this reality. For the time being we shall use the term "objective hermeneutics" (even though this may perhaps not be the most suitable choice), in order to illustrate our concern with the painstaking, extensive explanation of the objective significance of interaction texts and of the latent meaning of interaction. Reconstructive methods of textual interpretation have nothing in common with an empathetic reconstruction of psychic processes, for example in the interpretation of questionnaire results or of answers obtained through projective tests. We remain convinced that reconstructive interpretations of the objective significance of interaction texts come first; only then can we turn to the internal realities of actors.

We can conclude that, as an empirical science of objective social structures, sociology has interaction *texts* as its central subject matter. It may also serve as a theoretical frame for the sciences of action, such as the social and the cultural sciences, the humanities, and even economics.

Perhaps surprisingly, we shall mention Karl Popper as a chief witness for the approach of objective hermeneutics. We take this position even if a close union between behaviorist reductionism and critical rationalism is currently regarded as more compelling. Popper's conception of "world three" — the world of the structures of argumentation and proof — corresponds to our concept of latent structures of meaning. Popper applies it to empirical questions, in his historical reconstruction of science. The application of "world three" concepts permits a reconstruction of the original situation in which the problem arose and to which the sciences in question responded. Popper employs the methods of textual interpretation in the pursuit of these issues. This has nothing in common with the psychological analysis of mental processes. To give an example: Popper reconstructs the situation of inquiry which underlay Galileo's argument. It is to be found in the context of a theory of tides, a theory which was already considered problematic in Galileo's own day. Popper demonstrates the strategic importance of Galileo's initial discoveries for the future of science. In the past, Galileo's approach was erroneously assumed to be the result of his dogmatic personality. Thus Popper adopts an approach similar to objective hermeneutics: we have argued that theoretical concepts must be elucidated in the language of the "reconstructed case" itself. This example, furthermore, indicates that such constructs of psychological motives as "authoritarian" or "dogmatic" have no independent explanatory power. They only illustrate the need for more complete explanations. Structural explanations formulated in the language of the case in question or of the historical event itself must always be the first step in any empirical analysis. This is so even for Popper, the critical rationalist. They cannot be replaced by measurement operations supposedly required by the unity of science as a principle of inquiry.

Cognitive representations of the world can be encountered only on a second level of reality which, as it were, lies beneath the level of latent structures of meaning. Cognitive representations are merely a segment of the reconstructed latent structure of meaning of an interaction text. Additional distinctions are needed here, such as distinctions between different mental/cognitive functions. Distinctions between subjective and intentional representations on the one hand, and collective patterns of interpretation on the other, belong to this second level of reality. Collective patterns manifest themselves only to a limited extent, but they control judgments about the appropriateness of action. These matters usually become thematic in critical discussions of behaviorism: for behaviorists never resort to an independently structured psychic reality for purposes of explanation. They restrict themselves to observing and recording external, "meaningless" events. Even symbolic interactionism, with its central concept of the social definition of the situation (or the social definition of reality), is in danger, in the final analysis, of making social reality dependent upon the subjective-intentional achievement of meaning. Thereby objective structures of meaning disappear from view.

Even in daily life we can encounter analogies that correspond to the level of reality claimed by the concept of the latent structure of meaning and that recognize the subjectively intended meaning entailed by the concept. We implicitly recognize subjective meanings entailed by latent structures, for instance when in the case of a misunderstanding we return to the original text and its significance. An example of such a misunderstanding is the breakdown of procedures for inferring the intentions of a speaker from the implications of the spoken text. In the same manner we refer to an objective level of reality (having subjective implications) when we want to ascertain the "actual" motives for a person's action: We interpret the person's interaction texts by relying upon the belief that they have a significance which is independent and separate from the initial intentions of the "speaker." We also assume that the actor will reveal her real nature in these additional meanings.

The psychoanalyst proceeds in an analogous manner when he regards neurotic symptoms, slips of the tongue, parapraxes, dreams, and free associations as structures of meaning. He treats them as texts, for the meaning of texts exceeds subjectively intended meanings. Only by using such methodological and theoretical assumptions can the psychoanalyst draw empirically valid conclusions about unconscious motives revealing themselves in those texts. We also discuss these phenomena because in such cases the ego is not entirely successful in exercising censorship. Neurotic symptoms, slips of the tongue, parapraxes, dreams, and free associations can be regarded as texts appropriate for the reconstruction of unconscious motives. We have already pointed to the affinity between objective hermeneutics and the psychoanalytic method of interpretation, as well as to similarities in their understanding of the unconscious. In objective hermeneutics, for example, we look upon the representations of unconscious motives as repressed derivations of the latent meanings of childhood scenes which have subsequently been reinterpreted. They share the attribute of timelessness with latent structures of meaning; as structures they are independent from the particular existential or historical moment of time in which they are decoded. Unconscious or latent meanings always manifest themselves behind the backs of the subjects. And quite apart from the exceptional ideal case of complete self-knowledge achieved by way of communication, the difference between latent structures of meaning and their intentional representations in the actor's thought represents the standard empirical case.

The difference can be caused by three distinct types of conditions:

1. During the child's primary process of socialization — in other words, until he takes on the roles typical of adult life or until puberty, depending on which theoretical criteria of development are relied upon — his capacity for the interpretation of meaning is limited by the level of development. As a result, the presuppositions for the full realization of the latent structures of meaning of interaction are, as a general principle, not yet met. While arguing the relevance of objective hermeneutics for socialization theory we recognize, of course, that the latent structures of interaction (and the ontogenetic structures of development) are for sociological theory nothing but the realm of objectively social phenomena, existing outside the actor. We also share the view that ontogenetic development depends upon interpretations of the latent structures of meaning by significant others, such as parents and teachers. Their interpretations take the place of the developing subject's own interpretations. In this way, objectively understandable motives for action can be transformed into subjective intentions. Interpretations such as these (substituting for the subjects' own interpretations of the objective meaning of their actions) do not occur only in the process of socialization. They are also typical of "resocializing" efforts made, for example, in therapy and in other pro-

cesses of social control.

Developmental shortcuts in the subjective-intentional realization of latent structures of meaning may, but need not have a distorting effect; rather, they essentially imply simplifications. The more elementary the stage of development, the less explicitly will the latent structures of meaning be realized. The difference between subjective-intentional representations of latent structures of meaning and the structures themselves is the result of ontogenetic development and consists in the degree of explicitness of structures of significance.

We are now addressing problems belonging to a theory of the constitution of experience. Consequently we can take an important fact into account. Naturally, at an early stage in their development, children notice the significance of interaction for socialization only to a limited extent. They lack the interpretive competence and socialization required for differentiated constructions. However, they do perceive the natural, undistorted meaning of interaction, its "emotive truth," so to speak. Potential distortions in perception arise only later. They are caused by their acceptance of restrictive, ideological, or neurosis-producing social norms and interpretations. Pathological developments may originate in these distortions.

We shall attempt to illustrate this point of view by way of the following example of the relationship between an overprotective mother and her child. At a very early stage of development the child will clearly "recognize" the latent meaning of interaction with her mother. This latent meaning can be interpreted as the projection of maternal needs onto the child, who is abused as a surrogate in the satisfaction of the mother's own, repressed needs. It also entails a tendency to smother the child with affection. The child will be aware of what is going on "intuitively," and will realize the truth emotionally — with her almost physical capacities for perception. The child will often feel unwell simply because the mother's behavior toward the child, intentionally represented by her as a sacrifice of her own needs, has in fact little relation to the child's needs. The mother's behavior meets the child's needs in only a "technical" sense: for example, she may rigidly adhere to child care instructions. Here the child's comprehension of the latent meaning of interaction is not yet distorted. The child merely simplifies the meanings. But once the mother has succeeded in getting the child to internalize, in a general way, the significance of her actions as sacrifice, the child, as the "victim," will be obliged to be grateful. And then the child will interpret the latent meaning of her interaction with her mother not only in a simplified, but also in a systematically distorted manner. The subsequent process of becoming neurotic can then be corrected or undone during therapy. In this instance we assume that the condition of transference makes it possible for the therapist to reconstruct the latent meaning of the child's interactions with the mother and to offer alternative interpretations of the interaction and its structure.

The above example represents a case of *pathogenic* socialization. A successful process of socialization (formulated in an idealized model) consists in making latent meanings more and more conscious.

2. The second type of condition has already been introduced while explaining the first type. As a result of pathological constraints, latent meanings may be represented on the intentional level as systematically distorted, fragmented, or displaced interpretations. At the level of individual biography we refer to these factors as neuroses or psychoses, at the level of history as ideologies, dogmas, myths, or whatever. In the example of interaction discussed above, these were the factors we dealt with. They are responsible for producing slips of the tongue, parapraxes, action compromises, and symptomatic actions, as well as for concealing the objective meaning of these distortions. However, their decoding is the prerequisite of a cure. Thus the model of actions resulting from successful therapy is implied by the reconstructions of meanings latent in symptomatic behavior. It is implicit in the linguistic structure of interaction texts. Here we come upon the therapeutic potential of language. Once again we notice that it is the attitude acting subjects take toward latent meanings which may cause pathological deformations. But latent structures of meaning are not themselves pathological. Above all else, in the face of this fundamentally important distinction, we consider any talk about "damaged" or "destroyed language," or references to repression as "excommunication," to be muddled, if not in fact misleading.

3. Interpretive accomplishments and decodings of meanings naturally are also constitutive of the routine activities of everyday life. They are not a specifically scientific procedure. Objective hermeneutics, however, consists of a totally "impractical," detailed interpretation of the latent meaning of interaction texts. It involves the explication of "improbable readings" and of taken-for-granted assumptions. This is how the specific structures of interaction are made clear. In everyday life one proceeds in the opposite way: In interacting with others one attempts to make accurate conjectures about intentions and dispositions as quickly as possible. One responds to practical exigencies when accounting for the motives underlying everyday behavior. One pro-

ceeds similarly with respect to objective symbols which represent intentions. After all, one wants to achieve one's goals in practical life. But objective hermeneutics is to explicate structures of action with as much discrimination as possible.

Thus there are methods in everyday life for quickly decoding meanings and for understanding motives. These procedures generate the most probable interpretations. For the time being we shall refer to these interpretive methods of everyday life as features of practical action assuring its economy and efficiency. We include among these those basic systems of relevance that make intersubjective understanding possible. The phenomenological tradition within sociology has been particularly interested in them.

These features of practical action guarantee that, as a rule, the latent meanings of practical action are decoded "correctly" and without distortion (at least under the most likely sociohistorical conditions). But it must be taken into account that the interpretive methods of everyday life responsible for the achievement of economy and efficiency in action themselves rest upon background assumptions. They express the spirit of the age and the ideology of a particular stage of social development. They are deep-seated and historically specific patterns of interpretation, and in principle open to criticism. But within the sociocultural frame of reference found on a particular stage of social development, the features of practical action in question assure that an undistorted, essentially correct understanding of the meaning of interaction is achieved, albeit at a low level of explication. Therefore the understandings achieved in everyday life and within the framework of epochal assumptions cannot easily be criticized.

Interpretations of action in everyday life occur more or less naturally, without need for reflection. They reach their limit under unlikely conditions, for example, whenever actions have to be understood in an exceptional sense or whenever the standard interpretations of action have broken down because the underlying sociohistorical conditions have lost their validity. In any case, socialization *also* means the internalization of features of practical action in everyday life, which provide for its economy and efficiency.

Notes

1. The records of interactions discussed below originated in a research project on "Elternhaus und Schule (Home and School)," which was carried out at the Max-Planck-Institut für Bildungsforschung under the direction of Ulrich Oevermann, Lother Krappmann, and Kurt Kreppner. See Oevermann, Krappmann, and Kreppner, "Elternhaus und Schule," unpublished research proposal, Berlin 1968. The theoretical position advanced here is an elaboration of this earlier work.

2. On this point see the chapter by Ulrich Oevermann et al., "Beobachtungen zur Struktur der sozialisatorischen Interaktion," in M. Rainer Lepsius, ed., *Zwischenbilanz der Soziologie. Verhandlungen des 17. deutschen Soziologentages* (Stuttgart: Enke, 1976), pp. 274-295.

3. See Ulrich Oevermann, "Programmatische Überlegungen zu einer Theorie der Bildungsprozesse und zur Strategie der Sozialisationsforschung," in Klaus Hurrelmann, ed., *Sozialisation und Lebenslauf* (Reinbek: Rowohlt, 1976), pp. 34-52.

4. Ulrich Oevermann, "Sozialisationstheorie. Ansätze zu einer soziologischen Sozialisationstheorie und ihre Konsequenzen für die allgemeine soziologische Analyse," in Günther Lüschen, ed., *Deutsche Soziologie seit 1945*, [*Kölner Zeitschrift für Soziologie und Sozialpsychologie*, Sonderheft 21] (Opladen: Westdeutscher Verlag, 1979), pp. 143-168.

The Editors

VOLKER MEJA, born in 1940, studied sociology, economics, and philosophy in Frankfurt and at Brandeis University, where he obtained a Ph.D. He is presently professor of sociology at the Memorial University of Newfoundland, St. John's, Canada, after having previously taught in the United States. He is co-author, with David Kettler and Nico Stehr, of *Karl Mannheim* (London and New York: Tavistock, 1984), and *Politisches Wissen* (Frankfurt: Suhrkamp, 1987). His other publications include *Wissenssoziologie* (Opladen: Westdeutscher Verlag, 1981), *Der Streit um die Wissenssoziologie*, 2 vols. (Frankfurt: Suhrkamp, 1982). He is editor of the *Newsletter of the International Society for the Sociology of Knowledge*, and co-editor, with David Kettler and Nico Stehr, of several previously unpublished manuscripts by Karl Mannheim now published as *Structures of Thinking* (London: Routledge & Kegan Paul, 1982) and *Conservatism* (London: Routledge & Kegan Paul, 1986).

DIETER MISGELD, born in 1938, studied philosophy, law, psychology, and theology in Munich, Marburg, Bonn, and Heidelberg, where he obtained his doctorate in philosophy. He has taught in Canada since 1968 and presently teaches in the Department of Educational Theory, Ontario Institute for Studies in Education, and in the Department of Philosophy, University of Toronto. Among his publications are: "Critical Theory and Hermeneutics," in J. O'Neill, ed., *On Critical Theory* (New York: Seabury, 1976); "Critical Theory and Sociological Theory," *Philosophy of the Social Sciences* (1984); "Education as Cultural Invasion: Critical Social Theory, Education as Instruction and the Pedagogy of the Oppressed," in J. Forester, ed., *Critical Theory and Public Life* (Cambridge, Mass.: M.I.T. Press, 1985), "Critical Hermeneutics versus Neoparsonianism?" *New German Critique* (1985), vol. 35; "On Gadamer's Hermeneutics," in R. Hollinger, ed., *Hermeneutics and Praxis* (Notre Dame, Ind.: University of Notre Dame Press, 1985).

NICO STEHR, born in 1942, studied sociology and economics at the Universities of Cologne and Oregon (where he received his Ph.D.). He is professor of sociology at the University of Alberta, Edmonton, Canada. In 1984-85 he was Eric-Voegelin-Professor at the Ludwig-Maximilians-Universität in Munich. His research interests center on the sociology and philosophy of the social sciences, the history of sociological thought, the use of social science knowledge and the "knowledge society." He is a founding editor of the *Canadian Journal of*

Sociology and has co-edited, with René König, *Wissenschaftssoziologie: Studien und Materialien* (Opladen: Westdeutscher Verlag, 1975); with David Kettler and Volker Meja, Karl Mannheim's *Structures of Thinking* (London: Routledge & Kegan Paul, 1982) and *Conservatism* (London: Routledge & Kegan Paul, 1986); and, with Volker Meja, *Society and Knowledge: Contemporary Perspectives on the Sociology of Knowledge* (New Brunswick, N.J. and London: Transaction Books, 1984). With David Kettler and Volker Meja, he is co-author of *Karl Mannheim* (London and New York: Tavistock, 1984). He has held visiting appointments in Europe and the United States.

The Authors

THEODOR W. ADORNO (1903-1969) studied philosophy, music, psychology, and sociology at the University of Frankfurt, took his doctorate degree in 1924 and his *Habilitation* with a thesis on Kierkegaard in 1931. Adorno was an early member of the Frankfurt Institut für Sozialforschung, founded in 1925. He was forced to leave Germany in 1933. Having returned from the United States to West Germany in 1949, Adorno had a strong impact on German sociology, especially in the 1960s when critical theory was widely discussed and embraced by students. Together with Max Horkheimer and Herbert Marcuse, Adorno is one of the founders of critical social theory. He was director of the Institut für Sozialforschung until his death. Publications by Adorno available in English include: *The Authoritarian Personality*, co-author (New York: Harper, 1950); *Prisms: Cultural Criticism and Society* (London: Spearman, 1967); *Dialectic of Enlightenment*, with Max Horkheimer (New York: Herder & Herder, 1972); *The Jargon of Authenticity* (London: Routledge & Kegan Paul, 1973); *Negative Dialectics* (London: Routledge & Kegan Paul, 1973); *Philosophy of Modern Music* (London: Sheed & Ward, 1973); *Minima Moralia: Reflections from a Damaged Life* (London: New Left Books, 1974); *Introduction to the Sociology of Music* (New York: Seabury Press, 1976); *In Search of Wagner* (London: New Left Books, 1981); *Against Epistemology: a Metacritique* (Cambridge, Mass.: MIT Press, 1983); *Aesthetic Theory* (London: Routledge & Kegan Paul, 1984). Adorno's works have been published in his *Gesammelte Schriften*, 23 vols. (Frankfurt: Suhrkamp, 1970 ff.).

ULRICH BECK, born in 1944, studied sociology at the University of Munich. He became professor of sociology at the University of Münster in 1979 and, since 1981, has taught at the University of Bamberg. Beck is editor of *Soziale Welt*. His fields of interest include the theory of modernization, especially developments in labor relations and occupations, as well as forms of inequality in modern society. His publications include: *Objektivität und Normativität. Die Theorie-Praxis-Debatte in der modernen deutschen und amerikanischen Soziologie* (Reinbek: Rowohlt, 1974); *Soziologie der Arbeit und der Berufe* (Reinbek: Rowohlt, 1980); *Soziologie und Praxis*, ed. (Göttingen: Schwartz & Co., 1982); *Risikogesellschaft — Auf dem Wege in eine andere Moderne* (Frankfurt: Suhrkamp, 1986).

HELMUT DAHMER, born in 1937, is professor of sociology at the

Technische Hochschule in Darmstadt. He is editor of the psychoanalytic journal *Psyche*. His publications include: *Politische Orientierungen* (Frankfurt: Fischer, 1973); *Analytische Sozialpsychologie*, ed., 2 vols. (Frankfurt: Suhrkamp, 1980); *Libido und Gesellschaft. Studien über Freud und die Freudsche Linke* (Frankfurt: Suhrkamp, 1973), 2nd. rev. ed. 1982; *Zwischen Freud und Marx* (forthcoming, 1987); *Leo Trotzki, Schriften*, ed., 10 vols. (forthcoming, 1987 ff.).

RALF DAHRENDORF was born in 1929 as the son of a leading Social Democratic *Reichstag* deputy. He received his doctorate in philosophy and classical philology from the University of Hamburg and a Ph.D. degree from the University of London, becoming professor of sociology at the University of Constance in 1966. He has also taught at the Universities of Saarbrücken, Hamburg, and Tübingen as well as at Columbia, Harvard, and the University of Oregon. After a political career in the 1960s and early 1970s, initially as an FDP deputy in the West German parliament, Dahrendorf was appointed Director of the London School of Economics, which he left after a ten-year term in order return to the University of Constance. Dahrendorf's main publications are: *Class and Class Conflict in Industrial Society* (Stanford: Stanford University Press, 1959); *Gesellschaft und Freiheit* (Munich: Piper, 1961); *Die angewandte Aufklärung. Gesellschaft und Soziologie in Amerika* (Munich: Piper, 1963); *Essays in the Theory of Society* (Stanford: Stanford University Press, 1968); *Society and Democracy in Germany* (Garden City: Doubleday, 1969); *Homo Sociologicus* (Oxford: Basil Blackwell, 1975); *The New Liberty: Survival and Justice in a Changing World* (Stanford: Stanford University Press, 1975); *Life Chances* (Chicago: University of Chicago Press, 1980); *On Britain* (Chicago: University of Chicago Press, 1982); *Reisen nach innen und aussen: Aspekte der Zeit* (Stuttgart: Deutsche Verlagsanstalt, 1984); *Law and Order* (Boulder: Westview, 1985).

KLAUS EDER, born in 1946, studied sociology and political science at the universities of Erlangen, Frankfurt, and Paris. He received his doctorate in 1976 from the University of Constance with a thesis on the origins of state-societies, and his *venia legendi* in 1985 from the University of Düsseldorf with a study of the development of political modernity in nineteenth-century Germany. He is presently *Privatdozent* at the University of Düsseldorf and holds a research post at an institute for social research in Munich. Eder works on aspects of of social evolution in the tradition of critical theory, conceiving the problems of legitimization and rationalization in late capitalist societies as evolutionary processes to be analyzed with respect to their implicit rationality or pathology. His publications include: *Die Entstehung von*

Klassengesellschaften, ed. (Frankfurt: Suhrkamp, 1973); *Die Entstehung staatlich organisierter Gesellschaften. Ein Beitrag zu einer Theorie sozialer Evolution* (Frankfurt: Suhrkamp, 1976); *Genese und Struktur einer gesellschaftlichen Pathologie. Zur Entstehungs- und Entwicklungsgeschichte politischer Modernität in Deutschland* (Frankfurt: Suhrkamp, 1985).

NORBERT ELIAS was born in 1897 and worked, until 1984, at the Institute of Interdisciplinary Research at the University of Bielefeld (where he received an honorary degree). He studied medicine, philosophy (with Edmund Husserl, Karl Jaspers, and Richard Hönigswald), and psychology, and did postgraduate studies with Alfred Weber in Heidelberg. He taught in Frankfurt, where he was Karl Mannheim's assistant. After his forced emigration in 1933, he had a rough time in Paris, and later went on to posts at the London School of Economics and the University of Leicester. He also taught at the universities of Ghana, Amsterdam, Frankfurt, Constance, and others. In 1977 he received the Adorno Prize of the city of Frankfurt. Elias' human science applies sociological, historical, and social psychological approaches to the empirical and theoretical study of long-term social processes. He is best known for his books *The Civilizing Process,* 2 vols. (Oxford: Blackwell, 1979-1982), which was originally published in 1939, and *The Court Society* (Oxford: Blackwell, 1983). Other publications available in English include: *What Is Sociology?* (London: Hutchison, 1978); "Knowledge and Power," in N. Stehr and V. Meja, eds., *Society and Knowledge: Contemporary Perspectives on the Sociology of Knowledge* (New Brunswick, N.J. and London: Transaction Books, 1984); *The Loneliness of the Dying* (Oxford: Blackwell, 1985); *Involvement and Detachment* (Oxford: Blackwell, 1985). He has also published *Über die Zeit* (Frankfurt: Suhrkamp, 1984), *Humana Conditio* (Frankfurt: Suhrkamp, 1985), and he is presently working on a book on the power balance between the sexes.

ARNOLD GEHLEN (1904-1976) studied philosophy at Leipzig and Cologne, and was an assistant of Hans Freyer. He became a professor at the University of Königsberg (1938) and at the University of Vienna (1940). After World War II, Gehlen taught at Speyer and in Aachen. While his work on philosophical anthropology, sociology, and philosophy remains controversial, he is nevertheless an important figure in postwar German academic discourse. His writings focus upon the institutions constructed by humans in coping with a lack of inherent instincts that would guide their conduct. Institutions are seen by Gehlen as essential for stable and predictable social conduct. His publications include: *Der Mensch, seine Natur und seine Stellung in der Welt* [1940] (Bonn: Athenaeum, 1958), English edition forthcoming from Columbia University Press; *Urmensch und Spätkultur* (Frankfurt: Athenaeum, 1956); *Die Seele im technischen Zeitalter* (Reinbek: Rowohlt, 1957), also published in English as *Man in the Age of Technology* (New York: Columbia University Press, 1980); *Moral und Hypermoral* (Frankfurt: Athenaeum, 1969); *Studien zur Anthropologie und Soziologie* (Neuwied: Luchterhand, 1963). His collected works have been published in the *Arnold-Gehlen Gesamtausgabe* (Frankfurt: Klostermann, 1978 ff.).

JÜRGEN HABERMAS, born in 1929, studied philosophy, history, German literature, and economics at the universities of Göttingen, Zurich, and Bonn. He acquired his doctorate with a dissertation on Schelling's philosophy in 1954 in Bonn and his *venia legendi* in Marburg in 1961 with *Strukturwandel der Öffentlichkeit* (Neuwied: Luchterhand, 1962). After working at the Institute for Social Research in Frankfurt he became professor of philosophy in Heidelberg (1964) and was later appointed to Max Horkheimer's chair in Frankfurt as professor of sociology and philosophy (1971). From 1971 to 1983 he was director (jointly with the philosopher Karl Friedrich von Weizsäcker) of the Max-Planck-Institute in Starnberg. He is now professor of philosophy in Frankfurt. Habermas has been a visiting professor at a number of universities in the United States, including the New School for Social Research, Princeton University, the University of California at Berkeley, and Boston College. He has also lectured at the *Collège de France*. Habermas is the leading representative of the postwar generation of critical theorists. His work has been widely commented upon in North America and Britain, and his books have been translated into several languages. Publications by Habermas available in English include: *Toward a Rational Society* (Boston: Beacon Press, 1970); *Theory and Practice* (Boston: Beacon Press, 1974); *Legitimation Crisis* (Boston: Beacon Press, 1976); *Knowledge and Human Interests* (Boston: Beacon Press, 1979); *Communication and the Evolution of Society* (Boston: Beacon Press, 1979); *Philosophical-Political Profiles* (Cambridge, Mass.: MIT Press, 1983); *Observations on the Spiritual Situation of the Age* (Cambridge, Mass.: MIT Press, 1985); *The Theory of Communicative Action*, 2 vols. (Boston: Beacon Press, 1984-1987).

JÜRGEN KOCKA, born in 1941, is professor of history and social history at the University of Bielefeld, where he is also director of the Center for Interdisciplinary Studies. He was a fellow at Harvard University (1969), visiting member of the Institute of Advanced Studies, Princeton (1975-1976), and visiting professor at the University of Chicago (1984) and at the Hebrew University Jerusalem (1985). His publications include: *Unternehmensverwaltung und Angestelltenschaft am Beispiel Siemens 1847-1914* (Stuttgart: Klett, 1963); *Unternehmer in der deutschen Industrialisierung* (Göttingen: Vandenhoeck & Ruprecht, 1975); *Sozialgeschichte* (Göttingen: Vandenhoeck & Ruprecht, 1977); *Die Angestellten in der deutschen Geschichte, 1850-1980* (Göttingen: Vandenhoeck & Ruprecht, 1981); *Lohnarbeit und Klassenbildung. Arbeiter und Arbeiterbewegung in Deutschland 1800-1875* (Berlin: Dietz, 1983). His English publications include: *White-Collar Workers in America, 1890-1940* (London/Berkeley: Sage, 1980) and *Facing Total War: German Society 1914-1918* (Cambridge, Mass.: Harvard University Press, 1984). He is co-editor, since 1975, of *Geschichte und Gesellschaft. Zeitschrift für Historische Sozialwissenschaft* (Göttingen: Vandenhoeck & Ruprecht).

RENÉ KÖNIG, born in 1906, has had a strong impact on German postwar sociology. After studying philosophy, psychology, ethnology, and Roman and Islamic languages he received his doctorate in Berlin in 1930. In 1937 he emigrated to Switzerland, where he taught at the University of Zurich, returning to West Germany in 1949 as professor of sociology at the University of Cologne. He has been visiting professor at several universities, including the University of California at Berkeley and the University of Arizona. König has done work in the sociologies of the family, community, and social development, and became a leading proponent of empirical sociology during the phase of the reconstruction of sociology in West Germany. His publications include: *Soziologie* (Frankfurt: Fischer, 1958); *Handbuch der empirischen Sozialforschung* (Stuttgart: Enke, 1962); *Soziologische Orientierungen* (Opladen: Westdeutscher Verlag, 1965); *Emile Durkheim zur Diskussion. Jenseits von Dogmatismus und Skepsis* (Munich: Hanser, 1978); *Leben in Widerspruch. Versuch einer intellektuellen Autobiographie* (Munich: Hanser, 1980); *Menschheit auf dem Laufsteg. Zur Kulturgeschichte der Mode* (Munich: Hanser, 1985). He is an editor of the *Kölner Zeitschrift für Soziologie und Sozialpsychologie.*

KURT LENK, born in 1929, studied political science and sociology in Frankfurt and Marburg, receiving his doctorate in 1956. Since 1972 he has been professor of political science at the Technische Hochschule in Aachen. Lenk attempts to combine historical-genetic and systematic approaches and, in the tradition of the Frankfurt School, conceives of political studies as critical inquiry. His publications include: *Ideologie* (Neuwied: Luchterhand, 1961); *Marx in der Wissenssoziologie* (Neuwied: Luchterhand, 1972); *Politische Soziologie* (Stuttgart: Kohlhammer, 1982).

MARIO RAINER LEPSIUS, born in 1928, studied economics, sociology, and history and received his doctorate in 1955 at the University of Munich.

From 1963 to 1981 professor of sociology at the University of Mannheim, he is now at the University of Heidelberg and served as President of the German Sociological Society from 1971 to 1974. Lepsius' influence on German sociology is based on several contributions to general sociology, the sociology of sociology, industrial and political sociology, social stratification, and historical sociology. He is an editor of the collected works of Max Weber. His publications include: *Zwischenbilanz der Soziologie*, ed. (Stuttgart: Enke, 1976); *Soziologie in Deutschland und Österreich 1918-1945*, ed. (Opladen: Westdeutscher Verlag, 1981); *Sozialgeschichte der Bundesrepublik Deutschland* (Stuttgart: Klett-Cotta, 1983). Among his publications in English are: "From Fragmented Party Democracy to Government by Emergency Decree and National Socialist Takeover," in Juan J. Linz and Alfred Stepan, eds., *The Breakdown of Democratic Regimes* (Baltimore: Johns Hopkins University Press, 1978); "The Development of Sociology in Germany after World War II (1945-1968)," *International Journal of Sociology* (Fall 1983) 12(3).

THOMAS LUCKMANN, born in 1927, studied in Austria and in the United States (with Alfred Schutz). For almost ten years he taught at Hobart College and at the New School for Social Research. After his return to Germany in 1965 he became professor at the University of Frankfurt. In 1970, he moved to the University of Constance. Luckmann's research interests are in the sociology of religion, the relation between language, culture, and socialization as well as in the social construction of knowledge. With Alfred Schutz, whose unpublished *The Structures of the Life-World* (Evanston, Ill.: Northwestern University Press, 1973) he has completed, Luckmann is generally concerned with the foundations and applications of a Weberian "interpretive" sociology. His other publications include: with Peter Berger, *The Social Construction of Reality* (New York: Doubleday, 1966); *The Invisible Religion* (New York: Doubleday, 1967); *Phenomenology and Sociology*, ed. (Harmondsworth: Penguin, 1978); *Life World and Social Realities* (London: Heinemann, 1983); *Strukturen der Lebenswelt*, 2 vols. (Frankfurt: Suhrkamp, 1973-1984).

NIKLAS LUHMANN, born in 1927, is professor of sociology at the University of Bielefeld. He studied law at the University of Freiburg and sociology and public administration at Harvard University. Adopting a functionalist approach to social organization, his main concern is the complex nature of modern society and the role of social institutions in ordering and controlling this complexity. Among his main publications are *Funktionen und Folgen formaler Organisationen* (Frankfurt:

Suhrkamp, 1973); *Soziologische Aufklärung* [1970], 3 vols. (Opladen: Westdeutscher Verlag, 1975); *Gesellschaftsstruktur und Semantik* [1980], 2 vols. (Frankfurt: Suhrkamp, 1981); *Ausdifferenzierung des Rechts* (Frankfurt: Suhrkamp, 1981); *Soziale Systeme. Grundriss einer allgemeinen Theorie* (Frankfurt: Suhrkamp, 1984). His publications in English include: *Trust and Power* (New York: Wiley, 1979); *The Differentiation of Society* (New York: Columbia University Press, 1982); "The Differentiation of Advances in Knowledge: The Genesis of Science," in N. Stehr and V. Meja, eds., *Society and Knowledge: Contemporary Perspectives on the Sociology of Knowledge* (New Brunswick, N.J. and London: Transaction Books, 1984); *Religious Dogmatics and the Evolution of Society* (Lewiston, N.Y.: E. Mellen, 1984); *Love as Passion* (Oxford: Polity Press, 1985); *A Sociological Theory of Law* (London: Routledge & Kegan Paul, 1985).

ALEXANDER MITSCHERLICH (1908-1982) studied history and philosophy, medicine and psychology at different European universities. He was professor at the universities of Heidelberg (1948-1967) and Frankfurt (1967-1973) and, in the postwar period, emerged as the leading psychoanalytic social thinker in Germany. Until his death he was director of the Sigmund-Freud Institute in Frankfurt. Mitscherlich's research focused on the influence of institutions on the individual, on aggression, on cruelty, and on tolerance. His pathology of modern societies points to the psychological costs of socialization in industrial society and to the resulting forms of emotional impoverishment. His publications include: *Die Unfähigkeit zu Trauern* (Munich: Piper, 1967); *Die Entfaltung der Psychoanalyse. Das Wirken Sigmund Freuds in die Gegenwart* (Stuttgart: Klett, 1969); *Die Idee des Friedens und menschliche Aggressivität* (Frankfurt: Suhrkamp, 1970). His publications in English include: *Society Without the Father* (New York: Aronson, 1974) and, with Margarete Mitscherlich, *The Inability to Mourn: Principles of Collective Behavior* (New York: Grove, 1975). His collected works have been published as *Gesammelte Schriften*, 10 vols. (Frankfurt: Suhrkamp, 1983 ff.).

OSKAR NEGT, born in 1934, studied in Frankfurt and Göttingen. He was a visiting professor at Vienna, Berne, Milwaukee, and Madison, Wisconsin, before he became professor of sociology at the University of Hannover (1970). Negt's research interests, influenced by the Frankfurt School, include education, trade unions, political behavior, and Marxism. His publications include: *Soziologische Phantasie und exemplarisches Lernen. Zur Theorie und Praxis der Arbeiterbildung* (Frankfurt: Europäische Verlagsanstalt, 1968); *Öffentlichkeit und Erfahrung. Zur Organisationsanalyse von bürgerlicher und proletarischer Öffentlichkeit* (Frankfurt: Suhrkamp,

1972); with Alexander Kluge, *Geschichte und Eigensinn* (Frankfurt: Zweitausendeins, 1981); *Lebendige Arbeit, enteignete Zeit. Politische und kulturelle Dimensionen des Kampfes um die Arbeitszeit* (Frankfurt and New York: Campus, 1984).

ULRICH OEVERMANN, born in 1940, was an assistant of Jürgen Habermas (1964-1970). Since 1977 he has been professor of sociology at the University of Frankfurt. Oevermann's work has primarily been in the area of sociolinguistics, socialization (especially patterns of family interaction), and the sociological dimensions of developmental processes (including educational development). Best known are his proposals for a qualitative methodology, and an objective hermeneutics, which he has discussed in contributions to various volumes. His publications include: "Role Structure of the Family and its Implications for the Cognitive Development of Children," in Mathias Matthijssen, ed., *Education in Europe* (The Hague: Mouton, 1968); "Schichtenspezifische Formen des Sprachverhaltens und ihr Einfluss auf kognitive Prozesse," in H. Roth, ed., *Begabung und Lernen* (Stuttgart: Klett, 1971); *Sprache und soziale Herkunft* (Frankfurt: Suhrkamp, 1972); "Beobachtungen zur Struktur der sozialisatorischen Interaktion," in M. Rainer Lepsius, ed., *Zwischenbilanz der Soziologie. Verhandlungen des 17. deutschen Soziologentages* (Stuttgart: Enke, 1976); "Programmatische Überlegungen zu einer Theorie der Bildungsprozesse und zur Strategie der Sozialisationsforschung," in Klaus Hurrelmann, ed., *Sozialisation und Lebenslauf* (Reinbek: Rowohlt, 1976); "Sozialisationstheorie. Ansätze zu einer soziologischen Sozialisationstheorie und ihre Konsequenzen für die allgemeine soziologische Analyse," in Günther Lüschen, ed., *Deutsche Soziologie seit 1945*, Special issue 21 of the *Kölner Zeitschrift für Soziologie und Sozialpsychologie* (Opladen: Westdeutscher Verlag, 1979).

CLAUS OFFE, born in 1940, has been professor of political science and sociology at the University of Bielefeld since 1975. He received his doctorate in sociology at the University of Frankfurt in 1968. He has worked on political institutions, democratic theory, and sociopolitical aspects of labor markets. His publications include: *Berufsbildungsreform* (Frankfurt: Suhrkamp, 1975); *Strukturprobleme des kapitalistischen Staates* (Frankfurt: Suhrkamp, 1975); and *Arbeitsgesellschaft* (Frankfurt and New York: Campus, 1984). Apart from a large number of essays, he has published the following books in English: *Industry and Inequality* (New York: St. Martin's, 1977); *Contradictions of the Welfare State* (Cambridge, Mass.: MIT Press, 1984); *Disorganized Capitalism* (Oxford: Polity Press, 1985).

WOLFGANG SCHLUCHTER, born in 1938, studied at the universities of

Tübingen, Munich, and Berlin, where he received his doctorate in 1967. He received his second doctorate (*Habilitation*) from the University of Mannheim in 1972 and was professor of sociology at the University of Düsseldorf from 1973 to 1976. Since then he has been professor of sociology at the University of Heidelberg. Schluchter's work on sociological theory concentrates on bureaucracy, domination, rationality, state theory, and democracy, and is mainly devoted to a reconstruction and development of Max Weber's approach. His publications include: *Entscheidung für den Rechtsstaat* (Cologne: Kiepenheuer & Witsch, 1968); *Aspekte bürokratischer Herrschaft* (Munich: List, 1972), 2d ed. (Frankfurt: Suhrkamp, 1985); *Die Entwicklung des okzidentalen Rationalismus. Eine Analyse von Max Webers Gesellschaftsgeschichte* (Tübingen: J.C.B. Mohr, 1979). His English publications include: with Guenther Roth, *Max Weber's Vision of History* (Berkeley: University of California Press, 1979); and *The Rise of Western Rationalism* (Berkeley: University of California Press, 1981).

HELMUT SCHELSKY (1912-1984) was one of the most influential German postwar sociologists. His philosophical position was derived from the tradition of philosophical anthropology, hermeneutics and conservatism, as represented by his teachers Hans Freyer, Theodor Litt, and Arnold Gehlen. After World War II, Schelsky was among the first social scientists attempting to reconstruct German sociology and to stress the need for empirical social research. He became professor of sociology at Hamburg in 1949. Twenty years later, Schelsky became co-founder of Germany's largest sociology department at the University of Bielefeld. In the years before his death, Schelsky retreated from social science and criticized sociology from an "anti-sociological" perspective. His publications include: *Die skeptische Generation* (Düsseldorf-Cologne: Diederich, 1957); *Ortsbestimmung der deutschen Soziologie* (Düsseldorf-Cologne: Diederich, 1959); *Einsamkeit und Freiheit. Die deutsche Universität und ihre Reformen* (Hamburg: Reinbek, 1963); *Die Arbeit tun die anderen. Klassenkampf und Priesterherrschaft der Intellektuellen* (Opladen: Westdeutscher Verlag, 1975); *Rückblicke eines 'Anti-Soziologen'* (Opladen: Westdeutscher Verlag, 1981).

FRIEDRICH H. TENBRUCK, born in 1919, wrote his dissertation on Kant's *Critique of Pure Reason* in 1944, and shifted his interests from philosophy and history to sociology during his post-doctoral studies at the University of Virginia. After research and teaching periods at Hobart and Smith Colleges, Freiburg, and Frankfurt he became professor of sociology at the University of Tübingen in 1967. Throughout his work, he emphasizes the importance of an adequate understanding of European history for the sociological analysis of the spiritual condition of the present age. In this sense, studies in the history of sociology, in the sociologies of science, religion, and culture, but also analyses of role theory and of social change are according to Tenbruck always more than specialized efforts within an intellectual division of labor. They must be regarded as steps toward a sociologically and anthropologically informed explanation of the function of science, of rationality, and of religion in modern society. Tenbruck is known for his work on Max Weber, on the theory of action, and on the sociology of religion. He is presently working in the area of the sociology of science. His publications include: "Über Kultur im Zeitalter der Sozialwissenschaften," *Saeculum. Jahrbuch für Universalgeschichte* (Freiburg: Alber, 1963); *Zur Kritik der planenden Vernunft* (Freiburg: Alber, 1971); "Das Werk Max Webers," *Kölner Zeitschrift für Soziologie und Sozialpsychologie* (1975); "Der Fortschritt der Wissenschaft als Trivialisierungsprozess," *Kölner Zeitschrift für Soziologie und Sozialpsychologie*, Sonderheft 18 (Opladen: Westdeutscher Verlag, 1975); "Glaubensgeschichte der Moderne," *Zeitschrift für Politik* (1976); "Wahrheit und Mission," in H. Baier, ed., *Freiheit und Sachzwang* (Opladen: Westdeutscher Verlag, 1977); "Zur Anthropologie des Handelns," in H. Lenk, ed., *Handlungstheorien — interdisziplinär*, vol. 2 (Munich: Fink, 1978); "Die Aufgaben der Kultursoziologie," *Kölner Zeitschrift für Soziologie und Sozialpsychologie* (1979) 31; "Deutsche Soziologie im internationalen Kontext. Ihre Ideengeschichte und ihr Gesellschaftsbezug," *Kölner Zeitschrift für Soziologie und Sozialpsychologie*, Sonderheft 21 (Opladen: Westdeutscher Verlag, 1979); *Die unbewältigten Sozialwissenschaften* (Graz-Vienna-Cologne: Styria, 1984).

Index

Abendroth, Wolfgang, 272
Action, administrative, 224; analysis of, 437; capitalist rules of, 103; class, 249; communicative, 194, 198-199, 210-211; consensual, 194; control of, 178-179; criminal, 392; economic, 122-123; freedom of, 310, 333; individual, 49, 64, 66, 130, 372, 375, 412, 414, 416, 438; meaning of, 439; norms of, 93-94, 106, 395; organizational, 308; political, 77, 96, 146, 215, 277, 352; practical, 437, 446; rational, 64, 67, 117, 190, 384; revolutionary, 145-146, 261; science of, 441; social, 12, 18, 62, 64-65, 101, 117, 122, 126-136, 274, 277, 328, 352, 358, 375, 379-380, 411, 414, 416, 419, 421, 438; structure of, 188, 311, 446; theory of, 39, 151, 438, 440; theory of communicative, 188, 195-196, 198, 204, 206, 208, 210; value-related, 83
Adams, Robert McCormack, 290
Adler, Max, 40, 73, 104
Adorno, Theodor W., 1-2, 4, 6, 10, 14-19, 23-25, 27, 29, 35-36, 51, 53, 108-109, 111, 114-115, 118, 120, 139, 142-149, 174, 187, 196-197, 213-217, 232-247, 358, 361, 408-409, 451
Albert, Hans, 4, 24, 102, 111, 320
Albrecht, Günter, 55
Alemann, Heine von, 53
Alexander, Jeffrey, 26, 28
Alienation, 60, 63, 69, 76, 189, 192, 331-332, 343, 359-360, 378, 412, 418, 432-434; cultural, 15; dialectic of, 396, 399; theory of, 59, 71; universal, 69
Allert, Tilman, 436-447
Allport, Gordon, 410
Althusser, Louis, 107

Americanization of German sociology, 6
Analysis, causal, 408; class, 338, 342, 361; comparative, 189, 335; comprehensive, 54; conceptual, 61, 207; critical, 66-67, 76, 131, 135, 358; empirical, 23, 94, 127-129, 441; functional, 101, 128, 178, 335; genetic, 68; levels of, 364; Marxian, 215, 238; mechanical, 421; organizational, 315; phenomenological, 359; philosophical, 7, 24, 359; political, 274; program, 197; psychological, 408, 441; scientific, 49, 94, 105, 123; social, 17, 96; of social conditions, 427; of social developments, 324; of social processes, 251; sociological, 17, 50, 129, 132, 135, 273-274, 410, 433, 436; structural, 51, 178, 437; systematic, 49; systems, 278-290; theoretical, 117; *see also* Functionalism
Anomie, 192-193, 216, 289, 423
Anthropology, 139, 248, 362, 393, 434; cultural, 414-415, 419, 429, 432; philosophical, 9, 12, 27-28, 34, 36, 47, 68, 139, 359-360; social, 28, 280, 416; sociological, 28
Anti-sociology, 28, 49
Antrick, Otto, 55
Anwärter, Manfred, 29
Apel, Karl-Otto, 15, 24, 399, 401
Arendt, Hannah, 53
Arensberg, Conrad, 289
Aristotle, 11, 121, 173, 250-251
Arndt, Adolf, 267
Aron, Raymond, 52, 73
Ashby, W. Ross, 176
Aulard, Alphonse, 249
Authority, 251, 274, 376; analysis of functional, 298, 304; bureaucratic, 291; functional, 274, 291-299, 301,

472   INDEX